Fodor's 97

New York City

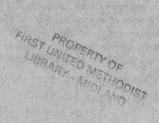

"When it comes to information on regional history, what to see and do, and shopping, these guides are exhaustive."

—*USAir Magazine*

"Usable, sophisticated restaurant coverage, with an emphasis on good value."

—Andy Birsh, *Gourmet Magazine* columnist

"Valuable because of their comprehensiveness."

—*Minneapolis Star-Tribune*

"Fodor's always delivers high quality...thoughtfully presented...thorough."

—*Houston Post*

"An excellent choice for those who want everything under one cover."

—*Washington Post*

Fodor's Travel Publications, Inc.
New York • Toronto • London • Sydney • Auckland
http://www.fodors.com/

Fodor's New York City

Editor: David Low

Editorial Contributors: Steven K. Amsterdam, Robert Andrews, Clair Berg, Hannah Borgeson, David Brown, Andrea Coller, Audra Epstein, Laura M. Kidder, Amy McConnell, Margaret Mittelbach, Linda Olle, Heidi Sarna, Helayne Schiff, Mary Ellen Schultz, M. T. Schwartzman (Gold Guide editor), Dinah Spritzer, J. Walman

Creative Director: Fabrizio La Rocca

Cartographer: David Lindroth

Cover Photograph: Francesco Ruggeri

Design: Between the Covers

Copyright

Special Sales

CONTENTS

ON THE ROAD WITH FODOR'S

WE'RE ALWAYS THRILLED to get letters from readers, especially one like this:

It took us an hour to decide what book to buy and we now know we picked the best one. Your book was wonderful, easy to follow, very accurate, and good on pointing out eating places, informal as well as formal. When we saw other people using your book, we would look at each other and smile.

Our editors and writers are deeply committed to making every Fodor's guide "the best one"—not only accurate but always charming, brimming with sound recommendations and solid ideas, right on the mark in describing restaurants and hotels, and full of fascinating facts that make you view what you've traveled to see in a rich new light.

About Our Writers

Our success in achieving our goals—and in helping to make your trip the best of all possible vacations—is a credit to the hard work of our extraordinary writers and editors.

The editor of *Fodor's New York City,* **David Low,** is a native New Yorker (born in Queens) who makes his living as a fiction writer and book editor. He also revised the Arts chapter and the Chelsea, Greenwich Village, East Village, and Rockfeller Center exploring tours. Mr. Low has had an obsessive interest in theater, movies, and other performing arts in the city since he saw his first Broadway play, *Baker Street,* a musical about Sherlock Holmes, in the 1960s. His favorite theater is the Broadhurst, and his favorite places to see movies are the Film Forum, the Ziegfeld, and the Sony Lincoln Square complex. He lives around the corner from the Strand Book Store, where he has spent many hours searching for bargains.

Editor and freelance writer **Hannah Borgeson,** who revised many of the Manhattan exploring tours, has helped arrange scores of visitor itineraries from her Yorkville apartment, where she and her roommate act as concierges of a de facto youth hostel. One of her favorite activities in the city is bicycling, and she hopes that one day New York will realize its true potential as an auto-free haven.

Gotham native **Andrea Coller** revised the Nightlife chapter. She has lived in three out of the five boroughs and has written on the city's people, places, and flings for such publications as *Metropolis, New York Newsday,* and *Swing* magazine. She recommends dawn at the Empire Diner in summer. Due to bouts of insomnia, she has often been awake in the wee hours when the garbage trucks arrive.

Fodor's editor **Amy McConnell** revised the chapter on Exploring the Other Boroughs. She also updated the SoHo, Chinatown, Little Italy, and Central Park exploring tours. Ever since she wrote about the outer boroughs for *The Berkeley Guides' New York City '97,* she has been a passionate defender of those parts of the city less visited by tourists. When she's not at her desk in the Random House building, you might find her riding the ferry to Staten Island or the No. 7 train to Queens—or running in the park.

Freelance writer **Margaret Mittelbach** is a Los Angeles native who has lived in New York for the past eight years. She updated the chapters on Exploring New York City with Children and Outdoor Activities and Sports. Because she is currently co-authoring a book about New York's wildlife and wild places, she has been spending a lot of time in the city's marshes, woods, and underground passageways. Her favorite spots in New York are Brooklyn's Park Slope, where she lives and works in a brownstone, and the Jamaica Bay Wildlife Refuge, where she has been seen stalking butterflies without a net.

Mary Ellen Schultz, who updated the Lodging chapter, has worked on many Fodor's guides. She loves visiting hotels around the globe. She hopes to win the lottery so that she can give up her Manhattan apartment and stay in a different hotel every night.

Syndicated travel, food, and wine journalist **J. Walman,** who wrote the Dining chapter, dispenses culinary advice to the 2 million listeners of WEVD-AM, writes regularly for *Chocolatier* and *Troika Magazines,* and is president of Punch In–International Syndicate, an interactive electronic publishing company specializing in travel, restaurants, entertainment, and wine. He prefers to skip breakfast (rather than exercise), take vitamins (instead of giving up martinis), and is married to a beautiful and intelligent woman who shares his enthusiasm for travel, food, and wine—not necessarily in that order.

New This Year

This year we've reformatted our guides to make them easier to use. *New York City '97* has brand-new walking tours and a timing section that tells you exactly how long to allot for each tour—and what time of day, day of the week, or season of the year is optimal. You may also notice our fresh graphics, new in 1996. More readable and more helpful than ever? We think so—and we hope you do, too.

On the Web

Also check out Fodor's Web site (http://www.fodors.com/), where you'll find travel information on major destinations around the world and an ever-changing array of travel-savvy interactive features.

Let Us Do Your Booking

Our writers have scoured New York City to come up with a well-balanced list of the best hotels, both small and large, new and old. But you don't have to beat the bushes for a reservation. Now that we've teamed up with an established hotel-booking service, reserving a room at the property of your choice is easy. It's fast and free, and confirmation is guaranteed. If your first choice is booked, the operators can recommend others. Call 1–800/FODORS–1 or 1–800/363–6771 (0800–89–1030 in Great Britain; 0014–800–12–8271 in Australia; 1–800/55–9101 in Ireland).

How to Use This Book

Organization

Up front is the **Gold Guide.** Its first section, **Important Contacts A to Z,** gives addresses and telephone numbers of organizations and companies that offer destination-related services and detailed information and publications. **Smart Travel Tips A to Z,** the Gold Guide's second section, gives specific information on how to accomplish

what you need to in New York City as well as tips on savvy traveling. Both sections are in alphabetical order by topic.

The Exploring chapters are subdivided by neighborhood; each subsection recommends a walking tour and lists neighborhood sights alphabetically. Off the Beaten Path sights appear after the places from which they are most easily accessible. The remaining chapters are arranged in alphabetical order by subject (arts, dining, lodging, nightlife, outdoor activities and sports, and shopping).

At the end of the book you'll find Portraits, with a wonderful essay about New York City by V.S. Pritchett, followed by suggestions for pretrip reading, both fiction and nonfiction, and movies on tape with New York City as a backdrop.

Icons and Symbols

★	Our special recommendations
✕	Restaurant
☒	Lodging establishment
♨	Rubber duckie (good for kids)
☞	Sends you to another section of the guide for more information
✉	Address
☎	Telephone number
FAX	Fax number
☉	Opening and closing times
☜	Admission prices (those we give apply only to adults; substantially reduced fees are almost always available for children, students, and senior citizens)

Numbers in white and black circles—② and ❷, for example—that appear on the maps, in the margins, and within the tours correspond to one another.

Credit Cards

The following abbreviations are used: **AE,** American Express; **D,** Discover; **DC,** Diners Club; **MC,** MasterCard; and **V,** Visa.

Don't Forget to Write

You can use this book in the confidence that all prices and opening times are based on information supplied to us at press time; Fodor's cannot accept responsibility for any errors. Time inevitably brings changes, so always confirm information when it matters—especially if you're making a detour to visit a specific place. In addition, when making reservations be sure to mention if you have a disability or are traveling with children, if you prefer a private bath or a certain type of bed, or if you have specific dietary needs or any other concerns.

Were the restaurants we recommended as described? Did our hotel picks exceed your expectations? Did you find a museum we recommended a waste of time? If you have complaints, we'll look into them and revise our entries when the facts warrant it. If you've discovered a special place that we haven't included, we'll pass the information along to our correspondents and have them check it out. So send your feedback, positive *and* negative, to the New York City Editor at 201 East 50th Street, New York, New York 10022—and have a wonderful trip!

Karen Cure

Karen Cure
Editorial Director

New York City Area

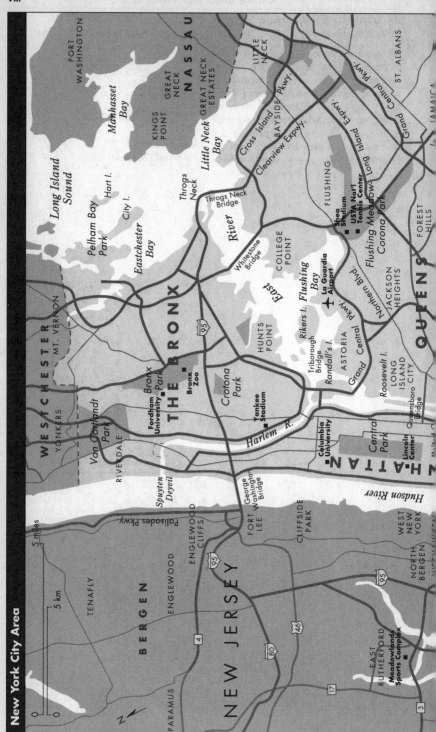

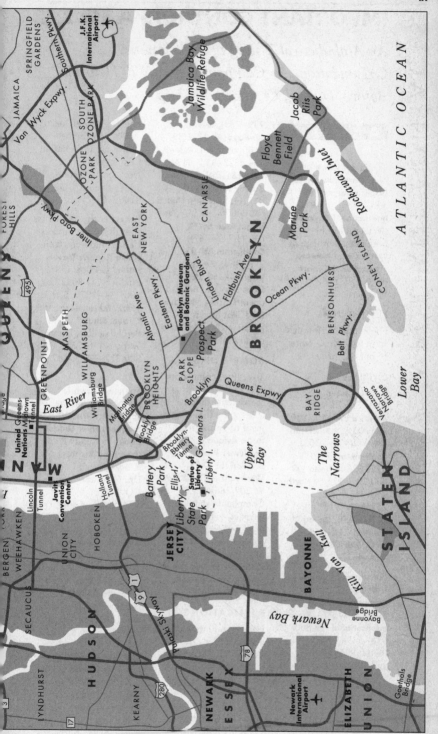

IMPORTANT CONTACTS A TO Z

An Alphabetical Listing of Publications, Organizations, & Companies That Will Help You Before, During, & After Your Trip

A

AIR TRAVEL

The major gateways to New York City are **La Guardia Airport** (☎ 718/533–3400) and **JFK International Airport** (☎ 718/244–4444), both in the borough of Queens; and **Newark International Airport** (☎ 201/961–6000) in New Jersey.

FLYING TIME

Flying time is 1½ hours from Chicago, 5 hours from Los Angeles.

CARRIERS

Carriers serving New York City include **America West** (☎ 800/235–9292), **American** (☎ 800/433–7300), **Continental** (☎ 800/525–0280), **Delta** (☎ 800/221–1212), **Northwest** (☎ 800/225–2525), **TWA** (☎ 800/221–2000), **United** (☎ 800/241–6522), and **USAir** (☎ 800/428–4322).

For inexpensive, no-frills flights, contact **Carnival Air Lines** (☎ 800/824–7386), **Kiwi International** (☎ 800/538–5494), **Midway** (☎ 800/446–4392), and **Midwest Express** (☎ 800/452–2022).

FROM THE U.K.

Seven airlines fly to La Guardia, Kennedy, or Newark airports from Heathrow: **Air India** (☎ 0181/745–1000), **American** (☎ 0345/789–789), **British Airways** (☎ 0181/897–4000; outside London, 0345/222–111), **El Al** (☎ 0181/759–9771), **Kuwait Airways** (☎ 0171/412–0006), **United** (☎ 0800/888–555), and **Virgin Atlantic** (☎ 01293/747–747). **Continental** (☎ 0800/776–464), **BA**, and **Virgin Atlantic** depart from Gatwick. **BA** also operates from Manchester. Flight time is approximately eight hours on all routes.

COMPLAINTS

To register complaints about charter and scheduled airlines, contact the U.S. Department of Transportation's **Aviation Consumer Protection Division** (✉ C-75, Washington, DC 20590, ☎ 202/366–2220). Complaints about lost baggage or ticketing problems and safety concerns may also be logged with the **Federal Aviation Administration (FAA) Consumer Hotline** (☎ 800/322–7873).

PUBLICATIONS

For general information about charter carriers, ask for the Department of Transportation's free brochure **"Plane Talk: Public Charter Flights"** (✉ Aviation Consumer Protection Division, C-75, Washington, DC 20590, ☎ 202/366–2220). The Department of Transportation also publishes a 58-page booklet, **"Fly Rights,"** available from the Consumer Information Center (✉ Supt. of Documents, Dept. 136C, Pueblo, CO 81009; $1.75).

For other tips and hints, consult the Consumers Union's monthly **"Consumer Reports Travel Letter"** (✉ Box 53629, Boulder, CO 80322, ☎ 800/234–1970; $39 1st year) and the newsletter **"Travel Smart"** (✉ 40 Beechdale Rd., Dobbs Ferry, NY 10522, ☎ 800/327–3633; $37 per year).

Some worthwhile publications on the subject are **The Official Frequent Flyer Guidebook,** by Randy Petersen (✉ Airpress, 4715-C Town Center Dr., Colorado Springs, CO 80916, ☎ 719/597–8899 or 800/487–8893; $14.99 plus $3 shipping); **Airfare Secrets Exposed,** by Sharon Tyler and Matthew Wunder (✉ Studio 4 Productions, Box 280400, Northridge, CA 91328, ☎ 818/700–2522 or 800/408–7369; $16.95 plus $2.50 shipping); **202 Tips Even the Best Business Travelers May Not Know,** by Christopher McGinnis (✉ Irwin Professional Publishing, 1333 Burr Ridge Pkwy., Burr Ridge, IL 60521, ☎ 800/634–3966; $11 plus $3.25 shipping); and **Travel**

Rights, by Charles Leocha (✉ World Leisure Corporation, 177 Paris St., Boston, MA 02128, ☎ 800/444–2524; $7.95 plus $3.95 shipping).

Travelers who experience motion sickness or ear problems in flight should get the brochures **"Ears, Altitude, and Airplane Travel"** and **"What You Can Do for Dizziness & Motion Sickness"** from the American Academy of Otolaryngology (✉ 1 Prince St., Alexandria, VA 22314, ☎ 703/836–4444, FAX 703/683–5100, TTY 703/519–1585).

TICKET OFFICES

Many airlines have ticket offices in convenient midtown and lower Manhattan locations. American, Continental, Delta, Northwest, and Virgin Atlantic, for example, all have offices at the **Airlines Building** (✉ 100 E. 42nd St.), and United, USAir, and TWA have offices in the other **Airlines Building** next door at 101 Park Avenue. Offices are generally open weekdays 8–7, weekends 9–5, but hours vary among carriers.

Ticket offices are also clustered in eight other Manhattan locations: the **New York Hilton and Towers** at 1335 6th Avenue (American, Continental, and Delta) and the **Satellite Airlines Ticket Company** locations at 1 East 59th Street (American, Continental, Delta, TWA, United, and USAir), **1 World Trade Center** (American, British

Airways, Continental, Delta, Northwest, TWA, United, and USAir), **Grand Central Station** (American, Continental, Delta, Midwest Express, Northwest, Virgin Atlantic), **555 7th Avenue** (American, Continental, Delta, USAir), **174 Water St.** at the South Street Seaport (American, Continental, DHL), **166 West 32nd Street** (American, Continental, Delta, TWA, United, USAir), and **1843 Broadway** at Columbus Circle (American, United). Many foreign carriers have ticket offices along 5th Avenue north of 50th Street.

AIRPORT TRANSFERS

BY BUS

Bus companies serving one or all of the area airports include **Carey Transportation** (☎ 718/632–0500, 800/456–1012, or 800/284–0909), **Gray Line Air Shuttle** (☎ 212/315–3006 or 800/451–0455), **Metropolitan Transportation Authority** (☎ 718/330–1234), **New Jersey Transit Airlink** and **Airport Express** (☎ 201/762–5100), and **Olympia Airport Express** (☎ 212/964–6233 or 718/622–7700).

CAR SERVICES

Try **All State Car and Limousine Service** (☎ 212/741–7440), **Carey Limousines** (☎ 212/599–1122 or 800/336–4646), **Carmel Car and Limousine Service** (☎ 212/666–6666), **Dav-El Services** (☎ 212/645–4242 or 800/922–0343),

Eastside Limo Service (☎ 212/744–9700), **Greenwich Limousine** (☎ 800/385–1033 or 212/868–4733), **London Towncars** (☎ 212/988–9700 or 800/221–4009), **Manhattan International Limo** (☎ 718/729–4200), **Sherwood Silver Bay Limousine Service** (☎ 718/472–0183), and **Skyline** (☎ 212/741–3711). **American Media Tours** (☎ 212/255–5908) provides car services exclusively for international visitors.

BY HELICOPTER

For helicopter service, contact **New York Helicopter** (☎ 800/645–3494).

BY SUBWAY

For information on subway service from JFK, contact the MTA (☎ 718/330–1234). From Newark, you can take a **PATH Train** (☎ 800/234–7284).

B

BETTER BUSINESS BUREAU

For local contacts, consult the **Council of Better Business Bureaus** (✉ 4200 Wilson Blvd., Suite 800, Arlington, VA 22203, ☎ 703/276–0100, FAX 703/525–8277).

BUS TRAVEL

Long-haul and commuter bus lines feed into the **Port Authority Terminal** (☎ 212/564–8484). Individual bus lines serving New York include **Greyhound Lines Inc.** (☎ 800/231–2222); **Adirondack, Pine Hill,** and **New York Trailways** from upstate

New York (☎ 800/225–6815); **Bonanza Bus Lines** from New England (☎ 800/556–3815); **Martz Trailways** from northeastern Pennsylvania (☎ 800/233–8604); **New Jersey Transit** from around New Jersey (☎ 201/762–5100); **Peter Pan Trailways** from New England (☎ 800/343–9999 or 413/781–2900); and **Vermont Transit** from New England (☎ 802/864–6811 or 800/552–8737).

The **George Washington Bridge Bus Station** (☎ 212/564–1114) is at Fort Washington Avenue and Broadway between 178th and 179th streets in the Washington Heights section of Manhattan. Six bus lines, serving northern New Jersey and Rockland County, New York, make daily stops there from 5 AM to 1 AM. The terminal connects with the 175th Street Station on the A subway, making it slightly more convenient for travelers going to and from the West Side.

WITHIN NEW YORK

For information about routes, bus stops, and hours of operation, call the **MTA** (☎ 718/330–1234) daily 6–9.

C

CAR RENTAL

The major car-rental companies represented in New York are **Avis** (☎ 800/331–1212; in Canada, 800/879–2847), **Budget** (☎ 800/527–0700; in the U.K., 0800/181181), **Dollar** (known as Eurodollar

outside North America, ☎ 800/800–4000; in the U.K., 0990/565–656), **Hertz** (☎ 800/654–3131; in Canada, 800/263–0600; in the U.K., 0345/555–888), and **National InterRent** (☎ 800/227–7368; in the U.K., where National is known as Europcar InterRent, 01345/222525). Rates in New York begin at $58 a day and $208 a week for an economy car with unlimited mileage. This does not include tax on car rentals, which is 13¼%.

RENTAL WHOLESALERS

Contact **Auto Europe** (☎ 207/828–2525 or 800/223–5555).

CHILDREN & TRAVEL

BABY-SITTING

The **Babysitters' Guild** (✉ 60 E. 42nd St., Suite 912, ☎ 212/682–0227) can take your children on sightseeing tours. Rates start at $12 an hour for one or two children over age one; $14.50 an hour for an infant, plus a $4.50 transportation charge ($7 after midnight); minimum booking is for four hours. The **Avalon Registry** (✉ Box 1362, Radio City Station, New York, NY 10101, ☎ 212/245–0250) is prepared to take very young children off your hands—at least for the day. Rates are $8 an hour for children over age seven months; $9 for babies seven weeks–six months; and $10 for newborns, plus a $2.50 transportation charge ($6 after 8 PM).

FLYING

Look into **"Flying with Baby"** (✉ Third Street Press, Box 261250, Littleton, CO 80163, ☎ 303/595–5959; $4.95 includes shipping), cowritten by a flight attendant. **"Kids and Teens in Flight,"** free from the U.S. Department of Transportation's Aviation Consumer Protection Division (✉ C-75, Washington, DC 20590, ☎ 202/366–2220), offers tips on children flying alone. Every two years the February issue of **Family Travel Times** (☞ Know-How, *below*) details children's services on three dozen airlines. **"Flying Alone, Handy Advice for Kids Traveling Solo"** is available free from the American Automobile Association (AAA) (✉ send stamped, self-addressed, legal-size envelope: Flying Alone, Mail Stop 800, 1000 AAA Dr., Heathrow, FL 32746).

KNOW-HOW

Family Travel Times, published quarterly by Travel with Your Children (✉ TWYCH, 40 5th Ave., New York, NY 10011, ☎ 212/477–5524; $40 per year), covers destinations, types of vacations, and modes of travel.

The **Family Travel Guides** catalog (✉ Carousel Press, Box 6061, Albany, CA 94706, ☎ 510/527–5849; $1 postage) lists about 200 books and articles on traveling with children. Also check **Take Your Baby and Go! A Guide for**

Traveling with Babies, Toddlers and Young Children, by Sheri Andrews, Judy Bordeaux, and Vivian Vasquez (⊠ Bear Creek Publications, 2507 Minor Ave. E, Seattle, WA 98102, ☎ 206/322–7604 or 800/326–6566; $5.95 plus $1.50 shipping).

LOCAL INFORMATION

Consult the lively by-parents, for-parents *Where Should We Take the Kids? Northeast* ($17; Fodor's Travel Publications, ☎ 800/533–6478 and in bookstores).

RESOURCES

For calendars of children's events, consult *New York* magazine, *Time Out New York,* and the weekly *Village Voice* newspaper, available at newsstands. The Friday *New York Times* "Weekend" section also provides a good listing of children's activities. Other good sources of information on happenings for kids are the monthly magazines *New York Family* (⊠ 141 Halstead Ave., Suite 3D, Mamaroneck, NY 10543, ☎ 914/381–7474) and the *Big Apple Parents' Paper* (⊠ 36 E. 12th St., New York, NY 10003, ☎ 212/533–2277), which are available free at toy stores, children's museums and clothing stores, and other places around town where parents and children are found.

STROLLER RENTAL

AAA-U-Rent (⊠ 861 Eagle Ave., Bronx, NY 10456, ☎ 718/665–6633).

TOUR OPERATORS

Contact **Grandtravel** (⊠ 6900 Wisconsin Ave., Suite 706, Chevy Chase, MD 20815, ☎ 301/986–0790 or 800/247–7651), which has tours for people traveling with grandchildren ages 7–17.

CUSTOMS

CANADIANS

Contact **Revenue Canada** (⊠ 2265 St. Laurent Blvd. S, Ottawa, Ontario K1G 4K3, ☎ 613/993–0534) for a copy of the free brochure **"I Declare/Je Déclare"** and for details on duty-free limits. For recorded information (within Canada only), call 800/461–9999.

U.K. CITIZENS

HM Customs and Excise (⊠ Dorset House, Stamford St., London SE1 9NG, ☎ 0171/202–4227) can answer questions about U.K. customs regulations and publishes a free pamphlet, **"A Guide for Travellers,"** detailing standard procedures and import rules.

D

DISABILITIES & ACCESSIBILITY

For brochures and further information, contact the **Mayor's Office for People with Disabilities** (⊠ 52 Chambers St., Office 206, New York, NY 10007, ☎ 212/788–2830, TTY 212/788–2842).

The **Andrew Heiskell Library for the Blind and Physically Handicapped** (⊠ 40 W. 20th St., New York, NY 10001,

☎ 212/206–5400) has a large collection of Braille, large-print, and recorded books, housed in a layout specially designed for easy access by the visually impaired.

COMPLAINTS

To register complaints under the provisions of the Americans with Disabilities Act, contact the U.S. Department of Justice's **Disability Rights Section** (⊠ Box 66738, Washington, DC 20035, ☎ 202/514–0301 or 800/514–0301, FAX 202/307–1198, TTY 202/514–0383 or 800/514–0383). For airline-related problems, contact the U.S. Department of Transportation's **Aviation Consumer Protection Division** (☞ Air Travel, *above*). For complaints about surface transportation, contact the Department of Transportation's **Civil Rights Office** (☎ 202/366–4648).

ORGANIZATIONS

TRAVELERS WITH HEARING IMPAIRMENTS➤ The **American Academy of Otolaryngology** (⊠ 1 Prince St., Alexandria, VA 22314, ☎ 703/836–4444, FAX 703/683–5100, TTY 703/519–1585) publishes a brochure, "Travel Tips for Hearing Impaired People."

TRAVELERS WITH MOBILITY PROBLEMS➤ Contact the **Information Center for Individuals with Disabilities** (⊠ Box 256, Boston, MA 02117, ☎ 617/450–9888; in MA, 800/462–5015; TTY 617/424–6855); **Mobility International USA** (⊠ Box 10767, Eugene, OR 97440,

THE GOLD GUIDE / IMPORTANT CONTACTS

☎ TTY 541/343–1284, FAX 541/343–6812), the U.S. branch of a Belgium-based organization (☞ *below*) with affiliates in 30 countries; **MossRehab Hospital Travel Information Service** (☎ 215/456–9600, TTY 215/456–9602), a telephone information resource for travelers with physical disabilities; the **Society for the Advancement of Travel for the Handicapped** (⊠ 347 5th Ave., Suite 610, New York, NY 10016, ☎ 212/447–7284, FAX 212/725–8253; membership $45); and **Travelin' Talk** (⊠ Box 3534, Clarksville, TN 37043, ☎ 615/552–6670, FAX 615/552–1182), which provides local contacts worldwide for travelers with disabilities.

TRAVELERS WITH VISION IMPAIRMENTS➤ Contact the **American Council of the Blind** (⊠ 1155 15th St. NW, Suite 720, Washington, DC 20005, ☎ 202/467–5081, FAX 202/467–5085) for a list of travelers' resources or the **American Foundation for the Blind** (⊠ 11 Penn Plaza, Suite 300, New York, NY 10001, ☎ 212/502–7600 or 800/232–5463, TTY 212/502–7662), which provides general advice and publishes "Access to Art" ($19.95), a directory of museums that accommodate travelers with vision impairments.

IN THE U.K.

Contact the **Royal Association for Disability and Rehabilitation** (⊠ RADAR, 12 City Forum, 250 City Rd.,

London EC1V 8AF, ☎ 0171/250–3222) or **Mobility International** (⊠ rue de Manchester 25, B-1080 Brussels, Belgium, ☎ 00–322–410–6297, FAX 00–322–410–6874), an international travel-information clearinghouse for people with disabilities.

PUBLICATIONS

Several publications for travelers with disabilities are available from the **Consumer Information Center** (⊠ Box 100, Pueblo, CO 81009, ☎ 719/948–3334). Call or write for its free catalog of current titles. The Society for the Advancement of Travel for the Handicapped (☞ Organizations, *above*) publishes the quarterly magazine **"Access to Travel"** ($13 for 1-year subscription).

Fodor's *Great American Vacations for Travelers with Disabilities* (available in bookstores, or ☎ 800/533–6478; $18) details accessible attractions, restaurants, and hotels in U.S. destinations. The 500-page *Travelin' Talk Directory* (⊠ Box 3534, Clarksville, TN 37043, ☎ 615/552–6670, FAX 615/552–1182; $35) lists people and organizations that help travelers with disabilities. For travel agents worldwide, consult the *Directory of Travel Agencies for the Disabled* (⊠ Twin Peaks Press, Box 129, Vancouver, WA 98666, ☎ 360/694–2462 or 800/637–2256, FAX 360/696–3210; $19.95 plus $3 shipping).

Access for All ($5), published by Hospital Audiences, Inc. (⊠ 220

W. 42nd St., 13th floor, 10036, ☎ 212/575–7660, TTY 212/575–7673), exhaustively covers New York City's cultural institutions.

TRAVEL AGENCIES & TOUR OPERATORS

The Americans with Disabilities Act requires that all travel firms serve the needs of all travelers. That said, you should note that some agencies and operators specialize in making travel arrangements for individuals and groups with disabilities, among them **Access Adventures** (⊠ 206 Chestnut Ridge Rd., Rochester, NY 14624, ☎ 716/889–9096), run by a former physical-rehab counselor.

TRAVELERS WITH MOBILITY PROBLEMS➤ Contact **Hinsdale Travel Service** (⊠ 201 E. Ogden Ave., Suite 100, Hinsdale, IL 60521, ☎ 708/325–1335, a travel agency that benefits from the advice of wheelchair traveler Janice Perkins; and **Wheelchair Journeys** (⊠ 16979 Redmond Way, Redmond, WA 98052, ☎ 206/885–2210 or 800/313–4751), which can handle arrangements worldwide.

TRAVELERS WITH DEVELOPMENTAL DISABILITIES➤ Contact the nonprofit **New Directions** (⊠ 5276 Hollister Ave., Suite 207, Santa Barbara, CA 93111, ☎ 805/967–2841) and **Sprout** (⊠ 893 Amsterdam Ave., New York, NY 10025, ☎ 212/222–9575), which specializes in custom-designed itineraries for groups but also books vacations for individual travelers.

TRAVEL GEAR

The **Magellan's** catalog (☎ 800/962–4943, FAX 805/568–5406) includes a range of products designed for travelers with disabilities.

DISCOUNTS & DEALS

AIRFARES

For the lowest airfares to New York, call 800/FLY–4–LESS. Also try 800/FLY–ASAP.

CLUBS

Contact **Entertainment Travel Editions** (✉ Box 1068, Trumbull, CT 06611, ☎ 800/445–4137; $28–$53, depending on destination), **Great American Traveler** (✉ Box 27965, Salt Lake City, UT 84127, ☎ 800/548–2812; $49.95 per year), **Moment's Notice Discount Travel Club** (✉ 7301 New Utrecht Ave., Brooklyn, NY 11204, ☎ 718/234–6295; $25 per year, single or family), **Privilege Card** (✉ 3391 Peachtree Rd. NE, Suite 110, Atlanta, GA 30326, ☎ 404/262–0222 or 800/236–9732; $74.95 per year), **Travelers Advantage** (✉ CUC Travel Service, 49 Music Sq. W, Nashville, TN 37203, ☎ 800/548–1116 or 800/648–4037; $49 per year, single or family), or **Worldwide Discount Travel Club** (✉ 1674 Meridian Ave., Miami Beach, FL 33139, ☎ 305/534–2082; $50 per year for family, $40 single).

HOTEL ROOMS

For discounts on hotel rates, contact **Express Hotel Reservations** (☎ 800/356–1123) or **Quickbook** (☎ 800/789–9887).

STUDENTS

Members of Hostelling International–American Youth Hostels (☞ Students, *below*) are eligible for discounts on car rentals, admissions to attractions, and other selected travel expenses.

PUBLICATIONS

Consult *The Frugal Globetrotter,* by Bruce Northam (✉ Fulcrum Publishing, 350 Indiana St., Suite 350, Golden, CO 80401, ☎ 800/992–2908; $15.95). For publications that tell how to find the lowest prices on plane tickets, *see* Air Travel, *above.*

E

EMERGENCIES

Dial 911 for **police, fire,** or **ambulance** in an emergency (TTY is available for the hearing impaired).

DOCTOR

Doctors On Call, 24-hour house-call service (☎ 212/737–2333). Near midtown, 24-hour emergency rooms are open at **St. Luke's-Roosevelt Hospital** (59th St. between 9th and 10th Aves., ☎ 212/523–6800) and **St. Vincent's Hospital** (7th Ave. and 11th St., ☎ 212/604–7997).

DENTIST

The **Dental Emergency Service** (☎ 212/679 3966 or 212/679–4172 after 8 PM) will make a referral.

HOT LINES

Victims' Services (☎ 212/577–7777), **Mental Health** (☎ 212/566–5222 or 800/527–7474 after 5 PM), **Sex Crimes Report Line** (☎ 212/267–7273).

24-HOUR PHARMACY

Kaufman's Pharmacy (Lexington Ave. and 50th St., ☎ 212/755–2266) is convenient, but its prices are exorbitant; **Genovese** (2nd Ave. at 68th St., ☎ 212/772–0104) is less expensive. Before 10 or 11 PM, look for a pharmacy in a neighborhood that keeps late hours, such as Greenwich Village or the Upper West Side for better deals.

ENTERTAINMENT

Call **Moviephone** (☎ 212/777–3456) to find out what movies are playing around town, including exact times and locations. Call **New York City On Stage** (☎ 212/768–1818) for up-to-the-minute information on tickets for theater, music, and dance performances.

G

GAY & LESBIAN TRAVEL

ORGANIZATIONS

The **International Gay Travel Association** (✉ Box 4974, Key West, FL 33041, ☎ 800/448–8550, FAX 305/296–6633), a consortium of more than 1,000 travel companies, can supply names of gay-friendly travel agents, tour operators, and accommodations.

THE GOLD GUIDE / IMPORTANT CONTACTS

PUBLICATIONS

Fodor's Gay Guide to the USA ($19.50; Fodor's Travel Publications, ☎ 800/533–6478 and in bookstores) covers the Big Apple in a detailed chapter.

Metro Source (✉ 180 Varick St., 5th floor, New York, NY 10014, ☎ 212/691–5127; $15 for 4 issues) has up-to-date news on gay- and lesbian-oriented hotels, restaurants, shops, and nightspots in New York City.

The premier international travel magazine for gays and lesbians is ***Our World*** (✉ 1104 N. Nova Rd., Suite 251, Daytona Beach, FL 32117, ☎ 904/441–5367, FAX 904/441–5604; $35 for 10 issues). The 16-page monthly newsletter ***"Out & About"*** (✉ 8 W. 19th St., Suite 401, New York, NY 10011, ☎ 212/645–6922 or 800/929–2268, FAX 800/929–2215; $49 for 10 issues and quarterly calendar) covers gay-friendly resorts, hotels, cruise lines, and airlines.

TOUR OPERATORS

Toto Tours (✉ 1326 W. Albion Ave., Suite 3W, Chicago, IL 60626, ☎ 312/274–8686 or 800/565–1241, FAX 312/274–8695) offers group tours to worldwide destinations.

TRAVEL AGENCIES

The largest agencies serving gay travelers are ***Advance Travel*** (✉ 10700 Northwest Fwy., Suite 160, Houston, TX 77092, ☎ 713/682–2002 or 800/292–0500), ***Islanders/Kennedy Travel*** (✉ 183 W. 10th St., New York, NY 10014, ☎ 212/242–3222 or 800/988–1181), ***Now Voyager*** (✉ 4406 18th St., San Francisco, CA 94114, ☎ 415/626–1169 or 800/255–6951), and ***Yellowbrick Road*** (✉ 1500 W. Balmoral Ave., Chicago, IL 60640, ☎ 312/561–1800 or 800/642–2488). ***Skylink Women's Travel*** (✉ 2460 W. 3rd St., Suite 215, Santa Rosa, CA 95401, ☎ 707/570–0105 or 800/225–5759) serves lesbian travelers.

I

INSURANCE

IN THE U.S.

Travel insurance covering baggage, health, and trip cancellation or interruptions is available from ***Access America*** (✉ 6600 W. Broad St., Richmond, VA 23230, ☎ 804/285–3300 or 800/334–7525), ***Carefree Travel Insurance*** (✉ Box 9366, 100 Garden City Plaza, Garden City, NY 11530, ☎ 516/294–0220 or 800/323–3149), ***Near Travel Services*** (✉ Box 1339, Calumet City, IL 60409, ☎ 708/868–6700 or 800/654–6700), ***Tele-Trip*** (✉ Mutual of Omaha Plaza, Box 31716, Omaha, NE 68131, ☎ 800/228–9792), ***Travel Guard International*** (✉ 1145 Clark St., Stevens Point, WI 54481, ☎ 715/345–0505 or 800/826–1300), ***Travel Insured International*** (✉ Box 280568, East Hartford, CT 06128, ☎ 203/528–7663 or 800/243–3174), and ***Wallach & Company*** (✉ 107 W. Federal St., Box 480, Middleburg, VA 22117, ☎ 540/687–3166 or 800/237–6615).

IN CANADA

Contact ***Mutual of Omaha*** (✉ Travel Division, 500 University Ave., Toronto, Ontario M5G 1V8, ☎ 800/465–0267 (in Canada) or 416/598-4083).

IN THE U.K.

The ***Association of British Insurers*** (✉ 51 Gresham St., London EC2V 7HQ, ☎ 0171/600–3333) gives advice by phone and publishes the free pamphlet ***"Holiday Insurance,"*** which sets out typical policy provisions and costs.

L

LIMOUSINES

Several recommended companies are ***All State Car and Limousine Service*** (☎ 212/741–7440); ***Bermuda Limousine International*** (☎ 212/249–8400); ***Carey Limousines*** (☎ 212/599–1122); ***Carmel Car and Limousine Service*** (☎ 212/662–2222); ***Chris Limousines*** (☎ 718/356–3232 or 800/542–1584); ***Concord Limousine Inc.*** (☎ 212/230–1600 or 800/255–7255); ***Eastside Limo Service*** (☎ 212/744–9700); ***Greenwich Limousine*** (☎ 800/385–1033); ***London Towncars*** (☎ 212/988–9700); and ***Sherwood Silver Bay Limousine Service*** (☎ 718/472–0183).

LODGING

APARTMENT & VILLA RENTAL

Among the companies to contact are ***Property Rentals International*** (✉ 1008 Mansfield Crossing Rd., Richmond, VA 23236, ☎ 804/378–6054 or

800/220–3332, FAX 804/379–2073) and **Rent-a-Home International** (⊠ 7200 34th Ave. NW, Seattle, WA 98117, ☎ 206/789–9377 or 800/488–7368, FAX 206/789–9379, hmaria@aol.com). Members of the travel club **Hideaways International** (⊠ 767 Islington St., Portsmouth, NH 03801, ☎ 603/430–4433 or 800/843–4433, FAX 603/430–4444; $99 per year) receive two annual guides plus quarterly newsletters and arrange rentals among themselves.

HOME EXCHANGE

Some of the principal clearinghouses are **HomeLink International/Vacation Exchange Club** (⊠ Box 650, Key West, FL 33041, ☎ 305/294–1448 or 800/638–3841, FAX 305/294–1148; $70 per year), which sends members three annual directories, with a listing in one, plus updates; **Intervac International** (⊠ Box 590504, San Francisco, CA 94159, ☎ 415/435–3497, FAX 415/435–7440; $65 per year), which publishes four annual directories.

M

MONEY

ATMS

For specific **Cirrus** locations in the United States and Canada, call 800/424–7787. For U.S. **Plus** locations, call 800/843–7587 and enter the area code and first three digits of the number from which you're calling (or of the calling area in which

you want to locate an ATM).

CURRENCY EXCHANGE

Foreign travelers visiting New York can exchange foreign currency and traveler's checks at a number of offices around Manhattan. Large banks—Chase Manhattan, Chemical, and Citibank, for example—accommodate travelers during weekday business hours. Other companies provide exchange services up to seven days a week and often quote rates over the phone. They include:

American Express Travel Service (822 Lexington Ave., ☎ 212/758–6510; Bloomingdale's, 59th St. and Lexington Ave., ☎ 212/705–3171; 150 E. 42nd St., ☎ 212/687–3700; 374 Park Ave., ☎ 212/421–8240; American Express Tower, 200 Vesey St., ☎ 212/640–5130; Macy's Herald Sq., 151 W. 34th St., ☎ 212/695–8075). Hours vary among locations.

Chequepoint USA (609 Madison Ave., between 57th and 58th Sts., ☎ 212/750–2255, ◷ Weekdays 8–8, Sat. 9:30–8, Sun. 10–7; 22 Central Park S at 59th St., ☎ 212/750–2400, ◷ Daily 8–8; 1568 Broadway at 47th St., ☎ 212/869–6281, ◷ Weekdays and Sat. 9–10:30, Sun. 9–7; and 708 7th Ave. ☎ 212/262–1030, ◷ Sun.–Thurs. 9–7, Fri.–Sat. 9–10:30.

Harold Reuter & Co. (Metropolitan Life Building, 200 Park Ave., Room 332 E, 3rd Floor,

☎ 212/661–0826, ◷ Weekdays 8–4; Stern's, 32nd St. and 6th Ave., 6th Floor, ☎ 212/268–8517, ◷ Mon.–Sat., 10–6, Sun. 11–6; Grand Central Terminal, 42nd St., between Vanderbilt and Lexington Aves., ☎ 212/661–7600, ◷ Weekdays 7–7, Sat. 8–3).

New York Foreign Exchange (61 Broadway, Suite 805, ☎ 212/248–4700, ◷ Weekdays 9–5).

People's Foreign Exchange (19 W. 44th St., Suite 306, ☎ 212/944–6780, ◷ Weekdays 9–6 and weekends 10–3).

Thomas Cook Currency Service (511 Madison Ave., ☎ 212/757–6915, ◷ Mon.–Sat. 9–5; 41 E. 42nd St., ☎ 212/883–0400, ◷ Weekdays and Sat. 9–5; 29 Broadway, ☎ 212/363–6208, ◷ Weekdays 9–5; 1271 Broadway, ☎ 212/679–4365, ◷ Mon.–Sat. 10–6; and 1590 Broadway, ☎ 212/265–6049, ◷ Mon.–Sat. 9–7, Sun. 9–5). There are also seven branch offices in JFK International Airport.

P

PACKING

For strategies on packing light, get a copy of **The Packing Book,** by Judith Gilford (⊠ Ten Speed Press, Box 7123, Berkeley, CA 94707, ☎ 510/559–1600 or 800/841–2665, FAX 510/524–4588; $7.95).

PASSPORTS & VISAS

U.K. CITIZENS

For fees, documentation requirements, and to

request an emergency passport, call the **London Passport Office** (☎ 0990/210–410). For U.S. visa information, call the **U.S. Embassy Visa Information Line** (☎ 01891/200–290; calls cost 49p per minute or 39p per minute cheap rate) or send a self-addressed, stamped envelope to the **U.S. Embassy Visa Branch** (✉ 5 Upper Grosvenor St., London W1A 2JB). If you live in Northern Ireland, write to the **U.S. Consulate General** (✉ Queen's House, Queen St., Belfast BTI 6EO).

The **Kodak Information Center** (☎ 800/242–2424) answers consumer questions about film and photography. The *Kodak Guide to Shooting Great Travel Pictures* (available in bookstores; or contact Fodor's Travel Publications, ☎ 800/533–6478; $16.50) explains how to take expert travel photographs.

S

"Trouble-Free Travel," from the AAA, is a booklet of tips for protecting yourself and your belongings when you're away from home. Send a stamped, self-addressed, legal-size envelope to Flying Alone (✉ Mail Stop 75, 1000 AAA Dr., Heathrow, FL 32746).

EDUCATIONAL TRAVEL

The nonprofit **Elderhostel** (✉ 75 Federal St., 3rd Floor, Boston, MA 02110, ☎ 617/426–

7788), for people 60 and older, has offered inexpensive study programs since 1975. Courses cover everything from marine science to Greek mythology and cowboy poetry. Fees for programs in the United States and Canada, which usually last one week, run about $300, not including transportation.

ORGANIZATIONS

Contact the **American Association of Retired Persons** (✉ AARP, 601 E St. NW, Washington, DC 20049, ☎ 202/434–2277; annual dues $8 per person or couple). Its Purchase Privilege Program secures discounts for members on lodging, car rentals, and sightseeing, and the AARP Motoring Plan (☎ 800/334–3300) furnishes domestic triprouting information and emergency roadservice aid for an annual fee of $39.95 ($59.95 for a premium version).

Additional sources for discounts on lodgings, car rentals, and other travel expenses, as well as helpful magazines and newsletters, are the **National Council of Senior Citizens** (✉ 1331 F St. NW, Washington, DC 20004, ☎ 202/347–8800; annual membership $12) and Sears's **Mature Outlook** (✉ Box 10448, Des Moines, IA 50306, ☎ 800/336–6330; annual membership $9.95).

PUBLICATIONS

The 50+ Traveler's Guidebook: Where to Go, Where to Stay, What to Do, by Anita Williams

and Merrimac Dillon (✉ St. Martin's Press, 175 5th Ave., New York, NY 10010, ☎ 212/674–5151 or 800/288–2131; $13.95), offers many useful tips. **"The Mature Traveler"** (✉ Box 50400, Reno, NV 89513, ☎ 702/786–7419; $29.95), a monthly newsletter, covers all sorts of travel deals.

BOAT TOURS

One of the best ways to get a crash orientation to Manhattan is aboard a **Circle Line Cruise** (✉ Pier 83, west end of 42nd St., ☎ 212/563–3200). Once you've finished the three-hour, 35-mile circumnavigation of Manhattan, you'll have a good idea of where things are and what you want to see next. Narrations are as interesting and individualized as the guides who deliver them. The fare is $18. The Circle Line operates daily March–mid-December.

For a shorter excursion, **Express Navigation's** hydroliner (✉ Pier 11, 2 blocks south of South St. Seaport, ☎ 800/262–8743) will show you the island of Manhattan in 75 minutes. The fare is $15. Boats depart April–September weekdays and Saturday at noon and 2 PM.

The Spirit of New York (✉ Pier 62, at W. 23rd St. and 12th Ave. on the Hudson River, ☎ 212/742–7278) sails on lunch ($29–$34), dinner ($53–$65), and moonlight cocktail ($20) cruises.

World Yacht Cruises
(✉ Pier 81, W. 41st St.
at Hudson River, ☎
212/630–8100) serves
Sunday brunch ($39)
on two-hour cruises,
and dinner (Sun.–Fri.
$62; Sat. $75; drinks
extra) on three-hour
cruises. The Continental
cuisine is restaurant
quality, and there's
music and dancing on
board. The cruises run
daily year-round,
weather permitting.

At South Street Sea-
port's Pier 16 you can
take hour-and-a-half-
or three-hour voyages to
New York's past aboard
the cargo schooner
Pioneer (☎ 212/748–
8786); cruises depart
daily May–September.
Seaport Liberty Cruises
(☎ 212/630–8888) also
offers daily, hour-long
sightseeing tours of New
York Harbor and Lower
Manhattan, as well as
two-hour cruises with
live jazz and blues on
Wednesday and Thurs-
day nights. Boats run
between March and
December.

BUS TOURS

Gray Line New York
(✉ 900 8th Ave., ☎
212/397–2620) offers
a taste of yesteryear
with its "NY Trolley
Tour" on coaches
replicating New York
trolleys of the '30s, in
addition to a number
of standard city bus
tours in various lan-
guages, plus cruises
and day trips to At-
lantic City. On week-
days between May and
October, Gray Line's
**Central Park Trolley
Tour** tempts visitors to
explore parts of the
park that even native
New Yorkers may
never have seen.

**New York Doubledecker
Tours** (✉ Empire State
Building at 34th St. and
5th Ave., ☎ 212/967–
6008) runs authentic
London double-deck
buses year-round, 9–6
in summer, 10–3 in
winter, making stops
every 15–30 minutes at
the Empire State Build-
ing, Greenwich Village,
SoHo, Chinatown, the
World Trade Center,
Battery Park, the South
Street Seaport, the
United Nations, and
Central Park. Tickets,
which are valid for
boarding and reboard-
ing all day for two
days, cost $15 and can
be purchased at the
Empire State Building.
An uptown loop, which
costs $25, makes stops
at Lincoln Center, the
Museum of Natural
History, Harlem, Mu-
seum Mile, and Central
Park. Hop on and off to
visit attractions as often
as you like.

New York Visions (✉
Broadway and W. 53rd
St., 10019 ☎ 212/956–
0517) has tours ranging
from two to nine hours,
including "New York
Lights at Night,"
featuring dinner in
Chinatown, a tour of
downtown New York,
and a glittering skyline
from the Empire State
Building.

HELICOPTER TOURS

Island Helicopter (✉
Heliport at E. 34th St.
and East River, ☎ 212/
683–4575) offers four
fly-over options, from
$44 per person (for
7 miles) to $129 per
person (for 34 miles).

From the West Side,
Liberty Helicopter Tours
(✉ Heliport at W. 30th
St. and Hudson River,
☎ 212/465–8905) has

four tours ranging from
$45 to $129 per person.

SPECIAL-INTEREST
TOURS

Art Tours of Manhattan
(☎ 609/921–2647) ·
custom-designs walking
tours of museum and
gallery exhibits as well
as artists' studios and
lofts.

Backstage on Broadway
(☎ 212/575–8065) is
a talk about the Broad-
way theater held in an
actual theater, given by
a theater professional.
Reservations are manda-
tory; tour groups of 25
or more only.

Bite of the Apple Tours
(☎ 212/541–8759 or
212/603–9750) orga-
nizes two-hour-long
bicycle trips through
Central Park with
several stops along the
way, including Straw-
berry Fields and the
Belvedere Castle.

**Gracie Mansion Conser-
vancy Tour** (☎ 212/
570–4751) will show
you the 1799 house,
official residence of New
York City mayors since
1942. The mansion is
open to the public on
Wednesdays; reserva-
tions are mandatory.

Grand Central Station
(☎ 212/986–9217)
provides the setting for
architectural tours that
take you high above the
crowds and into the
Beaux Arts building's
rafters.

Harlem Your Way!
(☎ 212/690–1687),
Harlem Spirituals, Inc.
(☎ 212/757–0425),
and **Penny Sightseeing
Harlem Tours** (☎ 212/
410–0080) offer bus
and walking tours and
Sunday gospel trips to
Harlem. Also, in

Harlem, you can trace the history of jazz backstage at the **Apollo Theater** (☎ 212/222–0992).

Louis Singer (☎ 718/875–9084), an encyclopedia of New York trivia, provides tours of Brooklyn and Manhattan, including a "Noshing in Brooklyn/Manhattan" tour.

The **Lower East Side Tenement Museum** (☎ 212/431–0233) offers tours through former immigrant communities.

Madison Square Garden (☎ 212/465–6080) has tours of the sports mecca's inner workings.

Manhattan Tours (☎ 212/563–2570) leads customized, behind-the-scenes tours inside fashion and interior-design showrooms, theaters, restaurants, and artists' lofts.

The **Metropolitan Opera House Backstage** (☎ 212/769–7020) offers a tour of the scenery and costume shops, stage area, and rehearsal facilities.

Radio City Music Hall Productions (☎ 212/632–4041) schedules behind-the-scenes tours of the theater.

River to River Downtown Walking Tours (☎ 212/321–2823) specializes in lower Manhattan for two-hour walking tours.

Rock and Roll Tours of New York (☎ 212/941–9464) visits the places where rock stars hung out, recorded, lived, and died.

Sax & Company (☎ 212/832–0350) tours include visits to museums, theaters, and artists' studios and private collections.

The **South Street Seaport Museum** (☎ 212/748-8590) has tours of historic ships and the waterfront, as well as predawn forays through the bustling Fulton Fish Market.

WALKING TOURS

Adventure on a Shoestring (☎ 212/265–2663) is an organization dating from 1963 that explores New York neighborhoods. Tours are scheduled periodically and cost $5 per person.

Big Onion Walking Tours (☎ 212/439–1090) has theme tours: try "From Naples to Bialystock to Beijing: A Multi-Ethnic Eating Tour."

Citywalks (☎ 212/989–2456) offers two-hour walking tours exploring various neighborhoods in depth; weekends at 1 PM for $12.

The **Municipal Art Society** (☎ 212/935–3960) operates a series of bus and walking tours on both weekdays and weekends. Weekday tours highlight the city's architecture and history.

The **Museum of the City of New York** (☎ 212/534–1672) sponsors primarily architectural walking tours on Sunday afternoons.

New York City Cultural Walking Tours (☎ 212/979–2388) focuses on the city's architecture, landmarks, memorials, outdoor art, and historic sites, including 5th Avenue's "Millionaires' Mile."

The **92nd Street Y** (☎ 212/996–1100) often has something special to offer on weekends and some weekdays.

Sidewalks of New York (☎ 212/517–0201) hits the streets from various thematic angles—"Famous Murder Sites" and "Greenwich Village Ghost" tours—on weekends year-round and daily May–Sept.; tours are also available by appointment.

Urban Explorations (☎ 718/721-5254) runs tours with an emphasis on architecture and urban planning; Chinatown is a specialty.

The **Urban Park Rangers** (☎ 212/427–4040) offer free weekend walks and workshops in city parks.

Walks of the Town (☎ 212/222–5343) strolls through neighborhoods of historic and architectural interest; tours are available by appointment only.

Among other knowledgeable walking-tour guides are **Joyce Gold** (☎ 212/242–5762), whose many history tours include "The Vital Heart of Harlem," "Colonial New York: The Financial District," and "When China and Italy Moved to New York"; and **Arthur Marks** (☎ 212/673–0477), who creates customized tours on which he sings about the city.

SELF-GUIDED WALKING TOURS

A free "Walking Tour of Rockefeller Center"

pamphlet is available from the information desk in the lobby of the **GE Building** (30 Rockefeller Plaza).

Heritage Trails New York (☎ 212/767–0637) is a wanderer's version of connect-the-dots. Four color-coded sidewalk trails wind through the downtown area, guiding visitors to the New York Stock Exchange, Trinity Church, and other points of interest.

Guides-on-Tape (✉ 21 E. 90th St., Suite 7B, New York, NY 10128, ☎ 212/289–8805, $9.95 per tape) will lead you on a tour of Greenwich Village's colorful past.

Another option is to pop one of the **Talk-a-Walk** cassettes (✉ Sound Publishers, 30 Waterside Plaza, New York, NY 10010-26301, ☎ 212/686–0356; $9.95 per tape, plus $2.90 packing and shipping for up to four tapes) into your Walkman and start strolling to an in-your-ear history of lower Manhattan or the Brooklyn Bridge.

GROUPS

A major tour operator specializing in student travel is **Contiki Holidays** (✉ 300 Plaza Alicante, Suite 900, Garden Grove, CA 92640, ☎ 714/740–0808 or 800/466–0610).

HOSTELING

In the United States, contact **Hostelling International–American Youth Hostels** (✉ 733 15th St. NW, Suite 840, Washington, DC 20005, ☎ 202/783–6161 or 800/444–6111 for reservations at selected hostels, FAX 202/783–6171); in Canada, **Hostelling International–Canada** (✉ 205 Catherine St., Suite 400, Ottawa, Ontario K2P 1C3, ☎ 613/237–7884); and in the United Kingdom, the **Youth Hostel Association of England and Wales** (✉ Trevelyan House, 8 St. Stephen's Hill, St. Albans, Hertfordshire AL1 2DY, ☎ 01727/855215 or 01727/845047). Membership (in the U.S., $25; in Canada, C$26.75; in the U.K., £9.30) gives you access to 5,000 hostels in 77 countries that charge $5–$30 per person per night.

ID CARDS

To be eligible for discounts on transportation and admissions, get either the **International Student Identity Card,** if you're a bona fide student, or the **GO 25: International Youth Travel Card,** if you're not a student but are under age 26. Each includes basic travel-accident and illness coverage, plus a toll-free travel hot line. In the United States, either card costs $18; apply through the Council on International Educational Exchange (☞ Organizations, *below*). In Canada, cards are available for $15 each ($16 by mail) from Travel Cuts (☞ Organizations, *below*), and in the United Kingdom for £5 each at student unions and student travel companies.

ORGANIZATIONS

A major contact is the **Council on International**

Educational Exchange (✉ mail orders only: CIEE, 205 E. 42nd St., 16th Floor, New York, NY 10017, ☎ 212/661–1450, info@ciee.org), with walk-in locations in Boston (✉ 729 Boylston St., 02116, ☎ 617/266–1926), Miami (✉ 9100 S. Dadeland Blvd., 33156, ☎ 305/670–9261), Los Angeles (✉ 10904 Lindbrook Dr., 90024, ☎ 310/208–3551), 43 other college towns in the United States, and in the United Kingdom (✉ 28A Poland St., London W1V 3DB, ☎ 0171/437–7767). Twice per year, it publishes *Student Travels* magazine.

The **Educational Travel Centre** (✉ 438 N. Frances St., Madison, WI 53703, ☎ 608/256–5551 or 800/747–5551, FAX 608/256–2042) offers rail passes and low-cost airline tickets, mostly for flights that depart from Chicago.

In Canada, contact **Travel Cuts** (✉ 187 College St., Toronto, Ontario M5T 1P7, ☎ 416/979–2406 or 800/667–2887).

For information about routes, schedules, and hours of operation, call the **MTA** (☎ 718/330–1234) daily 6–9.

T

Among the companies that sell tours and packages to New York, the following are nationally known, have a proven reputation, and offer plenty of options.

GROUP TOURS

DELUXE➤ **Globus** (⊠ 5301 S. Federal Circle, Littleton, CO 80123-2980, ☎ 303/797-2800 or 800/221-0090, FAX 303/795-0962), **Maupintour** (⊠ Box 807, Lawrence, KS 66047, ☎ 913/843-1211 or 800/255-4266, FAX 913/843-8351), and **Tauck Tours** (⊠ Box 5027, 276 Post Rd. W, Westport, CT 06881, ☎ 203/226-6911 or 800/468-2825, FAX 203/221-6828).

FIRST CLASS➤ **Collette Tours** (⊠ 162 Middle St., Pawtucket, RI 02860, ☎ 401/728-3805 or 800/832-4656, FAX 401/728-1380), **Gadabout Tours** (⊠ 700 E. Tahquitz Canyon Way, Palm Springs, CA 92262, ☎ 619/325-5556 or 800/952-5068), and **Mayflower Tours** (⊠ Box 490, 1225 Warren Ave., Downers Grove, IL 60515, ☎ 708/960-3430 or 800/323-7064).

BUDGET➤ **Cosmos** (☞ Globus, *above*).

PACKAGES

Independent vacation packages to New York are available from **Adventure Vacations** (⊠ 10612 Beaver Dam Rd., Hunt Valley, MD 21030-2205, ☎ 410/785-3500 or 800/638-9040, FAX 410/584-2771), **Continental Vacations** (☎ 800/634-5555), **Delta Dream Vacations** (☎ 800/872-7786), **SuperCities** (⊠ 139 Main St., Cambridge, MA 02142, ☎ 800/333-1234 or 617/621-9911), **United**

Vacations (☎ 800/328-6877), and **USAir Vacations** (☎ 800/455-0123). **Gogo Tours**, based in Ramsey, New Jersey, sells tours to New York City only through travel agents. For rail packages that combine air, hotel, and tour options, contact **Amtrak's Great American Vacations** (☎ 800/321-8684).

FROM THE U.K.

Tour operators offering packages to New York City include **Americana Vacations Ltd.** (⊠ Morley House, 320 Regent St., London W1R 5AD, ☎ 0171/637-7853), **Jetsave** (⊠ Sussex House, London Rd., East Grinstead, West Sussex RH19 1LD, ☎ 01342/312033), **Key to America** (⊠ 1-3 Station Rd., Ashford, Middlesex, TW15 2UW, ☎ 01784/248-777), **Premier Holidays** (⊠ Westbrook, Milton Rd., Cambridge CB4 1YQ, ☎ 01223/516-688), **Trailfinders** (⊠ 42-50 Earls Court Rd., London W8 6FT, ☎ 0171/937-5400; ⊠ 58 Deansgate, Manchester M3 2FF, ☎ 0161/839-6969), and **Travelpack** (⊠ Clarendon House, Clarendon Rd., Eccles, Manchester M30 9AL, ☎ 0990/747-101).

Travel agencies that offer cheap fares to New York City include **Trailfinders** (⊠ 42-50 Earls Court Rd., London W8 6FT, ☎ 0171/937-5400), **Travel Cuts** (⊠ 295a Regent St., London W1R 7YA, ☎ 0171/637-3161; ☞ Students, *above*), and **Flightfile** (⊠ 49 Tottenham Court Rd.,

London W1P 9RE, ☎ 0171/700-2722).

THEME TRIPS

PERFORMING ARTS➤ Contact **Dailey-Thorp Travel** (⊠ 330 W. 58th St., #610, New York, NY 10019-1817, ☎ 212/307-1555 or 800/998-4677, FAX 212/974-1420) and **Keith Prowse Tours** (⊠ 234 W. 44th St., #1000, New York, NY 10036, ☎ 212/398-1430 or 800/669-8687, FAX 212/302-4251. Also try **Sutherland Hit Show Tours** (⊠ 370 Lexington Ave., #411, New York, NY 10017, ☎ 212/532-7732 or 800/221-2442, FAX 212/532-7741).

TENNIS➤ For packages that include tickets to September's U.S. Open tennis championship, call **Championship Tennis Tours** (⊠ 7350 E. Stetson Dr., #106, Scottsdale, AZ 85251, 85251, ☎ 602/990-8760 or 800/468-3664, FAX 602/990-8744), **Esoteric Sports Tours** (⊠ 3450 Breckinridge Blvd., #1624, Duluth, GA 30136, ☎ 800/321-8008, FAX 770/921-8009), **Spectacular Sport Specials** (⊠ 5813 Citrus Blvd., New Orleans, LA 70123-5810, ☎ 504/734-9511 or 800/451-5772, FAX 504/734-7075), and **Steve Furgal's International Tennis Tours** (⊠ 11828 Rancho Bernardo Rd., #123-305, San Diego, CA 92128, ☎ 619/487-7777 or 800/258-3664).

ORGANIZATIONS

The **National Tour Association** (⊠ NTA, 546 E. Main St., Lexington, KY 40508, ☎ 606/226–4444 or 800/755–8687) and the **United States Tour Operators Association** (✉ USTOA, 211 E. 51st St., Suite 12B, New York, NY 10022, ☎ 212/750–7371) can provide lists of members and information on booking tours.

PUBLICATIONS

Contact the USTOA (☞ Organizations, *above*) for its **"Smart Traveler's Planning Kit."** Also get a copy of the Better Business Bureau's **"Tips on Travel Packages"** (✉ Publication 24-195, 4200 Wilson Blvd., Arlington, VA 22203; $2). The National Tour Association will send you **"On Tour,"** a listing of its member operators, and a personalized package of information on group travel in North America.

TRAIN TRAVEL

For schedules and information on national and regional rail service to New York City, contact **Amtrak** (☎ 800/872–7245), the **Long Island Railroad** (☎ 718/217–5477), **Metro-North Commuter Railroad** (☎ 212/340–3000), **New Jersey Transit** (☎ 201/762–5100),

and **PATH** (☎ 800/234–7284).

TRAVEL GEAR

For travel apparel, appliances, personal-care items, and other travel necessities, get a free catalog from **Magellan's** (☎ 800/962–4943, FAX 805/568–5406), **Orvis Travel** (☎ 800/541–3541, FAX 703/343–7053), or **TravelSmith** (☎ 800/950–1600, FAX 415/455–0554).

TRAVEL AGENCIES

For names of reputable agencies in your area, contact the **American Society of Travel Agents** (✉ ASTA, 1101 King St., Suite 200, Alexandria, VA 22314, ☎ 703/739–2782), the **Association of Canadian Travel Agents** (✉ Suite 201, 1729 Bank St., Ottawa, Ontario K1V 7Z5, ☎ 613/521–0474, FAX 613/521–0805), or the **Association of British Travel Agents** (✉ 55-57 Newman St., London W1P 4AH, ☎ 0171/637–2444, FAX 0171/637–0713).

V

VISITOR

INFORMATION

The **New York Convention and Visitors Bureau** (✉ 2 Columbus Circle, New York, NY 10019,

☎ 212/397–8222 or 212/484–1200, FAX 212/484–1280) is open weekdays 9–6, weekends and holidays 10–3. The **New York State Division of Tourism** (✉ 1 Commerce Plaza, Albany, NY 12245, ☎ 518/474–4116 or 800/225–5697) offers a free series of "I Love New York" booklets listing New York City attractions and tour packages.

In the United Kingdom, also contact the Port Authority of New York and New Jersey (☎ 0171/481–8909, FAX 0171/265–0674).

W

WEATHER

For current conditions and forecasts, plus the local time and helpful travel tips, call the **Weather Channel Connection** (☎ 900/932–8437; 95¢ per minute) from a Touch-Tone phone.

The **International Traveler's Weather Guide** (✉ Weather Press, Box 660606, Sacramento, CA 95866, ☎ 916/974–0201 or 800/972–0201; $10.95 includes shipping), written by two meteorologists, provides month-by-month information.

SMART TRAVEL TIPS A TO Z

*Basic Information on Traveling in New York &
Savvy Tips to Make Your Trip a Breeze*

A

AIR TRAVEL

If time is an issue, **always look for nonstop flights,** which require no change of plane. If possible, **avoid connecting flights,** which stop at least once and can involve a change of plane, even though the flight number remains the same; if the first leg is late, the second waits.

For better service, **fly smaller or regional carriers,** which often have higher passenger-satisfaction ratings. Sometimes they have such in-flight amenities as leather seats or greater legroom, and they often have better food.

CUTTING COSTS

MAJOR AIRLINES➤ The least-expensive airfares from the major airlines are priced for round-trip travel and are subject to restrictions. Usually, you must **book in advance and buy the ticket within 24 hours** to get cheaper fares, and you may have to **stay over a Saturday night.** The lowest fare is subject to availability, and only a small percentage of the plane's total seats is sold at that price. It's smart to **call a number of airlines,** and **when you are quoted a good price, book it on the spot**—the same fare may not be available on the same flight the next day. Airlines generally allow you to change your return date for a $25 to $50 fee. If you don't use your ticket, you can apply the cost toward the purchase of a new ticket, again for a small charge. However, most low-fare tickets are nonrefundable. To get the lowest airfare, **check different routings.** If your destination has more than one gateway, **compare prices to different airports.**

FROM THE U.K.➤ To save money on flights, **look into an APEX or Super-Pex ticket.** APEX tickets must be booked in advance and have certain restrictions. Super-PEX tickets can be purchased right at the airport.

ALOFT

AIRLINE FOOD➤ If you hate airline food, **ask for special meals when booking.** These can be vegetarian, low-cholesterol, or kosher, for example; commonly prepared to order in smaller quantities than standard fare, they can be tastier.

SMOKING➤ Smoking is banned on all flights of less than six hours' duration within the United States and on all Canadian flights; the ban also applies to domestic segments of international flights aboard U.S. and foreign carriers. Delta has banned smoking system-wide. On U.S. carriers flying to New York and other destinations abroad, a seat in a no-smoking section must be provided for every passenger who requests one, and the section must be enlarged to accommodate such passengers as long as they have complied with the airline's deadline for check-in and seat assignment. If smoking bothers you, request a seat far from the smoking section.

AIRPORT TRANSFERS

LA GUARDIA AIRPORT➤ Taxis cost $17–$29 plus tolls (which may be as high as $4) and take 20–40 minutes. Group taxi rides to Manhattan are available at taxi dispatch lines just outside the baggage-claim areas during most travel hours (except on Saturday and holidays). Group fares run $9–$10 per person (plus a share of tolls).

Carey Airport Express buses depart for Manhattan every 20 minutes from 6 AM to midnight, from all terminals. It's a 40-minute ride to 42nd Street and Park Avenue, directly opposite Grand Central Terminal. The bus continues from there to the Port Authority Bus Terminal, the New York Hilton, Sheraton Manhattan, Holiday Inn Crowne Plaza, and Marriott Marquis hotels. Other midtown hotels are a short cab ride away. The bus fare is $9; pay the driver. The Gray Line Air Shuttle

Minibus serves major Manhattan hotels directly to and from the airport. The fare is $13 per person; make arrangements at the airport's ground transportation center or use the courtesy phone.

The most economical way to reach Manhattan is to ride the M-60 bus (there are no luggage facilities on this bus) to 116th Street and Broadway, across from Columbia University. From there, you can catch the No. 1 or 9 subway to midtown. Alternatively, you can take the Q-33 bus to either the Roosevelt Avenue–Jackson Heights station, where you can catch the E or F subway, or the 74th Street–Broadway station, where you can catch the No. 7 subway. Allow 90 minutes for the entire trip to midtown; the total cost is two tokens ($3.00). You can use exact change for your bus fare, but you will have to purchase a token to enter the subway.

JFK INTERNATIONAL AIRPORT➤ Taxis cost $30–$38 plus tolls (which may be as much as $4) and take 35–60 minutes.

Carey Airport Express buses depart for Manhattan every 30 minutes from 6 AM to midnight, from all JFK terminals. The ride to 42nd Street and Park Avenue (Grand Central Terminal) takes about one hour. The bus continues from there to the Port Authority Bus Terminal, the New York Hilton, Sheraton Manhattan, Holiday Inn Crowne

Plaza, and Marriott Marquis hotels; it's a short cab ride to other midtown hotels. The bus fare is $13; pay the driver.

The Gray Line Air Shuttle Minibus serves major Manhattan hotels directly from the airport; the cost is $16 per person. Make arrangements at the airport's ground transportation counter or use the courtesy phone.

New York Helicopter offers private charter flights between the airport and the heliport at East 34th Street and the East River. Helicopters leave from the General Aviation Terminal and set you down in Manhattan 10 minutes later. The one-way fare is $299–$495.

The cheapest but slowest means of getting to Manhattan is to take the Port Authority's free shuttle bus, which stops at all terminals, to the Howard Beach subway station, where you can catch the A train into Manhattan. Alternatively, you can take the Q-10 bus (there are no luggage facilities on this bus) to the Union Turnpike–Kew Gardens station, where you can catch the E or F subway. Or you can take the B-15 bus to New Lots station and catch the No. 3 subway. Allow at least two hours for the trip; the total cost is one token ($1.50) if you use the shuttle or two tokens ($3) if you use the Q-10 or B-15. You can use exact change for your fare on the Q-10 and B-15, but you will need to pur-

chase a token to enter the subway.

NEWARK AIRPORT➤ Taxis cost $34–$38 plus tolls ($10) and take 20–45 minutes. "Share and Save" group rates are available for up to four passengers between 8 AM and midnight; make arrangements with the airport's taxi dispatcher.

NJ Transit Airport Express buses depart for the Port Authority Bus Terminal, at 8th Avenue and 42nd Street every 15 minutes from 6 AM to midnight and every hour thereafter. From there, it's a short cab ride to midtown hotels. The ride takes 30–45 minutes. The fare is $7; buy your ticket inside the airport terminal.

Olympia Airport Express buses leave for Grand Central Terminal, Penn Station, and 1 World Trade Center (WTC) about every 30 minutes from around 6 AM to midnight. The trip takes 35–45 minutes to Grand Central and Penn Station, 20 minutes to WTC. The fare is $7.

The Gray Line Air Shuttle Minibus serves major Manhattan hotels directly to and from the airport. You pay $18 per passenger; make arrangements at the airport's ground transportation center or use the courtesy phone.

If you are arriving in Newark, you can take New Jersey Transit's Airlink buses, which leave every 20 minutes from 6:15 AM to 2 AM, to Penn Station in Newark. The

THE GOLD GUIDE / SMART TRAVEL TIPS

ride takes about 20 minutes; the fare is $4. From there, your can catch PATH Trains, which run to Manhattan 24 hours a day. The trains run every 10 minutes on weekdays, every 15–30 minutes on weeknights, every 20–30 minutes on weekends, and stop at the WTC and at five stops along 6th Avenue—Christopher Street, 9th Street, 14th Street, 23rd Street, and 33rd Street. The fare is $1.

CAR SERVICES➤ Car services are a great deal, because the driver will often meet you on the concourse or in the baggage-claim area and help you with your luggage. You ride in late-model American-made cars that are comfortable, if usually a bit worn. New York City Taxi and Limousine Commission rules require that all be licensed and pick up riders only by prior arrangement. Call 24 hours in advance for reservations, or at least a half day before your flight's departure.

B

BUS TRAVEL

Most buses follow easy-to-understand routes along the Manhattan grid. Routes go up or down the north–south avenues, or east and west on the major two-way crosstown streets. Most bus routes operate 24 hours, but service is infrequent late at night. Buses are great for sightseeing, but traffic jams—a potential threat at any time or place in Manhattan—can make

rides maddeningly slow. Certain bus routes now offer "Limited-Stop Service"; buses on these routes stop only at major cross streets and transfer points and can save traveling time. The "Limited-Stop" buses usually run on weekdays and during rush hours.

Bus fare is the same as subway fare: $1.50 at press time, in coins (no change is given) or a subway token or Metro-Card (by the end of 1996, all buses will accept MetroCards). When you get on the bus, you can ask the driver for a free transfer coupon, good for one change to an intersecting route. Legal transfer points are listed on the back of the slip. Transfers have time limits of at least two hours, often longer. You cannot use the transfer to enter the subway system.

Route maps and schedules are posted at many bus stops in Manhattan and at major stops throughout the other boroughs. Each of the five boroughs of New York has a separate bus map, and they are scarcer than hens' teeth. They are available from some subway token booths, but never on buses. The best places to obtain them are the Convention and Visitors Bureau at Columbus Circle or the information kiosks in Grand Central Terminal and Penn Station.

BUSINESS HOURS

New York is very much a 24-hour city. Its subways and buses run around the clock, and plenty of services

are available at all hours and on all days of the week. It's always a good idea to check ahead.

Banks are open weekdays 9–3 or 9–3:30, although a few branches in certain neighborhoods may stay open late on Friday or open on Saturday morning.

Post offices are generally open weekdays 10–5 or 10–6. The main post office on 8th Avenue between 31st and 33rd streets is open daily 24 hours.

Museum hours vary greatly, but most of the major ones are open Tuesday–Sunday and keep later hours on Tuesday or Thursday evenings.

Stores are generally open Monday–Saturday from 10 AM to 5 or 6 PM, but neighborhood peculiarities do exist. Most stores on the Lower East Side and in the diamond district on 47th Street close on Friday afternoon and all day Saturday for the Jewish Sabbath while keeping normal hours on Sunday. Sunday hours, also common on the West Side and in Greenwich Village and SoHo, are the exception on the Upper East Side.

C

CAMERAS, CAMCORDERS, & COMPUTERS

LAPTOPS

Before you depart, **check your portable computer's battery;** at security you may be asked to turn on the computer to prove that it is what it appears to be. At the airport, you may prefer to **request a manual inspection,** although security X-rays do not harm hard-disk or floppy-disk storage.

PHOTOGRAPHY

The chances of your film growing cloudy increase with each pass through an X-ray machine. To protect against this, carry it in a clear plastic bag and **ask for hand inspection at security.** Don't depend on a lead-lined bag to protect film in checked luggage—the airline may increase the radiation to see what's inside.

VIDEO

Be prepared to turn on the camcorder for airport security personnel to prove that it's what it appears to be.

Videotape is not damaged by X-rays, but it may be harmed by the magnetic field of a walk-through metal detector, so **ask that videotapes be hand-checked.**

Children under 6 travel free on subways and buses; children over 6 must pay full fare.

When traveling with children, **plan ahead** and **involve your youngsters** as you outline your trip. When packing, **include a supply of things to keep them busy** en route (☞ Children & Travel *in* Important Contacts A to Z). On sightseeing days, try to **schedule activities of**

special interest to your children, like a trip to a zoo or a playground. If you **plan your itinerary around seasonal festivals,** you'll never lack for things to do. In addition, **check local newspapers for special events** mounted by public libraries, museums, and parks.

BABY-SITTING

For recommended local sitters, **check with your hotel desk.**

DRIVING

If you are renting a car, don't forget to **arrange for a car seat when you reserve.** Sometimes they're free.

FLYING

On domestic flights, children under 2 not occupying a seat travel free, and older children are charged at the lowest applicable adult rate.

BAGGAGE➤ In general, the adult baggage allowance applies to children paying half or more of the adult fare.

FACILITIES➤ When making your reservation, **request children's meals or freestanding bassinets** if you need them; the latter are available only to those seated at the bulkhead, where there's enough legroom. If you don't need a bassinet, **think twice before requesting bulkhead seats**—the only storage space for in-flight necessities is in inconveniently distant overhead bins.

SAFETY SEATS➤ According to the FAA, it's a good idea to **use safety seats aloft** for children weighing less than 40 pounds. Airline policies

vary. U.S. carriers allow FAA-approved models but usually require that you buy a ticket, even if your child would otherwise ride free, since the seats must be strapped into regular seats.

LODGING

Most hotels allow children under a certain age to stay in their parents' room at no extra charge; others charge them as extra adults. Be sure to **ask about the cutoff age.**

IN NEW YORK

Visitors from outside the United States who are age 21 or older may import the following: 200 cigarettes or 50 cigars or 2 kilograms of tobacco; one U.S. liter of alcohol; gifts to the value of $100. Restricted items include meat products, seeds, plants, and fruits. Never carry illegal drugs.

IN CANADA

If you've been out of Canada for at least seven days, you may bring in C$500 worth of goods duty-free. If you've been away for fewer than seven days but more than 48 hours, the duty-free allowance drops to C$200; if your trip lasts between 24 and 48 hours, the allowance is C$50. You cannot pool allowances with family members. Goods claimed under the C$500 exemption may follow you by mail; those claimed under the lesser exemptions must accompany you.

Alcohol and tobacco products may be included in the seven-day and 48-hour exemptions but not in the 24-hour exemption. If you meet the age requirements of the province or territory through which you reenter Canada, you may bring in, duty-free, 1.14 liters (40 imperial ounces) of wine or liquor *or* 24 12-ounce cans or bottles of beer or ale. If you are 16 or older, you may bring in, duty-free, 200 cigarettes, 50 cigars or cigarillos, and 400 tobacco sticks or 400 grams of manufactured tobacco. Alcohol and tobacco must accompany you on your return.

An unlimited number of gifts with a value of up to C$60 each may be mailed to Canada duty-free. These do not affect your duty-free allowance on your return. Label the package "Unsolicited Gift— Value Under $60." Alcohol and tobacco are excluded.

IN THE U.K.

From countries outside the EU, including the United States, you may import, duty-free, 200 cigarettes, 100 cigarillos, 50 cigars, or 250 grams of tobacco; 1 liter of spirits or 2 liters of fortified or sparkling wine or liqueurs; 2 liters of still table wine; 60 milliliters of perfume; 250 milliliters of toilet water; plus £136 worth of other goods, including gifts and souvenirs.

D

DISABILITIES & ACCESSIBILITY

Many buildings in New York City are now wheelchair-accessible. The subway is still hard to navigate, however; people in wheelchairs do better on public buses, most of which have wheelchair lifts at the rear door and "kneel" at the front to facilitate getting on and off.

When discussing accessibility with an operator or reservationist, **ask hard questions.** Are there any stairs, inside *or* out? Are there grab bars next to the toilet *and* in the shower/tub? How wide is the doorway to the room? To the bathroom? For the most extensive facilities, meeting the latest legal specifications, **opt for newer accommodations,** which more often have been designed with access in mind. Older properties or ships must usually be retrofitted and may offer more limited facilities as a result. Be sure to **discuss your needs before booking.**

DISCOUNTS & DEALS

You shouldn't have to pay for a discount. In fact, you may already be eligible for all kinds of savings. Here are some time-honored strategies for getting the best deal.

LOOK IN YOUR WALLET

When you **use your credit card to make travel purchases,** you may get free travel-accident insurance, collision-damage insurance, medical or legal assistance, depending on the card and bank that issued it. Visa and MasterCard provide one or more of these

services, so **get a copy of your card's travel benefits.** If you are a member of the AAA or an oil-company-sponsored road-assistance plan, always **ask hotel or car-rental reservationists for auto-club discounts.** Some clubs offer additional discounts on tours, cruises, or admission to attractions. And don't forget that auto-club membership entitles you to free maps and trip-planning services.

SENIOR CITIZENS & STUDENTS

As a senior-citizen traveler, you may be eligible for special rates, but you should mention your senior-citizen status up front. If you're a student or under 26 you can also get discounts, especially if you have an official ID card (☞ Senior-Citizen Discounts *and* Students on the Road, *below*).

DIAL FOR DOLLARS

To save money, **look into "1-800" discount reservations services,** which often have lower rates. These services use their buying power to get a better price on hotels, airline tickets, and sometimes even car rentals. When booking a room, always **call the hotel's local toll-free number** (if one is available) rather than the central reservations number—you'll often get a better price. Ask the reservationist about special packages or corporate rates, which are usually available even if you're not traveling on business.

JOIN A CLUB?

Discount clubs can be a legitimate source of savings, but you must use the participating hotels and visit the participating attractions in order to realize any benefits. Remember, too, that you have to pay a fee to join, so **determine if you'll save enough to warrant the membership fee.** Before booking with a club, **make sure the hotel or other supplier isn't offering a better deal.**

DRIVING

If you plan to drive into Manhattan, try to time your arrival for late morning or early afternoon. That way you'll avoid the morning and evening rush hours (a problem at the crossings into Manhattan) and lunch hour.

The deterioration of the bridges linking Manhattan, especially those spanning the East River, is a serious problem, and repairs will be ongoing for the next few years. Don't be surprised if a bridge is entirely or partially closed.

Driving within Manhattan can be a nightmare of gridlocked streets and predatory motorists. Free parking is difficult to find in midtown, and violators may be towed away literally within minutes. All over town, parking lots charge exorbitant rates—as much as $15 for two hours in some neighborhoods. If you do drive, **don't plan to use your car much for traveling within Manhattan.**

I
INSURANCE

BAGGAGE

Airline liability for baggage is limited to $1,250 per person on domestic flights. On international flights, it amounts to $9.07 per pound or $20 per kilogram for checked baggage (roughly $640 per 70-pound bag) and $400 per passenger for unchecked baggage. Insurance for losses exceeding the terms of your airline ticket can be bought directly from the airline at check-in for about $10 per $1,000 of coverage; note that it excludes a rather extensive list of items, shown on your airline ticket.

COMPREHENSIVE

Comprehensive insurance policies include all the coverages described above plus some that may not be available in more specific policies. If you have purchased an expensive vacation, especially one that involves travel abroad, comprehensive insurance is a must; **look for policies that include trip-delay insurance,** which will protect you in the event that weather problems cause you to miss your flight, tour, or cruise. A few insurers will also sell you a waiver for preexisting medical conditions. Some of the companies that offer both these features are Access America, Carefree Travel, Travel Insured International, and TravelGuard (☞ Important Contacts A to Z).

FLIGHT

You should **think twice before buying flight insurance.** Often purchased as a last-minute impulse at the airport, it pays a lump sum when a plane crashes, either to a beneficiary if the insured dies or sometimes to a surviving passenger who loses his or her eyesight or a limb. Supplementing the airlines' coverage described in the limits-of-liability paragraphs on your ticket, it's expensive and basically unnecessary. Charging an airline ticket to a major credit card often automatically provides you with coverage that may also extend to travel by bus, train, and ship.

U.K. TRAVELERS

According to the Association of British Insurers, a trade association representing 450 insurance companies, it's wise to **buy extra medical coverage when you visit the United States.** You can buy an annual travel insurance policy valid for most vacations during the year in which it's purchased. If you are pregnant or have a preexisting medical condition, make sure you're covered before buying such a policy.

TRIP

Without insurance, you will lose all or most of your money if you cancel your trip regardless of the reason. Especially if your airline ticket, cruise, or package tour is nonrefundable and cannot be changed, it's essential that you **buy trip-cancellation-and-inter-**

ruption insurance.
When considering how
much coverage you
need, look for a policy
that will cover the cost
of your trip plus the
nondiscounted price of
a one-way airline ticket
should you need to
return home early. Read
the fine print carefully,
especially sections that
define "family member"
and "preexisting medi-
cal conditions." Also
**consider default or
bankruptcy insurance,**
which protects you
against a supplier's
failure to deliver. Be
aware, however, that if
you buy such a policy
from a travel agency,
tour operator, airline,
or cruise line, it may
not cover default by the
firm in question.

L
LIMOUSINES

If you want to ride
around Manhattan in
style, you can rent a
chauffeur-driven car
from one of many
limousine services.
Companies usually
charge by the hour or
offer a flat fee for
sightseeing excursions.

LODGING

APARTMENT &
VILLA RENTAL

If you want a home
base that's roomy
enough for a family and
comes with cooking
facilities, **consider
taking a furnished
rental.** This can also
save you money, but
not always—some
rentals are luxury
properties (economical
only when your party is
large). Home-exchange
directories list rentals—
often second homes
owned by prospective
house swappers—and

some services search for
a house or apartment
for you (even a castle if
that's your fancy) and
handle the paperwork.
Some send an illustrated
catalog; others send
photographs only of
specific properties,
sometimes at a charge;
up-front registration
fees may apply.

HOME EXCHANGE

If you would like to
find a house, an apart-
ment, or some other
type of vacation prop-
erty to exchange for
your own while on
holiday, **become a
member of a home-
exchange organization,**
which will send you its
updated listings of
available exchanges for
a year, and will include
your own listing in at
least one of them.
Arrangements for the
actual exchange are
made by the two parties
involved, not by the
organization.

M
MONEY

ATMS

ATMs are numerous in
the Big Apple. It's good
to **be cautious in de-
serted areas and at
night.**

COSTS

There's no doubt that
New York is an expen-
sive city to visit. Hotel
rooms with views of
Central Park can easily
run as high as $250 a
night; dinner for two at
a moderate restaurant,
plus orchestra seats at a
Broadway show, can set
you back $150–$200
(☞ Chapters 5, 6, and
7). If you're on a bud-
get, don't despair. New
Yorkers themselves
know how to find

bargains; they **comb
discount clothing outlets,
grab food at corner
delis, walk just about
everywhere, and attend
free concerts and plays
in the parks.** You, too,
can moderate the cost
of your visit if you do
as they do (☞ Discount
Tickets *in* Chapter 5).

P
PACKING FOR
NEW YORK

Jackets and ties are
required for men in a
number of restaurants.
For sightseeing and
casual dining, jeans and
sneakers are acceptable
just about anywhere in
the city. Always **come
with sneakers or other
flat-heeled walking
shoes** for pounding the
New York pavements;
you may even see busi-
nesspeople in button-
down office attire lacing
them on for the sprint
from one appointment
to another.

Do **pack light,** because
porters and luggage
trolleys can be hard to
find at New York
airports. And **bring a
fistful of quarters to rent
a trolley.**

Bring an extra pair of
eyeglasses or contact
lenses in your carry-on
luggage, and if you
have a health problem,
**pack enough medica-
tion** to last the trip.
It's important that
you **don't put prescrip-
tion drugs or valuables
in luggage to be
checked,** for it could
go astray.

LUGGAGE

Airline baggage al-
lowances depend on the
airline, the route, and
the class of your ticket;

ask in advance. In general, on domestic flights you are entitled to check two bags. A third piece may be brought on board, but it must fit easily under the seat in front of you or in the overhead compartment. In the United States, the FAA gives airlines broad latitude regarding carry-on allowances, and they tend to tailor them to different aircraft and operational conditions. Charges for excess, oversize, or overweight pieces vary.

SAFEGUARDING YOUR LUGGAGE➤ Before leaving home, **itemize your bags' contents** and their worth, and label them with your name, address, and phone number. (If you use your home address, cover it so that potential thieves can't see it readily.) Inside each bag, **pack a copy of your itinerary.** At check-in, **make sure that each bag is correctly tagged** with the destination airport's three-letter code. If your bags arrive damaged—or fail to arrive at all—file a written report with the airline before leaving the airport.

PASSPORTS &
VISAS

CANADIANS

No passport is necessary to enter the United States.

U.K. CITIZENS

British citizens need a valid passport to enter the United States. If you are staying for fewer than 90 days and traveling on a vacation, with a return or on-ward ticket, you probably will not need a visa. However, you will need to fill out the Visa Waiver Form, 1-94W, supplied by the airline.

It is advisable that you **leave one photocopy of your passport's data page** with someone at home and keep another with you, separated from your passport, while traveling. If you lose your passport, promptly call the nearest embassy or consulate and the local police; having the data page information can speed replacement.

PERSONAL
SECURITY &
COMFORT

Despite New York's bad reputation in the area of crime, most people live here for years without being robbed or assaulted. Nevertheless, as in any large city, travelers make particularly easy marks for pickpockets and hustlers, so **be cautious.**

Do **ignore the panhandlers** on the streets (some aggressive, many homeless); people who offer to hail you a cab (they often appear at Penn Station, Port Authority, and Grand Central Terminal); and limousine and gypsy cab drivers who offer you a ride. Someone who appears to have had an accident at the exit door of a bus may flee with your wallet or purse if you attempt to give aid; the individual who approaches you with a complicated story is probably playing a confidence game and hopes to get some-thing from you. Also **beware of strangers jostling you in crowds,** or someone tapping your shoulder from behind. Never play or place a bet on a sidewalk card game, shell game, or guessing game—they are all rigged to get your cash.

Keep jewelry out of sight on the street; better yet, **leave valuables at home.** Don't wear gold chains or gaudy jewelry, even if it's fake. Women should **never hang a purse on a chair in a restaurant** or on a hook in a restroom stall. Men are advised to **carry wallets in front pants pockets** rather than in their hip pockets.

Avoid deserted blocks in out-of-the-way neighborhoods. If you end up in an empty area or a side street that feels unsafe, it probably is. A brisk, purposeful pace helps deter trouble wherever you go.

Although the subway runs round the clock, it is usually safest during the day and evening. Most residents of the city have a rough cut-off time—9 or 10 PM—past which they avoid riding the subway trains. The subway system is much safer than it once was, but to **err on the side of caution,** you may want to travel by bus or taxi after the theater or a concert. If you do take the subway at night, ride in the center car, with the conductor, and wait among the crowds on the center of the platform or right in front of the token clerk. Watch out for unsavory characters lurking around the inside or outside of stations, particularly at night. When you're waiting for a train, **stand away from the edge of the subway platform,** especially when trains are entering or leaving the station. Once the train pulls into the station, **avoid empty cars.** When disembarking from a train, **stick with the crowd** until you reach the comparative safety of the street.

Though they're slower, buses are often more pleasant than subways, particularly when you sit next to a window and can view the passing street life. Buses are usually safer than the subways.

R
REST ROOMS

Public rest rooms in New York run the gamut when it comes to cleanliness. Facilities in Penn Station, Grand Central Terminal, and the Port Authority bus terminal are often quite dirty and are inhabited by homeless people. Rest rooms in subway stations have largely been sealed off because of vandalism and safety concerns.

As a rule, the cleanest bathrooms are in midtown department stores such as Macy's, Lord & Taylor, and Bloomingdale's, in museums, or in the lobbies of large hotels. Public atriums, such as the Citicorp Center and Trump Tower, also provide good public facilities, as does the newly renovated Bryant Park. Restaurants, too, have

rest rooms, but usually just for patrons. If you're dressed well and look as if you belong, you can often just sail right in. Be aware that cinemas, Broadway theaters, and concert halls have limited amenities, and there are often long lines before performances, as well as during intermissions.

S
SENIOR-CITIZEN DISCOUNTS

To qualify for age-related discounts, **mention your senior-citizen status up front** when booking hotel reservations, not when checking out, and before you're seated in restaurants, not when paying the bill. Note that discounts may be limited to certain menus, days, or hours. When renting a car, **ask about promotional car-rental discounts**—they can net even lower costs than your senior-citizen discount.

STUDENTS ON THE ROAD

To save money, **look into deals available through student-oriented travel agencies.** To qualify, you'll need to have a bona fide student ID card. Members of international student groups are also eligible (☞ Students *in* Important Contacts A to Z).

SUBWAYS

The 714-mile subway system operates 24 hours a day, and especially within Manhattan, serves most of the places you'll want to visit. It's cheaper than a

cab and, during the workweek, often faster than either cabs or buses. The trains have been rid of their graffiti (some New Yorkers, of course, miss the colorful old trains), and sleek, new air-conditioned cars predominate on every line. Still, the New York subway is not problem-free. Many trains are crowded and noisy. Although trains usually run frequently, especially during rush hours, you never know when some incident somewhere on the line may stall traffic. Don't write off the subway—some 3.5 million passengers ride it every day without incident—but stay alert at all times (☞ Personal Security & Comfort, *above*).

Subway fares are $1.50, although reduced fares are available for people with disabilities and senior citizens during nonrush hours. If you're just taking a few trips, you should pay with tokens; they are sold at token booths that are *usually* open at each station, as well as at token vending machines. It is advisable to **buy several tokens at one time** to avoid having to wait in line later. For four or more subway trips, you might find it easier to use the MTA's new MetroCard, a thin, plastic card with a magnetic strip. Most major subway stations accept the cards, and all 469 stations are scheduled to accept Metro-Card by the end of 1997. They are sold at all subway stations where they are accepted and at some stores— look for an "Authorized Sales Agent" sign. You can buy a card for a minimum of $6 (4 trips) and a maximum of $80, in $6 increments. You can add more money to a card, and more than one person can use the same card: Swipe it through the turnstile once for each rider. Both tokens and MetroCards permit unlimited transfers within the system. There are no discounts offered for either tokens or MetroCards.

Most subway entrances are located at street corners and are marked by lampposts with globe-shaped green lights. Subway lines are named for numbers and letters, such as the No. 3 line or the A line. Some lines run "express" and skip lots of stops; others are "locals" and make all stops. Each station entrance has a sign indicating the lines that run through the station; some stations are also marked "uptown only" or "downtown only." Before entering subway stations, **read the signs carefully**—one of the most frequent mistakes visitors make is taking the train in the wrong direction—although this can be an adventure, it can also be frustrating if you're in a hurry. This book's subway map covers the most-visited parts of Manhattan. Maps of the full subway system are posted on trains near the doors and at stations. You can usually pick up free maps at token booths, too.

For route information, **ask the token clerk or a transit policeman** or a

fellow rider. Once New Yorkers realize you're harmless, most bend over backward to be helpful.

T

TAXIS

Taxis are usually easy to hail on the street or from a taxi rank in front of major hotels. You can tell if a cab is available by checking its rooftop light; if the center panel is lit, the driver is ready to take passengers. Taxi fares cost $2.00 for the first ⅕ mile, 30¢ for each ⅕ mile thereafter, and 20¢ for each minute not in motion. A 50¢ surcharge is added to rides begun between 8 PM and 6 AM. There is no charge for extra passengers, but you must pay any bridge or tunnel tolls incurred during your trip (sometimes a driver will personally pay a toll to keep moving quickly, but that amount will be added to the fare when the ride is over). Taxi drivers also expect a 15% tip. Barring performance above and beyond the call of duty, don't feel obliged to give them more.

To avoid unhappy taxi experiences, **try to have a general idea of where you want to go.** A few cab drivers are dishonest; some are ignorant; some can barely understand English. If you have no idea of the proper route, you may be taken for a long and costly ride.

TELEPHONES

There are more than 58,000 public telephones in New York

City, nearly 25,000 of which are in Manhattan. A visitor should never have to hunt more than three or four blocks before finding a coin-operated phone. If you're making a brief call—and don't mind the cacophonous sound of traffic or subways rumbling in the background—street phones are probably your best bet. **Make sure that the pay phone is labeled as a NYNEX telephone;** the unmarked variety are notorious change-eaters. There are also public credit card phones scattered around the city. If you want to consult a directory or make a more leisurely call, pay phones in the lobbies of office buildings or hotels (some of which take credit cards) are a better choice.

The area code for Manhattan is 212; for Brooklyn, Queens, the Bronx, and Staten Island, it's 718. Pay telephones cost 25¢ for the first three minutes of a local call (this includes calls between 212 and 718 area codes); an extra deposit is required for each additional minute.

TIPPING

The customary tipping rate is 15%–20% for taxi drivers and waiters (☞ Chapter 6 for further tipping advice); bellhops are usually given $2 in luxury hotels, $1 elsewhere. Hotel maids should be tipped around $1 per day of your stay.

TOUR OPERATORS

A package or tour to New York can make

your vacation less expensive and more hassle-free. Firms that sell tours and packages reserve airline seats, hotel rooms, and rental cars in bulk and pass some of the savings on to you. In addition, the best operators have local representatives available to help you at your destination.

A GOOD DEAL?

The more your package or tour includes, the better you can predict the ultimate cost of your vacation. Make sure you know exactly what is covered, and **beware of hidden costs.** Are taxes, tips, and service charges included? Transfers and baggage handling? Entertainment and excursions? These can add up.

Most packages and tours are rated deluxe, first-class superior, first class, tourist, or budget. The key difference is usually accommodations. If the package or tour you are considering is priced lower than in your wildest dreams, **be skeptical.** Also, **make sure your travel agent knows the accommodations** and other services. Ask about the hotel's location, room size, beds, and whether it has a pool, room service, or programs for children, if you care about these amenities. Has your agent been there in person or sent others you can contact?

BUYER BEWARE

Each year a number of consumers are stranded or lose their money when operators—even very large ones with excellent reputations—go out of business. To avoid becoming one of them, take the time to **check out the operator**—find out how long the company has been in business and ask several agents about its reputation. Next, **don't book unless the firm has a consumer-protection program.** Members of the USTOA and the NTA are required to set aside funds for the sole purpose of covering your payments and travel arrangements in case of default. Non-member operators may instead carry insurance; look for the details in the operator's brochure—and for the name of an underwriter with a solid reputation. Note: When it comes to tour operators, **don't trust escrow accounts.** Although there are laws governing the accounts of charter-flight operators, no governmental body prevents tour operators from raiding the till.

Next, **contact your local Better Business Bureau and the attorney general's offices** in both your own state and the operator's; have any complaints been filed? Finally, **pay with a major credit card.** Then you can cancel payment, provided that you can document your complaint. Always **consider trip-cancellation insurance** (☞ Insurance, *above*).

BIG VS. SMALL➤ Operators that handle several hundred thousand travelers per year can use their purchasing power to give you a good price. Their high volume may also indi-cate financial stability. But some small companies provide more personalized service; because they tend to specialize, they may also be more knowledgeable about a given area.

USING AN AGENT

Travel agents are excellent resources. In fact, large operators accept bookings made only through travel agents. But it's good to **collect brochures from several agencies** because some agents' suggestions may be skewed by promotional relationships with tour and package firms that reward them for volume sales. If you have a special interest, **find an agent with expertise in that area;** ASTA can provide leads in the United States. (Don't rely solely on your agent, though; agents may be unaware of small-niche operators, and some special-interest travel companies only sell direct.)

SINGLE TRAVELERS

Prices are usually quoted per person, based on two sharing a room. If traveling solo, you may be required to pay the full double-occupancy rate. Some operators eliminate this surcharge if you agree to be matched up with a roommate of the same sex, even if one is not found by departure time.

U

U.S. GOVERNMENT

The U.S. government can be an excellent source of travel information. Some of this is free and some is available for a nominal charge. When planning your trip, **find out what government materials are available.**

W
WALKING

The cheapest, sometimes the fastest, and usually the most interesting way to explore this city is by walking. Because New Yorkers by and large live in apartments rather than in houses, and travel by cab, bus, or subway rather than by private car, they end up walking quite a lot. As a result, street life is a vital part of the local culture. On crowded sidewalks, people gossip, snack, browse, cement business deals, make romantic rendezvous, encounter long-lost friends, and fly into irrational quarrels with strangers. It's a wonderfully democratic hubbub. Also sharing some streets, however, are panhandlers, some aggressive, some friendly, and others more or less insane.

The typical New Yorker, if there is such an animal, walks quickly, dodging around cars, buses, bicycle messengers, construction sites, and other pedestrians. Although the natives seem hurried and rude, they will often cheerfully come to the aid of a lost pedestrian, so don't hesitate to ask a passerby for directions.

WHEN TO GO

At one time, it seemed New York's cultural life was limited to the months between October and May, when new Broadway shows opened, museums mounted major exhibitions, and formal seasons for opera, ballet, and concerts held sway. Today, however, there are Broadway openings even in mid-July, and a number of touring orchestras and opera and ballet companies visit the city in summer. In late spring and summer, the streets and parks are filled with ethnic parades, impromptu sidewalk concerts, and free performances under the stars. Except for regular closing days and a few holidays (such as Christmas, New Year's Day, and Thanksgiving), the city's museums are open year-round.

CLIMATE

Although there's an occasional bone-chilling winter day, with winds blasting in off the Hudson, snow only occasionally accumulates in the city. Summer is the only unpleasant time of year, especially the humid, hot days of August, when many Manhattanites vacate the island for summer homes. Most hotels are air-conditioned, but if you're traveling in the summer and choosing budget accommodations, it's a good idea to ask whether your room has an air conditioner. Air-conditioned stores, restaurants, theaters, and museums provide respite from the heat; so do the many green expanses of parks. Subways and buses are usually air-conditioned, but subway stations can be as hot as saunas.

When September arrives—with its dry "champagne-like" weather—the city shakes off its summer sluggishness. Mild and comfortable, autumn shows the city off at its best, with yellow and bronze foliage displays in the parks.

The following table shows each month's average daily highs and lows:

Climate in New York City

Jan.	38F	3C	May	72F	22C	Sept.	76F	24C
	25	−4		54	12		60	16
Feb.	40F	4C	June	80F	27C	Oct.	65F	18C
	27	−3		63	17		50	10
Mar.	50F	10C	July	85F	29C	Nov.	54F	12C
	35	2		68	20		41	5
Apr.	61F	16C	Aug.	84F	29C	Dec.	43F	6C
	44	7		67	19		31	−1

1 Destination: New York City

DISCOVERING NEW YORK

I N 1925, THE YOUTHFUL song-writing team of Richard Rodgers and Larry Hart wrote "Manhattan," arguably the loveliest city anthem ever. "We'll have Manhattan, the Bronx, and Staten Island, too," it promises, drawing its images from the merry scramble that was the city more than 60 years ago: "sweet pushcarts," "baloney on a roll," a subway that "charms," Brighton Beach, Coney Island, and the popular comedy *Abie's Irish Rose.* "We'll turn Manhattan into an isle of joy," coos the refrain.

Several decades later, in 1989, an album called simply *New York,* by aging enfant terrible rocker Lou Reed, viewed the same city with glasses fogged by despair and cynicism: Drugs, crime, racism, and promiscuity reigned in what Reed considered to be a sinkhole of "crudity, cruelty of thought and sound." His voice brittle with weary irony, he sang, "This is no time for celebration." Manhattan's "sweet pushcarts" now apparently overflow with deadly vials of crack.

So, whom to believe—Larry or Lou?

The truth of the matter is slippery, for New York has long been a mosaic of grand contradictions, a city for which there has never been—nor ever will be—a clear consensus. Hart himself took the city to task in another song, "Give It Back to the Indians," whose lyrics count off a litany of problems that still exist: crime, dirt, high prices, traffic jams, and all-around urban chaos. Yet for all that, millions live here, grumbling but happy, and millions more visit, curious as cats to find out what the magnificent fuss is all about.

I was in eighth grade in suburban Detroit when I first really became aware of New York. A friend's Manhattan-born mother subscribed to the Sunday *New York Times,* and at their house I'd pore over the "Arts and Leisure" section, as rapt as an archaeologist with a cave painting. The details of what I read there have blurred, but I remember vividly the sensation I felt while reading: a combined anticipation and nostalgia so keen it bordered on pain. Although I had never been there, I was homesick for New York.

It's my home now, yet I can still appreciate the impulse that draws visitors here. In a city so ripe with possibilities, we are all more or less visitors.

I think of this on an uncharacteristically warm day in late March, as fellow New Yorkers and I escape from the hives of offices and homes to celebrate spring's first preview. We unbutton our jackets, leave buses a stop or two before our usual destinations, quicken our resolve to visit that new exhibit at the Met or jog around the Central Park Reservoir. A jubilant sense of renewal infects us all, and I overhear one happy fellow saying to a friend, "I felt just like a tourist yesterday."

Whenever I get the New York blues, the best tonic for me is to glimpse the city through the eyes of a visitor. One day, after subway construction had rerouted me well out of my usual path, I found myself in the grimy Times Square station—hardly the place for a spiritual conversion. As usual I had that armor of body language that we New Yorkers reflexively assume to protect ourselves from strangers bent on (1) ripping us off, (2) doing us bodily harm, (3) converting us, (4) making sexual advances, or (5) being general pains-in-the-butt just for the hell of it. But that day, tucked away in a corner, was a group of musicians—not an uncommon sight in New York—playing the guitar, organ, and accordion with gusto and good spirits behind a homemade sign that dubbed them the Argentinian Tango Company. Like many street musicians in Manhattan, they were *good,* but I was only half listening, too intent on cursing the city. Just as I passed the band, however, I noticed four teenagers drawn to the music—visitors, surely, they were far too open and trusting to be anything else. Grinning as widely as the Argentinians, they began to perform a spontaneous imitation of flamenco dancing—clapping hands above their heads, raising their heels, laughing at themselves, and only slightly self-conscious. Passersby, myself included, broke into smiles. As I made my way to the subway platform, buoyed by the impromptu show, I once again forgave New York. This minor piece of magic was apology enough.

I wonder whether that was the moment one of those teenagers happened to fall in love with the city. It *can* happen in a single moment, to a visitor or to a longtime resident. Perhaps it hits during a stroll through Riverside Park after a blanketing snowfall, when trees have turned to crystal and the city feels a hush it knows at no other time; or when you turn a corner and spy, beyond a phalanx of RVs and a tangle of cables and high-beam lights, the filming of a new movie.

That moment could also come when the house lights dim at the Metropolitan Opera, and the chandeliers make their magisterial ascent to the ceiling; or when you first glimpse the Prometheus statue in Rockefeller Center, gleaming like a giant present under the annual Christmas tree as dozens of skaters cut swirls of seasonal colors on the ice below. You may even be smitten in that instant when, walking along the streets in the haze of a summer afternoon, you look up above the sea of anonymous faces to see—and be astonished by—the lofty rows of skyscrapers, splendid in their arrogance and power. At times like these it is perfectly permissible to stop for a moment, take a breath, and think, "Wow! *This is New York!*" We who live here do it every so often ourselves.

For some, of course, that special moment comes when they spot a street or building made familiar by movies or television, from *I Love Lucy* to *On the Waterfront*. At the Empire State Building, who can help but remember King Kong's pathetically courageous swing from its pinnacle? Or at the brooding Dakota, the chilling destiny created for Rosemary's baby within those fortresslike walls? In the mind's eye, Audrey Hepburn is eternally pairing diamonds and a doughnut as she wends her swank way down 5th Avenue to have breakfast at Tiffany's. And the miniature park on Sutton Place will always be where Woody Allen and Diane Keaton began their angst-ridden *Manhattan* love affair, with the 59th Street bridge gleaming beyond and Gershwin music swelling in the background.

THERE'S A MOMENT OF sudden magic when a New York stereotype, seen so often on screen that it seems a joke, suddenly comes to life: when a gum-cracking waitress calls you "hon," or a stogie-sucking cabbie asks, "How 'bout them Yankees, Mac?" There's also the thrill of discovering one of New York's cities-within-the-city: Mulberry Street in Little Italy; Mott Street in Chinatown; Park Avenue's enclave of wealth and privilege; SoHo and TriBeCa, with their artistic types dressed in black from head to toe; or Sheridan Square, the nexus of the city's prominent lesbian and gay communities. The first glimpse of a landmark could excite the visitor's infatuation, too: frenetic Grand Central Station, abustle with suburban commuters; the concrete caverns of Wall Street, throbbing with power and ambition; or the Statue of Liberty, which neither cliché nor cheap souvenir can render common.

As you ready yourself to take on New York's contradictions, prepare to wonder and to exult. Here, on a single day, you might catch a glimpse of John Kennedy, Jr., or Rollerena, the gloriously tacky drag-queen-cum-fairy-godmother on roller skates, who waves her magic wand to bestow blessings on select public events. Here you can eat sumptuously at a hot-dog stand or at a world-celebrated gourmet shrine.

Excess and deprivation mingle here: As a limousine crawls lazily to take its pampered passengers to their luxe destination, it rolls past a beggar seeking the warmth that steams from the city's belly through an iron grate. It's a ludicrously bright cartoon and a sobering documentary, New York—almost too much for one city to be. It's maddening and it's thrilling; monstrous, yet beautiful beyond parallel.

And I envy anyone their first taste of it.

—*Michael Adams*

Writer Michael Adams finally moved to his hometown, New York City, 15 years ago.

WHAT'S WHERE

Rockefeller Center and Midtown

Apart from sweeping panoramas from the Hudson River or the New York Bay, no other city scene so clearly says "New York" than this 19-building complex known as Rockefeller Center. These 22 acres of prime real estate (between 5th and 7th avenues and 47th and 48th streets) with the Channel Gardens; the GE, Time & Life, and Associated Press buildings; and plazas, concourses, and street-level shops form a city within a city. St. Patrick's Cathedral, Saks Fifth Avenue, and the rest of midtown's gleaming skyscrapers are just steps away.

5th Avenue and 57th Street

One of the world's great shopping districts, 5th Avenue north of Rockefeller Center and 57th Street between Lexington Avenue and 7th Avenue is where you'll find some of the biggest names in New York retailing as well as the crème de la crème of designer boutiques. Fifty-seventh Street also is home to several theme restaurants, such as the Motown Cafe, Planet Hollywood, and the Hard Rock Cafe.

Times Square, 42nd Street, and the Theater District

The place where the ball drops on New Year's Eve, Times Square is still one of the city's principal energy centers. The Times Tower itself, from which the neighborhood took its name, is at the intersection of Broadway, 7th Avenue, and 42nd Street. Thirty or so major Broadway theaters are all nearby, in an area bounded roughly by 41st and 53rd streets between 6th and 9th Avenues. Also just a short walk away are Theater Row, a string of intimate Off-Broadway houses on the south side of 42nd Street between 9th and 10th avenues, and Restaurant Row (46th St. between 8th and 9th avenues), where critics, actors, directors, playwrights, and spectators come to dine before and after the show. Going much farther east on 42nd Street, past 5th Avenue, you'll discover the Beaux Arts beauty of Grand Central Terminal, with its main entrance between Vanderbilt and Lexington avenues. East of Grand Central is the United Nations complex on a lushly landscaped riverside tract just east of 1st Avenue between 42nd and 48th streets.

Murray Hill to Union Square

Three distinct neighborhoods east of 5th Avenue between 20th and 40th streets—Murray Hill, Madison Square, and Gramercy Park—have preserved some of the historic charm of 19th-century New York: brownstone mansions and town houses, the city's earliest "skyscrapers," shady parks, and, yes, even in New York, some quiet streets. South of Gramercy Park lies Union Square, with its restored park, wonderful green market, and trendsetting restaurants.

Museum Mile and the Upper East Side

Once Manhattan's Millionaire's Row, the stretch of 5th Avenue between 79th and 104th streets has been renamed Museum Mile because of the startling number of world-class collections of art and artifacts scattered along its length (some housed in the former mansions of some of the Upper East Side's more illustrious industrialists and philanthropists). Whatever you do, don't leave New York without visiting at least one or two galleries in the largest art museum in the Western Hemisphere, the Metropolitan Museum of Art, on the Central Park side of 5th Avenue at 82nd Street.

Central Park

This 843-acre patch of rolling countryside is where Manhattanites go to escape from the urban jungle and reconnect with nature. Named a National Historic Landmark in 1965, Central Park offers the city's most soothing vistas and opportunities for just about any activity that a city dweller might engage in outdoors. All this right in the heart of the city: The Park is bordered by 59th Street (called Central Park South between 5th and 8th avenues), 5th Avenue, 110th Street, and Central Park West.

The Upper West Side

The ornate prewar buildings that line the boulevards of Broadway, West End Avenue, Riverside Drive, and Central Park West provide a stately backdrop for glitzy boutiques and the scads of wanna-be soap actors hustling off to their auditions at ABC-TV and hopeful performers and aficionados making the pilgrimage to Lincoln Center. A stroll up tony Columbus Avenue should stretch at least as far as the Museum of Natural History, whose lavish grounds and pink-granite corner towers occupy a four-block tract. Farther uptown in Morningside Heights are the ivied buildings of Columbia University and the Cathedral of St. John the Divine, a magnificent Episcopal church.

Harlem

An important influence on American culture, this once-quiet country village grew into a suburb of apartment houses and brownstones for succeeding waves of German, Irish, Jewish, and Italian immigrants. For nearly a hundred years now it has been a mecca for African-American and Hispanic-American culture and life. Harlem extends north from 110th Street to about 145th Street (the border of Manhattanville); the most interesting sights on the tourist trail fall roughly between 116th Street and 135th Street.

Chelsea

Like its London district namesake, New York's Chelsea maintains a villagelike personality, with a number of quiet streets graced by lovingly renovated town houses. The neighborhood stretches from 5th Avenue west to the Hudson River, and from 14th to 23rd streets. Chelsea has always been a haven for writers and artists, and it has also embraced a multicultural population for decades; it now includes an active gay community that frequents the lively stores and restaurants on 8th Avenue. In recent years, the area has witnessed an economic boost with the opening of 6th Avenue superstores and the Chelsea Piers Sports and Entertainment Complex on the Hudson.

Greenwich Village

Extending from 14th Street south to Houston Street and from the piers of the Hudson River to 5th Avenue, the crazy-quilt pattern of narrow, tree-lined streets known to New Yorkers simply as "the Village" remains true to its 19th-century heritage as a haven for immigrants, bohemians, students, artists, actors, carousers, and tourists. It's one of the best parts of the city to wander for hours. The Village is still home to one of the largest gay communities in the country (centered around Sheridan Square and Christopher Street).

The East Village

Many regard the East Village—an area bounded by 14th Street on the north, 4th Avenue or the Bowery on the west, Houston Street on the south, and the East River—as the island's most colorful neighborhood. Here holdouts from the 1960s coexist with a deeply entrenched Eastern European community. Artists, punks, and account executives move freely between the Polish and Ukrainian coffee shops, galleries, trendy pasta bars, offbeat shops, and St. Mark's Place—a local thoroughfare for sidewalk vendors.

SoHo and TriBeCa

SoHo (South of Houston Street) is bounded on the other four sides by Broadway, Canal Street, and 6th Avenue. TriBeCa (the Triangle Below Canal Street) extends roughly as far south as Murray Street and east to West Broadway. Over the past 20 years both neighborhoods have gradually been transformed into lively realms of loft dwellers, galleries, and trendy shops and cafés.

Little Italy and Chinatown

Little Italy—a few blocks south of Houston Street between Broadway and the Bowery—is today not as Italian as it used to be. Still, Mulberry Street and its famous—and, in some cases, infamous—eateries are rife with atmosphere. If you head east along Canal Street (the southern border of Little Italy), you will run into the ever-expanding and frenetic Chinatown (the area south of Canal on the east side), which has over the years spilled over into much of the Lower East Side's Jewish neighborhood. One of the biggest attractions in Chinatown is simply the carnival-like atmosphere on the small streets, which are packed with shoppers and purveyors of untold varieties of pungent fish and exotic vegetables.

Wall Street and the Battery

Wall Street is both an actual street and a shorthand name for the financial community that clusters downtown around the New York and American stock exchanges. From Battery Park at the very tip of the island you can view New York Harbor with its two most famous sights: the Statue of Liberty and Ellis Island.

New York's days as a great 19th-century haven for clipper ships are preserved in lower Manhattan at South Street Seaport, centered on Fulton Street between Water Street and the East River. Just blocks away, you can experience another slice of New York history by walking the streets of the City Hall district, with its majestic court edifices.

PLEASURES AND PASTIMES

Fine Dining

The old reliable four-star French restaurants, steak houses, delis, and diners are of course still doing what they've been doing best for years (and in some cases, decades), but there's plenty new afoot. For one thing, the bistro/trattoria mania that broke out a few years ago is going strong: The French are downtown, the Italians on the Upper East Side. The mix of small ethnic eating spots reflects shifting immigration patterns, and the newest national cuisines to make their mark are Austrian, Afghan, Brazilian, Thai, Turkish, and Jamaican. Chinatown, not to be undone, is extending its borders, and noodle shops, complete with hanging ducks, heaping bowls of fried rice, and low prices are sprouting up everywhere.

Nightlife

New York's vibrant nightlife has something to please everyone. Much of the club life is concentrated downtown—in one night you can go to a grungy East Village dance dive, a classic West Village jazz joint, a sleekly decorated TriBeCa celebrity trap, or a preppy Wall Street hangout. Uptown's the place to go to listen to a romantic singer in a sophisticated setting like the Algonquin's Oak Room, the Cafe Carlyle, or Rainbow and the Stars, with its awesome backdrop of Manhattan lights. If you just want a drink, you can frequent an unpretentious neighborhood saloon in jeans or a vintage hotel bar in your tux. You can also write your novel in a coffee bar or laugh yourself silly at a comedy club.

Shopping

Whether you're planning to run your credit cards up to the max or just window-shop, New York offers a veritable orgy of options. Try the South Street Seaport for its unique combination of upscale, high-tech, and kitsch retail shops (and a spectacular view of the Brooklyn Bridge); the Lower East Side for inexpensive clothing and shoes; SoHo for art and antiques, avant-garde gifts and decorative items, gourmet foods, and funky clothes; 5th Avenue for haute couture; Herald Square for the biggest department stores; Columbus Avenue for some of the city's glitziest upscale if not top-of-the-line shops (and one of biggest flea markets in the city); and the Upper East Side for unique and stylish items for the home, fine antiques, and designer clothing.

Summer Arts

In summer the open spaces of the city become outdoor concert halls. Lincoln Center's Out-of-Doors and Lincoln Center Festival transform Manhattan's performing-arts centerpiece into a virtual state fair of the arts; while the theaters fill up with music, dance, and theater productions, stages set up in the plaza accommodate jazz dancers, chamber orchestras, Broadway lyricists and composers, mimes, dance bands, children's theater, and more. Metropolitan Opera in the Parks works its way throughout the five boroughs. The New York Shakespeare Festival stages two plays every summer. Summerstage fills the Naumberg Bandshell in Central Park with free programs ranging from grand opera to polka to experimental rock.

Walking

New York is a walker's city. It's hard to get lost, except in the Village, where New York's rigid grid pattern of streets falls apart. So step into your best walking shoes, choose any avenue or street, and follow it from one end to the other or from river to river, observing how the neighborhoods shade gradually into one another. Or hike across one of the city's many bridges for a fresh look at scenery that usually speeds by in a blur. Some of our favorite walks are: 5th Avenue from 40th Street to Central Park; the path through the Park from Grand Army Plaza to the Bethesda Fountain; Broadway on the Upper West Side from Lincoln Center to 86th Street; east to west on Bleecker Street in Greenwich Village;

the Brooklyn Bridge from Manhattan to Brooklyn Heights and its Esplanade.

FODOR'S CHOICE

Views to Remember

★ **The lower Manhattan skyline seen from the Brooklyn Heights Promenade.** This quiet, 3-mile-long sliver of park hanging over the ferry district offers both a respite from the urban din and one of the most stunning urban panoramas: the Brooklyn Bridge, South Street Seaport, and the glittering skyscrapers of lower Manhattan that seem to float on the water.

★ **Midtown Manhattan and New York Bay from the observation deck of the World Trade Center.** Elevators glide a quarter of a mile into the sky (107 stories) to the world's highest outdoor observation platform, where, on a clear day, you can see as far as 55 miles.

★ **The vista of skyscrapers ringing Central Park.** Perhaps the best spot from which to admire this picture-postcard view (midtown's jumble of high-rises looks like a surreal two-dimensional stage set rising from the trees) is the reservoir's northwest corner or the second-floor outdoor sculpture court at the Metropolitan Museum.

★ **A moonlit look at the harbor from the Staten Island Ferry.** Still one of the cheapest thrills available, this ride is even more breathtaking at night with the billions of lights of Manhattan twinkling in the distance.

★ **The Hudson River from the tower at Riverside Church.** Just 21 stories above street level, this perch nevertheless affords a dramatic unobstructed view of the river, the George Washington Bridge, and the Palisades of New Jersey to the west.

Architecture

★ **The Woolworth Building, the Flatiron Building, the Empire State Building, and the World Trade Center's twin towers.** Each is noteworthy for its own style and architectural features, and each, in its time, was the world's tallest building.

★ **The Chrysler Building.** One of the most graceful of the city's skyscrapers, this stainless-steel tower is famous for its Art Deco pinnacle, its radiator-cap ornaments and gargoyles, and for its graceful African marble lobby.

★ **Rockefeller Center.** A 22-acre city within the city, this complex is as remarkable for its smooth limestone structures as for its plazas, concourses, and public spaces.

★ **The Dakota.** The grande dame of New York apartment houses, this brick-and-stone urban castle outclasses all the other residences of Central Park West.

★ **The unbroken front of cast-iron beauties along Greene Street in SoHo.** The architectural rage of the second half of the 19th century, these facades are as functional as they are attractive.

★ **The graceful town houses along St. Luke's Place in the West Village.** These brownstones from the 1850s still rank among the most successful ensembles of urban residential architecture anywhere.

★ **The Cathedral of St. John the Divine.** This immense limestone-and-granite Gothic house of worship supported entirely by stonemasonry is still a work in progress.

Museums

★ **American Museum of Natural History.** There's something for everyone in this collection of more than 30 million artifacts. The lifelike dioramas and newly restored dinosaur collection are especially popular with children.

★ **Guggenheim Museum.** Since the opening of the new Tower Galleries annex in 1992, the Guggenheim has been able to display some of the extraordinarily large pieces from its phenomenal collection of modern art.

★ **The Cloisters.** The Metropolitan Museum's medieval collection is housed in an annex on a peaceful wooded hilltop in Washington Heights, near Manhattan's northernmost tip. Don't miss the unicorn tapestries.

★ **Metropolitan Museum of Art.** Simply one of the world's greatest museums. Select one or two galleries, but don't leave without visiting the European Sculpture Court.

★ **National Museum of the American Indian.** Opened in fall 1994, this is the first national museum dedicated to Native American culture; housed in the Alexander Hamilton Custom House in lower Manhattan.

⭐ **Pierpont Morgan Library.** The repository of one of the world's finest collections of rare books, prints, and incunabula. Don't miss J.P.'s own study and library within.

Restaurants

⭐ **Lespinasse.** Chef Gray Kunz works his magic in the Louix XV dining room of the elegant St. Regis Sheraton. *$$$$*

⭐ **San Domenico.** Terra-cotta floors, leather chairs, and warm earth help create the Mediterranean atmosphere at this Central Park South restaurant that is taking Italian cuisine to new heights. *$$$$*

⭐ **Ben Benson's.** A first-rate steak house, this is the place in midtown for chops and prime rib, Maryland crab cakes, and oversize cocktails. *$$$*

⭐ **American Place.** Executive chef Larry Forgione celebrates new American cooking in this stylish dining spot with kindly service; it just may be the country's finest regional American restaurant. *$$$*

⭐ **Hudson River Club.** This clubby, comfortable spot in lower Manhattan's Financial District combines flawless preparations of traditional dishes with an outstanding selection of American regional wines. *$$$*

⭐ **Trattoria Dell'Arte.** Across 7th Avenue from Carnegie Hall, this upbeat restaurant with its quirky, controversial decor attracts lively crowds with its creative take on traditional Italian recipes. *$$*

⭐ **Follonico.** In this Chelsea charmer, unusual pastas that change with the seasons. *$$*

⭐ **Boca Chica.** In this East Village hot spot for a (spicy) sampling of Latin America. *$*

⭐ **Turkish Kitchen.** Manhattan's best Turkish restaurant has a striking, brightly colored multilevel dining room where you can sample delicate, authentic cuisine. *$*

Hotels

⭐ **The Carlyle.** A truly grand hotel in the Old World sense, the Carlyle combines elegance and good taste with friendly, reliable service. Its serene lobby is just steps away from the fashionable shops of Madison Avenue. *$$$$*

⭐ **The Lowell.** This privately run landmark hotel has the feel of a hidden pied-à-terre. You won't want to leave your exquisite guest room with Chinese porcelains, champagne and biscuits at the minibar, a blazing fireplace, and a furnished terrace where you can eat breakfast overlooking Park Avenue. *$$$$*

⭐ **The Peninsula.** Sumptuous rooms and stylish furnishings on the swankiest stretch of 5th Avenue right in the heart of midtown. *$$$$*

⭐ **The Ritz-Carlton.** New York's Ritz somehow manages to be both grand and clubby. *$$$$*

⭐ **The Dorals.** That's as in Doral Court, Doral Park Avenue, and Doral Tuscany— three quiet, gracious sister hotels in Murray Hill, slightly off the beaten tourist track. *$$$*

⭐ **U.N. Plaza–Park Hyatt.** Popular among businesspeople, diplomats, and families with children, this hotel offers great value for its price category. All the rooms have dazzling views of the East Side. *$$$*

⭐ **The Royalton.** Hip, offbeat, and funky, this theater-district oddity (from French designer Philippe Starck) is definitely *not* for those who want their hotels to resemble English manor houses. *$$$*

⭐ **Mayflower.** This venerable spacious hotel on Central Park West makes its guests feel very much at home; just ask any of the many repeat visitors. *$$*

⭐ **The Fitzpatrick.** Good value and charm are what this amiable Irish boutique is all about. *$$*

⭐ **Hotel Beacon.** It's hard to beat the large, comfortable rooms just three blocks from Central Park, Zabar's, or Lincoln Center. *$*

⭐ **The Gershwin.** Cartoons, sculptures, and avant-garde prints dominate the public areas of this dormitory-style hotel that's popular with backpackers. *$*

⭐ **Gramercy Park.** This is a fetching Queen Anne–style hotel in an elegant, rarely visited neighborhood just southeast of midtown. Guests are provided with a key to the eponymous park. *$*

2 Exploring Manhattan

Around the next corner, a visitor to New York always has something new to discover uptown and down—world-class museums and unusual galleries, breathtaking skyscrapers, historic town houses, churches and synagogues, indoor plazas, outdoor parks and gardens. From the Battery in the south to Harlem in the north, this chapter uncovers the essential places to see in each neighborhood, as well as worthwhile sights off the tourist track. Be sure to stop and rest along the way so that you can observe the fabulous street life that makes this city so unique.

MANHATTAN IS, ABOVE ALL, A WALKER'S CITY.
Along its busy streets there's something else to
look at every few yards. Attractions, many of
them world-famous, are crowded close together on this narrow island,
and because it has to grow up, not out, new layers are simply piled on
top of the old. The city's character changes every few blocks, with quaint
town houses shouldering sleek glass towers, gleaming gourmet super-
markets sitting around the corner from dusty thrift shops, and soot-
smudged warehouses inhabited at street level by trendy neon-lit bistros.
Many a visitor has been beguiled into walking a little farther, then a
little farther still—"Let's just see what that copper dome and steeple
belongs to. . . ."

Revised by
Hannah
Borgeson,
David Low,
and Amy
McConnell

Our walking tours cover a great deal of ground, yet they only scratch
the surface. If you plod dutifully from point to point, nose buried in
this book, you'll miss half the fun. Look up at the tops of skyscrapers
and you'll see a riot of mosaics, carvings, and ornaments. Go inside
an intriguing office building and study its lobby decor; read the directory
to find out what sorts of firms have their offices there. Peep around
corners, even in crowded midtown, and you may find fountains, greenery, and sudden bursts of flowers. Find a bench or ledge to perch on,
and take time just to watch the people passing by. New York has so
many faces that every visitor can discover a different one.

Orientation

The map of Manhattan has a Jekyll-and-Hyde aspect. The rational,
Dr. Jekyll part prevails above 14th Street, where the streets form a regular grid pattern imposed in 1811. Consecutively numbered streets run
east and west (crosstown), while broad avenues, most of them also numbered, run north (uptown) or south (downtown). The chief exceptions
are Broadway (which runs on a diagonal from East 14th to West 79th
streets) and the thoroughfares that hug the shores of the Hudson and
East rivers.

Fifth Avenue is the east–west dividing line for street addresses: In both
directions, numbers increase in regular increments from there. For example, on 55th Street, the addresses 1–99 East 55th Street run from
5th, past Madison, to Park (the equivalent of 4th) avenues, 100–199
East 55th would be between Park and 3rd avenues, and so on; the addresses 1–99 West 55th Street are between 5th and 6th avenues, 100–
199 West 55th would be between 6th and 7th avenues, and so forth.
Above 59th Street, where Central Park interrupts the grid, West Side
addresses start numbering at Central Park West, an extension of 8th
Avenue. Avenue addresses are much less regular, for the numbers begin
wherever each avenue begins and increase at different increments. An
address at 552 3rd Avenue, for example, will not necessarily be anywhere near 552 2nd Avenue. Many New Yorkers themselves cannot
master the complexities of this system, so in their daily dealings they
usually include cross-street references along with avenue addresses
and rely on the handy Manhattan Address Locator found in the front
of the local phone book.

Below 14th Street—the area that was already settled before the 1811
grid was decreed—Manhattan streets reflect the disordered personality of Mr. Hyde. They may be aligned with the shoreline or they may
twist along the route of an ancient cow path. Below 14th Street you'll
find West 4th Street intersecting West 11th Street, Greenwich Street
running roughly parallel to Greenwich Avenue, Leroy Street turning

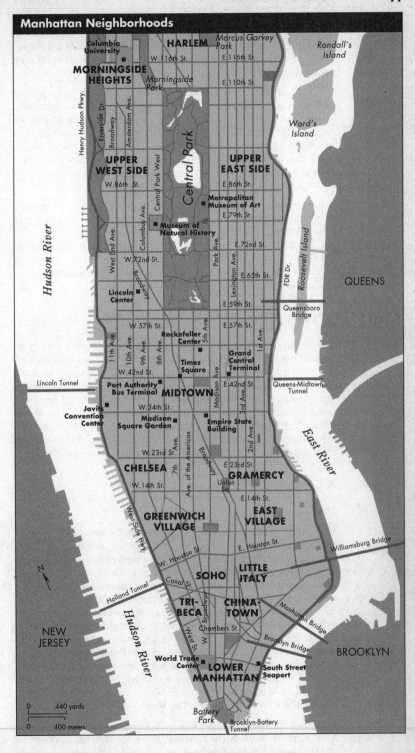

Manhattan Neighborhoods

into St. Luke's Place for one block and then becoming Leroy again. There's an East Broadway and a West Broadway, both of which run north–south and neither of which is an extension of plain old Broadway. Logic won't help you below 14th Street; only a good street map and good directions will.

You may also be confused by the way New Yorkers use "uptown" and "downtown." These terms refer both to locations and to directions. Uptown means north of wherever you are at the moment; downtown means to the south. But Uptown and Downtown are also specific parts of the city (and, some would add, two very distinct states of mind). Unfortunately, there is no consensus about where these areas are: Downtown may mean anyplace from the tip of lower Manhattan through Chelsea; it depends on the orientation of the speaker.

A similar situation exists with "East Side" and "West Side." Someone may refer to a location as "on the east side," meaning somewhere east of 5th Avenue. A hotel described as being "on the west side" may be on West 42nd Street. But when New Yorkers speak of the East Side or the West Side, they usually mean the respective areas above 59th Street, on either side of Central Park. Be prepared for misunderstandings.

ROCKEFELLER CENTER AND MIDTOWN SKYSCRAPERS

Athens has its Parthenon and Rome its Coliseum. New York's temples, which you see along this mile-long tour along six avenues and five streets, are its concrete-and-glass skyscrapers. Many of them, including the Lever House and the Seagram Building, have been pivotal in the history of modern architecture, and the 19 warm-hued limestone and aluminum buildings of Rockefeller Center are world-renowned. When movies and TV shows are set in Manhattan, they often start with a panning shot of this amazing architectural complex, because no other city scene—except perhaps the downtown skyline—so clearly says "New York."

A Good Walk
Numbers in the text correspond to numbers in the margin and on the Midtown map.

The heart of midtown Manhattan is **Rockefeller Center,** one of the greatest achievements in 20th-century urban planning. A fun way to navigate among its myriad buildings is to move from east to west following a trail punctuated by three famous statues from Greek mythology. Atlas stands sentry outside the classically inspired **International Building** ①, on 5th Avenue between 50th and 51st streets. Head one block south on 5th Avenue and turn west to walk along the **Channel Gardens** ②, a complex of rock pools and seasonally replanted flower beds. Below these is the **Lower Plaza** ③ and, towering heroically over it from an eternal ledge, the famous gold-leaf statue of Prometheus. The backdrop to this scene is the 70-story **GE Building** ④, originally known as the RCA Building, whose entrance is guarded by a striking statue of Prometheus. Straight across bustling 50th Street is America's largest indoor theater, the titanic **Radio City Music Hall** ⑤.

Two other notable Rockefeller Center buildings on the west side of 6th Avenue are the **McGraw-Hill Building** ⑥ between 48th and 50th streets and the **Time & Life Building** between 50th and 51st streets.

Continue north on 6th Avenue, leaving Rockefeller Center. On the east side of 6th Avenue between 52nd and 53rd streets, the monolithic black

CBS Building ⑦ (a.k.a. Black Rock) stands out from the crowd. From here, it's a short stroll to three museums enshrining contemporary culture. Go east on 52nd Street to the **Museum of Television and Radio** ⑧ devoted to the two key mediums of the modern era; here, you can screen favorite television shows from your childhood from the museum's huge library. A shortcut through a shopping arcade at 666 5th Avenue takes you to 53rd Street's other museums: on the south side, the **American Craft Museum** ⑨, which mounts changing exhibits of contemporary crafts from the 50 states and around the world, and, on the north side, the **Museum of Modern Art (MoMA)** ⑩, home of one of the world's most important collection of 20th-century art. Not far from MoMA, across 5th Avenue at 3 East 53rd Street is **Paley Park,** a small public space with a waterfall.

The true muse of midtown is not art but business, however, as you'll see on a brisk walk east on 53rd Street across 5th Avenue, where you'll encounter four office towers named after their corporate owners. First head north on Madison Avenue to 55th Street and the elegant rose granite tower known as the **Sony Building** ⑪, immediately recognizable from afar by its Chippendale-style pediment. Farther east and a little south on Park Avenue stand two prime examples of the functionalist International Style: **Lever House** ⑫ (between 53rd and 54th streets) and the **Seagram Building** ⑬ (between 52nd and 53rd streets), the only New York building by the celebrated Ludwig Mies van der Rohe. Finally, go one block east to Lexington Avenue where, between 53rd and 54th streets, the luminous white shaft of the **Citicorp Center** ⑭ houses thousands more New Yorkers engaged in the daily ritual that built the city—commerce. To end your walk on a less material note, return to Park Avenue and turn south to 51st Street and **St. Bartholomew's Church** ⑮, an intricate Byzantine temple struggling to be heard in the home of the skyscraper.

TIMING

To see only the buildings, block out an hour and a half. Expand your allotment depending on your interest in the museums en route. At minimum, you might spend 45 minutes in the American Craft Museum (depending on your interest in the exhibit); the same in the Museum of Television and Radio (depending on how many vintage TV shows you screen); and three and a half hours in the Museum of Modern Art (and even then you'll only dip briefly into the collections—and it would be easy to pass an entire day there, ending with a movie in the museum's theater).

Start early so as to arrive at the Museum of Television and Radio when it opens, so that you won't have to wait for a TV console to watch your shows on; break up your MoMA visit with lunch in its café.

Sights to See

⑨ **American Craft Museum.** Distinctions between "craft" and "high art" become irrelevant here, for much of this work created by contemporary American and international artisans is provocative and fun to look at. You'll see works in clay, glass, fabric, wood, metal, paper, even chocolate. ✉ *40 W. 53rd St.,* ☎ *212/956–3535.* ✆ *$5.* ☾ *Tues. 10–8, Wed.–Sun. 10–5.*

⑦ **CBS Building.** Designed by Eero Saarinen, this 38-story building has a concrete frame covered with dark gray granite. The so-called Black Rock, built in 1965, towers over the cluster of museums in the neighborhood: the Museum of Television and Radio, the American Craft Museum, and the Museum of Modern Art. ✉ *6th Ave., between 52nd and 53rd Sts.*

Algonquin Hotel, **34**

American Craft Museum, **9**

Bergdorf Goodman, **24**

Bryant Park, **37**

Carnegie Hall, **28**

CBS Building, **7**

Channel Gardens, **2**

Chrysler Building, **41**

Citicorp Center, **14**

Daily News Building, **42**

Duffy Square, **32**

FAO Schwartz, **27**

Ford Foundation Building, **43**

GE Building, **4**

Grand Army Plaza, **25**

Grand Central Terminal, **39**

Henri Bendel, **21**

International Building, **1**

ICP Midtown, **33**

Lever House, **12**

Lower Plaza, **3**

McGraw-Hill Building, **6**

Mechanics' and Tradesmen's Institute Building, **36**

Museum of Modern Art (MoMA), **10**

Museum of Television and Radio, **8**

New Amsterdam Theatre, **30**

New Victory Theatre, **29**

New York Public Library, **38**

The Plaza, **26**

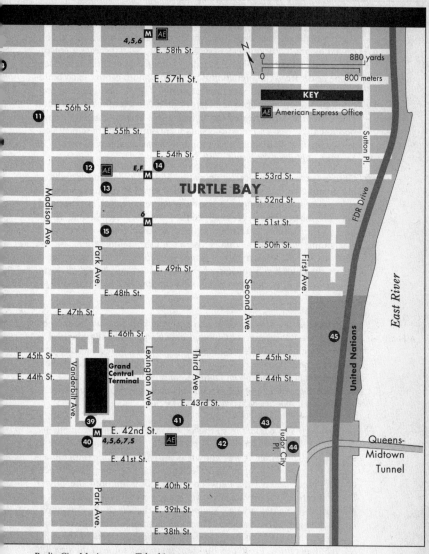

E. 58th St.
4,5,6 M AE
E. 57th St.

N
0 _____ 880 yards
0 _____ 800 meters

KEY
AE American Express Office

E. 56th St.
11

E. 55th St.

E. 54th St.
12 AE E,F 14
13 M

TURTLE BAY

E. 53rd St.
E. 52nd St.
E. 51st St.
E. 50th St.

6
15 M

E. 49th St.

E. 48th St.

E. 47th St.

E. 46th St.

E. 45th St.

E. 44th St.

E. 43rd St.

Grand
Central
Terminal

39
40 M
4,5,6,7,S

E. 42nd St.
41
AE
42
43
44

Tudor City Pl.

45

United Nations

East River

FDR Drive

Sutton Pl.

First Ave.

Second Ave.

Third Ave.

Lexington Ave.

Vanderbilt Ave.

Park Ave.

Madison Ave.

Queens-
Midtown
Tunnel

E. 41st St.
E. 40th St.
E. 39th St.
E. 38th St.

Radio City Music
Hall, **5**
Royalton Hotel, **35**
St. Bartholomew's
Church, **15**
St. Patrick's
Cathedral, **17**
St. Thomas
Church, **18**
Saks Fifth Avenue, **16**
Seagram Building, **13**
Sony Building, **11**

Takashimaya
New York, **20**
Tiffany & Co., **23**
Times Square, **31**
Trump Tower, **22**
Tudor City, **44**
United Nations
Headquarters, **45**
University Club, **19**
Whitney Museum of
American Art at
Phillip Morris, **40**

❷ **Channel Gardens.** This Rockefeller Center promenade, leading from 5th Avenue to a stair connected to the ☞ Lower Plaza, has six pools surrounded by flower beds filled with seasonal plantings and was conceived by artists, floral designers, and sculptors—10 shows a season. The area, called the Channel Gardens, separates the British building to the north from the French building to the south (above each building's entrance is a national coat of arms). The French building contains among other shops the Metropolitan Museum of Art gift shop and, of course, **Librairie de France**, which sells French-language books, periodicals, tapes, and recordings; its surprisingly large basement contains a Spanish bookstore and a foreign-language dictionary store. ⊠ *5th Ave., between 49th and 50th Sts.*

⓮ **Citicorp Center.** The most striking feature of this 1977 design of architect Hugh Stubbins & Associates is the angled top. The immense solar-energy collector it was designed to carry was never installed, but the building's unique profile forever changed the New York City skyline. At the base of the building you'll find a pleasant atrium mall of restaurants and shops, where occasionally there's music at lunchtime, and **St. Peter's Church,** known for its Sunday afternoon jazz vespers at 5; below the church is a theater where various acting troupes perform. ⊠ *Lexington Ave., between 53rd and 54th Sts.,* ☎ *212/935–2200 for St. Peter's.*

OFF THE
BEATEN PATH

BEEKMAN PLACE – This secluded and exclusive East Side two-block-long thoroughfare has an aura of unperturbably elegant calm. Residents of its refined town houses have included the Rockefellers, Alfred Lunt and Lynn Fontanne, Ethel Barrymore, Irving Berlin, and, of course, Auntie Mame, a character in the well-known Patrick Dennis play of the same name. Go down the steps at 51st Street to reach a walkway along the East River. ⊠ *East of 1st Ave., between 49th and 51st Sts.*

❹ **GE Building.** The backdrop to the ☞ Channel Gardens, Prometheus, and the ☞ Lower Plaza, this 70-story building is the tallest tower in ☞ Rockefeller Center. It was known as the RCA Building until GE acquired its namesake company in 1986. The block-long street called Rockefeller Plaza, which runs between the GE Building and the Lower Plaza, is officially a private street (to maintain that status, it closes to all traffic on one day a year); each year it is the site of the ever-popular Rockefeller Christmas tree. The thoroughfare is often choked with celebrities' black limousines, for this is the headquarters of the NBC television network. From this building emanated some of the first TV programs ever, including the *Today* show. It's now broadcast from a ground-floor, glass-enclosed studio on the southwest corner of 49th Street and Rockefeller Plaza, so if you're in the area between 7 and 9 AM, your face may show up on TV behind the *Today* show hosts. To see what goes on inside, sign up for a one-hour tour of the NBC Studios. ⊠ *30 Rockefeller Plaza,* ☎ *212/664–4000. Departures from street level of GE Building every 15 mins, 9:30–4:30, Mon.–Sat., and on Sun. in summer.* ▣ *$8.25. Children under 6 not permitted.*

As you enter the GE Building from Rockefeller Plaza, look up at the striking sculpture of Zeus above the entrance doors, executed in limestone cast in glass by Lee Lawrie, the same artist who sculpted the big Atlas in front of the ☞ International Building on 5th Avenue. Inside, crane your neck to see the dramatic ceiling mural entitled *Time,* by José Maria Sert. From the lobby information desk, go down the escalator in the right-hand corner and turn right to find a detailed exhibit on the history of the center. ▣ *Free.* ☽ *Weekdays 9–5.*

After leaving the exhibit, take some time to wander around the marble catacombs that connect the various components of Rockefeller Center. There's a lot to see: restaurants in all price ranges, from the chic American Festival Café to McDonald's; a post office and clean public rest rooms (scarce in midtown); and just about every kind of store. To find your way around, consult the strategically placed directories or obtain the free "Shops and Services Guide" at the GE Building information desk. Before leaving the GE Building lobby, you might also take an elevator to the 65th floor to enjoy the spectacular view with drinks or a meal at the **Rainbow Room** (☞ Chapter 6). When you've seen all there is to see, leave the GE Building on 6th Avenue to view the allegorical mosaics above that entrance. ⊠ *Bounded by Rockefeller Plaza, 6th Ave., and 49th and 50th Sts.*

NEED A
BREAK?   **Dean & Deluca** (⊠ 1 Rockefeller Plaza at 49th St., ☎ 212/664–1363) is near the GE Building. You can relax here with a cup of coffee, tea, or hot chocolate, and cookies, cakes, and small sandwiches.

---

❶ International Building. A huge statue of Atlas supporting the world stands sentry before this heavily visited ☞ Rockefeller Center structure, which houses many foreign consulates, international airlines, and a U.S. passport office. The lobby is fitted with Grecian marble. ⊠ *5th Ave., between 50th and 51st Sts.*

⑫ Lever House. Architect Gordon Bunshaft, of Skidmore, Owings & Merrill, created this seminal skyscraper, a sheer, slim glass box resting on one end of a one-story-thick shelf that is balanced on square chrome columns and seems to float above the street. Because the tower occupies only half of the space above the lower floors, a great deal of airspace is left open, and the tower's side wall displays a reflection of its neighbors. It was built in 1952. ⊠ *390 Park Ave., between 53rd and 54th Sts.*

❸ Lower Plaza. Sprawled on his ledge above this ☞ Rockefeller Center plaza, you will see one of the most famous sights in the complex (if not all of New York): the great gold-leaf statue of the fire-stealing Greek hero **Prometheus.** A quotation from Aeschylus is carved into the red granite wall behind, and 50 jets of water spray around the statue. The plaza's trademark ice-skating rink is open from October through April; the rest of the year, it becomes an open-air café. In December an enormous live Christmas tree towers above this area. On the Esplanade above the plaza, flags of the United Nations' members alternate with flags of the states. ⊠ *Between 5th and 6th Aves. and 49th and 50th Sts.*

❻ McGraw-Hill Building. Built in 1972, this ☞ Rockefeller Center skyscraper is notable for its street-level plaza with a 50-foot steel sun triangle that points to the seasonal positions of the sun at noon and a pool that demonstrates the relative size of the planets. ⊠ *6th Ave., between 48th and 49th Sts.*

★ ⑩ Museum of Modern Art (MoMA). In its second- and third-floor galleries of painting and sculpture, MoMA displays some of the world's most famous modern paintings: Van Gogh's *Starry Night,* Picasso's *Les Demoiselles d'Avignon,* Matisse's *Dance.* The bright and airy six-story structure, built around a secluded sculpture garden, also includes photography, architecture, decorative arts, drawings, prints, illustrated books, and films. Afternoon and evening film shows, mostly of foreign productions and classics, are free with the price of admission; tickets, distributed in the lobby on the day of the performance, often go fast. Programs change daily; call 212/708–9491 for a schedule. Free jazz concerts are given in the café on Friday evenings. And leave time to sit outside in that wonderful Sculpture Garden, which hosts contemporary music concerts during the summer. ⊠ *11 W. 53rd St., ☎ 212/708–9480. ☑ $8; pay what you wish Thurs. and Fri. 5:30–8:30. ☉ Sat.–Tues. 11–6, Thurs. and Fri. noon–8:30.*

⑧ Museum of Television and Radio. Three galleries of photographs and artifacts document the history of broadcasting in this new limestone building by Philip Johnson and John Burgee. But most visitors come here to sit at the museum consoles and watch TV: The collection includes more than 75,000 television shows and radio programs, as well as several thousand commercials. ⊠ *25 W. 52nd St., ☎ 212/621–6800 for daily events or 212/621–6600 for other information. ☑ Suggested contribution: $6. ☉ Tues.–Sun. noon–6, Thurs. noon–8.*

Paley Park. A boon to midtown's weary, this memorial to former CBS executive Samuel Paley was the first of New York's "pocket parks" to be inserted among the high-rise behemoths, placed on the site of the former society night spot the Stork Club. A waterfall blocks out traffic noise, and feathery honey locust trees provide shade. There's a snack bar that opens when weather permits. The public space is across the street from the Museum of Modern Art. ⊠ *3 E. 53rd St.*

⑤ Radio City Music Hall. Part of ☞ Rockefeller Center, this 6,000-seat Art Deco masterpiece is America's largest indoor theater, with a 60-foot-high foyer and two-ton chandeliers. Home of the fabled Rockettes chorus line (which actually started out in St. Louis in 1925), Radio City was built as a movie theater with a stage suitable for live shows as well. Its days as a first-run movie house are long over, but after an announced closing in 1978, Radio City has had an amazing comeback, producing concerts, awards presentations, and special events, along with its own Christmas and Easter extravaganzas. On most days you can take a one-hour tour of the premises. ⊠ *6th Ave. at 50th St., ☎ 212/247–4777; tour information, 212/632–4041. ☑ $12 (tour). ☉ Tours usually leave from main lobby every 30–45 mins Mon.–Sat. 10–5, Sun. 11–5.*

Rockefeller Center. Begun during the Great Depression of the 1930s by John D. Rockefeller, this 19-building complex occupies nearly 22 acres of prime real estate between 5th and 7th avenues and 47th and 52nd streets. Its central cluster of buildings are smooth shafts of warm-hued limestone, streamlined with glistening aluminum. The real genius of the complex's design was its intelligent use of public space: Its plazas, concourses, and street-level shops create a sense of community for the nearly quarter of a million human beings who use it daily. Restaurants, shoe-repair shops, doctors' offices, barbershops, banks, a post office, bookstores, clothing shops, variety stores—all are accommodated within the center, and all parts of the complex are linked by underground passageways.

Rockefeller Center helped turn midtown into New York City's second "downtown" area, which now rivals the Wall Street area in the number of its prestigious tenants. The center itself is a capital of the communications industry, containing the headquarters of a TV network (NBC), several major publishing companies (Time-Warner, McGraw-Hill, and Simon & Schuster), and the world's largest news-gathering organization, the Associated Press. Some of the complex's major sights include ☞ Radio City Music Hall, the ☞ International Building, the ☞ Channel Gardens, the ☞ Lower Plaza, and the ☞ GE Building.

OFF THE
BEATEN PATH

DIAMOND DISTRICT – The relatively unglitzy jewelry shops at street level on 47th Street between 5th and 6th avenues are just the tip of the iceberg; upstairs, millions of dollars' worth of gems are traded, and skilled craftsmen cut precious stones. Wheeling and dealing goes on at fever pitch, all rendered strangely exotic by the presence of a host of Hasidic Jews in severe black dress, beards, and curled side locks. During the day, this street becomes one of the slowest to navigate by foot in Manhattan because of all the people. Amid the jewelry stores, you'll also find one of New York's best bookstores, the Gotham Book Mart (⊠ 41 W. 47th St.).

★ ⑮ **St. Bartholomew's Church.** Church fathers have been eager to sell the airspace over this 1919 structure with rounded arches and an intricately tiled Byzantine dome, to take advantage of the stratospheric property values in this part of town. So far, fortunately, landmark forces have prevented any such move. ⊠ *Park Ave., between 50th and 51st Sts.*

⑬ **Seagram Building.** Architect Ludwig Mies van der Rohe, a leading interpreter of the International Style, built this simple bronze and glass boxlike tower in 1958. Its ground-level plaza, an innovation at the time, has since become a common element in urban skyscraper design. Inside is one of New York's most venerated restaurants, **The Four Seasons** (☞ Chapter 6). ⊠ *Park Ave., between 52nd and 53rd Sts.*

⑪ **Sony Building.** Unlike the sterile ice-cube-tray buildings of 6th Avenue, Sony's rose granite columns, its regilded statue of the winged *Golden Boy* in the lobby, and its peculiar "Chippendale" roof have made this design of architect Philip Johnson an instant landmark for New Yorkers, who consider it the first postmodern skyscraper. Former tenant AT&T has moved to New Jersey. The first floor, Sony Plaza, includes a public seating area, cafés, a newsstand, a music store where you can purchase recordings, and the new **Sony Wonder Technology Lab,** outfitted with tremendously entertaining interactive exhibits such as a recording studio, a video-game production studio, and a TV production studio. ⊠ *550 Madison Ave., between 55th and 56th Sts. Sony Wonder Technology Lab:* ☎ *212/833–8830.* ☜ *Free.* ☉ *Tues.–Sat. 10–6, Sun. noon–6. Plaza:* ☉ *Daily 7 AM–11 PM.*

The "21" Club. A trademark row of jockey statuettes parades along the wrought-iron balcony of this landmark restaurant. Now wonderfully restored after an extensive renovation, it still has a burnished men's-club atmosphere, a great downstairs bar, and a power-broker clientele. In the movie *The Sweet Smell of Success,* Burt Lancaster as a powerful Broadway columnist held court at his regular table here, besieged by Tony Curtis as a pushy young publicist. (☞ Chapter 6.) ⊠ *21 W. 52nd St.,* ☎ *212/582–7200.*

5TH AVENUE AND 57TH STREET

The stretch of 5th Avenue upward from Rockefeller Center glitters with elegant shops, but the rents are even higher along East 57th Street, a parade of very exclusive smaller stores and upmarket art galleries. This is one of the world's great shopping districts, and every year more and more international fashion firms try to muscle in on this turf. If your goal here is to spend a lot of money, *see* Chapter 10 for more details.

Theme restaurants, the most recent additions to the neighborhood, dominate 57th Street west of 5th Avenue (☞ Chapter 6 for more details).

A Good Walk

Numbers in the text correspond to numbers in the margin and on the Midtown map.

Start right across the street from Rockefeller Center's Channel Gardens (☞ Rockefeller Center and Midtown Skyscrapers, *above*), at renowned **Saks Fifth Avenue** ⑯, the flagship of the national department store chain. Across 50th Street is Gothic-style **St. Patrick's** ⑰, the Roman Catholic Cathedral of New York. From outside, catch one of the city's most photographed views: the ornate white spires of St. Pat's against the black glass curtain of **Olympic Tower,** a multiuse building of shops, offices, and luxury apartments.

Cartier, Inc., displays its wares in a jewel-box, turn-of-the-century mansion on the southeast corner of 52nd Street and 5th Avenue; similar houses used to line this street, and many of their residents were parishioners of **St. Thomas Church** ⑱, an Episcopal institution that has occupied the site at the northwest corner of 53rd Street and 5th Avenue since 1911. Continuing north, you'll see the imposing bulk of the **University Club** ⑲ at the northwest corner of 5th Avenue and 54th Street; this granite palace was built by New York's leading turn-of-the-century architects, McKim, Mead & White. Across the street is **Takashimaya New York** ⑳ (✉ 593 5th Ave.), a branch of Japan's largest department store chain.

Fifth Avenue Presbyterian Church, a grand brownstone church (1875), sits on the northwest corner of 5th Avenue and 55th Street. On the same block is **Henri Bendel** ㉑, a bustling fashion store organized like a little tower of intimate boutiques. Next door is **Harry Winston** (✉ 718 5th Ave.), with a spectacular selection of fine jewelry. Across the street, on the northeast corner of 5th Avenue and 55th Street, is the new **Disney Store.**

Trump Tower ㉒, on the east side of 5th Avenue between 56th and 57th streets, is an exclusive 68-story apartment and office building named for its developer, Donald Trump. Just north of it, the intersection of 5th Avenue and 57th Street is ground zero for high-class shopping. And what more fitting resident for this spot than **Tiffany & Co.** ㉓, the renowned jewelers. Around the corner on 57th, **Nike** recently opened a sporting goods superstore, next to what everyone still calls the **IBM Building,** a five-sided, 20-story sheath of dark gray-green granite and glass by Edward Larrabee Barnes. In 1996, the company sold the building, which is at the corner of 57th Street and Madison Avenue.

Cross 57th Street and head back toward 5th Avenue on the north side of the street, with its stellar lineup of boutiques: the French shop **Hermès** (✉ 11 E. 57th St.), the English shop **Burberrys Ltd.** (✉ 9 E. 57th St.), the German shop **Escada** (✉ 7 E. 57th St.), and the French classic **Chanel** (✉ 5 E. 57th St.). Regular folk are less likely to feel outclassed at the newer additions to the block: the **Original Levi's Store** (✉ 3 E. 57th St.), with the usual jeans, and the **Warner Brothers Studio Store** (✉ 1 E. 57th St.), with loads of movie, television, and cartoon paraphernalia. From outside the Warner Brothers store, you can watch a larger than life Superman pushing up the elevator. Across 5th Avenue (at 754, to be exact), you can visit the elegant **Bergdorf Goodman** ㉔. The extravagant women's boutiques are on the west side of the avenue and the men's store on the east side, both between 57th and 58th streets. **Van Cleef & Arpels** jewelers is located within Bergdorf's 57th Street corner.

Cross 58th Street to **Grand Army Plaza** ㉕, the open space along 5th Avenue between 58th and 60th streets. Appropriately named **The Plaza** ㉖, the famous hotel (☞ Chapter 7) at the western edge of this square is a registered historical landmark built in 1907. Across the street, on the southeast corner of 58th Street and 5th Avenue is the legendary **F.A.O. Schwarz** ㉗ toy store ensconced in the General Motors Building.

Now return to 57th Street and head west, where the glamour eases off a bit. The large red **No. 9** on the sidewalk, in front of the curving headquarters of Chanel, was designed by Ivan Chermayeff, noted for saying, "If it's big and ugly, it's not big enough." You'll also pass the excellent **Rizzoli** bookstore (✉ 31 W. 57th St.), and beyond that is arguably the handsomest McDonald's in the land, with an elegant blue-neon decorating scheme that's definitely not standard-issue for the burger chain. From the corner of 57th Street and 5th Avenue you can see the sleek **Harley-Davidson Cafe** (✉ 1370 6th Ave. at 56th St.), one of many contenders in the trendy burger-joint olympics, and the playfully menacing **Jekyll and Hyde Club** (✉ 1409 6th Ave. at 57th St.).

Across 6th Avenue (remember, New Yorkers *don't* call it Avenue of the Americas, despite the street signs), you'll know you're in classical-music territory when you peer through the showroom windows at **Steinway** (✉ 109 W. 57th St.). But before you get to Carnegie Hall, grab a bite (or at least steal a peek) at the **Motown Cafe** (✉ 104 W. 57th St.) or **Planet Hollywood** (✉ 140 W. 57th St.), where you'll find everything from Humphrey Bogart's Maltese Falcon to *Star Wars'* R2D2 and C-3PO robots. A few doors down from Planet Hollywood is the site of the famed **Russian Tea Room** restaurant (✉ 150 W. 57th St.), which is being renovated.

An old joke says it all: A tourist asks an old guy with a violin case, "How do you get to Carnegie Hall?" His reply: "Practice, practice, practice." Presiding over the southeast corner of 7th Avenue and 57th Street, **Carnegie Hall** ㉘ has been considered a premier international concert hall for decades. Devotees of classical music may want to head from here up to nearby Lincoln Center (☞ The Upper West Side, *below*). If rock-and-roll music is more to your liking, head west one more block to the **Hard Rock Cafe** (✉ 221 W. 57th St.), New York City's outpost of the restaurant chain.

A few blocks south and west is the old **Ed Sullivan Theater** (✉ 1697 Broadway, between 53rd and 54th Sts.), now home to the *David Letterman Show.* Many shopkeepers and restaurateurs on this block have become minor late-night celebrities as a result of the talk-show host's habit of wandering out onto the street to harass his neighbors.

TIMING

This walk isn't long and can be completed in about 1½ hours. Add at least an hour for basic browsing around stores, and several more hours for serious shopping. Make sure the stores are open beforehand (☞ Chapter 10). If you want to eat at your favorite memorabilia-decked restaurant, plan on waiting up to an hour just for a table. Fifth Avenue is jam-packed around the Christmas holiday until New Year's.

Sights to See

㉔ **Bergdorf Goodman.** Good taste reigns supreme in this understated department store with dependable service—at a price. The Home Department has room after exquisite room of wonderful linens, tabletop items, and gifts. The expanded men's store across the street is the place to go for that special gift. ✉ *754 5th Ave., between 57th and 58th Sts.,* ☎ *212/753–7300.*

NEED A
BREAK?   **Mangia** (✉ 50 W. 57th St., ☎ 212/582–3061), an Italian and American food shop, is a great place to stop for coffee and a snack on a very busy street. The salad bar is exceptional.

28 Carnegie Hall. Musical headliners have been playing here since 1891, when its first concert was conducted by no less than Tchaikovsky. Outside it's a stout, square brown building with a few Moorish-style arches added, almost as an afterthought, to the facade. Inside, however, is a simply decorated 2,804-seat auditorium that is considered one of the finest in the world. It was extensively restored before its gala 1990–1991 centennial season, but something was wrong with the main auditorium's acoustics. In mid-September 1995, the culprit was identified—concrete was found filling what should have been a hollow space under the stage's wood floor. The concrete was removed and the floor underpinnings were restored to what they should have been all along. The restoration also increased the size of the lobby, and a museum has been added just east of the main auditorium, displaying memorabilia from the hall's illustrious history. Guided tours of Carnegie Hall are available (they last about 45 minutes). ⊠ *Carnegie Hall Museum: 881 7th Ave.,* ☎ *212/903–9629.* ☎ *Free.* ☉ *Mon., Tues., Thurs.–Sun. 11–4:30; guided tours (*☎ *212/247–7800) offered Mon., Tues., Thurs., and Fri. 11:30, 2, and 3 (performance schedule permitting);* ☎ *$6.*

☝ **27 F.A.O. Schwarz.** The famous toy emporium has its fantastic mechanical clock right inside the front doors. Bigger than it looks from outside, the toy-o-rama offers a vast, wondrously fun selection, although it definitely tends toward expensive imports. Browsing here tends to bring out the child in everyone, as it did in the movie *Big,* when Tom Hanks and his boss got caught up in tap-dancing on a giant keyboard. ⊠ *767 5th Ave. at 58th St.,* ☎ *212/644–9400.*

25 Grand Army Plaza. Just before you get to Central Park, you'll reach this open space along 5th Avenue between 58th and 60th streets. The southern block features the **Pulitzer Fountain,** donated by publisher Joseph Pulitzer of Pulitzer Prize fame. Appropriately enough for this ritzy area, the fountain is crowned by a female figure representing Abundance. The block to the north holds a gilded (some say *too* gilded) equestrian statue of Civil War general William Tecumseh Sherman; beyond it is a grand entrance to Central Park (☞ Central Park, *below*). ☞ **The Plaza,** an internationally famous hotel, is at the western edge of the square. East of Grand Army Plaza on 5th Avenue at 58th Street stands the **General Motors Building,** a 50-story tower of Georgia marble. One section of the main floor is the flagship of the legendary ☞ **F.A.O. Schwarz** toy store.

21 Henri Bendel. Shoppers always seem to have a good time at this beautiful store, which continues to delight with its inventive displays and sophisticated boutiques. The facade's René Lalique art-glass windows from 1912 can be viewed at close range from balconies ringing the four-story atrium. The second floor café is particularly charming. ⊠ *712 5th Ave., between 55th and 56th Sts.,* ☎ *212/247–1100.*

26 The Plaza. This world-famous hotel is a registered historical landmark built in 1907. Its architect, Henry Hardenbergh, was the same man who designed the Dakota apartment building (☞ The Upper West Side, *below*); here he achieved a sprightly birthday-cake effect with white-glazed brick busily decorated and topped off with a copper-and-slate mansard roof. The hotel is home to the fictional children's-book star Eloise and has been featured in many movies, from Alfred Hitchcock's *North by Northwest* to more recent films such as *Arthur, Crocodile Dundee, Home Alone 2,* and, of course, *Plaza Suite.* Among the many upper-crust parties that have taken place in the Plaza's ballroom was Truman Capote's Black and White Ball of 1966, attended by everyone who was anyone—all dressed, naturally, in black and white. ⊠ *5th Ave. at 59th St.,* ☎ *212/759–3000.*

⑯ Saks Fifth Avenue. The flagship of the national department store chain moved here in 1926, solidifying midtown 5th Avenue's new status as an upscale shopping mecca. At the time, this branch's name was meant to distinguish it from its earlier incarnation on Broadway. It remains a civilized favorite among New York shoppers. ⊠ *611 5th Ave., between 49 and 50th Sts.,* ☎ *212/753–4000.*

⑰ St. Patrick's Cathedral. The Gothic-style house of worship is the Roman Catholic Cathedral of New York. Dedicated to the patron saint of the Irish—then and now one of New York's principal ethnic groups—the white marble and stone structure was begun in 1858, consecrated in 1879, and completed in 1906. The congregation purposely chose the 5th Avenue location for their church, claiming a prestigious spot for themselves at least on Sundays—otherwise they would be in the neighborhood largely as employees of the wealthy. Among the statues in the alcoves around the nave is a modern interpretation of the first American-born saint, Mother Elizabeth Seton. ⊠ *5th Ave. at 50th St.,* ☎ *212/753–2261 (rectory).*

⑱ St. Thomas Church. This Episcopal institution with a striking French Gothic interior has occupied its present site since 1911. The impressive huge stone reredos behind the altar holds the statues of more than 50 apostles, saints, martyrs, missionaries, and church figures; these were designed by Lee Lawrie. Christmas Eve services here have become a seasonal star. ⊠ *5th Ave. at 53rd St.,* ☎ *212/757–7013.*

⑳ Takashimaya New York. This elegant yet somewhat austere branch of Japan's largest department store chain features a garden atrium, a two-floor gallery, a tearoom, and three floors of men's and women's clothing and household items that combine Eastern and Western styles. ⊠ *693 5th Ave., between 54th and 55th Sts.,* ☎ *212/350–0100.*

㉓ Tiffany & Co. The renowned jewelers, with the Fort Knox–like Art Deco entrance and dramatic miniature window displays, moved uptown from Herald Square at the beginning of the century, helping to set the standard for what this neighborhood was to become. A quintessential New York movie, *Breakfast at Tiffany's,* opens with Audrey Hepburn dressed in a Givenchy evening gown and emerging from a yellow cab at dawn to stand here window-shopping with a coffee and Danish. ⊠ *727 5th Ave. at 57th St.,* ☎ *212/755–8000.*

㉒ Trump Tower. As he has done with other projects, developer Donald Trump named this exclusive 68-story apartment and office building after himself. The grand 5th Avenue entrance leads into a glitzy six-story shopping atrium paneled in pinkish-orange marble and trimmed with lustrous brass. A fountain cascades against one wall, drowning out the clamor of the city. ⊠ *5th Ave., between 56th and 57th Sts.*

⑲ University Club. New York's leading turn-of-the-century architects, McKim, Mead & White, designed this granite palace for an exclusive midtown men's club, one of several that only recently have begun accepting women members. Pick out the crests of various prestigious universities above its windows. ⊠ *1 W. 54th St.*

42ND STREET

As midtown Manhattan's central axis, 42nd Street ties together several major points of interest, from the United Nations on the East River, past Grand Central Terminal, to Times Square. Despite being one of the world's busiest streets, some of its blocks have fallen upon hard times recently. Revitalization began in the late 1980s, however, with the help of business improvement districts, or BIDs, that tax local businesses and residents in order to provide greater levels of sanitation, security, and tourist services, among others. Bryant Park has been touted as the success of one such organization, and the blocks of 42nd Street west of Times Square are next.

Having acquired a reputation as a den of pickpockets, porno houses, prostitutes, and destitutes, the area is working to reclaim its fame as the metaphorical Broadway. After years of talks, plans, and proposals, there is finally action, and now it's hard to keep up with the pace of change. Several old theaters are in different stages of being readied for reopening. New stores, hotels, and restaurants, many with entertainment themes, are moving in as well, sure to capitalize on the tourists who can't seem to get enough of the area. In Times Square itself, the neon lights shine brighter than ever, and the ads become as creative, and even interactive, as technology allows. Some critics decry the Disney-fication of this part of town, but really, what area is more appropriate for this over-the-top treatment?

A Good Walk
Numbers in the text correspond to numbers in the margin and on the Midtown map.

The block of 42nd Street between 9th and 10th avenues is home to a string of thriving Off-Broadway playhouses, called **Theatre Row** (☞ Chapter 5). The monolithic **Port Authority Bus Terminal,** itself much improved over the last few years, sits on the next block. At No. 330, between 8th and 9th avenues, you should peek in. Originally the **McGraw-Hill Building,** it was designed in 1931 by Raymond Hood, who later worked on Rockefeller Center. The lobby is an Art Deco wonder of opaque glass and stainless steel.

The block past Port Authority is one of those that are most obviously being improved. Many of its buildings stood unused for years, and many others were functional only as X-rated bookstores, peep shows, or movie theaters. All this is changing, however. The **Harris Theater** (✉ 226 W. 42nd St.) is the temporary home of a new tourist information center; the office will be moving around the block as buildings are renovated and the Times Square redevelopment project continues. The currently dark **Times Square Theater** is across the street. Be sure to stop for a minute to read the sayings posted on its marquee, and the others not used for advertising performances. The sometimes thought-provoking lines, such as "You can tell the ideas of a nation by its advertisements," are the result of the efforts of the 42nd Street Art project. Next to it is a rehabilitated treasure that opened in December 1995, the **New Victory** ㉙, the first theater in New York to feature productions by and for children. If you still can't erase the image of 42nd Street as a sleazy strip, consider the new tenant of the **New Amsterdam** ㉚—the Walt Disney Company. The city claimed victory when the company agreed to rehabilitate this site (across the street from the New Victory), and it is probably Disney's presence that convinced other developers and retailers that the neighborhood really was changing.

Although it may not exactly be the Crossroads of the World, as it is often called, **Times Square** ㉛ is one of New York's principal energy centers, not least because of its dazzling billboards. Heading east from Times Square on 42nd Street, you'll pass **Hotaling's News,** a bustling little shop where you can buy print news from around the world. The triangle north of Times Square between 46th and 47th Streets is named

Duffy Square ㉜ after World War I hero Father Francis P. Duffy, the "Fighting Chaplain," who later was pastor of Holy Cross Church on West 42nd Street. At the intersection of 42nd Street and 6th Avenue, look north to see, on the side of a low 43rd Street building, the **National Debt Clock,** an electronic display established by the late real-estate developer Seymour Durst to remind passersby of how much deeper in debt the United States gets every second. At 6th Avenue and 43rd Street you can visit a branch of the International Center of Photography (☞ Museum Mile, *below*), **ICP Midtown** ㉝.

A block north of that is a rather clubby section of 44th Street that you might want to peek into before returning to 42nd Street. First, you'll see the surprisingly unpretentious **Algonquin Hotel** ㉞, a celebrity haunt. Next door is the more humble (and cheaper) **Iroquois Hotel** (⊠ 49 W. 44th St.), where struggling actor James Dean lived in the early 1950s. Across the street from them is the **Royalton Hotel** ㉟, where unless your clothes are suitably trendy, you'll be eyed suspiciously by the staff. Its neighbor, at 42 West 44th Street, is the **Association of the Bar of the City of New York,** with a neoclassical facade resembling the courthouses where its members spend so much of their time. Back on the north side of the street, at 37 West 44th Street, is the **New York Yacht Club,** and at No. 27, the redbrick **Harvard Club.** The newer **Penn Club** (⊠ 30 W. 44th St.), with its elegant blue awning, is on the other side of the street. And yes, something on this block is open to the general public: the **Mechanics' and Tradesmen's Institute Building** ㊱, at 20 West 44th St.

At the southwest corner of 5th Avenue and 44th Street, notice the large **sidewalk clock** on a pedestal set in the 5th Avenue sidewalk, a relic of an era when only rich people could afford watches.

At 42nd Street at 6th Avenue, steps rise into the shrubbery and trees of the handsomely renovated **Bryant Park** ㊲, named for the poet and editor William Cullen Bryant (1794–1878). Full of benches and lawn chairs, this is a perfect place to relax for a few minutes. Though the park has been adopted as the backyard of all midtown workers, it's directly behind the magnificent Beaux Arts central research building of the **New York Public Library** ㊳, and the library houses part of its collections under the green lawn.

Continue east on 42nd Street to **Grand Central Terminal** ㊴. This Manhattan landmark was saved from the wrecking ball in a precedent-setting case that established the legality of New York's landmark preservation law. Stop on the south side of 42nd Street to admire the three huge windows separated by columns, and the Beaux Arts clock and sculpture (*Transportation*) crowning the facade above the elevated roadway (Park Avenue is routed around Grand Central's upper story). Go in the side doors on Vanderbilt Avenue to enter the cavernous main concourse.

On the southwest corner of Park Avenue and 42nd Street, directly opposite Grand Central, the **Whitney Museum of American Art at Philip Morris** ㊵ occupies the ground floor of the Philip Morris Building. The company keeps threatening to pull its headquarters out of the city in response to ever-stricter smoking regulations, but so far it has not left. The southeast corner of 42nd and Park is a major departure point for buses to the three New York area airports, and upstairs at 100 East 42nd Street is the **Satellite Airlines Terminal,** where you'll find ticket counters for most major U.S. airlines. Next door is the **Green Point Savings Bank,** also known as **Bowery Savings Bank** (⊠ 110 E. 42nd St.), whose massive arches and 70-foot-high marble columns give it a commanding presence; it more closely resembles a church than a bank. At the end of the block is the **Chanin Building** (✉ 122 E. 42nd St.), notable for the geometric Art Deco patterns that adorn its facade. Across the street you'll see the **Grand Hyatt** (✉ Park Ave. at Grand Central Terminal), which was created by wrapping a new black glass exterior around the former Commodore Hotel.

Ask New Yorkers to name their favorite skyscraper and most will choose the Art Deco **Chrysler Building** ㊶ at 42nd Street and Lexington Avenue. Although the Chrysler Corporation itself moved out a long time ago, this graceful shaft culminating in a stainless-steel spire still captivates the eye and the imagination. On the other side of 42nd Street, the **Daily News Building** ㊷, where the newspaper was produced until spring 1995, is another Art Deco tower with a lobby worth visiting. The **Ford Foundation Building** ㊸, on the next block, is more modern and encloses a 12-story, ⅓-acre greenhouse.

Climb the steps along 42nd Street between 1st and 2nd avenues to enter **Tudor City** ㊹, a self-contained complex of a dozen buildings featuring half-timbering and lots of stained glass. From it, you have a great view of the **United Nations Headquarters** ㊺, which occupies a lushly landscaped 18-acre riverside tract just east of 1st Avenue between 42nd and 48th streets.

TIMING

This long walk covers vastly different types of sites, from crazy Times Square to bucolic Bryant Park to majestic Grand Central Terminal to the inspiring United Nations. Make sure you allow ample time to see it all—more than half a day. Do this tour during daylight hours, but return to Times Square at night, perhaps for a meal or a show, to truly appreciate the neon spectacle.

Sights to See

㉞ **Algonquin Hotel.** Considering its history as a haunt of well-known writers and actors, this hotel is surprisingly unpretentious. Its most famous association is with a witty group of literary Manhattanites who gathered in its lobby and dining rooms in the 1920s—a clique that included short-story writer and critic Dorothy Parker, humorist Robert Benchley, playwright George S. Kaufman, and actress Tallulah Bankhead. One reason they met here was the hotel's proximity to the former offices of *The New Yorker* magazine at 28 West 44th (now at 20 West 43rd Street). Come here for tea in the lobby, a drink at the bar, or dinner and cabaret performances in the intimate Oak Room (☞ Chapter 7). ✉ *59 W. 44th St.,* ☎ *212/840–6800.*

★ ㉟ **Bryant Park.** The New York Public Library keeps an incredible stash of books underneath this lovely stretch of green. The park has been lovingly restored and teems with well-dressed professionals who snatch up the lawn chairs for their brown-bag power lunches. Named for the poet and editor William Cullen Bryant (1794–1878), this was the site of America's first World's Fair, the Crystal Palace Exhibition of 1853–54. The **Bryant Park Dance and Music Tickets Booth** in a setup similar to that of TKTS sells tickets for music and dance performances throughout the city (☞ Chapter 5). The park also has an elegant restaurant and a café.

★ ㊶ **Chrysler Building.** It'd be a shame to make New Yorkers pick one favorite skyscraper, but if they had to, this Art Deco masterpiece (1928–30) would probably be it. The Chrysler Corporation moved out a long time ago, but fortunately for publicity's sake the building still has its name and many details from the company's cars—check out the elevator cabs, for example. The stainless-steel spire (polished in late 1995 to shine even brighter) was kept secret during the building's construction so other builders wouldn't know what height to try to top. The building held the world's-tallest title only briefly, and architectural spies knew about its spire before it was hoisted up to crown the building, but it still captivates the eye and the imagination, glistening in the sun during the day, glowing geometrically at night. The Chrysler Building has no observation deck, but you can go into its elegant dark lobby, which is faced with African marble and covered with a ceiling mural that salutes transportation and human endeavor. ⊠ *405 Lexington Ave. at 42nd St.*

㊷ Daily News Building. This Raymond Hood–designed Art Deco tower has brown-brick spandrels and windows to make it seem loftier than its 37 stories. The newspaper moved out in spring 1995, but the famous revolving illuminated globe, 12 feet in diameter, is still there. The floor is laid out as a gigantic compass, with bronze lines indicating air mileage from principal world cities to New York. ⊠ *220 E. 42nd St.*

㉜ Duffy Square. This triangle north of 42nd Street is named after World War I hero Father Francis P. Duffy, the "Fighting Chaplain," who later was pastor of a theater district church on West 42nd Street. Besides the suitably military statue of Father Duffy, there's also one of George M. Cohan, the indomitable trouper who wrote "Yankee Doodle Dandy." Today Duffy Square is an important place to visit for the **TKTS discount ticket booth,** which sells half-price and 25%-off tickets to Broadway and Off-Broadway shows. Some days it seems that almost every show in town is up for grabs; at other times there may be nothing available but a few long-running shows on their last legs and some sleepers. Even when lines are long they move surprisingly fast. ⊠ *Between 46th and 47th Sts.*

OFF THE
BEATEN PATH
WORLDWIDE PLAZA – This massive, rose-colored multiuse complex sits on the former site of the second Madison Square Garden. An impressive office tower on 8th Avenue is followed by a pleasing mid-block plaza with a fountain; lower-scaled residential units and movie theaters (showing films for 🎬 $3) fill the block through to 9th Avenue. It was built in 1989 following a design by Skidmore, Owings & Merrill and Frank Williams. *50th–51st Sts., between 8th and 9th Aves.*

㊸ Ford Foundation Building. A 12-story, ⅓-acre greenhouse is this building's lobby and its claim to fame. With a terraced garden, a still pool, and a couple of dozen full-grown trees, the Ford atrium is open to the public—for tranquil strolling, not for picnics—weekdays from 9 to 5. ⊠ *320 E. 43rd St., with an entrance on 42nd St.*

★ **㊴ Grand Central Terminal.** Stop on the south side of 42nd Street to admire the three huge windows separated by columns, and the Beaux Arts clock and sculpture, *Transportation,* crowning the facade above the elevated roadway (Park Avenue is routed around Grand Central's upper story). Go in the side doors on Vanderbilt Avenue to enter the cavernous main concourse, with its 12-story-high ceiling displaying the constellations of the zodiac, and consider how well the space works. It's enormous but not intimidating, bustling but calming, and its human scale somehow keeps people from bumping into each other. Constructed between 1903 and 1913, this Manhattan landmark was originally designed by a Minnesota architectural firm and later gussied up with Beaux Arts ornamentation. Neglected for a time in the 1970s and 1980s, the building is now being renovated to become a destination in its own right, with more shops and restaurants (à la Union Station in Washington, DC). The section of the ceiling that looks spotlighted, in the southeast corner of the building, is merely clean, and within the next couple of the years the rest of it will be done. The waiting room by the 42nd Street entrance hosts exhibits and seasonal markets, and musicians often play in the concourse. The best time to visit is at rush hour, when this room crackles with the frenzy of scurrying commuters, dashing every which way. (Remember the scene in the movie *The Fisher King*, when the crowd stopped running for trains, turned to each other, and waltzed instead?) ✉ *Main entrance: E. 42nd St. at Park Ave. Tours conducted every Wed. at 12:30 PM (meet in front of Chemical Bank inside terminal on main level). The tour is free, but donations to the Municipal Art Society accepted,* ☎ *212/935–3960.*

Hotaling's News. This bustling little shop carries more than 220 daily newspapers from throughout the United States, most issues only a day or two old. ✉ *142 W. 42nd St.,* ☎ *212/840–1868.*

㉝ ICP Midtown. The midtown branch of the International Center of Photography uptown presents several photography shows a year in an ultracontemporary, multilevel space. ✉ *1133 6th Ave.,* ☎ *212/768–4680.* 🎟 *$4; Tues. 6–8 pay as you wish.* ☉ *Tues. 11–8, Wed.–Sun. 11–6.*

㊱ Mechanics' and Tradesmen's Institute Building. In its turn-of-the-century prep-school building, this institute has a wonderful library in a three-story-high hall. You can also look at displays of ancient trunks, Civil War paraphernalia, and locks and keys as old as the United States. ✉ *20 W. 44th St.,* ☎ *212/840–1840.* 🎟 *Free.* ☉ *Weekdays 10–4, except 1st Wed. of every month.*

㉚ New Amsterdam. Starting in 1903, the likes of Eddie Cantor, Will Rogers, Fanny Brice, and the Ziegfeld Follies packed the crowds into this wonderful Art Nouveau theater. Like the rest of 42nd Street between 7th and 8th avenues, its heyday was long gone until the area was rejuvenated by recent renovation, and the unlikely new tenant here is the Walt Disney Company. Broadway productions should soon be on this theater's stage again. ✉ *214 W. 42nd St.*

★ **㉙ New Victory.** Previously known as the Theater Republic and the Belasco Theater, this is the oldest surviving theater in New York (it opened in 1899), but its lovely Georgian facade was buried under smut and then scaffolding for so long that people nearly forgot the treasure that was underneath. After a superb restoration job and modernization, this jewel reopened in late 1995 as the only Big Apple theater for kids; the magical interior will take you back to the beginning of this century. ✉ *209 W. 42nd St.,* ☎ *212/239–6255.*

★ **㊳ New York Public Library.** This 1911 masterpiece of Beaux Arts design was financed largely by John Jacob Astor, whose previous library building downtown has since been turned into the Joseph Papp Public Theater (☞ East Village, *below*). Its grand front steps are guarded by two crouching marble lions—dubbed "Patience" and "Fortitude" by Mayor Fiorello La Guardia, who said he visited the facility to "read between the lions." After admiring the white marble neoclassical facade (crammed with statues, as is typical of Beaux Arts buildings), walk through the bronze front doors into the grand marble lobby with its sweeping double staircase. Turn left and peek into the Periodicals Room, decorated with trompe l'oeil paintings by Richard Haas commemorating New York's importance as a publishing center. Then take a (quiet) look upstairs at the huge, high-ceilinged main reading room, a haven of scholarly calm, or visit changing exhibitions and the art gallery. Among the treasures you might see are Gilbert Stuart's portrait of George Washington, Charles Dickens's desk, and Thomas Jefferson's own handwritten copy of the Declaration of Independence. Free one-hour tours, each as individual as the library volunteer who leads it, are given

Tuesday–Saturday at 11 AM, 12:30 PM, and 2:30 PM. ⊠ *5th Ave., between 40th and 42nd Sts.,* ☎ *212/930–0800.* ⊙ *Tues.–Wed. 11–7:30, Thurs.–Sat. 10–6.*

New York Yacht Club. Former longtime home of the America's Cup trophy, this Beaux Arts building is appropriately nautical. Notice its swelling window fronts, looking just like the sterns of ships, complete with stone-carved water splashing over the sill. ⊠ *37 W. 44th St.*

㉟ **Royalton Hotel.** Chicly redone to resemble a Deco dungeon by French designer Philippe Starck, this hotel is a midtown hot spot. You may want to step into its lobby for a peek, but you'll feel more comfortable if you're well dressed. ⊠ *44 W. 44th St.,* ☎ *212/212/869–4400.*

★ ㉛ **Times Square.** Love it or hate it, you can't deny that this is one of New York's principal energy centers. Like many New York City "squares," it's actually triangles formed by the angle of Broadway slashing across a major avenue—in this case, crossing 7th Avenue at 42nd Street. In exchange for having its name grace the area, the *New York Times,* then a less prestigious paper, moved into what had been a relatively quiet area known as Longacre Square when the subway opened. It built the Times Tower and opened its headquarters here on December 31, 1904 (the building is now resheathed in white marble and called **One Times Square Plaza**), publicizing the event with a fireworks show at midnight and thereby starting a New Year's Eve tradition. Each December 31, workmen on this roof lower a 200-pound ball down the flagpole by hand—a tradition since 1908. The huge intersection below is mobbed with revelers, and when the ball hits bottom on the stroke of midnight, pandemonium ensues.

The present headquarters of the *New York Times* (⊠ 229 W. 43rd St.) occupies much of the block between 7th and 8th avenues; look for the blue delivery vans lined up along 43rd Street. From 44th to 51st streets, the cross streets west of Broadway are lined with some 30 major theaters (☞ Chapter 5). This has been the city's main theater district since the turn of the century; movie theaters joined the fray beginning in the 1920s. As the theaters drew crowds of people in the evenings, advertisers began to mount huge electric signs here, which gave the intersection its distinctive nighttime glitter. Even the developers who want to change this area intend to preserve the signs, and the current zoning actually requires buildings to have enormous ads. The ads themselves only get bigger and brighter with new technology. One of the newer ones, which features a 42-foot-tall bottle of Coca-Cola hanging over Broadway and 47th Street, uses 60 miles of optical tubing.

The triangle north of 42nd Street between 46th and 47th streets is named ☞ **Duffy Square.**

Times Square Theater. For two decades after its 1920 opening, the Times Square, now dark, staged top hits such as *Gentlemen Prefer Blondes, The Front Page,* and *Strike Up the Band;* Noël Coward's *Private Lives* opened here with Gertrude Lawrence, Laurence Olivier, and the author himself. ⊠ *215 W. 42nd St.*

㊹ **Tudor City.** A dozen buildings featuring half-timbering and lots of stained glass comprise this self-contained complex. Constructed between 1925 and 1928, two of the apartment buildings of this residential enclave originally had no east-side windows, lest the tenants be forced to gaze at the slaughterhouses, breweries, and glue factories then located along the East River. Today, however, they're missing a wonderful view of the United Nations Headquarters; you'll have to walk to the terrace at the end of 43rd Street to overlook the United Nations. This will place you at the head of the **Sharansky Steps** (named for Natan—formerly Anatoly—Sharansky, the Soviet dissident), which run along the **Isaiah Wall** (inscribed "They Shall Beat Their Swords Into Plowshares"); you'll also look down into **Ralph J. Bunche Park** (named for the African-American former UN undersecretary) and **Raoul Wallenberg Walk** (named for the Swedish diplomat and World War II hero who saved many Hungarian Jews from the Nazis). ✉ *40th to 43rd Sts., between 1st and 2nd Aves.*

★ ㊺ **United Nations Headquarters.** Now more than 50 years old, this symbol of global cooperation occupies a lushly landscaped 18-acre riverside tract just east of 1st Avenue between 42nd and 48th streets. Its rose garden is especially pleasant to stroll in, although picnicking is strictly forbidden. A line of flagpoles with banners representing the current roster of member nations stands before the striking 550-foot-high slab of the Secretariat Building, with the domed General Assembly Building nestled at its side. The headquarters were designed in 1947–53 by an international team of architects led by Wallace Harrison. You can enter the General Assembly Building at the 46th Street door; the interior corridors overflow with imaginatively diverse artwork donated by member nations. Free tickets to assemblies are sometimes available on a first-come, first-served basis before sessions begin; pick them up in the General Assembly lobby. (The full General Assembly is in session from the third Tuesday in September to the end of December.) Visitors can take lunch in the Delegates Dining Room (jackets required for men) or eat from 9:30 to 4:30 in the public coffee shop. ✉ *Visitor entrance: 1st Ave. and 46th St.,* ☎ *212/963–7713,* ☎ *212/963–7113 for meeting schedule.* 🎟 *$6.50 (tour).* ⊘ *Tours offered daily 9:15–4:45 (weekdays only in Jan. and Feb.); 45-min tours in English leave the General Assembly lobby every 30 min. Children under 5 not permitted.*

OFF THE   **JAPAN SOCIETY GALLERY** – This wonderfully serene setting holds exhibi-
BEATEN PATH tions from well-known Japanese and American museums, as well as private collections. Also offered are movies, lectures, classes, concerts, and dramatic performances. *333 E. 47th St.,* ☎ *212/832-1155.* 🎟 *$3 (suggested contribution).* ⊘ *Tues.–Sun. 11–5.*

㊵ **Whitney Museum of American Art at Philip Morris.** Each year this free branch of the Upper East Side Whitney Museum, on the ground floor of the Philip Morris Building, presents five successive exhibitions of 20th-century painting and sculpture. An espresso bar and seating areas make it an agreeable place to rest. ✉ *120 Park Ave.,* ☎ *212/878-2550.* 🎟 *Free.* ⊘ *Sculpture court: Mon.–Sat. 7:30 AM–9:30 PM, Sun. 11–7; gallery: Mon.–Wed. and Fri. 11–6, Thurs. 11–7:30.*

MURRAY HILL TO UNION SQUARE

As the city grew progressively north throughout the 19th century, one neighborhood after another had its fashionable heyday, only to fade from glory. But three neighborhoods, east of 5th Avenue roughly between 20th and 40th streets, have preserved much of their historic charm: Murray Hill's brownstone mansions and town houses; Madison Square's classic turn-of-the-century skyscrapers; and Gramercy Park's London-like leafy square. The only "must-see" along this route is the Empire State Building, but the walk as a whole is worth taking for the many moments en route when you may feel as if you've stepped back in time.

A Good Walk

Numbers in the text correspond to numbers in the margin and on the Murray Hill to Union Square map.

Begin on East 36th Street, between Madison and Park avenues, at the **Pierpont Morgan Library** ①, known as much for its incredible interior as for its contents—Old Master drawings, medieval manuscripts, illuminated books, and original music scores. As you proceed south on Madison Avenue, at 35th Street you'll pass the **Church of the Incarnation** ②, a broodingly dark brownstone version of a Gothic chapel. Across the street and taking up the entire next block is the landmark **B. Altman Building** ③, home of the famous department store from 1906 to 1989.

At 5th Avenue and 34th Street, you can't miss the **Empire State Building** ④. It may no longer be the world's tallest building, but it is certainly one of the world's best-loved skyscrapers, and you'll understand why when you see the view from its upper decks. Leaving the Empire State Building, continue south on 5th Avenue to 29th Street and the **Marble Collegiate Church** ⑤ (1854), a marble-fronted Romanesque Revival structure. Cross the street and head east on 29th Street to the **Church of the Transfiguration** ⑥, better known as the Little Church Around the Corner. Continuing south along Madison Avenue now, you'll come to the **New York Life Insurance Building** ⑦, which occupies the block between 26th and 27th streets on the east side of Madison, its distinctive gold top visible from afar. The limestone Beaux Arts courthouse next door, at 25th Street, is the **Appellate Division of the State Supreme Court** ⑧. The **Metropolitan Life Insurance Tower** ⑨, between 23rd and 24th streets, is another lovely, classical-inspired insurance company tower.

You've probably been wondering about the green space along which you've been walking and the oddly shaped building across it. The park, bordered by 5th Avenue, Broadway, Madison Avenue, 23rd and 26th streets, is **Madison Square** ⑩, no longer the site of Madison Square Garden. You can walk through it to get to one of New York's most photographed buildings—the Renaissance-style **Flatiron Building** ⑪, by architect Daniel Burnham. This distinguished building has lent its name to the once seedy, now trendy Flatiron District that lies to the south between 5th Avenue and Park Avenue South. The neighborhood's massive buildings, the last of the pre-skyscraper era, have had their ornate Romanesque facades gleamingly restored; hip boutiques and restaurants occupy their street levels, while advertising agencies, publishing houses, architects' offices, graphic design firms, residential lofts, and multimedia companies fill the upper stories.

Continue south on Broadway and turn east on 20th Street to the **Theodore Roosevelt Birthplace** ⑫, a reconstruction of the Victorian brownstone where Teddy lived until he was 15 years old. What is probably the prettiest part of this residential district lies farther east, at the top of Irving Place, between 20th and 21st streets—**Gramercy Park** ⑬, a picture-perfect city park complete with flower beds, bird feeders, sundials, and cozy benches. Wander the streets around the park (you can't get in without a key, which is available only to residents) and continue down **Irving Place** ⑭, taking time to admire the charming brownstones here, too.

Another option is to make a detour east, to the **Police Academy Museum** ⑮, predictably full of law-enforcement memorabilia. If you're really energetic, wander up to Lexington Avenue in the high 20s, a neighborhood affectionately known as **Little India**, where Indian restau-

Murray Hill to Union Square

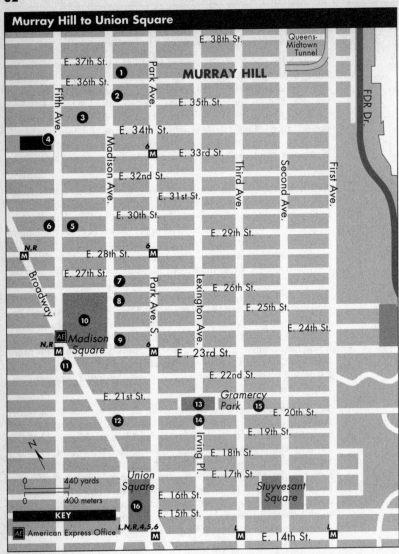

E. 38th St.

Queens-Midtown Tunnel

E. 37th St. **1**

E. 36th St. **2**

Park Ave.

MURRAY HILL

E. 35th St.

3

Fifth Ave.

Madison Ave.

E. 34th St.

4

6 M E. 33rd St.

E. 32nd St.

Third Ave.

Second Ave.

First Ave.

FDR Dr.

E. 31st St.

E. 30th St.

6 **5**

E. 29th St.

N,R M

E. 28th St.

6 M

Broadway

E. 27th St.

7

8

Park Ave. S.

Lexington Ave.

E. 26th St.

E. 25th St.

10

E. 24th St.

AE Madison Square

N,R M

9 **6**

11

6 M E. 23rd St.

E. 22nd St.

E. 21st St.

13 Gramercy Park **15**

E. 20th St.

12

14 E. 19th St.

N

Irving Pl.

E. 18th St.

E. 17th St.

0   440 yards

Union Square

Stuyvesant Square

0   400 meters

E. 16th St.

16

E. 15th St.

KEY

L,N,R,4,5,6

L M

L M

AE American Express Office

M E. 14th St.

Appellate Division of the State Supreme Court, **8**

B. Altman Building, **3**

Church of the Incarnation, **2**

Church of the Transfiguration, **6**

Empire State Building, **4**

Flatiron Building, **11**

Gramercy Park, **13**

Irving Place, **14**

Madison Square, **10**

Marble Collegiate Church, **5**

Metropolitan Life Insurance Tower, **9**

New York Life Insurance Building, **7**

Pierpont Morgan Library, **1**

Police Academy Museum, **15**

Theodore Roosevelt Birthplace, **12**

Union Square, **16**

rants, spice shops, imported-video stores, and clothing stores abound. The area also plays host to Middle Eastern, Indonesian, and Vietnamese restaurants. In this multicultural part of town, better seen during the day, don't be surprised to find a Spanish-language playhouse across the street from an Islamic bookstore.

Our walk ends at **Union Square** ⑯, which lies between Park Avenue South and Broadway and 14th and 17th streets, one block west of Irving Plaza. The neighborhood around it has improved so much recently that it now has several fashionable restaurants and stores. If possible, visit the **Greenmarket** on Monday, Wednesday, Friday, or Saturday, when the north side of the park bustles with friendly people and good, locally grown food.

TIMING

This tour will take an entire day. Allow 1½ hours each for the Empire State Building and the Morgan Library. Some of the office buildings included in the walk are open only during the week, so if you want to peek inside you should keep that in mind. Additionally, the Union Square Greenmarket really shouldn't be missed; it's open all day every Monday, Wednesday, Friday, and Saturday. The weather, and how it affects visibility from the Empire State Building, is something else you may want to consider. Sunsets from the top of the building are spectacular, so you may want to adjust your schedule to end your day there (but be sure to include time for the line you'll have to wait in to get to the top).

Sights to See

⑧ **Appellate Division of the State Supreme Court.** The roof balustrade of this imposing Corinthian structure depicts great lawmakers of the past: Moses, Justinian, Confucius, and others, although a statue of Muhammed had to be removed because it offended the Islamic religion. Rooms inside are furnished with pieces designed by Herter Brothers. ☒ *35 E. 25th St. at Madison Ave.*

③ **B. Altman Building.** One of New York's grand old department stores moved here in 1906, doing much to transform the neighborhood into a shopping district. What you see from Madison Avenue was the store's back; along 34th Street and 5th Avenue, elaborate entrances are graced by green canopies reminiscent of old subway kiosks. After the B. Altman chain declared bankruptcy in August 1989, the landmark building sat vacant until 1995, when Oxford University Press moved into its eastern office tower. The Science, Industry, and Business divisions of the New York Public Library claimed more of the building's east side, opening in 1996. ☒ *34th and 35th Sts., between Madison and 5th Aves.*

OFF THE
BEATEN PATH

SNIFFEN COURT – This is an easily overlooked cul-de-sac of 19th-century brick stables converted into town houses, with an atmosphere that's equal parts old London and New Orleans. Sniffen Court was for many years the home of sculptor Malvina Hoffman. ☒ *Off 36th St., between Lexington and 3rd Aves.*

② **Church of the Incarnation.** Outside this Episcopal church is a broodingly dark brownstone version of a Gothic chapel. Inside, however, there's enough jewel-like stained glass to counteract the dour effect. Look especially for the north aisle's 23rd Psalm Window, by the Tiffany Glass works, or the south aisle's two Angel windows dedicated to infants, which are by the 19th-century English writer-designer William Morris. ☒ *205 Madison Ave. at 35th St.*

6   Church of the Transfiguration. Known as the Little Church Around the Corner, this Gothic Revival church complex is set back in a shrub-filled New York version of an old English churchyard. It won its memorable appellation in 1870 when other area churches refused to bury actor George Holland, a colleague of well-known thespian Joseph Jefferson. Jefferson was directed to the "little church around the corner" to accomplish the burial, and the Episcopal institution has welcomed literary and theater types ever since. Go inside to see the south transept's stained-glass window, by John LaFarge, depicting 19th-century superstar actor Edwin Booth as Hamlet, his famous role. ⊠ *1 E. 29th St.*

★ **4   Empire State Building.** It may no longer be the world's tallest building, but it is certainly one of the world's best-loved skyscrapers, its pencil-slim silhouette a symbol for New York City. The Art Deco playground for King Kong opened in 1931 after only about a year and a half of construction—many floors were completely unfinished, however, so that tenants could have them custom-designed. The Depression delayed this process and critics deemed it the "Empty State Building." The crowning spire was originally designed as a mooring mast for dirigibles, but none ever docked here; in 1951, a TV transmittal tower was added to the top, raising the total height to 1,472 feet. Today more than 16,000 people work in the building, and more than 2½ million people a year visit the 86th- and 102nd-floor observatories. At night the top 30 stories are illuminated with colors appropriate to the season (green for St. Pat's Day, red and green around Christmas; orange and brown for Halloween). In 1956, revolving beacons named the Freedom Lights were installed. These lights are illuminated from dusk to midnight.

Pass beneath the stainless-steel canopy on 34th Street to enter the three-story-high marbled lobby, where illuminated panels depicting the Seven Wonders of the World brazenly add the Empire State as number eight. Go to the concourse level to buy a ticket for the observation decks. The 102nd-floor spot is glassed in; the 86th floor is open to the air. In the movie *An Affair to Remember,* Cary Grant waited here impatiently for his rendezvous with Deborah Kerr, an event around which Nora Ephron built the entire screenplay of her 1993 hit, *Sleepless in Seattle.*

The newest attraction in the building (second floor) is the **New York Skyride.** It consists of a three-minute Comedy Central TV presentation on the virtues of New York, followed by a seven-minute motion-simulator ride above and around some of New York's top attractions projected on a screen in the front of the room—you'll actually feel as if you're swooping between the twin towers of the World Trade Center. The show leaves you feeling a little dizzy and disoriented: It's not recommended for anyone who has trouble with motion sickness, and pregnant women are not admitted. ⊠ *350 5th Ave. at 34th St., Observations decks:* ☎ *212/736–3100.* ▭ *$4.* ☉ *Daily 9:30 AM–midnight; last elevator up leaves at 11:30 PM. New York Skyride:* ☎ *212/279–9777.* ▭ *$7.95.* ☉ *Daily 10–10.*

11   Flatiron Building. Like the Empire State Building and a host of other structures in the city, this was the tallest building in the world when it opened in 1902. Architect Daniel Burnham is responsible for the design that made ingenious use of the triangular plot of land and created very nontraditional office spaces inside—its rounded front point is only 6 feet wide, but gentle waves built into the molded limestone-and-terra-cotta side walls soften the wedge effect. Winds invariably swooped down its 20-story, 286-foot height, billowing up the skirts of women pedestrians on 23rd Street, and local traffic cops had to shoo away male gawkers—coining the phrase "23 Skiddoo." Originally named the Fuller Building, it was instantly rechristened by the public because of its resemblance to a flat-iron, and eventually the nickname became official. ✉ *175 5th Ave., bordered by 22nd and 23rd Sts., 5th Ave., and Broadway.*

NEED A BREAK?   A good stop for coffee, hearty soups, salads, or wonderful sandwiches on thick, crusty bread is **La Boulangère** (✉ 49 E. 21st St., ☎ 212/475-8582). You can either sit at one of the tiny tables or order takeout (enjoy a picnic on a bench in either Madison Square or Union Square to the south).

---

⑬ Gramercy Park. This picture-perfect park complete with flower beds, bird feeders, sundials, and cozy benches looks too good to be true, and in many ways it is—it stays nice largely because of the locked cast-iron fence that surrounds it. Only residents of the property around the park can obtain keys. Laid out in 1831 according to a design inspired by London's residential squares, Gramercy Park is surrounded by interesting buildings.

On the south side of the square, peek inside the park and you'll see a statue of actor Edwin Booth playing Hamlet. Booth lived at No. 16, which he remodeled in the early 1880s to serve as an actors' club, the **Players Club.** Stanford White, the architect for the renovation, was a member of the club, as were many other nonactors. Members over the years have included Mark Twain, Booth Tarkington, John and Lionel Barrymore, Irving Berlin, Winston Churchill, Lord Laurence Olivier, Frank Sinatra, Walter Cronkite, Jack Lemmon, and Richard Gere.

The **National Arts Club** (15 Gramercy Park S.) was once the home of Samuel Tilden, a governor of New York and the Democratic presidential candidate who, in 1876, received more popular votes than Rutherford B. Hayes, who won more electoral college votes—and the election. Calvert Vaux, codesigner of Central Park, remodeled this building in 1874, conjoining two houses. Among its Victorian Gothic decorations are medallions portraying Goethe, Dante, Milton, and Benjamin Franklin; early club members included Woodrow Wilson and Theodore Roosevelt. The Club now houses the Poetry Society of America, which sponsors poetry readings (☞ Readings and Lectures *in* Chapter 5).

On the west end of the square, note the row of redbrick Greek Revival town houses, with their fanciful cast-iron verandas looking like something out of New Orleans's French Quarter. Mayor James Harper (elected in 1888) lived at No. 4, behind the pair of street lanterns. The actor John Garfield died in 1952 while staying at No. 3.

At the northeast corner, the ornate white terra-cotta apartment building at **36 Gramercy Park East** is guarded by concrete knights in silver-paint armor. The turreted redbrick building at **34 Gramercy Park East** was one of the city's first cooperative apartment houses; its tenants have included actors James Cagney, John Carradine, and Margaret Hamilton, who played the Wicked Witch in *The Wizard of Oz.* The austere gray-brown Friends Meeting House at 28 Gramercy Park South became the **Brotherhood Synagogue** in 1974, and a narrow plaza just east of the synagogue contains a Holocaust memorial. No. **19 Gramercy Park South** was the home in the 1880s of society doyenne Mrs. Stuyvesant Fish, a fearless iconoclast who shocked Mrs. Astor and Mrs. Vanderbilt when she reduced the time of formal dinner parties from several hours to 50 minutes, thus ushering in the modern social era.

⑭ Irving Place. Like the neighboring Gramercy Park, this short street is lined with charming row houses and **Pete's Tavern** (✉ 18th St. and Irving Pl.), which claims that O. Henry (pseudonym of William Sidney Porter), wrote "The Gift of the Magi" while sitting in the second booth to the right. It also claims to be the oldest saloon in New York (1864); both facts are disputed, but stop here anyway for a casual drink and absorb the atmosphere of the Gaslight Era. O. Henry lived at 55 Irving Place, in a building long ago demolished.

The street takes its name from another famous New York chronicler, Washington Irving (1783–1859), who wrote *The Legend of Sleepy Hollow* more than a century before O. Henry was there. A plaque on the redbrick house at 17th Street and Irving Place proclaims it as the home of Washington Irving, but it was his nephew's house, though the famous writer did visit there often. Walk south to 40 Irving Place, where you'll see a huge bust of the writer outside **Washington Irving High School**, alma mater of Claudette Colbert and Whoopi Goldberg.

⑩ Madison Square. New York's first baseball games were played here circa 1845. On the north end, an imposing 1881 statue by Augustus Saint-Gaudens memorializes Civil War naval hero Admiral Farragut. A statue of William Henry Seward (the Seward of the phrase "Seward's folly"—as Alaska was originally known) sits in the park's southwestern corner, though it's rumored that the sculptor placed the statesman's head on Abraham Lincoln's body. ⊠ *23rd to 26th Sts., between 5th and Madison Aves.*

⑤ Marble Collegiate Church. Built in 1854 for the Reformed Protestant Dutch Congregation first organized in 1628 by Peter Minuit, the canny Dutchman who bought Manhattan from the Native Americans for $24, this impressive limestone church takes its name from the Tuckahoe marble that covers it. Dr. Norman Vincent Peale (*The Power of Positive Thinking*) was Marble Collegiate's pastor from 1932 to 1984.⊠ *1 W. 29th St. at 5th Ave.*

⑨ Metropolitan Life Insurance Tower. The tower made this building the world's tallest when it was added in 1909. At 700 feet, it re-creates the campanile of St. Mark's in Venice. The four dials of its clock are each three stories high, and their minute hands weigh half a ton each; wait for the quarter hour to hear it chime. Met Life's North Building, between 24th and 25th streets, is connected by a skywalk. Its Art Deco loggias have attracted many film crews—it appeared in such films as *After Hours, Radio Days,* and *The Fisher King.* Step into the lobby of the South Building during weekday business hours to see a fine set of Wyeth murals; the guard may stop you, but if you explain what you want to see, you should be issued a pass. ⊠ *1 Madison Ave., between 23rd and 24th Sts.*

⑦ New York Life Insurance Building. Cass Gilbert, better known for the Woolworth Building (☞ Wall Street and the Battery, *below*), designed this in 1928. Its birthday-cake top is capped by a gilded pyramid that is stunning when lit at night. Go inside to admire the soaring lobby's coffered ceilings and ornate bronze doors. This was formerly the site of P. T. Barnum's Hippodrome, and after that (1890–1925) Madison Square Garden, designed by architect and playboy Stanford White. White was shot in the Garden's roof garden by Harry K. Thaw, the jealous husband of actress Evelyn Nesbit—a lurid episode more or less accurately depicted in the movie *Ragtime.* ⊠ *51 Madison Ave., between 26th and 27th Sts.*

★ ① Pierpont Morgan Library. The core of this small, patrician museum is the famous banker's own study and library, completed in 1905 by McKim, Mead & White. If you walk east past the museum's main entrance on 36th Street, you'll see the original library's neoclassical facade, with what is believed to be Charles McKim's face on the sphinx in the right-hand sculptured panel. Around the corner, at 37th Street and Madison Avenue, is the latest addition to the library, an 1852 Italianate brownstone that was once the home of Morgan's son, J. P. Morgan, Jr. The elder Morgan's own house stood at 36th Street and Madison Avenue; it was torn down after his death and replaced with the simple neoclassical annex that today holds the library's main exhibition space. Go inside and visit the galleries for rotating exhibitions; go straight to see items from the permanent collection, principally drawings, prints, manuscripts, and rare books, and to pass through the new glass-roofed garden café court to the fine bookstore. Turn right just past the entrance and go down a long cloister corridor for the library's most impressive rooms: the elder Morgan's personal study, its red-damask-lined walls hung with first-rate paintings, and his majestic personal library with its dizzying tiers of handsomely bound rare books, letters, and illuminated manuscripts. It's hard to say which is more spectacular—the museum's collections or its interiors. ⊠ *29 E. 36th St.,* ☎ *212/685–0008.* ☎ *$5 (suggested contribution).* ☉ *Tues.–Fri. 10:30–5, Sat. 10:30–6, Sun. noon–6.*

⑮ Police Academy Museum. The second floor of the city's police academy is full of law-enforcement memorabilia—uniforms, firearms, batons, badges, even counterfeit money—dating back to the time of the Dutch. ⊠ *235 E. 20th St.,* ☎ *212/477–9753.* ☎ *Free.* ☉ *Weekdays 9–3 by advance (2 days) appointment only.*

⑫ Theodore Roosevelt Birthplace. The original brownstone was torn down, but this is a near-perfect reconstruction of the Victorian brownstone where Teddy lived until he was 15 years old. Before becoming president, Roosevelt was New York City's police commissioner and the governor of New York State. He's still the only president from New York City. The house contains Victorian period rooms and Roosevelt memorabilia; a selection of videos about the namesake of the teddy bear can be seen on request. Saturday-afternoon chamber-music concerts are offered each fall, winter, and spring. ⊠ *28 E. 20th St.,* ☎ *212/ 260–1616.* ☎ *$2.* ☉ *Wed.–Sun. 9–5; guided tours 9:30–4.*

⑯ Union Square. Its name, originally signifying the fact that two main roads merged here, proved doubly apt in the early 20th century when the square became a rallying spot for labor protests and mass demonstrations; many unions, as well as fringe political parties, moved their headquarters nearby. Over the years the area deteriorated into a habitat of drug dealers and kindred undesirables, until a massive renewal program in the 1980s transformed it. If possible, visit on **Greenmarket** day (Monday, Wednesday, Friday, and Saturday), when farmers from all over the Northeast, including some Pennsylvania Dutch and latter-day hippies, bring their goods to the big town: fresh produce, homemade bakery goods, cheeses, cider, New York State wines, even fish and meat.

The trendy, Warhol-founded *Interview* has its offices here, while the most recent developments have included renovation of the 1932 **Pavilion,** now flanked by playgrounds and an open-air café run by the Coffee Shop, and much new restaurant and retail activity. The handsome **Century Building** (built in 1881, ⊠ 33 E. 17th St.) has been beautifully restored and brought back to life as a Barnes & Noble bookstore; go inside to admire its cast-iron columns and the view over Union Square.

MUSEUM MILE

Once known as Millionaire's Row, the stretch of 5th Avenue between 79th and 104th streets has been fittingly renamed Museum Mile, for it now contains an impressive cluster of cultural institutions. The connection is more than coincidental: Many museums are housed in what used to be the great mansions of merchant princes and wealthy industrialists. A large percentage of these buildings were constructed of limestone (it's cheaper than marble) and reflect the Beaux Arts style, which was very popular among the wealthy at the turn of the century.

A Good Walk
Numbers in the text correspond to numbers in the margin and on the Museum Mile, Upper East Side map.

You won't need a map for this tour; it's a simple, straight walk up 5th Avenue, from 70th Street to 105th. Walking the Museum Mile actually covers closer to two miles. If you walk up the west side of the street (crossing over to visit museums, of course), you'll be under the canopy of Central Park and have a good view of the mansions and apartments across the street. If you're not sure whether you're interested in a particular museum, stop in its gift store; museum shops are usually good indicators of what's in the rest of the building.

Begin at 5th Avenue and 70th Street with the **Frick Collection** ①, housed in an ornate, imposing Beaux Arts mansion built in 1914 for coke-and-steel baron Henry Clay Frick. It's a few blocks north before you get to the next stop. On your way, be sure to admire the former mansions, some of them now converted into multiple-family dwellings, among them the Gothic Revival facade of what's now the **Ukrainian Institute,** on the southeast corner of 5th Avenue at 79th Street. One block north is the **American Irish Historical Society** ②, another fine example of the French-influenced Beaux Arts style that was so popular at the turn of the century.

From here, you can't miss the **Metropolitan Museum of Art** ③, the largest art museum in the Western Hemisphere, encroaching on Central Park's turf. The goings on around the steps that sweep you up into the museum are worthy of at least casual observation—its a favorite spot for performance artists and musicians as well as sophisticated souvenir sellers.

Across from the Met, between 82nd and 83rd streets on 5th Avenue, one Beaux Arts town house stands its ground amid newer apartment blocks. It now belongs to the Federal Republic of Germany, which has installed a branch of the Goethe Institute here—called **Goethe House** ④. At the corner of 85th Street is 1040 5th Avenue, former home of Jacqueline Kennedy Onassis, from which she could easily walk into Central Park and to the reservoir that now bears her name. Up at 86th Street and 5th Avenue, a brightly embellished limestone-and-redbrick mansion, designed by Carrère and Hastings to echo the buildings on the Place des Vosges in Paris, was once the home of Mrs. Cornelius Vanderbilt III.

Frank Lloyd Wright's **Guggenheim Museum** ⑤ (opened in 1959) is a controversial piece of architecture—even many of those who like its assertive six-story spiral rotunda will admit that it does not result in the best space in which to view art. A block north stands the **National Academy of Design** ⑥, housed in a stately 19th-century mansion and a pair of town houses on 89th Street. At 91st Street you'll find the former residence of industrialist Andrew Carnegie, now a museum named after him that's devoted to contemporary and historic design—the **Cooper-Hewitt Museum** ⑦. Across 91st Street, the **Convent of the Sacred Heart** is in a huge Italianate mansion originally built in 1918 for financier Otto Kahn, a noted patron of the arts.

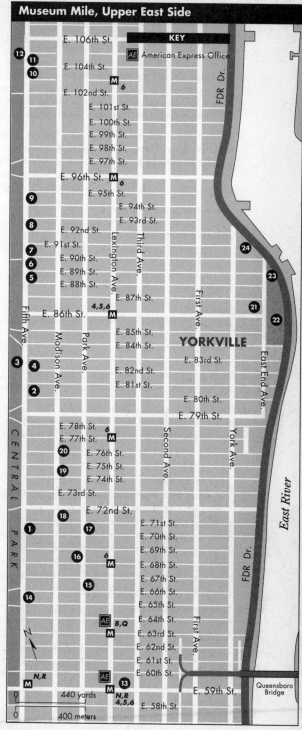

Museum Mile, Upper East Side

Continuing north, the next museum you'll come to is at 92nd Street, the **Jewish Museum** ⑧, which opened its expanded and renovated facilities in 1993. The handsome, well-proportioned Georgian-style mansion on the corner of 5th Avenue and 94th Street was built in 1914 for Willard Straight, founder of the *New Republic* magazine. Today it is the home of the **International Center of Photography** ⑨. As you proceed north on 5th Avenue, for architectural variety you may want to walk a few paces east on 97th Street to see the onion-domed tower of the **Russian Orthodox Cathedral of St. Nicholas,** built in 1902.

Between 98th and 101st streets, 5th Avenue is dominated by the various buildings of **Mount Sinai Hospital,** which was founded in 1852 by a group of wealthy Jewish citizens and moved here in 1904. The 1976 addition, the Annenberg Building, is a looming tower of Cor-Ten steel that has deliberately been allowed to develop a patina of rust.

The **Museum of the City of New York** ⑩, which traces the course of Big Apple history, is one of the homier museums on this tour. Another is **El Museo del Barrio** ⑪, founded in 1969, concentrating on Latin culture in general, with a particular emphasis on Puerto Rican art. Having completed this long walk, you may want to reward yourself by crossing the street to Central Park's **Conservatory Garden** ⑫, a formal, enclosed tract in the otherwise rambling park.

TIMING

It would be impossible to do justice to all these collections in one outing; the Metropolitan Museum alone contains too much to see in a day. You may want to select one or two museums or exhibits to linger in and simply walk past the others, appreciating their exteriors (this in itself constitutes a minicourse in modern architecture). Save the rest for another day—or for your next trip to New York.

Do be sure to pick the right day of the week for this tour: Most of these museums are closed on Monday, but a few have free admission during extended hours on Tuesday or Thursday evening. Others have drinks, snacks, and/or music during late weekend hours. The Jewish Museum is closed on Saturday.

Sights to See

❷ **American Irish Historical Society.** U.S. Steel president William Ellis Corey, who scandalized his social class by marrying musical comedy star Mabelle Gilman, once owned this Beaux Arts town house with its ornamentation and mansard roof. The society's library holdings chronicle people of Irish descent who became successful in the United States, and the society hosts talks of interest to this contingency approximately once a week in the summer. ⊠ *991 5th Ave. at 80th St.,* ☎ *212/288–2263.* ▢ *Free by appointment.* ⏱ *Weekdays 10:30–5:30.*

★ ⑫ **Conservatory Garden.** The entrance, at 105th Street, leads through elaborate wrought-iron gates that once graced the mansion of Cornelius Vanderbilt II. In contrast to the deliberately rustic effect of the rest of the park, these six acres comprise a symmetrical, formal garden. The central lawn is bordered by yew hedges and flowering crab-apple trees, leading to a reflecting pool flanked by a large wisteria arbor. To the south is a high-hedged flower garden named after Frances Hodgson Burnett, author of the children's classic *The Secret Garden.* To the north is the Untermeyer Fountain, with its three spirited girls dancing at the heart of a huge circular bed where 20,000 tulips bloom in the spring, and 5,000 chrysanthemums in the fall. Many a New York wedding party stops here for photos. ⊠ *Entrance at 105th St. and 5th Ave.* ⏱ *Daily 8 AM–dusk.*

⑦ Cooper-Hewitt Museum (officially the Smithsonian Institution's National Museum of Design). Andrew Carnegie sought comfort more than show when he built this 64-room house on what were the outskirts of town in 1901; he administered his extensive philanthropic projects from the first-floor study. (Note the low doorways—Carnegie was only 5 feet 2 inches tall.) The core of the museum's collection was begun in 1897 by the three Hewitt sisters, granddaughters of inventor and industrialist Peter Cooper; major holdings include drawings, prints, textiles, furniture, metalwork, ceramics, glass, woodwork, and wall coverings. The Smithsonian rescued the museum from financial ruin in 1963, and the Carnegie Corporation donated the mansion in 1972. The museum closed for renovations in 1995, but it was scheduled to reopen in September 1996. The changing exhibitions, which focus on various aspects of contemporary or historical design, are invariably well researched, enlightening, and often amusing. ✉ *2 E. 91st St.,* ☎ *212/ 860–6868.* 🎫 *$3; free Tues. 5–9.* 🕐 *Tues. 10–9, Wed.–Sat. 10–5, Sun. noon–5.*

⑪ El Museo del Barrio. *El barrio* is Spanish for "the neighborhood," and the museum is positioned on the edge of Spanish Harlem, a largely Puerto Rican neighborhood. Though the museum focuses on Latin American and Latino culture, and has objects from the Caribbean and Central and South America, its collection of Puerto Rican art is particularly strong. The 8,000-object permanent collection includes numerous pre-Columbian artifacts. ✉ *1230 5th Ave. at 104th St.,* ☎ *212/831– 7272.* 🎫 *$4 (suggested contribution).* 🕐 *Wed.–Sun. 11–5; Thurs. May–Sept. noon–7.*

① Frick Collection. Coke-and-steel baron Henry Clay Frick found a home for the superb art collection he was amassing to be kept far from the soot and smoke of Pittsburgh, where he'd made his fortune. The mansion was designed by architects Carrère and Hastings (also responsible for the New York Public Library on 5th Avenue at 42nd Street) and built in 1914. Opened as a public museum in 1935 and expanded in 1977, it still resembles a gracious private home, albeit one with a bona fide masterpiece or two in almost every room. Strolling through the mansion, one can imagine how it felt to live with Vermeers by the front stairs, Gainsborough and Reynolds portraits in the dining room, canvases by Constable and Turner in the library, and Titians, Holbeins, a Giovanni Bellini, and an El Greco in the living room. Some of the collection's best pieces include Rembrandt's *The Polish Rider* and Jean-Honoré Fragonard's series *The Progress of Love.* You can rest in the tranquil indoor court with a fountain and glass ceiling. ✉ *1 E. 70th St.,* ☎ *212/288–0700.* 🎫 *$5. Children under 10 not admitted.* 🕐 *Tues.– Sat. 10–6, Sun. 1–6, closed holidays.*

④ Goethe House. This German institute offers a changing series of art exhibitions as well as lectures, films, and chamber-music concerts; its extensive library (closed in the summer) includes current issues of German newspapers and periodicals. ✉ *1014 5th Ave. at 82nd St.,* ☎ *212/ 439–8700. Gallery* 🎫 *Free.* 🕐 *Tues., Thurs. 10–7, Wed., Fri. 10–5, Sat. noon–5.*

⑤ Guggenheim Museum. Frank Lloyd Wright eschewed cities, and this building of his (opened in 1959) is a controversial work of architecture that is either praised as his crowning achievement or criticized as looking like a giant toilet. You can't help admiring his attention to detail, however, evident in the circular pattern of the sidewalk outside the museum, for example, and the porthole-like windows on its south side. Inside, the assertive six-story spiral rotunda makes for challenging viewing: Under a 92-foot-high glass dome, a quarter-mile-long ramp spirals down past changing exhibitions of modern art. The museum has especially strong holdings in Wassily Kandinsky, Paul Klee, and Pablo Picasso; the oldest pieces are by the French Impressionists. The Tower Galleries opened in 1992, creating additional gallery space to display the recently acquired Panza di Buomo collection of Minimalist art, among other works. The 10-story annex designed by Gwathmey Siegel and based on Wright's original designs offers four spacious galleries that can accommodate the extraordinarily large art pieces that the Guggenheim owns but previously had no room to display. In 1992 the museum also received a gift from the Robert Mapplethorpe Foundation of more than 200 of the photographer's works, some of which are displayed in the Guggenheim's SoHo branch (☞ SoHo and TriBeCa, *below*). ⊠ *1071 5th Ave. at 88th St.,* ☎ *212/423–3500.* ⊞ *$7; pay what you wish Fri. 6–8.* ⊞ *$10 (to both Guggenheim branches).* ☽ *Sun.–Wed. 10–6, Fri. and Sat. 10–8.*

❾ International Center of Photography (ICP). A relatively young institution—founded in 1974—ICP is building a strong collection of 20th-century photography. Its changing exhibitions, both here and at its midtown branch (☞ 42nd Street, *above*) often focus on the work of a single prominent photographer or one photographic genre (portraits, architecture, etc.). The bookstore carries an impressive array of photography-oriented books, prints, and postcards. The imposing Georgian Revival exterior here belies the quaintness (meant in the best possible sense) of the museum inside. ⊠ *1130 5th Ave. at 94th St.,* ☎ *212/860–1777.* ⊞ *$4; pay what you wish Tues. 6–8.* ☽ *Tues. 11–8, Wed.–Sun. 11–6.*

❽ Jewish Museum. The permanent two-floor exhibition, presented alongside temporary shows, traces the development of Jewish culture and identity over 4,000 years. The exhibition draws on the museum's enormous collection of artwork, ceremonial objects, and electronic media. An expansion completed in 1993 preserved the gray-stone Gothic-style 1908 mansion occupied by the museum since 1947 and enlarged the 1963 addition; a café and a larger shop were also added. At the same time, the mansion facade was extended, giving the museum the appearance of a late–French Gothic château. ⊠ *1109 5th Ave. at 92nd St.,* ☎ *212/423–3230.* ⊞ *$7; pay what you wish Tues. after 5.* ☽ *Sun., Mon., Wed., Thurs. 11–5:45; Tues. 11–8. Closed national and Jewish holidays.*

★ ❸ Metropolitan Museum of Art. Billing itself as "New York's number-one tourist attraction," the Met may be selling itself short: The quality and range of its holdings make it one of the world's greatest museums. It's the largest art museum in the Western Hemisphere (1.6 million square feet), and its permanent collection of more than 2 million works of art from all over the world includes objects from prehistoric to modern times. The museum, founded in 1870, moved to this location in 1880, but the original redbrick building by Calvert Vaux has since been encased in other architecture, which in turn has been encased by other architecture. The majestic 5th Avenue facade, designed by Richard Morris Hunt, was built in 1902 of gray Indiana limestone; later additions eventually surrounded the original building on the sides and back. (On a side wall of the new ground-floor European Sculpture Court, you can glimpse the museum's original redbrick facade.)

The 5th Avenue entrance leads into the Great Hall, a soaring neoclassical chamber that has been designated a landmark. Past the admission booths, a vast marble staircase leads up to the European painting galleries, whose highlights include Botticelli's *The Last Communion of St. Jerome*, Pieter Brueghel's *The Harvesters*, El Greco's *View of*

Toledo, Johannes Vermeer's *Young Woman with a Water Jug,* and Rembrandt's *Aristotle with a Bust of Homer.* The arcaded European Sculpture Court includes Auguste Rodin's massive bronze *The Burghers of Calais.*

American art has its own wing, back in the northwest corner; the best approach is on the first floor, where you enter through a refreshingly light and airy garden court graced with Tiffany stained-glass windows, cast-iron staircases by Louis Sullivan, and a marble Federal-style facade taken from the Wall Street branch of the United States Bank. Take the elevator to the third floor and begin working your way down through the rooms decorated in period furniture—everything from a Shaker retiring room to a Federal-era ballroom to the living room of a Frank Lloyd Wright house—and excellent galleries of American painting.

In the realm of 20th-century art, the Met was a latecomer, allowing the Museum of Modern Art and the Whitney to build their collections with little competition until the Metropolitan's contemporary art department was finally established in 1967. The big museum has been trying to make up for lost time, however, and in 1987 it opened the three-story Lila Acheson Wallace Wing, in the southwest corner. Pablo Picasso's 1906 portrait of Gertrude Stein is the centerpiece of this collection.

There is much more to the Met than paintings, however. Visitors with a taste for classical art should go immediately to the left of the Great Hall on the first floor to see the Greek and Roman statuary, not to mention a large collection of rare Roman wall paintings excavated from the lava of Mount Vesuvius. Directly above these galleries, on the second floor, you'll find room after room of Grecian urns and other classical vases. The Met's awesome Egyptian collection, spanning some 3,000 years, is on the first floor, directly right of the Great Hall. Its centerpiece is the Temple of Dendur, an entire Roman-period temple (circa 15 BC) donated by the Egyptian government in thanks for U.S. help in saving ancient monuments. Placed in a specially built gallery with views of Central Park to refresh the eye, the temple faces east, as it did in its original location, and a pool of water has been installed at the same distance from it as the river Nile once stood. Another spot suitable for contemplation is directly above the Egyptian treasures, in the Asian galleries: The Astor Court Chinese garden reproduces a Ming Dynasty (1368–1644) scholar's courtyard, complete with water splashing over artfully positioned rocks.

There's also a fine arms and armor exhibit on the first floor (go through the medieval tapestries, just behind the main staircase, and turn right). The Met's medieval collection here is lovely, but to see the real medieval treasures, don't miss a trip to **The Cloisters,** the Met's annex in Washington Heights (☞ Morningside Heights, *below*). Keep going straight from the medieval galleries until you enter the cool skylit white space of the Lehman Pavilion, where the small but exquisite personal collection of the late donor, investment banker Robert Lehman, is displayed in rooms resembling those of his West 54th Street town house. This is one of the lesser-known wings of the Met (perhaps because it's tucked away behind so many other galleries), so it's a good place to go when the other galleries begin to feel crowded.

Although it exhibits only a portion of its vast holdings, the Met offers more than can reasonably be seen in one visit. The best advice for tackling the museum itself is to take it in manageable chunks, and know that somewhere, in some wing, there's an empty exhibit that just might be more interesting than the one you can't see for all the people. Walking tours and lectures are free with your admission contribution. Tours covering various sections of the museum begin about every 15 minutes on weekdays, less frequently on weekends; they depart from the Tour Board in the Great Hall. Self-guided audio tours can also be rented at a desk in the Great Hall. Lectures, often related to temporary exhibitions, are given frequently. ⊠ *5th Ave. at 82nd St.,* ☎ *212/879–5500.* ⊠ *$7 (suggested contribution).* ☉ *Tues.–Thurs. and Sun. 9:30–5:15, Fri. and Sat. 9:30–8:45.*

NEED A
BREAK?

Although the Metropolitan has a good museum café, only a block away is a friendly, sparkling-clean coffee shop: **Nectar of 82nd** (⊠ 1090 Madison Ave. at 82nd St., ☎ 212/772-0916), where you can stop for a quick refreshment. If you're looking for something more substantial, the menu has omelets, salads, soups, burgers—the portions are generous and the prices quite reasonable.

★ ⑩ **Museum of the City of New York.** From the Dutch settlers of Nieuw Amsterdam to the present day, with period rooms, dioramas, slide shows, prints, paintings, sculpture, and clever displays of memorabilia, this museum's got it all. An exhibit on the Port of New York illuminates the role of the harbor in New York's rise to greatness; the noteworthy Toy Gallery has several meticulously detailed dollhouses. Weekend programs appeal especially to children. Currently undergoing a $36 million renovation, and contemplating a merger with the New-York Historical Society across town, the massive Georgian mansion that houses the museum should be considerably brightened by the year 2000. ⊠ *1220 5th Ave. at 103rd St.,* ☎ *212/534–1672.* ⊠ *$5 (suggested contribution).* ☉ *Wed.–Sat. 10–5, Sun. 1–5; closed Mon. and holidays, Tues. open for tour groups only.*

⑥ **National Academy of Design.** The academy, which was founded in 1825, required each elected member to donate a representative work of art, which has resulted in a strong collection of 19th- and 20th-century American art. Members have included Mary Cassatt, Samuel F. B. Morse, Winslow Homer, John Singer Sargent, Frank Lloyd Wright, and Robert Rauschenberg. The collection's home is a stately 19th-century mansion and a pair of town houses. ⊠ *1083 5th Ave. at 89th St.,* ☎ *212/369–4880.* ⊠ *$5; free Fri. 5–8.* ☉ *Wed.–Sun. 11:30–5:30, Fri. until 8.*

THE UPPER EAST SIDE

The words "Upper East Side" leave a bad taste in the mouths of many New Yorkers, connoting old money, conservative values, and snobbery. For others, those same qualities make this neighborhood the epitome of the high-style, high-society way of life often associated with the Big Apple. It is true that between 5th and Lexington avenues, up to about 96th Street or so, the trappings of wealth are apparent: well-kept buildings, children in private school uniforms, nannies wheeling grand baby carriages, dog walkers, limousines, doormen in braided livery. This is the territory where Sherman McCoy, protagonist of Tom Wolfe's *The Bonfire of the Vanities,* lived in pride before his fall, and where the heroine of Woody Allen's movie *Alice* felt suffocated despite her money.

But like all New York neighborhoods, this one is diverse, and plenty of local residents live modestly. The northeast section particularly, which is known as **Yorkville,** is more affordable and ethnic, a jumbled mix of high and low buildings, old and young people. Until the 1830s, when the New York & Harlem Railroad and a stagecoach line began racing through, this was a quiet, remote hamlet with a large German population. Over the years it has also welcomed waves of immigrants from Austria, Hungary, and Czechoslovakia, and local shops and restaurants still bear reminders of this European heritage.

A Good Walk

Numbers in the text correspond to numbers in the margin and on the Museum Mile, Upper East Side map.

A fitting place to begin your exploration of the moneyed Upper East Side is that infamous shrine to conspicuous consumption, **Bloomingdale's** ⑬, at 59th Street between Lexington and 3rd avenues. Serious shoppers can get a lot accomplished here, while others may have more fun just watching. Leaving Bloomingdale's, head west on 60th Street toward 5th Avenue. As you cross **Park Avenue,** stop for a moment on the wide, neatly planted median strip. Railroad tracks once ran here; they were covered with a roadway just after World War I, and the grand, sweeping street that resulted became a distinguished residential address. Look south toward midtown and you'll see the Met Life Building, which New Yorkers will probably always refer to as the Pan Am Building, since the letters were changed only when that venerable airline went under in 1992. Squished up against it, the Helmsley Building looks small and frilly by comparison. Then turn to look uptown, and you'll see a thoroughfare lined with massive buildings that are more like mansions stacked atop one another than apartment complexes. Decorations such as colorful tulips in the spring and lighted pine trees in December in the "park" proclaimed by the street's name are paid for by residents.

On the northwest corner of 60th Street and Park Avenue is **Christ Church United Methodist Church,** built during the Depression but designed to look centuries old, with its random pattern of limestone blocks. Inside, the Byzantine-style sanctuary (open Sundays and holidays) glitters with golden handmade mosaics. Continue west on 60th Street to pass a grouping of clubs, membership-only societies that cater to the privileged. Their admirable architecture, on the other hand, is there for all to see. Ornate grillwork curls over the doorway of the scholarly **Grolier Club,** on the north side of 60th Street. On the block right before the park is the **Harmonie Club,** one of several private men's clubs (many of which now admit women) in this area. Across the street is the even more lordly **Metropolitan Club.**

Take a right at 5th Avenue. At 61st Street you'll pass **The Pierre** (☞ Chapter 7), a hotel that opened in 1930; notice its lovely mansard roof and tower. At 800 5th Avenue is an innocuous office with a little sign letting you know that dermatologist Dr. Zizmor practices here. There are many doctors in the area, and that name may not mean anything to you, but take note: He's famous for his ads ("Tired of that tatoo?") that plaster the city's public-transit system, and they bring him patients by the dozen. As you cross 62nd Street, look at the elegant brick-and-limestone mansion at 2 East 62nd, the home of the **Knickerbocker Club,** another private social club.

Across the street is the **Fifth Avenue Synagogue,** a limestone temple built in 1959. Its pointed oval windows are filled with stained glass in striking abstract designs. You may want to detour down this elegant block of town houses; take special note of No. 11, which has elaborate Corinthian pilasters and an impressive wrought-iron entryway. Farther up 5th Avenue, at 65th Street, is another notable Jewish house of worship: **Temple Emanu-El** ⑭, the world's largest Reform Jewish synagogue. If you walk east from 5th Avenue on 65th Street, you'll reach the **China House Gallery** (✉ 125 E. 65th St.), which houses displays of Chinese art.

Turn right on 66th Street, past the site of the house (⊠ 3 E. 66th St.) where Ulysses S. Grant spent his final years, before moving permanently up to Grant's Tomb (☞ Morningside Heights, *below*). (If you are interested in presidential homes, you may want to detour over to 65th Street between Madison and Park avenues to Nos. 45 and 47 East 65th Street, a pair of town houses built in 1910 for Sara Delano Roosevelt and her son, Franklin; FDR once lay recovering from polio at No. 47.) Next door, at 5 East 66th Street, is the **Lotos Club,** a private club whose members are devoted to arts and literature.

Continue east across Madison Avenue to Park Avenue. The large apartment building on the northeast corner of Madison Avenue and 66th Street was built from 1906 to 1908 with lovely Gothic-style detail. The red Victorian castle-fortress at 66th Street and Park Avenue is the **Seventh Regiment Armory** ⑮, now used as a meeting and exhibition space.

Though houses have generally been replaced by apartment buildings along Park Avenue, a few surviving mansions give you an idea of how the neighborhood once looked. The grandly simple silvery limestone palace on the southwest corner of 68th Street, built in 1920, now houses the prestigious **Council on Foreign Relations** (⊠ 58 E. 68th St.). The dark-red brick town house on the northwest corner was built for Percy Pyne in 1909–1911 by McKim, Mead & White and is now the **Americas Society** ⑯, which has an art gallery that is open to the public. The three houses to the north—built during the following decade, and designed by three different architects—carried on the Pyne mansion's Georgian design to create a unified block. Today these buildings hold the **Spanish Institute** (⊠ 684 Park Ave.), the **Italian Cultural Institute** (⊠ 686 Park Ave.), and the **Italian Consulate** (⊠ 690 Park Ave.). Two blocks north, on the east side of Park Avenue, is the **Asia Society** ⑰, a museum and educational center.

At this point shoppers may want to get down to business back on Madison Avenue (☞ Chapter 10). The catchphrase "Madison Avenue" no longer refers to the midtown advertising district (most major agencies have moved away from there anyway) but instead to uptown's fashion district, between 59th and 79th streets, an exclusive area of haute-couture designer boutiques, patrician art galleries, and unique specialty stores. For the most part, these shops are small, intimate, expensive— and almost invariably closed on Sunday. Even if you're just window-shopping, it's fun to step inside the tony digs of **Ralph Lauren** ⑱, which hardly seems like a store at all. The **Whitney Museum of American Art** ⑲, a striking building whose base is smaller than its upper floors, looms on the right at 75th Street, its collection well worth seeing. At Madison Avenue and 76th Street is the **Carlyle Hotel** ⑳, one of the city's most elite and discreet properties (☞ Chapter 7).

The final leg of this tour is several blocks away. How you get through Yorkville is up to you, but we suggest walking east on 78th Street, then north on 2nd Avenue, and east again on 86th. The blocks of 78th between Lexington and 2nd avenues are home to rows of well-maintained, landmark Italianate town houses from the mid-1800s. On 2nd Avenue there are plenty of shops and restaurants at street level to entertain you, some of them reflecting the area's Eastern European heritage. There are also a lot of secondhand stores that sell all sorts of odds and ends including the **Irvington Institute Thrift Shop,** at the southeast corner of 80th Street and 2nd Avenue.

On 86th Street at East End Avenue, the **Henderson Place Historic District** ㉑ includes 24 small-scale town houses built in the 1880s in the Queen Anne style, which was developed in England by Richard Norman Shaw. As if these beautiful dwellings weren't enough, residents here are doubly blessed by the view of and easy access to **Carl Schurz Park** ㉒, across the street and overlooking the East River. **Gracie Mansion** ㉓, the mayor's house, sits at its northern end. The park comes to a narrow stop at 90th Street, but the greenery continues at the **Asphalt Green** ㉔, a concrete parabolic former asphalt plant that's now protected by landmark status and part of a fitness center.

TIMING

This tour covers a lot of ground, but many of the sites require looking, not stopping. Allow about three leisurely hours for the walk. The art institutions—the Americas Society, Asia Society, and the Whitney Museum—make take more of your time, if you'd like them to, so watch their opening hours.

Sights to See

⑯ **Americas Society.** Percy Pyne, the grandson of noted financier Moses Taylor, pioneered Park Avenue when he had this McKim, Mead & White–designed house built in 1909–1911. From 1948 to 1963, the mansion was the Soviet Mission to the United Nations; when the Russians moved out, developers wanted to raze the town house, but in 1965 the Marquesa de Cuevas (a Rockefeller descendant) acquired the property and presented it to the Center for Inter-American Relations, now called the Americas Society. It has an art gallery that's open to the public. ⊠ *680 Park Ave.,* ☎ *212/249–8950.* ☞ *$3 (suggested gallery contribution).* ☉ *Tues.–Sun. noon–6.*

⑰ **Asia Society.** The eight-story red granite building that houses this museum and educational center pleasantly complements the older, more traditional architecture of Park Avenue. This nonprofit educational society, founded in 1956 and headquartered here offers a regular program of lectures, films, and performances, in addition to exhibitions. These feature Asian art, including South Asian stone and bronze sculptures; art from India, Nepal, Pakistan, and Afghanistan; bronze vessels, ceramics, sculpture, and paintings from China; Korean ceramics; and paintings, wood sculptures, and ceramics from Japan. ⊠ *725 Park Ave. at 70th St.,* ☎ *212/288–6400.* ☞ *$3; free Thurs. 6–8.* ☉ *Tues., Wed., Fri. Sat. 11–6, Thurs. 11–8, Sun. noon–5.*

㉔ **Asphalt Green.** You probably won't think this building is beautiful, but the design was rather unique considering its original, unglorious tenant—an asphalt plant. When it was built between 1941–1944, it was the country's first reinforced concrete arch, and it will be here for the ages thanks to landmark status. The plant is now part of a fitness complex—there are often games on the bright green lawn out front, and the natatorium next door houses the city's largest pool. ⊠ *90th St., between York Ave. and FDR Dr.*

⑬ **Bloomingdale's.** This block-long behemoth is noisy, trendy, and crowded; you'll find everything from designer clothes to high-tech teakettles in slick, sophisticated displays. Most selections are high quality, and sale prices on designer goods can be extremely satisfying. Not one to shrink from the limelight, Bloomie's has appeared in more than a few Manhattan movies. Diane Keaton and Michael Murphy shared a perfume-counter encounter here in Woody Allen's *Manhattan;* Robin Williams, playing a Russian musician, defected to the West in *Moscow on the Hudson;* and mermaid Darryl Hannah, in *Splash,* took a crash course in human culture in front of a bank of TVs in the electronics department. ⊠ *59th St., between Lexington and 3rd Aves.,* ☎ *212/705–2000.*

ABIGAIL ADAMS SMITH MUSEUM – Once the converted carriage house of the home of President John Adams's daughter Abigail and her husband, Colonel William Stephen Smith, this 18th-century treasure is now owned by the Colonial Dames of America. Nine rooms display furniture and articles of the Federal and Empire periods, and an adjoining garden is designed in 18th-century style. ✉ *421 E. 61st St.,* ☏ *212/838–6878.* ▨ *$3.* ◷ *Mon.–Fri. noon–4, Sun. 1–5. Closed Aug.*

ROOSEVELT ISLAND – This 2½-mile-long East River island was taken over by a completely self-sufficient residential complex in the 1970s, although only half of the high-rise buildings originally planned have been built. Some fragments remain of the asylums and hospitals once clustered here, when it was known as Welfare Island. Walkways along the edge of the island provide fine river views, and it's surprisingly quiet, considering that the city is so close. The real treat, however, is the 3½-minute ride over on an aerial tram; the entrance is at 2nd Avenue and 60th Street. The island can also be reached by subway (Mon.–Fri., Q train, 7 AM–8 PM; B train, late evening hours; weekends, all day, B train only). The one-way fare is $1.50. ✉ *East River, 48th to 85th Sts.*

★ ㉒ **Carl Schurz Park.** During the American Revolution, a house on this promontory was used as a fortification by the Continental Army, then was taken over as a British outpost. In more peaceful times, the land became known as East End Park. It was renamed in 1911 to honor Carl Schurz (1829–1906), a famous 19th-century German immigrant who eventually served the United States as a minister to Spain, a major general in the Union Army, and a senator of Missouri. During the Hayes administration, Schurz was Secretary of the Interior; he later moved back to Yorkville and worked as editor of the *New York Evening Post* and *Harper's Weekly.*

A curved stone staircase leads up to the wrought-iron railings at the edge of John Finley walk, which overlooks the churning East River— actually just an estuary connecting the Long Island Sound with the harbor. You can see the Triborough, Hell's Gate, and Queensboro bridges, Ward's, Randall's, and Roosevelt islands, and, on the other side of the river, Astoria, Queens. The view is so tranquil that you'd never guess you're directly above the FDR Drive. Behind you, along the walk, are raised flower beds planted with all sorts of interesting blooms; there are also a few recreation areas and a playground in the park. Though it doesn't compare in size with the West Side's Riverside Park, this area is a treasure to Upper East Siders.

Stroll up Carl Schurz Park to reach one of the city's most famous residences, ☞ **Gracie Mansion,** where the mayor of New York resides. ✉ *E. 84th to E. 90th St., between East End Ave. and the East River.*

㉓ **Carlyle Hotel.** The mood here is English manor house. The hotel has the elegant Cafe Carlyle, where top performers such as Bobby Short and Barbara Cook appear regularly, and the more relaxed Bemelmans Bar, with murals by Ludwig Bemelmans, the famed illustrator of the Madeline children's books. Stargazers take note: This elite and discreet hotel's current roster of rich-and-famous guests includes Elizabeth Taylor, George C. Scott, Steve Martin, and Warren Beatty and Annette Bening. In the early 1960s President John F. Kennedy frequently stayed here; rumor has it that he entertained Marilyn Monroe in his rooms. ✉ *35 E. 76th St. at Madison Ave.,* ☏ *212/744–1600.*

China House Gallery (China Institute). A pair of fierce, fat stone lions guards the doorway of this pleasant redbrick town house, where changing public exhibitions of Chinese art are held. ✉ *125 E. 65th St.,*

☎ *212/744–8181.* ✉ *$3 (suggested contribution).* ⊙ *Mon.–Sat. 10–5, Sun. 1–5.*

㉓ Gracie Mansion. This is official home of the mayor of New York. Surrounded by a small lawn and flower beds, this Federal-style yellow frame residence still feels like a country manor house, which is what it was built as in 1779 by wealthy merchant Archibald Gracie. The Gracie family entertained many notable guests at the mansion, including Louis Philippe (later king of France), President John Quincy Adams, the Marquis de Lafayette, Alexander Hamilton, James Fenimore Cooper, Washington Irving, and John Jacob Astor. The city purchased Gracie Mansion in 1887, and, after a period of use as the Museum of the City of New York, Mayor Fiorello H. La Guardia made it the official mayor's residence. A rather tall fence has been added since the Giulianis moved in. ✉ *Carl Schurz Park, East End Ave., opposite 88th St.,* ☎ *212/570–4751.* ✉ *$3. Guided tours mid-Mar.–mid-Nov., Wed; all tours by advance reservation only.*

Grolier Club. Founded in 1884, this private club is named after the 16th-century French bibliophile Jean Grolier. Its members are devoted to the bookmaking crafts; one of them, Bertram Grosvenor Goodhue, designed this neatly proportioned redbrick building in 1917. The club presents public exhibitions and has a specialized reference library that is open by appointment only. ✉ *47 E. 60th St.,* ☎ *212/838–6690.*

Harmonie Club. One of several private men's clubs (many of which now admit women) in this area, this was built in 1905 by McKim, Mead & White. The building, a pseudo-Renaissance palace stretched to highrise proportions, is closely guarded by a doorman, so it's best to admire it from afar. ✉ *4 E. 60th St.*

㉑ Henderson Place Historic District. Originally consisting of 32 small-scale town houses, Henderson Place still has 24 stone and brick buildings. They were built in the 1880s in the Queen Anne style, which was developed in England by Richard Norman Shaw. Designed to be comfortable yet romantic dwellings, they combine elements of the Elizabethan manor house with classic Flemish details. Note, especially, the lovely bay windows, the turrets marking the corner of each block, and the symmetrical roof gables, pediments, parapets, chimneys, and dormer windows. ✉ *East End Ave., between 86th and 87th Sts.*

NEED A BREAK?   **Rush'n Express** (✉ 306 E. 86th St., ☎ 212/517–4949) has unbeatable Russian food and real Russian tea, served from a samovar. You can indulge in wonderfully squishy blini, tart *kissel* (cranberry puree) borscht, and all sorts of other inexpensive items.

Lotos Club. Founded in 1870, this private club's members are devoted to the arts and literature. Its current home is a handsomely ornate French Renaissance mansion originally designed as a private residence by Richard Howland Hunt. ✉ *5 E. 66th St.*

Metropolitan Club. A lordly neoclassical edifice, this was built in 1891 by the grandest producers of such structures—McKim, Mead & White. Ironically, this exclusive club was established by J. P. Morgan when a friend of his was refused membership in the Union League Club; its members today include leaders of foreign countries and presidents of major corporations. ✉ *1 E. 60th St.*

⑱ Ralph Lauren. This store seems more like a private home. In fact, it's in the landmark Rhinelander Mansion and has preserved the grand house's walnut fittings, Oriental carpets, and family portraits as an aristocratic setting in which to display high-style preppy clothing (which is draped about casually, as though waiting to be put away). In the fourth-floor home-furnishings section, merchandise is arrayed in to-the-manor-born dream suites. ⊠ *867 Madison Ave. at 72nd St.,* ☏ *212/606–2100.*

⓯ **Seventh Regiment Armory.** This huge structure is no longer used as a military headquarters, but it has plenty of meeting and social space, which is used for a tennis club, a restaurant, a shelter for homeless people, and an exhibit hall that hosts, among other events, two posh annual antiques shows. Both Louis Comfort Tiffany and Stanford White helped design its surprisingly residential interior; go up the front stairs into the wood-paneled lobby and take a look around. Tours are available by appointment. ⊠ *643 Park Ave. Curator's office:* ☏ *212/744–2968.*

⓮ **Temple Emanu-El.** The world's largest Reform Jewish synagogue seats 2,500 worshipers. Built in 1929 of limestone, it is covered with mosaics and designed in the Romanesque style with Byzantine influences; the building features Moorish and Art Deco ornamentation. ⊠ *1 E. 65th St.,* ☏ *212/744–1400.* ☉ *Services Fri. 5 PM, Sat. 10:30 AM; weekday services Sun.–Thurs. 5:30 PM; guided group tours of synagogue by appointment.*

⓳ **Whitney Museum of American Art.** This museum grew out of a gallery in the studio of the sculptor and collector Gertrude Vanderbilt Whitney, whose talent and taste were fortuitously accompanied by the wealth of two prominent families. The current building, opened in 1966, is a minimalist gray granite vault separated from Madison Avenue by a dry moat; it was designed by Marcel Breuer, a member of the Bauhaus school, which prized functionality in architecture. Though part of the building is devoted to office space, the museum is planning to move these quarters to neighboring town houses to create more exhibit space. The monolithic exterior is much more forbidding than the interior, where changing exhibitions offer an intelligent survey of 20th-century American works; the second floor shows, among other exhibits, daring new work from American video artists and filmmakers, and the third-floor gallery features a sample of the permanent collection, including Edward Hopper's haunting *Early Sunday Morning* (1930), Georgia O'Keeffe's *White Calico Flower* (1931), and Jasper Johns's *Three Flags* (1958). Alexander Calder's *Circus,* a playful construction he tinkered with throughout his life (1898–1976), stands near the front entrance. In 1997 the museum will host its Biennial, an always controversial exhibition of new art. The Whitney also has a branch across from Grand Central Terminal (☞ 42nd Street). ⊠ *945 Madison Ave. at 75th St.,* ☏ *212/570–3641.* 🎫 *$8; free Thurs. 6–8.* ☉ *Wed. and Fri.–Sun. 11–6, Thurs. 1–8.*

CENTRAL PARK

Many people consider Central Park the greatest—and most indispensable—part of New York City. Without the park's 843 acres of meandering paths, tranquil lakes, ponds, and open meadows, New Yorkers might be a lot less sane. Every day, thousands of joggers, cyclists, in-line skaters, and walkers make their daily jaunts around "the loop," the reservoir, and various other parts of the park. Come summertime the park serves as Manhattan's Riviera, with sun-seekers crowding every available patch of grass. Throughout the rest of the year, pleasure-seekers of all ages come to enjoy horseback riding, softball, ice skating, roller-skating, croquet, tennis, bird-watching, boating, chess, checkers, theater, concerts, skateboarding, folk dancing, and more—or simply to escape from the rumble of traffic, walk through the trees, and feel—at least for a moment—far from the urban realities of the city.

Although it appears to be nothing more than a swath of rolling countryside exempted from urban development, Central Park was in fact the first artificially landscaped park in the United States. The design for the park was conceived in 1857 by park superintendent Frederick Law Olmsted and Calvert Vaux, one of the founders of the landscape architecture profession in the United States. Their design was one of 33 submitted in a contest arranged by the Central Park Commission—the first such contest in the country. The Greensward Plan, as it was called, combined pastoral, picturesque, and formal elements: Open rolling meadows complement fanciful landscapes and grand, formal walkways. Four transverse roads—at 66th, 79th, 86th, and 96th streets—were designed to carry crosstown traffic beneath the park's hills and tunnels so that park goers would not be disturbed, and 40 bridges were conceived—each with its own unique design and name—to give people easy access to various areas.

The task of constructing the park was monumental. Hundreds of residents of shantytowns were displaced, swamps were drained, and great walls of Manhattan schist were blasted. Thousands of workers were employed to remove some 5 million cubic yards of soil and plant thousands of trees and shrubs in a project that lasted nearly 20 years and cost $14 million.

In the years following the park's opening in 1857, more than half of its visitors arrived by carriage. Today, with a little imagination, you can still experience the park as they did, by hiring a horse-drawn carriage at Grand Army Plaza or any other major intersection of Central Park South (59th St., between 5th and 8th Aves.). Official rates are $34 for the first half hour, and $10 for every ¼ additional hour.

A Good Walk
Numbers in the text correspond to numbers in the margin and on the Central Park map.

If you want to explore the park on foot, begin at the southeast corner at Grand Army Plaza (at 59th St.). The first path off the main road (East Drive) leads to **The Pond** ①, where Gapstow Bridge provides a great vantage point for the oft-photographed midtown skyscrapers. Heading north on the main road you'll come to **Wollman Memorial Rink** ②, whose popularity is second only to the rink at Rockefeller Center. Turn your back to the rink and you'll see the historic **Dairy** ③, which now serves as the park's visitor center. As you walk up the hill to the Dairy, you'll pass the Chess and Checkers House to your left, where gamesters gather on weekends. (Playing pieces are available at the Dairy on Saturdays and Sundays, 11:30 AM to 3 PM.) Inside the Dairy, Central Park's history is explained through exhibits, models, and videos.

As you leave the Dairy, to your right (west) is the Playmates Arch—aptly named, since it leads to a large area of ball fields and playgrounds. Coming through the arch, you'll hear the jaunty music of the antique **Carousel** ④, the second oldest on the East Coast.

Turning your back to the Carousel, climb the slope to the left of the Playmates Arch and walk beside the Center Drive, which veers to the right. Stop for a look at **Sheep Meadow** ⑤, a 15-acre expanse that was used for grazing sheep until 1934, and the neighboring **Mineral Springs Pavilion** ⑥, one of the park's original refreshment stands. Continue along Center Drive about 200 yards to the circular garden at the foot of **The**

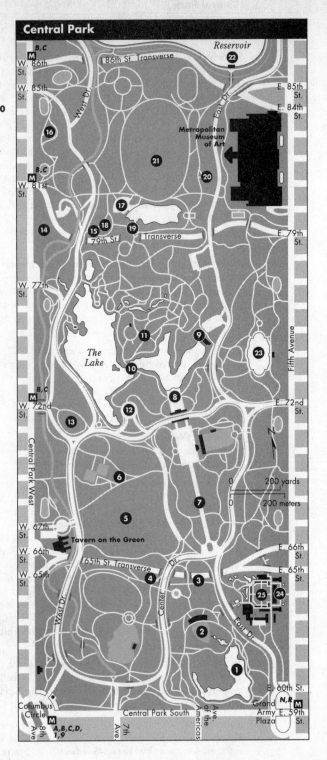

Central Park

Mall ⑦, the grand walkway whose "Literary Walk" is lined with statues of famous writers.

As you stroll down the Mall, note the contrast between the peaceful Sheep Meadow, to your left, and the buzzing path to your right, where joggers, rollerbladers, and cyclists speed by. This path is the 72nd Street transverse, the only crosstown street that connects with the East, Center, and West drives. The transverse cuts across the park at the west end of the Mall; you can either cross it or pass beneath it through a lovely tiled arcade—note the elaborately carved birds and fruit trees that adorn the upper parts of both staircases—to reach **Bethesda Fountain** ⑧, set on an elaborately patterned paved terrace on the edge of the **Lake.**

If you're in the mood for recreation, take the path east from the terrace to **Loeb Boathouse** ⑨, where in season you can rent rowboats and bicycles. The path to the west of the terrace leads to **Bow Bridge** ⑩, a splendid cast-iron bridge arching over a neck of the lake. Across the bridge is **The Ramble** ⑪, a heavily wooded, wild area laced with 37 acres of twisting, climbing paths. Then recross Bow Bridge and continue west along the lakeside path for a view of the lake from **Cherry Hill** ⑫.

Turn your back to the lake and follow the path back to the 72nd Street transverse; on the rocky outcrop across the road, you'll see a statue of a falconer gracefully lofting his bird. Turn to the right and you'll see a more prosaic statue, the pompous bronze figure of Daniel Webster with his hand thrust into his coat. Cross Center Drive behind Webster, being careful to watch for bikers hurtling around the corner. You've now come to **Strawberry Fields** ⑬, a lush, English-style garden memorializing John Lennon.

At the top of Strawberry Fields' hill, turn right through a rustic wood arbor thickly hung with wisteria vines. From here, follow the downhill path to Eaglevale Arch, the southern portal to **Naturalists' Walk** ⑭. After you've explored the varied landscapes of the Walk, head back toward the Park Drive, where directly across the street you will see the quaint wood **Swedish Cottage** ⑮, scene of marionette shows. Staying on the west side of the Drive, continue north along the path to **Summit Rock** ⑯, the highest natural point in the park. After you've enjoyed the view here, head down the other side of the promontory; a path will lead you back toward the Park Drive.

Cross the Park Drive and you'll find yourself at the north end of the Great Lawn (☞ *below*), at the Arthur Ross Pinetum, a collection of pine trees and evergreens from around the world. Follow the path south along the Great Lawn to the open-air **Delacorte Theater** ⑰, where the Joseph Papp Shakespeare Theater Company performs each summer. Just south of the theater is **Shakespeare Garden** ⑱, a lush, landscaped hill covered with flowers and plants that have figured in the writings of the bard. From the top of the hill you can follow a path to the aptly named **Vista Rock,** which is dominated by the circa-1872 **Belvedere Castle** ⑲. The castle is now used as a measurement station of the U.S. Weather Bureau; inside is a nature center.

From the castle's plaza, follow the downhill path east along Turtle Pond, populated by fish, ducks, and dragonflies, in addition to turtles. At the east end of the pond you'll pass a statue of King Jagiello of Poland; groups gather here for folk-dancing on weekends. Follow the path north to **Cleopatra's Needle** ⑳, an Egyptian obelisk just east of the **Great Lawn** ㉑. Vigorous walkers may want to continue north to the **Reservoir** ㉒ for a glimpse of one of the most popular and scenic jogging paths in the city. Others can return south from Cleopatra's Needle, following the path to the left under Greywacke Arch, which leads around the back corner of the Metropolitan Museum.

Continuing south on the path that runs along the east side of the park, you'll come to one of the park's most formal areas: the symmetrical stone basin of the **Conservatory Water** ㉓, which is usually crowded with model boats. Climb the hill at the far end of the water, cross the 72nd Street transverse, and follow the path south to the Children's Zoo; then pass under the Denesmouth Arch to the elaborately designed **Delacorte Clock.** A path to the left will take you around to the front entrance of the **Arsenal** ㉔, which houses various exhibits and some great WPA-era murals. Just past the clock is the **Central Park Zoo** ㉕, home to polar bears, sea lions, monkeys, and more.

TIMING

Allow three hours for this route so that you can enjoy its pastoral pleasures in an appropriately leisurely mood. Those who wish to stroll unharassed by traffic should bear in mind that the circular drive through the park is closed to auto traffic on weekdays 10 AM to 3 PM and 7 to 10 PM, and on weekends and holidays. Weekends are the liveliest time in the park—free entertainment is on tap, and the entire social microcosm is on parade. Weekend crowds make it safe to go into virtually any area of the park, although even on weekdays you should be safe anywhere along this tour. However, you're advised to take this walk during the day since the park is fairly empty after dark. Despite its bad reputation, Central Park has the lowest crime rate of any precinct in the city—though the spectacularly ugly and frightening attacks on joggers in September 1995 and April 1989 have reminded New Yorkers that the wisest course is to stay where the crowds are. The Ramble, a densely wooded, isolated section of the park, is best visited with a friend.

Before you set out for the park you may want to find out about scheduled events or ranger-led walks and talks. For park information and events, call 212/360–3444. For a schedule of weekend walks and talks led by Urban Park Rangers, call 212/427–4040 or 800/201–7275.

Food for thought: Although there are cafés connected with several attractions, as well as food stands near many entrances, most of the food choices are limited and predictable; a picnic lunch is usually a good idea. The Boathouse Cafe at the Loeb Boathouse (☞ *below*), however, is pleasant.

Sights to See

㉔ **The Arsenal.** The park's oldest building, the Arsenal dates from 1857, before Central Park was even created. It occupies a pre-Civil War arsenal and now serves as headquarters of the Parks and Recreation Department. At one time, it was the home of the American Museum of Natural History, which is now on Central Park West at 79th Street (☞ The Upper West Side, *below*). The downstairs lobby has some great WPA-era murals; an upstairs gallery features changing exhibitions relating to urban design and natural and organic themes; and a third-floor conference room houses the rendering of the Greensward Plan—the design that Olmsted and Vaux conceived for the park. ☎ *212/360–8111.* ☺ *Weekdays 9:30–4:30.*

⑲ **Belvedere Castle.** Standing regally atop Vista Rock, Belvedere Castle was built in 1872 of the same gray Manhattan schist that thrusts out of the soil in dramatic outcrops throughout the park. If you step through the pavilion out onto the lip of the rock, you can examine some of this schist, polished and striated by Ice Age glaciers. From here you can look down directly upon the stage of the Delacorte; you can also observe the picnickers and softball players on the Great Lawn.

The castle itself, a typically 19th-century mishmash of styles—Gothic with Romanesque, Chinese, Moorish, and Egyptian motifs—was deliberately kept small so that when it was viewed from across the lake, the lake would seem bigger. (The Ramble's forest now obscures the lake's castle view.) Since 1919 it has been a measurement station of the U.S. Weather Bureau; look up to see the twirling meteorological instruments atop the tower. Climb out onto its balconies for a dramatic view. On the ground floor, the new Henry Luce Nature Observatory has nature exhibits, children's workshops, and educational programs. ☎ 212/772–0210. ⌨ *Free.* ☉ *Mid-Feb.–mid-Oct., Wed.–Sun. 11–5; mid-Oct.–mid-Feb., 11–4* PM.

⑧ Bethesda Fountain. Built in 1863 to commemorate the soldiers who died at sea during the Civil War, the ornate, three-tiered Bethesda Fountain was named after the biblical Bethesda pool in Jerusalem, which was supposedly given healing powers by an angel—hence the statue of an angel rising from the center. This statue, called *The Angel of the Waters,* figured prominently in Tony Kushner's epic drama *Angels in America.* Perch on the low terrace wall or the edge of the fountain and watch the rowboaters stroke past on the lake.

⑩ Bow Bridge. This splendid cast-iron bridge arches over a neck of the lake to the ☞ Ramble. Stand here to take in the picture-postcard view of the water reflecting a quintessentially New York image of vintage apartment buildings peeping above the treetops.

Ⓒ ④ Carousel. Remarkable for the size of its hand-carved steeds—all 57 of them are three-quarters the size of real horses—this carousel was built in 1908 and later moved here from Coney Island. Today it's considered one of the best examples of turn-of-the-century folk art. The organ plays a variety of tunes, new and old. ☎ 212/879–0244. ⌨ *90¢.* ☉ *Summer, daily 10:30–8:00, weekends 10:30–6:30; winter, weekends and holidays, 10:30–5:00, weather permitting.*

Ⓒ ㉕ Central Park Zoo. Recently renamed the Central Park Wildlife Center, the zoo is a small but delightful menagerie. Clustered around the central Sea Lion Pool are separate exhibits for each of the earth's major environments; the Polar Circle features a huge penguin tank and polar-bear floe; the open-air Temperate Territory is highlighted by a pit of chattering monkeys; and the Tropic Zone contains the flora and fauna of a miniature rain forest. This is a good zoo for children and adults who like to take time to watch the animals; even a leisurely visit will take only about an hour, for there are only about 100 species on display. Go to the Bronx Zoo (☞ Chapter 3) if you need tigers, giraffes, and elephants—the biggest specimens here are the polar bears. ✉ *Entrance at 5th Ave. and 64th St.,* ☎ 212/439–6500. ⌨ *$2.50. No children under 16 allowed in without adult.* ☉ *Apr.–Oct., Mon.–Fri. 10–5:00, weekends and holidays 10:30–5:30; Nov.–Mar., daily 10–4:30.*

⑫ Cherry Hill. Originally a watering area for horses, this circular plaza with a small wrought-iron-and-gilt fountain is a great vantage point for the lake and the west-side skyline.

⑳ Cleopatra's Needle. This exotic, hieroglyphic–covered obelisk was a gift to the city in 1881 from the khedive of Egypt. The copper crabs supporting the huge stone at each corner almost seem squashed by its weight. The Needle is, appropriately, near the glass-enclosed wing of the Metropolitan Museum (☞ Museum Mile, *above*), which houses the Egyptian Temple of Dendur.

🕙 ㉓ **Conservatory Water.** At the symmetrical stone basin of this neo-Renaissance-style concrete basin you can watch some very sophisticated model boats being raced each Saturday morning at 10. (Unfortunately, model boats are not for rent here.) At the north end is one of the park's most beloved statues, José de Creeft's 1960 bronze sculpture of **Alice in Wonderland,** sitting on a giant mushroom with the Mad Hatter, White Rabbit, and leering Cheshire Cat in attendance. Children are encouraged to clamber all over it. On the west side of the pond, a bronze statue of **Hans Christian Andersen,** the Ugly Duckling at his feet, is the site of storytelling hours on summer weekends.

❸ **The Dairy.** As its name implies, this was originally an actual dairy built in the 19th century, when cows grazed in the area. In those days, toys could be rented and milk purchased at the Dairy, which lay within the so-called Children's District—the area below 65th Street where fanciful rustic shelters, the Carousel, and the Dairy attracted youngsters.

Today the Dairy's painted, pointed eaves, steeple, and high-pitched slate roof harbor the park's visitor center, offering informative exhibits and interactive videos on the history and construction of the park. Here you can buy maps and souvenirs, and a small research library lends out books about the park. ☎ *212/794–6565.* ⊙ *Winter, Tues.–Sun. 11–4, Fri. 1–4; summer, Tues.–Sun. 11–5, Fri. 1–5.*

🕙 **Delacorte Clock.** Set above a redbrick arch near the Central Park Zoo, this delightful glockenspiel was dedicated to the city by philanthropist George T. Delacorte. Its fanciful bronze face is decorated with a menagerie of mechanical animals, including a dancing bear, a kangaroo, a penguin, and monkeys that rotate and hammer their bells when the clock chimes its hourly tune.

⓱ **Delacorte Theater.** Some of the best plays in New York take place at this open-air theater-in-the-round, where the Joseph Papp Shakespeare Theater Company (☞ Chapter 5) performs each summer. Tickets are free, but expect an all-day wait in line to pick them up.

㉑ **Great Lawn.** This newly sodded 15-acre expanse of green is scheduled to reopen in 1997 after a two-year, $18 million restoration. The area hums with action on weekends and most summer evenings, when its softball fields and picnicking grounds provide a much-needed outlet for city dwellers of all ages. In summer, should you see a few hundred people sitting in a row around the oval edge of the lawn, you'll know they're waiting to pick up free tickets to a Shakespeare performance at the Delacorte Theater. (Call Joseph Papp Public Theater, ☎ 212/260–2400 for details).

❾ **Loeb Boathouse.** At the brick neo-Victorian boathouse you can rent bicycles as well as boats. Loeb also has a better-than-average restaurant, The Boathouse Cafe, where the characters dined in the movies *Three Men and a Little Lady, Postcards from the Edge,* and *The Manchurian Candidate.* The cafeteria end has a good cheap breakfast, including freshly made scones, and lunch. 🚣 *Boat rental $10 per hr, $20 deposit;* ☎ *212/517–4723.* 🚲 *Bicycle rental $8–$10 per hr, tandems $14 per hr;* ☎ *212/861–4137.* ⊙ *Mar.–Nov., weather permitting, Mon.–Fri. 10–6, weekends 9–6. Boathouse Cafe:* ☎ *212/517–2233.* ⊙ *Mar.-Sept., Tues.–Fri. noon–4, weekends 11:30–dusk.*

❼ **The Mall.** A broad, formal walkway where fashionable ladies and men used to gather to see and be seen around the turn of the century, the Mall looks as grand as ever. Its main path, the **"The Literary Walk,"** is lined with the largest group of American elms in the Northeast and statues of famous men, including Shakespeare, Robert Burns, and Sir Walter Scott.

❻ Mineral Springs Pavilion. The Moorish-style palace at the northern end of ☞ Sheep Meadow was designed by Calvert Vaux and J. Wrey Mould, who also designed Bethesda Terrace. Built as one of the park's four refreshment stands in the late 1860s, the pavilion still has a snack bar today.

Behind the pavilion are the **Croquet Grounds** and **Lawn Bowling Greens.** During the season (May–November) you can peer through gaps in the high hedges to watch the players, usually dressed in crisp white.

⓮ Naturalists' Walk. Starting at the new 79th Street entrance to the park across from the Museum of Natural History, this recently created nature walk is one of the best places to learn about local wildlife, bird life, flora, fauna, and geology. As you wind your way toward ☞ Belvedere Castle you'll find the spectacular rock outcrops of Geology Walk, a stream that attracts countless species of birds, a woodland area with various native trees, stepping-stone trails that lead over rocky bluffs, and a sitting area.

❶ The Pond. Swans and ducks can sometimes be spotted on the calm waters of the Pond. For an unbeatable view of the city skyline, walk along the shore to **Gapstow Bridge.** From left to right, you'll see the peak-roofed brown Sherry-Netherland hotel, the black-and-white General Motors Building, the rose-colored "Chippendale" top of the Sony Building, the black glass shaft of Trump Tower, and in front the green gables of the Plaza Hotel.

⓫ The Ramble. Across the Bow Bridge from the Lake, the Ramble is a heavily wooded, wild 37-acre area laced with twisting, climbing paths. This is prime bird-watching territory; a rest stop along a major migratory route, it shelters many of the 269 species of birds that have been sighted in the park. Because it is so dense and isolated, however, it is not a good place to wander alone.

㉒ The Reservoir. Quite possibly the most popular jogging path in all of New York City, this 1.58-mile track is also one of the most beautiful places to be come fall and spring, when the hundreds of trees around it burst into color. The Reservoir itself is more or less a holding tank; the city's main reservoirs are upstate. Dustin Hoffman ran here in the film *Marathon Man.*

⓲ Shakespeare Garden. One of the park's few formal flower plantings, this lushly landscaped, terraced hill is one of the more hidden spots in the park. Literary types may recognize some of the flowers that have figured in various plays.

❺ Sheep Meadow. Used as a sheep grazing area until 1934, this grassy 15-acre meadow is now a favorite of picnickers, sun bathers, and people seeking relaxation. It's an officially designated quiet zone; the most vigorous sports allowed are kite-flying and Frisbee-tossing.

Just west of the meadow, the famous **Tavern on the Green,** originally the sheepfold, was erected by Boss Tweed in 1870 and is now considered one of the glitziest, kitschiest restaurants in Manhattan.

⓭ Strawberry Fields. Called the "international peace garden," this memorial to John Lennon is one of the most visited sights in the park. Climbing up a hill, its curving paths, shrubs, trees, and flower beds—all donated from nearly every country of the world—create a deliberately informal pastoral landscape, reminiscent of the English parks Lennon may have been thinking of when he wrote the Beatles song "Strawberry Fields

Forever" in 1967. A black-and-white mosaic set into one of the sidewalks contains the word "Imagine," another Lennon song title. Just beyond the trees, at 72nd Street and Central Park West, is the Dakota (☞ The Upper West Side, *below*), where Lennon lived at the time of his death in 1980.

🕭 ⑮ **Swedish Cottage.** Looking like something straight out of Germany's Black Forest, this dark-wood chalet is used for marionette shows. ☎ 212/988–9093. ☞ *$5.* ☉ *Shows Tues.–Fri. 10:30 and noon; Sat., noon and 3; call for reservations.*

🕭 ❷ **Wollman Memorial Rink.** Now a beloved recreational facility, this was once a symbol of municipal inefficiency to New Yorkers. Fruitless and costly attempts by the city to repair the deteriorated rink kept it closed for years, until real-estate mogul Donald Trump adopted the project and quickly completed it in 1986. Even if you don't want to join in, you can stand on the terrace here to watch the skaters ice-skating throughout the winter. ☎ *212/396–1010.* ☞ *$6.50.* ☉ *Nov.–Mar., Mon. 10–5, Tues.–Thurs. 10–9:30, Fri. 10–11, Sat. 10–3 and 4–11, Sun. 10–3 and 4–9.*

OFF THE BEATEN PATH

CONSERVATORY GARDEN – Central Park's only formal garden is a gem. Named for the elegant old greenhouses that stood here before the Depression, the Conservatory Garden is a lavishly landscaped conglomerate: an ornate and manicured French garden, a classic Italian garden flanked by crabapple allées, and a densely planted perennial garden. It's a perfectly safe place to visit during the day—and very worthwhile. ✉ *5th Ave. and 105th St.* ☉ *Daily 8 AM–dusk.*

HARLEM MEER – Those who never venture beyond 96th Street miss out on one of the park's most unusual attractions: Harlem Meer, where as many as 100 people fish for stocked largemouth bass, catfish, golden shiners, and bluegills every day. The upper park's other main attraction is the **Charles A. Discovery Center,** at the north end of the meer. Here you can learn about geography, orienteering, ecology, and the history of the upper park. Within walking distance of the center are fortifications from the American Revolution and other historic sites, as well as woodlands, meadows, rocky bluffs, lakes, and streams. ✉ *5th Ave. and 110th St.*

THE UPPER WEST SIDE

The Upper West Side has never been as fashionable as the East Side, despite its many famous residents, past and present, and the fact that it has a similar mix of real estate—large apartment buildings along Central Park West, West End Avenue, and Riverside Drive, and town houses on the shady, quiet cross streets—much of which is now protected by landmark status. Unlike the East Side, this neighborhood's development largely followed the routes of mass transit, with an elevated train pioneering the way (1879) and subways coming around the turn of the century.

Once a haven for the Jewish intelligentsia, and still a liberal stronghold, the West Side in the 1960s had become a rather grungy multiethnic community. A slow process of gentrification began in the 1970s, however, when actors, writers, and gays began to move into the area. Today this neighborhood is quite desirable, with lots of restored brownstones and high-priced co-op apartments. Young professionals gravitate to its small apartments, and graduate to its larger ones when they become young families. On weekends they cram the sidewalks as they push babies around in their imported strollers, but in the evenings the action moves inside, where singles mingle in a growing number of restaurants and bars. Columbus Avenue is one such boutique-and-restaurant strip; Amsterdam Avenue is slowly following suit, its shop fronts a mix of bodegas and boutiques. Along upper Broadway, new luxury apartment towers are slowly blocking in the horizon. Many longtime West Siders decry the "yuppification" of their neighborhoods that began about 15 years ago, but now the good news is that small businesses thrive on blocks that a few years ago were not safe to walk on.

The popularity of the neighborhood is enhanced by the two parks— Central and Riverside—that form its eastern and western boundaries, respectively. Between them, Lincoln Center and the American Museum of Natural History always attract big crowds.

A Good Walk
Numbers in the text correspond to numbers in the margin and on the Upper West Side, Morningside Heights map.

The West Side story begins at **Columbus Circle** ①, the confusing intersection of Broadway, 8th Avenue, Central Park West, and Central Park South. This is a good place to start any tour of the city, for it is the headquarters of the **New York Convention and Visitors Bureau.** On the southwest quadrant of the circle is the **New York Coliseum,** a blank functional-looking white brick building that was the city's chief convention and trade-show venue before the opening of the Jacob Javits Center. A soaring multiuse complex proposed for the site was bitterly opposed by New Yorkers determined not to let its huge shadow be cast across Central Park; the site continues to be embroiled in suits and countersuits. On the northeast corner of the circle, an entrance to Central Park is presided over by the *Maine Monument,* with its florid bronze figures atop a stocky limestone pedestal. The piece-of-pie-shaped wedge of land between Central Park West and Broadway recently became the site of the **Trump International Hotel and Tower.**

Cross the intersection at your own discretion and head north on the west side of Broadway. At 61st Street is the world headquarters of the **American Bible Society,** which houses a library that is open to the public. A few blocks north is New York's major site for the performing arts: **Lincoln Center** ②.

Across the busy intersection on the east side of the street, at Columbus Avenue and 66th Street, the appreciation of culture continues at the **Museum of American Folk Art** ③. Around the corner on 66th Street is the headquarters of the ABC television network; ABC owns several buildings along Columbus Avenue as well, including some studios where news shows and soap operas are filmed, so keep an eye out for your favorite daytime doctors, tycoons, and temptresses.

Turn right from Columbus Avenue onto **West 67th Street** and head toward Central Park along this handsome block. Just inside Central Park is **Tavern on the Green** (☞ Chapter 6), a restaurant and cabaret that is very popular with tourists. Walk north on the east (park) side of the street for the best view of the stately apartment buildings that line Central Park West. Mixed among them is the **Spanish & Portuguese Synagogue, Shearith Israel,** thought to be the first synagogue built in the classical style of the Second Temple in Jerusalem. At 72nd Street, cross back over Central Park West to get a close view of **the Dakota** ④, the apartment building that presides over the block. Its neighbors to the north include several other famous apartment buildings and their famous residents: **The Langham** (⊠ 135 Central Park), an Italian Renaissance–style high-rise designed by leading apartment architect

American Museum of Natural History and Hayden Planetarium, **6**

Barnard College, **11**

Cathedral of St. John the Divine, **9**

Columbia University, **10**

Columbus Circle, **1**

The Dakota, **4**

Grant's Tomb, **15**

Jewish Theological Seminary, **14**

Lincoln Center, **2**

Museum of American Folk Art, **3**

New-York Historical Society, **5**

Riverside Church, **16**

Riverside Park, **8**

Subway kiosk, **7**

Teachers College, **12**

Union Theological Seminary, **13**

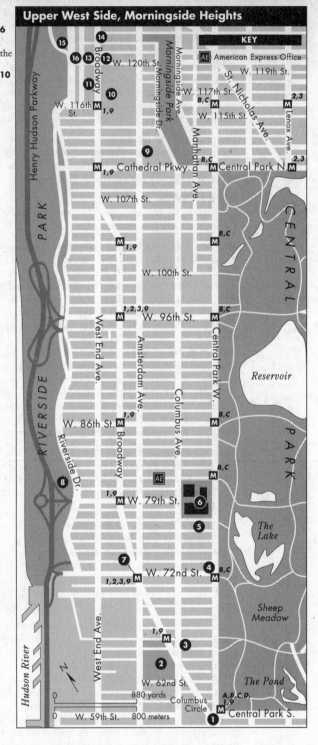

Upper West Side, Morningside Heights

KEY

AE American Express Office

Emery Roth in 1929–30; the twin-towered **San Remo** (⊠ 145–146 Central Park W), over the years home to Rita Hayworth, Dustin Hoffman, Raquel Welch, Paul Simon, Barry Manilow, Tony Randall, and Diane Keaton—but not to Madonna, whose application was rejected; and **The Kenilworth** (⊠ 151 Central Park W), with its immense pair of ornate front columns, once the address of Basil Rathbone, film's quintessential Sherlock Holmes, and Michael Douglas.

Now we're approaching the Museum of Natural History—the reason many people visit the neighborhood. Before dashing off to fight the crowds there, however, you can learn more about your host city inside the lovely neoclassical building on Central Park West between 76th and 77th streets (entrance on 77th), the headquarters of the **New-York Historical Society** ⑤. Past and present inhabitants of the entire world are the subject of the **American Museum of Natural History** ⑥. Along with the attached **Hayden Planetarium** and the surrounding grounds, the museum occupies a four-block tract bounded by Central Park West, Columbus Avenue, and 77th and 81st streets.

At this point you've covered the mandatory tourist itinerary for the neighborhood. If you've had enough sightseeing, you could forsake the rest of this tour for boutique-shopping along Columbus Avenue (☞ Chapter 10), which is directly behind the museum. If you're here on a Sunday, check out the **flea market** at the southwest corner of 77th Street and Columbus Avenue.

If you continue with this tour, you'll snake through the neighborhood past some institutions that figure prominently in the daily lives of New Yorkers. On the west side of Broadway, choose the shrine to which you'd like to make a pilgrimage: There's **Zabar's** (between 80th and 81st Sts.), where shoppers have to muscle for elbow room while trying to secure bargain prices on exquisite delicatessen items, prepared foods, gourmet groceries, coffee, and cheeses as well as the cookware, dishes, and small appliances; **H & H Bagels** (at 80th St., southwest corner), which sells (and ships around the world) several varieties of huge, chewy bagels hot from the oven; **Citarella's** store (at 75th St., southwest corner), with its intricate, often absurd arrangements of seafood on shaved ice in the front window; and the bountiful but unpretentious **Fairway Market** (2127 Broadway at 74th St.), where baby carriages bevy for space with snack food, cheeses, and produce that practically bursts onto the street.

At 73rd Street and Broadway on the west side of the street, look up at the white facade and fairy-castle turrets of the **Ansonia Hotel**, a turn-of-the-century luxury building. Here, where Broadway cuts across Amsterdam Avenue, the triangle north of 72nd is **Verdi Square** (named for Italian opera composer Giuseppe Verdi). In the 1970s this square was better known as Needle Park because of the drug addicts who hung out there. Now, elderly West Siders kibitz on the wood benches. The triangle south of 72nd Street is **Sherman Square** (named for Union Civil War general William Tecumseh Sherman); the **subway kiosk** ⑦ here is an official city landmark.

End your visit to the area with a walk through the park that many neighborhood residents consider to be their private backyard: **Riverside Park** ⑧, a long, slender green space along the Hudson River landscaped by Central Park architects Olmsted and Vaux.

TIMING

Part of this neighborhood's charm is its tree-lined blocks and the buildings that line them, and just walking past the ones on this tour would easily take two or three hours. To see some of what's inside the buildings lengthens the journey to the better part of a day. Plan according to which museums you'd like to visit, which days they're open, and how long you'd like to spend there. The exhibits at both the Museum of American Folk Art and the New-York Historical Society shouldn't take more than an hour or so to view. The American Museum of Natural History, on the other hand, is mammoth and often quite crowded. In bad weather, you might want to limit your itinerary to what's covered between Lincoln Center and the Museum of Natural History.

Sights to See

American Bible Society. A swirling staircase takes you to a little-known second-floor library that displays, among other things, Helen Keller's massive 10-volume braille Bible, a replica of the original Gutenberg press, and a Torah (Jewish scriptures) from China. ⊠ *1865 Broadway at 61st St.,* ☎ *212/408–1200).* ⊙ *Weekdays 9:30–4:30 (library).*

★ ☾ ❻ **American Museum of Natural History.** Approaching from the south, you can see the structure's original architecture in the pink granite corner towers, with their beehive crowns. Though the lines may be shorter at the south-side entrance, you should brave the crowds pouring in off Central Park West. Here, a more classical facade was added, its centerpiece an enormous equestrian statue of President Theodore Roosevelt, naturalist and explorer. Even if you don't want to visit the museum, you should look into **Theodore Roosevelt Rotunda,** a massive marble-laden, barrel-vaulted space where a five-story-tall cast of Barosaurus rears on its hind legs, protecting its fossilized baby from a fossil allosaurus.

With a collection of more than 30 million artifacts, the museum displays something for every taste, from a 94-foot blue whale to the 563-carat Star of India sapphire. Among the most enduringly popular exhibits are the wondrously detailed dioramas of animal habitat groups, on the first and second floors just behind the rotunda, and the fourth-floor halls full of dinosaur skeletons. These two new halls—of Saurischian and Ornithischian dinosaurs—opened in summer 1995 and use real fossils and interactive computer stations to present the most recent interpretations of how dinosaurs might have behaved. The Hall of Human Biology and Evolution investigates the workings of the human body and features a computerized archaeological dig and an electronic newspaper about human evolution. A Naturemax Theater projects films on a giant screen; the **Hayden Planetarium** (on 81st Street), which is slated for replacement, has two stories of exhibits, plus several different Sky Shows projected on 22 wraparound screens; its rock-music laser shows draw crowds of teenagers on Friday and Saturday nights. ⊠ *Central Park West at 79th St. Museum:* ☎ *212/769–5100;* ✉ *$7 (suggested contribution);* ⊙ *Sun.–Thurs. 10–5:45; Fri.–Sat. 10–8:45. Planetarium:* ☎ *212/769–5900;* ✉ *$7; $8.50 for laser show;* ⊙ *weekdays 12:30–4:45, Sat. 10–5:45, Sun. noon–5:45. Naturemax Theater film:* ✉ *$6,* ☎ *212/769–5650 for show times (joint tickets available).*

| NEED A BREAK? | For a diner-style cheeseburger or just a banana split, stop by **EJ's Luncheonette** (⊠ 447 Amsterdam Ave., between 81st and 82nd Sts., ☎ 212/873-3444). |

Ansonia Hotel. Now a residential condominium apartment building, the Ansonia was built in the Beaux Arts style as an apartment hotel, with suites without kitchens (and separate quarters for a staff who took care of the food). Designed to be fireproof, it has thick, soundproof walls that make it attractive to musicians; famous denizens of the past include Enrico Caruso, Igor Stravinsky, Arturo Toscanini, Florenz Ziegfeld, Theodore Dreiser, and Babe Ruth. ⊠ *2019 Broadway, between 73rd and 74th Sts.*

1 Columbus Circle. This confusing intersection has never had the grandeur or the definition of Broadway's major intersections to the south, but it does have a 700-ton monument capped by a statue of Christopher himself in the middle of a traffic island; it had to be elaborately supported when the land underneath was torn up during the construction of the Columbus Circle subway station in the early 1900s. The city perpetually tries to improve traffic conditions here, but it has yet to approve a concrete plan for all this concrete.

4 The Dakota. People once thought this building was so far from the city that it might as well be in the Dakotas; that's how the structure got its name. Indeed, the picturesque gables here housed some of the West Side's first residents, and their building (built in 1880–84) set a high standard for the apartments that followed. Resembling a buff-colored castle, with copper turrets, the Dakota is often depicted in scenes of Old New York, and it was by looking out of a window here that Si Morley was able to travel back in time in Jack Finney's *Time and Again.* Its slightly spooky appearance was played up in the movie *Rosemary's Baby,* which was filmed here.

The building's entrance is on 72nd Street, and you should look beyond the guard's station there into the surprisingly spacious, lovely courtyard. At this gate, in December 1980, a deranged fan shot John Lennon as he came home from a recording session. Other celebrity tenants have included Boris Karloff, Rudolf Nureyev, José Ferrer and Rosemary Clooney, Lauren Bacall, Rex Reed, and Gilda Radner. ⊠ *1 West 72nd St.*

2 Lincoln Center. A neighborhood was razed when Lincoln Center was built during the 1960s (*West Side Story* was filmed on the slum's gritty, deserted streets just before the demolition crews moved in), but that has long been forgotten by the artists who've since moved to the area, as well as their patrons. A unified complex of pale travertine marble, Lincoln Center can seat nearly 18,000 spectators at one time in its various halls (☞ Chapter 5).

Stand on Broadway, facing the central court with its huge fountain. The three concert halls on this plaza clearly relate to one another architecturally, with their symmetrical bilevel facades, yet each has slightly different lines and different details. To your left, huge honeycomb lights hang on the portico of the **New York State Theater,** home to the New York City Ballet and the New York City Opera. Straight ahead, at the rear of the plaza, is the **Metropolitan Opera House,** its brilliant-colored Chagall murals visible through the arched lobby windows; the Metropolitan Opera and American Ballet Theatre perform here. To your right, abstract bronze sculptures distinguish **Avery Fisher Hall,** host to the New York Philharmonic Orchestra.

Wander through the plaza, then angle to your left between the New York State Theater and the Metropolitan Opera House into **Damrosch Park,** where summer open-air festivals are often accompanied by free concerts at the **Guggenheim Bandshell.** Angle to your right from the plaza, between the Metropolitan and Avery Fisher, and you'll come to the North Plaza, with a massive Henry Moore sculpture reclining in a reflecting pool. To the rear is the **New York Public Library for the Performing Arts,** a branch library with an extensive collection of books, records, and scores on music, theater, and dance; visitors can listen to any of 50,000 records and tapes, or check out its four galleries. Next to the library is the wide glass-walled lobby of the **Vivian Beaumont Theater,** officially considered a Broadway house although it is far removed from the theater district. It was closed for renovation in early 1996 but was scheduled to reopen by the end of the year. Below it is the smaller **Mitzi E. Newhouse Theater,** where many award-winning plays originated.

An overpass leads from this plaza across 65th Street to the world-renowned **Juilliard School** (for music and theater). Check here to see if there's a concert or a play going on; actors Kevin Kline and Patti LuPone once performed here. Turn right for an elevator down to street level and **Alice Tully Hall,** home of the Chamber Music Society of Lincoln Center and the New York Film Festival. Or turn left from the overpass and follow the walkway west to Lincoln Center's newest arts venue, the **Walter Reade Theater,** opened in the fall of 1991, showing several unusual American and foreign films a day, seven days a week (☞ Chapter 5).

Visitors can wander freely through the lobbies of all these buildings. One-hour guided "Introduction to Lincoln Center" tours, given daily, cover the center's history and wealth of artwork and usually visit the three principal theaters, performance schedules permitting. ☎ *212/875–5350 for schedule and reservations.* 🎫 *$8.25.*

NEED A BREAK?	Before or after a Lincoln Center performance, the friendly **Cafe Mozart** (✉ 154 W. 70th St., ☎ 212/595-9797) is a good place to stop for conversation with a friend.

❸ Museum of American Folk Art. Its collection includes arts and crafts from all over the Americas: native paintings, quilts, carvings, dolls, trade signs, painted wood carousel horses, and a giant Indian-chief copper weather vane. ✉ *2 Lincoln Sq.,* ☎ *212/595–9533.* 🎫 *$2 (suggested contribution).* ☉ *Tues.–Sun. 11:30–7:30.*

New York Convention and Visitors Bureau. This weird pseudo-Byzantine structure was ostensibly modeled after the Doge's Palace in Venice but is locally nicknamed the Lollipop Building. Count on the bureau for brochures; bus and subway maps; hotel, restaurant, and shopping guides; a seasonal calendar of events; free TV-show tickets (sometimes) and discounts on Broadway theater; and sound advice. ✉ *2 Columbus Circle,* ☎ *212/397–8200.* ☉ *Weekdays 9–6, weekends and holidays 10–3.*

❺ New-York Historical Society. Founded back when New York was undistinguished enough to have to hyphenate its name (1804), this is the City's oldest museum; it moved to this site in 1908. Its collections and changing exhibits shed light on America's decorative art, history, and everyday life, with a special focus on New York—perhaps you'll see 18th-century roach traps, high-society punch bowls, or Tiffany lamps. The research library, which contains the original watercolors for Audubon's *Birds of America* and the architectural files of McKim, Mead, & White, is renowned in scholarly circles. Sadly, lack of funding closed the museum for a couple years, and despite the money raised by auctioning off some of its treasures, it has continued to struggle financially since reopening in spring 1995. ✉ *2 W. 77th St.,* ☎ *212/873–3400. Museum* ☉ *Wed.–Sun. noon–5;* 🎫 *$3 (suggested donation). Library* ☉ *Wed.–Fri. noon–5.*

❽ Riverside Park. Long and narrow, Riverside Park runs along the Hudson all the way from 72nd Street to 159th Street. The **Promenade,** a broad formal walkway with a stone parapet looking out over the river, extends from 80th Street to a few blocks north. Descend the steps here and go through the underpass beneath Riverside Drive to reach the **79th Street Boat Basin,** a rare spot in Manhattan, where you can walk right along the river's edge, smell the salt air, and watch a flotilla of houseboats bobbing in the water. Yes, these boats do actually sail—at least once a year when they have to prove their seaworthiness.

If you walk to the end of the Promenade, you'll see a patch of its median strip exploding with flowers tended by nearby residents. Look up to your right, where the Civil War **Soldiers' and Sailors' Monument**, an imposing circle of white marble columns, crests a hill along Riverside Drive. Climb to its base for a refreshing view of Riverside Park, the Hudson River, and the New Jersey waterfront.

OFF THE
BEATEN PATH

NICHOLAS ROERICH MUSEUM – Housed in an Upper West Side town house (built in 1898), this small, eccentric museum displays the work of the Russian artist who, among many other things, designed sets for Diaghilev ballets. Vast paintings of the Himalayas are a focal point of the collection. ✉ *319 W. 107th St.,* ☎ *212/864-7752.* ✍ *Free.* ⊙ *Tues.–Sun. 2–5.*

Spanish & Portuguese Synagogue, Shearith Israel (Orthodox Jewish). Built in 1897, this is the fifth home of the oldest Jewish congregation in the United States, founded in 1654. The adjoining "Little Synagogue" is a replica of Shearith Israel's Georgian-style first synagogue. ✉ *8 W. 70th St.*

➐ **Subway kiosk.** This brick and terra-cotta building with rounded neo-Dutch molding is one of two remaining control houses from the original subway line (the other is at Bowling Green). Built in 1904–1905, this was the first express station north of 42nd Street. ✉ *72nd and Broadway.*

Tavern on the Green. Originally built as a sheepfold, in the days when sheep grazed on the meadows of the park, it was converted into a restaurant in the 1930s. True, the high tone is not what it once was, but many of its dining rooms have fine park views; at night white lights strung through the surrounding trees create a magical effect. ✉ *Central Park W and 66th St.*

Trump International Hotel and Tower. The former headquarters of Paramount Communications, and before that the Gulf and Western Building, no longer resembles its previous selves. In fall 1995, all 45 of its stories were completely gutted as developer Donald Trump prepared to make his mark, aided by architects Philip Johnson and Costas Kondylis. When the $250 million project is finished sometime in 1997, the Trump-proclaimed "most important new address in the world" will be covered with tinted windows, V-shaped columns, and gold reflective glass, a fittingly garish addition to his real-estate collection. ✉ *106 Central Park S.*

West 67th Street. Between Columbus Avenue and Central Park West, many of the apartment buildings on West 67th Street were designed as "studio buildings," with high ceilings and immense windows that make them ideal for artists—these were the days when "studio apartment" meant much more than one room barely big enough for a futon. Look up at the facades and imagine the spaces within. Also notice the Gothic motifs, carved in white stone or wrought in iron, that decorate several of these buildings at street level. Perhaps the finest apartment building on the block is the **Hotel des Artistes**, built in 1918 on the corner of Central Park West, with its elaborate mock-Elizabethan lobby. Its tenants have included Isadora Duncan, Rudolph Valentino, Norman Rockwell, Noël Coward, Fannie Hurst, and contemporary actors Joel Grey and Richard Thomas and artist Leroy Neiman; another tenant, Howard Chandler Christy, designed the lush, soft-toned murals in the excellent ground-floor restaurant, **Café des Artistes** (☞ Chapter 6), where Louis Malle's *My Dinner with André* was filmed.

MORNINGSIDE HEIGHTS

On the high ridge just north and west of Central Park, a cultural outpost grew up at the end of the 19th century, spearheaded by a triad of institutions: the relocated Columbia University, which developed the mind; St. Luke's Hospital, which cared for the body; and the Cathedral of St. John the Divine, which tended the soul. Idealistically conceived of as an American Acropolis, the cluster of academic and religious institutions that developed here managed to keep these blocks stable during years when neighborhoods on all sides were collapsing. More recently, West Side gentrification has reclaimed the area to the south, while the areas north and east of here haven't changed as much. Yet within the gates of the Columbia or Barnard campus, or inside the hush of the cathedral or Riverside Church, the pace of life seems slower, more contemplative. Being a student neighborhood, the area has a casual atmosphere that is hip, friendly, and fun.

A Good Walk
Numbers in the text correspond to numbers in the margin and on the Upper West Side, Morningside Heights map.

You can't miss the massive **Cathedral of St. John the Divine** ⑨, its main entrance on Amsterdam Avenue at 112th, nor should you. You could easily spend an hour wandering through the church, inspecting its architecture, noticing different characters in its stained-glass windows, looking at its tapestry and art exhibits, and in its gift store. On the south side of the cathedral and also worth studying is the **Peace Fountain,** which sits in a circular plaza just off Amsterdam at 111th Street.

From here, swing east on 113th Street to secluded **Morningside Drive.** On 113th Street you can still see the baroque 1896 core of **St. Luke's Hospital,** which has grown rather awkwardly into a jumble of newer buildings. On Morningside Drive at 114th Street you'll find the **Church of Notre Dame,** much smaller than the other churches on this tour. At 116th Street you may want to pause on the overlook on the right to gaze out at the boxy skyline and down into **Morningside Park,** tumbling steeply into a wooded gorge. Designed by Olmsted and Vaux, of Central Park fame, the park is a lovely landscape, but since it is bordered by some rough blocks of Harlem, it would be safer not to get any closer.

At 116th Street and Amsterdam Avenue, you can pass through the campus gates of **Columbia University** ⑩. The university's renowned Journalism School, founded by Joseph Pulitzer (and the reason Columbia bestows Pulitzer Prizes each spring), holds classes in the building just south of the campus's west gates. Go through the gates and onto Broadway to find the official college bookstore at 115th Street and Broadway. Across Broadway from Columbia proper is its sister institution, **Barnard College** ⑪, another green oasis.

Institutes of higher learning abound as you follow Broadway on the east side of the street north to 120th Street, where on your right is **Teachers College** ⑫, a part of Columbia, and on your left, on the west side of the street, is the interdenominational **Union Theological Seminary** ⑬. At the northeast corner of 122nd Street and Broadway, behind a large blank-walled redbrick tower that fronts the intersection at an angle, is the **Jewish Theological Seminary** ⑭. Walk west on 122nd Street; between Claremont Avenue and Broadway, you'll see the prestigious

Manhattan School of Music on your right, with musical instruments carved into the stone beneath its upper-story windows. Between Claremont and Riverside Drive, you may want to sit for a moment in **Sakura Park**, a quiet formal garden.

Across Riverside Drive at W. 122nd Street, in Riverside Park, you can see for yourself who's buried in the immense General Grant Memorial, commonly known as **Grant's Tomb** ⑮. Just to the south, on Riverside Drive at 120th Street, our tour ends at **Riverside Church** ⑯.

TIMING

To get the true flavor of the neighborhood, which is often student-dominated, you'll want to visit during the week when classes are in session. You'll be able to visit campus buildings, sample café life as it's meant to be, and because the major churches on the tour are active weeklong, you won't miss seeing them in action. If you visit on a Sunday, however, you could attend church services and ascend the tower at Riverside Church. Allow yourself about two hours to leisurely walk the tour, stopping for at least a few minutes to look at the sites covered. To take any guided tours, allow longer.

Sights to See

⑪ **Barnard College.** Established in 1889 and one of the former Seven Sisters of women's colleges, Barnard has steadfastly remained single-sex and independent from Columbia, although its students can take classes there (and vice versa). Note the bear (the college's mascot) on the shield above the main gates at 117th Street. Through the gates is **Barnard Hall**, which houses classrooms, offices, a pool, and dance studios. Its brick-and-limestone design echoes Columbia University's buildings. To the right of Barnard Hall, a path leads through the narrow but neatly landscaped campus; to the left from the main gate is a quiet residential quadrangle. ⊠ *Tours:* ☎ *212/854–5262; Mon.–Sat. 10:30 and 2:30 year-round.*

★ ⑨ **Cathedral of St. John the Divine.** When New York's major Episcopal church is completed, it will be the world's largest Gothic cathedral; until then, you can have a rare, fascinating look at a cathedral in progress. Work on this immense limestone-and-granite church has progressed in spurts. Its first cornerstone was laid in 1892 and its second in 1925, but with the United States' entry into World War II, construction came to a "temporary" halt that lasted until 1982. St. John's follows traditional Gothic engineering—it is supported by stonemasonry rather than by a steel skeleton—so new stonecutters, many of them youngsters from nearby Harlem neighborhoods, had to be trained before work could proceed. That had to be abandoned, however, in 1993 due to lack of funding. The masons found other work, and the two front towers, transept, and great central tower remain unfinished. The proposed south transept is a radical conception: a "bioshelter" with branching columns, a glass roof, and an upper-level arboretum where sunlight will filter down through lush greenery, echoing the effect of stained glass. A model in the **gift shop** shows what the cathedral might look like when completed, probably quite a few years into the future. The superb shop (on the cathedral's north side, ☉ Daily 9–5) is known for its fine selection of international crafts, jewelry, religious artifacts, world music, and ecological literature.

On the wide steps climbing to the Amsterdam Avenue entrance, five portals arch over the entrance doors; the central one shows St. John having his vision of the Lord. The bronze doors he presides over open only twice a year—on Easter and in October for the Feast of St. Francis, so animals as large as an elephant and a camel can come in along with cats and dogs and be blessed. Looking at the doors, you can see scenes from the Old Testament on the left, the New Testament on the right. Statuary, much of it still not finished, is on the doorjambs, and this is currently the only part of the cathedral with "building" going on—during weekdays from approximately April to October, you can watch masons carving. Look closely at the pedestal of the third statue from the inside on the right-hand side of this center portal for a modern-day interpretation of Revelations: It's New York City's skyline under clouds resulting from a nuclear explosion.

The vast nave, the length of two football fields, can hold 6,000 worshipers. As is traditional in cathedrals, nothing inside is permanently fixed, except the pulpit. The small chapels that border the nave have a surprisingly contemporary outlook. The first bay on your left is devoted to sports; the second, the arts. Its **Poet's Corner** is modeled on the one in Westminster Abbey. One of the chapels of right-hand aisle movingly mourns the spread of AIDS.

Beneath the 155-foot-high central dome, tall enough even to give the Statue of Liberty and her torch some breathing room, you can see another quirk of the cathedral: Its original Romanesque-Byzantine design was scrapped in 1907, when architect Ralph Adams Cram took over and instated a Gothic style. Here, where the transept will someday cross the nave, note the rough granite walls of the original scheme (they will eventually be covered with limestone); note also that the side nearer the entrance has a pointed Gothic arch, while the arch near the altar is still rounded Romanesque. The altar area itself expresses the cathedral's interfaith tradition and international mission—with menorahs, Shinto vases, golden chests presented by the king of Siam, and in the ring of chapels behind the altar, dedicated to various ethnic groups. The **Saint Saviour Chapel** contains a three-panel plaster altar with religious scenes by New York artist Keith Haring. (This was his last work; he died of AIDS in 1990.) The **Baptistry,** to the left of the altar, is an exquisite octagonal chapel with a 15-foot-high marble font and a polychrome sculpted frieze commemorating New York's Dutch heritage.

A peaceful precinct of Gothic-style châteaus that includes the Bishop's House, the Deanery, and the Cathedral School, known as the **cathedral close,** lies to the south of the cathedral. The subject of the **Peace Fountain** is the struggle of good versus evil. The forces of good, embodied in the figure of the archangel Michael, triumph by decapitating Satan, whose head hangs from one side. The fountain is encircled by small, whimsical animal figures sculpted by children, also cast in bronze.

Along with Sunday services (8, 9, 9:30, 11 AM, and 1 and 7 PM), the cathedral operates a score of community outreach programs, has changing museum and art gallery displays, supports artists-in-residence and an early-music consortium, generates income through a tapestry works, and presents a full calendar of nonreligious (classical, folk, solstice) concerts. ⊠ 1047 Amsterdam Ave. at 112th St., ☎ 212/ 316–7540, box office ☎ 212/662–2133. ☉ Daily 7–5, Sun. to 8 PM; tours (reservations ☎ 212/932–7347) Tues.–Sat. 11, Sun. 1 (⊠ $3 requested); vertical tours 1st and 3rd Sat. every month at noon and 2 (⊠ $10 requested).

....

NEED A BREAK?   If your spiritual side has had enough and your stomach is crying out for its share, your best bets are two casual eating spots across Amsterdam Avenue, between 110th and 111th streets: **V & T Restaurant** (⊠ 1024 Amsterdam, ☎ 212/663–1708) for spicy pizza and Italian cooking;

and the **Hungarian Pastry Shop** (⊠ 1030 Amsterdam Ave., ☎ 212/866–4230) for luscious desserts and coffees.

Church of Notre Dame. A French neoclassical landmark building, this Roman Catholic church has a replica of the French grotto of Lourdes behind its altar. It once served a predominantly French community of immigrants, but like the neighborhood today's congregation is more diverse ethnically, with Irish, German, Italian, African-American, Hispanic, and Filipino members. ⊠ 405 W. 114th St., ☎ 212/866–1500.

⑩ Columbia University. This wealthy, private, coed Ivy League school was New York's first college when it was founded in 1754. Back then, before American independence, it was called King's College—note the gilded crowns on the black wrought-iron gates at the Amsterdam Avenue entrance. The herringbone-patterned brick paths of College Walk lead into the refreshingly green main quadrangle, dominated by massive neoclassical **Butler Library** to the south and the rotunda-topped **Low Memorial Library** to the north. Butler, built in 1934, holds the bulk of the university's 5 million books; Low, built in 1895–97 by McKim, Mead & White (who laid out the general campus plan when the college moved here in 1897) and modeled on the Roman Pantheon, is now mostly offices, but on weekdays you can go inside to see its domed, templelike former Reading Room. Low Library also houses the Visitors Center, where you can pick up a campus guide or arrange a tour. The steps of Low Library, presided over by Daniel Chester French's statue *Alma Mater,* have been a focal point for campus life, not least during the student riots of 1968. ⊠ *Visitor Center, N of W. 116th St., between Amsterdam Ave. and Broadway,* ☎ *212/854–4900,* ☉ *Mon.–Fri. 9–5.*

Before Columbia moved here, this land was occupied by the Bloomingdale Insane Asylum; the sole survivor of those days is **Buell Hall,** the gabled orange-red brick house just east of Low Library. Just north is **St. Paul's Chapel** (1907), an exquisite little Byzantine-style domed church laid out in the shape of a cross. Step inside to admire the tiled vaulting. ☎ *212/854–3574.* ☉ *Sept.–May, Sun.–Thurs. 10–10; Fri. 10–1 AM; noon–1 AM Sat., Sun. services, 10:30–2:30 and 7–10. Greatly reduced hrs June–Aug. and during winter intersession, so call ahead for Sun. schedule. Free organ recitals selected Thurs. noon.*

NEED A BREAK? The exterior of **Tom's Restaurant** (⊠ 2880 Broadway at 112th St., ☎ 212/864–6137) frequently appears on the TV show *Seinfeld,* and the place also figures in Suzanne Vega's song *Solitude Standing.* Whether or not you care about its fame, this diner is still a good place to unwind with a refreshment or a snack.

⑮ Grant's Tomb. Civil War general and two-term president Ulysses S. Grant and his wife, Julia Dent Grant, are buried here. The white mausoleum, constructed of more than 8,000 tons of granite, with imposing columns and a classical pediment, is modeled on a number of other famous mausoleums. It opened in 1897, almost 12 years after Grant's death—his remains sat in a temporary brick vault until the monument was completed. Under a small white dome, the Grants' twin black marble sarcophagi are sunk into a deep circular chamber visible from above; minigalleries to the sides display photographs and Grant memorabilia. You can walk downstairs to get a closer view of the tombs as well as busts of some of Grant's best generals, an added courtesy of the WPA. In contrast to this austere monument, the surrounding plaza features colorful 1960s-era mosaic benches designed by local schoolchildren. ⊠ *Riverside Dr. and 122nd St.,* ☎ *212/666–1640.* 🎟 *Free.* ☉ *Daily 9–5, 15–20-min tours free on request.*

⑭ **Jewish Theological Seminary.** The seminary was founded in 1887 as a training ground for rabbis, cantors, and scholars of Conservative Judaism, but this complex wasn't built until 1930. The tower, which housed part of the seminary's excellent library, was extensively renovated after a fire in 1966. ✉ *3080 Broadway at 122nd St.*

⑯ **Riverside Church.** A modern (1930) Gothic-style edifice, its smooth, pale limestone walls seem the antithesis of the Cathedral of St. John the Divine's rough gray hulk. Although most of the building is refined and restrained, the main entrance, on Riverside Drive, explodes with elaborate stone carvings (modeled on the French cathedral of Chartres, as are many other decorative details here). Inside, look at the handsomely ornamented main sanctuary, which seats only half as many people as St. John the Divine does; if you're here on Sunday, take the elevator to the top of the 22-story, 356-foot **tower**, with its 74-bell carillon, the largest in the world. Although it is affiliated with the Baptist church and the United Church of Christ, Riverside is basically nondenominational, interracial, international, extremely political, and socially conscious. Its calendar includes political and community events, dance and theater programs, and concerts, along with regular Sunday services at 10:45 AM. ✉ *Riverside Dr. and 122nd St.,* ☎ *212/222–5900.* 🕙 *Mon.–Sat. 9–5, Sun. noon–4; service each Sun. 10:45.* 🎫 *Free; $1 (tower);* 🕙 *12:30–4.*

⑫ **Teachers College.** Redbrick Victorian buildings house Columbia University's Teachers College, founded in 1887 and still the world's largest graduate school in the field of education. Names of famous teachers throughout history line the band of stone along the Broadway facade. ✉ *525 W. 120th St.*

⑬ **Union Theological Seminary.** Founded in 1836, the seminary moved here, to its rough gray collegiate Gothic quadrangle, in 1910; it has one of the world's finest theological libraries. Step inside the main entrance, on Broadway at 121st Street, and ask to look around the serene central quadrangle. ✉ *W. 120th to W. 122nd Sts., between Broadway and Claremont Ave.*

HARLEM

Harlem has been the mecca for African-American culture and life for nearly a century. Originally called Nieuw Haarlem and settled by Dutch farmers, Harlem was a well-to-do suburb in the 19th century; black New Yorkers began settling here in large numbers in about 1900, moving into a surplus of fine apartment buildings and town houses built by real-estate developers for a middle-class white market that never materialized. By the 1920s, Harlem (with one "a") had become the most famous black community in the United States, perhaps in the world. In an astonishing confluence of talent known as the Harlem Renaissance, black novelists, playwrights, musicians, and artists, many of them seeking to escape discrimination and worse in other parts of the country, gathered here. Black performers starred in chic Harlem jazz clubs—which, ironically, only whites could attend. Throughout the Roaring '20s, while whites flocked here for the infamous parties and nightlife, blacks settled in for the opportunity this self-sustaining community represented. But the Depression hit Harlem hard. By the late 1930s it was no longer a popular social spot for downtown New Yorkers, and many successful African-American families began moving out to houses in the suburbs of Queens and New Jersey.

By the 1960s Harlem's population had dropped dramatically, and many of those who remained were disillusioned enough to join in civil rights riots. A vicious cycle of crowded housing, poverty, and crime was choking the neighborhood, turning it into a simmering ghetto. Today, however, Harlem is well on its way to restoring itself. Mixed in with some of the seedy remains of the past are old jewels such as the refurbished Apollo Theatre and such newer attractions as the Studio Museum. A great number of Harlem's classic brownstones and limestone buildings are being restored and lived in by young families, bringing new life to the community.

Deserted buildings, burned-out shop fronts, and yards of rubble still scar certain parts; although a few whites live here, some white visitors may feel conspicuous in what is still a largely black neighborhood. But Harlemites are accustomed to seeing tourists—white and otherwise—on their streets; only common traveler's caution is necessary during daytime excursions to any of the places highlighted. For nighttime outings it's smart to take a taxi, as in many other parts of the city. Bus tours may be a good way to see Harlem, because they cover more areas than the central Harlem walk outlined below (☞ Tours *in* the Gold Guide).

Note that the city's north–south avenues acquire different names up here, commemorating heroes of black history: 6th Avenue becomes Lenox Avenue or Malcolm X Boulevard, 7th Avenue is Adam Clayton Powell Jr. Boulevard, and 8th Avenue is Frederick Douglass Boulevard; 125th Street, the major east–west street, is now Martin Luther King Jr. Boulevard. Many people still use the streets' former names, but the street signs use only the new ones.

A Good Walk

Numbers in the text correspond to numbers in the margin and on the Harlem map.

Beginning on West 115th Street and Adam Clayton Powell Jr. Boulevard, head west on the north side of the block to admire the facade of this branch of the **New York Public Library** ①. It's sufficiently interesting for you to make the trip even on Sundays, when the library is closed. The next two stops, however, are most worthwhile on Sundays, because church is in session and gospel singers are singing. Soulful, moving, often joyous gospel music blends elements from African songs and chants, American spirituals, and rhythm and blues. **Memorial Baptist Church** (✉ 141 W. 115th St., ☎ 212/663–8830) welcomes visitors at its soulful two-hour service that begins at 10:45. Gospel fans and visitors are also welcome at the 10:45 Sunday service at **Canaan Baptist Church of Christ** (✉ 132 W. 116th St., ☎ 212/866–0301), where Wyatt Tee Walker is pastor.

On the southwest corner of 116th Street and Lenox Avenue, notice the aluminum onion dome topping the **Malcolm Shabazz Mosque** (✉ 102 W. 116th St.), a former casino that was converted in the mid-1960s to a black Muslim temple (Malcolm X once preached here). Several Muslim stores are located nearby. Continuing north along Lenox Avenue and the east on 120th Street brings you to **Marcus Garvey Park** ②, which interrupts 5th Avenue between 120th and 124th streets. Stay outside the park, but be sure to notice its watchtower and the pretty row houses as you skirt its west side.

Harlem's main thoroughfare is **125th Street,** the chief artery of its cultural, retail, and economic life. Real-estate values here have never come close to those downtown along 5th Avenue or even Broadway, and many of the commercial buildings rise only a few stories. But never fear—Harlem isn't missing out on the malling of America, as new businesses—many of them branches of national chains—have moved in of late, bringing new shop fronts along a retail row that used to see many

72

Abyssinian Baptist
Church, **7**
Apollo Theater, **4**
Black Fashion
Museum, **5**
Marcus Garvey
Park, **2**
New York Public
Library, **1**
Schomburg Center for
Research in Black
Culture, **6**
Striver's Row, **8**
Studio Museum in
Harlem, **3**

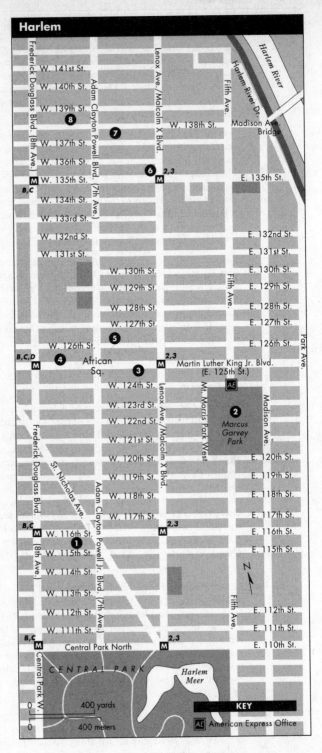

"For Rent" signs. Above the street-level stores is the home of the **National Black Theatre** (⊠ 2033 5th Ave., between 125th and 126th Sts., ☎ 212/722–3800), which produces new works by contemporary African-American writers. One block west, on Lenox Avenue between 126th and 127th streets, is **Sylvia's Soul Food Restaurant,** owned by Sylvia Woods, the self-proclaimed Queen of Soul Food in New York.

Continuing west along 125th Street, you can't help but notice the lovely **Theresa Towers** office building, at the southwest corner of Adam Clayton Powell Jr. Boulevard, and the modern, hulking State Office Building across the street, the latter temporarily housing the **Afro Arts Cultural Centre.** Both of these buildings tower over their neighbors. Farther down the street is another community showplace, the **Studio Museum in Harlem** ③, and on the next block across the street, the famous **Apollo Theatre** ④. One of Harlem's greatest landmarks, it was fantastically restored and brought back to life in 1986.

Return to Adam Clayton Powell Jr. Boulevard and head north. At 126th Street, the **Black Fashion Museum** ⑤ is housed in a brownstone. As you continue north, between 131st and 132nd streets you'll pass what is today the Williams Institutional (Christian Methodist Episcopal) Church. Once this was the **Lafayette Theater,** which presented black revues in the 1920s and housed the WPA's Federal Negro Theater in the 1930s. A tree outside the theater was considered a lucky charm for black actors; having fallen victim to exhaust fumes, it has been replaced by the colorful, abstract metal "tree" on the traffic island in the center of the street.

At 135th Street, cross back to Lenox Avenue, where you'll find the **Schomburg Center for Research in Black Culture** ⑥, a research branch of the New York Public Library that also functions as a community center of sorts. Another neighborhood landmark, the **Abyssinian Baptist Church** ⑦, was one of the first black institutions to settle in Harlem when it moved here in the 1920s; it was founded downtown in 1808. Across 7th Avenue from the church is St. Nicholas Historic District, a handsome set of town houses known as **Strivers' Row** ⑧.

TIMING

The walk takes about four hours, including stops at the Studio Museum and the Schomburg Center. Sunday is a good time to tour Harlem if you'd like to listen to gospel music at one of the area's many churches, and weekends in general are the liveliest time for walking around in this neighborhood. The Apollo tour and the Black Fashion Museum are by appointment only, so be sure to make those arrangements in advance if you're interested.

Sights to See

❼ **Abyssinian Baptist Church.** The Gothic-style bluestone church, which moved here in the 1920s, is further distinguished by its famous family of ministers—Adam Clayton Powell, Sr., and his son, Adam Clayton Powell, Jr., the first black U.S. congressman. Stop in on Sunday to hear the gospel choir and the fiery sermon of its present activist minister, the Reverend Calvin Butts. The baptismal font's Coptic Cross was a gift from Haile Selassie. ⊠ *132 Odell Clark Pl. (W. 138th St.),* ☎ *212/862–7474.* ☉ *Sun. services 9 and 11 AM.*

Afro Arts Cultural Centre. Artifacts from East, West, North, and Central Africa are on exhibit. The center is currently housed in the State Office Building while the permanent space at 2191 Adam Clayton Powell Jr. Boulevard undergoes renovation—call before you go to confirm its location. ✉ *163 W. 125th St., Room 913,* ☎ *212/749–0827.* *$3.75 (suggested contribution).* ⏲ *Daily 9–5.*

❹ **Apollo Theatre.** When it opened in 1913 it was a burlesque hall for white audiences only, but after 1934, music greats such as Billie Holiday, Ella Fitzgerald, Duke Ellington, Count Basie, and Aretha Franklin performed at the Apollo. The theater fell on hard times and closed for a while in the early 1970s but has been renovated and in use again since 1986. The current Apollo's roster of stars isn't as consistent as it was in the past, but its regular Wednesday-night amateur performances at 7:30 PM are as wild and raucous as they were in the theater's heyday. You can see the theater, its backstage, soundstage, TV control room, recording studio, and dressing rooms on a guided tour. ✉ *253 W. 125th St.,* ☎ *212/749–5838.* ⏲ *Call for performance schedules; tours by prior arrangement (☎ 212/222–0992, x205),* *$6 weekdays, $8 weekends (45 mins) and $3 weekdays, $4 weekends (25 mins).*

❺ **Black Fashion Museum.** Costumes from black theater and films are displayed, and the work of black fashion designers of the past century is highlighted. ✉ *155 W. 126th St.,* ☎ *212/666–1320.* *$3 (suggested contribution).* ⏲ *By appointment only.*

❷ **Marcus Garvey Park.** Originally Mount Morris Park, this rocky plot of land was renamed in 1973 after Marcus Garvey (1887–1940), who led the back-to-Africa movement. It's not known for being safe, so you should stay outside the park itself. From the street on its southern side, however, you can see its three-tiered, cast-iron fire **watchtower** (1856), the only remaining part of a now defunct citywide network useful in the days before the telephone. The handsome neoclassical row houses of the **Mount Morris Park Historic District** front the west side of the park and line side streets. *Interrupts 5th Ave., between 120th and 124th Sts., Madison Ave. to Mt. Morris Park W.*

NEED A BREAK? For a sweet treat, stop in at the **Ben & Jerry's** (✉ 125th St. at 5th Ave., ☎ 212/876-6909) ice cream parlor, a partnership with HARK homes, a shelter for young men. Another good place for sweets is **Googie's Pastry Shop** (✉ 50 W. 125th St., ☎ 212/831-0722), with excellent coconut pie and doughnuts.

❶ **New York Public Library 115th Street Branch.** This bubbly Beaux Arts row house was designed by McKim, Mead & White in 1903–1905. The money for the construction of this and more than 60 other branch libraries was donated by Andrew Carnegie in 1901, and almost all of these were narrow, mid-block structures—because Manhattan real estate is so expensive. ✉ *203 W. 115th St.,* ☎ *212/666–9393.* ⏲ *Mon., Thurs. 1–6; Tues. 1–8; Wed., Fri. 10–6; Sat. 1–5.*

★ ❻ **Schomburg Center for Research in Black Culture.** In 1926 the New York Public Library's Division of Negro History acquired the vast collection of Arturo Alfonso Schomburg, a scholar of black and Puerto Rican descent. In 1940, after Schomburg died, this collection, which included more than 10,000 books, documents, and photographs recording black history, was named after him. In 1972 the ever-growing collection was designated a research library, and in 1980 it moved into this modern redbrick building from the handsome Victorian one next door (designed by McKim, Mead & White), which is now a branch library. Today more than 5,000,000 items comprise the collection. The expansion and renovation of the original Schomburg building was completed in 1991 and includes the refurbished **American Negro Theatre** and increased gallery space. Just past the main entrance is an airy lobby, also the entrance to the **Langston Hughes Auditorium.** Inlaid in the floor is the artistic work *Rivers,* a memorial tribute to Hughes, whose remains are interred here. The center's resources include rare manuscripts, art and artifacts, motion pictures, records, and videotapes. Regular exhibits, performing-arts programs, and lectures continue to contribute to Harlem culture. ⊠ *515 Lenox Ave. at 135th St.,* ☎ *212/ 491–2200.* ⌨ *Free.* ⊙ *Mon.–Wed. noon–8, Thurs.–Sat. 10–6, Sun. 1–5 (to view exhibits only).*

❽ Strivers' Row. Since 1919 African-American doctors, lawyers, and other middle-class professionals have owned these elegant homes, designed by famous period architects such as Stanford White (his contributions are on the north side of 139th Street). Behind each row are service alleys, a rare luxury in Manhattan. Musicians W. C. Handy ("The St. Louis Blues") and Eubie Blake ("I'm Just Wild About Harry") were among the residents here. The area, now officially known as the **St. Nicholas Historic District,** got its nickname because less affluent Harlemites felt that its residents were "striving" to become well-to-do. These quiet, tree-lined streets are a remarkable reminder of the Harlem that used to be. ⊠ *W. 138th and W. 139th Sts., between 7th and 8th Aves.*

❸ Studio Museum in Harlem. One of the community's showplaces, this small art museum houses a large collection of paintings, sculpture, and photographs (including historic photographs of Harlem by James Van DerZee, popular in the 1930s). The museum often offers special lectures and programs, and its gift shop is full of black American and African-inspired books, posters, and jewelry. ⊠ *144 W. 125th St.,* ☎ *212/864–4500.* ⌨ *$5; sculpture garden free.* ⊙ *Wed.–Fri. 10–5, weekends 1–6.*

Sylvia's Soul Food Restaurant. Sylvia Woods remains most nights until 10 chatting with her customers, contributing to her restaurant's popularity among residents and tourists alike. Southern specialties and cordiality are the rule here. ⊠ *328 Lenox Ave., between 126th and 127th Sts.,* ☎ *212/996–0660.*

Theresa Towers. Its former incarnation as the Hotel Theresa is still evident from a sign painted on its west side, which literally towers over the neighboring buildings. Fidel Castro stayed here during his 1960 visit to the United Nations. ⊠ *2090 Adam Clayton Powell Jr. Blvd. at 125th St..*

OFF THE BEATEN PATH

AMERICAN NUMISMATIC SOCIETY – The society, founded in 1858, displays its vast collection of coins and medals, including many that date back to ancient civilizations, in one of several museums in the Audubon Terrace complex. ⊠ *Broadway at 155th St.,* ☎ *212/234–3130.* ⌨ *Free (donations accepted).* ⊙ *Tues.–Sat. 9–4:30, Sun. 1–4.*

THE CLOISTERS – Perched atop a wooded hilltop near Manhattan's northernmost tip, the Cloisters houses the Metropolitan Museum of Art's medieval collection in the style of a medieval monastery. Colonnaded walks connect authentic French and Spanish monastic cloisters, a French Romanesque chapel, a 12th-century chapter house, and a Romanesque apse. An entire room is devoted to a superb set of 15th- and 16th-century tapestries depicting a unicorn hunt. The view of the Hudson River and the New Jersey Palisades (an undeveloped Rockefeller family preserve) enhances the experience. From Morningside Heights, the Cloisters is easily accessible by public transportation. The M–4 "Cloisters–Fort Tryon Park" bus provides a lengthy but scenic ride; catch it along Broadway; or take the A subway to 190th Street. If you're traveling from below 110th Street, the M–4 bus runs along Madison Av-

enue. ⊠ *Fort Tryon Park,* ☎ *212/923–3700.* ☎ *$7 (suggested contri-
bution).* ⊙ *Tues.–Sun. 9:30–5:15. Closes at 4:45 Nov.–Feb.*

CHELSEA

Like the London district of the same name, New York's Chelsea has
preserved its villagelike personality. Both have their quiet nooks where
the 19th century seems to live on; both have been havens for artists,
writers, and bohemians. Although London's Chelsea is a much more
upscale chunk of real estate, New York's Chelsea is catching up, with
town-house renovations reclaiming block after block of the side streets.
Within the past few years, several historic cast-iron buildings on 6th
Avenue have also been restored, attracting superstore tenants that have
revitalized the area. Although 7th, 8th, and 9th avenues may never equal
the shopping mecca of King's Road in London's Chelsea, they have plenty
of hip, one-of-a-kind boutiques sprinkled among unassuming grocery
stores and other remnants of the neighborhood's immigrant past.

Precisely speaking, the New York neighborhood was named not after
Chelsea itself but after London's Chelsea Royal Hospital, an old soldiers' home. Running from 14th to 24th streets, from 8th Avenue
west, it was one family's country estate until the 1830s, when Clement
Clarke Moore saw the city moving north and decided to divide his land
into lots. With an instinctive gift for urban planning, he dictated a pattern of development that ensured street after street of graceful row houses.
A clergyman and classics professor, Moore is probably best known for
his 1822 poem "A Visit from St. Nicholas," which he composed while
bringing a sleigh full of Christmas treats from lower Manhattan to his
Chelsea home.

Today's Chelsea extends from 5th Avenue west, and from 14th Street to
23rd. Eighth Avenue now rivals Christopher Street in the West Village
as a gay concourse: Several bookstores, shops, fitness clubs, and restaurants cater to a gay clientele on both sides of the street. Yet the thriving
neighborhood also accommodates a multicultural population that has
lived here for decades as well as a burgeoning art community. Locals anticipate an economic boost as a result of the recent opening of the
Chelsea Piers Sports and Entertainment Complex on the Hudson.

A Good Walk

*Numbers in the text correspond to numbers in the margin and on the
Chelsea map.*

Begin your Chelsea tour by passing by some of its most popular stores.
On 7th Avenue between 16th and 17th streets is **Barneys New York** ①,
a longtime landmark Chelsea department store for fashion-conscious
men and women. Across 7th Avenue are branches of **Williams-Sonoma**
(gourmet cookware) and **Pottery Barn** (trendy home furnishings); a block
uptown, at 18th Street, you'll find one of the city's best children's bookstores, **Books of Wonder** (⊠ 132 7th Ave.).

Next, walk east from 7th Avenue on 18th Street to 6th Avenue, which
was once known as Ladies Mile for its concentration of major department
stores. After the stores moved uptown in the early 1900s, the neighborhood declined and the grand old store buildings stood empty and
dilapidated. The 1990s, however, brought the renaissance of the Flatiron District to the east (☞ Murray Hill to Union Square, *above*), and
several old buildings have been renovated all along 6th Avenue. Stand
at 6th Avenue and 18th Street and imagine it in the latter part of the
19th century, when the elevated tracks of the 6th Avenue El train still
cast their shadow along this street.

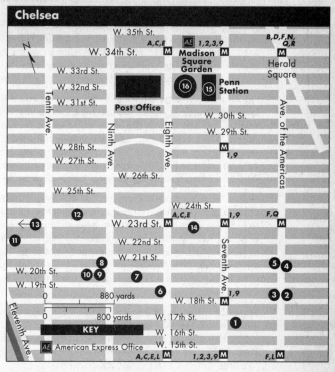

From the west side of the avenue you can look across at the embellished, glazed terra-cotta building between 18th and 19th streets. Originally constructed in 1896 as the **Siegel-Cooper Dry Goods Store** ②, it encompasses 15½ acres of space. Today one of its main tenants is **Bed, Bath & Beyond,** a massive emporium selling discounted items for the home. Branches of **Filene's Basement** and **T. J. Maxx** also occupy the site.

Between 18th and 19th streets on the west side of the avenue is the original, cast-iron **B. Altman Dry Goods Store** ③, built in 1877 and now home to **Today's Man,** a discount menswear store. Continue walking north to 20th Street. The **Church of the Holy Communion** ④, a former Episcopal house of worship dating from 1846, is on the northeast corner of the avenue. To the horror of some preservationists, it was converted a few years ago into **Limelight,** a popular nightclub. On the west side of the avenue between 20th and 21st streets stands another former cast-iron retail palace, the **Hugh O'Neill Dry Goods Store** ⑤. The recently renovated structure now houses the Elsevier Science Publishing Company and Goldman's Treasures.

If you're here on a weekend, you might like to take a **flea-market** break: 6th Avenue between 24th and 27th streets is the site of the city's longest-running outdoor market. Three hundred vendors sell antiques and memorabilia here from 9 to 5 on weekends.

Next, turn left from 6th Avenue on to 21st Street for a look at the **Third Cemetery of the Spanish & Portuguese Synagogue, Shearith Israel,** a private green oasis with a hardy old ailanthus tree. In use from 1829 to 1851, it is one of three graveyards created in Manhattan by this congregation (☞ Greenwich Village *and* Chinatown, *below*).

Continue west on 21st Street to 8th Avenue, where the **Chelsea Historic District** officially begins. Between 20th and 23rd streets, from 8th to 10th avenues, you'll find examples of all of Chelsea's architectural periods: Greek and Gothic Revival, Italianate, and 1890s apartment buildings. But before you start prowling around there, you may want to head down to 19th Street and 8th Avenue to see the Art Deco **Joyce Theater** ⑥, primarily a dance venue. Its presence has helped to attract several good, moderately priced restaurants to 8th Avenue.

On 20th Street, between 8th and 9th avenues, you'll find **St. Peter's Episcopal Church** ⑦, constructed between 1836 and 1838, behind some scaffolding. The church has three buildings: a rectory, a fieldstone church, and a brick parish hall, which now houses the Atlantic Theater Company, a showcase for new American plays. Next, head west on 20th Street to 9th Avenue; on the west side of the avenue, between 20th and 21st streets, is the **General Theological Seminary** ⑧.

Across the street from the seminary, at **404 West 20th Street** ⑨, is the oldest house in the historic district. The residences next door, from 406 to 418 West 20th, are called **Cushman Row** ⑩ and are excellent examples of Greek Revival town houses. Farther down West 20th Street, stop to look at the fine Italianate houses at **Nos. 446 to 450.** The arched windows and doorways are hallmarks of this style, which prized circular forms—not least because, being expensive to build, they showed off the owner's wealth.

West 22nd Street has a string of handsome old row houses just east of 10th Avenue. **No. 435** was the longtime residence of actors Geraldine Page and Rip Torn; they nicknamed this Chelsea town house the Torn Page. In 1987, a year after winning an Oscar for *The Trip to Bountiful,* Page suffered a fatal heart attack here.

On 22nd Street, between 10th and 11th avenues, you'll find the anchor of Chelsea's renaissance as an art community, the **Dia Center for the Arts** ⑪, which is dedicated to contemporary art. Also on the same block are the **Matthew Marks Gallery** (✉ 522 W. 22nd St.) and the **Pat Hearn Gallery** (✉ 530 W. 22nd St.), which showcases young conceptual artists.

From the galleries, return to 10th Avenue and start walking uptown. On the block spanning 23rd and 24th streets, between 9th and 10th avenues on the north side of the street, you can't miss the **London Terrace Apartments** ⑫, a vast 1930 complex containing 1,670 apartments. As you walk along 23rd Street, notice the lions on the arched entrances; from the side they look as if they're snarling, but from the front they display wide grins.

If you continue west on 23rd Street as far as you can go, you'll reach the mammoth **Chelsea Piers Sports and Entertainment Complex** ⑬, extending from 17th to 23rd Street along the Hudson River waterfront. With an entrance at 23rd Street, Chelsea Piers has a huge sports and fitness center, a golf club, skating rinks, roller rinks, a marina, and film and television studios.

Next, return east on 23rd Street. During the 1880s and Gay '90s, the street was the heart of the entertainment district, lined with theaters, music halls, and beer gardens. Today it is an undistinguished, even rundown, commercial thoroughfare, but there is one relic of its once-proud past: the **Chelsea Hotel** ⑭, between 7th and 8th avenues, which opened in 1884 as a cooperative apartment house and became a hotel in 1905. The Chelsea has always been known to attract creative types.

Go back to 7th Avenue and walk uptown a few blocks—you'll be leaving Chelsea and entering the garment district, where wheeled racks of clothing add to the traffic volume, and you may well stumble upon your dream designer sale (accept all flyers). Officially, the clothing quarter begins at 28th Street, but the bulk of the ateliers are farther up in the 30s, past **Penn Station** ⑮, stretching between 31st and 33rd streets. Manhattan's other Amtrak/LIRR station lies beneath the two-square-block Penn Plaza. Behind Penn Station on 8th Avenue stands the concrete-clad cylinder that is **Madison Square Garden** ⑯, host to numerous sporting events and major concerts.

TIMING

Allow yourself at least three to four hours to explore Chelsea. If your schedule permits, plan to spend the day so you can browse the stores and galleries.

Sights to See

③ **B. Altman Dry Goods Store.** Built in 1877 with additions in 1887 and 1910, this ornate cast-iron giant originally housed B. Altman Dry Goods until the business moved in 1906 to set up shop in its imposing quarters at 5th Avenue and 34th Street. The latter store closed in late 1989. ⊠ *621 6th Ave., between 18th and 19th Sts.*

① **Barneys New York.** Founded as a men's discounter some 60 years ago, Barneys is now one of the priciest stores in town. But even if you don't plan to buy, it's fun to browse. The wide selection of menswear ranges from made-to-measure and European and American designer labels to mass-market suits and outerwear. The women's department carries the latest fashions by top designers, and the ladies' accessories are très chic. The store is famous for its very hip window decorations around the Christmas holidays. There's a café on the lower level. ⊠ *106 7th Ave., between 16th and 17th Sts.,* ☎ *212/929–9000.*

⑭ **Chelsea Hotel.** Constructed of red brick with lacy wrought-iron balconies and a mansard roof, this neighborhood landmark opened in 1884 as a cooperative apartment house and became a hotel in 1905, although it has always catered to long-term tenants, with a tradition of broad-mindedness that has attracted many creative types. Its literary roll call of former live-ins includes Mark Twain, Eugene O'Neill, O. Henry, Thomas Wolfe, Tennessee Williams, Vladimir Nabokov, Mary McCarthy, Brendan Behan, Arthur Miller, Dylan Thomas, William S. Burroughs, and Arthur C. Clarke (who wrote the script for *2001: A Space Odyssey* while living here). In 1966 Andy Warhol filmed artist Brigid Polk in her Chelsea Hotel room, which eventually became *The Chelsea Girls,* considered by many to be Warhol's best film. More recently, the hotel was seen on screen in *Sid and Nancy* (1986), a dramatization of a true-life Chelsea Hotel murder, when drugged punk rocker Sid Vicious accidentally stabbed his girlfriend Nancy Spungeon to death. The shabby, seedy aura of the Chelsea Hotel is part of its allure. Read the commemorative plaques outside and then step into the lobby to look at the unusual artwork, some of it donated in lieu of rent by residents down on their luck. ⊠ *222 W. 23rd St., between 7th and 8th Aves.,* ☎ *212/243–3700.*

⑬ **Chelsea Piers Sports and Entertainment Complex.** Beginning in 1910, the Chelsea Piers was the launching point for a new generation of big ocean liners; it was also the destination of the *Titanic*, which never arrived, and the departure point for the last sailing of the *Lusitania*. During the past few decades, the piers were grimy, gloomy, and practically abandoned. All that has changed with the transformation of the old pier buildings along the Hudson River into this splendid 1.7-million-square-foot state-of-the-art facility that opened in 1995, providing an amazing selection of activities to the sports enthusiast. The $60 million complex has two year-round indoor ice-skating rinks for public skating; ice hockey and lessons; a gymnastic center accommodating indoor soccer, field hockey, lacrosse, basketball courts, and batting cages; two outdoor regulation-size in-line and roller skating rinks; the city's only year-round outdoor golf driving range, with four levels of heated stalls overlooking a 200-yard fairway by the river. The 150,000 square-foot Sports Center encompasses the world's longest indoor running track, the largest rock climbing wall in the Northeast, three basketball courts, a sand volleyball court, a huge weight training area, a 25-yard pool, a boxing ring, and a sports medicine center.

From the Maritime Center, the city's largest marina, with a 1.2-mile esplanade, Spirit Cruises runs two boats providing food, musical entertainment, dancing, and sightseeing around New York Harbor. Silver Screen Studios, an active film and television production center located on two levels in the Chelsea Piers, has provided a home to a number of network television series, including *Law and Order* and *The Cosby Mysteries*. The complex also has photography exhibits, sporting goods shops, and several dining areas with river views, including the Crab House seafood restaurant and the Chelsea Brewing Company, with its own microbrewery. ⊠ *Piers 59–62 on the Hudson River from 17th to 23rd Sts.; entrance at 23rd St.,* ☎ *212/366–6000.*

❹ Church of the Holy Communion. This unexceptional Gothic-style Episcopal house of worship was built in 1846 and designed by architect Richard Upjohn. To the horror of some preservationists, it was converted a few years ago into **Limelight,** a popular dance club with state-of-the-art sound and video systems. ⊠ *49 W. 20th St. at 6th Ave.*

❿ Cushman Row. Built by dry-goods merchant Don Alonzo Cushman, a friend of Clement Clarke Moore, who made a fortune developing Chelsea, this group of homes between 9th and 10th avenues represents some of the country's most perfect examples of Greek Revival town houses. The residences retain such original details as small wreath-encircled attic windows, deeply recessed doorways with brownstone frames, and striking iron balustrades and fences. Notice, too, the pineapples, a traditional symbol of welcome, atop the newels in front of Nos. 416 and 418. ⊠ *406–418 W. 20th St.*

★ ⓫ **Dia Center for the Arts.** This facility provides contemporary artists with the chance to develop new work or to mount an organized exhibit on a full floor for extended time periods, usually an entire year. Besides installations by diverse artists, you might find an exhibit from Dia's permanent collection, which includes creations by Joseph Beuys, Walter De Maria, Dan Flavin, Blinky Palermo, Cy Twombly, and Andy Warhol, among others. Outside on the roof there's a fascinating exhibition designed by Dan Graham, which consists of a two-way mirror glass cylinder inside a cube. ⊠ *548 W. 22nd St.,* ☎ *212/989–5912.* 🎫 *$3 (suggested donation).* ☉ *Thurs.–Sun. noon–6.*

NEED A BREAK?   If you're ready for a steaming cup of coffee and some apple pie, you'll be glad to see the shiny **Empire Diner** (⊠ 210 10th Ave., ☎ 212/243-2736) gleefully lighting up the corner of 22nd Street and 10th Avenue. Though it's somewhat overpriced, the authentic diner atmosphere here is cheerful and friendly, and it's open 24 hours.

---

❾ 404 West 20th Street. The oldest house in the historic district was built between 1829 and 1830 in the Federal style. It still has one clapboard side wall; over the years it acquired a Greek Revival doorway and Italianate windows on the parlor floor, and the roof was raised one story.

8 **General Theological Seminary.** When Chelsea developer Clement Clarke Moore divided up his estate, he began by deeding a large section to this Episcopal seminary where he taught Hebrew and Greek. At 9th Avenue and 20th Street, the religious oasis still occupies a block-long stretch. The stoutly fenced campus is accessible through the modern building on 9th Avenue; during off hours you can view the grounds from West 20th Street. The **West Building** (1836) is another early example of Gothic Revival architecture in the city. Most of the rest of the complex was completed in 1883–1902, when Eugene Augustus Hoffman, the school's third dean, hired architect Charles Coolidge Haight to design a campus that would rival those of most other American colleges of the day, in the style known as English Collegiate Gothic, which Haight had pioneered. The general campus plan is in an "E" shape, with the spine facing 21st Street. In the center is the **Chapel of the Good Shepherd,** with its 161-foot-high bell tower. **Sherred Hall,** a three-story classroom building flanked by dormitories, expresses beautifully the simple quality and uniform look Haight strove for. **Hoffman Hall,** the refectory-gymnasium, has an enormous dining hall that resembles a medieval knight's council chamber. A 1960s-era building facing 9th Avenue houses administrative offices, a bookstore, and the 210,000-volume **St. Mark's Library,** generally considered the nation's greatest ecclesiastical library; it has the world's largest collection of Latin bibles. ⊠ *175 9th Ave.,* ☎ *212/243–5150.* ☉ *Library: weekdays noon–3, Sat. 11–3, and by appointment; call ahead to visit the grounds.*

5 **Hugh O'Neill Dry Goods Store.** Constructed in 1875, this cast-iron building, originally an emporium, features Corinthian columns and pilasters; its corner towers were once topped off with huge bulbous domes. Look up at the pediment and you'll see the name of the original tenant proudly displayed. The recently renovated structure now houses the Elsevier Science Publishing Company and Goldman's Treasures, an antiques store. ⊠ *655–671 6th Ave., between 20th and 21st Sts.*

6 **Joyce Theater.** The former Elgin movie house built in 1942 was gutted and in 1982 transformed into this sleek modern theater that pays tribute to its Art Deco origins. If you have any interest in modern dance, it's well worth checking out who is performing at the Joyce during your stay. ⊠ *175 8th Ave. at 19th St.,* ☎ *212/242–0800.*

NEED A BREAK?	**The Big Cup** (⊠ 228 8th Ave., between 21st and 22nd Sts., ☎ 212/206–0059), a lively neighborhood meeting spot, serves good coffee, tea, and pastries.

12 **London Terrace Apartments.** When this huge brick complex first opened in 1930, the doormen dressed as London bobbies. London Terrace is actually made up of two rows of interconnected buildings, which enclose a block-long private garden. The complex contains 1,670 apartments with shops along the avenues it borders. ⊠ *W. 23rd to W. 24th Sts., between 9th and 10th Aves.*

16 **Madison Square Garden.** A concrete-clad cylinder serves as the 20,000-seat home of the New York Knicks and Rangers and also accommodates other sporting events and major concerts. Behind-the-scenes tours, from locker rooms to stage, are available. Much to the dismay of architects and preservationists, the ponderous Madison Square Garden was constructed on the site of the original vast Pennsylvania Station, which possessed a soaring Beaux Arts majesty until it was demolished in 1962. ⊠ *31st to 33rd Sts., between 7th and 8th Aves,* ☎ *212/465–6741.* ⊞ *$8 (tours).* ☉ *Tours offered weekdays 10, 11, noon, 1, 2, 3; Sat. 10, 11, noon, 1; Sun. and holidays 11, noon, 1.*

⑮ **Penn Station.** The original Pennsylvania Station contained a grand iron-and-glass train shed and an enormous Roman Revival waiting room, designed by McKim, Mead & White. Sadly destroyed in 1962, the widely admired terminal was replaced by the undistinguished (some call it ugly) Amtrak/LIRR station, which lies beneath the two-square-block Penn Plaza office building and Madison Square Garden. ⊠ *W. 31st to 33rd Sts., between 7th and 8th Aves.*

OFF THE
BEATEN PATH

GARMENT DISTRICT – This district teems with warehouses, workshops, and showrooms that manufacture and finish mostly women's and children's clothing. On weekdays the streets are crowded with trucks and the sidewalks swarm with daredevil deliverymen wheeling garment racks between factories and specialized subcontractors. ⊠ *7th Ave., between 31st and 41st Sts., also called Fashion Avenue.*

❼ **St. Peter's Episcopal Church.** Built between 1836 and 1838, St. Peter's has been hidden behind scaffolding for several years. The Greek Revival–style **rectory** (1832), to the right of the main church, originally served as the sanctuary. Four years after it was built, the congregation had already laid foundations for a bigger church when, it is said, a vestryman returned from England bursting with excitement over the Gothic Revival that had just taken hold there. The fieldstone **church** that resulted ranks as one of New York's earliest examples of Gothic Revival architecture. The church "welcomes all faiths and uncertain faiths." To the left of the church, the brick **parish hall** is an example of the so-called Victorian Gothic style; its churchlike front was added in 1871. It's now the home of the Atlantic Theater Company, founded by playwright David Mamet. The company stages small productions by emerging writers. The wrought-iron fence framing the three buildings once enclosed St. Paul's Chapel downtown (☞ Wall Street and the Battery, *below*). ⊠ *344 W 20th St.*

❷ **Siegel-Cooper Dry Goods Store.** Built much later than its neighbors in 1896, this impressive building adorned with glazed terra-cotta encompasses 15½ acres of space, yet it was built in only five months. In its retail heyday, the store's main floor featured an immense fountain—a circular marble terrace with an enormous white-marble-and-brass replica of *The Republic,* the statue Daniel Chester French displayed at the 1883 Chicago World's Fair—which became a favorite rendezvous point for New Yorkers. During World War I, the building was a military hospital. The structure was recently renovated, bringing attention to its splendid ornamentation: round wreathed windows, Corinthian and Doric pilasters, Romanesque rounded arches, lion heads, and more. Today one of its main tenants is **Bed, Bath & Beyond,** an impressive emporium with 11 sections of household items at discounted prices. Bed, Bath & Beyond has received a good share of the credit for revitalizing retail business in this area; it was the first superstore to open in Chelsea. **Filene's Basement** and **T. J. Maxx** are more recent retail additions to the building. ⊠ *620 6th Ave.*

GREENWICH VILLAGE

Greenwich Village, which New Yorkers almost invariably speak of simply as "the Village," enjoyed a raffish reputation for years. Originally a rural outpost of the city—a haven for New Yorkers during early 19th-century smallpox and yellow fever epidemics—many of its blocks still look somewhat pastoral, with brick town houses and low rises, tiny green parks and hidden courtyards, and a crazy-quilt pattern of narrow, tree-lined streets. In the mid-19th century, however, as the city spread north of 14th Street, the Village became the province of immigrants, bohemians, and students (New York University, today the nation's largest private university, was planted next to Washington Square in 1831). Its politics were radical and its attitudes tolerant, which is one reason it remains a home to such a large gay community.

Today Village apartments and town houses go for high rents, and several posh restaurants have put down roots there. Except for the isolated western fringe, where a string of tough gay bars along West Street attracts some drug traffic and prostitution, the Village is about as safe and clean as the Upper East Side. Nevertheless, something about the tangled street plan and the small buildings encourages anarchy. Shabby shop fronts, hole-in-the-wall restaurants, and non-mainstream arts groups persist and thrive here. There's still a large student population, and several longtime residents remain, paying cheap rents thanks to rent-control laws. The Village is no longer dangerous, but it still feels bohemian.

Several generations of writers and artists have lived and worked here: in the 19th century, Henry James, Edgar Allan Poe, Mark Twain, Walt Whitman, and Stephen Crane; at the turn of the century, O. Henry, Edith Wharton, Theodore Dreiser, and Hart Crane; and during the 1920s and '30s, John Dos Passos, Norman Rockwell, Sinclair Lewis, John Reed, Eugene O'Neill, Edward Hopper, and Edna St. Vincent Millay. In the late 1940s and early 1950s, the Abstract Expressionist painters Franz Kline, Jackson Pollock, Mark Rothko, and Willem de Kooning congregated here, as did the Beat writers Jack Kerouac, Allen Ginsberg, and Lawrence Ferlinghetti. The 1960s brought folk musicians and poets, notably Bob Dylan and Peter, Paul, and Mary.

A Good Walk
Numbers in the text correspond to numbers in the margin and on the Greenwich Village and the East Village map.

Begin your tour of Greenwich Village at the foot of 5th Avenue at **Washington Arch** in **Washington Square** ①, a hugely popular, 9½-acre park that provides a neighborhood oasis for locals and tourists alike. Most of the buildings bordering Washington Square belong to New York University (NYU). On Washington Square North, between University Place and MacDougal Street, stretches **The Row** ②, comprised of two blocks of lovingly preserved Greek Revival and Federal-style town houses.

On the east side of the square, you can take in a contemporary art exhibit at **Grey Art Gallery** ③, housed in NYU's main building. If you walk to the south side of the square, a trio of red sandstone hulks represents an abortive 1960s attempt to create a unified campus look for NYU, as envisioned by architects Philip Johnson and Richard Foster. At one time, plans called for all of the Washington Square buildings to be refaced in this red stone; fortunately, the cost proved prohibitive. At La Guardia Place and Washington Square South, the undistinguished modern **Loeb Student Center** stands on the site of a famous boardinghouse that had been nicknamed the House of Genius for the talented writers who lived there over the years: Theodore Drieser, John Dos Passos, and Eugene O'Neill, among others. A block west of the Student Center, at the corner of Washington Square South and Thompson Street, is the square-towered **Judson Memorial Church** ④.

From Washington Square Arch and the park, cross Washington Square North and head up 5th Avenue on the west side. Look to your right and note the small attractive garden behind the Row. A statue of Miguel de Cervantes, the author of *Don Quixote,* stands at the far end. The likeness, cast in 1724, was a gift from the mayor of Madrid to

Greenwich Village and the East Village

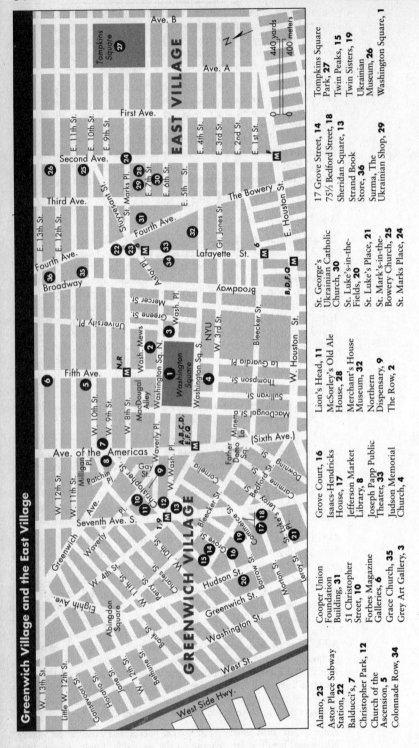

EAST VILLAGE

GREENWICH VILLAGE

440 yards
400 meters

Alamo, **23**
Astor Place Subway Station, **22**
Balducci's, **7**
Christopher Park, **12**
Church of the Ascension, **5**
Colonnade Row, **34**

Cooper Union Foundation Building, **31**
51 Christopher Street, **10**
Forbes Magazine Galleries, **6**
Grace Church, **35**
Grey Art Gallery, **3**

Grove Court, **16**
Isaacs-Hendricks House, **17**
Jefferson Market Library, **8**
Joseph Papp Public Theater, **33**
Judson Memorial Church, **4**

Lion's Head, **11**
McSorley's Old Ale House, **28**
Merchant's House Museum, **32**
Northern Dispensary, **9**
The Row, **2**

St. George's Ukrainian Catholic Church, **30**
St. Luke's-in-the-Fields, **20**
St. Luke's Place, **21**
St. Mark's-in-the-Bowery Church, **25**
St. Marks Place, **24**

17 Grove Street, **14**
75½ Bedford Street, **18**
Sheridan Square, **13**
Strand Book Store, **36**
Surma, The Ukrainian Shop, **29**

Tompkins Square Park, **27**
Twin Peaks, **15**
Twin Sisters, **19**
Ukrainian Museum, **26**
Washington Square, **1**

former NYC mayor Ed Koch. It stood in Bryant Park for several years, and has now found a home with NYU.

Another half a block north on the east side of 5th Avenue is **Washington Mews,** a cobblestone private street. A similar Village mews, **MacDougal Alley,** can be found between 8th Street and the square just off MacDougal Street, one block west.

Continue up the west side of 5th Avenue; you'll pass the **Church of the Ascension** ⑤ (⊠ 5th Ave. and W. 10th St.), a Gothic Revival brownstone building. At 5th Avenue and 12th Street, you can stop in the **Forbes Magazine Galleries** ⑥, which house the late publisher Malcolm Forbes's unusual personal collection.

Backtrack on 5th Avenue to **West 11th Street** and turn right to see one of the best examples of a Village town-house block. One exception to the general 19th-century redbrick look is the modern, angled front window of 18 West 11th Street, usually occupied by a stuffed bear whose outfit changes from day to day. This house was built after the original was destroyed in a 1970 explosion; members of the radical Weatherpeople Underground faction had started a bomb factory in the basement. At the end of the block, behind a low gray stone wall on the south side of the street, is the **Second Shearith Israel graveyard,** used by the country's oldest Jewish congregation after the cemetery in Chinatown (☞ Chinatown, *below*) and before the one in Chelsea (☞ Chelsea, *above*).

On Avenue of the Americas (6th Avenue), turn left to sample the wares at **Balducci's** ⑦ (⊠ 424 6th Ave. at 9th St.), a popular gourmet food store. Directly opposite, the triangle formed by West 10th Street, 6th Avenue, and Greenwich Avenue originally held a green market, a jail, and the magnificent towered courthouse that is now the **Jefferson Market Library** ⑧.

Just west of 6th Avenue on 10th Street is the wrought-iron gateway to a tiny courtyard called **Patchin Place;** around the corner, on 6th Avenue just north of 10th Street, is a similar cul-de-sac, **Milligan Place,** which few New Yorkers even know is there.

Next, proceed to Christopher Street, which veers off from the southern end of the library triangle. Christopher Street has long been the symbolic heart of New York's gay and lesbian community. Before you proceed just a few steps, you'll see **Gay Street** on your left. This quiet curved thoroughfare of early 19th-century row houses was immortalized in *My Sister Eileen,* a book of short stories by Ruth McKinney.

Continue west on Christopher Street, crossing Waverly Place; on your left, you'll pass the 1831 brick **Northern Dispensary** ⑨ building, which at one time provided health care to poor neighborhood residents. Across the street is **51 Christopher St.** ⑩, which used to be the site of a bar named the Stonewall Inn. At this address, a historic clash in 1969 between city police and gay men marked the beginning of the gay rights movement. Just a few doors west, steps lead down to the **Lion's Head** ⑪ (No. 59), a longtime writers' hangout. The restaurant faces a green triangle named **Christopher Park** ⑫, which is sometimes confused with another landscaped triangle to the south (between Washington Place, Barrow Street, and 7th Avenue) called **Sheridan Square** ⑬.

Across the busy intersection of 7th Avenue, Christopher Street has many bars and stores; several of them cater to a gay clientele, but the street is by no means off-limits to other people. Two shops worth a visit are **McNulty's Tea and Coffee Co.** (⊠ 109 Christopher St.), with a large variety of tea and coffee blends, and **Li-Lac Chocolate Shop** (⊠ 120

Christopher St.), a longtime favorite in the area for its homemade chocolate and butter crunch.

West of 7th Avenue, the Village turns into a picture-book town of twisting, tree-lined streets, quaint houses, and tiny restaurants. Follow Grove Street from Sheridan Square west past the house where Thomas Paine died (⊠ 59 Grove St.) and the boyhood home of poet Hart Crane (⊠ 45 Grove St.).

At this point you'll be close to the intersection of Grove and Bleecker streets. You may now choose to take a leisurely stroll along the portion of Bleecker Street that extends west of 7th Avenue from Grove to Bank Street, heading in the direction of Abingdon Square. This section of Bleecker Street is full of crafts and antiques shops, coffeehouses, and small restaurants.

If you choose to forego Bleecker Street, continue your walk west on Grove Street. The secluded intersection of Grove and Bedford streets seems to have fallen through a time warp into the 19th century. On the northeast corner stands **17 Grove Street** ⑭, one of the few remaining clapboard structures in the city. Behind it, at 102 Bedford Street, is **Twin Peaks** ⑮, an early 19th-century house that resembles a Swiss chalet. Heading west, Grove Street curves in front of the iron gate of **Grove Court** ⑯, a group of mid-19th-century brick-fronted residences.

Take a left from Grove Street and walk down Bedford Street a couple of blocks to the **Isaacs-Hendricks House** ⑰ (⊠ 77 Bedford St.), the oldest house in the Village. The place next door, **75½ Bedford Street** ⑱, at 9½ feet wide, is New York's narrowest house.

Heading west from Grove Street onto Commerce Street, you soon reach the **Cherry Lane Theater** (⊠ 38 Commerce St.), one of the original Off-Broadway houses and the site of American premieres of works by O'Neill, Beckett, Ionesco, and Albee. Across the street stand two nearly identical brick houses (⊠ 39 and 41 Commerce St.) separated by a garden and popularly known as the **Twin Sisters** ⑲. Across the street, **Grange Hall** (⊠ 50 Commerce St.) serves comfort food in an intriguing restored speakeasy.

Follow Barrow Street to Hudson Street, so named because this was originally the bank of the Hudson River. The block to the northwest is owned by **St. Luke's-in-the-Fields** ⑳, built in 1822 as a country chapel for downtown's Trinity Church. Writer Bret Harte once lived at 487 Hudson Street, at the end of the row.

East of Hudson Street, for the length of a block, Leroy Street becomes **St. Luke's Place** ㉑, a row of classic 1860s town houses shaded by graceful gingko trees. Across 7th Avenue, St. Luke's Place becomes Leroy Street again, which terminates in an old Italian neighborhood at Bleecker Street. Amazingly unchanged amid all the Village gentrification, Bleecker between 6th and 7th avenues seems more vital these days than Little Italy does. For authentic Italian ambience, stop into one of the fragrant Italian bakeries, such as **A. Zito & Sons** (⊠ 259 Bleecker St.) and **Rocco's** (⊠ 243 Bleecker St.), or look inside the old-style butcher shops such as **Ottomanelli & Sons** (⊠ 285 Bleecker St.) and **Faicco's** (⊠ 260 Bleecker St.). **John's Pizzeria** (⊠ 278 Bleecker St.) is one of those places that locals swear by. Be forewarned, however: no slices; whole pies only.

Head east on Bleecker and you'll come to **Father Demo Square** (Bleecker St. and 6th Ave.). Across Bleecker Street you'll see the **Church of Our Lady of Pompeii,** where Mother Cabrini, a naturalized Italian immigrant who became the first American saint, often prayed.

Head up 6th Avenue to 3rd Street and check out the playground caged there within a chain-link fence. NBA stars of tomorrow learn their moves on this patch of asphalt, where city-style basketball is played all afternoon and evening in all but the very coldest weather.

Return along Washington Square South to MacDougal Street and turn right. The **Provincetown Playhouse** (⊠ 133 MacDougal St.) premiered many of Eugene O'Neill's plays. Louisa May Alcott wrote *Little Women* while living at 130–132 MacDougal Street. The two houses at 127 and 129 MacDougal Street were built for Aaron Burr in 1829; notice the pineapple newel posts, a symbol of hospitality.

At **Minetta Tavern** (⊠ 113 MacDougal St.), a venerable Village watering hole, turn right onto **Minetta Lane,** which leads to narrow **Minetta Street,** another former speakeasy alley. Both streets follow the course of Minetta Brook, which once flowed through this neighborhood and still bubbles deep beneath the pavement.

The foot of Minetta Street returns you to the corner of 6th Avenue and Bleecker Street, where you will have reached the stomping grounds of 1960s-era folksingers (many of them performed at the now-defunct Folk City one block north on West 3rd Street). This area still attracts a young crowd—partly because of the proximity of NYU—to its cafés, bars, jazz clubs, coffeehouses, theaters, and cabarets (☞ Chapter 8), not to mention its long row of unpretentious ethnic restaurants.

TIMING
Allow yourself a full day to take this walk. Greenwich Village moves at a slower pace than the rest of city, and you'll want to take your time exploring back streets and stopping at shops and cafés.

Sights to See

7 **Balducci's.** From the vegetable stand of the late Louis Balducci, Sr., sprouted this full-service gourmet food store. Along with more than 80 Italian cheeses and 50 kinds of bread, the family-owned enterprise features imported Italian specialties, first-rate takeout foods, and a prodigious selection of fresh seafood. ⊠ 424 6th Ave. and 9th St., ☎ 212/673–2600.

12 **Christopher Park.** Sometimes mistaken for Sheridan Square, this pleasant triangular oasis contains a bronze statue of Civil War general Philip Sheridan and striking sculptures designed by George Segal of two women sitting on a bench and two men standing; both couples appear to be having a conversation. ⊠ Bordered by Washington Pl. and Grove and Christopher Sts.

5 **Church of the Ascension.** Inside this 1841 Gothic Revival–style brownstone designed by Richard Upjohn, you can admire a mural depicting the Ascension of Jesus and stained-glass windows by John LaFarge, as well as a marble altar sculpture by Louis Saint-Gaudens. In 1844 President John Tyler married Julia Gardiner here. ⊠ 36–38 5th Ave. at W. 10th St.

10 **51 Christopher Street.** On June 27, 1969, a gay bar at this address named the Stonewall Inn was the site of a clash between gay men (some in drag) and the New York City police. As these men were being forced into paddy wagons, sympathetic gay onlookers protested and started fighting back, throwing beer bottles and garbage cans. The Stonewall Riot is now commemorated each year in several American cities at the end of June with parades and celebrations that honor the gay rights movement. A clothing store now occupies the site of the event; a more recent bar named Stonewall is next door at No. 53.

★ ☾ ❻ **Forbes Magazine Galleries.** The late publisher Malcolm Forbes's idiosyncratic personal collection fills the ground floor of the limestone
Forbes Magazine Building, once the home of Macmillan Publishing.
Exhibits change in the large painting gallery and one of two autograph
galleries, while permanent highlights include U.S. presidential papers,
more than 500 intricate model boats, 12,000 toy soldiers, and some
of the oldest Monopoly game sets ever made. Perhaps the most memorable permanent display contains exquisite items created by the House
of Fabergé, including 12 jeweled eggs designed for the last of the Russian czars. ⊠ *62 5th Ave. at 12th St.,* ☎ *212/206–5548.* ⊡ *Free.*
☉ *Tues.–Wed. and Fri.–Sat. 10–4.*

NEED A BREAK?	If you're yearning for a pain au chocolat or a madeleine, stop by **Marquet Patisserie** (⊠ 15 E. 12th St., ☎ 212/243–7752), a sleek, friendly café that serves irresistible French pastries, great coffee, and satisfying sandwiches, salads, and quiches.

Gay Street. A curved lane lined with small row houses circa 1810, one-
block-long Gay Street was originally a black neighborhood and later
a strip of speakeasies. In the 1930s the short thoroughfare and nearby
Christopher Street became famous nationwide when Ruth McKinney
published her autobiographical stories in *The New Yorker,* based on
what happened when she and her sister moved to Greenwich Village
from Ohio. McKinney created her somewhat zany tales in the basement of No. 14, and they appeared in book form as *My Sister Eileen*
in 1938. Also on Gay Street, Howdy Doody was designed in the basement of No. 12. ⊠ *Between Christopher St. and Waverly Pl.*

❶❻ **Grove Court.** This enclave of brick-fronted town houses was built between 1853 and 1854. Intended originally as apartments for employees at neighborhood hotels, Grove Court used to be called Mixed Ale
Alley because of the residents' propensity to pool beverages brought
from work. It now houses a more affluent crowd: A town house there
recently sold for $3 million. ⊠ *10–12 Grove St.*

❸ **Grey Art Gallery.** On the east side of Washington Square, New York
University's main building contains a welcoming street-level space
with changing exhibitions usually focusing on contemporary art.
⊠ *33 Washington Pl.,* ☎ *212/998–6780.* ⊡ *$2.50 (suggested con-
tribution).* ☉ *Sept.–July, Tues., Thurs., and Fri. 11–6:30, Wed. 11–
8:30, Sat. 11–5.*

❶❼ **Issacs-Hendricks House.** Originally built as a Federal-style wood-frame
residence in 1799, this immaculate structure is the oldest remaining
house in Greenwich Village. Its first owner, Joshua Issacs, a wholesale
merchant, lost the farmhouse to creditors; the building then belonged
to copper supplier Harmon Hendricks. The village landmark was remodeled twice; it received its brick face in 1836, and the third floor
was added in 1928. ⊠ *77 Bedford St. at Commerce St.*

❽ **Jefferson Market Library.** Critics variously termed this magnificent
towered courthouse's hodgepodge of styles Venetian, Victorian, or
Italian; Villagers, noting the alternating wide bands of red brick and
narrow strips of granite, dubbed it the Lean Bacon Style. Over the years,
the structure has housed a number of government agencies (public works,
civil defense, census bureau, police academy); it was on the verge of
demolition when public-spirited citizens saved it and turned it into a
public library in 1967. Note the fountain at the corner of West 10th
Street and 6th Avenue, and the seal of the City of New York on the
east front; inside, look at the handsome interior doorways and climb
the graceful circular stairway. If the gate is open, visit the flower gar-

den behind the library, a project run by local green thumbs. ⊠ *425 6th Ave. at 10th St.,* ☎ *212/243–4334.*

❹ Judson Memorial Church. Designed by celebrated architect Stanford White, this Italian Roman-Renaissance church has long attracted a congregation interested in the arts and community activism. Funded by the Astor family and John D. Rockefeller and constructed in 1892, the yellow brick and limestone building was the brainchild of Edward Judson, who hoped to reach out to the poor immigrants in adjacent Little Italy. The church has stained-glass windows designed by John LaFarge and a 10-story campanile that serves as a New York University dormitory. ⊠ *51–54 Washington Sq. S at Thompson St.*

⓫ Lion's Head. Since the 1960s, this unpretentious cellar bar and restaurant has proved a popular hangout for performers, journalists, and literary types, such as Pete Hamill, Jimmy Breslin, and Lanford Wilson. Before she found stardom, Jessica Lange was a waitress here, and book covers by semiresident authors adorn the walls. ⊠ *59 Christopher St.,* ☎ *212/929–0670.*

❾ Northern Dispensary. Constructed for $4,700 in 1831, this triangular Georgian brick building originally served as a health care clinic for indigent Villagers. Edgar Allan Poe was a frequent patient. In more recent times, the structure has housed a dental clinic and a nursing home for AIDS patients. While the Dispensary has one side on two streets (Grove and Christopher where they meet), it has two sides facing one street— Waverly Place, which splits in two directions. ⊠ *165 Waverly Pl.*

Patchin Place. This charming cul-de-sac off 10th Street (between Greenwich and 6th Aves.) has 10 miniature row houses dating from 1848. Around the corner on 6th Avenue is a similar dead-end street, **Milligan Place,** consisting of four small homes completed in 1852. The houses in both quiet enclaves were originally built for the waiters (mostly Basques) who worked at the high-society Brevoort Hotel, long ago demolished, on 5th Avenue. Patchin Place later became home to several writers, including Theodore Dreiser, e.e. cummings, Jane Bowles, and Djuna Barnes. John Reed and Louise Bryant also lived there. Milligan Place eventually became the address for several playwrights, including Eugene O'Neill.

OFF THE BEATEN PATH

GANSEVOORT MARKET – Each morning otherwise undistinguished warehouse buildings become the meat market for the city's retailers and restaurants. Racks of carcasses make a fascinating, if not very pretty, sight. Action peaks on weekdays from 5 to 9 AM. ⊠ *Between 9th Ave. and the Hudson River, from Gansevoort St. north to 14th St.*

★ ❷ The Row. Built from 1829 through 1839, this series of beautifully preserved Greek Revival town houses along Washington Square North (on the two blocks between University Pl. and MacDougal St.) once belonged to merchants and bankers; now the buildings serve as New York University offices and faculty housing. Developers were not so tactful when they demolished 18 Washington Square North, once the home of Henry James's grandmother, which he later used as the setting for his novel *Washington Square* (Henry himself was born just off the square, in a long-gone house on Washington Place). The oldest building on the block, 20 Washington Square North, was constructed in 1829 in the Federal style. Notice its Flemish bond brickwork—alternate bricks inserted with the smaller surface (headers) facing out—which before 1830 was considered the best way to build stable walls. ⊠ *1–13 Washington Sq. N, between University Pl. and 5th Ave.; 19–26 Washington Sq. N, between 5th Ave. and MacDougal St.*

★ ⑳ **St. Luke's-in-the-Fields.** Constructed in 1822 as a country chapel for downtown's Trinity Church, St. Luke's first warden was Clement ("'Twas the Night Before Christmas") Clarke Moore, who figured so largely in Chelsea's history (☞ Chelsea, *above*). An unadorned structure of soft-colored brick, the chapel was nearly destroyed by fire in 1981, but a flood of donations, many quite small, from residents of the West Village financed restoration of the square central tower. Bret Harte once lived at 487 Hudson Street (today the St. Luke's Parish House), at the end of the row. The Barrow Street Garden on the chapel grounds is worth visiting. ⊠ *485 Hudson St., between Barrow and Christopher Sts.*

OFF THE BEATEN PATH

CHARLTON STREET – The city's longest stretch of redbrick town houses preserved from the 1820s and 1830s runs along the north side of this street (west of 6th Ave. and south of W. Houston St.), with high stoops, paneled front doors, leaded-glass windows, and narrow dormer windows all intact. While you're here, stroll along parallel King and Vandam streets for more fine Federal houses. This quiet enclave was once an estate called Richmond Hill, whose various residents included George Washington, John and Abigail Adams, and Aaron Burr.

NEW YORK CITY FIRE MUSEUM – Hand-pulled and horse-drawn apparatus, engines, sliding poles, uniforms, and fireboat equipment are featured in this comprehensive collection of authentic fire-fighting tools from the 18th, 19th, and 20th centuries. ⊠ *278 Spring St., near Varick St.* ☎ *212/691–1303.* ⊠ *$4 (suggested contribution).* ⊘ *Tues.–Sun. 10–4.*

㉑ **St. Luke's Place.** This often peaceful street (between Hudson St. and 7th Ave. S) has 15 classic Italianate brownstone and brick town houses (1852–53), shaded by graceful gingko trees. Novelist Theodore Dreiser wrote *An American Tragedy* at No. 16; poet Marianne Moore lived at No. 14, playwright Sherwood Anderson at No. 12. Mayor Jimmy Walker (first elected in 1926) lived at No. 6; the lampposts in front are "mayor's lamps," which were sometimes placed in front of the residences of New York mayors. This block is often used as a film location, too: No. 12 was shown as the Huxtables' home on *The Cosby Show* (although the family supposedly lived in Brooklyn), and No. 4 was the setting of the Audrey Hepburn movie *Wait Until Dark*. Before 1890 the playground on the south side of the street was a graveyard where, according to legend, the dauphin of France—the lost son of Louis XVI and Marie Antoinette—is buried.

NEED A BREAK?

At the corner of Hudson Street and St. Luke's Place, the **Anglers and Writers Café** (⊠ 420 Hudson St., ☎ 212/675–0810) lives up to its name with bookshelves, fishing tackle, and pictures of Door County, Wisconsin, hung on the walls. Weary wanderers may linger over a pot of tea and a slice of cake for an hour or so, absorbing the place's restful charm.

⑭ **17 Grove Street.** William Hyde, a prosperous window-sash maker, built this clapboard residence in 1822; a third floor was added in 1870. Hyde added a workshop behind the house in 1833. The building has since served many functions; it housed a brothel during the Civil War. The structure is the Village's largest remaining wood-frame house.

⑱ **75½ Bedford Street.** Rising real-estate rates inspired the construction of New York City's narrowest house—just 9½ feet wide—in 1873. It was built on a lot that was originally a carriage entrance of the Issacs-Hendricks House next door. Several celebrities have resided in this sliver of a building, including actor John Barrymore and poet Edna St. Vincent Millay, who wrote the Pulitzer Prize–winning *Ballad of the Harp-Weaver* during her stay here from 1923 to 1924.

⑬ Sheridan Square. At one time an unused asphalt space, this lovely green triangle was recently landscaped following an extensive dig by urban archaeologists, who unearthed artifacts dating back to the Dutch and Native American eras. ✉ *Bordered by Washington Pl. and W. 4th, Barrow, and Grove Sts.*

⑮ Twin Peaks. In 1925 financier Otto Kahn gave money to a Village eccentric named Clifford Daily to remodel an 1835 house for artists' use. The building was whimsically altered with stucco, half-timbers, and the addition of a pair of steep roof peaks. The result was something that might be described as an ersatz Swiss chalet. ✉ *102 Bedford St.*

⑲ Twin Sisters. These attractive Federal-style brick homes connected by a walled garden were said to have been erected by a sea captain for two daughters who loathed each other. Historical record insists that they were built in 1831 and 1832 by a milkman who needed the two houses and an open courtyard for his work. The striking mansard roofs were added in 1873. ✉ *39 and 41 Commerce St.*

★ Washington Arch. Designed by Stanford White, a wood version of Washington Arch was built in 1889 to commemorate the 100th anniversary of George Washington's presidential inauguration and was originally placed about half a block north of its present location. The arch was reproduced in marble in 1892, and the statues—*Washington at War* on the left, *Washington at Peace* on the right—were added in 1916 and 1918, respectively. The civilian version of Washington was the work of Alexander Stirling Calder, father of the renowned artist Alexander Calder. Bodybuilder Charles Atlas modeled for *Peace*. The arch is certainly one of the most photographed sites in Greenwich Village. ✉ *Washington Sq. at the foot of 5th Ave.*

Washington Mews. This cobblestone private street is lined on one side with the former stables of the houses on the Row on Washington Square North. Writer Walter Lippmann and artist-patron Gertrude Vanderbilt Whitney (founder of the Whitney Museum) once had homes in the mews; today it's mostly owned by New York University. ✉ *Between 5th Ave. and University Pl.*

★ ① Washington Square. The highly popular 9½-acre park started out as a cemetery, principally for yellow-fever victims, and an estimated 10,000–22,000 bodies lie below. In the early 1800s it was a parade ground and the site of public executions; bodies dangled from a conspicuous Hanging Elm that still stands at the northwest corner of the square. Later Washington Square became the focus of a fashionable residential neighborhood and a center of outdoor activity. By the early 1980s, Washington Square had deteriorated into a tawdry place only a drug dealer could love. Then community activism motivated a police crackdown that sent the drug traffic elsewhere and made Washington Square comfortable again for Frisbee players, street musicians, skateboarders, jugglers, stand-up comics, sitters, strollers, chess players, and a huge outdoor art fair each spring and fall. The park figures in Henry James's novel of the same name. ✉ *At the foot of 5th Ave.*

THE EAST VILLAGE

The gritty tenements of the East Village—an area bounded by 14th Street on the north, 4th Avenue or the Bowery on the west, Houston Street on the south, and the East River—provided inexpensive living places for artists, writers, and actors after real estate prices in SoHo

(☞ SoHo and TriBeCa, *below*) zoomed sky-high in the 1980s. New residents brought in their wake new restaurants, shops, and somewhat cleaner streets, while the old East Villagers maintained the trappings of the counterculture. Longtime bastions of the arts, such as the theaters Classic Stage Company and LaMaMa, and St. Mark's-in-the-Bowery Church were joined by newer institutions such as PS 122, and several "hot" art galleries opened in narrow East Village storefronts. But the East Village scene lasted only a couple of years—just long enough to drive up rents substantially on some blocks, but not long enough to drive out all of the neighborhood's original residents. Today an interesting mix has survived: artistic types in black leather and longtime members of various immigrant enclaves, principally Polish, Ukrainian, and Slovene. More recent arrivals come from the Dominican Republic, Japan, and the Philippines. The neighborhood also has its share of homeless people and drug addicts (more so as you head deeper east into the rundown buildings along Avenues A, B, C, and D).

A Good Walk

Numbers in the text correspond to numbers in the margin and on the Greenwich Village and the East Village map.

Begin at the intersection of East 8th Street, 4th Avenue, and Astor Place, where you'll see two traffic islands. One of these contains an ornate cast-iron kiosk, a replica of a Beaux Arts subway entrance, which provides access to the **Astor Place Subway Station** ㉒. Go down into the station to see the authentically reproduced wall tiles with a beaver motif. On the other traffic island stands the **Alamo** ㉓, a huge black cube sculpted by Bernard Rosenthal.

Go straight east from the Alamo to **St. Mark's Place** ㉔, the name given to 8th Street in the East Village. This often crowded thoroughfare has long attracted assorted fringe elements—punks, hyperkinetic clubcrawlers, and washed-out counterculturists.

Second Avenue, which St. Mark's crosses after one block, was called the **Yiddish Rialto** in the early part of this century. At this time several theaters between Houston and 14th streets presented Yiddish-language dramatic and musical productions. Two survivors from that period are the **Orpheum** (⊠ 126 2nd Ave.), and the former **Yiddish Arts Theatre,** now the multiscreen **Village East Cinemas** (⊠ 189 2nd Ave. at 12 St.).

Second Avenue is also home to a neighborhood landmark, **St. Mark's-in-the-Bowery Church** ㉕, a stately Episcopal church on the corner of 10th Street that serves as a community cultural center and public meeting hall. From in front of the church, you can take a quiet detour to investigate the facades of handsome redbrick row houses on **Stuyvesant Street,** which stretches southwest to 9th Street. If you continue north up 2nd Avenue from St. Mark's-in-the-Bowery Church, you'll reach the **Ukrainian Museum** ㉖ (⊠ 203 2nd Ave., between 12th and 13th Sts.), a modest upstairs gallery celebrating the cultural heritage of Ukraine.

Next, head east to 1st Avenue; walking south you'll pass at 9th Street **PS 122** (⊠ 150 1st Ave.), a former public school building transformed into a complex of spaces for avant-garde entertainment. Just west of the avenue on St. Mark's Place, the former location of the **Theater 80** repertory movie house is now host to the **Pearl Theatre Company** (⊠ 80 St. Mark's Pl.), which performs classic plays from around the world. Be sure to look down at the sidewalk, where you'll find the handprints, footprints, and autographs of such past screen luminaries as Joan Crawford, Ruby Keeler, Alexis Smith, and Gloria Swanson.

From 2nd Avenue, turn left (west) on St. Mark's Place and head east toward **Alphabet City,** the area's nickname; here the avenues are named A, B, C, and D. The blocks between 1st Avenue and Avenue A are lined with inexpensive cafés catering to a late-night younger crowd. Across from St. Mark's Place on Avenue A is the recently renovated **Tompkins Square Park** ㉗, a fairly peaceful haven from busy street life and sightseeing.

Next, head back west and follow 7th Street away from the southwest corner of Tompkins Square Park, studying the mix of small stores and restaurants to get a reading on the neighborhood's culture-in-flux. As you cross 2nd Avenue, notice **Love Saves the Day** (⊠ 119 2nd Ave.), which sells nostalgic toys, clothes, and jewelry. Right across 7th Street is **Kiev** (⊠ 117 2nd Ave.), a popular neighborhood hangout serving huge plates of potato pancakes, blintzes, or pierogi at bargain prices.

Walking on 7th Street west toward 3rd Avenue, you'll pass **McSorley's Old Ale House** ㉘ (⊠ 15 E. 7th St.), one of New York's oldest bars, and highly popular with New York University students. Just past Mc-Sorley's is **Surma, the Ukrainian Shop** ㉙ (⊠ 11 E. 7th St.), selling all sorts of Ukrainian-made goods. Across the street is the somewhat jarring sight of **St. George's Ukrainian Catholic Church** ㉚ (⊠ 16–20 7th St.) with its mosaic dome.

Across 3rd Avenue, the massive brownstone **Cooper Union Foundation Building** ㉛, a tuition-free school for artists, architects, and engineers, overlooks **Cooper Square,** a large open space. Across the street from the west side of the Cooper Union Building is the enormous **Carl Fischer Music Store** (⊠ 62 Cooper Sq.), where musicians select from an infinitude of sheet music and confer with the knowledgeable staff. Just south of this music store are the offices of the liberal downtown **Village Voice** newspaper (⊠ 36 Cooper Sq.).

If you're here from Sunday through Thursday, walk south on Cooper Square and turn left on 4th Street to visit the **Merchant's House Museum** ㉜ (⊠ 24 E. 4th St.), where 19th-century family life can be viewed thanks to the preservation of the original furnishings and architecture.

One block west of Cooper Square, you'll find Lafayette Street. The long block between East 4th Street and Astor Place contains on its east side a grand Italian Renaissance–style structure housing the New York Shakespeare Festival's **Joseph Papp Public Theater** ㉝ (⊠ 425 Lafayette St.); in the 19th century the city's first free library opened here. Across the street note the imposing marble Corinthian columns fronting **Colonnade Row** ㉞ (⊠ 428–434 Lafayette St.), a stretch of four 19th-century Greek Revival houses, whose facades are in need of a cleaning.

Walking north on Lafayette Street, you'll be back at Astor Place and the site of the Alamo, where you began your walk. West of Astor Place, you may choose to turn left (south) on Broadway to hit a trendy downtown shopping strip, with several clothing shops (some of them selling secondhand items); upscale chain stores such as Pottery Barn, Star Magic, and The Body Shop; and Tower Records. Above street level, the old warehouses here have mostly been converted into residential lofts.

Heading north on Broadway from Astor Place, you'll catch sight of the striking marble spire of **Grace Church** ㉟, a lovely Episcopal church on the corner of Broadway and 10th Street. If you continue north on the same side of the street as the church, you can end your walk at the popular **Strand Book Store** ㊱ (⊠ 828 Broadway at 12th St.), the largest secondhand bookstore in the city and an absolutely necessary stop for anyone who loves to read.

TIMING

Allow about 2½ hours for the walk. If you plan to stop at museums, add one hour, and at least another hour to browse in shops along the way. If you end your walk at the Strand Book Store, you may want to stop somewhere for coffee before perusing the bookshelves, which can easily take yet another hour of your time.

Sights to See

㉓ Alamo. Created by Bernard Rosenthal in 1967, this massive black cube made of steel was originally part of a temporary citywide exhibit, but it became a permanent installation thanks to a private donor. It was one of the first abstract sculptures in New York City to be placed in a public space. Balanced on a post, the "Cube," as it is locally known, rotates slowly when pushed. ⊠ *On traffic island at Astor Pl. and Lafayette St.*

Alphabet City. If you continue east on St. Mark's Place you'll see that the avenues are labeled with letters, not numbers, after you pass 1st Avenue. Until fairly recently, this area, nicknamed Alphabet City, meant a burned-out territory of slums and drug haunts, but some blocks and buildings were gentrified during the height of the East Village art scene in the mid-'80s. The reasonably priced restaurants with their bohemian atmosphere on St. Mark's Place and Avenue A (several of them serving ethnic cuisine) attract a large number of visitors "slumming it" from other parts of the city, as well as tourists. A close-knit Puerto Rican community lies east of Avenue A, lending a Latin flavor to many of the local dining spots and businesses. You'll also find a number of grungy bars and trendy, cheap cafés. During the day, make a stop at **San Isidro y San Leandro Orthodox Catholic Church of the Hispanic Rite** (⊠ 345 E. 4th St.), with a striking folk-art religious mural on its back wall, made from tiles and mirror shards. ⊠ *Alphabet City extends approximately from Ave. A to the East River, between 14th and Houston Sts.*

㉒ Astor Place Subway Station. At the entrance providing access to the uptown No. 6 subway line, you'll find an ornate cast-iron replica of a Beaux Arts kiosk; at the beginning of this century, almost every IRT subway entrance resembled this one. If you descend into the station, you'll see authentically reproduced ceramic wall tiles of beavers, a reference to the fur trade that contributed to John Jacob Astor's fortune. Milton Glaser, a Cooper Union graduate, designed the station's attractive abstract murals. ⊠ *On traffic island at 8th St. and 4th Ave.*

㉞ Colonnade Row. Marble Corinthian columns front this grand sweep of four Greek Revival mansions (originally nine) constructed in 1833, with stonework accomplished by Sing Sing penitentiary prisoners. Although sadly run-down today, in their time these once-elegant homes served as residences to millionaires John Jacob Astor and Cornelius Vanderbilt until they moved uptown. Writers Washington Irving, William Makepeace Thackeray, and Charles Dickens all stayed here at one time or another. Today three houses are occupied on street level by restaurants, while the northernmost building has the Astor Place Theatre as one of its residents. ⊠ *428–434 Lafayette St., between Astor Pl. and E. 4th St.*

㉛ Cooper Union Foundation Building. This impressive high-rise brownstone dominates **Cooper Square**, a large open space situated where 3rd and 4th avenues merge into the Bowery. A statue of industrialist Peter Cooper, by Augustus Saint-Gaudens, presides over the square. Cooper founded this college in 1859 to provide a forum for public opinion and free technical education for the working class; it still offers tuition-free education in architecture, art, and engineering. Cooper Union was the first structure to be supported by steel railroad rails—rolled in Cooper's own plant. Two galleries in the building are open to the public, presenting changing exhibitions during the academic year. ✉ *E. 7th St. to Astor Pl., 4th Ave. to the Bowery at Cooper Sq. Galleries:* ☎ *212/353–4155.* ☞ *Free.* ☉ *Weekdays 11–7, Sat. noon–5.*

★ ㉟ **Grace Church.** Topped by a finely ornamented octagonal marble spire, this remarkable Episcopal church, designed by James Renwick, Jr., has some excellent pre-Raphaelite stained-glass windows inside. The building—a fine mid-19th-century example of an English Gothic Revival church—fronts a small green yard in Greenwich Village. The church has been the site of many society weddings (including that of the P. T. Barnum show member Tom Thumb). ✉ *802 Broadway at E. 10th St.*

㉝ **Joseph Papp Public Theater.** In 1854 John Jacob Astor opened the city's first free library in this imposing redbrick Italian Renaissance–style building, which was renovated in 1967 as the Public Theater to serve as the permanent home of the New York Shakespeare Festival. The theater opened its doors with the popular rock musical *Hair.* Under the leadership of the late Joseph Papp, the Public's five playhouses built a fine reputation for bold and innovative performances; the long-running hit *A Chorus Line* had its first performances here, but so have many less commercial plays. Today director and producer George Wolfe heads the Public, which continues to present controversial modern works and imaginative Shakespeare productions. ✉ *425 Lafayette St.,* ☎ *212/260–2400.*

㉘ **McSorley's Old Ale House.** One of several claimants to the distinction of being New York's oldest bar, this often-crowded saloon attracts many collegiate types enticed by McSorley's own brands of ale. The mahogany bar, gas lamps, and potbelly stove all hark back to decades past. McSorley's opened in 1854 but didn't admit women until 1970. Joseph Mitchell immortalized the spot in short stories he wrote for *The New Yorker.* ✉ *15 E. 7th St.,* ☎ *212/473–9138.*

㉜ **Merchant's House Museum.** Come here for a rare glimpse of family life in the mid-19th century. Built in 1831–32, this house combining Federal and Greek-Revival styles was purchased in 1935 by Seabury Tredwell, a retired merchant, and remained the home of the Tredwell family from 1835 to 1933, when the last of the elderly Tredwell sisters died. The original furnishings and architectural features remain intact. Self-guided tour brochures are always available, and guided tours are given on Sunday. ✉ *29 E. 4th St.,* ☎ *212/777–1089.* ☞ *$3.* ☉ *Sun.–Thurs. 1–4.*

㉚ **St. George's Ukrainian Catholic Church.** Notable for its mosaic dome with stained-glass windows, this ostentatious modern church serves as a central meeting place for the old local Ukrainian population. Built in 1977, it took the place of the more modest Greek Revival–style St. George's Ruthenian Church. An annual Ukrainian folk festival occurs here in the spring. ✉ *16–20 E. 7th St.*

㉕ **St. Mark's-in-the-Bowery Church.** A Greek Revival steeple and a cast-iron front porch were added to this 1799 fieldstone country church, which occupies the former site of the family chapel of the old Dutch governor Peter Stuyvesant. St. Mark's is the city's oldest continually used Christian church building (Stuyvesant and Commodore Perry are buried here). Its interior had to be completely restored after a disastrous fire in 1978, and stained-glass windows were added to the balcony in 1982. Over the years St. Mark's has hosted much countercultural activity. In the 1920s a forward-thinking pastor injected the Episcopalian ritual with Native American chants, Greek folk dancing, and

Eastern mantras. William Carlos Williams, Amy Lowell, and Carl Sandburg once read here, and Isadora Duncan, Houdini, and Merce Cunningham also performed here. During the hippie era, St. Mark's welcomed avant-garde poets and playwrights, including Sam Shepard. Today dancers, poets, and performance artists cavort in the main sanctuary, where pews have been removed to accommodate them. ⊠ *Corner of 2nd Ave. and E. 10th St.*

㉔ St. Mark's Place. Starting at 3rd Avenue and going east, 8th Street changes its named to St. Mark's Place, the longtime hub of the hip East Village. During the 1950s, beatniks such as Allen Ginsberg and Jack Kerouac lived and wrote in the area; the 1960s brought Bill Graham's Fillmore East concerts, the Electric Circus, and hallucinogenic drugs. The black-clad, pink-haired or shaved-headed punks followed, and some remain today. St. Mark's Place between 2nd and 3rd avenues is lined with ethnic restaurants, jewelry stalls, leather shops, and stores selling books, posters, and eccentric clothing, although the arrival of a branch of The Gap seems to signal that this street has lost its countercultural relevance.

At 96–98 St. Mark's Place (between 1st Avenue and Avenue A), if you take a look up on your right, you may recognize these facades from the cover of the Led Zeppelin's *Physical Graffiti* album. The cafés between 1st Avenue and Avenue A attract customers late into the night; one of the best-known hangouts is **Sin-é** (⊠ 122 St. Mark's Pl.), an Irish-run café that books folk music; Sinead O'Connor has been spotted here.

㊱ Strand Book Store. Serious book lovers from around the world make pilgrimages to this secondhand book emporium with a stock of some 2 million volumes, including thousands of collector's items. (The slogan "Eight Miles of Books" calls out from the store's sign.) Opened in 1929 by Ben Bass, the Strand was originally found on 4th Avenue's Book Row until it moved to its present four-story location on Broadway in 1956. Review copies of new books sell for 50% off, and used books are often priced at much less. Don't be surprised if you wind up buying a book you weren't looking for; that's part of the fun of shopping here. ⊠ *828 Broadway at 12th St.,* ☎ *212/473–1452.*

Stuyvesant Street. This short thoroughfare angles southwest back to Astor Place. The area was once Governor Stuyvesant's "bouwerie," or farm; among the handsome redbrick row houses are the Federal-style **Stuyvesant-Fish House** (⊠ 21 Stuyvesant St.), which was built in 1804 as a wedding gift for a great-great-granddaughter of the governor, and **Renwick Triangle**, an attractive group of carefully restored one- and two-story brick and brownstone residences originally constructed in 1861.

㉙ Surma, The Ukrainian Shop. The exotic stock at this charming little store includes Ukrainian books, magazines, cassettes, and greeting cards, as well as musical instruments, painted eggs, and an exhaustive collection of peasant blouses. ⊠ *11 E. 7th St.,* ☎ *212/477–0729.*

㉗ Tompkins Square Park. This leafy oasis amid crowded apartment buildings received a much-needed renovation in 1992, making it a pleasant place to sit on a bench on a sunny afternoon. Several times old and new East Villagers have clashed around the park vicinity. The square's well-established tent city of homeless people provided the spark in the summers of 1988 and 1989, as police moved to rid the park of vagrants, and neighborhood residents vociferously took sides. Riots broke out, and tempers ran high. The homeless people have since moved on. ⊠ *Bordered by Aves. A and B and 7th and 10th Sts.*

㉖ **Ukrainian Museum.** At this small upstairs gallery, the cultural heritage of Ukraine is celebrated. Now that this country has become independent again, there's something especially poignant about this collection, nurtured in exile throughout the years of Soviet domination: ceramics, jewelry, hundreds of brilliantly colored Easter eggs, and an extensive collection of Ukrainian costumes and textiles. ⊠ *203 2nd Ave., between 12th and 13th Sts.,* ☎ *212/228–0110.* ⊡ *$1.* ☺ *Wed.–Sun. 1–5.*

Yiddish Rialto. Second Avenue in the East Village was known in the early part of this century as the Yiddish Rialto. Between Houston and 14th streets, eight theaters presented Yiddish-language productions of musicals, revues, and heart-wrenching melodramas. Two theaters from that golden era remain: the **Orpheum** (⊠ 126 2nd Ave.), still a legitimate playhouse, and the neo-Moorish **Yiddish Arts Theatre,** now the renovated multiscreen **Village East Cinemas** (⊠ 189 2nd Ave. at 12 St.), which has preserved the original ornate ceiling. Also, in front of the **Second Avenue Deli** (⊠ 2nd Ave. and 10th St.), Hollywood-style squares have been embedded in the sidewalk to commemorate Yiddish stage luminaries.

NEED A BREAK?

The East Village has some of the best Italian pastries in the city. **De Robertis Pasticceria** (⊠ 176 1st Ave., between 10th and 11th Sts., ☎ 212/674-7137) offers exceptional cheesecake and cappucinos in its original 1904 setting, complete with glistening mosaic tiles. Opened in 1894, the popular **Veniero Pasticceria** (⊠ 342 E. 11th St., ☎ 212/ 674-7264) has rows and rows of incredibly fresh cannoli, fruit tarts, cheesecakes, cookies, and other desserts on display in glass cases; there's a separate café section.

SOHO AND TRIBECA

Today the names of these two downtown neighborhoods are virtually synonymous with a certain eclectic elegance—an amalgam of black-clad artists, young Wall Streeters, track-lit loft apartments, hip art galleries, and restaurants with a minimalist approach to both food and decor. It's all very urban, very cool, very now.

Twenty-five years ago, they were virtual wastelands. SoHo (so named because it is the district *So*uth of *Ho*uston Street, bounded by Broadway, Canal Street, and 6th Avenue) was regularly referred to as "Hell's Hundred Acres" because of the many fires that raged through the untended warehouses that crowded the area. It was saved by two factors: (1) preservationists here discovered the world's greatest concentration of cast-iron architecture and fought to prevent demolition; and (2) artists discovered the large, cheap, well-lit spaces that cast-iron buildings provide.

All the rage between 1860 and 1890, cast-iron buildings were popular because they did not require massive walls to bear the weight of the upper stories. Since there was no need for load-bearing walls, these buildings had more interior space and larger windows. They were also versatile, with various architectural elements produced from standardized molds to mimic any style—Italianate, Victorian Gothic, neo-Grecian, to name but a few visible in SoHo. At first it was technically illegal for artists to live in their loft studios, but so many did that eventually the zoning laws were changed to permit residence.

By 1980 SoHo's galleries, trendy shops, and cafés, together with its marvelous cast-iron buildings and vintage Belgian-block pavements (the 19th-century successor to traditional cobblestones) had made SoHo such a desirable residential area that only the most successful artists could afford it. Seeking similar space, artists moved downtown to another half-abandoned industrial district, for which a new, SoHo-like name was invented: TriBeCa (the *Tri*angle *Be*low *Ca*nal Street), although in effect it goes no farther south than Murray Street and no farther east than West Broadway). The same scenario played itself out again, and TriBeCa's rising rents are already beyond the means of most artists, who have moved instead to west Chelsea, Long Island City (☞ Queens in Chapter 3), areas of Brooklyn, or New Jersey. But despite their gentrification, SoHo and TriBeCa retain the gritty bohemianism—one local store terms it shabby chic—that has come to dominate the downtown scene.

A Good Walk
Numbers in the text correspond to numbers in the margin and on the SoHo, TriBeCa, Little Italy, Chinatown map.

Starting at Houston (pronounced *how*-ston) Street, walk down Broadway to Prince Street, stopping at the many museums that crowd this block. The most noteworthy of these is the **Guggenheim Museum SoHo** ①, which opened in 1992—but also worthwhile are the **Alternative Museum** ②, whose political and sociopolitical themes make for lively discussion; the **Museum for African Art** ③, whose handsome two-story building complements its high-quality exhibits; and the **New Museum of Contemporary Art** ④, which is devoted exclusively to living artists. Several art galleries (☞ Chapter 10) share this block as well, most notably **586 Broadway,** a multigallery space whose bottom floor houses the trendy **Armani Exchange** store.

Just south of Prince Street, **560 Broadway** on the east side of the block is another popular exhibit space. Across the street, the 1907 **Singer Building** (✉ 561 Broadway) shows the final flower of the cast-iron style, with wrought-iron balconies, terra-cotta panels, and broad expanses of windows. On the bottom floor of this building is **Kate's Paperie,** where handmade paper is elevated to a high art form.

If you have youngsters with you, take them over to the **Children's Museum of the Arts** ⑤ at 72 Spring Street between Crosby and Lafayette streets. The exhibits here are largely interactive and should provide a welcome respite from SoHo's mostly grown-up pursuits.

One block south (downtown) of the Singer Building, between Spring and Broome streets, a cluster of lofts that were originally part of the 1897 **New Era Building** (✉ 495 Broadway) boast an Art Nouveau copper mansard. At the northeast corner of Broadway and Broome Street is the **Haughwout Building** ⑥, a newly restored classic of the cast-iron genre.

At the southeast corner of Broadway and Broome Street, note, at 486 Broadway, the Romanesque and Moorish Revival building with half-round brick arches; this is the former **Mechanics and Traders Bank.** At the northwest corner of Broadway and Grand Street, the popular **SoHo Antiques Fair** draws about 100 dealers to sell everything from used bicycles to vintage posters and prints on weekends from 9 to 5.

For a taste of pre-gentrified SoHo, detour west from Broadway to **Mercer Street** or east to **Crosby Street,** where Belgian street pavers, multiple loading docks, and a patchwork of fire escapes recall the days when these streets were used as service thoroughfares.

Go west from Broadway on Grand Street to **Greene Street,** where cast-iron buildings abound. Some of SoHo's best galleries are also on Greene Street: Try the **Andre Zarre Gallery** (✉ 48–50 Greene St.) or the **Jack Tilton Gallery** (✉ 49 Greene St.) for starters. For a look at one of the city's most artful retail stores, head to **Zona** (✉ 97 Greene St.); next door, **Shabby Chic** (✉ 97 Greene St.) defines the style so prevalent in this upscale bohemian neighborhood.

Greene Street between Prince and Spring streets is notable for the **SoHo Building** (✉ 104–110 Greene St.); towering 13 stories, it is SoHo's tallest building. On this block you'll also find **Anna Sui** (✉ 113 Greene St.), a boutique whose pricey avant-garde fashions are among New York's most cutting-edge. At Prince Street, walk one block west to Wooster Street, which, like a few other SoHo streets, still has its original Belgian pavers.

Going south on Wooster, shoppers will find a retail paradise in the block between Prince and Spring streets—most notably the whimsical **Todd Oldham** boutique (✉ 123 Wooster St.) and **Comme des Garçons** (✉ 116 Wooster St.), where high-style fashions are sold in a spartan setting.

Now head back north on Wooster Street, where you'll find exhibition spaces lining the block between Houston and Prince streets. Among the best are the minimalist-style **Chalk & Vermilion Gallery** (✉ 141– 145 Wooster St.), the **New York Earth Room** (✉ 141 Wooster St.), in which 140 tons of gently sculpted soil fill a second-floor gallery; and the **Gagosian Gallery** (✉ 136 Wooster St.), operated by prominent uptown dealer Larry Gagosian.

From Wooster Street, walk one block west on Prince Street to SoHo's main drag, **West Broadway,** whose range of galleries and stores puts other streets to shame. In the block between Prince and Spring streets alone, you'll find the gallery complex at **415 West Broadway,** which includes the Witkin Gallery for photography, and **420 West Broadway,** with six separate galleries including two of the biggest SoHo names, **Leo Castelli** and the **Sonnabend Gallery.**

Continuing south to Broome Streets, you'll find the immense **OK Harris** gallery (✉ 383 West Broadway); **Nahan Galleries** (✉ 381 West Broadway); the trendy robin's egg–blue **Dom** store (✉ 382 West Broadway), complete with rainbow-colored beads in the entrance; and **Smith & Hawken** (✉ 392 West Broadway), a gardener's emporium.

From here, TriBeCa is less than three blocks away; just follow West Broadway south to Canal Street, the neighborhood's official boundary. Stop to marvel at the life-size iron Statue of Liberty crown rising above the kitschy blue-tiled entrance to El Teddy's (✉ 219 W. Broadway), a gourmet Mexican restaurant. Continue south to Duane Street to reach the calm, shady **Duane Park** ⑦. Two blocks north, **Worth Street** was once the center of the garment trade, the 19th-century equivalent of today's 7th Avenue. The area to the west, near the Hudson River docks, became the heart of the wholesale food business; a few wholesalers such as Bazzini's (☞ below) still remain.

Back on West Broadway, walk one block north on Hudson Street. On your right you'll see the Art Deco **Western Union Building** (✉ 60 Hudson St.), where 19 subtly shaded colors of brick are laid in undulating patterns. Turn left from Hudson Street onto quiet Jay Street and pause at narrow **Staple Street,** whose green pedestrian walkway overhead links two warehouses. If you continue west on Jay Street you'll pass the loading docks of a 100-year-old food wholesaler, Bazzini's Nuts and Confections, where an upscale retail shop peddles nuts, coffee beans, and candies; there are also a few tables where you can enjoy a light snack.

On Greenwich Street near Harrison Street you'll find actor Robert De Niro's trendy restaurant, the **Tribeca Grill,** whose top floor houses the

100

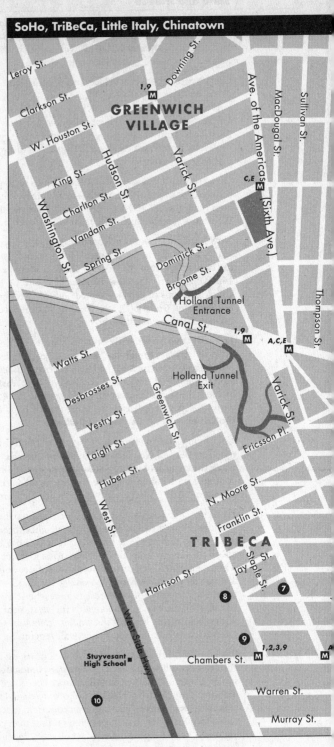

SoHo, TriBeCa, Little Italy, Chinatown

W. Houston St.

B,D,F,Q

E. Houston St.

Ⓜ

③

②

④

①

Prince St.

N,R

Ⓜ

SOHO

Spring St.

Lafayette St.

Mulberry St.

6

Ⓜ

⑤

West Broadway

Wooster St.

Greene St.

Mercer St.

Broadway

Crosby St.

Cleveland Pl.

Kenmare St.

Mott St.

Elizabeth St.

Chrystie St.

Forsyth St.

J,M

Ⓜ

Broome St.

⑥

Broome St.

LITTLE ITALY

B,D,Q

Ⓜ

Bowery

Grand St.

⑪

Howard St.

Hester St.

Lafayette St.

Centre St.

N,R

Ⓜ

Lispenard St.

Canal St.

Ⓜ 6

J,M,Z

Ⓜ

⑫

CHINATOWN

⑲

Walker St.

Baxter St.

⑬ Bayard St.

Pell St.

⑱

White St.

⑭

Mosco St.

Doyers St.

Broadway

Franklin St.

Park St.

Leonard St.

⑮

⑯

Worth St.

Thomas St.

Centre St.

Park Row

Pearl St.

⑰

West Broadway

Church St.

Duane St.

Reade St.

Duane St.

St. James's Pl.

N

City Hall Park

J,M,Z

Ⓜ

4,5,6

Ⓜ

N,R

Ⓜ

0 _____ 440 yards

0 _____ 400 meters

Tribeca Film Center (✉ 375 Greenwich St.), also owned by De Niro. As you walk south down Greenwich Street, notice on your right a surprising row of early 19th-century town houses nestled in the side of **Independence Plaza** ⑧, a huge high-rise apartment complex. Continuing south on Greenwich Street, you'll soon come to the 2½-acre **Washington Market Park** ⑨, a pleasant, landscaped oasis.

At the corner of the park, turn west on Chambers Street, heading west toward the Hudson River. A five-minute walk will bring you to the overpass across the West Side Highway. Here, behind the huge **Stuyvesant High School** building, you'll reach the north end of the recently landscaped **Hudson River Park** ⑩, a great place for a peaceful stroll.

TIMING
To see SoHo and TriBeCa at their liveliest, visit on a Saturday, when the fashionable art crowd is joined by smartly dressed uptowners and suburbanites who come down for a little shopping and gallery-hopping. If you want to avoid crowds, take this walk during the week. Keep in mind that most galleries are closed on Sundays and Mondays. Allowing time for leisurely browsing in several galleries and museums, as well as a stop for lunch, this tour can easily take up to an entire day.

Sights to See

② **Alternative Museum.** This small museum exhibits art with a sociopolitical twist, addressing issues such as homelessness, media manipulation, and gender stereotypes. ✉ 594 Broadway, ☎ 212/966–4444. ✉ $3 (suggested contribution). ◷ Tues.–Sat. 11–6.

⑤ **Children's Museum of the Arts.** In a loftlike space in SoHo, children ages 1 to 10 have the chance to become actively involved in visual and performing arts. They can play with brightly colored balls, draw on a computer, read in a special corner, and have fun in an art workshop. ✉ 72 Spring St., ☎ 212/941–9198. ✉ $4 weekdays and $5 weekends. ◷ Tues.–Sun. 11–5.

⑦ **Duane Park.** Preserved since 1800 as a calm, shady triangle, this little urban oasis is still surrounded by cheese, butter, and egg warehouses. ✉ Bordered by Hudson, Duane, and Staple Sts.

NEED A BREAK?   For a real New York story, duck into the **Odeon** (✉ 145 W. Broadway, ☎ 212/233–0507), the Art Deco restaurant/bar that figured in the novel *Bright Lights, Big City*. With black-and-red banquettes, chrome mirrors, neon-lit clocks, and ceiling fans, this place has a distinctively slick atmosphere. Come for a drink at the bar or a snack anytime from noon to 2 AM.

Greene Street. Cast-iron architecture is at its finest here; the block between Canal and Grand streets (✉ 8–34 Greene St.) represents the longest row of cast-iron buildings anywhere. Handsome as they are, these buildings were always commercial, containing stores and light manufacturing, principally textiles. Along this street notice the iron loading docks and the sidewalk vault covers that lead into basement storage areas.

Two of the standout buildings on Greene Street are the so-called **Queen of Greene Street** (✉ 28–30 Greene St.), whose dormers, columns, window arches, projecting central bays, and Second Empire roof have a grace that is indeed regal; and its more masculine counterpart, the **King of Greene Street** (✉ 72–76 Greene St.), two blocks north; it's a five-story Renaissance-style building with a magnificent projecting porch of Corinthian columns. Today the King (now painted yellow) houses the M-13 art gallery, Alice's Antiques, and Bennison Fabrics.

Even the lampposts on Greene Street are architectural gems: Note their turn-of-the-century bishop's-crook style, adorned with various cast-iron curlicues from their bases to their curved tops.

① Guggenheim Museum SoHo. Since it opened in 1992, this downtown branch of the uptown museum has displayed a revolving series of exhibitions, both contemporary work and pieces from the Guggenheim's permanent collection. The museum occupies space in a landmark 19th-century redbrick structure with its original cast-iron storefronts and detailed cornice. Arata Isozaki designed the two floors of stark, loft-like galleries as well as the museum store facing West Broadway. ⊠ *575 Broadway,* ☎ *212/423–3500.* ▨ *$8.* ☉ *Wed.–Fri. and Sun. 11–6, Sat. 11–8.*

NEED A BREAK?

Right around the corner from the Guggenheim Museum SoHo down a small flight of stairs, you'll find **T Salon Restaurant and Tea Emporium** (⊠ 142 Mercer St., ☎ 212/925–3700), one of the nicest places to have an afternoon tea in Manhattan. In a grand yet restful space, you can order fine teas and coffees, accompanied by rich desserts. The tiny, down-home **Olive's** (⊠ 120 Prince St., ☎ 212/941–0111) outdoes even its glitzy neighbor Dean & Deluca in the spectacular sandwich stakes, but aside from a rustic wood bench and two or three stools, it's takeout only. For a taste of SoHo shabby chic, head for **Scharmann's** (⊠ 386 W. Broadway, ☎ 212/219–2561), where the hip drink tea from gleaming brass pots on oversize couches, mismatched chairs, and a bean bag or two.

⑥ Haughwout Building. Nicknamed the Parthenon of Cast Iron, this Venetian palazzo-style structure was built in 1857 to house Eder Haughwout's china and glassware business. Inside, the building once contained the world's first commercial passenger elevator, a steam-powered device invented by Elisha Graves Otis. ⊠ *488 Broadway.*

⑩ Hudson River Park. At the corner of Chambers and West streets, this spacious recreational area includes a river promenade, basketball courts, playgrounds, playing fields, and even handball courts. Area residents come out in droves on sunny days to enjoy the beautiful views of the water and to run, walk, or skate along the river. Note the whimsical sculptures that line the promenade—monkeys, turtles, and countless other creatures. North of Stuyvesant High School the promenade continues as far as Gansevoort Street in the West Village.

⑧ Independence Plaza. These high-rise towers at the intersection of Greenwich and Harrison streets are the fruit of a pleasant, if somewhat utilitarian, project of the mid-1970s that was supposed to be part of a wave of demolition and construction—until the preservationists stepped in. For several years Independence Plaza remained a middle-class island stranded downtown, far from stores, schools, and neighbors. With TriBeCa's increasingly chic reputation, however, plus the development of Battery Park City to the south, it has become a much more desirable address.

The three-story redbrick houses that share Harrison Street with Independence Plaza were moved here from various sites in the neighborhood when, in the early 1970s, the food-wholesalers' central market nearby was razed and moved to the Bronx. ⊠ *Greenwich St., between Duane and N. Moore Sts.*

③ Museum for African Art. Dedicated to contemporary and traditional African art, this small but expertly conceived museum is housed in a handsome two-story space designed by Maya Lin, who also designed the Vietnam Veterans Memorial in Washington, DC. Exhibits may include contemporary sculpture, ceremonial masks, architectural details, costumes, and textiles. The entertaining museum store features African crafts, clothing, and jewelry. ⊠ *593 Broadway,* ☎ *212/966–1313.* ⊞ *$4.* ☉ *Tues.–Fri. 10:30–5:30, weekends noon–6.*

❹ **New Museum of Contemporary Art.** The avant-garde exhibitions here, all by living artists, are often radically innovative and socially conscious. Past exhibitions have included "alt.youth.media," in which videotapes, web sites, and interactive computer projects explored issues concerning today's youths; and "A Labor of Love," in which the handmade folk and craft works of more than 40 contemporary artists was meant to question the definition of high art. ⊠ *583 Broadway,* ☎ *212/219–1222.* ⊞ *$4; free Sat. 6 PM–8 PM.* ☉ *Wed., Thurs., Fri., and Sun. noon–6, Sat. noon–8.*

Staple Street. Little more than an alley, Staple Street was named for the staple products unloaded here by ships in transit that didn't want to pay duty on any extra cargo. Framed at the end of the alley is the redbrick **New York Mercantile Exchange,** its square corner tower topped by a bulbous roof. On the ground floor is the acclaimed French restaurant, Chanterelle (☞ Chapter 6).

Tribeca Film Center. Robert De Niro created this complex of editing, screening, and production rooms, where Stephen Spielberg, Quincy Jones, and De Niro himself keep offices. Like many of the chic buildings in this area, it's inside a former factory, the old Martinson Coffee Building. On the ground floor is the trendy Tribeca Grill (☞ Chapter 6), also owned by Robert De Niro. ⊠ *375 Greenwich St., between Franklin and Moore Sts.*

❾ **Washington Market Park.** This much-needed recreation space for TriBeCa was named after the great food market that once sprawled over the area. It is now a green, landscaped oasis with a playground and a gazebo. Just across Chambers Street from the park, **PS 234,** a public elementary school, has opened to serve TriBeCa's younger generation. At the corner, a stout little red tower resembles a lighthouse, and iron ship figures are worked into the playground fence—reminders of the neighborhood's long-gone dockside past. ⊠ *Greenwich St., between Chambers and Duane Sts.*

LITTLE ITALY

Mulberry Street is the heart of Little Italy; in fact, at this point it's virtually the entire body. In 1932 an estimated 98% of the inhabitants of this area were of Italian birth or heritage, but since then the growth and expansion of neighboring Chinatown have encroached on the Italian neighborhood to such an extent that merchants and community leaders of the Little Italy Restoration Association (LIRA) negotiated a truce in which the Chinese agreed to let at least Mulberry remain an all-Italian street.

In the second half of the 19th century, when Italian immigration peaked, the neighborhood stretched from Houston Street to Canal Street and the Bowery to Broadway. During this time Italians founded at least three Italian parishes, including the Church of the Transfiguration (now almost wholly Chinese); they also operated an Italian-language newspaper, *Il Progresso.*

In 1926 immigrants from southern Italy celebrated the first Feast of San Gennaro along Mulberry Street—a 10-day street fair that still takes place every September. Dedicated to the patron saint of Naples, the festival transforms Mulberry Street into a virtual al fresco restaurant, as wall-to-wall vendors sell traditional fried sausages and pastries. Today the festival is one of the few reminders of Little Italy's vibrant history, as the neighborhood continues to be overwhelmed by the ever-expanding Chinatown, and as Italians continue to move out of Manhattan. If you want the flavor of a complete Italian neighborhood, you'd do better to visit Carroll Gardens in Brooklyn or Arthur Avenue in the Bronx (☞ Chapter 3)—or rent a video of the Martin Scorsese movie *Mean Streets,* which was filmed in Little Italy back in the early 1970s.

Still, the neighborhood is full of enticing eateries and historical sights of interest. Note the many tenement buildings with fire escapes projecting over the sidewalks. Most of these are of the late-19th-century New York style known as railroad flats: six-story buildings on 25-by-90-foot lots, with all the rooms in each apartment placed in a straight line like railroad cars. This style was common in the densely populated immigrant neighborhoods of lower Manhattan until 1901, when the city passed an ordinance requiring air shafts in the interior of buildings.

A Good Walk

Numbers in the text correspond to numbers in the margin and on the SoHo, TriBeCa, Little Italy, Chinatown map.

Start your tour at the intersection of Spring and Mulberry streets, which still has a residential feel. Take a moment to poke your nose into the **D & G Bakery** (⊠ 45 Spring St.), one of the last coal-oven bakeries in the United States. Walk down Mulberry Street to **Broome Street,** a major gastronomic thoroughfare.

To see the ornate Renaissance Revival building that is the original **New York City Police Headquarters** ⑪, walk west on Broome Street to Centre Street, between Hester and Grand streets. Then work your way back to the corner of Grand and Mulberry streets and stop to get the lay of the land. Facing north (uptown), on your right you'll see a series of wide, four-story houses from the early 19th century, built long before the great flood of immigration hit this neighborhood between 1890 and 1924. Turn and look south along the east side of Mulberry Street to see Little Italy's trademark railroad-flat-style tenement buildings.

On the southeast corner of Grand Street, **E. Rossi & Co.** (⊠ 191 Grand St.), established in 1902, is an antiquated little shop that sells housewares, espresso makers, embroidered religious postcards, and jocular Italian T-shirts. Two doors east on Grand Street is **Ferrara's** (⊠ 195 Grand St.), a 100-year-old pastry shop that ships its creations—cannoli, peasant pie, Italian rum cake—all over the world. Another survivor of the pretenement era is the two-story, dormered brick Van Rensselaer House, now **Paolucci's Restaurant** (⊠ 149 Grand St.)—built in 1816, it is a prime example of the Italian Federal style.

One block south of Grand Street, on the corner of Hester and Mulberry streets, you'll reach **Umberto's Clam House** (⊠ 129 Mulberry Street), best known as the place where mobster Joey Gallo was munching scungilli in 1973 when he was fatally surprised by a task force of mob hit men. Turn left onto Hester Street to visit yet another Little Italy institution, **Puglia** (⊠ 189 Hester St.), a restaurant where guests sit at long communal tables, sing along with house entertainers, and enjoy southern Italian specialties with quantities of homemade wine. (For other Little Italy restaurants, ☞ Chapter 6.)

One street west, on Baxter Street about three-quarters of a block toward Canal Street, stands the **San Gennaro Church** ⑫, which each year around mid-September sponsors Little Italy's keynote event, the annual Feast of San Gennaro.

TIMING

Since Little Italy consists of little more than one street, this tour shouldn't take more than one hour. Since most attractions are food-related, plan on visiting around lunchtime. Another fun time to visit is during the 10-day San Gennaro festival, around mid-September.

Sights to See

Broome Street. Crowded with restaurants, cafés, bakeries, imported-food shops, and souvenir stores, Broome Street is where Little Italy lives and breathes. Especially on weekends, this is a street for strolling, gawking, and inhaling the aroma of garlic and olive oil. Some restaurants and cafés display high-tech Eurodesign; others seem dedicated to staying exactly as their old customers remember them.

At the southwest corner of Broome and Mulberry streets, stairs lead down through a glass entrance to what seems to be a blue-tiled cave—and, appropriately enough, it is the **Grotta Azzurra** (Blue Grotto) restaurant, a longtime favorite for both the hearty food and the very Italian ambience. ⊠ *387 Broome St.,* ☎ *212/925–8775.*

East of Mulberry Street, the building at 375 Broome Street is known for its sheet-metal cornice that bears the face of a distinguished, albeit anonymous, bearded man.

NEED A BREAK?	You can savor cannoli and other sweet treats at **Caffè Roma** (⊠ 385 Broome St., ☎ 212/226–8413), a traditional neighborhood favorite with wrought-iron chairs and a pounded-tin ceiling.

⓫ **New York City Police Headquarters.** The fabulously ornate building that served as the New York City police headquarters until 1973 was converted into a high-priced condominium complex in 1988; big-name residents have included Cindy Crawford, Winona Ryder, and Steffi Graf, among others. Notice the baroque touches that embellish its classical Renaissance Revival design. ⊠ *240 Centre St.*

⓬ **San Gennaro Church.** Every year around mid-September, San Gennaro Church—officially called the Most Precious Blood Church, National Shrine of San Gennaro—sponsors the feast of San Gennaro, the biggest event in Little Italy. (The community's other big festival celebrates St. Anthony of Padua in June; that church is at Houston and Sullivan streets, in what is now SoHo.) During the feasts, Little Italy's streets are closed to traffic, arches of tinsel span the thoroughfares, the sidewalks are lined with booths offering games and food, and the whole scene is one noisy, crowded, kitschy, delightful party. ⊠ *113 Baxter St.*

CHINATOWN

Visibly exotic, Chinatown is a popular tourist attraction, but it is also a real, vital community where about half of the city's population of 300,000 Chinese still live. Its main businesses are restaurants and garment factories; some 55% of its residents speak little or no English. Theoretically, Chinatown is divided from Little Italy by Canal Street, the bustling artery that links the Holland Tunnel (to New Jersey) and the Manhattan Bridge (to Brooklyn). However, in recent years an influx of immigrants from the People's Republic of China, Taiwan, and especially Hong Kong has swelled Manhattan's Chinese population, and Hong Kong residents, anticipating the return of the British colony to PRC domination in 1997, have been investing their capital in Chinatown real estate. Consequently, Chinatown now spills over its traditional borders into Little Italy to the north and the formerly Jewish Lower East Side to the east.

Its prolific expansion is a relatively recent development. The first Chinese immigrants were primarily railroad workers who came from the West in the 1870s to settle in a limited section of the Lower East Side. For nearly a century, anti-immigration laws prohibited most men from having their wives and families join them; the neighborhood became known as a "bachelor society," and for years its population remained static. It was not until the end of World War II, when Chinese immigration quotas were increased, that the neighborhood began the outward expansion that is still taking place today.

As a result of its rapid growth, Chinatown has become more lively than ever. Where once there was just a handful of businesses in Chinatown, today it's a virtual marketplace, crammed with souvenir shops and restaurants in funky pagoda-style buildings and crowded with pedestrians day and night. Here you can find every imaginable type of Chinese cuisine, from fast-food noodles or dumplings to sumptuous Hunan, Szechuan, Cantonese, Mandarin, and Shanghai feasts (☞ Chapter 6). You can also stroll among countless sidewalk markets bursting with stacks of fresh seafood and strange-shaped vegetables in extraterrestrial shades of green. Food shops proudly display their wares: If America's motto is "a chicken in every pot," then Chinatown's must be "a roast duck in every window."

A Good Walk

Numbers in the text correspond to numbers in the margin and on the SoHo, TriBeCa, Little Italy, Chinatown map.

A good place to get oriented is the **Museum of Chinese in the Americas** ⑬, in a century-old schoolhouse at the corner of Bayard and Mulberry streets. For a taste of Chinatown-style commercialism, walk one block north to Canal Street, where restaurants and markets abound. If Chinese food products intrigue you, stop to browse in **Kam Man** (⊠ 200 Canal St.), then head east to Mott Street, the principal business street of the neighborhood.

Turn right from Canal Street onto Mott Street and walk three blocks. On the corner of Mott and Mosco streets, you'll find the **Church of the Transfiguration** ⑭ (⊠ 25 Mott St.), where the faithful have worshiped since 1801. From here, turn right from Mott Street onto Mosco Street, proceeding downhill to Mulberry Street, where you'll see **Columbus Park** ⑮. This peaceful spot occupies the area once known as the Five Points, a tough 19th-century slum ruled by Irish gangs.

Across the street from the Church of the Transfiguration is **Quong Yuen Shing & Co.** (⊠ 32 Mott St.), also known as the Mott Street General Store; it is one of Chinatown's oldest curio shops, with porcelain bowls, teapots, and cups for sale. Three doors up from the store, you'll see a sign for Pell Street, a narrow lane of wall-to-wall restaurants whose neon signs stretch halfway across the thoroughfare.

Halfway up Pell is **Doyers Street,** the site of turn-of-the-century gang wars. At the end of Doyers you'll find the Bowery. Cross the street to **Chatham Square** ⑯, where the **Kum Lau Arch** honors Chinese casualties in American wars. From Chatham Square, cross over the east side, past Park Row. Take a sharp right turn onto St. James Place to find two remnants of this neighborhood's pre-Chinatown past. On St. James Place is the **First Shearith Israel graveyard** ⑰, the first Jewish cemetery in the United States. Walk a half block farther, turn left on

James Street, and you'll see **St. James Church** (✉ 32 James St.), a stately 1837 Greek Revival edifice where Al Smith, who rose from this poor Irish neighborhood to become New York's governor and a 1928 Democratic presidential candidate, once served as altar boy.

Return to Chatham Square once again and walk north up the **Bowery** to **Confucius Plaza** ⑱, where a statue of the Chinese sage stands guard. Across the Bowery at the corner of Pell Street, **18 Bowery** is one of Manhattan's oldest homes—a Federal and Georgian structure built in 1785 by meat wholesaler Edward Mooney. Farther north up the Bowery, a younger side of Chinatown is shown at the **Asian American Arts Centre** ⑲ (✉ 26 Bowery), which displays current work by Asian-American artists. For some exotic shopping, duck into the Canal Arcade, a passage linking the Bowery and Elizabeth Street.

Continue north. At the intersection of the Bowery and Canal Street, a grand arch and colonnade mark the entrance to the Manhattan Bridge, which leads to Brooklyn. This corner was once the center of New York's diamond district. Today most jewelry dealers have moved uptown, but you can still find some pretty good deals at jewelers on the Bowery and the north side of Canal Street.

TIMING

Come on a weekend to see the neighborhood at its liveliest; locals crowd the streets from dawn until dusk, along with a slew of tourists. If you're looking for a more relaxed experience, opt for a weekday instead. Allowing for stops at the two local museums and a lunch break, this tour will take about three hours.

Sights to See

⑲ **Asian American Arts Centre.** This place may look like a hole in the wall, but it does offer impressive contemporary works by Asian-American artists, annual Chinese folk-art exhibitions during the Chinese New Year, performances by the Asian American Dance Theater, and videotapes of Asian American art and events. There's no sign out front and the door reads "KTV-City"; ring buzzer No. 1. ✉ *26 Bowery,* ☎ *212/233–2154.* ✆ *Free.* ☼ *Tues.–Fri. noon–6, Sat. 3–6.*

The Bowery. Now a commercial thoroughfare lined with stores selling light fixtures and secondhand restaurant equipment, in the 17th century this broad boulevard was a farming area north of the city; its name derives from *bowerij,* the Dutch word for farm. As the city's growing population moved northward the Bowery became a broad, elegant avenue lined with taverns and theaters.

In the late 1800s the placement of an elevated subway line over the Bowery and the proliferation of saloons and brothels led to its demise as an elegant commercial thoroughfare; by the early 20th century it had become infamous as a skid row full of indigents and crime. After 1970, efforts at gentrification had some effect, and the neighborhood's indigent population dispersed. Today the Bowery is a major, if forgotten, artery through lower Manhattan.

⑯ **Chatham Square.** Ten streets converge at this labyrinthine intersection, creating pandemonium for cars and a nightmare for pedestrians. A memorial, the **Kim Lau Arch,** honoring Chinese casualties in American wars, stands on an island in the eye of the storm. On the far end of the square, at the corner of Catherine Street and East Broadway, there's a **Republic Bank for Savings**—originally a branch of the Manhattan Savings Bank. It was built to resemble a pagoda.

⑭ **Church of the Transfiguration.** Built in 1801 as the Zion Episcopal Church, this is an imposing Georgian structure with Gothic windows. It is now a Chinese Catholic church distinguished by its trilingualism: Here Mass is said in Cantonese, Mandarin, and English. ✉ *25 Mott St.*

A colorful flag hangs outside the entrance of the **Chinatown Ice Cream Factory** (✉ 65 Bayard St., between Mott and Elizabeth Sts., ☎ 212/608–4170), where the flavors range from red bean to lychee to green tea. Prepare to eat your scoop on the run, since there's no seating here. At 35 Pell St. is **May May Chinese Gourmet Bakery** (☎ 212/267–0733), a local favorite, with Chinese pastries, rice dumplings wrapped in banana leaves, yam cakes, and other sweet treats.

⑮ Columbus Park. Today this shady, paved urban space is where children play and elderly Chinese gather to reminisce about their homeland. One hundred years ago, the then-swampy area was known as the Five Points—after the intersection of Mulberry Street, Anthony (now Worth) Street, Cross (now Park) Street, Orange (now Baxter) Street and Little Water Street (no longer in existence)—and was notoriously ruled by dangerous Irish gangs. In the 1880s a neighborhood-improvement campaign brought about the creation of the park.

⑱ Confucius Plaza. At this open area at an intersection, a bronze statue of Confucius presides in front of the redbrick high-rise apartment complex named for him. The statue was originally opposed by leftist Chinese immigrants, who considered the sage a reactionary symbol of old China. That the statue is there tells you something about Chinatown's political makeup. ✉ *Intersection of Bowery and Division St.*

Doyers Street. The "bloody angle"—an unexpected sharp turn halfway down this little alleyway—was the site of turn-of-the-century battles between Chinatown's Hip Sing and On Leon *tongs,* gangs who fought for control over the local gambling and opium trades. Today the street is among the most colorful in Chinatown, lined with tea parlors and barbershops.

⑰ First Shearith Israel graveyard. Consecrated in 1656 by the country's oldest Jewish congregation, this small burial ground bears the remains of Sephardic Jews (of Spanish-Portuguese extraction) who emigrated from Brazil in the mid-17th century. The second and third Shearith Israel graveyards are in Greenwich Village and Chelsea, respectively. ✉ *55 St. James Pl.*

⑬ Museum of Chinese in the Americas. In a century-old schoolhouse that once served Italian-American and Chinese-American children, the former Chinatown History Museum recently underwent a yearlong renovation and a change of name. A new permanent exhibit entitled "Where's Home? Chinese in the Americas" explores the Chinese diaspora, and a new gallery designed by Billie Tsien improves the museum. In addition, there are interactive photographic exhibitions on Asian-American labor history, and a library and bookstore with books on the history of Chinese-Americans. Historical walking tours of Chinatown are offered by appointment only. ✉ *70 Mulberry St., 2nd floor,* ☎ *212/619–4785.* 🎫 *$3.* 🕙 *Weekdays and Sun. noon–5.*

WALL STREET AND THE BATTERY

Lower Manhattan doesn't cover many acres, but it is packed with attractions, for it has always been central to the city's networks of power and wealth. It was here that the Nieuw Amsterdam colony was established by the Dutch in 1625; in 1789 the first capital building of the United States was located here. The city did not really expand beyond these precincts until the middle of the 19th century. Today this historic heart of New York is increasingly being abandoned by companies for cheaper and better-equipped buildings in midtown and the suburbs, but all sorts of tax breaks, rezonings, and incentives, including plans to convert parts of some buildings to residences, are being worked up to help the area maintain its vitality. Still, lower Manhattan is in many ways dominated by Wall Street, which is both an actual street and a shorthand name for the vast, powerful financial community that clusters around the New York and American stock exchanges. A different but equally awe-inspiring type of site can be found at the tip of the island, as you look out across the great silvery harbor and see enduring symbols of America: the Statue of Liberty and Ellis Island, port of entry for countless immigrants to a new land.

A Good Walk
Numbers in the text correspond to numbers in the margin and on the Lower Manhattan map.

Our tour begins at the southernmost point of Manhattan, at the **Staten Island Ferry Terminal** (for subway riders, that's just outside the South Ferry station on the No. 1 line). The **Staten Island Ferry** ① is still the best deal in town: The 20- to 30-minute ride across New York Harbor provides great views of the Manhattan skyline, the Statue of Liberty, the Verrazano-Narrows Bridge, and the New Jersey coast—and it's free if you don't get off in Staten Island (otherwise it costs only 50¢ round-trip). To the west of South Ferry lies **Battery Park** ②, a verdant landfill, loaded with monuments and sculpture, at Manhattan's green toe. **Castle Clinton** ③ is one such monument; now it's where you buy tickets for the boats to the **Statue of Liberty** ④ and **Ellis Island** ⑤.

As you leave the park, across State Street you'll see the imposing **Alexander Hamilton Custom House,** home of the first national museum dedicated to Native American culture, the **National Museum of the American Indian** ⑥. The museum faces onto **Bowling Green,** an oval greensward at the foot of Broadway that became New York's first public park in 1733. From Bowling Green, head south on State Street. A stunning semicircular office tower in reflective glass, most eye-catching from the harbor, hugs the bend of the street at 17 State Street. Next door is the **Shrine of St. Elizabeth Ann Seton,** in what was built in 1793 as a private home.

Continue left and around onto Water Street, passing on your right, on either side of Broad Street, **New York Plaza,** a complex of high-tech office towers linked by an underground concourse. Just beyond it is the **Vietnam Veterans Memorial** ⑦, where moving passages from the letters of servicemen and servicewomen have been etched into a wall of greenish glass set on a large brick plaza. Return to Broad Street, noticing the old row houses on the right before you get there. These used to front the water—thus, the street's name. One block farther inland (north) is **Fraunces Tavern** ⑧ (✉ 54 Pearl St.), a complex of five largely 19th-century buildings housing a museum, restaurant, and bar (☞ Chapter 6). History is integrated more subtly in the lobby of the high-rise office building at **85 Broad Street,** which, paying due homage to urban archaeology, traces the course of the old Dutch Stone Street with a line of brown paving stones (the lobby is open to the public). At the side of the building, on Pearl Street, peer through the transparent panel in the sidewalk to see the excavated foundations of the 17th-century Stadt Huys, the Old Dutch City Hall.

Head up north on Pearl Street to **Hanover Square,** a quiet tree-lined plaza that stood on the waterfront when the East River reached Pearl Street. Walk inland up Hanover Square to the rounded corner of South

William and Beaver streets. Two blocks farther north, William Street crosses **Wall Street,** so called because it traces the course of a wood wall built across the island in 1653 to defend the Dutch colony against the Native Americans. Ironically, now it's practically walled in by the towering buildings on either side of it. Developers' greed backfired here—they built on every inch of land only to have property values decrease once people realized how stultifying the results were.

One block west on Wall Street, where Broad Street becomes Nassau Street, you'll find on your right a regal statue of George Washington on the steps of the **Federal Hall National Memorial** ⑨. This 1883 statue, by noted sculptor and relative of the president, John Quincy Adams Ward, marks the spot where Washington was sworn in as the first U.S. president in 1789. Across the street is an investment bank built by J. P. Morgan in 1913. By building only four stories Morgan was in effect declaring himself above the pressures of Wall Street real estate values. Now **Morgan Guaranty Trust,** the building bears pockmarks near the fourth window on the Wall Street side; these were created when a bomb that had been placed in a pushcart exploded in 1920. Perhaps the heart of the area is the **New York Stock Exchange** ⑩ at 20 Broad Street. From its visitor center you can watch stressed-out traders gesture wildly in the name of making deals.

Trinity Church ⑪, which cuts off Wall Street two blocks west of Nassau Street, was established as an Anglican parish in 1697. The present structure (1846), by Richard Upjohn, ranked as the city's tallest building for most of the second half of the 19th century. Just north of the church is tiny Thames Street, where a pair of skyscrapers playfully called the **Thames Twins**—the Trinity and U.S. Realty buildings—display early 20th-century attempts to apply Gothic decoration to skyscrapers. Across the street at 120 Broadway, the 1915 **Equitable Building** rises 30 stories straight from its base with no setback; its overpowering shadow on the street helped convince the city government to pass the nation's first zoning law. Large public plazas around the bases of skyscrapers have helped to alleviate this problem, and a good example is between Cedar and Liberty streets, where the black-glass **Marine Midland Bank** (1971) features in its street-level plaza a red-and-silver Noguchi sculpture, *Cube.* Two blocks east at William and Pine streets, the plaza surrounding the 65-story **Chase Manhattan Bank Building** holds a striking black-and-white sculpture, *Group of Four Trees,* by Jean Dubuffet.

Liberty Street converges with William Street and Maiden Lane at the triangular **Louise Nevelson Plaza,** which contains four black welded-steel abstract Nevelson sculptures, three middle-size pieces and one huge 70-footer. Sit in the plaza and contemplate the **Federal Reserve Bank** ⑫ directly across the street, which looks the way a bank ought to look: gray, solid, imposing, absolutely impregnable.

Go back west again on Maiden Lane, which turns into Cortlandt Street, to the **World Trade Center** ⑬, a 16-acre, 12-million-square-foot complex that contains New York's two tallest buildings (1,350 feet high). More than a million cubic yards of rock and soil were excavated for the World Trade Center—and then moved across West Street to help beget the 100-acre **Battery Park City** development, a complete neighborhood built from scratch. Take the pedestrian overpass north of 1 World Trade Center to Battery Park City's centerpiece, the **World Financial Center** ⑭, a four-tower complex designed by Cesar Pelli, with some heavy-duty corporate tenants. Just north of the basin is the terminal for **ferry service** to Hoboken, New Jersey. Beyond the ferry terminal is the southern end of the **Hudson River Park.** To the south, a

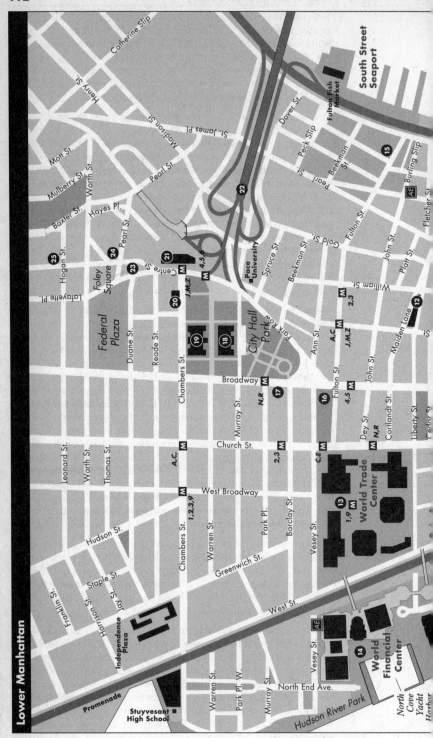

Lower Manhattan

South Street Seaport

Fulton Fish Market

Catherine Slip

Henry St.

Madison St.

St. James Pl.

Dover St.

Peck Slip

Burling Slip

15

Mott St.

Worth St.

Mulberry St.

Baxter St.

Pearl St.

Pearl St.

Fletcher St.

Beekman St.

Pearl St.

Fulton St.

John St.

Platt St.

22

Hayes Pl.

Pearl St.

Spruce St.

Gold St.

Beekman St.

William St.

John St.

Maiden Lane

25

Hogan Pl.

24

Foley Square

23

Lafayette Pl.

21

Centre St.

4,5,6

Pace University

M

J,M,Z

2,3

A,C

J,M,Z

12

Federal Plaza

20

Duane St.

Reade St.

Chambers St.

19

18

City Hall Park

Park Row

Ann St.

Fulton St.

John St.

St.

Broadway

17

N,R

Murray St.

M

16

Fulton St.

4,5

Dey St.

N,R

Cortlandt St.

Liberty St.

Cedar St.

Leonard St.

Worth St.

Thomas St.

A,C

M

Church St.

2,3

M

C,E

M

West Broadway

M

1,2,3,9

West Broadway

Warren St.

Park Pl.

Barclay St.

13

1,9

World Trade Center

Hudson St.

Vesey St.

Staple St.

Harrison St.

Jay St.

Greenwich St.

Chambers St.

Franklin St.

Independence Plaza

West St.

A,E

Promenade

Stuyvesant High School

Warren St.

Park Pl. W.

Murray St.

North End Ave.

Vesey St.

14

World Financial Center

North Cove Yacht Harbor

Hudson River Park

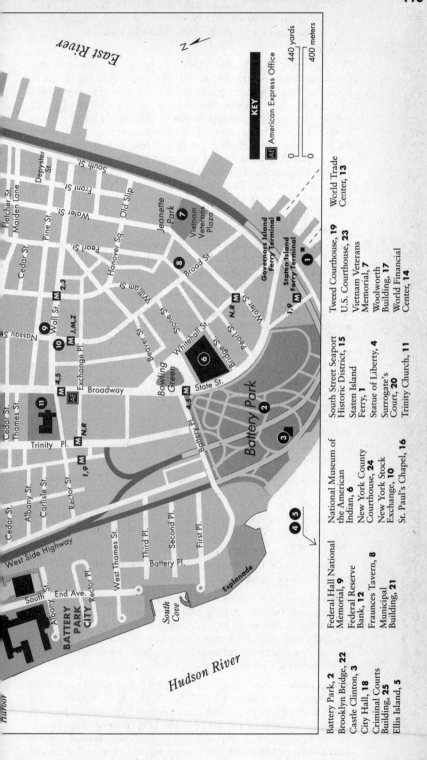

East River

N

KEY

▆ American Express Office

AE American Express Office

0 — 440 yards

0 — 400 meters

Depyster St.
Fletcher St.
Maiden Lane
South St.
Front St.
Water St.
Pine St.
Cedar St.
Old Slip
Pearl St.
Jeanette Park
Hanover Sq.
Vietnam Veterans Plaza
Broad St.
7
8
William St.
M 2,3
Wall St.
9
M 1,M,Z
10
Nassau St.
Exchange Pl.
M 4,5
Stone St.
Beaver St.
Whitehall St.
Broadway
AE
11
Trinity Pl.
Cedar St.
Thames St.
M N,R
Bridge St.
6
State St.
Bowling Green
Battery Pl.
M 4,5
Governors Island Ferry Terminal
Staten Island Ferry Terminal
M 1,9
M N,R
Water St.
1
2
3
Battery Park

M 1,9
Rector St.
Carlisle St.
Albany St.
Cedar St.
West Side Highway
West Thames St.
Battery Pl.
Third Pl.
Second Pl.
First Pl.
Rector Pl.
End Ave.
South St.
Albany
BATTERY PARK CITY
South Cove
Esplanade

4 5

Hudson River

Harbor

Battery Park, **2**
Brooklyn Bridge, **22**
Castle Clinton, **3**
City Hall, **18**
Criminal Courts Building, **25**
Ellis Island, **5**

Federal Hall National Memorial, **9**
Federal Reserve Bank, **12**
Fraunces Tavern, **8**
Municipal Building, **21**

National Museum of the American Indian, **6**
New York County Courthouse, **24**
New York Stock Exchange, **10**
St. Paul's Chapel, **16**

South Street Seaport Historic District, **15**
Staten Island Ferry, **1**
Statue of Liberty, **4**
Surrogate's Court, **20**
Trinity Church, **11**

Tweed Courthouse, **19**
U.S. Courthouse, **23**
Vietnam Veterans Memorial, **7**
Woolworth Building, **17**
World Financial Center, **14**

World Trade Center, **13**

longer riverside **Esplanade** that eventually will connect with Battery Park accompanies the residential part of Battery Park City.

This tour takes an entire day. Visit on a weekday to capture the district's true vitality—but expect to be jostled on the crowded sidewalks if you stand too long, peering at the great buildings that surge skyward on every corner. If you visit on a weekend, on the other hand, you'll feel like a lone explorer among a canyon of buildings. Either way, winds from the harbor whipping around the buildings can make this area feel markedly colder than other parts of the city, so dress accordingly. Start early, preferably making the first ferry, to try to beat the crowds to Liberty and Ellis islands. You should also get tickets by lunchtime if you plan to visit the Stock Exchange, though it's open until 4, weekdays only. The best place to end the day is anywhere overlooking the Hudson, for the sunset.

Sights to See

2 **Battery Park.** Jutting out as if it were Manhattan's green toe, this verdant landfill is loaded with monuments and sculpture. The park's name refers to a line of cannons once mounted here to defend the shoreline (which ran along what is currently State Street). Starting near the Staten Island ferry terminal, head north along the water's edge to the **East Coast Memorial,** a statue of a fierce eagle that presides over eight granite slabs inscribed with the names of U.S. servicemen who died in the Western Atlantic during World War II. Climb the steps of the East Coast Memorial for a fine view of the main features of **New York Harbor;** from left to right: **Governors Island,** a Coast Guard installation that is looking for a new tenant for 1998 and beyond, when the Coast Guard will leave it; hilly **Staten Island** in the distance; the **Statue of Liberty** on Liberty Island; **Ellis Island,** gateway to the New World for generations of immigrants; and the old railway terminal in **Liberty State Park,** on the mainland in Jersey City, New Jersey. On crystal-clear days, you can see all the way to Port Elizabeth's cranes, which seem to mimic the stance of Lady Liberty.

Continue north past a romantic **statue of Giovanni da Verrazano,** the Florentine merchant who piloted the ship that first sighted New York and its harbor in 1524. The **Verrazano-Narrows Bridge** between Brooklyn and Staten Island—so long that the curvature of the earth had to be figured into its dimensions—is visible from here, just beyond Governors Island.

Battery Park is also home to ☞ **Castle Clinton,** the takeoff point for ferries to the ☞ **Statue of Liberty** and ☞ **Ellis Island.**

Battery Park City. An impressive feat of urban planning, this complete 92-acre neighborhood was built from scratch on lower Manhattan landfill near the Hudson River. Its residential parts, a mix of high-rises, town houses, shops, and green squares, does a surprisingly good job of duplicating the rhythms of the rest of the city. Its commercial centerpiece is the ☞ **World Financial Center.**

Bowling Green. This oval greensward at the foot of Broadway became New York's first public park in 1733. On July 9, 1776, a few hours after citizens learned about the signing of the Declaration of Independence, rioters toppled a statue of British king George III that had occupied the spot for 11 years; much of the statue's lead was melted down into bullets. In 1783, when the occupying British forces fled the city, they defiantly hoisted a Union Jack on a greased, uncleated flagpole so it couldn't be lowered; patriot John Van Arsdale drove his own cleats into the pole to replace the flag with the Stars and Stripes. The entrance to the subway station here is original, built in 1904–05.

MUSEUM OF AMERICAN FINANCIAL HISTORY – On the site of Alexander Hamilton's law office (today the Standard Oil Building), this one-room museum displays artifacts of the financial markets' history, including a vintage ticker-tape machine. ⊠ *24 Broadway,* ☎ *212/908–4519.* ▦ *Free.* ⊙ *Weekdays 11:30–2:30 or by appointment.*

❸ Castle Clinton. In Battery Park, this circular brick fortress was first built as a defense for New York Harbor on an island 200 feet from shore. In 1824 it became Castle Garden, an entertainment and concert facility that reached its zenith in 1850 when more than 6,000 people (the capacity of Radio City Music Hall) attended the U.S. debut of the Swedish Nightingale, Jenny Lind. After landfill connected it to the city, Castle Clinton became, in succession, an immigrant processing center, an aquarium, and now a restored fort, museum, and ticket office for ferries to the ☞ **Statue of Liberty** and ☞ **Ellis Island.** The ferry ride is one loop; you can get off at Liberty Island, visit the statue, then reboard any ferry and continue on to Ellis Island, boarding another boat once you have finished exploring the historic immigration facility there.

Outside the landward entrance to Castle Clinton is a statue titled *The Emigrants,* at the beginning of a broad mall that leads back across the park to the Netherlands Memorial, a quaint flagpole depicting the bead exchange that bought from the Native Americans the land to establish Fort Amsterdam in 1626. Inscriptions describe the event in English and Dutch. ⊠ *Battery Park. Castle Clinton:* ☎ *212/269–5755.* ⊙ *Tours hourly 10:35–3:35 daily. Ferry information:* ☎ *212/269–5755;* ▦ *$7 (round-trip).* ⊙ *Departures every 45 min on weekdays and every 30 min on weekends 9:15, 10–3:30 (more departures and extended hrs in summer).*

❺ Ellis Island. Approximately 17 million men, women, and children entered the country at this federal immigration facility between 1892 and 1954—the ancestors of more than 40% of Americans living today. After a $140 million restoration, the center opened in September 1990 to record crowds. Now a national monument, the island's main building contains the **Ellis Island Immigration Museum,** with exhibits detailing not only the island's history but the whole history of immigration to America. Perhaps the most moving exhibit is the American Immigrant Wall of Honor, where the names of nearly 400,000 immigrant Americans are inscribed along an outdoor promenade overlooking the Statue of Liberty and the Manhattan skyline. The names include Miles Standish, Priscilla Alden, George Washington's grandfather, and Irving Berlin, and possibly an ancestor of yours. For ferry information, ☞ Castle Clinton, *above.* ☎ *212/363–3200; for Wall of Honor info,* ☎ *212/883–1986.* ▦ *Free.*

❾ Federal Hall National Memorial. On the steps of this Greek Revival building stands a regal statue of George Washington, who on that site—then also Federal Hall—was sworn in as the nation's first president in 1789. The likeness was made by noted sculptor and presidential relative John Quincy Adams Ward. After the capital moved to Philadelphia in 1790, the original Federal Hall became New York's City Hall, then was demolished in 1812 when the present City Hall (☞ The Seaport and the Courts, *below*) was completed. The clean and simple lines of the current structure, built as a U.S. Customs House in 1842, were modeled on the Parthenon, a potent symbol for a young nation striving to emulate classic Greek democracy. It's now a museum featuring exhibits on New York and Wall Street. Guided site tours are sometimes available on request, and you can also pick up brochures that lead you on differently themed self-guided walking tours of downtown. ⊠ *26 Wall St.,* ☎ *212/264–8711.* 🖾 *Free.* ☉ *Weekdays 9–5.*

⑫ Federal Reserve Bank. Gray, solid, imposing, and absolutely impregnable, this is how a bank should look. Built in 1935, this neo-Renaissance structure made of sandstone, limestone, and ironwork goes five levels underground. Vaults here reputedly contain a third of the world's gold reserves. ⊠ *33 Liberty St.,* ☎ *212/720–6130.* 🖾 *Free.* ☉ *1-hr tour by advance (at least 5 days) reservation, weekdays at 10:30, 11:30, 1:30, and 2:30.*

⑧ Fraunces Tavern. A museum, restaurant, and bar (☞ Chapter 6) comprise this historic five-building complex. The main building is a Colonial home (brick exterior, cream-colored marble portico and balcony) built in 1719 and converted to a tavern in 1762. It was the meeting place for the Sons of Liberty up until the Revolutionary War. This was also the site where, in 1783, George Washington delivered a farewell address to his officers celebrating the British evacuation of New York; later, the building housed some offices of the fledgling U.S. government. Today Fraunces Tavern contains two fully furnished period rooms and other displays of 18th- and 19th-century American history. The museum also offers family programs (such as a scavenger hunt), lectures, workshops, and concerts. ⊠ *54 Pearl St. at Broad St.,* ☎ *212/ 425–1778.* 🖾 *Museum: $2.50.* ☉ *Museum: Weekdays 10–4:45, Sat. noon–4.*

NEED A
BREAK?

The **brick plaza behind 85 Broad Street** is flanked by a variety of small restaurants. Order a take-out meal or snack and eat it out here on the benches, where you can watch busy office workers milling past and enjoy not being one of them.

Hanover Square. The East River once reached Pearl Street, and this quiet tree-lined plaza stood on the waterfront then. This was the city's original printing-house square; on the site of 81 Pearl Street, William Bradford established the first printing press in the colonies. The pirate Captain Kidd lived in the neighborhood, and the graceful brownstone **India House** (1837), a private club at No. 1, used to house the New York Cotton Exchange.

★ Hudson River Park. A landscaped oasis with playgrounds, promenades and walkways, handball and basketball courts, and grassy areas, this park on the river north of the World Financial Center is strewn with downtown residents soaking up rays on sunny days. *The Real World* sculpture garden at its north end, by Tom Otterness, playfully pokes fun at the area's capitalist ethos. The fairly new Stuyvesant High School building is also at this end of the park; on the far side of it begins the paved river promenade that extends to Gansevoort Street in the West Village. The promenade is full of skaters, joggers, and strollers at all hours, and the benches along the path are terrific spots from which to watch the sunset over New Jersey. You'll notice the small **Hudson River Sculpture Center** at Pier 25. These pieces are exhibited by local artists—unrepresented elsewhere—and are available for sale. For information about the sculptures, call Stephen Mann at 212/587–1030. The park is part of plans for a park to extend north to midtown, managed by the Hudson River Park Conservancy.

⑥ National Museum of the American Indian. Constructed in 1907 in the ornate Beaux Arts style fashionable at the time, the museum building originally functioned as the **Alexander Hamilton Custom House.** Above the base, the facade features massive columns rising to a pediment topped by a double row of statuary. Daniel Chester French, better known for the statue of Lincoln in the Lincoln Memorial in Washington, DC, sculpted the lower statues, which symbolize various continents (left to right: Asia, the Americas, Europe, Africa); the upper row represents the major trading cities of the world.

The national museum is the first of its kind to be dedicated to Native American culture, with well-mounted exhibits that examine the history and the current cultures of native peoples from all over the Americas through literature, dance, lectures, film, and crafts. The collections were largely amassed by George Gustav Heye, a wealthy New Yorker, and include pottery and basketry from the Southwestern United States, painted hides from the Plains Indians of North America, carved jade from the Mexican Olmec and Maya cultures, and contemporary Native American paintings. There are two souvenir shops. ⊠ *1 Bowling Green,* ☎ *212/668–6624.* 🎫 *Free.* 🕑 *Daily 10–5.*

⑩ New York Stock Exchange. The stock exchange nearly bursts from this little building, constructed before modern technology came to Wall Street. Compared with the Federal Hall memorial, this neoclassical building is much more elaborately decorated, as befitted the more grandiose national image of 1901, when it was designed. Inside, after what may be a lengthy wait, you can take an elevator to the third-floor visitor center. A self-guided tour, informative slide shows, video displays, and guides may help you interpret the seeming chaos you'll see from the visitors' gallery overlooking the immense (50-foot-high) trading hall. ⊠ *Tickets available at 20 Broad St.,* ☎ *212/656–5165.* 🎫 *Free tickets distributed beginning at 9:00; come before 1 PM to assure entrance.* 🕑 *Weekdays 9:15–4.*

Shrine of St. Elizabeth Ann Seton. The rectory of the shrine is a redbrick Federal-style town house with a distinctive wood portico shaped to fit the curving street. This house was built in 1793 as the home of the wealthy Watson family; Mother Seton and her family lived here from 1801 to 1803. She joined the Catholic Church in 1805, after the death of her husband, and went on to found the Sisters of Charity, the first American order of nuns. In 1975 she became the first American-born saint. Masses are held here daily. ⊠ *7–8 State St.*

❶ Staten Island Ferry. The best deal in town is right here. The 20- to 30-minute ride across New York Harbor provides great views of the Manhattan skyline, the Statue of Liberty, the Verrazano-Narrows Bridge, and the New Jersey coast—and it's free as long as you stay on the boat for the round trip (if you board in Staten Island you'll only be out 50¢). Boats embark on various schedules: every 15 minutes during rush hours, every 20–30 minutes most other times, and every hour after 11 PM and on weekend mornings. A word of advice, however: Although commuters love the ferry service's swift, new low-slung craft, the boats ride low in the water and have no outside deck space. Wait for one of the higher, more open old-timers. Once you're on Staten Island (☞ Chapter 3, *below*), you can, of course, stay as long as you like, though most tourists return immediately. ☎ *718/390–5253.*

★ ❹ Statue of Liberty. After arriving on Liberty Island (☞ Castle Clinton for ferry information, *above*), you have two ways to get from the ground-floor entrance to the monument: You can take an elevator 10 stories to the top of the 89-foot-high pedestal, or if you're strong of heart and limb, you can climb 354 steps (the equivalent of a 22-story building) to the crown. (Visitors cannot go up into the torch.) It usually takes two to three hours to walk up to the crown because of the wait beforehand. Erected in 1886 and refurbished for its centennial, the Statue of Liberty weighs 225 tons and stands 151 feet from her feet to her torch. Exhibits inside illustrate the statue's history, including videos of the view from the crown for those who don't make the climb. There is also a model of the statue's face for the blind to feel and a pleasant outdoor café. ⊠ *Liberty Island,* ☎ *212/363–3200 or 212/363–8340.* 🎫 *Free.*

⓫ Trinity Church. Established as an Anglican parish in 1697, the present structure (1846), by Richard Upjohn, ranked as the city's tallest building for most of the second half of the 19th century. Its three huge bronze doors were designed by Richard Morris Hunt to recall Lorenzo Ghiberti's doors for the Baptistery in Florence, Italy. After the exterior sandstone was restored in 1991, New Yorkers were amazed to discover that a church they had always thought of as black was actually a rosy pink. The church's Gothic Revival interior is surprisingly light and elegant. On the church's north side is a 2½-acre graveyard: Alexander Hamilton is buried beneath a white stone pyramid; and a monument commemorates Robert Fulton, the inventor of the steamboat (he's actually buried in the Livingstone family vault, with his wife).The church, which has many theater people in its congregation, does a popular dramatic midnight Mass at Christmas. ⊠ *Broadway and Wall St.*

❼ Vietnam Veterans Memorial. At this 14-foot-high, 70-foot-long, rectangular memorial (1985), moving passages from news despatches and the letters of servicemen and servicewomen have been etched into a wall of greenish glass set on a large brick plaza. ⊠ *On the bed of Coenties Slip, between Water and South Sts.*

Wall Street. The street is named after a wood wall built across the island in 1653 to defend the Dutch colony against the native Indians. Arguably the most famous thoroughfare in the world, though only a third of a mile long, Wall Street began its financial career with stock traders conducting business along the sidewalks or at tables beneath a sheltering buttonwood tree. Today it's a dizzyingly narrow canyon—look to the east and you'll glimpse a sliver of East River waterfront; look to the west and you'll see the spire of Trinity Church, tightly framed by skyscrapers at the head of the street.

To learn the difference between Ionic and Corinthian columns, look at the **Citibank Building** (⊠ 55 Wall St.). The lower stories were part of an earlier U.S. Customs House, built in 1836–42, and it was literally a bullish day on Wall Street when oxen hauled its 16 granite Ionic columns up to the site. When the National City Bank took over the building in 1899, they hired architects McKim, Mead & White to redesign the building, and in 1909 they added the second tier of columns but made them Corinthian.

⓮ World Financial Center. At this four-tower complex designed by Cesar Pelli, the heavy-duty corporate tenants include Merrill Lynch, American Express, and Dow Jones. You'll come out into the soaring **Winter Garden Atrium,** its mauve marble cascade of steps spilling down into a vaulted plaza with 16 giant palm trees, framed by a vast arched window overlooking the Hudson. This stunning space has become a popular venue for free performances by top-flight musicians and dancers. Surrounding the atrium are several upscale shops and a skylit food court.

The outdoor plaza right behind the atrium curls around a tidy little yacht basin; take in the view of the Statue of Liberty and read the stirring quotations worked into the iron railings. Just north of the basin is the terminal for **ferry service** to Hoboken, New Jersey (☎ 908/463–3779; 🎫 $2), on the other side of the Hudson River. It's an eight-minute ride to Frank Sinatra's hometown, with a spectacular view of lower Manhattan.

To the south, a longer riverside **Esplanade** that eventually will connect with Battery Park accompanies the residential part of Battery Park City. Especially noteworthy among the artwork populating the Esplanade are Ned Smyth's columned plaza with chessboards and the South Cove (a collaborative effort), a romantic curved stage set of wood piers and a steel-frame lookout. ⊠ *World Financial Center, West St., Battery Park City,* ☏ *212/945–0505.*

NEED A
BREAK?

While the World Financial Center courtyard also offers several full-service restaurants, for a quick bite head for **Minters** (☏ 212/945–
4455)—and be sure to leave room for great ice cream cones.

★ ⑬ **World Trade Center.** The only way to grasp just how big these build-ings are is to crane your neck and look straight up at them from the base. This 16-acre, 12-million-square-foot complex contains New York's two tallest buildings (1,350 feet high). To reach the **Top of the World** observation deck on the 107th floor of 2 World Trade Center, elevators glide a quarter of a mile into the sky—in only 58 seconds. The view potentially extends 55 miles, although signs at the ticket win-dow disclose how far you can see that day and whether the outdoor deck is open. In February 1993, the Center was the site of a bombing by terrorists that killed six people and caused extensive damage to the area. However, the Center has, for the most part, returned to normal operations, though security has been tightened considerably within the complex. ☏ *Observation Deck:* ☏ *212/323–2340.* ☑ *$6.* ☉ *June–Sept., daily 9:30 AM–11:30 PM; Oct.–May, daily 9:30 AM–9:30 PM.*

Some 50,000 people work in this seven-building complex, and at street level and underground it contains more than 60 stores, services, and restaurants, the adjacent New York Vista hotel (☞ Chapter 7), and a skating rink. There's a TKTS booth selling discount tickets to Broad-way and Off-Broadway shows (☞ Chapter 5) in the mezzanine of 2 World Trade Center (☉ Weekdays 11–5:30, Sat. 11–1), and on the ninth floor of 4 World Trade Center, a visitors' gallery overlooks the trading floor of the Commodities Exchange (☏ 212/748–1000. ☉ Week-days 9:30–3). ⊠ *Church to West Sts., Liberty to Vesey Sts.*

THE SEAPORT AND THE COURTS

New York's role as a great seaport is easiest to understand downtown, with both the Hudson River and East River waterfronts within walk-ing distance. While the deeper Hudson River came into its own in the steamship era, the more sheltered waters of the East River saw most of the action in the 19th century, during the age of clipper ships. This era is preserved in the South Street Seaport restoration, centered on Fulton Street between Water Street and the East River. Only a few blocks away, you can visit another seat of New York history: the City Hall neighborhood, which includes Manhattan's magisterial collection of court buildings.

A Good Walk

Numbers in the text correspond to numbers in the margin and on the Lower Manhattan map.

Begin at the intersection of Water and Fulton streets. The latter thor-oughfare was named after the ferry to Brooklyn that once docked at its foot (the ferry itself was named after its inventor, Robert Fulton), while Water Street was once the shoreline. On the 19th-century landfill across the street is the 11-block **South Street Seaport Historic District** ⑮, which was created in 1967 to preserve the area's heritage as a port and prevent it from being overtaken by skyscrapers. You could easily spend a few hours here, looking at the Seaport museum, boats, shops, and restaurants.

When you're ready to leave, return to Fulton Street and walk away from the river to Broadway, to **St. Paul's Chapel** ⑯, the oldest (1766) surviving church in Manhattan. Forking off to your right is **Park Row,** which was known as Newspaper Row from the mid-19th to early 20th century, when most of the city's 20 or so daily newspapers had offices there. In tribute to that past, a statue of Benjamin Franklin (who was, after all, a printer) stands in front of Pace University farther up on Park Row. Two blocks north on Broadway is the so-called Cathedral of Commerce, the ornate white terra-cotta **Woolworth Building** ⑰.

Between Broadway and Park Row is triangular **City Hall Park,** originally the town common, which gives way to a slew of government offices. **City Hall** ⑱, built between 1803 and 1812, is unexpectedly sedate, small-scale, and charming. Lurking directly behind it is the **Tweed Courthouse** ⑲, named after notorious politician "Boss" William Marcy Tweed, under whose corrupt management this building took millions and nine years to complete. East of the Tweed Courthouse is a space that's used as a **Farmers' Market** (Tues. Apr.–Dec. and Fri. year-round) and a Big Apple novelty that just might be worth the 25¢ it costs to get in—a **public toilet.** The design is subject to so many stipulations— the toilet cleans itself after every use, and people who stay too long need to be kicked out, for example—that so far this is the only one in the city that's in service. On the north side of Chambers Street directly across from the Tweed Courthouse is the **Surrogate's Court** ⑳, also called the **Hall of Records** (✉ 31 Chambers St.), which is one of the most ornate City Hall–area courts.

On the east side of Centre Street is the city government's first skyscraper, the **Municipal Building** ㉑, built in 1914 by McKim, Mead & White. Just south of the Municipal Building, a ramp curves up into the pedestrian walkway over the **Brooklyn Bridge** ㉒, definitely worth walking over for the views.

To see more courts, head north up Centre Street to **Foley Square,** a name that has become synonymous with the New York court system; the district attorneys on the TV series *Law and Order* frequently hold their on-screen colloquies in this vicinity. The **U.S. Courthouse** ㉓ at 40 Centre Street has marble steps climbing to a massive columned portico. With its stately columns, pediments, and 100-foot-wide flight of marble steps, the **New York County Courthouse** ㉔ has an impressive grandeur. Turn to look across Foley Square at **Federal Plaza,** which sprawls in front of the gridlike skyscraper of the **Javits Federal Building.** The black glass box to the left houses the **U.S. Court of International Trade.**

Continue north up Centre Street past neoclassical civic office buildings to 100 Centre Street, the **Criminal Courts Building** ㉕, a rather foreboding construction with Art Moderne details. In contrast, the **Civil and Municipal Courthouse** across the way at 111 Centre Street is an uninspired modern cube, although it, too, has held sensational trials. On the west side of this small square is the slick black-granite **Family Court** (✉ 60 Lafayette St.), with its intriguing angular facade.

Turn left onto Leonard Street, which runs just south of the Family Court, and take a look at the ornate Victorian building that runs the length of the block on your left. This is the old New York Life Insurance Company headquarters (✉ 346 Broadway), an 1870 building that was remodeled and enlarged in 1896 by McKim, Mead & White. The ornate clock tower facing Broadway is now occupied by the avant-garde **Clocktower Gallery,** which is currently used as rehearsal space by various artists and is therefore not open to the public.

TIMING

You can easily spend a half day at the Seaport, or longer if you browse in shops. The rest of the tour is just walking and takes about 1½ hours. The real Seaport opens well before the sun rises and clears out not much after, when fishmongers leave to make way for the tourists. Unless you're really interested in wholesale fish, however, you're best off visiting the Seaport when its other attractions are open. Try to do this during the week, so that the government offices will be open too.

Sights to See

★ ㉒ **Brooklyn Bridge.** Its Great Bridge promenade takes a half hour to walk and is a New York experience on a par with the Statue of Liberty trip or the Empire State Building ascent. Before this bridge was built, Brooklynites had to rely on the Fulton Street ferry to get to Brooklyn—a charming way to travel, surely, but unreliable in fog and ice. After some 50 years of talk about a bridge, John Augustus Roebling, a respected engineer, was handed a construction assignment in 1867. As the project to build the first steel suspension bridge slowly took shape over the next 15 years, it captured the imagination of the city; on its completion in 1883, it was called the Eighth Wonder of the World. Its twin Gothic-arched towers rise 268 feet from the river below. The roadway is supported by a web of steel cables, hung from the towers and attached to block-long anchorages on either shore. It is hardly the longest suspension bridge in the world anymore, but it remains a symbol of what man can accomplish. As you look south from the walkway, the pinnacles of downtown Manhattan loom on your right, Brooklyn Heights stands sentinel on your left, and before you yawns the harbor, with Lady Liberty showing herself in profile. Turn about for a fine view up the East River, spanned within sight by the Manhattan and Williamsburg bridges. You don't need binoculars to enjoy the vistas, but you'd do well to bring a hat or scarf, because the wind whips through the cables like a dervish.

⑱ **City Hall.** For a city as overwhelming as New York, this main government building, built between 1803 and 1812, is unexpectedly sedate, small-scale, and charming. Its exterior columns reflect the classical influence of Greece and Rome, and the handsome cast-iron cupola is crowned with a statue of Lady Justice. Originally its front and sides were clad in white marble while the back was faced in cheap brownstone, because the city fathers assumed New York would never grow farther north than this. (Limestone now covers all four sides.) The major interior feature is a domed rotunda from which a sweeping marble double staircase leads to the second-floor public rooms. The Victorian-style City Council Chamber in the east wing is small and clubby, with mahogany detailing and ornate gilding; the Board of Estimate chamber to the west has colonial paintings and church-pew-style seating; and the Governor's Room at the head of the stairs, used for ceremonial events, is filled with historic portraits and furniture, including a writing table that George Washington used in 1789 when New York was the U.S. capital. The blue room, which was traditionally the mayor's office, is on the ground floor; the room is now used for mayoral press conferences.

On either side of City Hall are free interactive video machines that dispense information/propaganda to both tourists and residents on area attractions, civic procedures, City Hall history, mass transit, and other topics. ⊠ *City Hall Park,* ☎ *212/788–6879 (tour info).*

City Hall Park. Originally the town common, in its day this green spot has hosted hangings, riots, and demonstrations; it is also the finish line for ticker-tape parades up lower Broadway (though ticker tape is nowadays replaced with perforated margin strips torn off from computer paper). A bronze statue of patriot Nathan Hale, who was hanged as a spy by the British troops occupying New York City, stands on the Broadway side of the park. ⊠ *Between Broadway and Park Row/Centre St., from Vesey St./Ann St. to Chambers St.*

㉕ Criminal Courts Building. This rather grim Art Deco tower may be familiar to fans of the television show *NYPD Blue,* connecting by a skywalk (New York's Bridge of Sighs) to the detention center known as "The Tombs." In *The Bonfire of the Vanities,* Tom Wolfe wrote a chilling description of this court's menacing atmosphere. ⊠ *100 Centre St.*

㉑ Municipal Building. Who else but the venerable architecture firm McKim, Mead, & White would the city government trust to build its first skyscraper in 1914? The roof section alone is 10 stories high, bristling with towers and peaks and topped by a gilt statue of Civic Fame. This is where New Yorkers come to pay parking fines and get marriage licenses. An immense arch straddles Chambers Street (traffic used to flow through here); the vaulted plaza in front was the site of a scene in the movie *Crocodile Dundee,* in which the Aussie hunter coolly scares off would-be muggers with his bowie knife. ⊠ *1 Centre St.*

㉔ New York County Courthouse. With its stately columns, pediments, and 100-foot-wide flight of marble steps, built in 1926, this structure set the precedent for neoclassical grandeur. It's actually more eccentric than it looks, having been built in a hexagonal shape to fit an irregular plot of land. That quintessential courtroom drama *Twelve Angry Men* was filmed here, as was the unpopular film *Legal Eagles.* The Courthouse also hosts thousands of marriages a year. ⊠ *Foley Sq.*

⑯ St. Paul's Chapel. The oldest (1766) surviving church in Manhattan, this was the site of the prayer service following George Washington's inauguration as president. Built of rough Manhattan brownstone, it was modeled on London's St. Martin-in-the-Fields. It's open until 3 every day except Saturday for prayer and meditation; look in the north aisle for Washington's pew. ⊠ *Broadway and Fulton St.*

★ ⑮ **South Street Seaport Historic District.** Had it not been declared a historic district in 1967, this charming, cobblestone corner of the city would likely have been gobbled up by skyscrapers. The Rouse Corporation, which had already created slick so-called "festival marketplaces" in Boston (Quincy Market) and Baltimore (Harborplace), was hired to restore and adapt the existing historic buildings, preserving the commercial feel of centuries past.

The little white lighthouse at Water and Fulton streets is the **Titanic Memorial,** commemorating the sinking of the RMS *Titanic* in 1912. Beyond it, Fulton Street, cobbled in blocks of Belgian granite, is a pedestrian mall that swarms with visitors, especially on fine-weather weekends. Immediately to your left is the **Cannon's Walk Block,** which contains 15 restored buildings.

At 211 Water Street is **Bowne & Co.,** a reconstructed working 19th-century print shop. Around the corner, a narrow court called Cannon's Walk, lined with shops, opens onto Fulton Street; follow it around to Front Street. Directly across Front Street is the **Fulton Market Building,** a modern building, full of shops and restaurants, that re-creates the bustling atmosphere of the old victual markets that occupied this site from 1822 on. On the south side of Fulton Street is the seaport's architectural centerpiece, **Schermerhorn Row,** a redbrick terrace of Georgian- and Federal-style warehouses and countinghouses built in 1811–12. Today the ground floors are occupied by upscale shops, bars, and restaurants, and the **South Street Seaport Museum.** ⊠ *12 Fulton St.,* ☎ *212/669–9400; 212/732–7678 for events and shopping information.* ⊡ *$6 (to ships, galleries, walking tours, Maritime Crafts Center, films, and other seaport events).* ⊙ *Daily 10–5.*

Cross South Street under an elevated stretch of the FDR Drive to **Pier 16,** where the historic ships are docked, including the *Peking,* the second-largest sailing ship in existence; the full-rigged *Wavertree;* and the lightship *Ambrose.* The Pier 16 ticket booth provides information and sells tickets to the museum, the ships, tours, and exhibits. Pier 16 also hosts frequent concerts and performances and is the departure point for the one-hour **Seaport Liberty Cruise.** ☎ *212/630–8888.* ⊡ *$12 (fare); $15 (combination fares for cruise and other attractions).* ⊙ *Runs late Mar.–Nov.*

To the north is **Pier 17,** a multilevel dockside shopping mall. Its weathered-wood rear decks make a splendid spot from which to sit and contemplate the river; look north to see the Brooklyn, Manhattan, and Williamsburg bridges, and look across to see Brooklyn Heights.

As your nose may already have surmised, the blocks along South Street north of the museum complex still house a working fish market, which has been in operation since the 1770s. Although the city has tried to relocate the hundreds of fishmongers of the **Fulton Fish Market** to the South Bronx, the area remains a beehive of activity. Get up early (or stay up late) if you want to see it: The action begins around midnight and ends by 8 AM. *Tours by reservation only,* ☎ *212/748–8590.* ⊡ *$10.* ⊙ *1st and 3rd Thurs. every month Apr.–Oct. at 6 AM.*

NEED A BREAK? | If you're hungry, head for the fast-food stalls on Pier 17's third-floor **Promenade Food Court.** The cuisine is nonchain eclectic: Seaport Fries, Pizza on the Pier, Wok & Roll, the Simply Seafood, and the Salad Experience. What's really spectacular is the view from the tables in a glass-walled atrium.

㉑ Surrogate's Court. Also called the **Hall of Records,** this building is the most ornate of the City Hall court trio. In true Beaux Arts fashion, sculpture and ornament seem to have been added wherever possible to the basic neoclassical structure, yet the overall effect is graceful rather than cluttered. Filmmakers sometimes use its ornate lobby in opera scenes. A courtroom here was the venue for *Johnson v. Johnson,* where the heirs to the Johnson & Johnson fortune waged their bitter battle. ⊠ *31 Chambers St.*

㉒ Tweed Courthouse. Under the corrupt management of notorious politician "Boss" William Marcy Tweed, this building took some $12 million and nine years to build (it was finally finished in 1872, but the ensuing public outrage drove Tweed from office). Although it is imposing, with its columned classical pediment outside and seven-story rotunda inside, almost none of the boatloads of marble that Tweed had shipped from Europe made their way into this building. Today it houses municipal offices; it has also served as a location for several films, most notably *The Verdict.* ⊠ *52 Chambers St.*

㉓ U.S. Courthouse. Cass Gilbert built this in 1936, convinced that it complemented the neighboring Woolworth Building, which he had built earlier. Marble steps climb to a massive columned portico; above this rises a 32-story tower topped by a gilded pyramid, not unlike that with which Gilbert crowned the New York Life building uptown. This courthouse has been the site of such famous cases as the tax-evasion trial of hotel queen Leona Helmsley. ⊠ *26 Foley Sq.*

★ ⑰ **Woolworth Building.** Called the Cathedral of Commerce, this ornate white terra-cotta was, at 792 feet, the world's tallest building when it opened in 1913; it still houses the Woolworth corporate offices. Take a peek at the **lobby:** Among its extravagant Gothic-style details are sculptures set into arches in the lobby ceiling; one of them represents an elderly F. W. Woolworth pinching his pennies, while another depicts the architect, Cass Gilbert, cradling in his arms a model of his creation. ⊠ *Park Pl. and Broadway.*

3 Exploring the Other Boroughs

Many of New York's treasures await visitors who venture to the outer boroughs. The Bronx has a world-renowned zoo and a beautiful botanical garden. In Brooklyn you can relax in verdant Prospect Park and take in the wonderful river views of the Brooklyn Heights Promenade. Queens has the artists' enclave of Long Island City and the lively Greek neighborhood, Astoria. And if you take the pleasant ferry ride to Staten Island, you can visit historic Richmondtown.

MANY VISITORS TO MANHATTAN notice the four outer boroughs—Brooklyn, Queens, the Bronx, and Staten Island—only from a Circle Line cruise, leaving those areas to remain ciphers. *"Don't fall asleep on the subway,"* the unschooled tourist tells himself, *"or you may end up in the Bronx!"*

Revised by
Amy
McConnell

Manhattanites themselves, many driven over the river by astronomical rents, discovered the outer boroughs some years back. They found sky, trees, and living space among the 19th-century brownstones, and converted industrial lofts, Art Deco apartment palaces, and tidy bungalows. They also found fascinating ethnic enclaves and a host of museums and parks.

The reality is that Manhattan is only a small part of New York City. Its population of about 1.5 million is smaller than that of either Brooklyn (2.3 million) or Queens (2 million), and only slightly larger than that of the Bronx (1.2 million). Staten Island may be less populous (391,000), but it's 2½ times the size of Manhattan.

There are things to see and do in the outer boroughs that you simply won't find in Manhattan, and most are just a subway ride away from midtown. Manhattanites may try to put you off such a journey, but don't be daunted. After a couple of beers, those same people may rave about their favorite place for cheesecake (Junior's on Flatbush Avenue in Brooklyn), or a great outdoor barbecue they had at their sister-in-law's mock-Tudor brick house (in Forest Hills Gardens, Queens); you may even have to listen to a story about their life's peak experience—found in the bleachers of Yankee Stadium in . . . the Bronx.

THE BRONX

The only borough attached to the North American mainland, the Bronx was first settled by Dutch, French, English, and Swedish country squires, who established manorial holdings there while fighting off Native Americans. Little now remains from the Colonial era, but the area does dramatically illustrate another aspect of New York City history—the influx of immigrant groups from the 1840s onward: first the Irish, then the Germans, Italians, and Jews. Later waves included African-Americans, Greeks, Hispanics, Russians, Albanians, Koreans, and Cambodians.

In the 1920s the Bronx experienced a short-lived golden age. The building of the elevated subway line attracted an upwardly mobile population of average but improving means; Yankee Stadium was built; and the mile-long Grand Concourse was fashioned as New York's Champs Élysées, lined with elaborate Art Deco buildings.

Those days are history. Today crime and urban decay are the words most often associated with the Bronx. Certain areas, such as the South Bronx, have long been considered unsafe—especially for unfamiliar visitors—even though recent neighborhood improvement efforts by various community development groups are starting to pay off.

Fordham and the Bronx Zoo

Now a busy urban center with a major university, several major tourist attractions, and nonstop street activity, this neighborhood in the northwestern Bronx used to be a sleepy village. It was settled by the Dutch

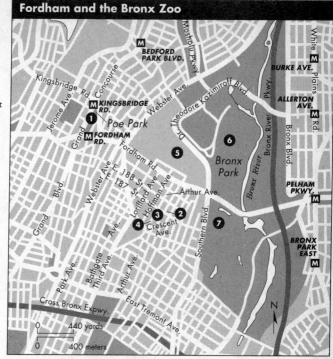

Fordham and the Bronx Zoo

in the 17th century and was later favored by writer Edgar Allan Poe for its fresh country air.

A Good Walk

Numbers in the text correspond to numbers in the margin and on the Fordham and the Bronx Zoo map.

Take the D or C subway to Kingsbridge Road, where you'll find a fine stretch of the **Grand Concourse,** once called the Bronx Champs Élysées. Alternatively, take the Metro North to Fordham Road and start the tour just past the **Edgar Allan Poe Cottage** ①, situated in the small Poe Park, at East Kingsbridge Road and the Grand Concourse. This is where Poe spent the final years of his life.

A couple blocks south of the bottom of Poe Park, at the intersection of Fordham Road and the Grand Concourse, is chaotic Fordham Plaza, nicknamed the Times Square of the Bronx. Walk one block farther south on the Grand Concourse and turn west on East 188th Street to peek at the **Creston Avenue Baptist Church** (⊠ 114 E. 188th St.), built in 1905 and looking as if it belongs in a rural town in England rather than amid the commercial chaos of Fordham Road.

From Fordham Plaza, the Bx 12 bus will take you east along Fordham Road to Arthur Avenue and **Belmont.** If you prefer the easy walk, you'll pass myriad coffee shops and discount stores, the Metro North train's Fordham stop, 1 Fordham Plaza (a modern green-and-white birthday-cake-like construction), the looming Theodore Roosevelt High School, and an enormous library construction site next to the Metro North station. Fordham University broke ground here in 1994 for a new campus library, scheduled for completion in 1997.

Centering around the intersection of Arthur Avenue and East 187th Street, Belmont feels like an old New York neighborhood. On East 187th

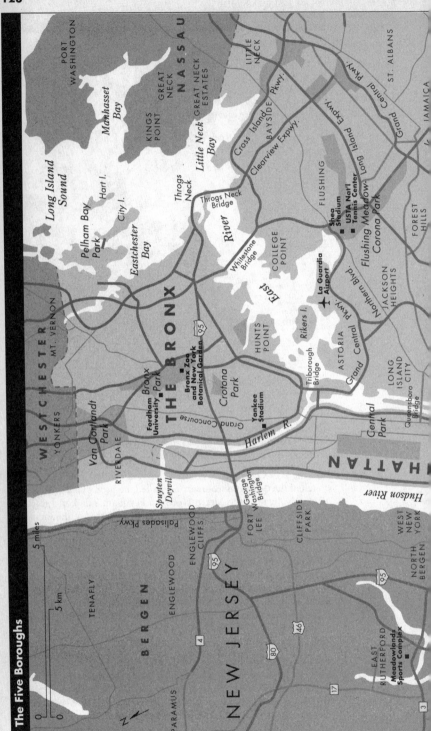

The Five Boroughs

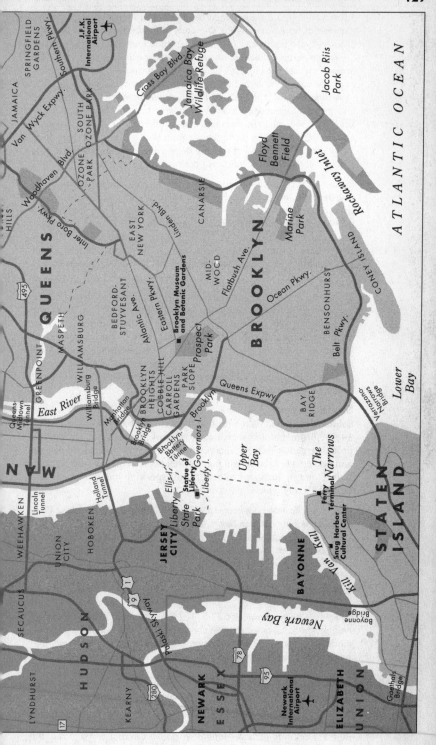

J.F.K.
International
Airport

SPRINGFIELD
GARDENS

Southern Pkwy.

JAMAICA

Van Wyck Expwy.

Cross Bay Blvd.

Jamaica Bay
Wildlife Refuge

ATLANTIC OCEAN

Jacob Riis
Park

SOUTH
OZONE PARK

OZONE
PARK

Woodhaven Blvd.

Inter Boro Pkwy.

Floyd
Bennett
Field

Rockaway Inlet

Rockaway

QUEENS

I-495

GREENPOINT

MASPETH

WILLIAMSBURG

EAST
NEW YORK

Linden Blvd.

BEDFORD-
STUYVESANT

Atlantic Ave.

Eastern Pkwy.

CANARSIE

Marine
Park

MID-
WOOD

Flatbush Ave.

Ocean Pkwy.

BENSONHURST

Belt Pkwy.

CONEY ISLAND

Queens-
Midtown
Tunnel

East River

Williamsburg
Bridge

Manhattan
Bridge

BROOKLYN
HEIGHTS

COBBLE
HILL

CARROLL
GARDENS

Brooklyn Museum
and Botanic Gardens

Prospect
Park

PARK
SLOPE

BROOKLYN

Queens Expwy

BAY
RIDGE

Lower
Bay

Verrazano
Narrows
Bridge

N E W

Lincoln
Tunnel

WEEHAWKEN

Holland
Tunnel

HOBOKEN

Brooklyn
Bridge

Brooklyn-
Battery
Tunnel

Ellis I.

Statue of
Liberty

Liberty
State
Park

Governors I.

Liberty I.

Upper
Bay

The
Narrows

Ferry
Terminal

Snug Harbor
Cultural Center

STATEN
ISLAND

SECAUCUS

UNION
CITY

JERSEY
CITY

Pulaski Skway

9

11

HUDSON

LYNDHURST

KEARNY

17

280

NEWARK

ESSEX

78

95

Newark
International
Airport

ELIZABETH

UNION

BAYONNE

Kill Van Kull

Newark Bay

Bayonne
Bridge

Goethals
Bridge

Street you'll find family-owned food stores, a luncheonette, and the community house of worship, **Our Lady of Mt. Carmel Roman Catholic Church** ②. On the corner of Hughes Avenue and East 186th Street is the **Enrico Fermi Cultural Center/Belmont Branch New York Public Library** ③, where the Heritage Collection contains several volumes outlining the contributions of Italians and Italian-Americans. Continue back to **Arthur Avenue,** the belly of Belmont, where every kind of Italian gourmet food specialty is available. At the Arthur Avenue Retail Market (No. 2344), a skylit shopping mart with 70 stalls, Italian sausages and cheeses hang from on high and mounds of fresh fruit and produce weigh down the tables. For the true Belmont experience, **Dominick's** ④, a family-style Italian restaurant on Arthur Avenue, is a must.

Return to Fordham Road to explore the 85-acre campus of **Fordham University** ⑤, with its Gothic-style buildings and cathedral whose church was immortalized by Poe. The university's main entrance faces the **New York Botanical Garden** ⑥, one of the world's most important botanical research centers and a delight at any time of year. Also in Bronx Park is the 265-acre **Bronx Zoo** ⑦, the nation's largest urban zoo, recently renamed the **International Wildlife Conservation Park.**

TIMING

To see the Bronx Zoo and the New York Botanical Garden in depth, you may want to visit each one for two to three hours on a separate trip. Alternatively, you might combine one of these destinations with a visit to Fordham and Belmont. If you choose to do the latter, set aside an entire day. Saturday is the best day to see Belmont; on Sunday most stores are closed. The zoo and the botanical gardens are less crowded on weekdays—except Wednesdays, when admission to both is free and crowds rush to snatch up the bargain.

Sights to See

Belmont. Often called the Little Italy of the Bronx, this is where some 14,500 Bronx families socialize, shop, work, and eat, eat, eat. On Saturday afternoons, as residents rush around buying freshly baked bread and homemade salami, you may as well be in a small market town in Italy. Don't be surprised to hear people speaking Italian in the neighborhood's tidy streets.

On Arthur Avenue, between 188th and 187th streets, **Ciccarone Playground** has a huge Italian flag painted on a backboard. East 187th Street is the place to pick up Italian provisions. On one stellar block between Hughes and Belmont avenues you'll find **Danny's Pork Store** (✉ 626 E. 187th St.); the **Catholic Goods Center** (✉ 630 E. 187th St.), which sells Italian greeting cards and religious art; and **Borgatti's Ravioli & Egg Noodles** (✉ 632 E. 187th St.).

NEED A
BREAK?

At **Egidio's Pastry Shop** (✉ 622 E. 187th St., ☎ 718/295–6077), the neighborhood favorite, you can choose from 55 different kinds of handmade Italian pastries, washed down with a strong shot of espresso. The homemade gelatos are top-notch.

★ ㋡ ❼ **Bronx Zoo.** Opened in 1899, this zoo is one of the nation's largest, with 265 acres and more than 4,000 animals representing more than 600 species. Always in the vanguard, the Bronx Zoo was one of the first zoos to use naturalistic, parklike settings instead of caged enclosures. Witness exhibits such as "Jungle World," an indoor tropical rain forest complete with five waterfalls, millipedes, flowering orchids, and pythons; "Wild Asia," where tigers and elephants roam free on nearly 40 acres of open meadows and dark forests; and "World of Birds," a huge glassed-in aviary where birds cozy up to visitors. Three different rides, including a shuttle bus, a monorail, and a tram, offer various perspectives of the grounds.

The **Children's Zoo** has many hands-on learning activities, as well as a large petting zoo. At the **Zoo Center,** visitors will find a rare black rhino.

To get to the Bronx Zoo, take the No. 2 subway to Pelham Parkway and walk three blocks west to the zoo; or take the Liberty Line Bx M 11 express bus from mid-Manhattan. Call 718/652–8400 for schedule and fares. ⊠ *Bronx Park, S of E. Fordham Rd.,* ☎ *718/367–1010.* *Thurs.–Tues. $6.75; free Wed.* ☉ *Mar.–Oct., weekdays 10–5, weekends and holidays 10–5:30; Nov.–Feb., daily 10–4:30. Children's Zoo:* *$2;* ☉ *Apr.–Oct.*

❹ **Dominick's.** There are no menus and no wine lists at this wildly popular family-style restaurant, where the question "What do you have?" is most often answered with "What do you want?" What you'll want is a heaping dish of traditional spaghetti with meatballs—some of the best you'll find in New York City—along with crusty bread and wine poured from a jug. The same family has been cooking at Dominick's for 30 years, serving their loyal fans at congested communal tables with red-and-white checked cloths. Expect to pay about $50 for two people. ⊠ *2335 Arthur Ave.,* ☎ *718/733–2807. Closed Tues.*

❶ **Edgar Allan Poe Cottage.** It was here that Poe and his sickly wife, Virginia, sought refuge from Manhattan and from the vicissitudes of the writerly life between 1846 and 1849. He wandered the countryside on foot and listened to the sound of the church bells at nearby St. John's College Church (now Fordham University); word has it that these bells inspired one of his most famous poems, "The Bells." The cottage, maintained by the Bronx Historical Society, is in the middle of a small patch of green called Poe Park. ⊠ *E. Kingsbridge Rd. and the Grand Concourse,* ☎ *718/881–8900.* *$2.* ☉ *Sat. 10–4, Sun. 1–5. Closed Jan.*

❸ **Enrico Fermi Cultural Center/Belmont Branch New York Public Library.** Housed within the Belmont branch of the New York Public Library is this cultural center with the Italian Heritage Collection, for researching everything from Italy's immigrants to art to opera and food. The library also has a large supply of circulating Italian-language books (including books for children) and videos. ⊠ *610 E. 186th St. at Hughes St.,* ☎ *718/933–6410.* ☉ *Mon. 1–6, Tues. noon–8, Wed.–Thurs. 10–6, Fri. 1–6, Sat. 10–5. Closed Sun.*

❺ **Fordham University.** A small enclave of distinguished Collegiate Gothic architecture in the midst of urban sprawl, this university opened in 1841 as a Jesuit college. Fordham now has an undergraduate enrollment of 6,800 and an auxiliary campus near Lincoln Center. Enter the grounds via Bathgate Avenue, three blocks west of Arthur Avenue (the security guard may require you to show ID), to see **Old Rose Hill Manor Dig,** the **University Church,** whose stained glass was donated by King Louis Philippe of France (1773–1850), the pleasant **Edward's Parade** quadrangle in the center of campus, and **Keating Hall,** sitting like a Gothic fortress in the center of things. Maps are posted around the campus or are available in the security office on your left inside the gate.

Grand Concourse. Like a semaphore of Bronx history, this major thoroughfare has reflected the social and economic changes in central Bronx ever since it was built at the turn of the century. Back then the 4-mile-long, 11-lane-wide concourse was a parade route of sorts, the axis of the then-thriving shopping and entertainment district, and the site of many elegant apartment buildings belonging to the wealthiest residents of the Bronx. Today the concourse is home to a completely different crowd of mostly non-English-speaking residents, and its striking Art Deco buildings are in sad disrepair.

★ ❻ **New York Botanical Garden.** Considered one of the leading botany centers of the world, this 250-acre botanical garden built around the dramatic gorge of the Bronx River is one of the best reasons to make a trip to the Bronx. The garden was founded by Dr. Nathaniel Lord Britton and his wife, Elizabeth. After visiting England's Kew Gardens in 1889, they returned full of fervor to create a similar haven in New York. In 1991 the New York Botanical Garden celebrated its centennial.

On the botanical garden grounds is the historic **Lorillard Snuff Mill,** built by two French Huguenot manufacturers in 1840 to power the grinding of tobacco for snuff. Nearby, the Lorillards grew roses to supply fragrance for their blend.

A walk along the Bronx River from the mill leads the visitor to the garden's 40-acre **Forest,** the largest remnant of the forest that once covered New York City. Outdoor plant collections include the **Peggy Rockefeller Rose Garden,** with 230 different kinds of roses. The luminous **Enid A. Haupt Conservatory** (scheduled to reopen in mid-April 1997) displays ferns, tropical flora, and Old and New World deserts. At the **Museum Building** there's a gardening shop, a library, and a world-renowned herbarium holding 5.7 million dried plant specimens.

To get to the Botanical Garden, take the Metro North train to the Garden from Grand Central Terminal; or take the D or No. 4 subway to the Bedford Park Boulevard stop and walk eight blocks west to the entrance on Bedford Park Boulevard. ✉ *Bronx Park, 200th St. and Southern Blvd.,* ☎ *718/817–8705.* ✐ *$3; free Sat. 10–noon and Wed. Parking: $4.* ⊗ *Nov.–Mar., Tues.–Sun., and holidays on Mon. 10–4; Apr.–Oct., Tues.–Sun., and Mon. holidays 10–6.*

❷ **Our Lady of Mt. Carmel Roman Catholic Church.** Rising like a beacon of faith above all the neighboring food stores and restaurants, this is the spiritual center of Belmont. Built in 1907, it is an imposing brick structure with columned arches and four jutting flagpoles; inside, amid the marble columns and the intricate stained-glass windows, you're sure to find a number of local devotees at prayer. ✉ *627 E. 187th St.*

BROOKLYN

New York City's most populous borough is also its most popular—aside from Manhattan, that is. More people visit Brooklyn than any of the other outer boroughs; and several Brooklyn neighborhoods, particularly Brooklyn Heights, Park Slope, Cobble Hill, and Carroll Gardens, are consistently desirable as places to live, with dignified brownstones, water views, lush urban parks, and a friendly atmosphere.

Brooklyn Heights, Cobble Hill, and Carroll Gardens

"All the advantages of the country, with most of the conveniences of the city." So ran the ads for a real-estate development that sprang up in the 1820s just across the East River from downtown Manhattan. Brooklyn Heights—named for its enviable hilltop position—was New York's first suburb, linked to the city first by ferry and later by the Brooklyn Bridge. Feverish construction quickly transformed the airy heights into a fashionable upper-middle-class community. Happily, some 600 buildings more than 100 years old remain intact today, making Brooklyn Heights a kind of picture book of 19th-century American architecture.

In the 1940s and 1950s, the neighborhood was said to be home to the city's largest number of writers outside Greenwich Village, among them Carson McCullers, W. H. Auden, Arthur Miller, and Truman Capote. Given the neighborhood's peaceful yet convenient setting, it's not hard to imagine why they came.

Cranberry and Pineapple are just two of the unusual street names around here. Word has it that these names were created by a certain Miss Sarah Middagh, who despised the practice of naming streets for the town fathers and instead named them after various fruits.

A few miles south of Brooklyn Heights, Cobble Hill is a peaceful residential area of leafy streets lined with notable town houses of varying architectural styles. The neighborhood is popular with young families, and on most days you can see an assortment of people pushing strollers, walking dogs, or returning home with grocery-laden bags. Still farther south is the largely Italian neighborhood of Carroll Gardens, an area distinguished by unusually deep blocks that allow for front yards that are unusually large, at least by New York standards.

A Good Walk

Numbers in the text correspond to numbers in the margin and on the Brooklyn Heights, Cobble Hill, and Carroll Gardens map.

Take the No. 2 or 3 subway from Manhattan to Clark Street, or the No. 6 subway to Borough Hall and walk up Court Street to Clark Street. From Clark, turn left on Henry Street toward Pineapple Street. From here you'll be able to see the blue towers of the Manhattan Bridge linking Brooklyn to Manhattan; you'll have a view of the Brooklyn Bridge itself in a few minutes.

Turn left onto Orange Street. On the north side of the block (the right-hand side of the street) between Henry and Hicks streets is a formidable institution: the **Plymouth Church of the Pilgrims** ①, the vortex of abolitionist sentiment in the years before the Civil War. Turn right on Hicks Street and follow it to Middagh Street (pronounced *mid*-awe). At its intersection with Willow is **24 Middagh Street** ②, the oldest home in the neighborhood. Venture a few steps west on Middagh to watch neighborhood children and their parents playing at the pleasant **Harry Chapin Playground,** named after the late singer-songwriter.

Backtrack on Willow Street, noting the outstanding architecture between Clark and Pierrepont streets. As you turn right on Pierrepont heading toward the river, glance down Columbia Heights to your right, where the brownstones are particularly elegant.

Pierrepont Street ends at the **Brooklyn Heights Promenade** ③, one of the most famous vista points in all of New York City. This is a great place for a picnic, with provisions from the exotic food stores on nearby Atlantic Avenue; try Sahadi Importing (✉ 187–189 Atlantic Ave., ☎ 718/624–4550) in particular. As you leave the Promenade (via Montague Street), look left to see **Nos. 2** and **3 Pierrepont Place,** two brownstone palaces built in the 1850s by a China trader and philanthropist, and used as a location for John Huston's film *Prizzi's Honor.* On your right lies **Montague Terrace,** where Thomas Wolfe lived when he finished *You Can't Go Home Again.*

After you've soaked in the views from the Promenade, leave it via yuppified Montague Street, heading east past restaurants of every ethnicity. At the northeast corner of Montague and Clinton streets is the **Church of St. Anne and the Holy Trinity** ④, known for its historic stained-glass windows and performing-arts center.

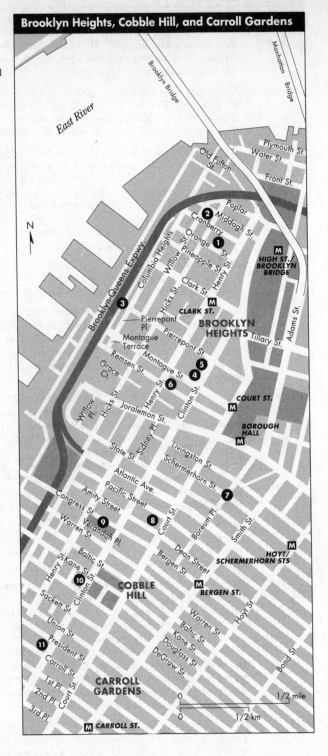

Brooklyn Heights, Cobble Hill, and Carroll Gardens

Beyond Clinton on the north side of Montague Street, note an interesting row of banks: **Chemical** (⊠ 177 Montague St.), a copy of the Palazzo della Gran Guardia in Verona, Italy; a **Citibank** (⊠ 181 Montague St.) that looks like a latter-day Roman temple; and the Art Deco **Municipal Credit Union** (⊠ 185 Montague St.). A block north of Montague, at the corner of Clinton and Pierrepont streets, the **Brooklyn Historical Society** ⑤ has a gallery full of Brooklyn memorabilia and a richly decorated and well-stocked research library.

Return south along Clinton Street, then turn right onto Remsen Street. At the corner of Remsen and Henry streets, stop to take in the Romanesque Revival **Our Lady of Lebanon Maronite Church** ⑥. If you want to see more of Brooklyn Heights, walk west on Rensen Street and then turn left onto Hicks Street to visit the Gothic Revival **Grace Church** at No. 254. Across Hicks Street is **Grace Court Alley,** a traditional mews with a score of beautifully restored carriage houses, where the stables used to be.

From Clinton Street, two blocks south of Remsen Street, turn right and stroll down **Joralemon Street,** noting Nos. 29–75, a row of Greek Revival brownstones that delicately sidestep their way down the hill toward the river and the piers. Follow **Willow Place** south along the peaceful block between Joralemon and State streets; in late afternoon, the houses take on the soft oranges and yellows of a faded quilt.

At the end of Willow Place, turn left on State Street and follow it past Hicks and Henry streets back to Clinton. If you're so inclined, turn left on Schermerhorn Street to visit the **New York City Transit Museum** ⑦. Otherwise continue down Clinton to Atlantic Avenue, a busy thoroughfare crowded with Middle Eastern restaurants and downscale antiques shops.

Atlantic Avenue is the official dividing line between the neighborhoods of Brooklyn Heights and **Cobble Hill.** For a taste of the latter, go two blocks south down Clinton Street to Amity. You may want to turn left to **197 Amity Street** ⑧, where Jennie Jerome, the mother of Winston Churchill, was born in 1854.

Return to Clinton and go one more block south, where on the west side of the street you'll find **Cobble Hill Park** ⑨, bordered by **Verandah Place,** a charming row of converted stable buildings where Thomas Wolfe once lived. Proceed south down Clinton Street to observe block after block of distinguished row houses, ranging from Romanesque Revival to neoclassical to Italianate brownstone. Three blocks south of the park, at 320 Clinton Street, is the Episcopal **Christ Church** ⑩ designed by Richard Upjohn.

About four blocks farther down Clinton, toward President Street, Cobble Hill gives way to the largely Italian **Carroll Gardens.** Wander down President, Carroll, 1st, and 2nd places to see the lovingly tended gardens; notice the abundance of religious statuary that attests to the largely Catholic makeup of the neighborhood.

Before leaving Clinton Street, stop for a look at the **Guido Funeral Home** ⑪ (on the northwest corner of Carroll and Clinton streets), possibly the finest example of a Greek Revival town house in the city. Then head left (east) on Carroll Street to **Court Street,** the main commercial thoroughfare of the neighborhood. Two blocks away at the corner of Sackett and Henry streets is the **Cammareri Brothers Bakery** (☎ 718/852–3606), where Nicolas Cage worked in the 1987 film *Moonstruck.*

If you have the stamina to continue on to the Park Slope tour, take the F train farther into Brooklyn to the 7th Avenue stop. You can also return to Manhattan on the F train. The subway station is at the intersection of Carroll and Smith streets.

TIMING

Allow three to four hours for a leisurely tour of these three neighborhoods, more if you plan on stopping for a picnic along the Promenade or along Montague Street for a meal. Try to come on a clear, sunny day, when the view from the Promenade is most spectacular.

Sights to See

★ ❸ **Brooklyn Heights Promenade.** Pierrepont Street ends at this ⅓-mile-long sliver of park, which hangs over the ferry district like one of Babylon's fabled gardens. Cantilevered over two lanes of the Brooklyn–Queens Expressway and a service road, the esplanade has benches offering views of the Manhattan skyline. Circling gulls squawk, tugboats honk, and the city seems like a vision from another planet. This is a terrific vantage point from which to admire the Brooklyn Bridge, the historic steel suspension bridge designed by John Augustus Roebling and completed in 1883 (☞ The Seaport and the Courts *in* Chapter 2). The small island to your left is Governors Island, a military installation.

❺ **Brooklyn Historical Society.** The 1989 Shellens Gallery housed inside this historical society has an eclectic collection that includes Brooklyn Dodgers' bats and balls, trick mirrors from Coney Island, and a 300-pound cast-zinc eagle saved from the offices of the *Brooklyn Eagle*. The society's library, with its rich carved bookcases and lustrous stained-glass windows, is a showcase of late-19th-century interior design; it also holds 33,000 Brooklyn photographs and 155,000 books. ✉ *128 Pierrepont St.,* ☎ *718/624–0890.* ⌨ *Library: research fee $5;* ☉ *Tues.–Sat. noon–4:45.* ⌨ *Gallery: $2.50; Wed. free;* ☉ *Tues.–Sat. noon–5.*

❿ **Christ Church.** This sandstone Episcopal church was designed by the prolific architect Richard Upjohn, who lived nearby at 296 Clinton Street. The pulpit, lectern, and altar are the work of Louis Comfort Tiffany. The setting, on a tree-embowered patch of green enclosed by a wrought-iron fence, has the tranquil air of an English churchyard. ✉ *320 Clinton St. at Kane St.*

❹ **Church of St. Ann and the Holy Trinity.** The stained-glass windows of this church, currently under restoration, were the first ever made in the United States. In 1980 the church created its own performing-arts center, "Arts at St. Ann's," referred to in *Rolling Stone* as "New York's hippest hall," and frequented by downtown Manhattan types. ✉ *157 Montague St. at Clinton St.,* ☎ *718/858–2424.* ☉ *Box office: Tues.–Sat. noon–6.*

☾ ❾ **Cobble Hill Park.** This small green oasis has a playground at one end. Bordering the park's south side is **Verandah Place**, a charming row of converted stable buildings where Thomas Wolfe once lived. ✉ *Congress St., between Clinton and Henry Sts.*

NEED A
BREAK?

Between Court and Clinton streets on Atlantic Avenue are a half-dozen Middle Eastern gourmet markets and eateries. The best of these is **Sahadi Importing** (✉ 187–189 Atlantic Ave., ☎ 718/624–4550), where serious cooks stock up on astonishingly cheap and delicious dried fruits, nuts, oils, olives, and spices, among other things. **Damascus Bread & Pastry** (✉ 195 Atlantic Ave., ☎ 718/625–7070) is a take-out joint with stellar spinach pie and baklava.

Columbia Heights. Among the majestic residences on this street, Nos. 210–220 comprise a brownstone grouping often cited as the most graceful in New York. Norman Mailer lives on this street, and from a rear window in **No. 111**, John Roebling's son Washington, who in 1869 succeeded his father as chief engineer for the Brooklyn Bridge, directed the building of the bridge from his sickbed.

Court Street. On this main commercial thoroughfare of Carroll Gardens, you can gather a few edible mementoes of the neighborhood. Fresh pasta, cheeses, sausages, olives, and prepared Italian dishes are available at a number of shops, including **Pastosa Ravioli** (⊠ 347 Court St.), where the gnocchi is particularly good, and **Caputo's Dairy** (⊠ 460 Court St.), with a wide selection of homemade pastas and sauces.

NEED A
BREAK?

At **Shakespeare's Sister** (⊠ 270 Court St. at Kane St., ☎ 718/694-0084) you can soothe yourself with any one of a great variety of teas and light snacks while viewing art exhibits by women.

⑪ Guido Funeral Home. Once the John Rankin Residence, this freestanding redbrick building, built in 1840, is considered one of the city's finest examples of a Greek Revival town house. ⊠ *440 Clinton St.*

⑦ New York Transit Museum. If you've always wanted to know what an old-fashioned subway car looked like, here's your chance to find out. Located inside a converted 1930s subway station, the museum displays 18 restored classic subway cars and has an operating signal tower. ⊠ *Boerum Pl. at Schermerhorn St.,* ☎ *718/243–3060.* 🖃 *$3.* ⊙ *Tues.–Fri. 10–4, Sat.–Sun. noon–5.*

⑧ 197 Amity St. Jennie Jerome, the mother of Winston Churchill, was born in this modest house in 1854. (Perversely, a plaque at 426 Henry Street, southwest of here, identifies *that* building as the famous woman's birthplace. The Henry Street address is actually where Jennie's parents lived before she was born.)

⑥ Our Lady of Lebanon Maronite Church. One of the oldest Romanesque Revival buildings in the country, this Congregational church was designed by Richard Upjohn in 1844. Its doors, which depict Norman churches, were salvaged from the 1943 wreck of the ocean liner *Normandie.* ⊠ *113 Remsen St. at Henry St.*

❶ Plymouth Church of the Pilgrims. Thanks to the stirring oratory of Brooklyn's most eminent theologian, Henry Ward Beecher, this house of worship was the vortex of abolitionist sentiment in the years before the Civil War. In the Underground Railroad, which smuggled slaves to freedom, Plymouth Church was more or less "Grand Central Station." Beside the church is a courtyard (locked, alas) with a statue of Beecher, which you can see through the gate. Nearby, at 22 Willow Street, Beecher's house still stands—a prim Greek Revival brownstone. ⊠ *Orange St., between Henry and Hicks Sts.*

❷ 24 Middagh Street. This 1824 Federal-style wood residence with a mansard roof is the oldest home in the neighborhood. Peer through a door in the wall on the Willow Street side for a glimpse of the cottage garden and carriage house in the rear.

Willow Street. One of the prettiest and most architecturally varied blocks in Brooklyn Heights is Willow Street between Clark and Pierrepont streets. **Nos. 155–159** are three distinguished brick Federal row houses that were allegedly stops on the Underground Railroad.

Park Slope

Park Slope grew up in the late 1800s and is today one of Brooklyn's most sought-after places to live. The largely residential neighborhood has row after row of dazzlingly well-maintained brownstones dating from the turn of the century. Aside from its handsome architecture, Park Slope offers several other worthwhile attractions. Prospect Park, a 526-acre urban playground, encompasses a zoo, concert grounds, a boathouse, and more. Then there's the remarkable Grand Army Plaza with its Arc de Triomphe–style Soldiers' and Sailors' Memorial Arch; the stately Brooklyn Museum and Brooklyn Library; and the scenic Brooklyn Botanic Garden, a favorite springtime destination.

A Good Walk

Numbers in the text correspond to numbers in the margin and on the Park Slope map.

Start your tour at **7th Avenue,** the neighborhood's commercial center, packed with wine stores, bakeries, and restaurants. Seventh Avenue is accessible by the D and F subway trains (7th Ave. stop) and by the No. 2 or 3 subway trains (Grand Army Plaza stop). The beginning of this walk is closer to the D, 2, or 3 subway. Turn east from 7th Avenue onto Lincoln Place to find the **Montauk Club** ① (⊠ 25 8th Ave.), whose sumptuous Venetian palace style belies its standing as one of Brooklyn's most prestigious men's clubs. Make your way south along 8th Avenue, sampling the brownstones on various streets along the way (President and Carroll streets are especially handsome), until you reach **Montgomery Place** ②, with its remarkable row of Romanesque Revival brownstones.

From Montgomery Place, walk one block east along Prospect Park West to **Grand Army Plaza** ③, whose center is dominated by the **Soliders' and Sailors' Memorial Arch,** patterned on the Arc de Triomphe in Paris. Southeast of the plaza is the main entrance to the 526-acre **Prospect Park,** designed by Frederick Law Olmsted and Calvert Vaux, who also created Manhattan's Central Park. Inside the entrance lies the 75-acre **Long Meadow,** usually full of picnickers and kite-fliers on weekends and the site of free New York Philharmonic and Metropolitan Opera performances in summer. Turn right and follow the circular drive to **Litchfield Villa** ④, an elaborate Italianate mansion built in 1857. If you take the main drive of the park to the left of the main entrance, you will come to the **Prospect Park Wildlife Conservation Center** ⑤, a small, child-oriented zoo. Just beyond the zoo is the **Lefferts Homestead Children's Museum** ⑥ and the nearby **carousel.**

Continue on the circular drive from the villa. A smaller central path that branches off to your right leads to the **Quaker Cemetery,** the burial place of a few celebrities. If you stay on the circular drive, you'll soon pass the **Boathouse** ⑦, which houses a visitor center and a café. Farther down the path is the giant, gnarled **Camperdown Elm,** which Marianne Moore immortalized in a poem in the 1960s. South of here is **Concert Grove** ⑧, site of outdoor summer performances near the shore of 60-acre **Prospect Lake,** inhabited by ducks and swans.

Return to Grand Army Plaza, to the east of the park's main entrance, where you will find the main branch of the **Brooklyn Public Library** ⑨. A couple hundred yards east on the grand **Eastern Parkway** lie the entrances to two of Brooklyn's most important cultural offerings: the **Brooklyn Botanic Garden** ⑩, which occupies 52 acres across Flatbush Avenue from Prospect Park, and the world-class **Brooklyn Museum** ⑪. To re-

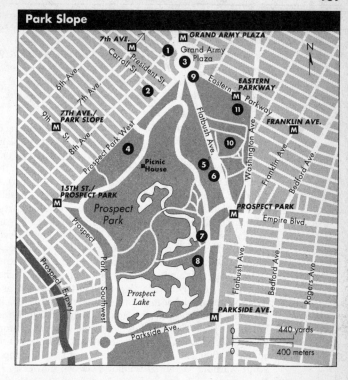

turn to Manhattan, you can take the No. 2 or 3 subway train from the station right in front of the museum.

TIMING

You could very well spend a whole day at the Brooklyn Museum alone—and another day exploring Prospect Park and the Brooklyn Botanic Garden. If you do choose to fit everything into one trip, break up your wanderings with a visit to 7th Avenue, where restaurants and cafés abound. Weekends are the best time to observe local life along 7th Avenue. The Botanic Garden reaches its prime during spring, when the cherry blossoms bloom like pink snow.

Sights to See

7 Boathouse. Styled after the Library of St. Mark's in Venice, this 1905 structure in Prospect Park now houses a café and a visitor center with a relief model of the park. ☎ 718/287–3474. ☿ Closed winter months.

★ **10 Brooklyn Botanic Garden.** A major attraction at this 52-acre botanic garden is the beguiling **Japanese Garden**—complete with a blazing red *torii* gate and a pond laid out in the shape of the Chinese character for "heart." The Japanese cherry arbor in the Japanese Garden turns into a heart-stopping cloud of pink every spring. You can also wander through the **Cranford Rose Garden** (5,000 bushes, 1,200 varieties); the **Fragrance Garden,** designed especially for the blind; the **Shakespeare Garden,** featuring more than 80 plants immortalized by the bard (including many kinds of roses); and **Celebrity Path,** Brooklyn's answer to Hollywood's Walk of Fame, with the names of homegrown stars—including Mel Brooks, Woody Allen, Zero Mostel, Barbra Streisand, and Mae West—inscribed on stepping-stones. A complex of handsome greenhouses called the **Steinhardt Conservatory** holds thriving desert, tropical, temperate, and aquatic vegetation, as well as a display charting the evolution of plants over the past 140 million years. The unique **C. V. Starr Bonsai Museum** in the Conservatory exhibits about 100 miniature Japanese specimens. Free tours are given weekends at 1 PM, except for holiday weekends. ✉ *1000 Washington Ave., between Empire Blvd. and S side of Brooklyn Museum,* ☎ 718/622–4433. ✐ *Free.* ☼ *Apr.–Sept., Tues.–Fri. 8–6, weekends and holidays 10–6; Oct.–Mar., Tues.–Fri. 8–4:30, weekends and holidays 10–4:30. Steinhardt Conservatory* ☼ *Apr.–Sept., Tues.–Sun. 10–5:30; Oct.–Mar., Tues.–Sun. 10–4.*

★ ⓫ **Brooklyn Museum.** Housed in a stunningly regal building designed by McKim, Mead & White in 1897, this world-class museum has huge statues of Brooklyn and Manhattan (as classical ladies) on its Eastern Parkway front. With approximately 1.5 million objects, the Brooklyn collection is the second-largest art museum in New York. Look especially for its Egyptian Art collection (third floor), considered one of the best of its kind, or the **African and Pre-Columbian Art** (first floor), another collection recognized worldwide. In the gallery of **American painting and sculpture** (5th floor) you'll find *Brooklyn Bridge* by Georgia O'Keeffe, as well as striking works by Winslow Homer, John Singer Sargent, Stuart Davis, and Gilbert Stuart. The **Period Rooms** (fourth floor) include the complete interior of the Jan Martense Schenck House, built in the Brooklyn Flatlands section in 1675, as well as a Moorish-style room from the 54th Street mansion of John D. Rockefeller. The museum's 1993 renovation by Japanese architect Arata Isozaki and New York firm James Stewart Polshek includes a new auditorium with a wavelike ceiling, and new galleries in the oldest part of the building, adding 30,000 square feet of exhibition space. Outdoors, the **Frieda Schiff Warburg Memorial Sculpture Garden** showcases architectural fragments from demolished New York buildings, including Penn Station. The museum also has excellent special exhibitions and dramatic views of Manhattan from its Eastern Parkway–Washington Avenue corner. ✉ *200 Eastern Pkwy.,* ☎ 718/638–5000. ✐ *$4 (suggested contribution).* ☼ *Wed.–Sun. 10–5.*

❾ **Brooklyn Public Library.** This grand neoclassical edifice has held its post near the Brooklyn Museum since 1941. Designed to resemble an open book, with a gilt-inscribed spine on Grand Army Plaza opening out to Eastern Parkway and Flatbush Avenue, it remains an architectural wonder, touted for its bright limestone walls, perfect proportions, and ornate decorative details. The 15 bronze figures over the entrance represent favorite characters in American literature; they were sculpted by Thomas Hudson Jones, who also designed the Tomb of the Unknown Soldier in Arlington National Cemetery. ✉ *Grand Army Plaza at the intersection of Flatbush Ave. and Eastern Pkwy.,* ☎ 718/780–7700. ☼ *Tues.–Thurs. 9–8; Mon., Fri., and Sat. 10–6; Sun. 1–5. Closed summer Sundays.*

❽ **Concert Grove.** One of the most visited parts of ☞ Prospect Park, this area was a happening place during World War II, when the sailors would come here to dance outdoors—and it still hosts free annual summer performances. It's also a scenic spot, with a Chinese pagoda providing shelter from sun and rain, busts of Shakespeare, and sculpted sandstone walls depicting various musical instruments. The grove is conveniently close to the popular **Wollman Memorial Skating Rink.**

Eastern Parkway. The first six-lane parkway in the world, this major boulevard mimics the grand sweep of the boulevards of Paris and Vienna; it originates at Grand Army Plaza. Frederick Law Olmsted and Calvert Vaux conceived the design in 1866; at that time the parkway ended at Ralph Avenue, then the border of Brooklyn. Today Eastern Parkway continues to play an important role in Brooklyn culture:

Every Labor Day weekend it hosts the biggest and liveliest carnival outside the Caribbean—a cacophony of calypso, steel band, and reggae music, with plenty of conch curry, spice bread, and meat patties to go around.

❸ **Grand Army Plaza.** Prospect Park West, Eastern Parkway, and Flatbush and Vanderbilt avenues radiate outward from this geographic star. At the center stands the **Soldiers' and Sailors' Memorial Arch,** honoring Civil War veterans and patterned on the Arc de Triomphe in Paris. Three heroic sculptural groupings adorn the arch: atop, a four-horsed chariot by Frederick MacMonnies, so dynamic that it almost seems on the verge of catapulting off the arch; to the sides, the victorious Union Army and Navy of the Civil War. Inside are bas-reliefs of presidents Abraham Lincoln and Ulysses S. Grant, sculpted by Thomas Eakins and William O'Donovan, respectively. Crossing the broad streets around here can be hazardous; beware.

To the northwest of the arch, Neptune and a passel of debauched tritons leer over the edges of the **Bailey Fountain,** where tulle-drenched brides and grooms in technicolor tuxes pose after exchanging vows.

☙ ❻ **Lefferts Homestead Children's Museum.** Built in 1783 and moved to ☞ Prospect Park in 1918, this gambrel-roofed Dutch colonial farmhouse contains a historic house museum for children. Adults will enjoy the two period rooms furnished with antiques, while children love playing in the four rooms with period reproduction furniture. Nearby is a restored 1912 **carousel.** *Museum:* ☎ *718/965–6505.* ▩ *Free.* ☉ *Mid-Apr.–mid-Dec., weekends 1–4:30; weekdays and mid-Dec.–Mar. by appointment. Hours vary, so call ahead. Carousel:* ▩ *50¢ per ride on weekends.* ☉ *Closed in winter.*

❹ **Litchfield Villa.** Dominating the west side of ☞ Prospect Park, this Italianate mansion built in 1857 was for many years the center of Brooklyn social life. It now holds the park's administrative offices, but visitors are welcome to step inside and view the domed foyer. Across the main drive from the Litchfield Villa is the **Picnic House** (☎ 718/965–6516), which has a year-round schedule of drama, dance, music, puppetry, yoga, and tai chi classes. ⊠ *Prospect Park W and 3rd St.*

❶ **Montauk Club.** Park Slope's most venerable edifice, this 1891 mansion is modeled on Venice's Ca' d'Oro. Notice the friezes of Montauk Indians and the 19th-century private side entrance for members' wives. ⊠ *25 8th Ave.*

❷ **Montgomery Place.** This block-long street between 8th Avenue and Prospect Park West is considered to be one of Park Slope's finest thoroughfares; it's filled with a picturesque variety of town houses designed by the Romanesque Revival genius C. P. H. Gilbert.

Prospect Park. When they built the park in 1866, Frederick Law Olmsted and Calvert Vaux considered it superior to their earlier creation, Central Park, because no streets divided it and no bordering skyscrapers broke its rural illusion. So beloved was Prospect Park that poet Marianne Moore, one of its chief advocates, termed her park-related campaigns her "only mortal engagement." Attractions within the park include ☞ Concert Grove, ☞ Litchfield Villa, the ☞ Boathouse, the ☞ Prospect Park Wildlife Conservation Center, and the ☞ Quaker Cemetery.

☙ ❺ **Prospect Park Wildlife Conservation Center.** Small, friendly, and educational, this children's zoo off the main road of ☞ Prospect Park has just the right combination of indoor and outdoor exhibits, and a number of unusual and endangered species among its 160 inhabitants. The central sea lion pool is a hit with youngsters, as are the indoor exhibits—

"Animal Lifestyles," which explains habitats and adaptations, and "Animals in Our Lives," showcasing animals that make good pets and animals used on the farm. In addition, there's an outdoor discovery trail with a simulated prairie dog burrow and a naturalistic pond. The zoo is run by the Wildlife Conservation Society, which also oversees the Bronx Zoo. ☎ *718/399–7339.* ⌑ *$2.50.* ☉ *Nov.–Mar., daily 10– 4:30; Apr.–Oct., weekdays 10–5, weekends 10–5:30.*

Quaker Cemetery. Montgomery Clift is just one of the famous people buried in this peaceful cemetery inside ☞ Prospect Park. The cemetery, which predates the park, is closed to the public, but the Urban Park Rangers lead periodic tours of the grounds. ☎ *718/287–3400.*

Seventh Avenue. Park Slope's main commercial street is popular with gourmets and gourmands. Here, among other interesting shops, you'll find a wine store of real distinction, **Leon Paley Ltd. Wines & Spirits** (⌧ 88 7th Ave.); **Cheese in the Park** (⌧ 446 9th St. at 7th Ave.), with a fine selection of imported cheeses; and a handful of diet-defying bakeries: **Connecticut Muffin** (⌧ 171 7th Ave.), **Cousin John's** (⌧ 70 7th Ave.), and the **New Prospect** (⌧ 52 7th Ave.). The corner of 7th Avenue and Sterling Place was the site of a horrendous plane crash in 1960 that leveled several buildings around the intersection.

NEED A
BREAK?

Second Street Café (⌧ 189 7th Ave. at 2nd St., ☎ 718/369–6928) is a homey restaurant and coffee bar with lunch on weekdays, brunch on weekends, and counter-service coffee-bar fare in late afternoons and evenings. Try the raisin-studded bread pudding or heart-warming soups such as curry pumpkin. The coffee house of choice around here is **Ozzie's Coffee & Tea** (⌧ 57 7th Ave. at Lincoln Pl., ☎ 718/398–6695), a converted drugstore with its apothecary cases still intact.

QUEENS

Astoria

Home to a vital community of some 35,000 Greeks, Astoria is a place where people socialize on their front lawns at dusk, and where mom-and-pop businesses thrive. Here you can buy Cypriot cured olives and feta cheese from store owners who will tell you where to go for the best spinach pie; or you can sit outside at one of the many *xaxaroplasteion* (pastry shops), eating baklava and watching the elevated subways speed by.

Originally German, then Italian, Astoria earned the nickname "Little Athens" in the late 1960s; by the early 1990s, Greeks accounted for slightly less than half the population. Today there are also substantial numbers of Asians, Eastern Europeans, Irish, and Hispanic immigrants in Astoria, not to mention a growing contingent of former Manhattan residents in search of cheaper rents and a safer, friendlier atmosphere.

It may seem ironic that such a melting pot made history as the center of one of America's most traditionally white-bread industries—namely, show business. Before Hollywood, in the 1920s, such stars as Gloria Swanson, Rudolph Valentino, and the Marx Brothers came to this neighborhood to work at "the Big House," Paramount's moviemaking center in the east. At that time the Kaufman-Astoria studios were the largest and most important filmmaking studios in the country; today they remain the largest in the East, and they're still used for major films and television shows.

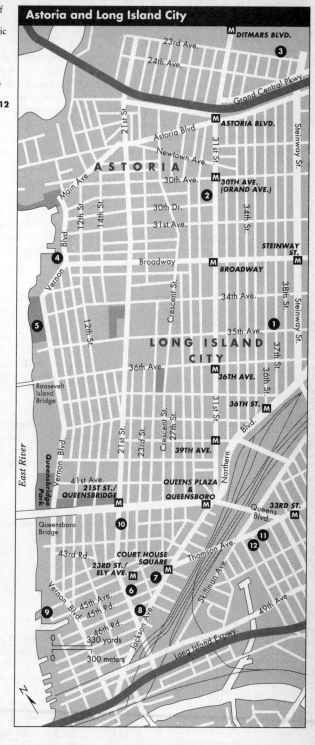

Astoria and Long Island City

A Good Walk

*Numbers in the text correspond to numbers in the margin and on the
Astoria and Long Island City map.*

From Manhattan, take the N train to 36th Street and walk north two
blocks to 35th Avenue (bear with the confusion of intersecting streets,
drives, and avenues). Here you'll find the **American Museum of the Moving Image** ①, the reason most people come to Astoria; you may
spend hours studying its exhibits on film production and catching bits of the
regularly scheduled film series and directors' talks. The 13-acre **Kaufman-Astoria Studios** next door is not open to the public, but you can
stop and look at the monumentally columned entrance.

Head for the heart of the Greek community by walking west on 35th
Avenue and then north on 31st Street to Broadway. Here Greek pas-
try shops and coffeehouses abound, and the elevated subway brings a
constant stream of activity. On the northeast corner of 31st Street and
Broadway is one of the neighborhood's few architectural landmarks,
a four-story building from the early 1860s that now houses Interbank.
Late into the night the Grecian Cave nightclub next door resounds with
Greek crooners and bouzouki music.

Walk north up 31st Street to 30th Drive. Here you'll find the Greek
Orthodox **St. Demetrios Cathedral** ②, which allegedly has the largest
Orthodox congregation outside Greece. Continue north on 31st Street
to reach 23rd Avenue, where Greek-owned businesses bustle. On the
way you'll pass **Elias Corner** (☞ Chapter 6), at 31st Street and 24th
Avenue, where crowds line up for seafood served without menus. At
23rd Avenue, turn right and walk five blocks east to the **St. Irene
Chrysovalantou Cathedral** ③, famous for its icon that reportedly weeps
tears.

If you're up for a hike, return to Broadway and head eight blocks west
until you reach the East River, at Vernon Boulevard. Before you is
Socrates Sculpture Park ④, 4.2 acres of large, abstract artwork that at
first almost appears to be an urban hallucination. Three blocks south
on the other side of Vernon Boulevard is the **Isamu Noguchi Sculpture
Museum** ⑤, where hundreds of Noguchi's works are displayed in an
indoor-outdoor setting.

TIMING

To see Greek Astoria at its finest, visit on a Saturday, when sidewalk
culture comes to life. Weekdays are also pleasant, however, as the
neighborhood's quiet pace offers a welcome alternative to frenetic
Manhattan. Allow at least three hours for a leisurely visit to the American Museum of the Moving Image and a tour of Greek Astoria; add
another hour or two if you plan to visit the more distant Socrates Sculpture Park and Isamu Noguchi Museum.

Sights to See

★ ☺ ❶   **American Museum of the Moving Image.** At this unique museum, a 195-
seat theater and a 60-seat screening room host fascinating film series—
among them tributes to Hollywood directors, cinematographers,
writers, and stars. Galleries feature exhibitions such as **Behind the Screen:
Producing, Promoting Motion Pictures and Television** and hands-on
displays that allow visitors to try their skills at film editing. Commis-
sioned artwork is on display, such as **Tut's Fever Movie Palace,** designed
by the Red Grooms and Lysiane Luong as a metaphorical recapitula-
tion of Egyptian-style picture palaces of the 1930s (you'll find lifelike
figures of Theda Bara at the ticket booth and Mae West serving up pop-
corn); and Gregory Barsamian's Stroboscopic Zoetrope, a giant spin-
ning disk that demonstrates the optics of animation. The museum's

collection of movie memorabilia includes 70,000 items; in the costume display you might find outfits worn by Marlene Dietrich and Robin Williams, among others. ⊠ *35th Ave., between 36th and 37th Sts.,* ☎ *718/784–0077.* ☞ *$5.* ⊙ *Tues.–Fri. noon–4, weekends noon–6.*

★ ❺ **Isamu Noguchi Sculpture Museum.** Some 30 years ago, Japanese sculptor Isamu Noguchi took studio space here in what was a photo-engraver's factory. Part of it now holds 12 galleries showcasing the sculptor's evocative work in stone and stage-set designs, with videos documenting his long career. A small sculpture garden adjoins the museum. ⊠ *32–37 Vernon Blvd., entrance on 33rd Ave.,* ☎ *718/204–7088.* ☞ *$4 (suggested contribution).* ⊙ *Apr.–Nov., Wed., Sat., and Sun. 11–6. Weekend bus service to Noguchi Museum leaves every hr on the ½ hr, 11:30–3:30, from the Asia Society, Park Ave. and 70th St. in Manhattan.* ☞ *$5.*

Kaufman-Astoria Studios. Though its heyday has passed, this former powerhouse in the American movie industry remains a principal player. Since 1977 scores of pictures have been produced here, including *The Age of Innocence, Sabrina, The Cotton Club, The Verdict, Arthur, The Wiz, Sesame Street,* and *The Cosby Show,* to name just a few. The studios are not open to the public, but peek through the windows of the monumentally columned entrance to see on-the-set stills of Rudolph Valentino, the Marx Brothers, Maurice Chevalier, and other stars. ⊠ *34–12 36th St.,* ☎ *718/392–5600.*

❷ **St. Demetrios Cathedral.** A brick building with a red-tile roof, gold domes, and the largest Orthodox community outside Greece, this is in some ways the heart of Astoria. ⊠ *30–11 30th Dr.,* ☎ *718/728–1718.*

❸ **St. Irene Chrysovalantou Cathedral.** At this independent Greek church, worshipers pray to an icon that reportedly wept real tears at the outbreak of the Persian Gulf War in 1991. There was an outcry when the icon was stolen several months later; it was mysteriously returned through the regular mail, wrapped in brown paper, minus its jewel-encrusted frame. Although the congregation rejoiced, the mainstream Greek Orthodox priests down at St. Demetrios took the opportunity to denounce the defectors once again and to deny that the icon ever wept. ⊠ *36–25 23rd Ave.*

❹ **Socrates Sculpture Park.** The ancient Greeks excelled in the art of sculpture, which was often displayed in outdoor temples. It is appropriate, then, that Astoria should have an outdoor sculpture park. At the end of Vernon Boulevard, down the street from the **Isamu Noguchi Sculpture Museum** where it meets the East River, this 4.2-acre collection of large, abstract artwork at first almost appears to be an urban hallucination. As its bleak surroundings suggest, it was once an illegal dump site; in 1985 locals rallied to transform it into a public art space. Today a view of the river and the Manhattan skyline beyond frames huge works of art made of scrap metal, old tires, and other recycled products. ⊠ *Vernon Blvd. at Broadway,* ☎ *718/956–1819.* ⊙ *Daily 10 AM–sunset.*

NEED A BREAK? **The Omonia Café** (⊠ 32–20 Broadway, ☎ 718/274–6650), one block east of the Broadway and 31st Street intersection, is the local hangout. If you don't want to sit at a table, you can still stop by the bakery counter to buy such pastries as cream-filled *ekmek* or flaky layered *pontikaki*.

Long Island City

In the 1800s, along the East River in Queens, a string of neighborhoods thrived due to their ferry links with Manhattan. One of the busiest ferries connected a finger of land called Hunters Point with East 34th Street, Manhattan. Here, a business district known as Long Island City burgeoned. (Queens is, after all, on the western end of Long Island, as is Brooklyn.) Factories, boardinghouses, municipal buildings, and restaurants clustered around the intersection of Vernon Boulevard and Jackson Avenue, while north along Vernon Boulevard tycoons built summer homes with boathouses and lawns that reached gracefully to the banks of the river. Today at the intersection, modest shingled homes, butcher shops, diners, and the Vernon–Jackson subway stop still crowd together beneath the huge, four-barreled stacks of the old Pennsylvania Railroad generating plant.

Another kind of industry has bloomed here as well. Ironically but appropriately, the gritty Long Island City became an outpost for America's glitziest industry, the motion pictures in the 1980s. Soundstages were created from converted warehouses and bakeries as the area experienced a small renaissance of sorts.

Like TriBeCa, another industrial district turned bohemian, Long Island City is now home to artists, who've migrated with their paint pots and welding tools to airy, low-rent studios. The area to the west of Vernon is slated to change dramatically when the Hunters Point Development plan turns 90 acres of riverfront and landfill between the Midtown Tunnel and Queensboro Bridge into an apartment complex.

Long Island City's streets puzzle cartographers and visitors alike; you'll find numbered streets running north and south, and numbered avenues, roads, and drives going east–west. Consider 45th Avenue: To its south lies 45th Road, and to its north is 44th Road, 44th Avenue, and 44th Drive. Your best bet is to go with a map—and don't be afraid to ask for directions.

A Good Walk
Numbers in the text correspond to numbers in the margin and on the Astoria and Long Island City map.

A 10-minute ride on the No. 7 subway from Times Square or Grand Central Terminal will take you to the 45th Road Court House Square station. You can also take the E or F train to the 23rd Street/Ely Avenue stop and walk to the Court House Square station exit. This will put you next to the towering green **Citicorp Building** and the more modest **New York State Supreme Court House** ⑥, site of several films. From here, walk one block north on 23rd Street and turn left onto 45th Avenue, where you'll find the **Hunters Point Historic District** ⑦, an immaculate row of brownstones dating from 1870. Walk north on 45th Avenue to 21st Street and turn left. Between 46th Road and 46th Avenue is **PS 1** ⑧, a contemporary art museum.

The white concrete block of a building that rises at the foot of 44th Drive is **Water's Edge Restaurant** ⑨, Queens's most famous dining establishment; from the pier outside you can survey the **Queensboro Bridge.** Now walk east from Vernon to the intersection of 21st Street and 43rd Avenue, and take a left to find **Silvercup Studios** ⑩, the center of Long Island City's short-lived filmmaking history.

Follow 43rd Avenue east to Thomson Avenue, which will lead you— via a covered sidewalk—over the mind-boggling mesh of the Long Island Railroad tracks. Just past here, Thomson Avenue merges into

Queens Boulevard, one of the borough's chief transverses. To your right lie the shells of several once-thriving industries: the **Sunshine Biscuit Company** (✉ Skillman Ave., between 29th and 30th Sts.), **American Eveready Building** (✉ 29–10 Thomson Ave.), **Adams Chewing Gum Factory** (✉ 30–30 Thomson Ave.), and **White Motor Company Factory** (✉ 31–10 Thomson Ave.), all built between 1914 and 1920 in a delightful mix of the practical and the ornamental. The Sunshine Building now has a parking lot in front, but the Eveready and the Adams buildings have had a more interesting fate—the **International Design Center of New York** ⑪, completed in 1985, now occupies these two structures. Also on Thomson but closer to the bridge, **La Guardia Community College** ⑫ occupies the old White Motor Company factory.

TIMING

Unless you want to linger at the PS 1 Museum, this tour will take no more than two hours, since most of the sights are seen from the outside only. The sidewalks are usually deserted and the area, although perfectly safe, feels quiet by comparison to Manhattan.

Sights to See

Citicorp Building. When this tower was built in 1989, Manhattan office space ran at $40–$95 per square foot, while in Queens you could rent at a cool $17–$27. I. M. Pei is responsible for the building's basic design, which carries over some general themes from Manhattan's Citicorp Building. The 48-story tower is New York City's tallest building outside of Manhattan.

❼ **Hunters Point Historic District.** The immaculate brownstone houses around 45th Avenue and 23rd Street date from 1870, and each one has its original stoops and cornices. Their fine condition is due partly to their having been faced in resilient Westchester stone. Two blocks down 45th Road at 21st Street, a small park offers benches (for pigeons and people) and a setting for a large metal sculpture called *Bigger Bird* by Daniel Sinclair. The warehouses surrounding the park are a warren of artists' studios; above their low roofs there's an unobstructed view of Manhattan.

⑪ **International Design Center of New York.** This vast marketplace (1 million square feet) for the products of interior designers was completed in 1985 at a cost of more than $125 million. Peek inside (the main entrance and information desk is between Thomson and 47th Aves.); there you'll see the ballooning central atrium, surrounded by showrooms ad infinitum. Gigantic elevators for unloading train cars occupied those central spaces back in the days when these buildings still turned out bubble gum and auto parts. ✉ *30–20 Thomson Ave.,* ☎ *718/937–7474.*

⑫ **La Guardia Community College.** Within this building lie the papers of the city's most colorful mayor, Fiorello H. La Guardia. New York's "Little Flower," as La Guardia came to be called, presided over the metropolis during the Depression. ✉ *31–10 Thomson Ave., Room E-238.* ☉ *Weekdays 9:30–4:30, but call 718/482–5065 for appointment to view documents.*

❻ **New York State Supreme Court House.** Built in 1909 in a jumbled Beaux Arts architectural style, the courthouse is being restored throughout the 1990s, but depending on where the work is being done, you may be able to step inside the four-story-high lobby to see the mosaic tile floors, elaborate iron banisters, and stained-glass ceiling. The courthouse's original construction entailed so much graft and corruption that the Queens borough president, Joseph Bermel, resigned, and the architect, Peter M. Coco, was tried for grand larceny in one of the very courtrooms he had designed. Today it's frequently used as a location by neighborhood movie studios. ⊠ *25–10 Court House Sq., across from Citicorp.*

❽ PS 1 Museum. The founders of this contemporary art museum were the first of the art-conscious to see the possibilities in the area; back in 1976 they turned the old school into one of the largest exhibition spaces in the world. A recent renovation has expanded it even more and added an outdoor sculpture courtyard. There are also studios for artists and lecture rooms. The emphasis is on emerging and mid-career artists, and European art not normally shown in the United States. ⊠ *46–01 21st St.,* ☎ *718/784–2084.*

Queensboro Bridge. Extending more than 7,000 feet from Manhattan's East 60th Street to Crescent Street, Queens, this bridge exacted a toll on its construction workers—50 died before it was completed in 1909. At the bridge's base, near Queens Plaza, there's a riverfront park, Queensbridge Park, and a lonely, empty remnant of the past century, the old **New York Architectural Terra Cotta Company** complete with Tudor Revival adornments and chimney pots.

❿ Silvercup Studios. Filmmakers began to gather in 1983 to make movies and commercials at this three-block-long complex, converted from a bakery into 16 soundstages. Such movies as *Godfather III*, *Sea of Love*, and *When Harry Met Sally* were shot within the walls of old Silvercup. The studios are not open to the public, but if you're passing by take a gander. ⊠ *42–22 22nd St.,* ☎ *718/784–3390.*

❾ Water's Edge Restaurant. In summertime umbrellas sprout up on the dock and boaters check in for quick drinks at this elegant Queens restaurant that charges Manhattan prices. The sophisticated clientele arrives via a complimentary ferry service from the city's 34th Street Marina Tuesday–Saturday in summer, weekends in winter. ⊠ *44th Dr. and East River,* ☎ *718/482–0033.*

NEED A BREAK?	Only locals know about **Café Vernon** (⊠ 46–18 Vernon Blvd., ☎ 718/472-9694), a tiny, unassuming Italian restaurant at Vernon Boulevard and 46th Road. Don't let its modesty fool you—in fact, it offers splendid, filling repasts of Italian sandwiches, soups, and pastas. Prices are moderate, and the atmosphere is friendly. Behind the restaurant you can glimpse the back of the Pepsi-Cola sign on the East River, a local landmark.

STATEN ISLAND

Even though Staten Island (SI) is officially a borough of New York City, many Staten Islanders refer to Manhattan as "the City." Perhaps that's because farms and vast woodlands have distinguished it from the more crowded and developed Manhattan since 1661, when it was permanently settled as a farming community by the Dutch (after several fatal battles with the native Indian tribes that already inhabited the area). When oystering became a thriving industry in the early 1800s, farmers brought free blacks up from Maryland to help plant new oyster beds. The black community on the south shore became known as Sandy Ground; descendants of the first black oystermen still live there. Factories came later, as did shipbuilding. Today Staten Island still feels more residential than the other boroughs. (A recent election revealed that an overwhelming majority of the SI natives support secession as a way to rid themselves of the many responsibilities of being part of "the City.") Getting around can be somewhat difficult for visitors because the various attractions are so spread out, but bus service is convenient.

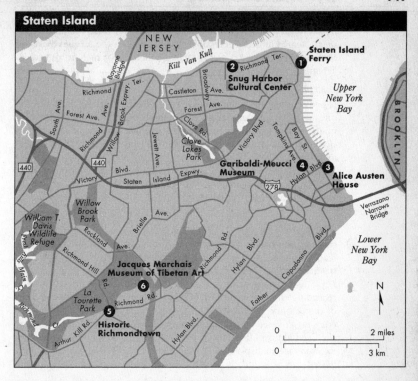

Snug Harbor and Historic Richmond Town

Though they're on opposite sides of the island, Snug Harbor and Richmond Town are both worth seeing—preferably by car. The two sites together will give you a great sense of Staten Island history, with some amazingly well-preserved remnants of its colonial and 18th-century past.

A Good Walk

Numbers in the text correspond to numbers in the margin and on the Staten Island map.

The best way to introduce yourself to Staten Island is by taking the 20-minute ride across New York Harbor on the **Staten Island Ferry** ①, which leaves regularly from the southern tip of Manhattan (☞ Wall Street and the Battery *in* Chapter 2). From the ferry terminal on Staten Island, a seven-minute (2-mile) ride on the S40 bus will take you to the **Snug Harbor Cultural Center** ②, an 83-acre complex with an art gallery, a botanical garden, a children's museum, and a colorful history. Signal the driver as soon as you glimpse the beginning of the black iron fence along the edge of the property.

If you're still feeling energetic and the day is young, return to the ferry terminal and catch the S51–Bay Street bus for the 15-minute ride to Hylan Boulevard to see the turn-of-the-century photographs displayed in the picturesque **Alice Austen House** ③. Italian history buffs should head to the **Garibaldi-Meucci Museum** ④, where war general Giuseppe Garibaldi lived in exile with his friend Antonio Meucci—the true inventor of the telephone.

Since it's on the other side of Staten Island, you may want to see **Historic Richmondtown** ⑤ on a separate trip: A unique museum village on the site of Staten Island's first permanent settlement, it merits at least the better part of a day. The best way to get there is the S74–Richmond Road bus, which leaves from the ferry terminal (about 35 minutes). Nearby and also accessible by the S74 bus is the **Jacques Marchais Museum of Tibetan Art** ⑥, the largest collection of such art outside of Tibet.

TIMING

If you're intent on seeing all of Staten Island's far-flung attractions in one day, plan on spending at least an hour on the bus, on the train, or in a car. (Few attractions are within walking distance of each other.) If you're short on time or energy, approach this tour in two parts: Richmondtown and the Tibetan Museum on one day; Snug Harbor, the Alice Austen House, and the Garibaldi-Meucci Museum on another. Keep in mind that on weekend mornings (until 11:30 AM), ferries leave the South Street Seaport only every hour; on weekdays and weekend afternoons you can catch one at least every half hour.

Sights to See

❸ **Alice Austen House.** Photographer Alice Austen (1866–1952) defied tradition when, as a girl of 10, she received her first camera as a gift from an uncle and promptly began taking pictures of everything around her. Austen went on to make photography her lifetime avocation, recording on film a vivid social history of Staten Island in the early part of the century; one of the local ferries is actually named for her. The cozy, ivy-covered Dutch-style cottage known as Clear Comfort, where she lived almost all her life, has been restored, and many of her photographs are on display. ⊠ *2 Hylan Blvd.,* ☎ *18/816–4506.* ☞ *$2 (suggested contribution).* ☉ *Thurs.–Sun. noon–5.*

❹ **Garibaldi-Meucci Museum.** Housed in an altered Federal farmhouse, this small museum is full of letters and photographs from the life of fiery Italian patriot Giuseppe Garibaldi; it also documents Antonio Meucci's claim that he invented the telephone before Alexander Graham Bell did. Appropriately, the museum is in the heart of the Italian neighborhood of Rosebank; the colorful, if kitschy, **Our Lady of Mount Saint Carmel Society Shrine** is just around the corner, at 36 Amity Street. Ask the curator for directions. ⊠ *420 Tompkins Ave., Staten Island,* ☎ *718/442–1608.* ☞ *$1 (suggested contribution).* ☉ *Tues.–Sun. 1–5.*

★ ❺ **Historic Richmondtown.** These 27 historic buildings founded in 1685 are on a 100-acre complex that was the site of Staten Island's original settlement. The buildings have been restored inside and out; some were here originally, while others were relocated from other spots on the island. Many of the buildings, such as the Greek Revival courthouse that serves as the **visitor center,** date from the 19th century; other architectural styles on site range from Dutch Colonial to Victorian Gothic Revival. During the warmer months, costumed interpreters demonstrate Early American crafts and trades such as printing, tinsmithing, and baking.

The **Voorlezer's House,** built in 1695, is the oldest elementary schoolhouse in the United States; it looks like the mold from which all little red schoolhouses were cast.

The **Staten Island Historical Society Museum,** built in 1848 as the second county clerk's and surrogate's office, now has in its archives American china, furniture, toys, and tools, plus a collection of Staten Island photographs.

During a summer visit, you might want to make reservations for the 19th-century dinner, cooked outdoors and served with utensils of the period. The Autumn Celebration shows off craftspeople demonstrating their skills;

the annual Encampment in July is a reenactment of a Civil War battle; December brings a monthlong Christmas celebration. Richmond Town regularly hosts other fairs, flea markets, and tours of the historic buildings. A tavern on the grounds of the historic village hosts a Saturday night concert series showcasing ethnic and folk music; call the visitor center for details. ☒ *441 Clarke Ave.,* ☎ *718/351–1611.* ☜ *$4.* ☉ *Jan.–Mar., Wed.–Fri. 1–5; Apr.–June, Wed.–Sun. 1–5; July–Aug., Wed.–Fri. 10–5, weekends 1–5; Sept.–Dec., Wed.–Sun. 1–5.*

❻ Jacques Marchais Museum of Tibetan Art. One of the largest private, nonprofit collections of Tibetan sculpture, scrolls, and paintings outside of Tibet is displayed in a museum resembling a Tibetan temple. Try to visit on a day when the monks bless the temple—and you. ☒ *338 Lighthouse Ave., Staten Island,* ☎ *718/987–3500.* ☜ *$3; occasionally, an additional $3 charge for special Sun. programs.* ☉ *Apr.–Nov., Wed.–Sun. 1–5; Dec.–Mar., by appointment only.*

❷ Snug Harbor Cultural Center. Once part of a sprawling farm, then a home for "aged, decrepit and worn-out sailors," this 83-acre property is based around a row of five columned Greek Revival temples, built between 1831 and 1880, and consists of 28 historic buildings, most of which have been restored. There are plans to renovate and reopen the Music Hall, the second-oldest hall in the city (after Carnegie); the hall has been closed since the early '70s and may reopen in 1997. The former chapel now houses the 210-seat **Veterans Memorial Hall,** site of many indoor concerts and gatherings, including an annual jazz festival.

Snug Harbor's Main Hall—the oldest building on the property, dating from 1833—holds the **Newhouse Center for Contemporary Art,** which features changing exhibitions. The building next door to the Newhouse Center houses the **John A. Noble Collection** of maritime art, with paintings, lithographs, photographs, and drawings. The complex has a gift shop and a cafeteria. The ☞ Staten Island Botanical Gardens and the ☞ Staten Island Children's Museum are also located on the grounds. ☒ *1000 Richmond Terrace,* ☎ *718/448–2500 (John A. Noble Collection,* ☎ *718/447–6490).* ☜ *Free to Cultural Center grounds, $2 (Newhouse Center suggested contribution), $2 (John A. Noble Collection; various charges for special events). Free guided tours weekends 2 PM.* ☉ *Grounds: 8 AM–dusk; Newhouse Center: Wed.–Sun. noon–5; John A. Noble Collection: Weekdays 9–2 and by appointment.*

Staten Island Botanical Gardens. On the grounds of the ☞ Snug Harbor Cultural Center, this haven includes a perennial garden, a greenhouse, 10 acres of natural marsh habitat, a fragrance garden for the physically challenged, and a new rose garden. An authentic Chinese Scholar's Garden, with a meditation area and a water garden, will probably be built within the next few years. ☒ *1000 Richmond Terr.,* ☎ *718/273–8200.* ☜ *Free.* ☉ *Dawn–dusk.*

♺ Staten Island Children's Museum. Four galleries at this popular museum are devoted to revolving hands-on exhibitions that introduce children to such diverse topics as news and media, storytelling, and insects. ☒ *Snug Harbor Cultural Center, 1000 Richmond Terr.,* ☎ *718/273–2060.* ☜ *$3.25.* ☉ *Tues.–Sun. noon–5.*

NEED A BREAK? Those with a powerful thirst should head straight to **Adobe Blues** (☒ 63 Lafayette Ave., just off Richmond Terr., ☎ 718/720–2583), a southwestern-style saloon and restaurant with more than 200 beers and a killer chili con carne.

🖐 **❶** **Staten Island Ferry.** Known as New York City's best bargain, the 50¢ (round-trip) ferry ride from the South Street Seaport to Staten Island provides close-up views of the Statue of Liberty, Ellis Island, and Manhattan's dazzling skyline. Try to get on one of the boats with outer decks so that you can sit outside. Bigger boats take ferries; call ahead to arrange (☎ 718/390–5253). ☎ *718/815–2628 for schedules and directions.*

Inside the ferry terminal on Staten Island, the **Staten Island Ferry Collection** is a small museum with an assortment of ferry memorabilia, including old black-and-white photos of commuters, a big wooden steering wheel, and a few other tidbits. ☎ *718/720–9268.* 🎟 *$1 (suggested contribution).* ⊙ *Daily 9 AM–2 PM.*

4 Exploring New York City with Children

New York is as magical a place for children as it is for adults. Although hotels and restaurants tend to be geared firmly to the grown-ups, when provision has been made for children, it is usually accomplished in a grand way. The world's best and largest toy shop, the biggest dinosaur skeletons, the biggest and best park, the nicest city seaport, the best burgers, and of course, some of the world's tallest buildings are here.

By Kate
Sekules

Updated by
Margaret
Mittelbach

BESIDES NEW YORK'S CHILD-PLEASING SIGHTS, there are rare ambient treats to stumble upon—from brightly colored pictograms in Chinatown to the spectacular four-story-high neon signs in Times Square, from Central Park squirrels to Greenwich Village street musicians good enough to appear on television (and sometimes they do).

To get children psyched up for a New York trip, give them *Eloise,* by Kay Thompson; *A Cricket in Times Square,* by George Selden; *From the Mixed-up Files of Mrs. Basil E. Frankweiler,* by E. L. Konigsburg; *My New York,* by Kathy Jakobsen; or *Stuart Little,* by E. B. White.

SIGHTSEEING

As far as outdoors sights are concerned, there is plenty to please; surprising pockets of street sculpture, graffiti art, strange building facades, and quirky shop windows may be found on almost every block. In no other city are you more likely to entertain offspring simply by wandering. Children get a kick from the sheer size of the buildings, and from riding cabs, or even buses and subways (especially the first or last car, with a view of the track and tunnels). You can also try taking more exotic transportation. To get a feeling for turn-of-the-century New York, try taking a **horse-drawn carriage** around Central Park (⊠ At Grand Army Plaza or intersections of Central Park S., between 5th and 7th Aves.; ▧ $34 for a half hour).

Set sail on the restored 19th-century schooner, **The Pioneer** (⊠ South St. Seaport, ☎ 212/748–8784; ▧ $16 adults, $6 children under 12, for 2 hours). For an aerial view of the city, take an **Island Helicopter** tour (⊠ 34th St. and East River, ☎ 212/683–4575; ▧ $44–$129).

For little more than the price of a subway token, the **Roosevelt Island Aerial Tramway** (⊠ 2nd Ave., at 60th St.) across the East River is a sure hit. Trams run every 15 minutes during regular hours, and every 7½ minutes during rush hours, which you might wish to avoid.

Ferry rides are great fun. For a close-up view of the boats, islands, and other sites of New York Harbor, try the bargain 50¢ ride on the **Staten Island Ferry** (⊠ Terminal in Battery Park).

Kids also enjoy New York's opportunities for vertical travel. Take the elevator to the 107th floor of the **World Trade Center** (⊠ 1 World Trade Center, ☎ 212/323–2340) for a panoramic view, 1,350 feet above the city (☞ Wall Street and the Battery *in* Chapter 2). The favorite midtown high-level view is from the 102nd floor of the **Empire State Building** (⊠ 350 5th Ave., ☎ 212/736–3100), where, on a clear day, you can see for 80 miles (☞ Murray Hill to Union Square *in* Chapter 2).

Museums

Although just about every major museum in New York City has something to interest children, certain ones hold special appeal. At the top of the list is the **American Museum of Natural History** (⊠ Central Park W, at W. 79th St., ☎ 212/769–5100), with its lifelike dioramas and newly restored collection of giant dinosaurs, including a huge Tyrannosaurus rex.

For young stargazers, the **Hayden Planetarium** (⊠ W. 81st St., at Central Park W, ☎ 212/769–5920) offers astronomical exhibits and sky shows; there is also a preschool show.

The **Children's Museum of Manhattan** is a kind of indoor playground for kids 2–10, where they can climb, crawl, paint, make collages, try on costumes, and even film their own newscasts. Daily workshops are included in the admission price. ⊠ *212 W. 83rd St.,* ☎ *212/721–1234.* ☞ *$5 adults and children, children under 2 free.* ☉ *Mon., Wed., and Thurs. 1:30–5:30, Fri.–Sun. 10–5.*

The **Children's Museum of the Arts,** in a loftlike space in SoHo, allows children ages 1 to 10 to become actively involved in visual and performing arts. Highlights include the Monet Ball Pond, where children can play with brightly colored balls near a water-lily mural; and the Creative Play area, which provides a reading corner, art activities, and cushions and futons. Weekend workshops, for children 6–10, are included in the admission price, plus a $1 materials fee. ⊠ *72 Spring St.,* ☎ *212/941–9198.* ☞ *$4 weekdays and $5 weekends for adults under 65 and children over 18 months.* ☉ *Tues.–Sun. 11–5.*

A big favorite—literally—with the younger generation is the *Intrepid Sea-Air-Space Museum,* an immense World War II aircraft carrier. On deck is a startling array of aircraft; inside there are aviation and military exhibits, as well as skinny hallways, winding staircases, and dozens of knobs, buttons, and wheels to manipulate. ⊠ *Pier 86, at 12th Ave. and W. 46th St.,* ☎ *212/245–0072.* ☞ *$10 adults; $5 children 6–11.* ☉ *Wed.–Sun. 10–5.*

In the nautical vein, the **South Street Seaport Museum** is an 11-square-block "museum without walls" with cobblestone streets, 19th-century architecture, an old print shop, a maritime crafts center, and a children's center with hands-on exhibits about the history of ships and the sea. *Museum Visitors' Center:* ⊠ *12 Fulton St.,* ☎ *212/748-8600.* ☞ *$6 adults, $3 children under 12.* ☉ *Daily, except major holidays; summer hrs 10–6; winter hrs 10–5.*

Kids tend to like the **Forbes Magazine Galleries** (⊠ *62 5th Ave., at 12th St.,* ☎ *212/206–5548*) for the collections of toy soldiers and boats, and rooms with the bejeweled Fabergé eggs (☞ Greenwich Village *in* Chapter 2). Aspiring heroes appreciate the **New York City Fire Museum** (⊠ *278 Spring St.,* ☎ *212/691–1303*), with displays of fire-fighting equipment and tours given by real firefighters (☞ Greenwich Village *in* Chapter 2). For children eight and older, the **Sony Wonder Technology Lab** (⊠ *550 Madison Ave., at 55th St.,* ☎ *212/833–8100*) is an interactive science and communications technology exhibit that allows kids to log on computers, play sound engineer, and be on TV.

Many "adult" museums in Manhattan offer special programs for kids. Meanwhile, don't ignore the city's outer boroughs and environs.

For children who like hands-on involvement, the place to go is the **Brooklyn Children's Museum,** considered one of the best in the world. This interactive museum is full of tunnels to crawl through and animals to pet. ⊠ *145 Brooklyn Ave.,* ☎ *718/735–4432.* ☞ *$3 (suggested contribution).* ☉ *June–Aug., Mon. and Wed.–Sun. noon–5; Sept.–May, Wed.–Fri. 2–5, weekends and holidays noon–5.*

Located underground in an old subway station in downtown Brooklyn, the **Transit Museum** houses full-size, turn-of-the-century and modern subway cars and working miniature subway trains. ⊠ *Boerum and Schermerhorn Sts.,* ☎ *718/243–3063.* ☞ *$3 adults, $1.50 children.* ☉ *Tues., Thurs., and Fri. 10–4, Wed. 10–6, weekends noon–5.*

In Queens, the **New York Hall of Science** in Flushing Meadows–Corona Park allows budding researchers access to 150 exhibits (many of them touchable). ⊠ *111th St., at 46th Ave.,* ☎ *718/699–0005.* ⛁ *$4 adults, $3 children; free Wed. and Thurs. 2–5.* ☉ *Wed.–Sun. 10–5.*

The **Staten Island Institute of Arts and Sciences** offers weekend kids' programs and wonderful exhibits covering natural history and the arts. ⊠ *75 Stuyvesant Pl.,* ☎ *718/727–1135.* ⛁ *$2.50 adults, $1.50 children (suggested contributions).* ☉ *Mon.–Sat. 9–5, Sun. 1–5.*

The hands-on exhibits of the **Staten Island Children's Museum** (⊠ 1000 Richmond Terr., ☎ 718/273–2060) on everything from the five senses to high technology will particularly enthrall younger kids (☞ Staten Island and Historic Richmondtown *in* Chapter 3). Children with a strong sense of the past may enjoy **Historic Richmondtown** (441 Clarke Ave., ☎ 718/351–1611), which has a Museum of Childhood with displays of antique dolls, toys, and children's furniture (☞ Staten Island and Historic Richmondtown *in* Chapter 3).

Just across the Hudson River in Liberty State Park, New Jersey, the **Liberty Science Center** is the largest science museum in the New York metropolitan area. Highlights include laser light and sound displays, an insect zoo, a 100-foot touch tunnel, an amazing 700-pound geodesic globe, and the Kodak OMNI Theater for viewing OMNIMAX movies on a gigantic screen. ⊠ *Liberty State Park, 251 Philip St., Jersey City, NJ,* ☎ *201/200–1000.* ⛁ *$9 adults, $6 children 2–12. OMNI Theater:* ⛁ *$7 adults, $5 children under 12; combined admission to exhibits and theater, $13 adults, $9 children 2–12; pay what you wish 1st Wed. of every month 1 PM–closing.* ☉ *Daily 9:30–5:30. Call the center for directions by car, the PATH train, or ferry.*

Parks and Playgrounds

New York's great outdoors sounds like a contradiction in terms, especially when you add children to the equation. But in **Central Park,** children can ride bicycles, play tennis, row boats, go horseback riding, ice-skate, roller-skate, rollerblade, skateboard, fly kites, feed ducks, throw Frisbees, and much more (☞ Central Park *in* Chapter 2). Favorite destinations include the **Conservatory Water,** which attracts owners of large, remote-controlled model boats and is located near the statues of Alice in Wonderland and Hans Christian Andersen. Younger children enjoy the hands-on activities at the park's fairy tale–like **Belvedere Castle** (☎ 212/772–0210). For horsing around, the antique **Carousel** (⊠ Central Park at 65th St., ☎ 212/879–0244), complete with painted steeds that prance to jaunty organ music, costs only 90¢ a ride. The pretty **Wollman Rink** (☎ 212/396–1010) has outdoor rollerblading classes and sessions—ice-skating in winter (☞ Chapter 9). At the beautifully restored **Harlem Meer,** kids of all ages are encouraged to fish along the shore for bass and sunfish. Free fishing poles and live bait are given out at the **Charles A. Dana Discovery Center** (☎ 212/860–1370).

At Brooklyn's 536-acre **Prospect Park,** kids enjoy kite flying and picnicking on the 90-acre Long Meadow (☞ Brooklyn *in* Chapter 3). The cherry trees, giant glass greenhouses, and spicy herbs at the **Brooklyn Botanic Garden** (⊠ 1000 Washington Ave., ☎ 622–4433) will please both kids and parents (☞ Brooklyn *in* Chapter 3).

In the Bronx, adjacent to the Bronx Zoo, the **New York Botanical Garden** (⊠ 200th St. and Southern Blvd., ☎ 212/817–8700) is one of the world's largest botanical gardens, with a large conservatory, 12 outdoor gardens, walking trails, and 40 acres of forest (☞ The Bronx *in* Chapter 3).

Manhattan has wonderful state-of-the-art playgrounds. **Central Park's** adventure playgrounds are full of slides, bridges, bars, swings, towers and tunnels; they're carpeted with sand or soft rubber matting and often cooled in summer by sprinklers, fountains, or running water. Good ones can be found along 5th Avenue at 67th Street near the zoo, at 71st and 77th streets, and at 85th Street near the Metropolitan Museum. Along Central Park West, the best ones are at 68th, 82nd, 85th, 93rd (with a Wild West theme), and 96th streets. The large **Hecksher Playground,** in Central Park at 62nd Street, is designed especially for toddlers.

Top-rated by Manhattan kids is the playground at **Hudson River Park** (⊠ West St. south of Vesey St.), which offers kid-size bronze sculptures of people and animals integrated into the parkscape. **Washington Square Park** (⊠ At foot of 5th Ave., between Waverly Pl. and W. 4th St.) has a popular and shady playground, as well as live jugglers and magicians in summertime. In **Riverside Park,** west of Riverside Drive, the best playgrounds are at 77th and 91st streets; the one at 77th Street has a circle of spouting elephant fountains. The **Asser Levy Playground** (⊠ 23rd St., 1 block from East River) is the first in Manhattan to cater fully to children with disabilities, with giant, multicolored mazelike structures, helter-skelter slides with wheelchair stations, and textured pavement for children who are blind.

At indoor playgrounds, kids can burn up energy—no matter what the weather is like. Seven days a week for $4.50 per person (including parents), **Playspace** (⊠ 1504 3rd Ave., at 85th St., ☎ 212/717–5200) provides sandboxes, toys, games, and room to run for youngsters 6 months–6 years. For kids aged 1–10, **WonderCamp** (⊠ 27 W. 23rd St., ☎ 212/243–9111) features a jungle gym, giant bouncing balls, organized games, and drama classes for $5.95 per visitor.

Zoos

Central Park Zoo (⊠ Off 5th Ave., at 64th St., ☎ 212/861–6030), recently renamed the **Central Park Wildlife Conservation Center,** is of a very manageable size, even for toddlers (☞ Central Park *in* Chapter 2). The antics of the Japanese snow monkeys—which live here on their own private island—are endlessly fascinating. But the diving and swimming polar bears steal the show.

The **Bronx Zoo** (⊠ 2300 Southern Blvd., ☎ 718/367–1010), renamed the **International Wildlife Conservation Park** (☞ The Bronx *in* Chapter 3) is the largest zoo in the United States. Most of the animals here live in replicas of their natural habitats. Don't miss the Children's Zoo area (☉ Apr.–Oct.).

Brooklyn's **Prospect Park Zoo** (⊠ Flatbush Ave., at Empire Blvd, ☎ 718/399–7339), now called the **Prospect Park Wildlife Conservation Center,** focuses on small animals, such as prairie dogs and red pandas.

The **Queens Zoo,** also known as the **Queens Wildlife Conservation Center,** shows North American animals in approximations of their natural habitat. The inhabitants include black bears, mountain lions, sea lions, bobcats, coyotes, bison, and elk. ⊠ 53–51 111th St., Flushing Meadows Park, ☎ 718/271–7761. ☒ $2.50 adults, 50¢ children 3– 12. ☉ Apr.–Oct., weekdays 10–5, weekends and holidays 10–5:30; Nov.–Mar., daily 10–4:30.

The **Staten Island Zoo** is small but of high quality and features one of the world's finest collections of snakes, as well as a separate Children's Zoo. ⊠ *Barrett Park, 614 Broadway, Staten Island,* ☎ *718/442–3100.* ☞ *$3 adults, $2 children 3–11; pay as you wish Wed. 2–4:45.* ☉ *Daily 10–4:45.*

Nearly 300 different marine creatures, including dolphins, sharks, walruses, and whales, are on display in Brooklyn at the **Aquarium for Wildlife Conservation.** Check out Discovery Cove, where kids can touch starfish and sea urchins and a 400-gallon "tidal wave" crashes every 30 seconds. ⊠ *Surf Ave., at W. 8th St., Coney Island,* ☎ *718/265–3474.* ☞ *$6.75 adults, children 2–12.* ☉ *June–Aug., weekdays 10–5, weekends and holidays 10–7; Sept.–May, daily 10–5.*

THE ARTS AND ENTERTAINMENT

In New York, theater groups exist just for children, art museums organize special programs, and kids can choose among art classes, summer courses, the circus, music concerts, storytelling, parades, and puppet shows.

Madison Square Garden (⊠ 7th Ave., between 31st and 33rd Sts., ☎ 212/465–6000) offers, besides sports events (☞ Chapter 9), some Disney and Sesame Street extravaganzas that appeal especially to children. There are major ice shows in winter, and each spring brings the **Ringling Bros. Barnum & Bailey Circus** (check local newspapers for dates, times, and ticket information). Meanwhile, the **Big Apple Circus** (⊠ 35 W. 35th St., ☎ 212/268–0055) charms the toughest New Yorkers in locations all over the five boroughs during spring and summer and is in residence at Lincoln Center from October through January.

Music

The **Little Orchestra Society** (⊠ 220 W. 42nd St., ☎ 212/704–2100) organizes concert series that introduce classical music to children ages 3–5 at Florence Gould Hall (55 E. 59th St.) and ages 5–12 at Lincoln Center. The **Metropolitan Opera** offers its **Growing Up with Opera** program (☎ 212/769–7008) and also sponsors an out-of-doors summer arts program, with plenty in it for children.

Theater

Henry Street Settlement (⊠ 466 Grand St., between Pitt and Willett Sts., ☎ 212/598–0400) has an Arts for Family weekend program. **Miss Majesty's Lollipop Playhouse** (⊠ Grove Street Playhouse, 39 Grove St., between W. 4th St. and 7th Ave., ☎ 212/741–6436) brings fairy tales and nursery rhymes to life on weekend afternoons. **New York Children's Theater** (⊠ Lincoln Sq. Theater, 250 W. 65th St., ☎ 212/496–8009) is determinedly realistic in style and explores topics such as literacy and aging. **New Victory Theater** (⊠ 209 W. 42nd St., ☎ 212/239–6255), the oldest surviving theater in New York, now presents a variety of plays and performances devoted solely to families. **Paper Bag Players** (☎ 212/362–0431) is the longest-running children's theater group in the nation (68th St., between Park and Lexington Aves., ☎ 212/772–4448). **Tada!** (⊠ 120 W. 28th St., ☎ 212/627–1732) is a popular children's group with a multiethnic perspective. **Theaterworks/USA** (⊠ Promenade Theater, Broadway, at 76th St., ☎ 212/677–5959) mounts classic stories and original productions. The **13th Street Theater** (⊠ 50 W. 13th St., ☎ 212/675–6677) presents its children's offerings on weekends.

Puppet Shows

The **International Festival of Puppet Theater,** sponsored by the Jim Henson Foundation, takes place in the summer at the Joseph Papp Public Theater (⊠ 425 Lafayette St., ☎ 212/539–8500). **Marionette Theater** (⊠ Swedish Cottage, Central Park at W. 81st St., ☎ 212/988–9093) features programs Tuesday–Saturday. **Puppet Playhouse** (⊠ Asphalt Green, 555 E. 90th St., ☎ 212/369–8890) offers weekend shows with puppets and marionettes. **Puppetworks** (⊠ 338 6th Ave., Park Slope, Brooklyn, ☎ 718/965–3391) presents marionettes performing classic children's stories.

Storytelling

Books of Wonder (⊠ 132 7th Ave., at 18th St., ☎ 212/989–3270) has storytelling on Sunday mornings. **Barnes & Noble** (⊠ 1280 Lexington Ave. at 86th St., ☎ 212/423–9900; Citicorp Building, ⊠ 54th St. at 3rd. Ave., ☎ 212750–8033; ⊠ 2289 Broadway at 82nd St., ☎ 212/362–8835; ⊠ 1972 Broadway at 66th St., ☎ 212/595–6859; ⊠ 605 5th Ave. at 48th St., ☎ 212/765–0590; ⊠ 675 6th Ave. at 22nd St., ☎ 212/727–1227; ⊠ 33 Union Sq., ☎ 212/253–0810; 4 Astor Pl., between Broadway and Lafayette, ☎ 212/420–1322) hosts readings for kids.

Film

Several museums sponsor special film programs aimed at families and children, including the Museum of Modern Art, the Museum of Television and Radio (☞ Rockefeller Center *in* Chapter 2), and the American Museum of the Moving Image (☞ Queens *in* Chapter 3). At the **Sony IMAX Theater** (⊠ 1998 Broadway, at 68th St., ☎ 212/336–5000) audience members strap on high-tech headgear that make nature and specially created feature films appear in 3-D. Kids thrill at the amazing nature films shown on the huge screen at the **Naturemax Theater** (⊠ Central Park W and 79th St., ☎ 212/769–5650) at the American Museum of Natural History. The immaculate **Walter Reade Theater** (⊠ 165 W. 65th St., ☎ 212/875–5600) shows feature films for children on weekends and sponsors children's film festivals.

DINING

In lower Manhattan, the younger ones should enjoy **Minter's Fun Food and Drink** (⊠ 4 World Financial Center, ☎ 212/945–4455) for chocolate beverages. At South Street Seaport, Pier 17's **Promenade Food Court** has a variety of quick foods. The surprising charms of the only **McDonald's** branch with doorman, pianist, and table service (⊠ 160 Broadway, between Maiden La. and Liberty St., ☎ 212/385–2063) are obvious. In TriBeCa, **Bubby's** (⊠ 120 Hudson St., at N. Moore, ☎ 212/219–0666) has casual dining and great baked goods. In Chinatown, don't miss the green-tea or red-bean ice cream at the **Chinatown Ice Cream Factory** (⊠ 65 Bayard St., ☎ 212/608–4170). Chinatown is also a good place to take the whole family for lunch or dinner at reasonable prices. **Mandarin Court** (⊠ 61 Mott St., ☎ 212/608–3838) serves dim sum every day until 3.

In SoHo, the airy decor at **Jerry's** (⊠ 101 Prince St., ☎ 212/966–9464) is popular with local artists and their young protégés. The **Cupping Room Café** (⊠ 359 W. Broadway, near Broome St., ☎ 212/925–2898) provides waffles throughout the day. In the West Village, **Arturo's** (⊠ 106 W. Houston St., at Thompson St., ☎ 212/677–3820) serves coal-fired pizza with child-friendly aplomb. **Aggie's** (⊠ 146 W. Houston St., at MacDougal St., ☎ 212/673–8994) is a funky coffee shop with sprightly soups and sandwiches. **Elephant and Castle** (⊠ 68 Greenwich Ave., near W. 11th St., ☎ 212/243–1400) has burgers and great french fries. For huge Cal-Tex servings at low prices, try **Benny's Burritos** (⊠ 113 Greenwich Ave., at Jane St., ☎ 212/727–0584). The **Cowgirl Hall of Fame** (⊠ 519 Hudson St., at W. 10th St., ☎ 212/633–1133) dishes up both Cajun cooking and cowgirl memorabilia.

In the East Village, the **Time Cafe** (⊠ 380 Lafayette St., below E. 4th St., ☎ 212/533–7000) is sunny, relaxed, and fantastic for brunch when they serve heavenly Southern-style biscuits. Kids will love **Stingy Lulus** (⊠ 129 St. Mark's Pl., between 1st Ave. and Ave. A, ☎ 212/674–3545), a raucous nouveau diner that raided the truck stops of middle America for its blue-plate-special decor. **Two Boots** (⊠ 37 Ave. A, between 2nd and 3rd Sts., ☎ 212/505–2276), which refers to the geographical "boots" of Italy and Louisiana, serves both pizza and jambalaya.

Just off Union Square is **America** (⊠ 9 E. 18th St., ☎ 212/505–2110), where everything is huge—menu, portions, spaces—except your check. The **Royal Canadian Pancake House** (⊠ 180 3rd Ave., between 16th and 17th Sts., ☎ 212/777–9288) has more than 50 flavors, including peanut-butter pancakes with real maple syrup. Chelsea offers the hip all-rounder **Empire Diner** (⊠ 210 10th Ave., at 22nd St., ☎ 212/243–2736). On Chelsea's bustling 6th Ave., the neon-decorated **Lox Around the Clock** (⊠ 676 6th Ave., at 21st St., ☎ 212/691–3535) serves up nice, juicy burgers.

Midtown, the **American Festival Café** (⊠ Rockefeller Center, 20 W. 50th St., ☎ 212/332–7620) is the essential NYC family dining experience. **Stage Delicatessen** (⊠ 834 7th Ave., at 54th St., ☎ 212/245–7850) will wow kids with its enormous piles of corned beef. If you're strolling to where 5th Avenue meets Central Park, the upscale ice cream parlor **Rumpelmayer's** (⊠ 50 Central Park S, near 6th Ave., ☎ 212/755–5800) is a nice place to cool off.

As you move west, prepare yourself for the "restaurant-as-theme park" district. Young music fans will be impressed by the **Hard Rock Café** (⊠ 221 W. 57th St., ☎ 212/459–9320) and **Planet Hollywood** (⊠ 140 W. 57th St., ☎ 212/333–7827). The motorcycle-oriented **Harley-Davidson Cafe** (⊠ 1370 6th Ave., at 56th St., ☎ 212/245–6000) bills itself as the "newest American legend." **Mickey Mantle's** (⊠ 42 Central Park S, near 6th Ave., ☎ 212/688–7777) excites ball-crazy kids. With its displays of famous designer gowns, **The Fashion Cafe** (⊠ 51st St, between 5th and 6th Aves., in Rockefeller Plaza, ☎ 212/765–3131) will enthrall would-be supermodels.

A good bet near Lincoln Center is **The Saloon** (⊠ 1920 Broadway, at 64th St., ☎ 212/874–1500), with a long menu and an occasional skating waiter. **Fiorello's Roman Café** (⊠ 1900 Broadway, near 63rd St., ☎ 212/595–5330) has individual pizzas and outside seating. Older kids will enjoy **Sidewalkers** (⊠ 12 W. 72nd St., ☎ 212/799–6070) for its buckets of spiced blue crabs and rollicking atmosphere. Fun, messy ribs and chicken entice youngsters at **Dallas BBQ** (⊠ 27 W. 72nd St., ☎ 212/873–2004). **Big Nick's** pizza joint (⊠ 2175 Broadway, at 77th St., ☎ 212/724–2010) gives out balloons that say "Big Nick Loves Me." Very child-friendly, the **Popover Cafe** (⊠ 551 Amsterdam Ave., at 87th St., ☎ 212/595–8555) has comfortable booths, hearty food, and teddy bears lurking in odd corners. At the brasserie-style **Boule-**

vard (⊠ 2398 Broadway, at 88th St., ☎ 212/874–7400), kids can eat spaghetti and draw on the tablecloths.

On the East Side, **Serendipity 3** (⊠ 225 E. 60th St., ☎ 212/838–3531), "the ice cream parlor to the stars," is perfect for a light meal or dessert. **Jackson Hole** (⊠ 232 E. 64th St., ☎ 212/371–7187) is a reliable, pleasant burger joint with other branches around town. Central Park's **Boathouse Café** (⊠ Near E. 72nd St., ☎ 212/517–3623) can be somewhat pricey, but it's wonderfully soothing. **Sarabeth's Kitchen** (⊠ 1295 Madison Ave., at 92nd St., ☎ 212/410–7335) serves whopping cakes and other desserts. **Barking Dog Luncheonette** (⊠ 1678 3rd Ave., at 94th St., ☎ 212/831–1800) has a special drinking fountain for dogs.

LODGING

Since the vast majority of hotels are in midtown Manhattan, your choice of which neighborhood to pick for a family stay is limited. If anything, it may be best to avoid the environs of seedy Times Square, just in case your offspring escapes alone or gets lost. Generally speaking, as in any other big city, most Manhattan hotels will provide an extra bed, babysitting, and stroller rental—all the common requirements of families traveling with young children—but call ahead.

Good bets for families, at the top end of the scale, include the following. Kids like the **Holiday Inn-Crown Plaza** (⊠ 1605 Broadway, ☎ 212/977–4000) for its swimming pool, and parents will like it for its lifeguard. Also good choices, thanks to their child-pleasing swimming pools, are the Sheraton Manhattan, the Vista, and the UN Plaza–Park Hyatt. The **Doubletree Guest Suites** (⊠ 1563 Broadway, at 47th St., ☎ 212/403–6300) has a "Kids Quarters" playroom with games and computers. Less costly, any of the **Manhattan Suites East** (☎ 212/465–3690) properties would make an excellent choice, since they resemble tiny apartments. At **The San Carlos** (⊠ 150 E. 50th St., ☎ 212/755–1800), the large suites have kitchen facilities. On the far Upper West Side, near Columbia University, **International House** (⊠ 500 Riverside Dr., ☎ 212/316–8436), formerly for students only, has 10 family-sized apartments for under $100 per night. The **Vanderbilt Y** (⊠ 224 E. 47th St., ☎ 212/756–9600) in midtown has some family rooms with two bunk beds apiece for $103 per night.

SHOPPING

Adults and children alike find shopping nirvana in New York. One of the world's best toy stores, **F.A.O. Schwarz** (⊠ 5th Ave., at 58th St., ☎ 212/644–9400)—where Tom Hanks danced on the giant keyboard in the movie *Big*—is probably highlight number one for young consumers (☞ Toys *in* Chapter 10). Even shopping for clothes, often resented by children, can be fun here.

In addition to the stores listed under Children's Clothing in Chapter 10, try the following. On the Upper West Side, **Monkeys & Bears** (⊠ 506 Amsterdam Ave., between 84th and 85th Sts., ☎ 212/873–2673) stocks all-age clothes, both hip and traditional. **Kids Are Magic** (⊠ 2293 Broadway, between 82nd and 83rd Sts., ☎ 212/875–9240) sports two stories of reasonably priced clothes and toys. **Shoofly** (⊠ 465 Amsterdam Ave., between 82nd and 83rd Sts., ☎ 212/580–4390) sells designer footwear, hats, knapsacks, and a huge assortment of hair ribbons. On the Upper East Side, Madison Avenue's boutiques offer an array of choices for dressing the well-heeled child. **Bebe Thompson** (⊠ 1216 Madison Ave., between 82nd and 83rd Sts., ☎ 212/249–4740) deals in prêt-à-porter,

European fashions for budding runway models, newborn to 12 years. **Chocolate Soup** (✉ 946 Madison Ave., between 74th and 75th Sts., ☎ 212/861–2210) sells hand-sewn and imported clothes for kids. **Jacadi** (✉ 787 Madison Ave., at 67th St., ☎ 212/535–3200 and 1281 Madison Ave., at 91st St., ☎ 212/369–1616) stocks toddler-sized clothes from Paris, as well as stuffed animals.

It's worth visiting the clothing and toy sections of **department stores.** Visit **Macy's** for the thrill of size and **Stern's** for the cool atrium plaza. Go to Macy's during the holiday season between Thanksgiving and Christmas, and enjoy the enchanting Christmas window displays for free. Don't miss the animated windows at **Lord & Taylor,** either; the elegant ones at **Bergdorf Goodman, Bloomingdale's, Saks Fifth Avenue** and, especially, at **Barneys New York** tend to be aimed squarely at adults, but kids usually enjoy them, too (☞ Department Stores *in* Chapter 10).

For stores featuring toys, games, magic, and general gizmos, *see* Fun and Games *in* Chapter 10. **Dollhouse Antics** (✉ 1343 Madison Ave., at 94th St., ☎ 212/876–2288) stocks miniature furnishings at 1-inch scale. Children should like the **Big City Kite Co.** (✉ 1210 Lexington Ave., at 82nd St., ☎ 212/472–2623), which has one of the best kite selections anywhere. **Children's General Store** (✉ 2473 Broadway, at 92nd St., ☎ 212/580–2723) sells a new breed of "educational" toys for infants and preteens; they're so fun and colorful, kids will actually enjoy them. It's easy to lose yourself in SoHo's **Enchanted Forest** (✉ 85 Mercer St., ☎ 212/925–6677), where the often handmade and always original games, toys, and stuffed animals will charm kids and parents alike. For older kids, **Forbidden Planet** (✉ 840 Broadway, at 13th St., ☎ 212/473–1576), stocks everything relating to science fiction and fantasy, such as comic books and monster masks. **Little Rickie** (✉ 49½ 1st Ave., at 3rd St., ☎ 212/505–6467) specializes in kitschy, oddball merchandise, from snowdomes and balloon modelling kits to legitimate folk art. At the **Pull Cart** ceramics studio (✉ 31 W. 21st St., 7th floor, ☎ 212/727–7089), kids can pick out and paint their own tablewares.

For children's books, **Books of Wonder** (✉ 132 7th Ave., at 18th St., ☎ 212/989–3270) has an extensive stock for all reading levels. **Twinkleberry and Nutkin** (✉ 311 E. 81st St., ☎ 212/794–2565) has a thoughtful selection, especially if you're a fan of the Madeline books. **Bank Street College Bookstore** (✉ 2875 Broadway, at 112th St., ☎ 212/678–1654) carries politically correct kids books. **Barnes & Noble**'s several branches around town all have large children's books sections ☞ Storytelling *in* The Arts and Entertainment, *above.*).

For comics, try **Village Comics** (✉ 163 Bleecker St., 2nd floor, ☎ 212/777–2770), for their enormous selection. **Funny Business Comics** (✉ 0660-B Amsterdam Ave., ☎ 212/799–9477) carries a delightful stock of old and new issues.

Babies have their own shopping needs, though they don't know it. On the Upper West Side, the comprehensively stocked **Albee's** (✉ 715 Amsterdam Ave., at 95th St., ☎ 212/662–5740) has clothes, cribs, and snappy-looking strollers. The very upscale **Bellini** (✉ 473 Columbus Ave., at 83rd St., ☎ 212/362–3700; 1305 2nd Ave., at 68th St., ☎ 212/517–9233) specializes in both infant fashions and baby-pleasing home furnishings. **Dinosaur Hill** (✉ 302 E. 9th St., ☎ 212/473–5850) sells unusual handmade clothes for infants, as well as discovery toys. **Hush-A-Bye** (✉ 1459 1st Ave., at 76th St., ☎ 212/988–4500) caters to Upper East Side small-fry with a mix of clothes and toys. **Schneider's** (✉ 20 Ave. A, at 2nd St., ☎ 212/228–3540) is a very well-stocked store for downtown infants and discount hunters.

5 The Arts

For lovers of the arts, New York is close to paradise. Theater fans can choose among big Broadway productions, stellar revivals of classics, and works by emerging playwrights Off Broadway. Music devotees have the chance to see the world's top performers, appearing in premier showcases such as Carnegie Hall and the Metropolitan Opera House. For dance aficionados, there are two first-rate ballet troupes and a fine selection of modern-dance venues. Film fanatics can indulge in Hollywood releases, classics, foreign movies, and independent works.

Revised by
David Low

IN A CITY AS LARGE AS NEW YORK, urban hassles sometimes appear insurmountable. When it's pouring rain,
every cab seems engaged or off-duty. Waiting at the post
office, supermarket, and even the cash machine almost always takes
longer than you expected. Even buying a pair of socks can become a
chore when a store is busy, which is usually the case. But in the end,
New Yorkers put up with all the stress for at least one obvious reason:
the city's unrivaled artistic life. Despite the immense competition and
the threat of cuts in city aid to the arts, artists from all disciplines continue to come to the city to find their peers and to produce their work.
Audiences benefit greatly.

New York has somewhere between 200 and 250 legitimate theaters,
and many more ad hoc venues—parks, churches, universities, museums, lofts, galleries, streets, and rooftops—where performances ranging from Shakespeare to sword-dancing take place. The city is, as well,
a revolving door of festivals and special events: Summer jazz, one-act
play marathons, international film series, and musical celebrations
from the classical to the avant-garde are just a few.

Arts Centers

New York's most renowned centers for the arts are tourist attractions
in themselves.

Carnegie Hall (⊠ 881 7th Ave., at 57th St., ☎ 212/247–7800) is
world famous as a premier hall for concerts, attracting great orchestras from around the world, and music masters such as Arturo Toscanini,
Leonard Bernstein, Isaac Stern, Yo-Yo Ma, Kathleen Battle, Frank
Sinatra, and the Beatles. Performances are held in both its main auditorium (opened in 1891 with a concert conducted by Tchaikovsky) and
in Weill Recital Hall, where rising young talents often make their first
New York debuts. Although the emphasis is on classical music, Carnegie
Hall also hosts jazz, cabaret, and folk-music series.

City Center (⊠ 131 W. 55th St., ☎ 212/581–1212; mailing address
for ticket orders: Citytix, 130 W. 56th St., 4th Floor, 10019), under
its eccentric, tiled Spanish dome (built in 1923 by the Ancient and Accepted Order of the Mystic Shrine and saved from demolition in 1943
by Mayor Fiorello La Guardia), presents dance troupes such as Alvin
Ailey and Paul Taylor, as well as concert versions of American musicals. The Manhattan Theatre Club (☞ Theater, *below*) also resides here,
with its highly regarded program of innovative contemporary drama.

Lincoln Center (⊠ W. 62nd to 66th Sts., Columbus to Amsterdam
Aves., ☎ 212/875–5000) is a 14-acre complex that houses the Metropolitan Opera, the New York Philharmonic, the Juilliard School, the New
York City Ballet, the American Ballet Theatre, the New York City Opera,
the Film Society of Lincoln Center, the Chamber Music Society of Lincoln Center, the Lincoln Center Theater, the School of American Ballet, and the New York Public Library's Library and Museum of the
Performing Arts. Tours of Lincoln Center are available (☎ 212/875–
5351; ☞ The Upper West Side *in* Chapter 2).

Madison Square Garden (⊠ W. 31st to W. 33rd Sts. on 7th Ave.,
☎ 212/465–6741), camped atop Penn Station, includes a renovated
20,000-seat arena and the sleek 5,600-seat Paramount Theater. In addition to sports events such as basketball, ice hockey, tennis, and boxing, the complex draws large crowds to pop music concerts by stars
as diverse as Barbra Streisand, Paul Simon, and Elton John. If your fa-

vorite rock band isn't appearing at Madison Square Garden, check out its suburban sister halls, **Nassau Veterans Memorial Coliseum** (✉ Uniondale, Long Island, ☎ 516/794–9300) and **Meadowlands Arena** (✉ East Rutherford, NJ, ☎ 201/935–3900).

Radio City Music Hall (✉ 1260 6th Ave., at 50th St., ☎ 212/247–4777), an Art Deco gem, opened in 1932; it has 6,000 seats, a 60-foot-high foyer, two-ton chandeliers, and a powerful Wurlitzer organ. On this vast stage you'll find everything from rock and pop concerts to Christmas and Easter extravaganzas (featuring the perennial Rockettes kick line), and star-studded TV specials. Tours (☎ 212/632–4041) are conducted daily (☞ Rockefeller Center and Midtown Skyscrapers *in* Chapter 2).

Brooklyn Academy of Music (BAM; ✉ 30 Lafayette Ave., Brooklyn, ☎ 718/636–4100), America's oldest performing arts center began in 1859, but its reputation today is far from stodgy thanks to its daring and innovative dance, music, opera, and theater productions. The main hall is the Opera House, a white Renaissance Revival palace built in 1908; other spaces at BAM are the Majestic Theatre (a partly restored vaudeville house around the corner), the Helen Owen Carey Playhouse, and the Lepercq Space.

Manhattan has several small-scale yet important arts centers. **Town Hall** (✉ 123 W. 43rd St., ☎ 212/840–2824), hosts a diverse program of chamber music, cabaret performances, and stand-up comedy. **Merkin Concert Hall** (✉ 129 W. 67th St., ☎ 212/362–8719) mainly features chamber music concerts. **Symphony Space** (✉ 2537 Broadway, at 95th St., ☎ 212/864–5400), a cavernous converted movie theater, schedules an eclectic offering that ranges from folk music to short stories read by celebrities. The **Sylvia and Danny Kaye Playhouse** (✉ Hunter College, 68th St., between Park and Lexington Aves., ☎ 212/772–4448), a lovely concert hall, has a varied calendar of music, dance, opera, and theater events. The **92nd Street Y** (✉ 1395 Lexington Ave., ☎ 212/996–1100), known for its classical music concerts, also sponsors readings by famous writers, and the Lyrics and Lyricists series. **The Kitchen** (✉ 512 W. 19th St., ☎ 212/255–5793), showcases avant-garde videos, music, performance art, and dance.

Getting Tickets

Ticket prices in New York, especially for Broadway shows, never seem to stop rising. Major concerts and recitals, however, can be equally expensive. The top Broadway ticket prices for musicals are $75; the best seats for nonmusicals can cost as much as $65.

On the positive side, tickets for New York City's arts events usually aren't too hard to come by—unless, of course, you're dead set on seeing the season's hottest, sold-out show. Generally, a theater or concert hall's box office is the best place to buy tickets, since in-house ticket sellers make it their business to know about their theaters and shows and don't mind pointing out (on a chart) where you'll be seated. It's always a good idea to purchase tickets in advance to avoid disappointment, especially if you're traveling a long distance. For advance purchase, send the theater or hall a certified check or money order, several alternate dates, and a self-addressed, stamped envelope.

You can also pull out a credit card and call **Tele-Charge** (☎ 212/239–6200) or **TicketMaster** (☎ 212/307–4100 or 212/307–7171) to reserve tickets for Broadway and Off-Broadway shows—newspaper ads generally will specify which you should use for any given event. Both services will give you seat locations over the phone upon request. A surcharge

($2–$5 per ticket) will be added to the total. You can arrange to have your tickets mailed to you or have them waiting for you at the theater.

For those willing to pay top dollar to see that show or concert everyone's talking about but no one can get tickets for, try a ticket broker. Recently, brokers charged $100–$150 for tickets to *Sunset Boulevard*; had the same seat been available at the box office, it would have sold for $70. Among the brokers to try are **N.Y. Theatre Tickets** (☎ 201/392–0999) and **Continental/Golden/Leblangs Theatre Tickets** (☎ 212/944–8910 or 800/299–8587). Also, check the lobbies of major hotels for ticket-broker outlets.

You may be tempted to buy from ticket scalpers. But beware: They have reportedly sold tickets to the big hits for up to $200, when seats were still available at the box office for much less. Bear in mind that ticket scalping is against the law in New York. Also, these scalpers may even sell you phony tickets.

Off- and Off-Off-Broadway theaters have their own joint box office called **Ticket Central** (⊠ 416 W. 42nd St., ☎ 212/279–4200). It's open between 1 and 8 PM. Although there are no discounts here, tickets to performances in these theaters are usually less expensive than Broadway tickets, and they cover an array of events, including legitimate theater, performance art, and dance.

Discount Tickets

The **TKTS booth** in Duffy Square (⊠ 47th St. and Broadway, ☎ 212/768–1818) is New York's best-known discount source. TKTS sells day-of-performance tickets for Broadway and Off-Broadway plays at discounts that, depending on a show's popularity, often go as low as 50% to 75% of the usual price, plus a $2.50 surcharge per ticket. The names of shows available on that day are posted on electronic boards in front of the booth. If you're interested in a Wednesday or Saturday matinee, go to the booth between 10 and 2, check out what's offered, and then wait in line. For evening performances, the booth is open 3–8; for Sunday matinee and evening performances, noon–8. *Note: TKTS accepts only cash or traveler's checks—no credit cards.*

The wait is generally pleasant (weather permitting), as the bright lights and babble of Broadway surround you. (Lines, however, can be particularly long on weekends.) You're likely to meet friendly theater lovers on line eager to share opinions about shows they've recently seen; often you'll even meet struggling actors who can give you the inside scoop. By the time you get to the booth, you may be willing to take a gamble on a show you would otherwise never have picked, and it just might be more memorable than one of the long-running hits.

So successful has TKTS proved that an auxiliary booth operates in the Wall Street area (⊠ 2 World Trade Center mezzanine). The World Trade Center Branch is open weekdays 11–5:30, Saturday 11–3:30. For matinees and Sundays, you have to purchase tickets the day before the performance. The lines at the downtown TKTS booth are usually shorter than those at Duffy Square, though the uptown booth usually has a larger selection of plays.

The **Bryant Park Music and Dance Tickets Booth,** located on 42nd Street and 6th Avenue in Bryant Park, just west of the New York Public Library, sells half-price day-of-performance tickets for several music and dance events around the city (and full-price tickets for other concerts as well). It's open Tuesday–Sunday noon–2 and 3–7. Unlike TKTS, the Bryant Park booth has a telephone information line (☎ 212/382–2323). It accepts only cash and traveler's checks.

Discounts on big-name, long-running shows (such as *Miss Saigon* and *Les Misérables*) are often available if you can lay your hands on a couple of **"twofers"**—discount ticket coupons found on various cash registers around town, near the lines at TKTS, at the Times Square visitor information office (at the northwest corner of 7th Ave. and 42nd St.), at the New York Visitors and Convention Bureau (at 2 Columbus Circle), and at the office of their producer, the **Hit Show Club** (⊠ 630 9th Ave., 8th floor, ☎ 212/581–4211; ☉ weekdays 9–4).

Some theaters, such as **Classic Stage Company** (⊠ 136 E. 13th St., ☎ 212/677–4210), offer reduced rates on unsold tickets the day of the performance, often one hour before curtain time. These special discounts are usually noted in the newspaper theater listings or ads.

Some Broadway and Off-Broadway shows sell reduced-priced tickets for performances scheduled before opening night. Look at newspaper ads for discounted previews, or consult the box office. Tickets may cost less at matinees, particularly on Wednesday.

Finding Out What's On

To find out who or what's playing where, your first stop should be the newsstand. The **New York Times** isn't a prerequisite for finding out what's going on around town, but it comes in pretty handy, especially on Friday, with its "Weekend" section. The Sunday "Arts and Leisure" section features longer articles on everything from opera to soap opera—and a lot more theater ads, plus a full, detailed survey of cultural events for the upcoming week.

For adventurous, more unconventional tastes, there's the free weekly paper the **Village Voice;** its club listings and "Choices" section are both reliable. When its club-tattler critic Michael Musto talks (in a column called "La Dolce Musto"), night prowlers and club crawlers listen. The *Voice* is published on Wednesday.

Time Out New York is a comprehensive guide to all kinds of entertainment happenings around town, with particularly good coverage of the downtown scene. **The New Yorker** magazine has long been known for its discerning and often witty listings called "Goings On About Town"—a section at the front of the magazine that contains ruthlessly succinct reviews of theater, dance, art, music, film, and nightlife. **New York** magazine's "Cue" listings are extremely helpful, covering everything from art to the written word. **Theater Week** has up-to-date theater and cabaret news. The **New York Native, Christopher Street,** and **Homo-Extra** illuminate the gay scene.

The League of New York Theatres and Producers and **Playbill** magazine publish a twice-monthly **Broadway Theatre Guide,** available in hotels and theaters around town. For information on the lower Manhattan cultural scene, write for a **Downtown Arts Activities Calendar** (⊠ Lower Manhattan Cultural Council, 1 World Trade Ctr., Suite 1717, 10048, ☎ 212/432–0900).

NYC/ON STAGE (☎ 212/768–1818) is the Theatre Development Fund's 24-hour information service.

THEATER

The theater—not the Statue of Liberty or South Street Seaport—is the city's number-one tourist attraction, and uptown or downtown you can spot theater folk pursuing their work with customary passion and panache. Delicate little ladies tottering about in their pillbox hats are really theatrical grande dames, with fast answers to the flashers on 8th Avenue; shifty-looking guys toting battered briefcases turn out to be famous directors; and the girls and boys scuttling through stage doors are chorus members rushing to exchange their Nikes for tap shoes.

Broadway Theater District

To most people, New York theater means **Broadway,** that region bounded by 42nd and 53rd streets, between 6th and 9th avenues, where bright, transforming lights shine upon porn theaters and jewel-box playhouses alike. Although the area's busy sidewalks contain more than their share of hustlers and pickpockets, visitors brave them for the playhouses' plentiful delights. Extravagant plans for redevelopment of the Times Square area continue to ricochet from marquee to marquee. With every thud of the wrecker's ball, theater devotees pray for the survival of the essence of Broadway—as Paul Goldberger put it in the *New York Times,* "the world of memory, the magical Times Square of old, the lively, glittering district of theaters, restaurants, cabarets, hotels, and neon signs that was in many ways the city's symbolic heart."

Some of the old playhouses are as interesting for their history as for their current offerings. The **St. James** (⊠ 246 W. 44th St.), for instance, is where Lauren Bacall served as an usherette in the '40s, and a sleeper of a musical called *Oklahoma!* woke up as a hit. The **Lyceum** (⊠ 149 W. 45th St.) is New York's oldest still-functioning theater, built in 1903 with a posh apartment on top that now holds the Shubert Archive (open to scholars by appointment only). At the **Shubert Theatre** (⊠ 225 W. 44th St.), Barbra Streisand made her 1962 Broadway debut in *I Can Get It for You Wholesale,* and the long-run record breaker, *A Chorus Line,* played for 15 years. The **Martin Beck Theatre** (⊠ 302 W. 45th St.), built in 1924 in Byzantine style, is the stage that served up premieres of Eugene O'Neill's *The Iceman Cometh,* Arthur Miller's *The Crucible,* and Tennessee Williams's *Sweet Bird of Youth.* Theater names read like a roll call of American theater history: **Booth, Ethel Barrymore, Eugene O'Neill, Gershwin, Lunt-Fontanne, Richard Rodgers,** and **Neil Simon,** among others.

Within the past two years, two 42nd Street houses have come back to life. The **New Victory** (⊠ 209 W. 42nd St.), previously known as the Theater Republic and the Belasco Theater, is the oldest surviving playhouse in New York with a lovely Georgian facade; now completely modernized, it stages exciting productions for kids. Across the street, the Walt Disney Company has refurbished the Art Nouveau **New Amsterdam** (⊠ 214 W. 42nd St.); Eddie Cantor, Will Rogers, Fanny Brice, and the Ziegfeld Follies once drew crowds here.

As you stroll around the theater district, you may also see: **Shubert Alley,** a shortcut between 44th and 45th streets where theater moguls used to park their limousines, today the site of a jam-packed Great White Way memorabilia store called One Shubert Alley; **Manhattan Plaza,** a largely subsidized apartment complex at 9th Avenue and 42nd Street inhabited primarily by theater people, whose rent in hard times is assessed at 30% of their income (whatever that comes to); **Theatre Row** (⊠ 42nd St. between 9th and 10th Aves.), a convivial collection of small Off-Broadway theaters; and **Restaurant Row** (⊠ 46th St., between 8th and 9th Aves.), which offers plenty of choices.

Beyond Broadway

Not all that long ago it was relatively simple to categorize the New York stage beyond Broadway. It was divided into **Off-Broadway** and **Off-Off-Broadway,** depending on a variety of factors that included

Theater District

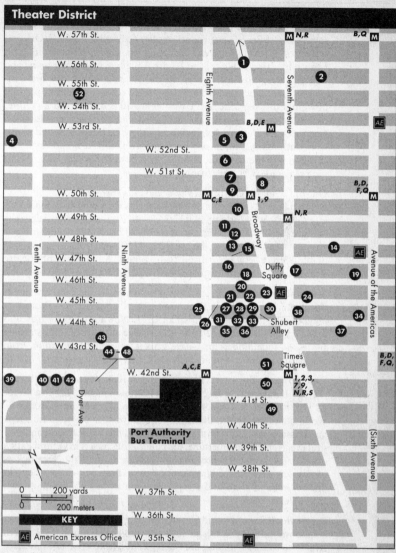

Ambassador, **10**
American Place, **19**
Belasco, **34**
Booth, **29**
Broadhurst, **32**
Broadway, **3**
Brooks Atkinson, **16**
Circle in the Square, **9**
Cort, **14**
Douglas Fairbanks, **42**
Ensemble Studio, **4**
Ethel Barrymore, **15**
Eugene O'Neill, **11**
Gershwin, **7**
Harold Clurman, **47**

Helen Hayes, **36**
INTAR, **45**
Imperial, **21**
John Golden, **26**
John Houseman, **40**
Judith Anderson, **44**
Kaufman, **39**
Lamb's, **37**
Lincoln Center
Theater: Vivian
Beaumont, Mitzi E.
Newhouse, **1**
Longacre, **13**
Lunt-Fontanne, **18**
Lyceum, **24**

Majestic, **31**
Manhattan Theatre
Club (City Center), **2**
Marquis, **23**
Martin Beck, **25**
Minskoff, **30**
Music Box, **22**
Nat Horne, **41**
Nederlander, **49**
Neil Simon, **6**
New Amsterdam, **50**
New Victory, **51**
Palace, **17**
Playwrights Horizons,
46

Plymouth, **28**
Richard Rodgers, **20**
Roundabout Theatre
Company (Criterion
Center), **38**
Royale, **27**
Samuel Beckett, **48**
St. James, **35**
Shubert, **33**
Theatre Four, **52**
Virginia, **5**
Walter Kerr, **12**
Westside, **43**
Winter Garden, **8**

theatrical contract type, location, and ticket price. Today such distinctions seem strained, as Off-Broadway prices have risen and the quality of some Off-Off-Broadway productions has decidedly improved. Off- and Off-Off-Broadway is where Eric Bogosian, Ann Magnuson, John Leguizamo, Danny Hoch, and Laurie Anderson make their home and where *Driving Miss Daisy, Steel Magnolias,* and *Jeffrey* were first conceived. Attendance and ticket sales remain relatively healthy, proving how vital this segment of the theater world is to New York culture. Recent long-running hits have included *Tubes* by the surreal Blue Man Group; *Death Defying Acts* by Woody Allen, David Mamet, and Elaine May; and *Stomp,* a percussion performance piece. Off-Broadway is also still home to the romantic musical *The Fantasticks,* the longest-running play in U.S. theater history.

One of the major Off-Broadway enclaves is **Theatre Row,** a collection of small houses (100 seats or less)—such as the **John Houseman Theatre** (⊠ 450 W. 42nd St., ☎ 212/967–9077), the **Douglas Fairbanks Theatre** (⊠ 432 W. 42nd St., ☎ 212/239–4321), and **Playwrights Horizons** (⊠ 416 W. 42nd St., ☎ 212/279–4200)—on the downtown side of 42nd Street between 9th and 10th avenues. A block east of Theatre Row is the **Westside Theatre** (⊠ 407 W. 43rd St., ☎ 212/307–4100).

Name actors appear in top-flight productions at the two theaters at **Lincoln Center:** the **Vivian Beaumont** (actually considered a Broadway playhouse) and the more intimate **Mitzi E. Newhouse** (⊠ 65th St. and Broadway, ☎ for both 212/239–6200), which has scored some startling successes, including John Guare's *Six Degrees of Separation,* Tom Stoppard's *Arcadia,* and an acclaimed revival of *Carousel.*

Downtown in the East Village, at the **Joseph Papp Public Theater** (⊠ 425 Lafayette St., ☎ 212/260–2400), renamed in 1992 to honor its late founder and longtime guiding genius, producer George C. Wolfe continues the tradition of innovative theater, mounting new and classic plays, along with dance concerts, literary readings, and musical events. In the summertime, the Public raises its sets in Central Park's open-air **Delacorte Theater** for Shakespeare in the Park. Free tickets for evening performances are handed out to those who have waited in line beforehand at around 1 PM downtown at the Public and uptown at the Delacorte.

Greenwich Village, around Sheridan Square, is another Off-Broadway neighborhood. Its theaters include the **Actors Playhouse** (⊠ 100 7th Ave. S, ☎ 212/239–6200); the **Cherry Lane Theatre** (⊠ 38 Commerce St., ☎ 212/989–2020); the **Lucille Lortel Theatre** (⊠ 121 Christopher St., ☎ 212/924–8782); the **Minetta Lane Theatre** (⊠ 18 Minetta La., ☎ 212/420–8000); the **Players Theater** (⊠ 115 MacDougal St., ☎ 212/254–5076); and the **Sullivan Street Playhouse** (⊠ 181 Sullivan St., ☎ 212/674–3838).

Many estimable **Off-Broadway theaters** are flung across the Manhattan map: the **Astor Place Theatre** (⊠ 434 Lafayette St., ☎ 212/254–4370); the **Orpheum Theatre** (⊠ 126 2nd Ave., at 8th St., ☎ 212/477–2477); the **Variety Arts Theatre** (⊠ 110 3rd Ave., at 14th St., ☎ 212/239–6200); the **Union Square Theatre** (⊠ 100 E. 17th St., ☎ 212/505–0700); the **WPA Theatre** (⊠ 519 W. 23rd St., ☎ 212/206–0523), showcasing new works by American playwrights; and the **Promenade Theatre** (⊠ Broadway at 76th St., ☎ 212/580–1313).

THEATER COMPANIES

Several Off- and Off-Off-Broadway theater groups are worth keeping your eye on:

American Jewish Theatre (✉ 307 W. 26th St., ☎ 212/633–9797) stages contemporary plays and revivals of musicals, more often than not with a Jewish theme.

Atlantic Theater Company (✉ 33 W. 20th St., ☎ 212/645–1242), founded by playwright David Mamet and actor William H. Macy, is dedicated to producing controversial new plays.

Circle Repertory Company (✉ 159 Bleecker St., ☎ 212/239–6200) presents plays and musicals by up-and-coming American talents.

Classic Stage Company (CSC, ✉ 136 E. 13th St., ☎ 212/677–4210) provides a showcase for the classics—some arcane, others European—in new translations and adaptations.

Ensemble Studio Theatre (✉ 549 W. 52nd St., ☎ 212/247–3405), with its tried-and-true roster of players, stresses new dramatic works. It also presents an annual one-act-play marathon.

Irish Arts Center (✉ 553 W. 51st St., ☎ 212/757–3318) stages classic and contemporary Irish plays.

Jean Cocteau Repertory (✉ Bouwerie Lane Theatre, 330 Bowery, ☎ 212/677–0060), founded in 1971, reinvents international classics, intelligently performed by its resident acting troupe.

Jewish Repertory Theatre (✉ Playhouse 91, 316 E. 91st St., ☎ 212/831–2000), begun in 1972, produces plays and musicals about Jewish life such as *Crossing Delancey,* the basis for the hit film.

Manhattan Theatre Club (✉ At City Center, 131 W. 55th St., ☎ 212/581–1212) stages some of the most talked-about new plays and musicals in town; Terrence McNally, Athol Fugard, and Stephen Sondheim have all had their work produced here.

New York Theater Workshop (✉ 79 E. 4th St., ☎ 212/460–5475) produces challenging new theater by American and international playwrights like Tony Kushner and Caryl Churchill.

Pan Asian Repertory Theatre (✉ Playhouse 46 in St. Clement's Church, 423 W. 46th St., ☎ 212/245–2660), a center for Asian and Asian-American artists, focuses on new works or adapted Western plays.

Pearl Theatre Company (✉ 80 St. Mark's Pl., ☎ 212/598–9802) is the intimate home of a troupe of resident players who concentrate on classics from around the globe; the works of such masters as Molière, Ibsen, Shakespeare, and Sophocles have found a new life here.

Primary Stages (✉ 354 W. 45th St., ☎ 212/333–4052) puts the spotlight on new work by American playwrights, such as David Ives, Charles Busch, and Donald Margulies.

Repertorio Español (✉ Gramercy Arts Theatre, 138 E. 27th St., ☎ 212/889–2850) is an Obie award–winning Spanish arts repertory theater; performances are in Spanish.

Second Stage (✉ McGinn/Cazale Theatre, 2162 Broadway, at W. 76th St., ☎ 212/873–6103) is committed to new works and recent plays that may not have been given a fair chance their first time around.

Signature Theatre Company (✉ Administrative office: 422 W. 42nd St., ☎ 212/967–1913) devotes each season to the sensitive productions of the works of one American playwright; past seasons have recognized the plays of Lee Blessing, Edward Albee, Horton Foote, and Adrienne Kennedy. In 1997, Sam Shepard's plays will be performed.

Vineyard Theater (✉ 108 E. 15th St., ☎ 212/353–3366) features innovative new plays and musicals by established and emerging artists.

York Theatre Company (✉ Theatre at St. Peter's Church, 54th St. at Lexington Ave., ☎ 212/935–5820) presents acclaimed revivals of plays and musicals in addition to new theater works.

Avant-Garde

Last, but not at all least, is New York's fabled theatrical avant-garde. The experimental theater movement's founders may no longer be the long-haired hippies they were when they first started doing mixed-media productions and promoting off-center playwrights (such as Sam Shepard) in the '60s, but they continue at the forefront.

Ellen Stewart, also known, simply and elegantly, as "La Mama," started the theater complex **La MaMa E.T.C.** (⊠ 74A E. 4th St., ☎ 212/ 475–7710) in 1961. Over the past three decades, her East Village organization has branched out to import European innovators and has grown physically as well. It now encompasses a First Floor Theater, an Annex theater, and a club. Productions include everything from African fables to New Wave opera to reinterpretations of the Greek classics; past triumphs have included the original performances of *Godspell* and *Torch Song Trilogy*.

A four-theater cultural complex is home to the experimentalist **Theater for the New City** (⊠ 155 1st Ave., ☎ 212/254–1109), which devotes its productions to new playwrights. The complex also sponsors a free street-theater program, arts festivals, and Christmas and Halloween spectacles. Founded by the late Charles Ludlam in 1972 and now led by actor Everett Quinton, the **Ridiculous Theatrical Company** (⊠ Actor's Playhouse, 100 7th Ave. S, ☎ 212/239–6200) keeps audiences laughing with its unique performance style: a blend of classical acting— usually in drag—and high camp.

Performance Art

At the vanishing point of the avant-garde is that curious mélange of artistic disciplines known as performance art. Intentionally difficult to categorize, it blends music and sound, dance, video and lights, words, and whatever else comes to the performance artist's mind, to produce events of erratic success—sometimes fascinating, sometimes deadening. Performance art is almost exclusively a downtown endeavor, though it is also showcased in the outer boroughs, especially Brooklyn, where the **Brooklyn Academy of Music** (⊠ 30 Lafayette Ave., Brooklyn, ☎ 718/636–4100) has built its considerable reputation on its annual Next Wave Festival, which features many performance works.

Manhattan has a few notable performance-art showcases:

Dixon Place (⊠ 258 Bowery, between Houston and Prince Sts., ☎ 212/ 219–3088) presents an eccentric, eclectic schedule, including comedy acts, musicians, and readings.

The Kitchen (⊠ 512 W. 19th St., ☎ 212/255–5793) is perhaps *the* Manhattan center for performance art, although video, dance, and music have their moments here, too.

PS 122 (⊠ 150 1st Ave., ☎ 212/477–5288) has been hailed by the *Village Voice* as "the petri dish of downtown culture." Occupying a former public school that was comedian George Burns's alma mater, PS 122 presents exhibitions and productions that come and go quickly, but they're never boring. Look especially for its annual marathon in February, in which scores of dazzling downtowners take part.

MUSIC

"Gentlemen," conductor Serge Koussevitzky once told the assembled Boston Symphony Orchestra, "maybe it's good enough for Cleveland or Cincinnati, but it's not good enough for New York." That's New York's place in the musical world, in a nutshell.

New York possesses not only the country's oldest symphony, the New York Philharmonic, but also three renowned conservatories—the Juilliard School, the Manhattan School of Music, and Mannes College of

Music—plus myriad musical performance groups. Since the turn of the century, the world's great orchestras and soloists have made Manhattan a principal stopping point.

If you're visiting the city for its music, New York has an overwhelming number of happenings to keep you busy. In an average week, between 50 and 150 events—everything from zydeco to Debussy, Cole Porter, Kurt Weill, and reggae—appear in newspaper and magazine listings, and weekly concert calendars are published in all of the major newspapers. Record and music shops serve as music information centers. Theses shops include the cavernous **Tower Records** (⊠ 692 Broadway, at 4th St., ☎ 212/505–1500); **Trump Tower** (⊠ 725 5th Ave., at 57th St., ☎ 212/838–8110; ⊠ 1961 Broadway, between 73rd and 74th Sts., ☎ 212/799–2500); **HMV** (⊠ 2081 Broadway, at 72nd St., ☎ 212/721–5900; ⊠ 1280 Lexington Ave., at 86th St., ☎ 212/348–0800; ⊠ 565 5th Ave. at 46th St., ☎ 212/681–6700; ⊠ 59 W. 34th St., ☎ 212/629–6900), **J & R Music World** (⊠ 15–33 Park Row, across from City Hall, ☎ 212/238–9000); the reliable **Bleecker Bob's Golden Oldies** (⊠ 118 W. 3rd St., ☎ 212/475–9677); and the classy **Patelson's** (⊠ 160 W. 56th St., ☎ 212/582–5840). The **Bryant Park Music and Dance Tickets Booth,** (⊠ 42nd St. just east of 6th Ave., ☎ 212/382–2323), also lists music around town.

Classical Music

Lincoln Center (⊠ W. 62nd St. to 66th Sts., Columbus to Amsterdam Aves.) remains the city's musical nerve center, especially when it comes to the classics. The **New York Philharmonic** (☎ 212/875–5656), led by Music Director Kurt Masur, performs at **Avery Fisher Hall** (☎ 212/875–5030) late September to early June. In addition to its magical concerts showcasing exceptional guest artists and the works of specific composers, the Philharmonic also schedules weeknight "Rush Hour" Concerts at 6:45 PM and Casual Saturdays Concerts at 2 PM; these special events, offered throughout the season, last one hour and are priced lower than the regular subscription concerts. "Rush Hour" Concerts are followed by receptions with the conductor on the Grand Promenade, and Casual Saturdays Concerts feature discussions after the performances. In summer, the popular **Mostly Mozart** concert series presents an impressive roster of classical performers.

A note for New York Philharmonic devotees: In season, and when conductors and soloists are amenable, Thursday orchestra rehearsals at 9:45 AM are open to the public for $10. Call 212/875–5656 for information.

Avery Fisher Hall, designed by Max Abramovitz, opened in 1961 as Philharmonic Hall, but underwent drastic renovation in 1976 to improve the acoustics (at a price tag of $5 million). The result is an auditorium that follows the classic European rectangular pattern. To its stage come the world's great musicians; to its boxes, the black-tie-and-diamond-tiara set.

Near Avery Fisher is **Alice Tully Hall** (⊠ Broadway at 65th St., ☎ 212/875–5050), an intimate "little white box," considered as acoustically perfect as concert houses get. Here the **Chamber Music Society of Lincoln Center** tunes up, along with promising Juilliard students, chamber music ensembles such as the Kronos Quartet, music on period instruments, choral music, famous soloists, and concert groups. Lincoln Center's outdoor **Damrosch Park,** and **Bruno Walter Auditorium** (in the Library of the Performing Arts, ☎ 212/870–1630) often offer free concerts. In 1996, Lincoln Center inaugurated a summer international performance festival under the direction of arts critic and writer

John Rockwell. The program includes classical music concerts, contemporary music and dance presentations, stage works, and non-Western arts.

While Lincoln Center is only some 30 years old, another famous classical music palace—**Carnegie Hall** (⊠ W. 57th St. at 7th Ave., ☎ 212/247–7800)—recently celebrated its 100th birthday. This is the place where the great pianist Paderewski was attacked by ebullient crowds (who claimed kisses and locks of his hair) after a performance in 1891; where young Leonard Bernstein, standing in for New York Philharmonic conductor Bruno Walter, made his triumphant debut in 1943; where Jack Benny and Isaac Stern fiddled together; and where the Beatles played one of their first U.S. concerts. When threats of the wrecker's ball loomed large in 1960, a consortium of Carnegie loyalists (headed by Isaac Stern) rose to save it; an eventual multimillion-dollar renovation in 1986 worked cosmetic wonders.

In addition to Lincoln Center and Carnegie Hall, the city has many other prime classical music locales around the city:

Aaron Davis Hall at City College (⊠ W. 133rd St. at Convent Ave., ☎ 212/650–6900) is an uptown venue for world music events and a variety of classical concerts and dance programs.

Bargemusic at the Fulton Ferry Landing in Brooklyn (☎ 718/624–4061) keeps chamber-music groups busy year-round on an old barge with a fabulous skyline view.

Brooklyn Academy of Music (⊠ 30 Lafayette Ave., ☎ 718/636–4100) continues to experiment with new and old musical styles, and it's still a showcase for the Brooklyn Philharmonic.

Grace Rainey Rogers Auditorium at the Metropolitan Museum of Art (⊠ 5th Ave. at 82nd St., ☎ 212/570–3949) offers performances of classical music in stately surroundings.

Merkin Concert Hall at the Abraham Goodman House (⊠ 129 W. 67th St., ☎ 212/362–8719) is almost as prestigious for performers as the concert halls at Lincoln Center.

Miller Theatre (⊠ Columbia University, Broadway at 116th St., 212/854–7799) features a varied program of classical performers, such as the New York Virtuosi Chamber Symphony.

92nd St. Y (⊠ 1395 Lexington Ave., ☎ 212/996–1100) showcases star recitalists and chamber music groups.

Sylvia and Danny Kaye Playhouse (⊠ Hunter College, 68th St., between Park and Lexington Aves., ☎ 212/772–4448) presents a varied program of events, including distinguished soloists and chamber music groups, in a small state-of-the-art concert hall.

Outdoor Concerts

Weather permitting, the city presents myriad musical events in the great outdoors. Each August, the plaza around Lincoln Center explodes with the **Lincoln Center Out-of-Doors** series. In the summertime, both the **Metropolitan Opera** and the **New York Philharmonic** appear in municipal parks to play free concerts, filling verdant spaces with the haunting strains of *La Bohème* or the thunder of the *1812 Overture* (for information call Lincoln Center, ☎ 212/875–5400, or the City Parks Special Events Hotline, ☎ 212/360–3456). **Summerstage** (⊠ Rumsey Playfield, Central Park at 72nd St., ☎ 212/360–2777 or 212/360–2756) presents free music programs, ranging from grand opera to experimental rock, generally on Saturday and Sunday afternoons from June through August. The **Museum of Modern Art** hosts free Friday and Saturday evening concerts of 20th-century music in their sculpture garden as part of the **Summergarden** series (☎ 212/708–9480), held from mid-June through August. A **Jazzmobile** (☎ 212/866–4900) transports jazz and Latin music to parks throughout the five boroughs in July and August; Wednesday evening concerts are held at Grant's Tomb (✉ Riverside Dr. and 122nd St.). **Prospect Park** comes alive with the sounds of its annual **Celebrate Brooklyn Concert Series** (✉ 9th St. Bandshell, 9th St. and Prospect Park W, Park Slope, Brooklyn, ☎ 718/965–8969). **Pier 16 at South Street Seaport** (☎ 212/732–7678) becomes the setting for a cornucopia of musical entertainment Thursday through Saturday evening from Memorial Day to Labor Day; it also sponsors holiday music concerts from late November through January 1 on weekday evenings and weekend afternoons.

Lunchtime Concerts

During the workweek, **lunchtime concerts** provide musical midday breaks at public atriums all over the city. Events are generally free, and bag-lunching is encouraged. Check out the **World Financial Center's Winter Garden Atrium** (across the West Side Highway from the World Trade Center) and the **Citicorp Center Marketplace** (✉ 54th St. and Lexington Ave.). And, of course, everywhere—in parks, on street corners, and down under in the subway—aspiring musicians of all kinds hold forth, with their instrument cases thrown open for contributions. True, some are hacks, but others are bona fide professionals: moonlighting violinists, Broadway chorus members indulging their love of the barbershop quartet, or horn players prowling up from clubs.

A midtown music break can be found at **St. Peter's Lutheran Church** (✉ 619 Lexington Ave., at the Citicorp Center, ☎ 212/935–2200), with its Wednesday series of lunchtime jazz at 12:30, organ concerts on Fridays at 12:45, and occasional events on Thursdays.

Downtown, the venerable **St. Paul's Chapel** (✉ Fulton St. and Broadway, ☎ 212/602–0874) presents free lunchtime concerts on Monday at noon. **Trinity Church** (✉ 74 Trinity Pl., ☎ 602–0873) also has free concerts on Thursday at 1 PM. Programs at both churches may include classical or contemporary music. A $2 contribution is suggested.

OPERA

Recent decades have sharply intensified the public's appreciation of grand opera—partly because of the charismatic personalities of such great singers as Luciano Pavarotti, Placido Domingo, and Cecilia Bartoli, and partly because of the efforts of New York's magnetic **Metropolitan Opera** (☎ 212/362–6000). A Met premiere draws the rich and famous, the critics, and the connoisseurs. At the Met's elegant Lincoln Center home, with its Marc Chagall murals and weighty Austrian-crystal chandeliers, the supercharged atmosphere gives audiences a sense that something special is going to happen, even before the curtain goes up. Luciano Pavarotti put it best: "When it comes to classical music, New York can truly be called a beacon of light—with that special quality that makes it *unico in mondo,* unique in the world."

The Metropolitan Opera performs its vaunted repertoire from October to mid-April, and though tickets can cost more than $100, many less expensive seats and standing room are available. The top-priced tickets are the center box seats, which are actually few in number and almost never available without a subscription. Unlike Broadway theaters, the Metropolitan Opera House has several different price levels, with some 600 seats sold at $23; bear in mind that weekday prices are slightly lower than weekend prices. Standing-room tickets for the week's performances go on sale on Saturday.

The **New York City Opera,** which performs from September through November and in March and April at Lincoln Center's **New York State Theater** (☎ 212/870–5570) continues its tradition of offering a diverse repertoire consisting of adventurous and rarely seen works as well as beloved classic opera and operetta favorites. City Opera has widened its program to include several time-honored musicals, such as *A Little Night Music, The Most Happy Fella, 110 in the Shade, On the Town,* and *Cinderella.* The company has a reputation for nurturing the talent of young American stars-to-be. (A surprising number of the world's finest singers, such as Placido Domingo, Frederica von Stade, and Beverly Sills, began their careers at City Opera.) The company maintains its ingenious practice of "supertitling"—electronically displaying, above the stage, line-by-line English translations of foreign-language operas. Recent seasons have included such old favorites as *Carmen, Madama Butterfly,* and *La Traviata* as well as premieres of challenging new works such as *The Times of Harvey Milk.*

Opera aficionados should also keep track of the **Carnegie Hall** (☎ 212/247–7800) schedule for debuting singers and performances by the Opera Orchestra of New York, which specializes in presenting rarely performed operas in concert form, often with star soloists. Pay close attention to provocative opera offerings at the **Brooklyn Academy of Music** (☎ 718/636–4100), which often premieres avant-garde works difficult to see elsewhere.

The city has a few lesser-known opera groups:

Amato Opera Theatre (✉ 319 Bowery, ☎ 212/228–8200) is an intimate showcase for rising singers.
New York Gilbert and Sullivan Players (✉ 302 W. 91st St., ☎ 212/769–1000; box office, ☎ 212/864–5400), presents lively productions of G & S classics, usually at Symphony Space (95th and Broadway).
New York Grand Opera (✉ 154 W. 57th St., Suite 125, ☎ 212/245–8837) mounts free summer performances of Verdi operas—with a full orchestra and professional singers—at Rumsey Playfield (Central Park at 72nd St.).

DANCE

Ballet
Visiting balletomanes live out their dreams in New York, where two powerhouse companies—the New York City Ballet and the American Ballet Theatre—continue to please and astonish.

The **New York City Ballet (NYCB),** a hallmark troupe for nearly 50 years, recently marked its 104th season with compelling examples of exceptional dances from the company's vast repertory, including works by George Balanchine, Jerome Robbins, Ballet Master-in-Chief Peter Martin, and others. NYCB performs in Lincoln Center's **New York State Theater** (☎ 212/870–5570). Its winter season runs from mid-November through February—with the beloved annual production of *George Balanchine's The Nutcracker* ushering in the December holiday season—while its spring season lasts from late April through June.

Founded by Lincoln Kirstein and Balanchine in 1948, NYCB continues to stress dance as a whole above individual ballet stars, though that hasn't stopped a number of principal dancers (such as Kyra Nichols, Darci Kistler, Damian Woetzel, and Jock Soto) from standing out. The company has more than 100 dancers and performs and maintains an active repertoire of 20th-century works unmatched in the world.

Across the plaza at Lincoln Center, the **Metropolitan Opera House** (☎ 212/362–6000) is home to **American Ballet Theatre,** renowned for its brilliant renditions of the great 19th-century classics (*Swan Lake, Giselle, The Sleeping Beauty,* and *La Bayardère*), as well as for the unique scope of its eclectic contemporary repertoire (including works by all the 20th-century masters—Balanchine, Tudor, Robbins, de Mille, among others). Since its inception in 1940, the company has included some of the greatest dancers of the century, such as Mikhail Baryshnikov, Natalia Makarova, Rudolf Nureyev, Gelsey Kirkland, and Cynthia Gregory. Since 1992, American Ballet Theatre has been directed by Kevin McKenzie, one of the company's leading male dancers in the 1980s. Its New York season runs from April to June.

Part of Lincoln Center's dance vitality is accounted for by the presence of the **School of American Ballet** (⊠ 70 Lincoln Plaza), the focus for the dreams of young dancers across the country. Some 2,000 of them vie for spots in SAB's summer session, and a talented handful of the 200 who make it into the summer group go on to join the school. Here the Balanchine legacy lives on, and soulful-eyed baby dancers are molded into professional performers. You can see SAB students dashing across 66th and Broadway with leotard-stuffed bags slung over their shoulders.

The varied bill at **City Center** (⊠ 131 W. 55th St., ☎ 212/581–1212) often includes touring ballet companies.

Modern Dance

At **City Center** (⊠ 131 W. 55th St., ☎ 212/581–1212), the moderns hold sway. In seasons past, the **Alvin Ailey Dance Company, Twyla Tharp and Dancers,** the **Martha Graham Dance Company,** the **Paul Taylor Dance Company,** the **Dance Theater of Harlem,** and the **Merce Cunningham Dance Company** have performed here. The **Brooklyn Academy of Music** (⊠ 30 Lafayette Ave., ☎ 718/636–4100) features both American and foreign contemporary dance troupes as part of its **Next Wave Festival** every fall.

A growing, international modern-dance center is the **Joyce Theater** (⊠ 175 8th Ave., ☎ 212/242–0800), housed in a former Art Deco movie theater. The Joyce is the permanent home of **Feld Ballets/NY,** founded in 1974 by an upstart ABT dancer who went on to become a principal fixture on the dance scene. Recent featured companies have included the startling **Parsons Dance Company,** the lyrical **Lar Lubovitch Dance Company,** the passionate **Ballet Hispanico,** and the acrobatic **Streb/Ringside.** The Joyce has an eclectic program, including tap, jazz, ballroom, and ethnic dance, and it also showcases emerging choreographers.

Manhattan has several other small-scale, mostly experimental and avant-garde dance forums:

Dance Theater Workshop (⊠ 219 W. 19th St., ☎ 212/924–0077) serves as one of New York's most successful laboratories for new dance.

Danspace Project (⊠ St. Mark's-in-the-Bowery Church, 10th St. and 2nd Ave., ☎ 212/674–8194) sponsors a series of avant-garde choreography that runs from September through June.

DIA Center for the Arts (⊠ 155 Mercer St., ☎ 212/431–9233) hosts a number of performances by highly talented local dancers.

Merce Cunningham Studio (⊠ 55 Bethune St., ☎ 212/691–9751) showcases performances by cutting-edge modern dance companies.

92nd St. Y Harkness Dance Center (⊠ 1395 Lexington Ave., ☎ 996–1100) presents emerging dance troupes with discussion following performances.

PS 122 (⊠ 150 1st Ave., ☎ 212/477–5288) programs dance events that often border on performance art.

Repertorio Español (⊠ 138 E. 27th St., ☎ 212/889–2850) is often visited by the famed Spanish stylist Pilar Rioja.

Sylvia and Danny Kaye Playhouse (⊠ Hunter College, 68th St., between Park and Lexington Aves., ☎ 212/772–4488) hosts up-and-coming dance companies.

Symphony Space (⊠ 2537 Broadway, ☎ 212/864–5400) often focuses on ethnic dance.

Tribeca Performing Arts Center (⊠ 199 Chambers St., ☎ 212/346–8500) presents dance troupes from around the world.

FILM AND VIDEO

On any given week, New York City might be described as a kind of film archive featuring all the major new releases, classics renowned and obscure, unusual foreign offerings, small independent flicks, and cutting-edge experimental works. Because you don't usually need to buy tickets in advance, except on Friday and Saturday evenings, moviegoing is a great spur-of-the-moment way to rest from sightseeing. You may have to stand awhile in a line that winds around the block, but even that can be entertaining—conversations overheard in such queues are generally just as good as the previews of coming attractions. Note, however, that these lines are generally for people who have already bought their tickets; be sure, as you approach the theater, to ask if there are separate lines for ticket *holders* and ticket *buyers*.

For information on first-run movie schedules and theaters, dial 212/777–3456, the **MovieFone** sponsored by WQHT 97 FM and the *New York Times*. You can also call this number to order tickets in advance with a credit card; not all movie theaters participate, however, and the surcharge is $1.50 per ticket.

Festivals

New York's numero uno film program remains the **New York Film Festival,** conducted by the Film Society of Lincoln Center every September and October at Alice Tully and Avery Fisher halls (☎ 212/875–5600). Its program includes exceptional movies, most of them never seen before in the United States; the festival's hits usually make their way into local movie houses over the following couple of months. This festival has presented the U.S. premieres of such memorable movies as Martin Scorsese's *Mean Streets,* François Truffaut's *Day for Night,* Robert Altman's *Short Cuts,* and Quentin Tarantino's *Pulp Fiction.* Each March the Film Society joins forces with the Museum of Modern Art to produce a **New Directors/New Films** series, where the best works by up-and-coming directors get their moment to flicker. Several movies included in this festival have gone on to become box-office successes. The series is held at MoMA's Roy and Niuta Titus theaters (⊠ 11 W. 53rd St., ☎ 212/708–9480).

Museums

The **American Museum of the Moving Image** (⊠ 35th Ave. at 36th St., Queens, ☎ 718/784–0077) is the only U.S. museum devoted to motion pictures, video, and digital media. Located on the site of the historic Kaufman Astoria Studios, it offers multiple galleries that are a movie buff's paradise, as are its 195-seat Riklis Theatre and 60-seat Warner Communications Screening Room. The museum presents changing exhibits and provocative film programs, including major artist-oriented retrospectives, Hollywood classics, experimental videos, and TV documentaries.

In midtown Manhattan, the **Museum of Television & Radio** (✉ 25 W. 52nd St., ☎ 212/621–6800) has a gigantic collection of 75,000 radio and TV shows, from the golden past to the present. The museum's library provides 96 consoles where you can watch or listen to whatever you wish for up to two hours at a time. The museum presents scheduled theater screenings, gallery exhibits, and series for children.

First-Run Houses

New suburban-style multiscreen complexes have sprung up all over town, even in such hip urban neighborhoods as SoHo (Houston and Mercer Sts.), the East Village (2nd Ave. at 12th St. and 3rd Ave. at 11th St.), the Flatiron District (890 Broadway, at 19th St.), and Hell's Kitchen (Worldwide Plaza, 320 W. 50th St.). Although the increase in the number of screens seems to have eased lines at the box office somewhat, these cinemas often seem to show the same mainstream commercial movies, so long lines still snake around the corner at the few theaters that show more offbeat fare. Manhattan's most impressive multiplex movie house, **Sony Theatres Lincoln Square** (✉ Broadway and 68th St., ☎ 212/336–5000), opened in November 1994. This complex has 12 state-of-the-art theaters designed to recall grand old movie palaces and an eight-story, 600-seat IMAX Theatre that is equipped not only for large-scale formatted films but also for 3-D imagery.

Besides the Lincoln Square, two other New York theaters preserve the size and allure of the great movie houses of the past. The **Ziegfeld** (✉ 141 W. 54th St., west of 6th Ave., ☎ 212/765–7600) has somewhat garish red decor and an awesome sound system. **Radio City Music Hall** (✉ 1260 6th Ave., ☎ 212/247–4777) with its art-deco setting, 34-foot-high screen, and 4,500-watt projector is unfortunately only rarely used for movie screenings these days.

Revival Houses

One of the best places to see old films in Manhattan is the **Walter Reade Theater** at Lincoln Center (✉ 70 Lincoln Plaza, Broadway at 65th St., ☎ 212/875–5600), operated by the Film Society of Lincoln Center. This comfortable movie house presents several fascinating series that run concurrently, devoted to specific themes or a certain director's body of work; movies for kids are featured on Saturday morning. The auditorium is a little gem with excellent sight lines, and tickets can be purchased at the box office weeks in advance.

Revivals can also be found at:

American Museum of the Moving Image (✉ 35th Ave. at 36th St., Queens, ☎ 718/784–0077) offers American film series, often in historical contexts. Programs often honor overlooked artists, such as cinematographers and screenwriters.
Anthology Film Archives (✉ 32 2nd Ave., at 2nd St., ☎ 212/505–5181) shows movies that have made a significant contribution to film history.
Film Forum (✉ 209 W. Houston St., ☎ 212/727–8110) has three screens showing often quirky series based on movie genres, directors, and other film artists.
The Museum of Modern Art (✉ 11 W. 53rd St., ☎ 212/708–9480) includes rare classic films in its many excellent revival series.

Foreign and Independent Films

Between the interest generated by the New York Film Festival, the city's population of foreign executives and diplomats, a resident corps of independent filmmakers, and a large contingent of cosmopolitan cinemaniacs, there's always an audience here for foreign films and for innovative new American films and videos that buck the Hollywood currents. New York has several cinemas that more or less specialize in such films.

Angelika 57 (✉ 225 W. 57th St., ☎ 212/586–1900) shows film programs similar to those of its downtown sister theater, the Angelika Film Center.

Angelika Film Center (✉ W. Houston and Mercer Sts., ☎ 212/995–2000) offers several screens devoted to offbeat independent and foreign films, as well as a lively café catering to a youthful crowd.

Anthology Film Archives (✉ 32 2nd Ave., at 2nd St., ☎ 212/505–5181) presents esoteric independent fare seldom shown elsewhere.

Carnegie Hall Cinemas (✉ 887 7th Ave., between 56th and 57th Sts., ☎ 212/265–2520) screens intriguing new films in two small theaters.

Cinema Village (✉ 12th St., between 5th Ave. and University Pl., ☎ 212/924–3363) schedules innovative independent features and occasional animation festivals. Programs concentrating on movies produced in Hong Kong are particularly popular.

Eastside Playhouse (✉ 3rd Ave., between 55th and 56th Sts., ☎ 212/755–3020) usually shows first-run art films.

Film Forum (✉ 209 W. Houston St., ☎ 212/727–8110) presents some of the best new independent films and hard-to-see foreign movies.

Lincoln Plaza (✉ Broadway, between 62nd and 63rd Sts., ☎ 212/757–2280) has six subterranean cinemas playing long-run foreign and independent hits.

Millennium (✉ 66 E. 4th St., ☎ 212/673–0090) focuses on the avant-garde.

Quad Cinema (✉ 13th St., between 5th and 6th Aves., ☎ 212/255–8800) plays first-run art and foreign films on very small screens.

68th Street Playhouse (✉ 3rd Ave. at 68th St., ☎ 212/734–0302) has exclusive extended runs of critically acclaimed films.

Sony Paris (✉ 58th St., between 5th and 6th Aves., ☎ 212/980–5656) is an exquisite showcase for much-talked-about new American and foreign entries.

Village East Cinemas (✉ 2nd Ave. at 12th St., ☎ 212/529–6799) presents cutting-edge independent features alongside mainstream Hollywood productions.

Foreign and independent films and videos frequently run at cultural societies and museums around town, including:

Asia Society (✉ 725 Park Ave. at 70th St., ☎ 212/288–6400) shows excellent films from countries all over Asia.

French Institute (✉ Florence Gould Hall, 55 E. 59th St., ☎ 212/355–6160) programs retrospectives of French movies, often devoted to a particular theme or director.

Goethe House (✉ 1014 5th Ave., between 82nd and 83rd Sts., ☎ 212/439–8700) screens movies by leading German filmmakers.

Japan Society (✉ 333 47th St., ☎ 212/832–1155) focuses on Japanese films rarely available in other parts of the city.

The Museum of Modern Art (✉ 11 W. 53rd St., ☎ 212/752-3015) frequently shows foreign classics and hard-to-see independent films.

Whitney Museum of American Art (✉ Madison Ave. at 75th St., ☎ 212/570–3676) is a reliable forum for experimental and independent films.

READINGS AND LECTURES

New York is the center of American publishing, and as a result many writers from around the world—however reclusive—eventually find reason to come here, either to visit or to live. If you're interested in the written word and catching a glimpse of the people who create books, a New York prose or poetry reading can be a lot of fun and often inspirational. Readings unfold all over the city—in bookstores, libraries, museums, bars, and legitimate theaters—attracting debuting talents and some of the top names in contemporary literature, writers such as E. L. Doctorow, Nadine Gordimer, Tony Morrison, Edna O'Brien, Seamus Heaney, Philip Roth, Kazuo Ishiguro, and many others.

Poetry Calendar (⊠ 611 Broadway, Suite 905, 10012, ☎ 212/260–7097), published monthly September through June, provides extensive listings of prose and poetry readings around the city. The calendar is available by subscription or for free at several Manhattan bookstores. Check also listings for readings in *New York* magazine, *The New Yorker, Time Out New York,* and the *Village Voice.*

Authors, poets, lyricists, and travelogue-spinners take the stage at the **92nd St. Y** (⊠ 1395 Lexington Ave., ☎ 212/996–1100). The **West Side YMCA** (⊠ 5 W. 63rd St., ☎ 212/875–4128) offers readings by major novelists, poets, and humorists. **Symphony Space** (⊠ Broadway at 95th St., ☎ 212/864–5400) holds a number of readings, including the Selected Shorts series of stories read by prominent actors. Manhattan Theatre Club sponsors **Writers in Performance** (⊠ 131 W. 55th St., ☎ 212/645–5848), a provocative program of dramatic readings and roundtable discussions that showcase novelists, poets, and playwrights from the United States and abroad.

Downtown, rising young scribes appear at **Limbo** (⊠ 47 Ave. A, between 3rd and 4th Sts., ☎ 477–5271), a coffee bar. **Dixon Place** (⊠ 258 Bowery, between Houston and Prince Sts., ☎ 212/219–3088) and **The Kitchen** (⊠ 512 W. 19th St., ☎ 212/255–5793) both sponsor readings regularly, some of which border on performance art.

Distinguished series of **poetry readings** are sponsored by several organizations in Manhattan, including **The Academy of American Poets** (⊠ 580 Broadway, ☎ 212/274–0343); **The Poetry Project** (⊠ St. Mark's-in-the-Bowery Church, E. 10th St. and 2nd Ave., ☎ 212/674–0910); **Poetry Society of America** (⊠ 15 Gramercy Park S, ☎ 212/254–9628); and **Poets House** (⊠ 72 Spring St., ☎ 212/431–7920).

Informal poetry readings, sometimes with an "open-mike" policy that allows audience members to read their own work, continue to crop up with frequency in New York City clubs and bars. These events are fairly popular, particularly with a younger crowd. There may be a low cover charge ($2–$5), and food and drink are usually available. Some reliable spots include **Ear Inn** (⊠ 326 Spring St., ☎ 212/226–9060) on Saturday afternoons; **Cornelia Street Café** (⊠ 29 Cornlia St., ☎ 212/989–9319); **The Knitting Factory** (⊠ 74 Leonard St., ☎ 212/721–0837); and **Nuyorican Poets Cafe** (⊠ 236 E. 3rd St., ☎ 212/505–8183), with a variety of multicultural poets scheduled weekly and a Poetry Slam competition each Friday.

Many **Manhattan bookstores** organize evening readings by authors of recently published books. Best bets are **Barnes & Noble** (⊠ 1280 Lexington Ave. at 86th St., ☎ 212/423–9900; Citicorp Building, ⊠ 54th St. at 3rd. Ave., ☎ 212750–8033; ⊠ 2289 Broadway at 82nd St., ☎ 212/362–8835; ⊠ 1972 Broadway at 66th St., ☎ 212/595–6859; ⊠ 605 5th Ave. at 48th St., ☎ 212/765–0590; ⊠ 675 6th Ave. at 22nd St., ☎ 212/727–1227; ⊠ 33 Union Sq., ☎ 212/253–0810; 4 Astor Pl., ☎ 212/420–1322), **Books & Co.** (⊠ 939 Madison Ave., near 74th St., ☎ 212/737–1450), **Posman Books** (⊠ 1 University Pl., between Waverly Pl. and 8th St., ☎ 212533–2665), **Rizzoli Bookstore** (⊠ 454 W. Broadway, between Prince and Houston Sts., ☎ 212/674–1616), **Three Lives and Co.** (⊠ 154 W. 10th St., ☎ 212/741–2069), and **Tower**

Books (⊠ 383 Lafayette St. at 4th St., ☎ 212/228–5100). For readings by gay and lesbian authors, try **A Different Light** (⊠ 151 W. 19th St., ☎ 212/989–4850).

A major reading and talk series held at the **Lincoln Center Library for the Performing Arts** (☎ 212/870–1630) specializes in musicians, directors, singers, and actors. Several branches of the **New York Public Library** present reading events, including the **main building of the New York Public Library** (⊠ 5th Ave., between 40th and 42nd Sts., ☎ 212/ 930–0800), the **Donnell Library** (⊠ 20 W. 53rd St., ☎ 212/ 621–0618), and the **Mid-Manhattan Library** (⊠ 455 5th Ave., ☎ 212/ 340–0833).

At the **Metropolitan Museum of Art** (⊠ 5th Ave. at 82nd St., ☎ 212/ 535–7710), seasonal lectures regularly draw sellout crowds. Artists and world eminent art historians speak here.

6 Dining

Dining out is one of New York's greatest pleasures. Because of the city's prominence as an international financial and cultural center, you can easily sample a multitude of foreign cuisines in the span of a week as well as regional dishes from around the United States. Manhattan has a restaurant to match any taste or pocketbook—from extravagant caviar and sushi bars to trendsetting TriBeCa haunts to affordable bistros, trattorias, coffee shops, and delis. If you're looking for innovative cuisine, you'll discover it prepared by some of the best chefs anywhere, and you can find places that serve traditional meals as well.

By J. Walman

NEW YORK CITY'S FRENCH AND ITALIAN restaurants cannot compare with the ones you'll find in France or Italy. While Paris boasts its Taillevent, London its Le Gavroche, and Brussels its Villa Lorraine, New York is conspicuously lacking a genuinely distinguished *grand luxe* restaurant, one that is glamorous and incredibly elegant, where food, wine, and service fulfill the promise of the decor. Although seafood restaurants are improving, there are still precious few outstanding ones, given that the city is a port. And despite the prevalence of small Indian restaurants, their menus and spicing tend to be similar. Alas, the Spanish kitchen has never taken flight in Manhattan. As for Brazilian fare, an authentic *feijoada,* the stew of black beans with smoked meats, is better described on menus than executed in the kitchen.

Still, that international appendage to the United States known as the Big Apple supports more good restaurants, and more kinds of them, than any other city in the world. And while it's possible to spend big bucks and eat badly, it's equally possible to dine like a king for a pittance. Food is one of the city's joys. Its restaurant mix also has an idiosyncratic charm. Hotel dining rooms—which have the resources to provide the professional service staff, fine china, comprehensive wine cellar, and top-flight kitchen required for serious dining—are increasingly common, with a life and often an entrance of their own. New York bistros and trattorias are as excellent as they are inexpensive and abundant, and the city is dotted with outstanding steak houses (meat has apparently made a comeback). Star chefs such as Larry Forgione, Daniel Boulud, David Burke, and Gray Kunz have given the city a coterie of innovative kitchens whose graduates have assured that even neighborhood eateries serve more than usually interesting fare.

New York's best breakfasts are not limited to so-called tablecloth restaurants. Dozens of Greek-owned coffee shops pride themselves on perfectly scrambled eggs, savory hash browns, and that New York institution, the toasted bagel. Chinatown's tea houses go nonstop from 8 AM till 5 PM, and "Little Korea," a string of amazingly inexpensive possibilities centered around West 32nd Street, between 5th and 7th avenues, is open around the clock. The coffeehouse explosion offers a civilized respite from Manhattan frenzy: Most offer restorative snacks in addition to a long list of java drinks (with or without caffeine).

Such small ethnic eating spots are legion in New York, their mix constantly changing with shifting immigration patterns; countries like Austria, Afghanistan, Thailand, Turkey, and Jamaica are currently adding culinary breadth to the dining scene. There are more Chinese options than ever, and you are no longer obliged to endure rude service and dingy surroundings: Brightening today's Chinatowns (which thrive in Brooklyn and Queens as well as Manhattan) are noisy, gaudy eating emporiums in the Hong Kong style, and Asian-inspired fare is available in modish spots, from Aja to Zoe (Lespinasse, one of Manhattan's best haute kitchens, has made a trademark of it). Szechuan may be out, but Cantonese home cooking, with its fresh ingredients and simple cooking, is in. The Chinese tea lunch known as dim (touch) sum (heart, thus "to touch one's heart")—consisting of various dumplings, small cooked dishes, rice, noodles, puffs, balls, claws, you name it—holds strong. (At a dim sum lunch or brunch, point to what you want as trolleys bearing these delicacies wheel past your table.) The next wave? Caribbean cuisine is currently popular. Malaysian, Burmese, Vietnamese, Korean, Spanish, Middle Eastern, and African cuisines may gain a stronghold, not to mention African-American cooking and some of the little-known regional foods of Italy and other European nations.

Bottom line? Take a chance. Not every venture will be a success. But the whole experience will be rewarding. That's a promise.

Planning Your Culinary Itinerary

In most great restaurant towns, there is generally one best restaurant; New York generously offers a variety of candidates. Times being what they are, top restaurants have short lives, chefs play musical kitchens, and today's star is often tomorrow's laggard. As in France, it's prudent to seek out restaurants on their way up and to approach celebrities with caution. Temper your visits to famous restaurants with informed selections from among lesser-knowns. Can a famous restaurant produce a really spectacular dinner? Probably. Will an unknown diner receive a great meal on the first visit to a fashionable restaurant? Probably not. Even in these recessionary times, the snob snub is not dead.

Our Selections

We firmly believe that everybody should be treated like somebody, and our recommendations take into account the reception as well as the food, decor, service, and wines. When there are several restaurants within a genre, we choose the most interesting. Some famous restaurants, elsewhere held in high regard, have not captured our accolades; others are omitted because they treat guests shabbily or are poor value. To familiarize you with the kitchen's style, we also mention dishes we have sampled. Menus change often (sometimes daily); signature dishes are becoming a thing of the past. It's the kitchen's style that counts, so look for similar preparations or ingredients.

Wine

New York won't disappoint on this score. Generally, the most expensive wines have the smallest markup, the mid-price spectrum offers the best values, and the least-expensive offerings are poor values. Half bottles are hard to find. Increasingly common instead is wine by the glass; younger restaurants as well as a number of old-timers offer serious vintages at sensible prices this way. If the wine list is large, have an aperitif and take your time in ordering. Remember: You're the buyer. Note that many restaurants allow you to bring your own bottle, charging a service fee ranging from $5 to about $25.

Tipping

Rules are simple. Never tip the maître d' unless you're out to impress your companion. In most restaurants, tip the waiter at least 15% to 20%. (To figure the amount quickly, just double the tax noted on the check—it's 8¼% of your bill—and round up or slightly down.)

In stylish establishments, give 5% to the captain, even if he did most of the work, and 15% to the waiter. To a busboy, a couple of dollars is appreciated but hardly expected. Give wine stewards about $5 per bottle, more if you order important wines that require decanting or other special services. Give the captain or sommelier his or her tip, palmed in your hand, with a friendly shake and a smile. Tip at least $1 per coat checked.

Prices

New York gets a bum rap. Of course, you can order caviar and champagne or Bordeaux of great years; you will pay accordingly. But you will also do that in Nashville and Los Angeles. Our point is that each price stratum has its own equilibrium. Translation: $20 is only inexpensive if you get $20 worth of value, and $100 may be a bargain.

CATEGORY	COST*
$$$$	over $60
$$$	$40–$59
$$	$20–$39
$	under $20

per person, excluding drinks, service, and sales tax (8¼%)

Restaurants marked with two prices ($–$$, for example) include modest restaurants where choosing the most expensive dishes can push your check into the next category and also pricier restaurants where you can lower your tab by opting for the less-expensive fare or choosing a prix-fixe meal such as $19.97 lunches or dinners found in many New York restaurants. Brunches are also price-wise. Most prix-fixe menus don't include coffee or drinks.

If you're watching your budget, always ask the price of the specials. Rather than being sensibly attached to the menu, European-style, specials are often recited by the waiter with no mention of cost. Ask.

Finally, always go over your bill. Mistakes do occur (and not always in the restaurant's favor).

Dress

Use common sense. Dress up for grand restaurants, and wear neat but casual clothes for casual spots. Midtown is more conservative than residential neighborhoods, SoHo and TriBeCa trendier than the Upper East and Upper West sides. Shorts are appropriate only in summer and in the most casual spots. When in doubt, call ahead.

Reservations

Make a reservation. If you change your mind, cancel—it's only courteous. Tables can be hard to come by between 7 and 9; if a restaurant tells you that it can seat you only before 6 or after 10, you may decide that it doesn't need you. Or you may be persuaded that eating early or late is okay. Eating after a play or concert is quite common in New York, and there's no shortage of options.

Smoking

New York is no longer smoker-friendly. Only restaurants with fewer than 35 seats legally allow smoking. Establishments may allow you to smoke at the bar or at a table outdoors, if such seating is available. Also speak up if you prefer to sit in a certain area or if you want a certain table.

MANHATTAN RESTAURANTS

Lower Manhattan

American

$$ ✕ **Fraunces Tavern.** Opened as a tavern in 1762 by Samuel Fraunces, George Washington's steward, this Georgian brick landmark dates back

to 1719; George Washington delivered his farewell address here when the British evacuated New York. Today the place has a clubby bar and faithful Colonial decor; it's a nice spot for cocktails (they're rather good) and for basic eggs-bacon-and-oatmeal breakfasts. Any other time, stick to steaks or, Wednesday, pot roast. ⊠ *54 Pearl St. at Broad St.,* ☎ *212/269–0144. Reservations essential. AE, DC, MC, V. Closed weekends.*

Contemporary

$$$–$$$$ ✕ **Hudson River Club.** This distinguished restaurant improves with
★ age. It has spacious wood-paneled rooms with paisley-print banquettes, spectacular views of the Hudson River and the Statue of Liberty, and a spirited bar with piano music. Always creative, chef Waldy Malouf celebrates Hudson River valley produce with a talent that speaks for itself in such hallmark dishes as mint cured apple-smoked salmon Napoleon and veal shank with horseradish mashed potatoes. Desserts—like the signature tower of chocolate (combining brownie, mousse, and meringue)—are edible sculptures, while the New York State cheese plate with walnut bread and nut muffins serves as a perfect foil to the magnificent wines from the regional American wine list. ⊠ *4 World Financial Center,* ☎ *212/786–1500. Reservations essential. AE, DC, MC, V. No lunch Sat.*

Chinese

$$$ ✕ **Au Mandarin.** One of the best bets in Manhattan for haute Chinese, this World Financial Center restaurant has a courtyard-like setting, an exotic fish tank, and classy furnishings. The dining experience combines a polished atmosphere with careful service. You might start with vegetarian dumplings or Shanghai buns, then move on to Shanghai prawns, followed by Peking duck, tangerine beef, and delicate rice noodles with julienne vegetables. ⊠ *200–250 Vesey St. (World Financial Center),* ☎ *212/385–0313. AE, DC, MC, V.*

Italian

$$$ ✕ **F. Ille Ponte Ristorante.** In a former hotel, this Italian eatery has exposed brick walls, ceramic-tile floors, and a wood-burning pizza oven. The more formal retreat upstairs comes with a view of the Hudson, and tables are set with handmade-paper menus and Frette linen napkins, endowed with a buttonhole so they can be worn. Portions tend to be on the gargantuan side; the Tuscan-style spit-roasted baby pig, grilled, aged porterhouse, and center cut veal chops are noteworthy. If you don't drive, consider a car service—the location is off the beaten track. ⊠ *39 Desbrosses St., near West St.* ☎ *212/226–4621. AE, DC, MC, V. Closed lunch weekends.*

Seafood

$$ ✕ **Gianni's.** This is the most earnest restaurant near South Street Seaport, an area not noted for gastronomic excellence. Pastas, salads, and seafood work best. Or try an out-of-the-ordinary sandwich. There's an outdoor café during the summer. ⊠ *15 Fulton St.,* ☎ *212/608–7300. AE, DC, MC, V.*

SoHo and TriBeCa

American Casual

$ ✕ **Lucky Strike.** One of Manhattan's funkiest small restaurants, this unadorned SoHo boîte doesn't look like much. In the crowded back room, specials and available wines are written on mirrors on the walls. You can have a terrific steak and *pommes frites* (french fries) at a bar-

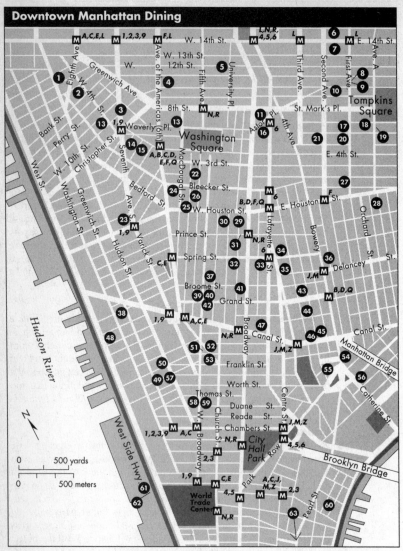

Downtown Manhattan Dining

Agrotikon, **7**
Arturo's, **25**
Au Mandarin, **62**
Boca Chica, **27**
Brothers Bar-B-Q, **23**
Cafe Fes, **13**
Caffè Lure, **26**
Capsouto Frères, **38**
Casa La Femme, **30**
Cendrillon
Asian Grill & Mamba
Bar, **41**
Chanterelle, **52**
Chez Jacqueline, **24**
C3, **12**
Da Nico, **43**
Diva, **40**
Dix et Sept, **3**

Duane Park Café, **58**
El Teddy's, **51**
Felix, **39**
F. Ille Ponte
Ristorante, **48**
First, **20**
Fraunces Tavern, **63**
French Roast, **4**
Global 33, **21**
Gianni's, **60**
Golden Unicorn, **56**
Gotham Bar & Grill, **5**
Grand Ticino, **22**
Home, **15**
Hudson River Club, **61**
Il Cortille, **46**
Inca Grill, **37**
Indochine, **16**

Kwanzaa, **35**
Lanza Restaurant, **9**
L'Auberge Du Midi, **2**
Layla, **53**
Le Jardin, **34**
Lucky Strike, **42**
Ludlow Street Cafe, **28**
L'Udo, **11**
Manila Garden, **6**
Match, **29**
Mi Cocina, **1**
Montrachet, **52**
New York
Noodletown, **54**
9 Jones Street, **14**
Nobu, **50**
Odeon, **59**
Pacifica, **47**

Penang Soho, **32**
Pisces, **19**
Roettelle A. G., **18**
Sammy's Roumanian
Steak House, **36**
Second Avenue Deli, **10**
S.P.Q.R., **44**
Spring Street Natural
Restaurant & Bar, **33**
Sweet 'n' Tart Cafe, **45**
Teresa's, **17**
Tribeca Grill, **49**
20 Mott, **55**
Xunta, **8**
Zoë, **31**

gain price, homey roasted chicken, good burgers, and great bread pudding; the homemade bread is also worth the trip. The crowd mobbing the bar is young and hip. ⊠ *59 Grand St., between Wooster St. and W. Broadway,* ☎ *212/941–0479 or 212/941–0772. Reservations not accepted. AE, DC, MC. V.*

Contemporary

$$$$ × **Chanterelle.** Soft peach walls, luxuriously spaced tables, towering
★   ceilings, and glorious displays of flowers set the stage for what is arguably New York's finest new-American restaurant. The unassuming, flawless service complements chef David Waltuck's inventions, which are carefully prepared and beautifully presented. Although the signature seafood sausage, charred on the outside and succulent within, and the Japanese-style raw seafood are both always available, other dishes on the menu are changeable, dictated by the bounty of the seasons. Trust your exceptional sommelier to find value in the discriminating, beautifully chosen wine list. Lunch and dinner are prix fixe. In TriBeCa. ⊠ *2 Harrison St., near Hudson St.,* ☎ *212/966–6960. Reservations essential. AE, DC, MC, V. Closed Sun.–Mon., lunch.*

$$–$$$ × **Tribeca Grill.** This cavernous brick-walled restaurant, subtly lighted and anchored by the bar from the old Maxwell's Plum, displays art by the late Robert De Niro, Sr., father of the actor, who opened it with various celebrity partners and now owns it with Montrachet's Drew Nieporent. The best dishes are the simple ones, such as crisp fried oysters with anchovy aïoli, and herb-crusted rack of lamb with oven-roasted vegetables; desserts are amicable (try banana tart with milk-chocolate ice cream), as is the staff. ⊠ *375 Greenwich St., near Franklin St.,* ☎ *212/941–3900. Reservations essential. AE, DC, MC, V. Closed Sat. lunch.*

$$–$$$ × **Zoë.** Thalia and Stephen Loffredo's colorful, high-ceilinged SoHo eatery with terra-cotta columns and floor is relatively noisy. But the open kitchen produces impressive food, such as grilled yellowfin tuna on wok-charred vegetables. Zoë also has an exceptionally well-organized wine list and a fine group of carefully tended wines by the glass. ⊠ *90 Prince St., between Broadway and Mercer St.,* ☎ *212/966–6722. Reservations essential. AE, DC, MC, V.*

$$ × **Duane Park Café.** This quiet TriBeCa find is owned by its Japanese chef, Seiji Maeda. It can spoil you with its comfortable seating, excellent service, serious but fairly priced wines, and international menu. Look for marinated duck and arugula salad and crispy skate with the Japanese-inspired *ponzu* sauce. The pleasing design incorporates dark columns, a salmon color scheme, maple-veneered walls, and an abundance of cherry wood. ⊠ *157 Duane St., between W. Broadway and Hudson St.,* ☎ *212/732–5555. AE, D, DC, MC, V. Closed Sat. lunch, Sun.*

$$ × **Match.** This bilevel restaurant-lounge is hot enough to scorch the heels of a seasoned fire walker. Open beams and machine fixtures, blond-wood paneling, and Old World booths hugging the wall preserve the memory of the building's industrial past (Match is housed in the former home of New York's oldest electrical company). Check out the raw bar, which teems with fabulous presentations of fresh shellfish, sushi, sashimi and caviar, or go for the dim-sum platter. There's also a Match Uptown (⊠ 33 E. 60th St., ☎ 212/906–9173.) ⊠ *160 Mercer St., between Houston and Prince Sts.,* ☎ *212/343–0020. AE, MC, V.*

$–$$ ✕ **Odeon.** Established in 1980, this was downtown's first "trendy" restaurant, and it's still one of the neighborhood's best. The Art Deco cafeteria setting includes plentiful neon, vinyl banquettes and Formica tables, and the pleasant service, low prices, and well-chosen wine list are all pluses. But let's not neglect the food: crab and potato fritters with soy-daikon sauce, and grilled lamb and leek sandwich on country bread, which still makes our mouth water. ⊠ *145 W. Broadway at Thomas St.,* ☎ *212/233–0507. AE, DC, MC, V.*

French

$$$–$$$$ ✕ **Montrachet.** This TriBeCa trendsetter, owned by Tribeca Grill's Drew Nieporent, is unpretentious in its decor: pastel walls, plush mauve banquettes, and engaging works of art. There's a choice of two three-course menus as well as a five-course tasting affair. A satisfying dinner might begin with endive salad, pears, and walnuts, followed by roasted veal kidney in sherry-vinegar sauce, and one of the noteworthy desserts, such as banana and chocolate gratin over linzer crust. Daniel Johnnes epitomizes the young, knowledgeable American sommelier and offers an interesting selection of wines from diminutive regional vineyards. ⊠ *239 W. Broadway, between Walker and White Sts.,* ☎ *212/ 219–2777. Reservations essential. AE. Closed Sun.; no lunch Mon.–Thurs. or Sat.*

$$–$$$ ✕ **Capsouto Frères.** You'd never guess this romantic spot with exposed brick walls, tall columns and wooden floors was once a warehouse. With its top-notch service, classical music, and reasonable prices, this 1891 TriBeCa landmark is also a winner. Chef Charles Tutino prepares classics with a solid, contemporary touch—for instance, terrine Provençale and Peking duck in cassis-ginger sauce. Dessert soufflés around town pale against the light, delicious versions here. ⊠ *451 Washington St., near Watts St.,* ☎ *212/966–4900. Reservations essential. AE, DC, MC, V. Closed Mon. lunch.*

$–$$ ✕ **Caffè Lure.** Owner Jean Claude Iacovelli earned his stripes at Bouley.
★ The room is small, rough, and raffish with its tin ceiling, tables topped with brown paper and flacons of water and walls festooned with vintage advertising signs and fishing lures—hence the name. The culinary emphasis here is on seafood; try baby lobster with spinach and port sauce or roast monkfish with black olive pureed potatoes and mushrooms. You can also play it simple and enjoy some of the best brick-oven-fired pizza imaginable. ⊠ *169 Sullivan St., between Houston and Bleecker Sts.,* ☎ *212/473–2642. No credit cards.*

$–$$ ✕ **Felix.** No, you haven't traveled 3,000 miles to Paris's Left Bank; this charming bistro is in SoHo, a taxi ride from midtown. Whether you dine inside or alfresco, the service is friendly, and the contemporary bistro fare is attractively presented. Try the steak with thin, crunchy french fries. ⊠ *340 W. Broadway at Grand St.,* ☎ *212/431–0021. AE. Closed Mon. lunch.*

$ ✕ **Le Jardin.** Gerard and Pamela Maurice's welcoming house with a lovely garden and grape arbor really belongs in a small French village. There's no pretention—just hearty portions of French food. The small, charming interior has a tin ceiling, ceiling fans, an antique mirror, and lace café curtains. The fine steak tartare comes with light and grease-free pommes frîtes. You can't go wrong with any of the pleasant house wines, or the homemade desserts. ⊠ *25 Cleveland Pl., near Spring St.,* ☎ *212/343–9599. Reservations essential. AE, DC, MC, V.*

Health

$–$$ ✗ **Spring Street Natural Restaurant & Bar.** This restaurant proves that healthy can taste heavenly. The big open room has ceiling fans, overhead globe lights, wood floors, a blackboard menu, and a long comfortable bar; in warm weather, there are also tables outside. Two vegetarian dishes are standouts: corn-fried organic *seitan* (a sort of wheat-gluten), in two dipping sauces; and a crispy tempeh. You can't go wrong with the fabulous desserts. ⊠ *62 Spring St. at Lafayette St.,* ☎ *212/966–0290. AE, DC, MC, V.*

Italian

$–$$ ✗ **Diva.** You need operatic training to converse above the din in this frenzied SoHo spot with its closely spaced tables and trendy convoy of models, artists, and actors. For tranquillity, arrive by 7:30 and stick around as the sidewalk café fills up. Dependable choices include spaghetti *frutti di mare* (seafood sauce), Gran Duca (filet mignon in cognac), and the ubiquitous tiramisù. ⊠ *341 W. Broadway, near Grand St.,* ☎ *212/941–9024. Reservations essential. AE, DC, MC, V.*

Japanese

$$–$$$$ ✗ **Nobu.** A curved wall of river-worn black pebbles, a 12-seat onyx-faced sushi bar (perfect for single diners), bare-wood tables, birch trees, and a hand-painted beech floor create drama as well as conversation. Sake is the drink of choice, and the clientele is as interesting as the kitchen, which is ruled by celebrity chef Nobu Matsuhisa, of Los Angeles. It's difficult to decide in which direction to go on his menu: rock-shrimp tempura; black cod with miso; new-style sashimi—all are tours de force. ⊠ *105 Hudson St., off Franklin St.,* ☎ *212/219–0500 or 212/219–8095 for same-day reservations. Reservations essential. AE, DC, MC, V. Closed Sun. and lunch.*

Latin

$$ ✗ **Inca Grill.** Stained-glass windows command your attention as you enter this open space with a white grand piano. The huge mahogany bar turns out exotic drinks, while executive-chef and co-owner Rafael Palomino, formally of Metropolis, creates exciting South American dishes. Try an intriguing free-range-chicken tamale (wrapped in banana leaves), or an earthy braised oxtail and potato stew. ⊠ *492 Broome St., near W. Broadway,* ☎ *212/966–3371. AE, DC, MC, V. Closed lunch, Sun. and Mon. dinner.*

Malaysian

$–$$ ✗ **Penang SoHo.** This is a technicolor fantasy with a dramatic waterfall, palm trees, tropical flowers, bar seats with backs made of hoe handles, and individual little huts for small groups. Relatively authentic culinary masterpieces include *roti canai,* flaky pancakes to dip in chicken curry; and *sarang burung,* a ring of fried taro filled with scallops, squid, shrimp, and vegetables. For dessert have *ice kacang,* made with ice cream, shaved ice, red beans, corn, palm seeds, herbs, lotus jelly, red-rose syrup, and milk. ⊠ *109 Spring St., between Greene and Mercer Sts.,* ☎ *212/274–8883. AE, MC, V.*

Mexican

$$ ✗ **El Teddy's.** The margaritas get high marks and the food is mostly wonderful, revealing both authentic Mexican subtleties and contemporary creativity, from the smoked chicken and goat-cheese quesadilla to the grilled rare yellowfin tuna. The roster of inventive desserts includes almond flan and flourless chocolate cake. This is a Mexican restaurant like no other, with its mirrors, tiles, glitter, and grotesque use of colors. In TriBeCa. ⊠ *219 W. Broadway, between Franklin and*

White Sts., ☎ *212/941–7070. Reservations essential. AE, MC, V. No lunch weekends.*

Middle Eastern

$$$ ✗ **Layla.** Mosaics made of pottery shards form exotic collages within this leviathan space. Owned by Drew Nieporent (of Tribeca Grill, Nobu, and Montrachet fame) and actor Robert De Niro, this campy takeoff on the Middle East comes complete with live belly dancers and lifelike mannequins of belly dancers and water-pipe smokers. The menu has a few Turkish and Mediterranean dishes, but most of the food is Moroccan. You can choose a three-course dinner or a chef's feast of various hot and cold Middle Eastern appetizers (served family-style for the entire table). Or better still, you can order piece by piece as your appetite dictates. Sample the delicious sardines, wrapped in phyllo to dip in black-olive aïoli; or the pomegranate-glazed lamb kebob over curried bulgur wheat. ⊠ *211 W. Broadway at Franklin St.,* ☎ *212/431–0700. Reservations essential. AE, DC, MC, V.*

$$–$$$ ✗ **Casa La Femme.** This enterprising restaurant changes its entire decor every six months. Currently the theme is Egyptian, with burgundy banquettes and tables under flowing white tents. In season, there's a sidewalk café. Standout dishes include *mezze,* the Middle Eastern equivalent of mixed hors d'oeuvres and Moroccan vegetarian *tagine* (a spicy stew). ⊠ *150 Wooster St., between Houston and Prince Sts.,* ☎ *212/505–0005. AE, DC, MC, V.*

Philippine

$$–$$$ ✗ **Cendrillon Asian Grill & Marimba Bar.** Cendrillon means Cinderella
★   in French, so the slipper-shaped bar is apropos. The all-exposed red-brick dining room has beautiful wood-tables with delicate inlay designs. Don't miss the spring rolls, Asian barbecues (duck, spareribs, chicken), black rice salad, and adobo—the national dish of the Philippines, prepared here with quail and rabbit in the traditional vinegar and garlic sauce. ⊠ *45 Mercer St., between Broome and Grand Sts.,* ☎ *212/343–9012. AE, DC, MC, V. Closed Sun.*

Soul

$ ✗ **Kwanzaa.** This SoHo restaurant decorated with vibrant wall hangings and African art serves what is best described as international soul food. The menu alternates Jamaican favorites such as jerk chicken wings and kingfish *escabeche* (pickled fish) and African-American specialties like southern fried chicken with macaroni and vegetarian collard greens. Try the scorching chicken curry and save room for the phenomenal carrot cake. ⊠ *19 Cleveland Pl., off Spring St., near Lafayette St.,* ☎ *212/941–6095. AE, MC, V.*

Chinatown, Little Italy, East Village, and Lower East Side

American

$–$$ ✗ **First.** Come here for in inner-city flavor, late-night dining, and intriguing food. The decor is luxurious, with an open kitchen, hammered-metal tables against silk horseshoe-shape banquettes, and a bar graced with a lovely display of photographs by local photographers. The wine list is carefully chosen (several fine vintages are available by the glass), and dinner can be assembled for a song and a half. Hot shrimp cocktail with horseradish crust, grilled lettuce and chili oil, hanger steak with seasonal garnishes, and an uncommonly nurturing warm chocolate-pudding cake are indicative of the culinary scenario. On Sunday, there's a fun brunch and a one-of-a-kind roast suckling pig dinner. ⊠ *87 1st Ave., between 5th and 6th Sts.,* ☎ *212/674–3823. Reservations essential. AE, MC, V. No lunch.*

$ ✕ **Ludlow Street Cafe.** The food is earthy, well-spiced, and cheap at this easygoing, down-home Lower East Side restaurant, filled with young people having a good time. You will, too, if you stick to uncomplicated Texas-inspired dishes like fried catfish. ✉ *165 Ludlow St., between E. Houston and Stanton Sts.,* ☎ *212/353–0536. AE. No Sat. lunch.*

Asian

$$ ✕ **Indochine.** Palm leafs painted on cream-colored walls, black-and-
★ white tile floors, mirrors, leather banquettes, and live palm trees team up with some of the most fascinating food this side of Saigon. Select from among such savory soups as *pho* (sliced fillet of beef, rice noodles, bean sprouts) and *noum protchok namya* (fish, scallops, shrimp, coconut milk, rice vermicelli). The *banh cuon* (steamed Vietnamese ravioli filled with chicken, shiitake, bean sprouts) is ethereal. And the lemon tart, chocolate truffle cake, and coconut crème brûlée, are celestial. ✉ *430 Lafayette St., between 4th St. and Astor Pl.,* ☎ *212/505–5111. Reservations essential. AE, DC, MC, V. No lunch.*

Barbecue

$. ✕ **Brothers Bar-B-Q.** This huge barnlike space on two levels has a lounge-area decorated in the offbeat style of the American South, with hair dryers, tacky period-plastic furniture circa 1949, Texaco, Esso, and Shell oil signs, and even a garage door. Monday nights, it's all-you-can-eat; sample puffy hush puppies with hot sauce, smoked sausage over black eyed peas, fried wings and smoked rib tips in bourbon sauce, shrimp po'boy sandwiches, and terrific chicken and ribs. There's enough of a selection of tequila shots to satisfy Pancho Villa, 11 bottled beers and seven on tap. ✉ *225 Varick St. at Clarkston St.* ☎ *212/727–2775. AE.*

Chinese

$$ ✕ **Golden Unicorn.** If you come to this Hong Kong–style restaurant with
★ at least nine other diners, you can divide the price of a 12-course banquet ($350) by 10, which is a real bargain. You must order it three days in advance and request a small private room. The 12-course banquet may include such dishes as roast suckling pig, scallops and seafood in a noodle nest, whole steamed fish, fried rice with raisins, lobster with ginger, and unusual desserts based on warm or chilled fruit or rice soups. If you can't muster the crowd, sit in the regular dining room and order from the everyday menu. ✉ *18 E. Broadway at Catherine St.,* ☎ *212/ 941–0911. AE, MC, V.*

$$ ✕ **Pacifica.** Holiday Inn houses this elegant Chinatown restaurant. Take the escalator to the second floor and pass through the tasteful lobby to a well-appointed room in shades of gold, salmon, and soft green. Ignore the pastas and order simple and classic dishes such as salt baked triple delight, consisting of shrimp, scallops, and calamari; or steamed fish with ginger and scallions. ✉ *138 Lafayette St., between Canal and Howard Sts.,* ☎ *212/941–4168. AE, DC, MC, V.*

$–$$ ✕ **New York Noodletown.** This unassuming place with a window full of hanging cooked ducks remains one of the best small Chinatown restaurants. Single diners may have to sit at communal round tables, and if you're not careful, you can spend more than the no-nonsense coffee shop decor suggests. Soup and noodles are the things to order here, and you'll find none better elsewhere. For under $5, you'll can get full on delicious shrimp, Chinese greens, and soft egg noodles served in a remarkably cultivated seafood-broth. ✉ *28½ Bowery at Bayard St.,* ☎ *212/349–0923. Reservations not accepted. No credit cards.*

$–$$ ✕ **20 Mott.** This three-story restaurant, an excellent choice for dim sum, is neat if nondescript, and the service rates a notch above average. To get food that's authentic, you must insist on it (look around and point), and when you do, you may be served fabulous steamed dumplings; deep-fried eel with orange peel and spicy XO sauce (a Hong Kong specialty that's rare here)—or different but equally novel dishes. ⊠ *20 Mott St., between Bowery and Pell St.,* ☎ *212/964–0380. AE, MC. V.*

$ ✕ **Sweet'n'Tart Cafe.** You step down into what looks like the inside
★ of a pink sea shell, furnished with Formica tables and a service counter to the right. The menu has some 20 curative soups: little white bowls composed of such exotica as quail eggs, almonds and Asian pears, snow fungi, and spooky-sounding herbs, which actually taste wonderful. This is the place to sample *congee,* that porridge-like concoction eaten for breakfast in Hong Kong. The friendly, somewhat intolerant waiters may advise you to accompany the congee with a sugarless cruller; follow their advice, because the crullers are terrific. Less adventurous souls can enjoy dim sum or fresh fruit shakes. ⊠ *76 Mott St. at Canal St.,* ☎ *212/334–8088. Reservations not accepted. No credit cards.*

Contemporary

$$ ✕ **Global 33.** It looks like an airport lounge furnished by Blooming-dale's, with vinyl, pewter, Lucite, and cast-concrete decor. In this hip space, would-be jet-setters can enjoy generous retro-cocktails. Even the blasting music becomes tolerable if you try the *bagna cauda,* a salad of grilled vegetables with a warm anchovy vinaigrette, followed by a luscious herbed rack of lamb with white bean stew and roasted tomato. ⊠ *93 2nd Ave., between 5th and 6th Sts.,* ☎ *212/477–8427. AE, D. MC, V. Closed lunch.*

Deli

$–$$ ✕ **Second Avenue Deli.** Here it is, the last of a dying breed. And it's not just pastrami and corned beef. There's a bevy of Eastern European Jewish classics, including chicken in the pot, matzo-ball soup, chopped liver, Romanian tenderloin and *cholent* (a central European Jewish dish of meat, bean, and grain)—they're alive and well and accompanied by humor-filled NY Jewish service from days of yore, as well as interesting memorabilia from the Yiddish theater. Try it, you'll like it. ⊠ *156 2nd Ave. at 10th St.,* ☎ *212/677–0606. AE.*

Eastern European

$$$–$$$$ ✕ **Sammy's Roumanian Steak House.** This Lower East Sider is not much to look at with signed endorsements and pictures of customers, newspaper clippings and other memorabilia plastered on the wall, an electric piano, and threadbare decor. Still, it gives new meaning to the word *party.* For starters, there's the live music and wisecracking co-owner Stanley Zimmerman. Then there are those Absolut bottles frozen in blocks of ice on the table. The chopped liver is the best you'll ever eat. And what eggplant salad, stuffed cabbage, half-sour pickles, and roasted peppers. ⊠ *157 Chrystie St. at Delancey St.,* ☎ *212/673–0330. Reservations essential. AE, DC, MC, V. No lunch.*

$ ✕ **Teresa's.** Prices at this Polish luncheonette are in the giveaway category, and the food is satisfying. A few stars: *bigos* (here simply called sauerkraut), the Polish national stew—sauerkraut layered with fresh and smoked meats and sausage—and the hearty, stick-to-the-ribs dumplings known as pierogi, filled with meat, fish, cheese, or mushrooms, boiled or fried and served with sour cream. Homesick Poles mix with cost-conscious students here. ⊠ *103 1st Ave., between 6th and 7th Sts.,* ☎ *212/228–0604. No credit cards.*

French

$–$$ ✕ **L'Udo.** This winning restaurant in historic Colonnade Row combines classy food, low prices, and warm management. Its name comes from the Latin term for "fresco." Walls have been bared to reveal the building's original stone foundation, creating a ruinlike feel to the entrance and lounge area. Art is everywhere, even in the rest rooms. An iron staircase leads to the main dining room with fireplaces, caricatures of alchemists, and French doors onto a garden. The seasonal menu may include onion soup with sourdough bread, and braised lamb shank with tarragon, garlic confit, and flageolets. ✉ *432 Lafayette St., near Astor Pl.*, ☎ *212/388–0978. Reservations essential. AE.*

Italian

$$–$$$ ✕ **Il Cortile.** The setting resembles an Italian palazzo with statues, a Roman brick wall, sprays of fresh flowers, plants, trees, and a skylit courtyard. Chef-owner Michael De Georgio creates food that is always good and often wonderful: lump crabmeat, celery root and radicchio salad and rack of veal De Georgio, with sausage, herbs, and prosciutto sauce. ✉ *125 Mulberry St., between Canal and Hester Sts.*, ☎ *212/226–6060. Reservations essential. AE, DC, MC, V.*

$$ ✕ **S.P.Q.R.** This inviting spot with spacious tables, brickwork, and lots of fresh flowers is one of the few earnest restaurants in Little Italy, an area more noted for fun than food. In addition to the good pasta, there's a terrific veal chop and a phenomenal wine list. ✉ *133 Mulberry St., between Hester and Grand Sts.*, ☎ *212/925–3120. AE, DC, MC, V.*

$ ✕ **Lanza Restaurant.** Ceiling fans, paintings of Italian scenes, and an inviting garden create the feel of an authentic trattoria. The good classic food offers one of Manhattan's greatest restaurant bargains, which explains the crowds of hungry New Yorkers. ✉ *168 1st Ave., between 10th and 11th Sts.*, ☎ *212/674–7014. AE, DC, MC, V.*

Latin

$ ★ ✕ **Boca Chica.** At this raffish East Villager start with a potent *caipirinha* (Brazilian rum, lime juice, and sugar). Assertively seasoned food from several Latin American nations at giveaway prices is Boca Chica's forte. Check out the plantains, served as croquettes or filled with spicy meat; soupy Puerto Rican chicken-rice stew; or Cuban sandwiches blending roast pork, ham, and pickles. Lively music and dancing has its way on weekends, and watch your step—there's often an equally lively boa constrictor by the bar. ✉ *13 1st Ave., near 1st St.*, ☎ *212/473–0108. AE, DC, MC, V. No lunch Mon.–Sat.*

Pizza

$–$$ ✕ **Da Nico.** This Little Italy restaurant deserves praise for its outstanding rotisserie grills and thin-crusted, charred, coal-oven pizza. The roast chicken is delicious, the roast suckling pig soul-stirring. You can dine up front by the marble bar or in a comfortable back room with a skylight. ✉ *164 Mulberry St., between Grand and Broome Sts.*, ☎ *212/343–1212. AE, DC, MC, V.*

Seafood

$–$$ ✕ **Pisces.** This striking restaurant, where tables near the open windows seem to spill out into Alphabet City, as this neighborhood of lettered avenues is called has fallen victim to the quick-change-chef syndrome. But a sophisticated menu combined with reasonable prices, still make it worthwhile. Brunch is served on weekends. ✉ *95 Ave. A at 6th St.*, ☎ *212/260–6660. AE, MC, V. No lunch weekdays.*

Spanish

$ ✕ **Xunta.** The dining room has wine barrels for tables, high stools (watch your balance), fish nets covering the ceiling, and a brick bar with overhanging dried peppers. Of the 32 tapas, don't miss the *tortilla Espanola con cebola* (classic potato omelet with onions)—it is superb. Other recommended dishes include grilled shrimp, tuna or codfish empanadas, and sautéed *cigalas* (a typical shellfish in white wine and cherry-tomato sauce). ✉ *174 1st Ave., between 10th and 11th Sts.* ☎ *212/614–0620. AE, DC, MC, V.*

Swiss

$ ✕ **Roettelle A. G.** If you hanker for hearty European cooking, you'll
★   love this charming East Village town house, where you can sit in a hidden nook in one of the several dining rooms, in the cozy bar, or under an arbor in the garden sipping Swiss wine and eating *viande de Grisons* (Swiss dried beef) or raclette (mild melted cheese served with boiled potatoes and tiny pickles). Sauerbraten with spaetzle and red cabbage is delicious, and it's rare to taste apple strudel and linzer torte this good. Prices are low anyway, but German-born owner Ingrid Roettelle also offers a bargain two-course fixed-price dinner. ⊠ *126 E. 7th St., between 1st Ave. and Ave. A,* ☎ *212/674–4140. Reservations essential. MC, V. Closed Sun.*

Greenwich Village

Contemporary

$$$–$$$$ ✕ **Gotham Bar & Grill.** Chef Alfred Portale originated the vertical style of food presentation here, which turns each plate into an artful edible tower. Rack of lamb is always dependable, and the Gotham chocolate cake, served with toasted almond ice cream should not be ignored. The lofty, multilevel space was the prototype of the new-style New York restaurant, with its warm salmon-and-green color scheme, diffuse lighting from shirred-fabric fixtures, and large window overlooking a courtyard. ⊠ *12 E. 12th St.,* ☎ *212/620–4020. Reservations essential. AE, DC, MC, V. No lunch weekends.*

$$ ✕ **Home.** In this sliver of restaurant, David Page cooks with rare authority and honesty, from the superb blue cheese fondue, caramelized shallots, and rosemary toast to the moist roast chicken and spiced onion rings served with homemade ketchup. Nor will you soon forget the creamy chocolate pudding and homemade cookies. Home also offers an interesting wine list and brunch on weekends. ⊠ *20 Cornelia St., between Bleecker and W. 4th St.,* ☎ *212/243–9579. AE. Closed Mon.*

$$ ✕ **9 Jones Street.** This quintessential Village restaurant has charming whitewashed exposed-brick walls, food-themed murals and lots of culinary bric-a-brac, like roosters in drag. The chef's style favors a deceptive simplicity coupled with the judicious use of ethnic ingredients and frolicsome twists: for example, marinated and grilled pork chops with glazed sweet potato stew with carrots, prunes, and dried fruits. Try the Sunday brunch. ⊠ *9 Jones St.,* ☎ *212/989–1220. Reservations essential. AE, DC, MC, V. No lunch Mon.–Sat.*

$ ✕ **C3.** The landmark Washington Square Hotel's slightly subterranean dining room, dating from 1902, has scenic murals of Washington Square Park, stylish tapestry banquettes, and changing displays of artwork. Typical dishes include grilled leg of lamb, with wild mushroom risotto cake, asparagus, and mint sauce; and the decadent and deadly Grand Marnier chocolate mousse cake. ⊠ *103 Waverly Pl., near Washington Sq.,* ☎ *212/254–1200. AE, DC, MC, V. No dinner Sun. and Mon.*

French

$–$$ ✕ **Chez Jacqueline.** This charming bistro feels just like France with its specials written on the blackboard outside and cast of regulars at the bar. Owner Jacqueline Zini greets you like an old friend, and you'll want to become part of her family after sampling the delectable Provençale dishes, such as *soupe de poisson,* a creamy puree of seafood and vegetables; *jarret de veau* or veal shank, braised with tomatoes, potatoes, zucchini, garlic, endive, and olives in marrow sauce; veal kidneys; and the celebrated upside-down apple tart. The prix-fixe dinner is a good buy. ⊠ *72 MacDougal St., between W. Houston and Bleecker*

Sts., ☎ 212/505–0727. *Reservations essential. AE, MC, V. Closed week-end lunch.*

$–$$ ✕ **Dix et Sept.** Named for its location at West 10th Street and 7th Avenue, this spot has a warm neighborhood feel, a cozy bar area, a comfortable back room with exposed brick walls and framed prints, and another, more formal room upstairs. Start with something simple like asparagus-and-leek vinaigrette. Then select from one of the interesting daily specials such as cassoulet of preserved duck, sausage and smoked ham or braised lamb shank with beans and vegetables. The roast chicken is a steal! ⊠ *181 W. 10th St., ☎ 212/645–8023. Reservations essential. AE, DC, MC, V. No lunch.*

$–$$ ✕ **L'Auberge Du Midi.** If you want the "perfect Greenwich Village restaurant," look no further than this seductive bistro with its French country atmosphere combining exposed brick, copper pots, and stone floors. The welcome couldn't be more ingratiating, and the food is relatively inexpensive and honest. Try the unblemished roast rack of lamb with fresh thyme and *gratin chaud de pommes au Calvados* (glazed hot apples and almond paste, flavored with apple brandy). There's a charming sidewalk café, weather permitting. ⊠ *310 W. 4th St., between W. 12th and Bank Sts., ☎ 212/242–4705. Reservations essential. AE, MC, V. Closed Mon. Nov.–Mar.; no lunch.*

$ ✕ **French Roast.** This casual, around-the-clock spot with a Left Bank ambience charges bargain prices for some very good bistro dishes rarely encountered, such as poached beef marrow finished with bread crumbs and served in broth. The *croque monsieur* (melted cheese sandwich, done in the style of French toast) is first-rate. Or just stop for coffee and dessert. ⊠ *458 6th Ave. at 11th St., ☎ 212/533–2233. AE, MC, V.*

Greek

$–$$ ✕ **Agrotikon.** Designed by artist Anna Lascari, this immaculate white, ★ blue, and green dining room with two fireplaces has been whimsically decorated with decals of fruit and tiny blue fish. Owner and executive chef Kostis Tsingas oversees the most inventive Greek restaurant in town. Don't miss the meatballs of baby calamari. Also worth your while is the whole red snapper, accompanied by delightfully crunchy dandelion greens. ⊠ *322 E. 14 St., between 1st and 2nd Aves., ☎ 212/473–2602. AE, DC, MC, V. Closed Mon.*

Italian

$–$$ ✕ **Grand Ticino.** Walk down a few stairs to enter this agreeable little restaurant with its hunter-green walls and romantic lighting that's named after the Swiss Canton of Ticino. It served its first meal in 1919. Home to artists and writers (Eugene O'Neill and Edna St. Vincent Millay were regulars), the Grand Ticino even made a cameo appearance in the movie *Moonstruck.* The menu includes excellent pasta, a wonderfully simple broiled chicken, and very good calves' liver. ⊠ *228 Thompson St., between W. 3rd and Bleecker Sts., ☎ 212/777-5922. Reservations essential. AE, DC, MC, V. Closed Sun.*

Mexican

$–$$ ✕ **Mi Cocina.** This unassuming Mexican restaurant is one of New York's most arresting, neat as a pin with its gay tiles and rosy walls. And what food: chunky guacamole, *crepas de cajeta* (dessert crepes filled with nuts and dried fruits,) and an unusual tamale *de rajas,* stuffed with spicy poblano chili, onion, and roasted tomato. ⊠ *57 Jane St., off Hudson St., ☎ 212/627–8273. AE, DC, MC, V.*

Moroccan

$–$$ ✕ **Cafe Fes.** This amiable Moroccan restaurant, situated on one of Greenwich Village's most charming streets, is named after co-owner and chef Drissa Rafael's hometown. She and husband Jean Roger have created a perfect setting with peach walls, Moroccan lanterns, a tin ceiling, and a small fountain. The cold mixed salad, made with pureed eggplant and spinach is a delectable beginning. The menu also includes the classic couscous, served in three variations, and *tajine,* a stewlike entrée made of lamb with prunes or artichokes and fava beans. ✉ *246 W. 4th St. at Charles St.,* ☎ *212/924–7653. AE, DC, MC, V. Closed lunch.*

Philippine

$ ✕ **Manila Garden.** Authentic Philippine cuisine, combining Asian and Spanish flavors, may be savored at this lovely spot, with a white grand piano, a seasonal garden, and fresh orchids on each table. Tuesdays, you can take advantage of the bargain buffet at lunch and dinner. Other times, enjoy escabeche, wonderful *lechon* (roasted pig), *lumpia Shanghai* (a delicious pork egg roll), and chicken adobo. For dessert, order the flan, which is richer than its Spanish counterpart, and *halo halo* (ice cream topped with fruit). ✉ *325 E. 14th St., between 1st and 2nd Aves.,* ☎ *212/777–6314. AE, DC, MC, V.*

Pizza

$ ✕ **Arturo's.** Few guidebooks list this brick-walled Village landmark, but the body-to-body crowds teetering on the wobbly wooden chairs suggest good things. The pizza is terrific, cooked in a coal-fired oven. Basic pastas as well as seafood, veal, and chicken concoctions with mozzarella and lots of tomato sauce come at giveaway prices. ✉ *106 W. Houston St., off Thompson St.,* ☎ *212/677–3820. AE, MC, V.*

Gramercy Park, Murray Hill, Chelsea, and the Flatiron District

American

$$$–$$$$ ✕ **Gramercy Tavern.** A 91-foot-long mural of fruit and vegetables wraps around the bar. Although the dining area is reminiscent of an English tavern, the food is best classified as new American: typical dishes include tuna tartar with sea urchin and cucumber vinaigrette and saddle of rabbit with olives, roasted garlic, shallots, and rosemary. Eight beers from American microbreweries on draught, a stellar wine list, smooth service, plus unrivaled media-hype make Gramercy Tavern a hard-to-get reservation. ✉ *42 E. 20th St., between Park Ave. S and Broadway,* ☎ *212/477–0777. Reservations essential. AE, DC, MC, V. Closed Sun. lunch.*

$$$ ✕ **Union Square Cafe.** In this spiffy restaurant where mahogany moldings outline white walls hung with bright modern paintings, the disposition is unpretentious, the service friendly, and the atmosphere pleasant. Breads are delicious and appetizers sparkle; we heartily endorse the iced oysters on the half shell, shucked to order, with shallot vinaigrette. While dinner entrées are conscientious, the sandwiches served at lunch—for example, fresh-tuna club on Tom Cat white bread with slab bacon, arugula, and homemade herb-potato chips—approach the divine. ✉ *21 E. 16th St.,* ☎ *212/243–4020. Reservations essential. AE, DC, MC, V. No lunch Sun.*

$$$ ✕ **Verbena.** In this small, cunning restaurant in the historic Inn at Irving Place, windows are dotted with small pots of herbs, and there are two small rooms with fireplaces and a diminutive garden. An olive, beige, and mustard color scheme plays backdrop to executive chef Diane Foley's inventive yet severely simple style, as evidenced in chopped endive salad with melted Taleggio cheese tart, beer-braised ribs of beef with horseradish dumplings, and bittersweet chocolate soufflé. ✉ *54 Irving Pl. at 17th St.,* ☎ *212/260–5454. Reservations essential. AE, DC, MC, V. Closed Mon.–Sat. lunch.*

$$$ ✕ **American Place.** This stylish establishment with kindly service gets
★ our vote as the country's finest regional American restaurant. Execu-
tive chef Larry Forgione is a leading supporter of new American cook-
ing. His seasonal menu ranges from fresh Maine deviled crab spring
roll to cedar-planked salmon with seasonal vegetables. The high-
ceilinged room with its Art Deco brasserie-style light fixtures, color-
ful Mikasa china, generously spaced tables, and Frank Stella paintings
represents luxury at its most effortless. ⊠ *2 Park Ave. at 32nd St.,*
☎ *212/684–2122. Reservations essential. AE, DC, MC, V. Closed Sat.
lunch, Sun.*

American Casual

$ ✕ **Alley's End.** This long sectioned space with laminated-copper table-
tops, a Japanese enclosed garden, and rock-bottom prices is a real dis-
covery. Customers appreciate the enthusiastic service, and the chef
succeeds best with unaffected but classy dishes, such as thyme-grilled
breast of chicken on fabulous garlic mashed potatoes. Don't skip the
wonderful desserts, including pumpkin crème brûlée. ⊠ *311 W. 17th
St.,* ☎ *212/627–8899. AE, DC, MC, V.*

Asian

$–$$ ✕ **Republic.** Downtown epicureans on the run flock to this innovative
Asian noodle emporium. At one of the two long bluestone bars, you
can simultaneously dine and enjoy the spectacle of chefs scurrying amid
clouds of steam in the open kitchen. The menu contains chiefly rice
dishes or noodles, stir-fried with hints of ginger, peanuts and coriander or served in savory broths, made with coconut milk, lemongrass,
Asian basil and lime leaf. ⊠ *37A Union Sq. W, between 16th and 17th
Sts.,* ☎ *212/627–7172. AE, DC, MC, V.*

Austrian

$ ✕ **Kaffeehaus.** This café-cum-restaurant with its upholstered ban-
quettes, marble-top tables, pastry display, and racks of newspapers and
magazines, re-creates old Vienna. There's also an inviting neighborhood feeling—not to mention terrific coffee, unusual organic and un-
filtered wheat beers, interesting Austrian wines, and food that will
surprise you with its finesse. Start with smoked trout with marinated
beets and horseradish cream. Then go for a classic Wiener schnitzel.
Desserts look better than they taste—smart customers order the homemade *milchram* strudel (cheese with vanilla cream). ⊠ *131 8th Ave.,
between 16th and 17th Sts.,* ☎ *212/229–9702. DC, MC, V.*

Contemporary

$$$ ✕ **Aja.** The mix of new American, Southwestern, Thai, Vietnamese,
Korean, and classic French cuisine is positively futuristic. Witness the
tuna tartare with a blend of sesame, avocado, and daikon; and the
steamed lobster–Penang curry, with roasted eggplant and grilled pineap-
ple. The decor is almost as quirky as the menu: distressed finishes and
natural woods, bold color combinations (brilliant chartreuse, deep
brick, and pale gold), and sofas and chairs covered in lush damask.
⊠ *937 Broadway at 22nd St.,* ☎ *212/473–8388. Reservations essential.
AE, DC, MC, V. Closed Sun.*

$$$ ✕ **Water Club.** This glass-enclosed barge in the East River is decidedly
★ dramatic, with its long wood-paneled bar, blazing fireplace, appetiz-
ing shellfish display, and panoramic water views. Food is ingeniously
presented. Tuna tartare with marinated shiitake mushrooms, wasabi,
spicy ocean salad, and flying fish roe arrives on a porthole with a tiny
anchor supporting a jar of caviar. Or order the exemplary sautéed red
snapper fillet with lobster dumpling fennel and saffron bouillon. Sample any dessert your conscience desires: Chocolate flourless cake with
peppermint-stick ice cream will sweeten even the sourest disposition.

Sunday brunch is winsome. ⊠ *500 E. 30th St.,* ☎ *212/683–3333. Reservations essential. Jacket required. AE, DC, MC, V.*

$$–$$$ ✕ **Flowers.** The intimate Tuscan-style dining room resembles a country-barn interior. Baskets of dried flowers adorn the walls and copper light-fixtures exude a comforting glow that dims as the evening progresses. Executive chef and co-owner Marc Salonsky incorporates such influences as Asian (crispy shrimp roll with soy-ginger vinaigrette and spaghetti vegetables), Caribbean (roasted baby lamb chops with Jamaican spices) and Italian (risotto of seasonal wild mushrooms, asparagus, rosemary, and white truffle oil). Desserts are lovely—especially Baked Alaska. ⊠ *21 West 17th St., between 5th and 6th Aves.* ☎ *212/691–8888. AE, DC, MC, V. Closed Sat. lunch, Sun.*

$$–$$$ ✕ **Lola.** Here, beautiful people dance to loud music when they're not sipping wine at the bar, or languishing romantically on striped banquettes in the main dinning room with bouquets of fresh flowers. There's a Sunday Gospel Brunch and an affordable lunch called Lola Bola, including noodles, rice dishes, and drinks. Perhaps start with a stack of ribbon onion rings, then follow with the signature Lola fried chicken and Cuban–style black beans. ⊠ *30 West 22nd St., between 5th and 6th Ave.,* ☎ *212/675–6700. AE, DC, MC, V. Closed Sat. lunch.*

French

$$$–$$$$ ✕ **CT.** This airy restaurant is named for the initials of the owner and
★   chef, Claude Troisgros, of the illustrious family of chefs. The signature jumbo ravioli, filled with taro root mousseline and white truffle oil, and prepared with wild mushroom sauce is unmatched; crispy red snapper with eggplant confit in honey and sherry vinegar is another winner. ⊠ *111 E. 22nd St., between Park Ave. S and Lexington Ave.,* ☎ *212/995–8500. Reservations essential. AE, DC, MC, V. No Sat. lunch.*

$$ ✕ **Les Halles.** Strikingly unpretentious, this French-American steak house has a homey interior, with posters plastered on antique walls, a tin ceiling, and a windowed kitchen. This is the place to go for crispy duck-leg confit and frisée salad, warm sausages with lentils, and heaping plates of garlicky cold cuts. A good bet is the extraordinary *côte de boeuf*, with béarnaise sauce, a massive rib steak for two served from a wooden board. ⊠ *411 Park Ave. S, between 28th and 29th Sts.,* ☎ *212/679–4111. AE, DC, MC, V.*

Indian

$–$$ ✕ **Mavalli Palace.** Service may a bit slow here, but the gentle prices and marvelous dishes more than compensate. Magnificent crepes made with lentils and rice flour are wrapped around potatoes and a fiery chutney. Fresh onions top *uttappam*, a rice and lentil pancake. This pretty place has exposed brick walls and blond wood chairs. ⊠ *46 E. 29th St.,* ☎ *212/679–5535. AE, DC, MC, V. Closed Mon.*

Italian

$$$ ✕ **Le Madri.** The Tuscan-style space with a vaulted ceiling and wood-burning pizza oven is the creation of Pino Luongo (of Coco Pazzo). Fried calamari and zucchini with spicy roast-pepper tomato sauce might be a prelude to braised veal shank with portobello mushrooms and saffron risotto. You're bound to enjoy the impeccable desserts, such as *tortino* (a warm chocolate-hazelnut cake), and the top-flight service. ⊠ *168 W. 18th St.,* ☎ *212/727–8022. Reservations essential. AE, DC, MC, V.*

$$–$$$ ✕ **Follonico.** You'll like the vintage wainscoting, muted Tuscan colors,
★   open kitchen, and wood-burning oven—but most of all, you will like the food, chef-owner Alan Tardi's personal interpretation of regional cuisine from Tuscany. The deep-fried oysters crowned with horseradish

cream and *osetra* caviar are so good you'll want to overindulge. But save room for one of the unusual pastas. *Fazzoletto,* a handkerchief pasta imprinted with fresh herbs, is sauced differently with each visit—but it's always inspired. Follow this with a whole red snapper, baked in a rock-salt crust. Fresh fruit granita is refreshing, but it would be a shame to leave without submerging a *biscotti* into a compatible dessert wine and some bracing espresso. ⊠ *6 W. 24th St.,* ☎ *212/691–6359. Reservations essential. AE, DC, MC, V. Closed Sat. lunch, Sun.*

$$-$$$ ✕ **I Trulli.** Nicola Marzovilla of Tempo, a successful Italian restaurant, created this intimate space with rough-hewn gold walls, a glass-enclosed fireplace, a garden for summer dining, and a whitewashed open grill with the traditional beehive-shape of early Pugliese houses. Start your dinner with an out-of-the-ordinary glass of wine from a little-known producer and one of the enticing appetizers, such as baked oysters with pancetta, Tallegio cheese, and bread crumbs. Next, try a split of pasta—perhaps ricotta dumplings with fresh tomato and arugula or *orecchiette* (ear shaped pasta) with broccoli rabe and roasted almonds. Other specialties use game, meat, and fish cooked in the wood-fired oven. ⊠ *122 E. 27th St., between Lexington and Park Aves.,* ☎ *212/481–7372. Reservations essential. AE, DC, MC, V. Closed Sat. lunch, Sun.*

$$ ✕ **Sal Anthony's.** Of the many Italian restaurants in this historic area, this town-house dining room is one of the best and most pleasant. Opened in 1966, long before a pasta palace anchored every other corner, Sal Anthony's has attracted a loyal cadre with its deferential service, superior wine list, thick veal chops, and pretty decor—oil paintings on brick walls, huge bouquets, and crisp white cloths on well-spaced tables. ⊠ *55 Irving Pl.,* ☎ *212/982–9030. Reservations essential. AE, DC, MC, V.*

$-$$ ✕ **Caffe Bondi Ristorante.** This fascinating small restaurant with a ★ garden boasts one of Manhattan's most authentic menus (a food historian helped re-create the cooking of southern Italy in the 18th and 19th centuries): artichokes braised in almond sauce, ravioli filled with pumpkin and ricotta, oven roasted boar chops, quail stuffed with grapes, and a chocolate almond torte you'll remember for a lifetime. The wine list is short, excellent, and fairly priced. ⊠ *7 W. 20th St.,* ☎ *212/691–8136. AE, MC, V. Closed Sun.*

Latin

$$$ ✕ **Patria.** Owned by Philip Suarez (of Vong and Jo Jo), this trendy trilevel ★ Caribbean café, painted in striking earth tones, has handsome mosaics and an open grill. The fluctuating menu offers variations of several ethnic entrées such as meat, vegetable, or seafood empanadas as well as soups and seafood (look for the crispy red snapper with coconut-conch rice). Even nonsmokers will want to indulge in the signature dessert, a chocolate-filled cigar with edible matches. The wine list focuses on Spain, Argentina, and California. ⊠ *250 Park Ave. S at 20th St.,* ☎ *212/777–6211. Reservations essential. AE, MC, V.*

Southwestern

$$$ ✕ **Mesa Grill.** Chef Bobby Flay and owner Jerome Kretchmer have Manhattan foodies in the palms of their hands in this former bank, now done with vinyl banquettes, green-and-yellow walls, and industrial fans. You can't go wrong with the small menu. Try the shrimp with a roasted garlic and corn tamale, the pumpkin soup with chili cream, or the chili-crusted rabbit with sweet potato polenta and caramelized mango sauce. Chocolate-peanut butter ice cream cake with roasted marshmallows is just one of the unbeatable desserts. ⊠ *102 5th Ave., between 15th and 16th Sts.,* ☎ *212/807–7400. Reservations essential. AE, MC, V.*

Spanish

$$ ✕ **Bolo.** With its tile-edged brick oven, vivid gold-red-cobalt color scheme, state-of-the-art open kitchen, and polished wood bar, the design here fuses Manhattan and Spain. The food aims at New York palates: Oven-roasted baby shrimp with toasted garlic is garnished with fragrant sprigs of thyme, and curried shellfish paella unites bivalves with sausage, chicken, and rice. If you're not in the mood for the perfect house sangria, choose from the well-chosen and well-priced wine list. ✉ *23 E. 22nd St.,* ☎ *212/228–2200. Reservations essential. AE, MC, V. Closed Sat. lunch, Sun.*

Turkish

$ ✕ **Turkish Kitchen.** Manhattan's best Turkish restaurant is housed in
★ a striking multilevel room with lipstick red walls, chairs with skirted slipcovers, framed prints, and kilims covering the walls and floor. The young staff dressed in long white chefs' aprons serves delicate and authentic food. For appetizers, choose from such delectable offerings as velvety char-grilled eggplant salad, pan-fried calves liver, and fried calamari. The stuffed cabbage and bulgur wheat patties, filled with ground lamb, pine nuts and currants, are both highly recommended. ✉ *386 3rd Ave., between 27th and 28th Sts.,* ☎ *212/679–1810. AE, DC, MC, V. No lunch weekends.*

Vegetarian

$–$$ ✕ **Zen Palate.** In this remarkable vegetarian restaurant walls are made from squares of fragile rice paper, and there are wooden beams and bamboo chairs. The resplendent appetizers include taro spring rolls, Vietnamese-style autumn rolls, and marinated seaweed. Entrées have poetic names like "Festival on a Roll"—seasoned spinach in soybean crepes with a spicy sauce, or "Dreamland"—layers of spinach linguine, bean sprouts, and shredded black mushrooms. ✉ *34 Union Sq. E at 16th St.,* ☎ *212/614–9291 and 212/614–9345. Reservations essential. AE, MC, V. No lunch Sun.*

Midtown

Afghan

$ ✕ **Pamir.** Afghan cuisine might be loosely described as a combination
★ of Italian, Chinese, and Middle Eastern cooking; for New Yorkers, it's exotic, healthy, and delicious. This attractive two-level restaurant has gold-leaf chandeliers, hanging brass pots, Asian rugs, and brass sconces. It serves such memorable dishes as delicate, deep-fried turnovers with stuffing of pumpkin or carrot; scallion-filled dumplings topped with yogurt and meat sauce; and a mélange of seasoned lamb garnished with pistachio nuts, almonds, orange strips, cardamom, and rose water. ✉ *1065 1st Ave.,at 58th St.,* ☎ *212/644–9258. AE, DC, MC, V. Closed lunch Sat., Sun., Mon.*

American

$$$$ ✕ **Rainbow Room.** This $25 million dinner-and-dancing room on the 65th floor remains a monument to glamour and fantasy with its state-of-the-art sound and lighting systems and colored lights beaming across a domed ceiling. Tables clad in silver lamé rise in tiers around a revolving dance floor lit by an immense chandelier; aubergine walls frame panoramic 50-mile views through floor-to-ceiling windows. The service is better than you'd expect; revamped retro-dishes including lobster Thermidor, oysters Rockefeller, a fresh shellfish extravaganza, and tournedos Rossini with truffle sauce are decorative and agreeable. If you indulge in dessert, let it be the stellar baked Alaska. ✉ *30 Rockefeller Plaza,* ☎ *212/632–5000 or 212/632–5100. Reservations es-*

sential. Jacket and tie. AE, DC, MC, V. Closed Mon. (Sun. and Mon., during the summer).

$$$$ ✕ **"21" Club.** Not all are treated equally in this four-story brownstone
★ landmark, a former speakeasy—if you're not known, the greeting can
be indifferent, even chilly. Once inside, though, service is seamless, and
it's exciting to hobnob with celebrities and tycoons and sip a well-made
cocktail in the lounge before dinner. Here is one of the world's great
wine cellars (with some 50,000 bottles). The Grill Room is *the* place
to be, with its banquettes, red checked tablecloths and a ceiling hung
with toys. Executive chef Michael Lomonaco can prepare a creditable
rendition of the signature "21" burger or chicken hash, but he can also
finesse more complex dishes, such as pan roasted lobster potpie, pep-
pered tuna steak, and roast squab with foie gras. ✉ *21 W. 52nd St.,*
☎ *212/582–7200. Reservations essential. Jacket and tie. AE, DC, MC,
V. Closed Sat. lunch, Sun.*

$$$–$$$$ ✕ **Fifty Seven Fifty Seven.** Designed by I. M. Pei, the Four Seasons Hotel
that houses this room is strikingly sleek, and its 22-foot coffered ceil-
ings, inlaid maple floors, and onyx-studded bronze chandeliers set the
tone for urbane food served superbly. Imaginative appetizers like lob-
ster-Caesar salad elevates this overworked dish to star status, and it's
hard to choose between the perfectly timed herb-roasted rack of lamb
and the moist rack of veal with its crispy onion garnish. ✉ *57 E. 57th
St.,* ☎ *212/758–5757. AE, DC, MC, V.*

$$–$$$ ✕ **Gloucester Cafe.** Copper and cobalt-blue light fixtures brighten this
updated remake of a traditional seafood house with an eclectic menu,
combining some excellent seafood dishes with trendy pastas, pizza, and
sandwiches. Stick with simple dishes and you won't go wrong. You sit
in the spacious downstairs area with an open kitchen and striking mu-
rals or on the balcony with a choice of TVs. ✉ *37 East 50th St.,
between Madison and Park Aves.,* ☎ *212/750–2233. Closed Sun.*

$$–$$$ ✕ **Judson Grill.** Another venture of Jerome Kretchmer (of Gotham Bar
★ and Grill fame), the airy space with a bar and balcony has red velour
banquettes, mirrored walls, lofty ceilings, engaging John Parks murals,
and immense gold vases. The open kitchen produces sumptuous ex-
pensive dishes like New York State foie gras, yet the more down-to-
earth dishes—salads, sandwiches, seafood platters as well as double
rib steak—are equally well executed. ✉ *152 W. 52nd St.,* ☎ *212/582–
5252. AE, DC, MC, V. Closed Sat. lunch, Sun.*

$$ ✕ **Ambassador Grill.** If it's Sunday, head for the Park Hyatt Hotel, which
★ houses this greenhouse-inspired model of modern elegance with black
and white tile floors, pink tablecloths, abundant plants, and an open
kitchen. The brunch buffet is one of the finest in the city. But then the
dining experience here is always first-class (and at less-than-first-class
prices). Favorite plates include Bourbon barbecued shrimp, rotisserie
five-spice duck, and pecan diamond with butterscotch glaze. There's
also an amazing prix-fixe dinner. ✉ *1 United Nations Plaza at 44th
St.,* ☎ *212/702–5014. Reservations essential. AE, DC, MC, V.*

$$ ✕ **Billy's.** In this quintessential New York neighborhood restaurant,
established in 1870, straightforward burgers, steaks, fish, and pasta
dishes take second place to such down-home specials as chicken pot-
pie, turkey with real mashed potatoes, and corned beef and cabbage.
Billy's neighborhood is unusually moneyed (it's the home of the ex-
clusive River House and the kind of people who are written up in *For-
tune* magazine and the society pages), so the people-watching is often
as satisfying as the comfort food and vintage setting. ✉ *948 1st Ave.,
between 52nd and 53rd Sts.,* ☎ *212/753–1870. AE, DC, MC, V.*

Midtown Manhattan Dining

Le Marais, **61**
Le Périgord, **48**
Les Célébrités, **17**
Les Halles, **94**
Lespinasse, **40**
Lola, **96**
Lutèce, **69**
Mangia e Bevi, **28**
Manhattan Ocean Club, **14**
March, **2**
Marichu, **75**
Mavalli Palace, **93**
Mesa Grill, **108**
Morton's, **83**
Monkey Bar, **43**
Motown Cafe, **15**
New York Kom Tang Soot Bul House, **87**
Oceana, **44**
Orso, **60**
Osteria al Droge, **63**
Otabe, **12**
Palio, **33**
Pamir, **4**
Patria, **102**
Peacock Alley, **67**
Pen & Pencil, **74**
Petrossian, **18**
Planet Hollywood, **16**
Pomaire, **56**
Rainbow Room, **77**
Remi, **26**
Republic, **106**
Rosa Mexicano, **3**
Ruth's Chris, **32**
Sal Anthony's, **103**
San Domenico, **21**
San Pietro, **42**
Sea Grill, **79**
Seryna, **41**
Shaan, **81**
Smith & Wollensky, **68**
Stage Deli, **27**
Tang Pavillion, **32**
Tapika, **23**
"21" Club, **50**
Trattoria Dell'Arte, **19**
Tse Yang, **65**
Turkish Kitchen, **91**
Uncle Nick's, **52**
Union Square Cafe, **107**
Verbena, **103**
Victor's Cafe 52, **34**
Virgil's, **63**
Vong, **48**
Water Club, **90**
Zen Palate, **111**

Basque

$$$ ✕ **Marichu.** Natural brick and old beams from Connecticut grace New York's only Basque restaurant, which has a lovely garden. The main dining room is simply furnished and understated. As prepared here, Basque cuisine is refined and elegant, with notable seafood offerings. There's no better way to start than with Rioja peppers, stuffed with a puree of cod. Order one of the changing house specials—you won't be disappointed. ⊠ *342 E. 46th St., between 1st and 2nd Aves.,* ☏ *212/370–1866. AE, DC, MC, V. Closed weekend. lunch.*

Chinese

$$$–$$$$ ✕ **Tse Yang.** There are Tse Yangs in Paris, Geneva, and Beverly Hills, but this one is perhaps the most dramatic, with its dark polished wood, dim lighting, elegant tableware, and an exotic fish tank. One of the joys of dining here is experimenting with wine and food combinations. Try the crisp whole sea bass with an equally crisp sauvignon blanc or the Peking duck, served traditionally with doilies (thin pancakes) and skin, with a spicy gewürztraminer. ⊠ *34 E. 51st St.,* ☏ *212/688–5447. Reservations essential. AE, DC, MC, V.*

$$–$$$ ✕ **Tang Pavillion.** Outside of Chinatown, this is the most authentic Chi-
★ nese restaurant in Manhattan, featuring the cuisine of Shanghai and Soo Chow. Don't be put off by language problems. Westernized dishes shine (shrimp toast, for example) and teasers of pickled vegetables and seasoned nuts are addictive. You're advised to request the Shanghai menu, which is presented in English as well as Chinese. Go with a group on your first visit and sample the crisp baby eel, drunken chicken, Tung-Po pork to stuff in incredibly light doughy buns, jumbo shrimp with walnuts in a slightly sweet, slightly spicy sauce, and green beans and tofu sheets (reminiscent of pasta). ⊠ *65 W. 55th St.,* ☏ *212/956–6888. Reservations essential. AE, DC, MC, V.*

$$–$$$ ✕ **Chiam.** Although purists argue that the only worthy Chinese eater-
ies are in Chinatown, such venues as this, with its polished service, make a persuasive case for the more westernized uptown experience. The stylish setting includes natural wood, an understated white and black motif, and a courtyard view. The wine list is extraordinary for a Chinese restaurant (inquire about special wine-tasting dinners). Enlist the services of your congenial captain, who will select from such diverse menu options as squab *soon* (minced pigeon in lettuce leaves), prawns Chiam (in a zesty chili sauce), and steamed lotus-wrapped chicken. ⊠ *160 E. 48th St.,* ☏ *212/371–2323. AE, DC, MC, V.*

$$–$$$ ✕ **Jimmy Sung's.** Four dramatic peacock-fountain chandeliers cast off restrained lighting at this elegant Chinese restaurant with rich carpeting, patterned wallpaper, gleaming cherry wood paneling and ornately carved wood arches. The menu concentrates on Manchurian, Shanghai, and Mandarin cuisine, all discreetly served on lovely china. Begin your dinner auspiciously with vegetarian pie with house pancake—crisp sheets of bean curd are stuffed in a puffy pancake, accompanied by plum sauce and scallions. Next, choose among such well-prepared entrées as salt baked fresh cuttlefish, shrimp or scallops with chili pepper (a dish rarely encountered uptown), or sliced prawn, barely cooked, and served with an ethereal egg white sauce. ⊠ *219 E. 44th St., between 2nd and 3rd Aves.,* ☏ *212/682–5678. AE, DC, MC, V.*

Contemporary

$$$$ ✕ **Lespinasse.** The pulchritudinous (some call it stuffy) Louis XV
★ decor of this St. Regis Sheraton dining room with its oil paintings and commodious seating in satin chairs is an ideal setting for the refined cuisine of Gray Kunz, who honed his craft under Switzerland's celebrated Frédy Girardet. Kunz's Singapore past and background as chef of Hong Kong's Regent Hotel dining room are felt in the Asian

touches—there is also an Asian tasting menu. A less adventurous repast might begin with herbed risotto and mushroom fricassee, move on to rack of lamb on curried eggplant tart, and conclude with warm chocolate tartlet with orange-grapefruit coulis. ⊠ *2 E. 55th St.,* ☎ *212/339– 6719. Jacket required. AE, DC, MC, V. Closed Sun.*

$$$–$$$$ ✕ **Four Seasons Grill Room.** This bastion of the power lunch offers one
★ of Manhattan's loftiest dinner experiences at a realistic price. Diners enjoy architect Philip Johnson's timeless contemporary design, inviting leather banquettes, rosewood walls, renowned floating sculpture, and one of the best bars in New York. The eclectic international fare changes often, but the tolerably priced wine list and smooth service are perennially present. A short stroll through the marble corridor leads to the celebrated Pool Room, where the check might flabbergast even a millionaire. ⊠ *99 E. 52nd St.,* ☎ *212/754–9494. Reservations essential. Jacket required. AE, DC, MC, V. No lunch Sat.; closed Sun.*

$$$–$$$$ ✕ **March.** With its travertine floor, working fireplace, and burled teak
★ and English elm wainscoting, this singular restaurant is elegantly understated. Co-owner Joseph Salice supervises the polished and inconspicuous service, and the cuisine of chef Wayne Nish is at once restrained and inspired, demonstrating a mastery of classical technique coupled with artful contemporary presentations. Dishes include Japanese-influenced sashimi of Japanese yellowfin tuna with olive oil and soy sauce and luxury offerings, such as the whimsical "Beggar's Purses," filled with lobster and truffles. ⊠ *405 E. 58th St.,* ☎ *212/754–6272. Reservations essential. AE, DC, MC, V. No lunch; closed Sun.*

$$$ ✕ **China Grill.** This huge restaurant has jade-color walls, cloudlike light fixtures, and an open kitchen. The Asian-inspired cuisine may make you overlook the noise: lobster or duck pancakes, sake-cured salmon rolls, duck in caramelized black vinegar, and, for dessert, coconut crème brûlée or chocolate hazelnut bombe. The wine list is full of pleasures; the dessert wines are perfect as aperitifs and with vinegar-based and sweet-and-sour sauces. Check out the flavored sakes. ⊠ *60 W. 53rd St.,* ☎ *212/333–7788. AE, DC, MC, V. No lunch weekends.*

$$$ ✕ **Monkey Bar.** Cobalt-blue bread plates and glasses, etched-glass
★ panels of the Manhattan skyline, velvet banquettes with a colorful palm-tree design, and cute little monkeys hanging from the lighting fixtures all contribute to the lively atmosphere of this fashionable restaurant with impeccable service. You can bypass the mobbed bar scene by entering through the subdued Hotel Elysée. There's no monkey business going on with the food; the fried shrimp, rolled in shredded-phyllo on a bed of cucumber may be the best appetizer in town. Among the signature entrées is a perfectly roasted cod with luscious mashed potatoes, carrots, and celery-root chips. ⊠ *60 E. 54th St.,* ☎ *212/838–2600. Reservations essential. Jacket required. AE, DC, MC, V. Closed weekend lunch.*

$$–$$$ ✕ **Bryant Park Grill, Roof Restaurant and BP Cafe.** Stone fountains, Parisian chairs, and a 200-seat outdoor garden precede the more formal Grill area, graced with rare lacquered woods, slate floors, and velvet leaf-patterned banquettes. The dining room has a large abstract mural of birds by Hunt Slonem and a chandelier with fireflies and brass curlicues. Executive chef Jonathan Waxman oversees the attractive looking food, which is reasonably good, considering the volume demand on the kitchen. A typical dinner: calamari salad, Joe's special (scrambled eggs, sautéed spinach, ground sirloin, and mushrooms), and chocolate soufflé. ⊠ *25 W. 40th St., between 5th and 6th Aves.,* ☎ *212/840–6500. AE, DC, MC, V.*

$$ ✕ **Vong.** Jean-Georges Vongerichten's stint at Bangkok's Oriental Hotel inspired this radiant restaurant with its potted palms and gold-leaf ceiling. While the menu changes often, reliable standbys include the lobster and daikon roll with rosemary-ginger dip; lobster in Thai spices; and the distinctive rabbit curry braised with carrots and cumin seed. Prices, though not bad, can be kept down by ordering a second appetizer in lieu of an entrée. Wines are well chosen, but you may favor beer. ☒ *200 E. 54th St.,* ☎ *212/486–9592. Reservations essential. AE, DC, MC, V. Closed weekend lunch.*

French

$$$$ ✕ **La Cote Basque.** A landmark in French dining has found a new home. Practically all the elements of the original restaurant have been imported, including the dark wooden cross beams, signature murals by Bernard Lamotte, faux windows, and even the revolving door. Executive chef-owner Jean-Jacques Rachou has lightened the cuisine; he's also hired Richard Leach, a young American pastry chef. Customers can partake of a fixed price, three-course dinner, with very few surcharges. If you order the signature roast duckling with honey, Grand Marnier, and black-cherry sauce, your waiter will deliver it whole for inspection, and then carve it before you. Desserts are no less dramatic; for instance, glazed pumpkin custard with crunchy walnuts and frozen pumpkin terrine comes with a flaming candle inside a pumpkin lantern. ☒ *60 W. 55th St., between 5th and 6th Ave.,* ☎ *212/688–6525. Reservations essential. Jacket and tie. Closed Sun. lunch. AE, DC, MC, V.*

$$$$ ✕ **Lutèce.** One of New York's most prestigious restaurants, Lutèce was sold in 1994 to the Ark Group (owner of B. Smith's, Ernie's, Jim Mc-Mullen, American Place, and others). It also has a new chef. The service ranges from friendly to somewhat distant; the menu retains signature dishes (the onion tart, for example) and favorites of the old regime alongside such contemporary creations as snapper tartare in Reisling wine sauce, lime juice, and cilantro. Most desserts are lighter than before, but you can still savor the classic soufflés. ☒ *249 E. 50th St.,* ☎ *212/752–2225. Reservations essential. Jacket required. AE, DC, MC, V. Closed Mon. and Sat. lunch, Sun., and Aug.*

$$$–$$$$ ✕ **Peacock Alley.** This luxurious Waldorf-Astoria salon offers the professional service, fine china, and comprehensive wine cellar that distinguish many of today's hotel restaurants. It also has tranquil lighting, lovely murals with a peacock motif, and cushy seating at banquettes and roomy tables. Chef de cuisine Laurent Manrique makes certain the kitchen lives up to the surroundings. Look for superlative game specials (including hare, pheasant and wood pigeon) and dishes from Manrique's native Gascony: an assortment of cold foie gras pâté; river trout, stuffed with Basque-style rice and served with Manilla clams and crispy chorizo; and warm chocolate cake with hazelnut sherbet. ☒ *301 Park Ave., between 49th and 50th Sts.,* ☎ *212/872–4895. Reservations essential. AE, DC, MC, V. Closed Sat. lunch, Sun.*

$$$–$$$$ ✕ **La Reserve.** This luxurious, exceedingly beautiful restaurant can be an excellent value if you go for the prix-fixe lunch. Lighting is soft, the flowers and murals lovely, the service smooth, and the wine list replete with great bottles from great châteaux in great years. The cuisine represents a contemporary side of the classical French kitchen; lobster salad, smoked salmon, saddle of rabbit, poached Dover sole with an artichoke mousse, and *panier Pompadour,* a basket of fresh raspberries and white and dark chocolate mousse—all artfully presented. ☒ *4 W. 49th St.,* ☎ *212/247–2993. Reservations essential. Jacket and tie. AE, DC, MC, V. Closed Sat. lunch, Sun.*

$$$ ✕ **Adrienne.** The graceful restaurant of the Peninsula Hotel offers extravagant comfort. The Belle Epoque decor, subdued lighting, spacious seating, and attention to detail afford a rare respite from the trendy at one extreme and tired at the other. Service is extraordinary. The kitchen is dependable with such dishes as smoked salmon, roast chicken breast

in pesto cream with seasonal vegetables, and Granny Smith apple tart. Sunday brunch is elegance itself, an elaborate buffet with harp music. ✉ *700 5th Ave. at 55th St.,* ☎ *212/903–3918. AE, DC, MC, V. Reservations essential. Closed Sun.–Mon. dinner and Sat. lunch.*

$$$ ✕ **Bouterin.** Baskets of apples and copper pans adorn the walls, adding a warm touch to the new home of chef-owner Antoine Bouterin, formerly of Le Périgord. Bouterin created this restaurant as a shrine to his grandmother Marguerite, whose restaurant in St. Remy de Provence, Le Café de l'Epicerie, was launched in 1915. She surely would have liked the farmhouse atmosphere, green and burnt orange color scheme, and table lamps (with shades or globes). The mix-and-match feel of the decor arises from Monsieur Bouterin's interest in antiques collecting. His grandmother would also have appreciated the short menu of unpretentious dishes, including dandelion omelet with turkey bacon and organic salad and old fashioned lamb stew, cooked for seven hours and best eaten with a spoon. ✉ *420 E. 59th St., off 1st Ave.,* ☎ *212/758–0323. Reservations essential. Jacket required. AE, DC, MC, V. Closed Sunday and lunch.*

$$$ ✕ **La Caravelle.** Rita and André Jammet's celebration of the good life is New York's most Parisian restaurant. The appealing main dining room comes alive with Jean Pagès murals, its colors spilling over to the pink-peach banquettes. Mirrors, flowers, and the Caravelle coat of arms add to the scene, as does the most professional service staff in town—captains in ceremonious black, waiters in immaculate white. The kitchen has embraced a multitude of gastronomic styles, ranging from new American to Asian; it's now at its highest level of excellence since this restaurant's inauguration in 1960. Order truffled pike dumplings in lobster sauce; stewed snails in brie and herb sauce; or the perfectly roasted chicken in a delicate bath of champagne and cream. While it would be hard to resist the cloudlike soufflés, the peanut-crunch, white-chocolate cake is equally compelling. ✉ *33 W. 55th St.,* ☎ *212/586–4252. Reservations essential. Jacket and tie. AE, DC, MC. V. Closed Sat. lunch, Sun.*

$$$ ✕ **Le Chantilly.** When executive chef David Ruggiero joined forces with owner–maître d'hôtel Camille Dulac, Le Chantilly joined the ranks of Manhattan's top French restaurants. Well-spaced tables, wall sconces, and unobtrusive colors lend an air of opulence. The creative Mr. Ruggiero has retained traditional dishes but also prepares everything from masterful napoleon of tomatoes and Maine crab with gazpacho puree to medaillons of New York State venison with gâteau of prune and root vegetables. But whatever entrée you choose, the edible chocolate piano will be playing your song when it's time for dessert. ✉ *106 E. 57th St.,* ☎ *212/751–2931. Reservations essential. Jacket and tie. AE, DC, MC, V. Closed Sun. lunch.*

$$$ ✕ **Le Périgord.** When you enter this luxurious restaurant, you're greeted with dusty rose walls and banquettes, green leather chairs, lovely flowers on each table in small silver vases, and an inviting display of hors d'oeuvres and desserts. The noise level is low; the mirrors and soft lighting create a warm glow. The international clientele demands first-class food at a fair price, and that's what owner-maître d'hôtel Georges Briguet and chef de cuisine Pascal Coudouy provide. Dinner in southwestern France often begins with fresh foie gras (goose liver). Here, it's decadent, delicious, and worth the modest surcharge on a prix-fixe dinner. There are comforting soups, a marvelous cassoulet with confit (preserved goose), and a luscious sautéed beef fillet in red wine and bone marrow sauce. Desserts are all tempting—fig pudding, tarts, cakes, and soufflés. ✉ *405 E. 52nd St.,* ☎ *212/755–6244. Reservations essential. Jacket and tie. AE, DC, MC, V. Closed Sat. lunch, Sun.*

$$ ✕ **Cafe Centro.** Reminiscent of a French brasserie with terrazzo floors, interior columns accented with gold leaf, and a glass-enclosed kitchen, this pleasant café has an eclectic menu, including an assertive Provençal fish soup with saffron–red pepper rouille, a good three-pound T-bone steak, and some compelling desserts, including a hot chocolate soufflé. The wine list is admirable. The separate beer bar offers over 30 selections and has its own attractively priced menu with fun snacks like salmon croquettes with cucumber-dill cream. ✉ *200 Park Ave., between 45th St. and Vanderbilt Ave., in the MetLife Building,* ☎ *212/818–1222. AE, DC, MC, V. Closed Sat. lunch, Sun.*

$$ ✕ **Cité.** Alan Stillman (of Smith & Wollensky, Manhattan Ocean Club, Post House, and Park Avenue Cafe) offers an incredible deal. His Art Deco Parisian-style brasserie with crystal chandeliers and imported grillwork (not to be confused with the more casual adjoining bistro) pours four wines with dinner free of charge. The wines change, but they're always top-drawer. An excellent three-course dinner is served from 8 PM to midnight. The food ranges from American steak house to Mediterranean, and since there's a real chef in the kitchen, you needn't stick to the excellent roast beef and sparkling shrimp or lobster cocktail. ✉ *120 W. 51st St.,* ☎ *212/956–7100. AE, DC, MC, V.*

Indian

$$–$$$ ✕ **Dawat.** One of the city's finest Indian restaurants, this classy, un-
★   derstated spot has roomy tables and consultant Madhur Jaffrey's creative cuisine. Provocative choices include shrimp in mustard seeds with curry leaves, and Parsi-style salmon, steamed in a banana leaf with coriander chutney. The *kulcha,* an onion-stuffed bread flavored with fresh coriander, is particularly good. Dawat demonstrates the charms of Indian sweets; try the puddinglike carrot halvah, the *kheer* (rice pudding) with pistachios, and *kulfi,* a delicate frozen dessert. ✉ *210 E. 58th St.,* ☎ *212/355–7555. Reservations essential. AE, DC, MC, V. No lunch Sun.*

$$ ✕ **Jewel of India.** Since its opening in 1990, this glittering restaurant—with its attractive lounge and bar area and popular luncheon buffet—has had a loyal following. The main dining room shimmers with hammered silver, mother of pearl, and brass, and overflows with wall hangings, exotic sculptures and carved rosewood screens. In the subcontinent's exotic cookery, each dish must exhibit its distinct flavor; spice plays against spice. Jewel of India specializes in the fare of the north, which trades in the south's vegetarian dishes for subtle meat preparations. The marvelous herb-scented breads and knockout tandoori show off the kitchen's prowess. ✉ *15 W. 44th St.,* ☎ *212/869–5544. Reservations essential. AE, DC, MC, V.*

Italian

$$$$ ✕ **Bruno.** One of the top three on swank Italian row, Bruno has an art deco look, with maroon carpets, dusty rose walls, three working fireplaces, art by Giancarlo Impelgia, and etched-glass renderings of the restaurant's logo: a man and woman proposing a toast. Customers like the service, which is as smooth as the fine wines that grace the extensive list. Highlights on the classy, traditional menu include penne *alla vodka* (in a vodka-cream sauce), roast rack of veal, and marinated grilled tuna. ✉ *240 E. 58th St.,* ☎ *212/688–4190. Reservations essential. AE, DC, MC, V. Closed weekend lunch.*

$$$$ ✕ **Felidia.** Manhattanites frequent this celebrated bilevel *ristorante* as much for the winning enthusiasm of Lidia Bastianich, who owns it with her husband Felix, as for the food, whose style is evidenced by osso buco with barley risotto, angel hair pasta with seafood, and apple strudel. Guests dine in an attractive front room with a wooden bar, in the rustic room beyond, and in a skylit balcony with terra-cotta floor, hanging tapestry, and lovely plants. ⊠ *243 E. 58th St.,* ☎ *212/758–1479. Reservations essential. Jacket and tie. AE, DC, MC, V. Closed Sat. lunch, Sun.*

$$$–$$$$ ✕ **Il Nido.** This fashionable restaurant, with wood beams set in rough plaster walls, strives to create the interior of a Tuscan farmhouse. Hands-on restaurateur Adi Giovanetti finishes pastas, whisks zabaglione, and prepares the masterful blend of Gorgonzola and cognac to spread on toast. Dishes will please traditionalists: salmon carpaccio, *malfatti* (a raviolilike pasta), baked red snapper. Be prepared to wait for your table. ⊠ *251 E. 53rd St.,* ☎ *212/753–8450. Reservations essential. AE, DC, MC, V. Closed Sat. lunch, Sun.*

$$$–$$$$ ✕ **San Pietro.** The stylish San Pietro, like its counterpart, Sistina (⊠ 1555 2nd Ave.), highlights specialties of the Amalfi Coast. Baked cylinders of eggplant topped with tomatoes and fresh herbs come served on a bed of mushrooms. Also masterful is the roast suckling pig, rolled in fresh herbs and white wine sauce. Paintings of sunny Italy and trays of fresh vegetables complement the yellow color scheme. ⊠ *18 E. 54th St.,* ☎ *212/753–9015. Reservations essential. Jacket and tie. AE, DC, MC, V. Closed Sun.*

$$$ ✕ **Girafe.** This Italian restaurant, with its name spelled in French, has a 20-foot-high metal statue of its namesake waiting outside to greet you. Inside, you can sample a northern Italian traditional meal: hay and straw (green and white vermicelli) in a bath of cream, prosciutto, and peas, served with a thick, juicy veal chop. The house tiramisù definitely qualifies as one of Manhattan's best. ⊠ *208 E. 58th St., between 2nd and 3rd Aves.,* ☎ *212/752–3054. Reservations essential. Jackets required. AE, DC, MC, V. Closed Sat. lunch, Sun.*

$$ ✕ **Anche Vivolo.** Austrian shades and big clay pots of fresh flowers help create the feel of an enclosed garden. This is one of the best deals in an expensive part of town. Huge portions of such well prepared dishes as linguine *Francesco* (with garlic, anchovies, basil, tomatoes, and oregano) would cost at least 50% more at most of the other restaurants on this Italianate block. The best entrée is often a special. ⊠ *222 E. 58th St., between 2nd and 3rd Aves.,* ☎ *212/308–0112. AE, DC, MC, V. Closed Sat. lunch, Sun.*

Japanese

$$$$ ✕ **Otabe.** The sleek dining room has attractive wall prints and spacious seating. Among the appealing appetizers, try grilled eel on a bed of cucumber with a bouquet of fresh ginger or deep-fried tofu and eggplant. Adventurous souls will love the sparkling slices of raw tuna sashimi, brushed with garlic-flavored soy sauce. Traditional Kyoto cuisine (a tasting menu of several small dishes) can be ordered, and in a room in back, you can experience superbly authentic *teppan* (barbecue-style grill) cooking. Here, you can spoil yourself with Kobe beef, so tender knives are unnecessary. ⊠ *68 E. 56th St.,* ☎ *212/223–7575. AE, DC, MC, V. Closed Sat. lunch, Sun.*

$$$$ ✕ **Seryna.** This lovely restaurant vividly evokes Tokyo with its digni-
★ fied air, earth tones, and comfortable seating at big wooden tables. Although the sushi is superbly fresh, the specialty is steak *ishiyaki,* cooked table-side on a smoldering rock. In the six-course *wagyu* dinner, you can choose between it and *shabu shabu,* another mealtime dish-cum-event: You begin with a broth to which you add meat (which you then eat), then vegetables, then noodles; and conclude by sipping the bracing soup. Cocktails are served in small carafes that come buried in crushed ice. Service is superb. ⊠ *11 E. 53rd St.,* ☎ *212/980–9393. Reservations essential. AE, DC, MC, V. Closed Sat. lunch, Sun.*

Korean

$$ ✕ **Empire Korea.** This vast, strikingly upscale restaurant with crystal chandeliers and silk banquettes has a sushi bar, an hibachi-grill area, and a third section with wood tables inset with gas grills for the outstanding Korean barbecue. First-timers should enjoy the traditional *chapche* (stir-fried, thin, clear noodles with vegetables, meat, and bonito, a dried fish with a smoky taste). Of course, you must sample at least one of the 13 barbecue dishes; *kal-bee* (No. 1), marinated beef short ribs, is a safe bet. As your waiter cooks it, savor the *kimchi* (peppery Korean pickle) and any or all of the gratis side dishes. Then wrap the barbecue in crisp romaine lettuce and add condiments to your liking. ⊠ *6 E. 32nd St.,* ☎ *212/725–1333. AE, DC, MC, V.*

$ ✕ **New York Kom Tang Soot Bul House.** Specializing in barbecue, this is one of the best Korean restaurants on a street jammed with them, and dinner is a show. So come ready for charades (little English is spoken); wear clothes you don't mind getting smoky (from the hibachis in the center of the communal tables); and insist on the attractive second floor. Dinner starts with 10 delicious side dishes, including kimchi. Afterward there's soup, then the main event: You cook thin slices of beef or chicken over red-hot coals, top them with hot chilies and raw garlic, and wrap it all up with lettuce. ⊠ *32 W. 32nd St.,* ☎ *212/947–8482. AE, MC, V.*

Latin

$ ✕ **Ipanema.** This snug, modern restaurant has white and peach-colored walls covered with vivid oil paintings of Rio and Bahia. It's a comfortable place to sample Brazil's exotic cuisine. Feijoada, the national meal—black beans with smoked meats, collard greens, oranges, chili peppers, and a comforting grain called *farofa*—is good here. Shrimp sautéed in the shell and codfish fritters are tasty, as is the boiled cod and vegetable platter with herb-infused olive oil. And don't miss the great drinks made with *cachaça* (Brazilian rum)—*batidas* (with coconut milk) and caipirinhas. ⊠ *13 W. 46th St.,* ☎ *212/730–5848. Reservations accepted. AE, DC, MC, V.*

Mexican

$$–$$$ ✕ **Rosa Mexicano.** Owner Josefina Howard is serious about her profession, and her authentic restaurant is a delight. The food is carefully executed, including guacamole prepared table-side and a cold seafood platter. A number of its regional dishes are unavailable elsewhere. How often do you see duck enchiladas? Chicken in parchment steamed in beer? Or a *pozole,* that delectable soupy stew of hominy, pork, and chicken? If only the margaritas were better! ⊠ *1063 1st Ave. at 58th St.,* ☎ *212/753–7407. Reservations essential. AE, DC, MC, V. Closed lunch.*

$ ✕ **Alamo.** The facade mimics the entrance to a ranch, but the scene inside is cosmopolitan. Wall Street types at the bar imbibe fabulous margaritas served in beautiful Mexican glasses. There's an unpretentious main dining room a few steps up, decorated with piñatas and colorful Mexican posters, and an even more comfortable second level, with a brass railing, big comfy booths, and streamers hanging from the ceiling. Here you can enjoy creative riffs on Mexican and Texas-style cooking. Guacamole is chunky and made to order at your table. Several vegetarian dishes stand out, such as *chili relleno* (green chili pepper stuffed with cheese and batter fried). ⊠ *304 E. 48th St.,* ☎ *212/759–0590. AE, DC, MC, V. Closed Sat. lunch, Sun.*

Scandinavian

$$$ ✕ **Aquavit.** Although you can dine in the delightful café upstairs for half the price, the striking downstairs room in the late Nelson Rockefeller's town house—with its atrium, Roger Smith kites, and water-fall—*is* Aquavit. Swedish fare has been stripped of its homeyness and decked out in contemporary garb, with impressive results. Order roasted-lobster salad or the more traditional herring plate as appetizers. Then explore cherry-crusted rack of lamb or an uncommon tea-smoked duck breast. Triangles of gingerbread with mascarpone ice cream or an out-of-the-ordinary cheese plate make stellar desserts. New York's largest selection of aquavits keeps company with the standout wine list. ⊠ *13 W. 54th St.,* ☎ *212/307–7311. Reservations essential downstairs. AE, DC, MC, V. Closed Sat. lunch, Sun. dinner.*

Seafood

$$$–$$$$ ✕ **Manhattan Ocean Club.** This sophisticated bilevel restaurant with comfortable seating is embellished with Picasso ceramics from the collection of owner Alan Stillman. Shellfish by the piece, a good starter, is impeccably fresh. Tuna arrives seared and raw inside, with lattice potatoes and a green salsa. Other admirable entrées may include roasted blackfish with shiitake mushrooms, shallots, and penne pasta, or perfectly grilled swordfish. A luscious, warm chocolate tart and a butterscotch sundae deserve their awards. ⊠ *57 W. 58th St.,* ☎ *212/ 371–7777. Reservations essential. AE, DC, MC, V. Closed weekend lunch.*

$$$–$$$$ ✕ **Oceana.** Seafood for the civilized. Neither trendy nor snobby,
★ Oceana is also pretty, with its warm wood decor, contemporary lighting, bright murals, and posters of luxury oceanliners. You can dine upstairs and down as well as in the wine cellar; service is smooth. The kitchen gets high marks for salmon tartare wrapped in smoked salmon, crab cakes, lobster ravioli, and bouillabaisse. The wine list (with over a hundred whites) is first-rate; the white Bordeaux are recommended. The three-course dinner offers good value, as does the six-course tasting menu. ⊠ *55 E. 54th St.,* ☎ *212/759–5941. Reservations essential. Jacket required. AE, DC, MC, V. Closed Sat. lunch, Sun.*

$$$–$$$$ ✕ **Sea Grill.** Famous restaurants with extraordinary views are often
★ suspect when it comes to the food. But *this* famous restaurant, with a spectacular view of the Rockefeller Center ice rink in winter and captivating patio dining in summer, can stand tall. The kitchen, under the direction of one of Manhattan's master chefs, Ed Brown (of Tropica and Judson Grill), creates some of Manhattan's best seafood dishes. Charred, moist, sugarcane shrimp on skewers with buttery rice is a simple composition; the complementing fresh herbs, spices, and subtle sauce allow each creature of the deep to give its life in honor, not in vain. We applaud the best lime pie this side of the Keys. ⊠ *19 W. 49th St.,* ☎ *212/332–7610. Reservations essential. AE, DC, MC, V. Closed Sat. lunch, Sun.*

$$–$$$ ✕ **Captain's Table.** To be truly distinguished, a seafood restaurant must use scrupulously fresh fish and cook it precisely and with some inventiveness. This unpretentious spot, an eclectic room with Murano chandeliers and starched white linens, scores on all counts. In addition to straightforward grilled, sautéed, and poached offerings, there are preparations with international twists; some reflect the chefs' Thai and Mexican backgrounds (shrimp Bangkok style or wrapped in jalapeños). Others draw on owner Gino Musso's Italian heritage (grilled whole snapper or striped bass with an herbed olive oil–garlic lemon sauce). The wine list is that rarity, one with a few real bargains. ⊠ *860 2nd Ave. at 46th St.,* ☎ *212/697–9538. Reservations essential. AE, DC, MC, V. Closed Sat. lunch, Sun.*

$$ ✕ **Docks.** The large brass-trimmed bar of this striking, high-ceilinged
★ art deco bilevel brasserie displays scrupulously fresh shellfish, which are presented on tiered platters. Cooked preparations run the gamut

from traditional American to inventive-eclectic. Steamers in beer broth and Maryland crab cakes are generally available as appetizers. For the main course, you can order grilled or fried wolffish, monkfish, snapper, and other seafood, depending on what's fresh that day. Lobster is as good as it gets in Manhattan. ⊠ *633 3rd Ave. at 40th St.,* ☎ *212/ 986–8080. Reservations required AE, DC, MC, V. No lunch Sat.*

Steak

$$$–$$$$ ✕ **Morton's.** Although famous for its steaks, New York has never seen anything like this branch of Chicago's famous steak house, in a masculine, dimly lit room that's easy on the spirit. Service is enthusiastic, the bar knows how to make a drink, and oh, those steaks and chops, that double-cut prime rib, and those 4½-pound lobsters! Potato skins, hash browns, and fresh asparagus are also terrific; for dessert, go straight to the cheesecake or the rich chocolate-velvet cake. The wine list offers hundreds of extraordinary reds, and there is an excellent single-malt Scotch list. ⊠ *551 5th Ave. at 45th St.,* ☎ *212/972–3315. Reservations essential. AE, DC, MC, V. Closed weekend lunch.*

$$$–$$$$ ✕ **Pen & Pencil.** It's hard to beat this civilized and thoroughly pleasant restaurant with its comfortable bar area, fitted out with leather banquettes, and intimate main dining room, recalling a private club—lunch is particularly pleasant. Here's a steak house where grilled swordfish and sole stand out, and from time to time there's a special menu featuring low-cholesterol buffalo meat. ⊠ *205 E. 45th St.,* ☎ *212/682– 8660. Reservations essential. AE, DC, MC, V. No lunch weekends.*

$$$–$$$$ ✕ **Smith & Wollensky.** This archetypal New York–style steak house, with its bold and unabashedly masculine setting, gargantuan portions, and lofty list of wines (strong in red Bordeaux and California cabernets) is one of the best. Meat is dry-aged in-house, and sirloin, porterhouse, and double sirloin arrive cooked to a turn. Order a side of hash browns or cottage fries and creamed or sautéed spinach, but skip the perfunctory appetizers and desserts. There is a generous selection of single-malt Scotch. The bustling, less-pricey Wollensky's Grill next door has pleasant sidewalk seating in summer. ⊠ *201 E. 49th St.,* ☎ *212/753–1530 (Grill* ☎ *212/753–0444). Reservations essential. AE, DC, MC, V. Restaurant closed weekend lunch.*

Vietnamese

$$–$$$ ✕ **Le Colonial.** The dining room here comes straight out of Somerset Maugham with its rattan chairs, potted palms, ceiling fans, shutters, and period photographs. The food, although westernized, is usually well prepared; start with the superb *bahn cuon*—steamed Vietnamese ravioli with chicken, shrimp, and mushrooms, and move on to crispseared whole snapper with spicy and sour sauce. The sorbets, ice creams, and fruit-based puddings are right on. Don't miss the Vietnamese coffee—strong black brew over a layer of condensed milk. Nirvana in a cup! You can't fault the wine selection. ⊠ *149 E. 57th St.,* ☎ *212/ 752–0808. Reservations essential. AE, DC, MC, V.*

Theater District and Carnegie Hall

American Casual

$–$$ ✕ **Hard Rock Cafe.** This restaurant with the fins of a vintage Cadillac as a marquee is best known for its loud rock music, rock-star memorabilia, and teenyboppers. Truth be told, the food is amazingly tasty. The pork barbecue, listed as pig sandwich, is as good as you often find in North Carolina. Or try the club sandwich—crispy bacon, roast chicken, lettuce, tomato, and mayo between huge slabs of ice-box bread. Because portions are huge, everything can be split. To avoid waits, go at opening hours and avoid school holidays. ⊠ *221 W. 57th St.,* ☎ *212/489–6565. AE, MC, V.*

$–$$ ✕ **Joe Allen.** With its brick walls, dark-wood bar, and showbiz posters, it looks like a pub, but the food warrants the smart white tablecloths. The menu has several satisfying offerings: delicious black bean soup, fresh fish or pasta specials, a marvelous meat-loaf sandwich, and an exceptional grilled calves' liver, thinly cut and served with creamy mashed potatoes. You might even glimpse a celebrity or two. ⊠ *326 W. 46th St.,* ☎ *212/581–6464. Reservations essential. MC, V.*

$ ✕ **Film Center Cafe.** Customers dine at vintage Formica tables and in cozy booths, surrounded by authentic Art Deco decor, pink neon lights, old radios, film reels, and wall murals of 20th Century Fox, Paramount, and MGM logos. For dinner, your friendly waiter will bring you good diner food, such as chili, meat loaf with soothing mashed potatoes, or calves' liver cooked just right. From 11 AM to 4 PM on Sundays, a limited retro-price menu offers unlimited cocktails, home-style brunch, and a hot cup of java. ⊠ *635 9th Ave., between 44th and 45th Sts,* ☎ *212/262–2525. AE, DC, MC, V. Closed Sat. lunch.*

$ ✕ **Motown Cafe.** On three floors, you're surrounded by the history of musical recording. You'll also see the biggest record in the world: a classic 45 that is 27 feet in diameter and revolves on the ceiling. The stairway to the mezzanine is actually a ladder of gold records honoring Motown singers. While the food isn't Grammy material, desserts really rock and roll—the homemade ice-cream sandwich plays lead, while a fabulous peach cobbler and sweet potato–pecan pie do great backup. ⊠ *104 W. 57th St., near 6th Ave.,* ☎ *212/581–8030. AE, DC, MC, V.*

$ ✕ **Planet Hollywood.** This café is fun; its owners and shareholders include Bruce Willis, Demi Moore, Sylvester Stallone, Keith Barish, and Arnold Schwarzenegger. The walls are full of celebrity handprints outside and movie memorabilia inside; check out the gremlin. Who cares that the place rates a 10 on the decibel scale? The food is adequate, but you'll be happiest if you stick with the Southwestern-style nachos, the fajitas, and the playful pizzas. ⊠ *140 W. 57th St.,* ☎ *212/333–7827. AE, DC, MC, V.*

Barbecue

$ ✕ **Virgil's.** This massive roadhouse in the Theater District has clever neon-and-Formica decor. Start perhaps with stuffed jalapeños, buttermilk onion rings with blue-cheese dip, or the flaky buttermilk biscuits. Then go for the "pig out": a rack of pork ribs, Texas hot links, pulled pork, rack of lamb, chicken, and more. Memphis pork ribs wet or dry, with a choice of five sauces. Most entrées can serve two and come with two excellent side dishes—mustard slaw, Georgia rice (laced with pecans), mashed potatoes and gravy, and the like. ⊠ *152 W. 44th St.,* ☎ *212/921–9494. Reservations essential. AE, MC, V.*

Caribbean

$ ★ ✕ **Island Spice.** This spotless and altogether delightful spot, with green walls and plastic tablecloths, serves some of New York's best Caribbean fare. The kitchen's gastronomic reggae shows up in such dishes as the zesty jerk pork and chicken curry; delicious whole red snapper, panfried then steamed with peppers, onions, and tomatoes; and the tender, curried goat, which you stuff into Indian flat bread—what a terrific sandwich. Brunch on Sunday. ⊠ *402 W. 44th St.,* ☎ *212/765–1737,* ☎ *212/807–6411. Reservations essential. AE, DC, MC, V.*

Contemporary

$$$ ✕ **Halcyon.** Peacock green banquettes line the perimeter of the room, dominated by a domed ceiling painted to resemble the sky; looking up, you'll see gold star bursts and an antique brass chandelier. Despite the

elaborate setting, the food is refreshingly simple, including such standards as hearts of romaine Caesar salad and roasted rack of lamb. Sunday brunch in the Marketplace in the Sky on the 53rd floor offers one of the best views (and buffets) in town. ⊠ *151 W. 54th St., in the Rihga Royal Hotel,* ☎ *212/468–8888. AE, DC, MC, V.*

Deli

$ ✕ **Carnegie Deli.** Although not what it was, this no-nonsense spot is still one of midtown's two best delis, a species distinguished by crowds, noise, impatient service, and jumbo sandwiches. Ask the counterman to hand-slice your corned beef or pastrami; the extra juiciness and superior texture warrant the extra charge. To drink? Try cream soda or celery tonic. ⊠ *854 7th Ave., between 54th and 55th Sts.,* ☎ *212/757–2245. No credit cards.*

$ ✕ **Stage Deli.** One taste of its chopped liver and pickles and you'll know why this monument to corned beef and pastrami, founded in 1936 by Max Asnas, a Russian immigrant, transcends the tourist-trap syndrome. It personifies the New York theater culture. Bossy waiters and regular guests like Milton Berle and Eddie Cantor were legion. Today the waitpersons seem almost genteel, but the sandwiches are more gargantuan than ever. ⊠ *834 7th Ave., between 53rd and 54th Sts.,* ☎ *212/245–7850. AE, DC, MC, V. Closed Sat. lunch.*

French

$$$$ ✕ **Le Bernardin.** Since 1986, this French seafood restaurant has been a trendsetter with inventive fish creations carefully prepared. The plush, expansive, and softly lit teak-paneled room with its well-spaced tables, late-19th-century French oil paintings, and low noise level is as popular as ever. Service is impeccable, and the food can still dazzle, with such recommended offerings as fricassee of mussels, clams, and oysters in their broth with sweet garlic and tomato butter; and pan-roasted yellowtail snapper on balsamic-glazed artichokes. ⊠ *155 W. 51st St.,* ☎ *212/489–1515. Reservations essential. Jacket required. AE, DC, MC, V. Closed Sat. lunch, Sun.*

$$$$ ✕ **Les Célébrités.** From the moon-shaped banquettes and the plush red carpets to the careful lighting and paintings by celebrity artists, this intimate restaurant in the Essex House hotel is definitely lavish; the china is Limoges, the silver Christophle. The glassed-in kitchen, discretely hidden by a painting on canvas (of the fabled French ocean liner the *Normandy*), opens from time to time to reveal executive chef Christian Delouvrier busily preparing such specialties as a playful foie-gras burger, in which slices of Granny Smith apple replace bread and elegant goose-liver subs for beef. The six-item tasting dinner showcases his strengths. The wine list is extensive (and expensive), but there is also a good selection by the glass. ⊠ *160 Central Park S,* ☎ *212/484–5113. Reservations essential. Jacket and tie. AE, DC, MC, V. Closed Sun.–Mon. and lunch.*

$$$–$$$$ ✕ **Petrossian.** This Art Deco caviar bar and restaurant is like no other
★ New York dining spot, with its fur-trimmed banquettes, granite bar, profusion of marble, and contributions of Erté and Lalique. You'll probably want to start with gobs of fresh caviar: beluga (the largest egg and most popular with Americans), sevruga (smaller and a favorite of the British), or osetra (yellowish and highly prized by Russians on buttered toast or blini (a puffy pancake), with no competing garnishes. Petrossian offers an outstanding prix-fixe dinner (one of the world's great bargains in luxury dining) all evening; the supplement for 30 grams of sevruga is relatively small. You may drink vodka with the caviar or champagne throughout. ⊠ *182 W. 58th St.,* ☎ *212/245–2214. Reservations essential. AE, DC, MC, V.*

$$ ✕ **Café Botanica.** With its high ceilings, wicker chairs, soft-green table-cloths and ravishing views of Central Park, this glorious café, airy as a country garden, serves inventive and elegant food. The pre-theater dinner is an exceptional value. You'll find the service neither intimi-dating or overbearing, while the wine list is priced fairly. If you can't make it for dinner, try the equally splendid fixed-price lunch or Sunday brunch. ⊠ *160 Central Park S,* ☎ *212/484–5120. Reservations essential. AE, DC, MC. V.*

$$ ✕ **Jean Lafitte.** Owned by Eric Demarchelier (of the successful Le Select and Demarchelier), this popular spot has an attractively priced prix-fixe menu. The à la carte menu also lists Creole dishes, in deference to the Jean Lafitte–New Orleans connection. The ambience and decor, with lots of wood, mirrors, brass railings, and Art Nouveau tulip-shaped lighting fixtures is straight out of Paris. You'll also welcome the sprightly bar scene. ⊠ *68 W. 58th St.,* ☎ *212/751–2323. Reservations essential. AE, DC, MC, V. Closed weekend lunch.*

Greek

$ ✕ **Uncle Nick's.** Here's the best Greek restaurant in Manhattan, an
★ inexpensive taverna with a long room, a navy-blue pipe-lined tin-ceil-ing, an exposed kitchen, and a wood floor. Note the appetizing dis-plays of whole red snapper, porgy, and striped bass. Uncle Nick's owners, Tony and Mike Vanatakis prepare each fish selection with simplicity and care. Be sure to try as many of the excellent appetizers as your tummy can handle, including crispy fried smelts, tender grilled baby octopus, marvelous sweetbreads, and giant lima beans with tomatoes and herbs. ⊠ *747 9th Ave., between 50th and 51st Sts.,* ☎ *212/315–1726. MC, V.*

Indian

$$–$$$ ✕ **Shaan.** The name of this restaurant means "pride" in Hindi, and owners Victor Khubani and Bhushan Arora have good reason to be proud of their elegant palace with a deep-burgundy marquee, hand-carved doors, Italian and Portuguese marble, hand-embroidered tapestries, and roomy banquettes. The spicing in the unusual dishes ranges from subtle to fiery. The Bengali-born chef prepares splendid tandoori lobster, rack of lamb, or quail, which are marinated in yo-gurt and spices and cooked in a clay oven. ⊠ *57 W. 48th St.,* ☎ *212/ 977–8400. AE, DC, MC, V.*

Italian

$$$–$$$$ ✕ **Barbetta.** The 18th-century Venetian harpsichord in the foyer sets
★ the mood for New York's oldest restaurant still operated by its found-ing family (opened in 1906). This island of civility in two distinguished, antique-furnished town houses has an enchanting garden, verdant with century-old trees and perfumed with magnolia, wisteria, and jas-mine. Its kitchen was one of the first to produce northern Italian food in America, and it retains its simplicity and fidelity to tradition. The *carne cruda* (hand-chopped raw veal with lemon juice and olive oil) dusted with white truffles (season permitting), and handmade *ag-nolotti* (pasta cut into small round pieces, filled with a stuffing of meat or vegetables, and folded in half like turnovers) are superb. In addi-tion to the well-priced, beautifully selected short wine list, there is a long version offering many bottles dating from 1880. ⊠ *321 W. 46th St.,* ☎ *212/246–9171. Reservations essential. AE, DC, MC, V. Closed Sun., Mon. lunch.*

$$$–$$$$ ✕ **Palio.** Named after the 800-year-old Italian horse race that celebrates
★ the Assumption of the Virgin, this exceptional restaurant has an im-pressive 13-foot mural by Sandro Chia. Your name is discretely requested as you're ushered to an elevator and the second-floor dining room with

light oak paneling and luxuriously spaced tables set with Frette linen and Riedel crystal. Food and service to match such a high tone must be unblemished, and Palio meets the challenge. Here you'll experience authentic Italian cuisine elevated to greatness, from a regional six-course menu from Siena, to one based on aged balsamic vinegar. In Italy you will not find a better Tuscan bean soup with sage and virgin olive oil, nor homemade squid-ink spaghettini with garlic, oil, and *peperocino*. And the osso buco is impeccable. ⊠ *151 W. 51st. St.,* ☎ *212/245–4850. Reservations essential. Jacket and tie. AE, DC, MC, V. Closed Sat. lunch, Sun.*

\$\$\$–\$\$\$\$ ✕ **San Domenico.** Owner Tony May has raised American conscious-
★ ness of the Italian *cucina,* and executive chef Theo Schoenegger exe-
cutes with authority such dishes as soft egg ravioli with truffle butter and loin of veal in smoked-bacon cream sauce. For dessert, try polenta *nera* (chocolate hazelnut dessert soufflé). The setting is like a private villa, with terra-cotta floors, sumptuous leather chairs, and lots of warm, earthy hues. The huge wine list showcases Italy's great vintages. Your tab drops if you stick to prix-fixe dinners, especially on Sunday; throw caution to the winds, and you may have to thumb a ride home. ⊠ *240 Central Park S,* ☎ *212/265–5959. Reservations essential. Jacket and tie required except on Sun. AE, MC, DC, V. Closed weekend lunch.*

\$\$\$ ✕ **Remi.** This stylish Italian restaurant—designed by architect Adam Tihany, who co-owns it with chef Francesco Antonucci—is striking with its nautical decor, skylighted open atrium-garden, blue and white striped banquettes, Venetian-glass chandeliers, and soaring room-length mural of Venice by Paulin Paris. The accompanying contemporary Venetian cuisine is beautifully presented. Fresh sardines make a lovely beginning with their contrasting sweet and sour onion garnish, and you can't go wrong with the ravioli Marco Polo (tuna and ginger filled) in a light tomato sauce, the expertly prepared rack of lamb, or any of the wonderful desserts. ⊠ *145 W. 53rd St.,* ☎ *212/581–4242. Reservations essential. AE, DC, MC, V. Closed weekend lunch.*

\$\$–\$\$\$ ✕ **Lattanzi Ristorante.** Although not kosher, the cuisine here derives from the Jewish ghetto with such dishes as baby artichokes flattened like a pancake and parchment-fried, so that even the leaves are edible. Noteworthy pastas include homemade noodles with artichoke sauce and *Pecorino* cheese. Breads are remarkable, especially a huge flat un-leavened sheet of homemade matzo and the garlicky bread sticks. Don't ignore the homemade napoleon. You'll dine in an elegant town house with several exposed-brick rooms, candles, flowers, and one of Manhattan's most romantic gardens. ⊠ *361 W. 46th St.,* ☎ *212/315–0980. Reservations essential. AE, DC, MC, V. Closed Sat. lunch, Sun.*

\$\$–\$\$\$ ✕ **Trattoria Dell'Arte.** This popular trattoria near Carnegie Hall still
★ displays the controversial oversize renderings of body parts, alongside portraits of Italian artists, in its three dining rooms. But you'll probably be more interested in the mouthwatering antipasti on the bar and the tasty pasta, pizza, hot focaccia sandwiches and the house spe-
cialty, a grilled double veal chop (skip the sauce) with a mountain of shoestring potatoes. The cannoli are the best you'll ever taste, but all desserts are worthwhile. Check out the great wine list and flavored grap-
pas. ⊠ *900 7th Ave., between 56th and 57th Sts.,* ☎ *212/245–9800. Reservations essential. AE, DC, MC, V.*

\$\$ ✕ **Orso.** Stylish and unpretentious, with two smallish rooms and easy-on-the-eye colors, Orso serves outrageously delicious fare and bargain-priced wines. All of the variations of pizza are recommended, especially the paper-thin version with garlic, rosemary, and oil (called pizza bread) or the flat pizza with pesto, roasted peppers, olives, baby moz-
zarella, onions, and chopped tomatoes. Pasta comes thick, thin, long, short, fresh or dried, and sauced according to what's fresh in the mar-

ket that day. Usually available are the grilled portobello mushrooms, spicy sausage, and the stupendous sliced pan-fried calves' liver. ⊠ *322 W. 46th St.,* ☎ *212/489–7212. Reservations essential. MC, V.*

$–$$ ✕ **Frico Bar.** Owned by Lidia Bastianich of Felidia and son Joseph of Becco, this casual place serves an array of tempting snacks ranging from thin-crust pizza to the house specialty, *frico,* a crustless pizza of griddle-crisped cheese stuffed with potatoes and vegetables. Other good bets are home-style pastas like rigatoni with oxtail ragout; and the casserole of braised lamb shank osso buco with barley, served in rustic earthenware. As in the Friulian countryside, wine comes on tap, along with 10 excellent beers. The restaurant has an engaging decor: tile floors and the moon and star logo displayed on the attractive wooden tables and in metal cutouts above the ceiling moldings. ⊠ *402 W. 43rd St., off 9th Ave.,* ☎ *212/564–7272. AE, DC, MC, V.*

$–$$ ✕ **Osteria al Droge.** Warm yellow walls and a two-tiered room with a charming balcony, long mahogany bar, colorful framed posters, and bare oak family tables conjure Tuscany in Times Square. You are bound to enjoy thin-crusted pizza with mozzarella, fresh tomatoes, arugula, and prosciutto and marvelous risottos. Leave room for warm pecan tart and cinnamon ice cream. ⊠ *142 W. 44th St.,* ☎ *212/944– 3643. Reservations essential. AE, DC, MC,V.*

$ ✕ **Mangia e Bevi.** This down-to-earth slice of Naples features murals of Italy, ceiling fans, checkered tablecloths, an open kitchen, and a woodburning oven. Pizza fans are kept happy (try the white four-cheese pizza), and there's also good bread to smear with virgin olive oil and foccacia with herb-marinated Mediterranean olives. Among the bargain priced pasta, perhaps try rigatoni *Amatriciana*—brimming with homemade tomato sauce, Italian bacon, and spices. Waiters in T-shirts are helpful as the music blares and customers slap tambourines and join in the fun. ⊠ *800 9th Ave. at 53rd St.,* ☎ *212/956–3976. AE, DC, MC, V.*

Latin

$$ ✕ **Victor's Café 52.** This technicolor Cuban restaurant has big highback booths, a tile floor, and a raised back room with skylight. The blasting Latin American music and an atmosphere harking back to movie musicals set in old Havana seem not to bode well for serious dining. But fear not, the food is mostly wonderful, a contemporary transcription of Cuban, Puerto Rican, and Latino signature dishes. Recommended appetizers range from golden-fried plantain gourds, to filled spicy shrimp in peanut-coconut sauce, to fresh Cuban corn tamales with a pungent Antillean three-pepper sauce. Entrées, some served in colorful, oversized bowls, are equally enticing. ⊠ *236 W. 52nd St.,* ☎ *212/586–7714. AE, DC, MC, V.*

$ ✕ **Pomaire.** Named after a small village renowned for its pottery (in which many of the dishes are served), this uncommon restaurant with exposed brick, handmade rugs, a faux skylight, and attractive paintings sometimes offers live music. The menu lists several intriguing dinner options, such as *pastel de choclo,* a casserole of beef, olives, chicken, onions, and egg that is covered with a corn puree, dusted with sugar, and baked in a clay pot. Leave room for *torta de mil hojas*—leaves of pastry layered with caramel. ⊠ *371 W. 46th St., off 9th Ave.,* ☎ *212/ 956–3055. AE, DC, MC, V.*

Southwestern

$$ ✕ **Tapika.** The design of the relaxed dining room by architect David Rockwell pays a fanciful tribute to the American West: adobe-brown walls, colored picket fencing around the windows, faux pony-skin bar stools, branded wood, and steel light fixtures with Native American cutout designs. Chef David Walzog expertly reinvents Southwestern cuisine with such dishes as barbecued short ribs falling off the bone, wild-mushroom tamale, and incendiary-yet-scrumptious ground vegetable chili rellenos served with smoked tomato salsa and crumpled cheese. The margaritas are terrific. ⊠ *950 8th Ave. at 56th St.,* ☎ *212/ 397–3737. DC, MC, V.*

Steak

$$$–$$$$ ✕ **Ben Benson's.** Not only are steaks, chops, and accompaniments first-
★   rate here, there is also a real chef in the kitchen. Witness such contemporary steak-house fare as cold lobster cocktail and Maryland crab cakes, steaks, chops, and the fabulous prime rib, and such excellent daily specials as Friday's crusted fish hash. Don't miss the horseradish-mashed potatoes or the excellent home fries. The wine list improves with each visit. This convivial spot has a masculine interior— brass plaques inscribed with names of celebrities, framed pictures of animals and game birds. ⊠ *123 W. 52nd St.,* ☎ *212/581–8888. Reservations essential. AE, DC, MC, V. Closed weekend lunch.*

$$$–$$$$ ✕ **Gallagher's.** The most casual of New York steak houses, with checkered tablecloths and photos of sports greats on the walls, Gallagher's has almost no pretensions and nothing to hide. Look for the meat-aging room, visible through the window. You won't be disappointed with the famous aged sirloin steaks, oversize lobsters, or any of the fabulous potato dishes (try the O'Brien with its sweet pepper and onion flavor). Don't miss the creamy rice pudding. ⊠ *228 W. 52nd St.,* ☎ *212/245–5336. Reservations essential. AE, DC, MC, V*

$$$–$$$$ ✕ **Le Marais.** The appetizing display of raw meats and terrines at the entrance and the bare wood floors may remind you of a Parisian bistro. Tables covered with butcher paper, French wall posters, and maroon banquettes reinforce that image. Yet the clientele (mostly male) is strictly kosher. A cold *terrine de boeuf en gelée façon pot au feu* (marinated short ribs) starts the meal on the right note, and rib steak for two is cooked to a turn, tender, and juicy. The accompanying fries are perfect. ⊠ *150 W. 46th St.,* ☎ *212/869–0900. AE, DC, MC, V. Closed Fri. dinner, Sat. lunch.*

$$$–$$$$ ✕ **Ruth's Chris.** Manhattan's genteel addition to this group of more than 40 around the world is giving other steak houses around town a run for their money. With its Impressionistic oil paintings, dark red walls, and crisp white napery on well-spaced tables, it's much more inviting than its location at the base of a nondescript office tower might suggest. Moreover, the steaks and chops, served sizzling in butter unless you specify otherwise, are tops. The menu defines degrees of doneness according to temperature and color, and the kitchen gives you just what you request. ⊠ *148 W. 51st St.,* ☎ *212/245–9600. Reservations essential. AE, DC, MC, V. No lunch weekends.*

Upper East Side

American Casual

$ ✕ **Hi-Life Restaurant and Lounge.** Young East Siders wait in line to sit down at one of the spacious half-moon-shaped booths at this bilevel Art Deco café and then strain to hear the music or the conversation of their dining companions. The draw? Soothing prices for huge portions of food that is far better than it has to be in such a hot spot. Join the crowd—you can drink some of the best martinis in town and polish off sushi, or something from the raw bar, before you proceed to the filet mignon, sliced and served with potato salad; pad thai noodles with chicken or shrimp; or the decadent chocolate mud pie. ⊠ *1340 1st Ave. at 72nd St.,* ☎ *212/249–3600. AE, DC, MC, V.*

$ ✕ **Serendipity 3.** This whimsical store-cum-café has been producing excellent burgers, sandwiches, salads, and other interesting if overly complicated plates since 1954. But most people come for the fantasy sundaes—huge, naughty, and decadent. You'll love the thick frozen hot chocolate. ✉ 225 E. 60th St., ☎ 212/838–3531. Reservations accepted. AE, DC, MC, V. BYOB.

$ ✕ **Seventh Regiment Mess and Bar.** The fourth floor of the historic Seventh Regiment Armory is home to this unusual restaurant with high ceilings, wooden beams, and appropriately militaristic motifs. You won't find fancy cooking—just homey food such as chicken à la king, pork chop, roast beef, and mustardy deviled beef bones—at rock-bottom prices. ✉ 643 Park Ave. at 66th St., ☎ 212/744–4107. Reservations accepted. AE, MC, V. Closed Sun. and Mon.

Chinese

$–$$ ✕ **Evergreen Cafe.** Come here for the "Chinatown-style" dumplings (try asparagus or seafood fillings) and the full range of noodle and rice dishes, such as Singapore-style curry flavored noodles or diced chicken in salted fish-flavor fried rice. This attractive restaurant has blond wood tables, ceiling fans, and an illuminated emerald sculpture; the back dining room tends to be more quiet. ✉ 1288 1st Ave. at 69th St. ☎ 212/744–3266. AE, DC, MC, V.

Contemporary

$$$$ ✕ **Aureole.** Charles Palmer's fashionable restaurant with its alluring bas-reliefs, baskets of dried flowers and swank town-house location, is one of the town's toughest reservations. Appetizers are generally trustworthy; desserts are visual masterpieces. Wine prices are high, and the ventilation and ambience upstairs are sub-par. ✉ 34 E. 61st St., ☎ 212/ 319–1660. Reservations essential. AE, DC, MC, V. Closed Sat. lunch, Sun.

$$$ ✕ **Jo Jo.** New York's most fashionable bistro, this classy restaurant
★ with an upstairs dining area has burgundy banquettes, a black and white tile floor, and the obligatory etched glass and gilt-edge mirrors. Celebrity-chef Jean-Georges Vongerichten follows a culinary approach that is personal (French with Asian accents), healthy (infused oils, juices, and reduction rather than heavy sauces) and classic (hardy bistro dishes freely updated). As in many Manhattan gastronomic temples, lunch costs less. Goat cheese-and-potato terrine is typical of Vongerichten's culinary range, as are the signature shrimp in spiced-carrot juice and Thai lime leaves, and the simple chicken roasted with ginger, green olives, and ginger juice, accompanied by chickpea-tahini fritters. ✉ 160 E. 64th St., ☎ 212/223–5656. Reservations essential. AE, MC, V. Closed Sat. lunch, Sun.

$$–$$$ ✕ **Matthew's.** This popular café is airy and attractive with its white shutters, ceiling fans, rattan chairs, jumbo potted plants, and warm colors. Young chef Matthew Kenny has an eclectic contemporary style. You'll relish the tuna tartare (more coarsely chopped here than in most new American restaurants), served with a Mediterranean-green-olive condiment. There's also a terrific Moroccan-spiced lamb shank with dried fruits and couscous, and a soft-centered chocolate-hazelnut cake that makes life worth living. ✉ 1030 3rd Ave. at 61st St., ☎ 212/838–4343. Reservations essential. AE, DC, MC, V.

$$$ ✕ **Park Avenue Cafe.** American folk art, antique toys, and sheaves of dried wheat decorate this unpretentious pacesetter. The Flag Room, to the left of the bar, is more sedate. David Burke's imaginative presentations are often whimsical. Salmon is cured like pastrami and arrives on a marble slab, with warm corn blini (pancakes), while the signature swordfish "chop" comes dressed with a numbered tag (save the tag, sign the book, and you may win a all-inclusive holiday). The

Uptown Manhattan Dining

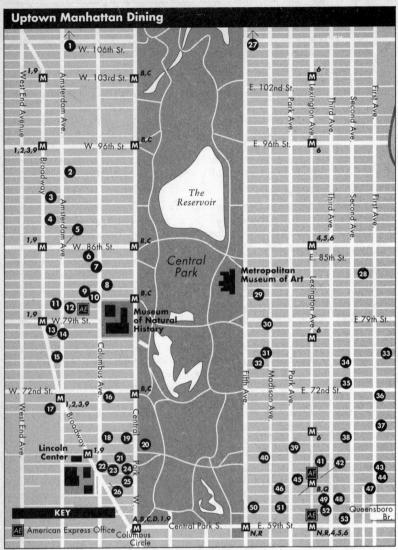

Arizona 206, **53**
Aureole, **51**
Bar Anise, **52**
Boonthai, **35**
Café des Artistes, **19**
Café Luxembourg, **17**
Café Pierre, **50**
Carmine's, **3**
Coco Pazzo, **32**
Daniel, **31**
Emily's, **27**
Ernie's, **15**
Evergreen Cafe, **37**
Ferrier, **40**

Fiorello's Roman
Café, **26**
Firehouse, **6**
Fishin Eddie, **16**
Fujiyama Mama, **8**
Gabriela's, **2**
Hi-Life Restaurant
and Lounge, **36**
Jo Jo, **42**
L'Absinthe, **38**
L'Auberge, **43**
Le Select, **7**
Lincoln Tavern, **23**
Mad Fish, **14**
Main Street, **10**
Manhattan Café, **44**

Matthew's, **49**
Montien, **47**
Parioli
Romanissimo, **29**
Park Avenue Cafe, **45**
Persepolis, **34**
Picholine, **24**
Popover Café, **5**
Post House, **46**
Rain, **9**
Red Tulip, **33**
Sarabeth's Kitchen, **12**
The Savannah Club, **4**
Serendipity 3, **48**
Seventh Regiment
Mess and Bar, **39**

Sfuzzi, **22**
Shun Lee West, **21**
Sign of the Dove, **41**
Sofia Fabulous Pizza, **30**
Stingray, **11**
Tavern on
the Green, **20**
Terrace, **1**
Triangolo, **28**
Two Two Two, **13**
Vince & Eddie's, **18**
West 63rd Street
Steakhouse, **25**

pastry chef's masterpieces include a milk-chocolate crème brûlée and "opera in the park," a cake decorated to mimic Central Park. ✉ *100 E. 63rd St.,* ☎ *212/644–1900. Reservations essential. AE, DC, MC, V. Closed Sat.lunch.*

$$$ ✕ **Sign of the Dove.** Skylights, stunning floral arrangements, well-
★ spaced tables, brick arches, and piano music lend a distinctive char-
acter to each of the dining rooms here, some the prettiest in town. From Andrew D'Amico's distinguished kitchen, don't miss the arugula salad with shaved Parmesan, papaya, celery and balsamic vinaigrette; the singular pan-seared tuna in aromatic broth; and braised bok choy and Asian vegetables. Warm chocolate soufflé cake with house-made vanilla ice cream is intense without being overpowering. Prix-fixe menus put this place squarely among the city's best famous-restaurant values. ✉ *1110 3rd Ave. at 65th St.,* ☎ *212/861–8080. Reservations essential. AE, DC, MC, V. No lunch Mon.*

Eastern European

$–$$ ✕ **Red Tulip.** With the gypsy violins and high-back wooden booths, the atmosphere is early Budapest (via MGM), heavy on the gemütlichkeit. The food is a bit more contemporary; try the celebrated chicken paprika with egg dumplings, the crispy roast goose, the stuffed cabbage, or the sausage with onions, green peppers, and tomato sauce. *Palacsinta* (dessert crepes) with assorted fillings are a graceful example of this time-honored dessert. ✉ *439 E. 75th St.,* ☎ *212/734–4893. AE, DC, MC, V. Closed Mon. and Tues.*

French

$$$$ ✕ **Café Pierre.** The long room is a jewel, with its ornate mirrors, overhead cloud murals, and tables fitted with gold lamé skirts under crisp white cloths. The selection of glass wines is admirably suited to the tasting menu. Cosmopolitan dishes worth exploring include risotto with wild mushrooms and chervil; Maine crab with lemon confit and chive vinaigrette; and breast of chicken with braised leeks, potatoes, and truffles. Save some space for hot chocolate fudge cake with espresso ice cream. You can have coffee or an after dinner drink at the sophisticated piano bar, where there's dancing Thursday, Friday, and Saturday nights. ✉ *2 E. 61st St.,* ☎ *212/940–8185. Reservations essential. Jacket and tie. AE, DC, MC, V.*

$$$$ ✕ **Daniel.** At Daniel Boulud's $1.9 million restaurant, large flower arrangements and antique mirrors decorate the main dining room, with exquisite table settings by Limoges, gold-tinted walls, and red-checked banquettes. The celebrity clientele (Barbara Walters, Henry Kissinger) dazzles, and the cuisine (at once contemporary and classic) is among the best in New York. Note the uncommon tuna tartare, with a touch of curry; the delicate nine-herb ravioli accompanied by bitter greens with artichokes, tomato confit and sheep ricotta; and the signature black sea bass, wrapped in a crispy potato shell, with leeks and a red-wine sauce. Spoil yourself with the all-chocolate or all-fruit dessert menu. Daniel also has a well-chosen, albeit expensive, wine list, a pleasant sidewalk café, and accommodating, if slightly serendipitous, service. ✉ *20 E. 76th St.,* ☎ *212/288–0033. Reservations essential. Jacket required. AE, DC, V, MC, D. Closed Sun., Mon. lunch.*

$$–$$$ ✕ **L'Absinthe.** The wonderful Art Nouveau bistro decor of the former
★ tenant, Le Comptoire, remains—etched glass, huge gilt-framed mirrors, and tile floors. A few sidewalk tables have been added, and the front room is now more spacious. Expect a warm greeting, helpful service, and a welcoming bar. Chef-owner Jean-Michel Bergougnoux takes shellfish and cheese seriously, and they are both beautifully presented. Highlights on the menu include a fine foie gras terrine, salmon Moroccan-style, poached free-range chicken in truffle broth, and a thin,

crisp apple tart or warm chocolate cake. ⊠ *227 E. 67th St.,* ☎ *212/ 794–4950. Reservations essential. AE, MC, V. Closed lunch.*

$$ ✕ **Ferrier.** There are a few tables at its sidewalk café in the summer, but any time of the year, this very popular bistro will give you some idea of how tinned sardines must feel. So tuck in your tummy and turn up your hearing aid (the noise level tests one's tolerance for audio excess). The service and reception are so friendly and the food so delicious and copious you won't even mind the relatively high prices. Savor steak au poivre, grilled tuna "Ferrier," and profiteroles. Alas, the wine list is so out of shape, it would benefit from a personal trainer. ⊠ *29 E. 65th St.,* ☎ *212/772–9000. Reservations essential. AE, DC, MC, V.*

Italian

$$$$ ✕ **Parioli Romanissimo.** In a splendid town house, this special restau-
  ★   rant is one of Manhattan's last bastions of civility. You enter through a small bar and make your way down a long corridor, where you'll see one of New York's most astounding selections of imported cheese. The exquisite main dining area overlooking an enclosed garden room features a marble fireplace, the original plaster-molded ceiling, and spacious tables. Pasta is always wonderful here, as are such graceful offerings as sautéed sea scallops seared in peppercorns, in a discreet watercress sauce, and roasted rack of young lamb, marinated in spicy oil, herbs, and garlic. The wine list showcases jewels from Italy, France, and California, and 12 kinds of tea are available, presented in apothecary jars. Such luxury has a price, and new customers have at times been disappointed by a less than solicitous reception. Yet like a fine Brunello, Parioli Romanissimo improves each year and is ideally savored, shared, and enjoyed on special occasions. ⊠ *24 E. 81st St.,* ☎ *212/288–2391. Reservations essential. Jacket required. AE, DC, MC, V. Closed Sun. and lunch.*

$$–$$$ ✕ **Coco Pazzo.** One of New York's celebrity-spotting restaurants, the
  ★   main dining room is aglow with ecru walls, yellow tablecloths, colorful murals, and huge urns of flowers. All pastas and risottos are splendid, and it's hard to resist the *maccheroncini al pepolino*—rectangles of fresh egg pasta in a rich tomato sauce with thyme and grated aged pecorino cheese. If push comes to shove (or waistline challenges impulse), the entrée of choice is the roasted whole fish of the day: Carefully boned, it is garnished with deep-fried fresh herbs. *Crosta di frutta fresca* (open-faced fruit tart) changes its face often, but never disappoints, nor do the marvelous homemade biscotti. And be sure to take a sip of grappa, the clear Italian brandy. ⊠ *23 E. 74th St.,* ☎ *212/794– 0205. Reservations essential. AE, MC, V.*

$ ✕ **Triangolo.** A bowl of pasta is a bona fide bargain at this bustling trattoria with peach walls and colorful Itzhak Tarkay prints—but you may have to stand in line for it, since reservations are only taken for four or more. The sensibly short menu offers huge portions of homemade pasta dishes, such as *rotolo di pasta Montanalo* (homemade rolled noodles, stuffed with spinach, porcini mushrooms, and Parmesan cheese) and *caserecci alla Norma* (twisted pasta in a sauce of light cream, sausages, and sun-dried tomatoes). Flourless chocolate cake is the dessert of choice. There's an inexpensive wine list. ⊠ *345 E. 83rd St.,* ☎ *212/472–4488. No credit cards. Closed lunch.*

Mediterranean

$ ✕ **Bar Anise.** Anise, that exotic herb of the carrot family, is pictured in the blue wall tiles and the colorful print fabric on the banquettes. It also appears in several dishes, such as spicy tuna tartare with Moroccan anise bread and a sensuous anise-crusted duck with clementines (tangerines), almonds, and capers; even an apple-almond upside-down cake is topped with a silky anise-perfumed pistachio ice cream. ⊠ *1022 3rd Ave., between 60th and 61st Sts.,* ☎ *212/355–1112. AE, DC, MC, V.*

Middle Eastern

$ ✕ **L'Auberge.** With its flattering lighting and elegant decor, L'Auberge recalls Paris more than Beirut, with snowy white linens and fresh flowers on the well-spaced tables, and a gleaming cherry wood wine cabinet along the wall. You'll know it's Lebanese when you dig into the delicious hummus, *baba ghanoush* (warm eggplant pureed and mixed with *kashk,* a haunting spice), and kibbee. Most Middle Eastern entrées are letdowns, but French influences elevate Lebanon's, as is evident in L'Auberge's skewered lamb meatballs, cassoulet-like white bean and lamb stew, and whole grilled sea bass with zesty red sauce. The low-priced all-you-can-eat weekday lunch buffet is a steal. ⊠ *1191 1st Ave., between 64th and 65th Sts.,* ☎ *212/288–8791. AE, DC, MC, V.*

$ ✕ **Persepolis.** Manhattan's only authentic Persian restaurant has been artfully decorated with smoked-glass mirrors, huge globe light fixtures, and carpeted banquettes. Make an effort to order as many appetizers as you can handle, and don't omit baba ghanoush, *torshi* (pickled carrots, eggplant, celery, garlic, and parsley), and the olive salad. The Persepolis kabab (filet mignon, chopped steak, and chicken) on skewers is a good example of this delicate and choice cuisine. ⊠ *1423 2nd Ave., between 74th and 75th Sts.,* ☎ *212/535–1100. AE, DC, MC, V.*

Pizza

$ ✕ **Sofia Fabulous Pizza.** Mediterranean-colored friezes grace this
★ trendy café with wine racks, a vaulted ceiling, and wall sconces made of Japanese paper. Here you'll sample the best pizza and variations on focaccia in Manhattan. In the breathtaking thin-crusted pizza, prepared with filtered water to resemble the dough of Naples, Sofia uses mozzarella made daily with fresh milk. For a singular treat, try the mashed potatoes slathered with homemade tomato sauce and Parmesan cheese and then baked in the oven. ⊠ *1022 Madison Ave., near 79th St.,* ☎ *212/734–2676. AE, DC, MC, V.*

Southwestern

$$–$$$ ✕ **Arizona 206.** Santa Fe meets Manhattan at this seemingly casual eatery, which also incorporates the less-expensive adjacent Arizona Café. There's a cozy nook with a working fireplace as you enter and an inviting bar with superb margaritas, 18 premium tequilas, 22 microbrewery beers, and 11 wines by the glass. Stucco walls mimic an adobe hut, and colorful Native American prints cover the chair cushions. But no Mojave truck stop aspired to serving cuisine so urbane and inventive, such as the lipstick chili relleno, a seasonal chili of crab, fresh corn, carrot-ginger butter, black beans and habanera sauce, which bursts with flavor. The lobster tamale stuffed with diced meat, wild mushrooms, chili, and cactus, is another wonder. ⊠ *206 E. 60th St.,* ☎ *212/838–0440. AE, DC, MC, V. No Sun. lunch.*

Steak

$$$–$$$$ ✕ **Manhattan Café.** You enter this steak house through a bronze door-
★ way that belonged to the old Biltmore hotel. The bar room has a 110-year-old mahogany and oak bar with the original moldings from the former Astor hotel ballroom. Cut flowers, Art Deco chandeliers, Persian carpets and deep hunter green upholstery are a far cry from the rush-and-crush atmosphere of most of its competitors. If you're not a carnivore, you can order well-prepared seafood dishes, along with lyonnaise potatoes and potato pancakes. There's a good selection of Italian specialties and an expansive dessert tray. Sunday brunch is a

pleasure. ☒ *1161 1st Ave., between 63rd and 64th Sts.,* ☎ . *212/888–6556. AE, DC, MC, V. No Sat. lunch.*

$$$–$$$$ ✕ **Post House.** Superior grilling and first-rate ingredients are only half the appeal. Good service, inventive daily specials, and the inordinately comfortable main dining room, with leather armchairs, capacious tables, and parquet floor, complete the story. Triple lamb chops are prima, Caesar salad perfection. Frozen crème brûlée rejuvenates this tired dish, and the signature chocolate box—Belgian chocolate filled with white and dark chocolate mousse—may be copied by others but not duplicated. The wine list is vast, full of wines unavailable elsewhere. ☒ *28 E. 63rd St.,* ☎ *212/935–2888. Reservations essential. Jacket required. AE, DC, MC, V. Closed Sat. lunch, Sun.*

Thai

$–$$ ✕ **Montien.** Not only will you find the Thai cuisine extremely fresh, flavorful, and impeccably prepared and presented, you'll also dine in a lovely room with mirrors, white walls, flowers, and wood carvings of exotic birds. Choose delicate puffs of diced chicken, potato, and curry; a remarkable salad of roasted duck, cashews, apple, chilis, and lemon juice; boned chicken wings, stuffed with ground shrimp; deep fried whole red snapper, topped with sweet and spicy sauce; the classic *pad thai* (soft noodles); curried rice; or a red, green, or yellow chicken curry. Dining with a group of at least four makes the above banquet wondrously affordable. ☒ *1134 1st Ave. , between 62nd and 63rd Sts.,* ☎ *212/421–4433. AE, DC, MC, V.*

$ ✕ **Boonthai.** At this mirrored, softly lit charmer with its pretty paintings, crisply set tables, and handsome breakfront, Julie, the owner, greets you warmly. Your dining experience can be tempered to your taste. If you like your food hot, sample the deep-fried whole fish with chili sauce. Or order the chicken in not-so-spicy *masman* (red Muslim curry) sauce, the pad thai, or the obliging deep-fried duck. ☒ *1393A 2nd Ave., between 72nd and 73rd Sts.,* ☎ *212/249–8484. Reservations essential. AE, MC, V. Closed weekend lunch.*

Lincoln Center

American Casual

$$ ✕ **Vince & Eddie's.** This bucolic restaurant offers realistic prices, generous portions, and friendly service. It encompasses a series of small rooms and a seasonal garden patterned on a country inn. Executive chef Scott Campbell's new American fare is always a pleasure. Lamb shank with dried cherries and mashed turnips has deservedly become a classic. Save room for the magnificent desserts: Sorbets, ice creams, and even humble cobblers take on a new dimension. ☒ *70 W. 68th St,* ☎ *212/721–0068. Reservations essential. AE, DC, MC, V.*

$–$$ ✕ **Lincoln Tavern.** At this classic pub with high ceilings, wood walls, leather banquettes, and vintage black and white photographs, you have a good choice of American entrées, typified by chicken quesadilla with fresh roasted corn and jalapeño jack cheese, braised lamb shank with seasonal vegetables, and a chocolate macadamia nut brownie for dessert. ☒ *51 W. 64th St.,* ☎ *212/721–8271. AE, DC, MC, V.*

Chinese

$$–$$$ ✕ **Shun Lee West.** It's a dramatically lighted study in black, accented by white dragons and monkeys. Service is good, and considering the number of people the restaurant serves, the food can be excellent. Shanghai steamed dumplings and giant prawns make stellar starters. Then try the Peking duck, sweetbreads with hot peppers and scallions, or rack of lamb Szechuan style. Fresh fruit makes an ideal dessert. The food at Shun Lee Palace (☒ *155 E. 55th St.,* ☎ *212/371–8844*), under the same management, is equally good. ⊠ *43 W. 65th St.,* ☎ *212/595–8895. Reservations essential. AE, DC, MC, V.*

Contemporary

$$$ ✕ **Tavern on the Green.** The reception can be perfunctory and the service polite but inept. Nevertheless, Warner LeRoy's lavish restaurant is a visual fantasy, and careful selection can yield a satisfying meal. Try the jumbo lump crab cakes, chili and red pepper sauce, or roast double rack of pork with Cheddar cheese mashed potatoes and braised cabbage. There's also jazz, dancing, and cabaret. Request the brilliant Crystal Room, for its view of the twinkle-lighted trees, or opt for alfresco dining in the engaging garden. Prix-fixe menus lower the tab. ⊠ *In Central Park at 67th St.,* ☎ *212/873–3200. Reservations essential. AE, DC, MC, V.*

$$ ✕ **Sfuzzi.** The professionalism and appealing style exhibited here juxtaposes traditional (trompe l'oeil walls) and high-tech (video monitors, loud music). Commence with a Sfuzzi, a Bellini–frozen margarita hybrid. Then go for one of the designer pizzas, eclectic pastas, or contemporary Italian or new American entrées. A Cruvinet keeps the nice selection of open wines fresh. ⊠ *58 W. 65th St.,* ☎ *212/873–3700 (also* ⊠ *2 World Financial Center,* ☎ *212/385–8080). Reservations essential. AE, DC, MC, V.*

Continental

$$$–$$$$ ★ ✕ **Café des Artistes.** Writer–restaurant consultant George Lang's masterpiece, this most European of cafés provides a snug and beautiful ambience with its polished oak woodwork and rosy Howard Chandler Christy murals of nymphs at play. The cuisine is as refined as the setting. Four-way salmon, with tidbits of the fish that are smoked, poached, dill-marinated, and tartare, is a perfect introduction, and it would be hard to find a better pot-au-feu, a French variation on pot roast, here beautifully presented with bone marrow and traditional accompaniments. Desserts are appealing: toasted orange savarin and frozen mocha praline. Champagnes come by the carafe. Customers adore the especially festive brunch. ⊠ *1 W. 67th St.,* ☎ *212/877–3500. Reservations essential. Jacket required. AE, DC, MC, V.*

French

$$ ✕ **Café Luxembourg.** With its well-heeled clientele, this bustling, sophisticated bistro with airy arched windows, a zinc-top bar, and racks of newspapers is a bit of SoHo on the Upper West Side. Here's the place for steak frîtes, soothing roasted free-range chicken with mashed potatoes, or a robust cassoulet. Desserts are mostly fine, especially the mouthwatering profiteroles. Several prix-fixe menus lower the tab. There is a very good selection of wines. ⊠ *200 W. 70th St.,* ☎ *212/873–7411. Reservations essential. AE, DC, MC, V. Closed Mon. lunch*

Italian

$–$$ ✕ **Fiorello's Roman Café.** Although Trattoria Dell'Arte's corporate cousin gets better with each visit, it is largely unsung. (Perhaps people still remember it as a place for deep-dish pizza, or perhaps it's the prices, which are high by West Side standards, that intimidate.) Those in the know enjoy fabulous thin-crust pizza, good pastas, excellent baby chicken (roasted in a clay pot with vegetables), lovely salads, and grand desserts. There's a sidewalk café in summer and a bargain wine list. ⊠ *1900 Broadway, between 63rd and 64th Sts.,* ☎ *212/595–5330. AE, MC. V.*

Mediterranean

$$$–$$$$ ★ ✕ **Picholine.** Named for a small green Mediterranean olive, this mellow restaurant is patterned on a Provençal farmhouse, with soft col-

ors, wood floors, and dried flowers. There's a small bar in front, a narrow second room, and best of all, an attractive rear area with green and white checked wallpaper and comfortable banquettes. Chef-proprietor Terrance Brennan's food is among the finest in Manhattan. Among the top dishes are the signature grilled octopus with fennel, potato, and lemon-pepper dressing; Moroccan-spiced loin of lamb with vegetable couscous and mint-yogurt sauce; and tornados of salmon with horseradish crust, cucumbers, and salmon caviar. A cheese selection of some 30 varieties, in prime condition and served at room temperature, is indicative of Brennan's commitment to quality. The wine list offers outstanding wines by the glass. ⊠ *35 W. 64th St.,* ☎ *212/724– 8585. Reservations essential. AE, DC, MC, V. Closed Mon. lunch, Sun.*

Mexican

$ ✕ **Gabriela's.** This small cantina with mirrors, ceramic parrots hang-
★   ing from the ceiling, and a desert mural may be modest, but it will reward lovers of authentic Mexican cuisine. The menu has wonderful tacos, stuffed with beef-tongue and *chicharron* (deep-fried pork skins) in a haunting bath of tomatillo and serrano sauce. Guacamole arrives as a chunky-salad of avocado, tomatoes, chilies, fresh cilantro, and onions. And where else in town can you find an unusual Vera Cruz–style tamale, filled with shrimp, olives, and capers in a roasted tomato sauce? The house specialty is a whole rotisserie chicken, Yucatan style, with rice, beans, and plantains. ⊠ *685 Amsterdam Ave. at 93rd St.,* ☎ *212/961–0574. AE, DC, MC, V.*

Seafood

$$ ✕ **Fishin Eddie.** Well prepared seafood in a variety of styles shows up in this playful spot, designed by the noted set designer Sam Lopata. There's a cozy, low-ceilinged bar flanked by a sofa up front and a skylighted main dining room filled with painted furniture and farmhouse tables. Try the tuna steak au poivre with french fries. For dessert, you can't beat the triple-chocolate brownie nestled beside a scoop of white-chocolate ice cream. ⊠ *73 W. 71st St.,* ☎ *212/874–3474. AE, DC, MC, V. Closed lunch.*

Steak

$$–$$$ ✕ **West 63rd Street Steakhouse.** An elevator takes you to the mezzanine of this sumptuous steak house, located in the Radisson Empire hotel. The leopard carpeting extends to the main dining room, which is lined with floral banquettes. A prime porterhouse for two is always a test of the management's commitment to first-rate preparation, and the kitchen triumphs in the art of grilling: Steaks are charred, pink, juicy, warm, sliced on the bone, and delicious. ⊠ *44 W. 63rd St.,* ☎ *212/246–6363. Reservations essential. AE, DC, MC, V.*

Upper West Side

American Casual

$$ ✕ **Ernie's.** This restaurant brought downtown to the Upper West Side, but now it's just a typical Upper West Side dining spot with a large menu. It has a cavernous dining room, exposed brick walls, ceiling fans, and a killer noise level. Order with care and you can assemble a good meal. Portions are large. ⊠ *2150 Broadway, between 75th and 76th Sts.,* ☎ *212/496–1588. AE, DC, MC, V.*

$–$$ ✕ **Main Street.** Bring kids, friends, and an appetite—everything is served family style. Picture a whole roast chicken and a really good meat loaf. This American-as-apple-pie restaurant prepares them all well.

Since every order comes large enough to split four ways, don't let the prices turn you off (just divide by four). Check out the terrific puddings and stupendous pies. The lighting is a bit uncharitable, and the decibel level can be unfortunate. ⊠ *446 Columbus Ave., between 81st and 82nd Sts.,* ☏ *212/873–5025. AE, DC, MC, V. Closed weekday lunch.*

$–$$ ✕ **Popover Café.** There's a certain captivating, innocent quality to the honest American food in this vintage West Side tearoom-cum-restaurant full of teddy bears. Besides the superb popovers (you'll swear they're no less than the best in creation), you'll admire the terrific soups and the delectable sandwiches with names like Mad Russian. Sunday brunch packs 'em in, and the dinner menu stars fried catfish breaded in pecans and cornmeal, good lamb chops, and a half beef-half veal burger. There's also a health-watch prix-fixe menu and an inexpensive wine and beer list. ⊠ *551 Amsterdam Ave., between 86th and 87th Sts.,* ☏ *212/595–8555. Reservations essential. AE, MC, V.*

$–$$ ✕ **Sarabeth's Kitchen.** Despite the bric-a-brac and homespun charm, this is more than a tearoom, with a menu that embraces Italianate smoked-salmon bruschetta, homespun American chicken potpie, and pan seared salmon on wild rice. Desserts such as cranberry-pear bread pudding and homemade ice creams and sorbets are worthwhile. This is a fine place for breakfast and brunch. ⊠ *423 Amsterdam Ave., between 80th and 81st,* ☏ *212/496–6280. AE, DC, MC, V.*

$ ✕ **Firehouse.** There's a reason this find calls itself a firehouse: The sauce they use gives the plain chicken enough kick to get you to Jamaica without an airplane, and the pizza topped with that chicken is not much milder. Still, you can get tamer varieties, too, and the crust is high, crisp, and delicious. You'll also find good buffalo wings and chili. Or you can try the so-called sexy fries with cheese dipping sauce, and burgers (mild, medium, or inferno). Be sure to check out the microbrewery beers and the brownies. ◷ Until 4 AM. ⊠ *522 Columbus Ave., between 85th and 86th Sts.,* ☏ *212/ 595-3139 AE, MC, V.*

Asian

$ ✕ **Rain.** Conjuring up memories of the writings of Somerset Maugham, who wrote a short story called "Rain," this pleasant restaurant has a friendly bar, rattan chairs with pillows in chintz, and wooden floors covered with Oriental runners. The raised dining area features wooden booths and back-lit Asian glass prints. This is a good place to come with a group so you can share first-rate Thai and Vietnamese inspired food: steamed ravioli called *bahn cuon,* with lump crab, bean sprouts and chili sauce; crispy whole fish in three-flavor sauce; and tantalizing charred beef salad. ⊠ *100 W. 82nd St.,* ☏ *212/501–0776. Reservations essential. AE, DC, MC, V. Closed lunch.*

Contemporary

$$$ ✕ **Two Two Two.** On the ground level of a brownstone, this oak-paneled dining room with its skylight, polished-wood floor, and massive chandelier is classy for any neighborhood—and the garden is a pleasure. Representative offerings include spicy salmon tartare with red caviar, lobster risotto with black truffles, filet mignon with wild mushrooms in a red wine sauce, and baked apple in phyllo with raspberry coulis. ⊠ *222 W. 79th St.,* ☏ *212/799–0400. Reservations essential. AE, DC, MC, V. Closed lunch.*

$–$$ ✕ **Le Select.** This bustling bistro from Eric Demarchelier has a large bar and dining room in front with amusing sconces, globe lights, ceiling fans, and the au courant exposed brick walls and wood floors as well as changing photography exhibitions. The back area is separated by transparent bamboo shades, creating an intimate dining space. The all-French bar room serves hardy bistro dishes like pâté, escargot, and steak frîtes, while the back area concentrates on Thai-inspired dumplings, spring rolls, and sensuous *satays* (skewered and grilled meats or chicken) in light *masman* (lemongrass curry) sauces. ⌂ *507 Columbus Ave., between 84th and 85th Sts.,* ☎ *212/875–1993. AE, MC, V.*

Continental

$$$ ✕ **Terrace.** About as off the beaten path as you can get (unless you happen to go to Columbia University), this Old World charmer on the 16th floor possesses a studied elegance reminiscent of Eastern Europe circa the late 1930s. Diners enjoy two large dining rooms, a wraparound balcony, staggering views, occasional harp music, and a rose on each table. The Terrace is ideal for special occasions (like popping the question). And the out-of-fashion hybrid cuisine once referred to as Continental is not bad. ⌂ *400 W. 119th St., between Amsterdam and Morningside Aves.,* ☎ *212/666–9490. Jacket required. AE, MC, V. Closed Sat. lunch, Sun. and Mon.*

Italian

$–$$ ✕ **Carmine's.** Dark woodwork and old-fashioned black and white
★ tiles make this hot spot look like an old-timer. It isn't. Still, savvy West Siders are only too glad to line up for its home-style cooking, served family style. Yet despite the crowds and the low prices, Carmine's is good. Kick off a meal with fried calamari or stuffed artichoke; then move on to the pastas (perhaps rigatoni in a rollicking broccoli, sausage, and white-bean sauce) or lobster *fra diabolo* (in a spicy tomato sauce). ⌂ *2450 Broadway, between 90th and 91st Sts.,* ☎ *212/362–2200. Reservations only for 6 or more. AE. No lunch.*

Japanese

$$ ✕ **Fujiyama Mama.** White-slipcovered side chairs line up like statues in the vitrine of this creative restaurant with a high-tech design. In the startling spirit of the place, dishes have names like Poseidon Adventure and Bermuda Triangle. But the food is serious, inventive, and invariably first-rate, including marinated chicken in a blue Curaçao sauce; and sparkling toro, tuna, fluke, yellowtail, sea trout and salmon sushi, sashimi, and hand rolls. Tell the waiter it's your birthday and your tempura deep-fried ice cream comes with flickering sparklers, while the DJ lays on a "Happy Birthday to You" from his collection of weird recordings of the classic tune. ⌂ *467 Columbus Ave., between 82nd and 83rd Sts.,* ☎ *212/769–1144. Reservations essential. AE. Closed lunch.*

Seafood

$$ ✕ **Mad Fish.** This seafood spot has a skylit shingled roof and amusing murals depicting cocktail parties with fish as the guests. At the long mahogany bar, patrons can sample boiled periwinkles, steamed lobster, seasonal oysters, and more. The kitchen produces stylish food, such as barbecued bluefish and fish and chips—cured fresh cod, gently coated with tempura and quickly deep-fried. Be sure to sample one of the desserts, especially the warm flourless chocolate cake, with a soft center, à la mode. ⌂ *2182 Broadway, between 77th and 78th Sts.,* ☎ *212-787-0202. AE, DC, MC, V. Closed lunch.*

$–$$ ✕ **Stingray.** This trendy restaurant has mottled gold walls, a copper-colored tin ceiling, and comfortably upholstered red wood chairs. The most commanding area is the lounge with its cane chairs, colorful tile mosaics, and small cocktail tables. Snackers will think they've gone to heaven—what with the dumplings, salads, pizza, pasta, and sandwiches. Don't miss the fabulous seafood burger, topped with *sofrito,* the spicy Spanish condiment, mayo, and seasonal greens and served on homemade sourdough bread. The guava tart with its shortbread-like crust and crème anglaise merits raves. ✉ *428 Amsterdam Ave., between 80th and 81st Sts.,* ☎ *212/501–7515. AE, DC, MC, V.*

Soul

$ ✕ **Emily's.** At this neat and pleasant eatery, the bare Formica tables, paper napkins, and minimalist decor obviously aren't the draw. This bargain-priced Harlem discovery serves some of the best chopped barbecue sandwiches, deep-fried chicken livers (dunk them into the zesty house sauce), corn-bread stuffing (spiked with hot peppers and spices), and homemade potato salad this side of the Mason–Dixon Line. It's hard to choose among such extraordinary dishes as batter-fried whiting, Southern-fried chicken, and gutsy Harlem chicken and waffles with maple syrup. Desserts are also fabulous: peach cobbler, carrot cake, and sweet-potato pie. A good bet for breakfast and brunch. ✉ *1325 5th Ave. at 111th St.,* ☎ *212/996–1212. AE, DC, MC, V.*

Southern

$–$$ ✕ **The Savannah Club.** Lightened up soul food is dished out to an attractive crowd at this airy restaurant with ceiling fans, French doors opening to the street, and a bar flanked by columns rimmed with colored neon. Homemade corn bread and biscuits are giveaways, served with onion jam and sweet potato butter. But leave room for fried oysters, and the house specialty: a bowl of tender chicken and puffy dumplings. For dessert, the dark chocolate pie with a brownielike texture and whipped cream is a must. ✉ *2420 Broadway at 89th St.* ☎ *212/496–1066. AE, DC, MC, V. Closed lunch.*

Worth a Special Trip

Contemporary

$$$$ ✕ **River Café.** This is one of New York's most romantic restaurants.
★ Sipping a perfect cocktail or a glass of wine from the extensive list and watching the sun set over lower Manhattan, just across the East River, is one of the city's great treats. So is the food by Rick Laakkonen. Favorite dishes include fruitwood smoked salmon and grilled jumbo quail on white hominy puree. Desserts are dramatic, such as the Brooklyn Bridge, sculpted out of a chocolate-mousse cake. Although prices are high—there's a three-course dinner or a more elaborate six-course tasting—the service is among the best in the business. Sunday brunch is a joy, lunch less hectic. ✉ *1 Water St. at the East River,* ☎ *718/522–5200. Reservations essential. Jacket required. AE, DC, MC, V.*

COFFEE BARS AND CAFÉS

Cafés have been a New York institution since beat days. Yet only recently have coffee bars on the Seattle model taken off. Still, they're multiplying at an exponential rate. Plain and decaffeinated drip coffee and espresso are standard. (Note: "Regular coffee" in New York comes with milk or cream; you must add your own sugar if you want your brew sweetened.) You will also find appellations that were never uttered in Italy: *ristretto,* a highly refined espresso; *macchiato,* espresso with just a bit of foam; caffè latte, espresso with steamed milk; cappuccino, half espresso and half steamed milk, with foam; caffè mocha, espresso with steamed chocolate milk; *mochaccino,* cappuccino flavored with chocolate. Most come in a decaf variant or with skim, low-fat, and soy milk, half-and-half, and cream as well as plain whole milk. Many offer snacks; others are restaurants in coffee-bar drag. While prices can top more than $2 for an espresso, all offer a bit of civilized sipping.

Starbuck's, Timothy's, and New World Coffee are among the upscale coffee-bar chains around the city. The listings below serve desserts and snacks and cater to tea drinkers as well.

Greenwich Village

✕ **Caffè Dell'Artista** (⊠ 46 Greenwich Ave., ☎ 212/645–4431). This West Village Italian café has dark, romantic back rooms, delirium-inducing desserts, and mismatched wooden writing desks doubling as tables, complete with past patron's poems discarded in the drawers.

✕ **Caffè Dante** (⊠ 79–81 Macdougal St., between Houston and Bleecker Sts., ☎ 212/982–5275). A longtime Village hangout, this convivial spot has superlative espresso and knockout tiramisù.

✕ **Caffè Reggio** (⊠ 119 MacDougal St., between 3rd and Bleecker Sts., ☎ 212/475–9557). In the neighborhood's oldest coffeehouse, where a huge, antique machine steams forth espresso, the tiny tables are close together, perfect for eavesdropping on the interesting crowd.

✕ **Caffè Vivaldi** (⊠ 32 Jones St. at Bleecker St., ☎ 212/691–7538). Soak up West Village atmosphere in this peaceful café serving coffee, tea, cannoli, and lovely toasted sandwiches.

East Village, Little Italy, SoHo

✕ **Caffè Roma** (⊠ 385 Broome St. at Mulberry, ☎ 212/226–8413). At Manhattan's most authentic Italian coffeehouse with worn walls and marble tables, the cappuccino is strong, bracing, and foamy.

✕ **Dean & Deluca** (⊠ 121 Prince St., ☎ 212/254–8776). The owner of a gourmet market operates this spacious, skylit café, where you can join the well-heeled SoHo shoppers and gallery hoppers and have coffee, a brie baguette, or a wicked sweet.

✕ **Internet Cafe** (⊠ 82 E. 3rd St., between 1st and 2nd Aves., ☎ 212/614–0747). Relax in cyberspace with a PC or Mac, munch sandwiches with names like NetScape, and enjoy computer magazines over a cup of java.

✕ **Le Gamin** (⊠ 50 MacDougal St., between Houston and Prince Sts., ☎ 212/254–4678). Enjoy this hip little haven for surprisingly good crepes, café au lait, and conversation.

✕ **Marquet Patisserie** (⊠ 15 E. 12th St., between 5th Ave. and University Pl., ☎ 212/229–9313). At this friendly café, you can savor a French pastry and a steaming bowl of café au lait; the menu also includes inventive salads, thick sandwiches, healthy soups, and croque monsieur.

✕ **T Salon** (⊠ 143 Mercer St. at Prince St., ☎ 212/925–3700). At this exquisite tearoom near the SoHo Guggenheim, you'll adore the sushi bar, the marvelous choice of exotic teas and coffees, and the special snacks and desserts.

✕ **Veniero's Pasticceria** (⊠ 342 E. 11th St., near 1st Ave., ☎ 212/674–7264). Now a century old, this bustling bakery-café sells every kind of Italian *dulce,* plus irresistible cheesecakes and pies.

Chelsea

✕ **Big Cup** (⊠ 228 8th Ave., between 21st and 22nd Sts. ☎ 212/206–0059). *The* place to meet in Chelsea—grab a chair or sofa, hang out for hours, sip café au lait, and start writing that novel.

✕ **Milan Café and Coffee Bar** (⊠ 120 W. 23rd St., ☎ 212/807–1801). A serious chef makes knockout sandwiches, salads, and desserts in this striking eatery with knotty pine tables and a ceiling of flags.

✕ **Newsbar** (⊠ 2 W. 19th St., ☎ 212/255–3996). This ultracasual resting place with four other Manhattan locations has good coffee and tea, a generous offering of magazines, and even Cable News Network.

East Side

✕ **Café Bianco** (✉ 1486 2nd Ave., between 77th and 78th Sts., ☎ 212/988–2655). White tables fill this popular meeting place with excellent coffee, sinful desserts, and small meals; in warm weather, try the back garden.

✕ **Columbus Bakery** (✉ 957 1st Ave., between 52nd & 53rd Sts., ☎ 212/421–0334; ✉ 474 Columbus Ave., between 82nd & 83rd Sts., ☎ 212/724–6880). In an airy space with chandeliers that look like a loaf of bread, you can enjoy the same delicious bread, muffins, and pastries that are served at Lutèce.

✕ **Corrado Café** (✉ 1013 3rd Ave., between 60th and 61st Sts., ☎ 212/753–5100). A branch of a successful West Side restaurant, this convenient spot near cinemas and Bloomingdale's has pastries, cookies, and cakes that outshine the coffee.

✕ **Fleur de Jour** (✉ 348 E. 62nd St., ☎ 212/355–2020). Lace curtains, patterned wallpaper, wonderful wicker baskets full of cookies, and an owner who seems to be everybody's best friend make this New York's most welcoming café; there are just five small tables and four high-back stools.

✕ **Sant Ambroeus** (✉ 1000 Madison Ave., between 77th and 78th Sts., ☎ 212/570–2211). You'll swear you're in Milan at this very Italian café with red leather banquettes and Maurano chandeliers, where you can enjoy magnificent coffee and desserts, including gelato (Italian ice cream).

✕ **Trois Jean** (✉ 154 E. 79th St., between Lexington and 3rd Aves., ☎ 212/988–4858). Straight out of Paris, this lower-level patisserie in an expensive bistro provides a romantic respite from the standard coffeehouse, with sensational and classy desserts.

West Side

✕ **Café La Fortuna** (✉ 69 W. 71st St., ☎ 212/724–5846). Weary Columbus Avenue strollers have long flocked to this comforting refuge offering Italian pastries, serious coffee, and opera music.

✕ **Café Lalo** (✉ 201 W. 83rd St., ☎ 212/496–6031). Linger over cappuccino, cake, and crossword puzzles at this flashy, Lautrec-themed spot just off Broadway.

✕ **The Coffee Pot** (✉ 350 9th Ave. at 49th St., ☎ 212/265–3566). Overstuffed sofas and chairs, mirrors, brass chandeliers, good deals on coffee of the day, and pleasant service make this joint one of the theater district's most pleasant options.

✕ **Cupcake Café** (✉ 522 9th Ave. at 39th St., ☎ 212/465–1530). Although it's in a desolate neighborhood, this funky place is worth the trek for the old-fashioned cupcakes, doughnuts, coffee cake, and hearty soup, accompanied by strong coffee.

✕ **French Roast Café** (✉ 2340 Broadway at 85th St., ☎ 212/799–1533). In a re-creation of a Parisian Left Bank café, you can relax over light bistro fare, decent sweets, and coffee; open around the clock.

7 Lodging

New York visitors have a fine choice of places to stay—from elegant grand old hotels and bustling modern giants to friendly boutique hotels and money-saving bed-and-breakfasts. Several of the city's best restaurants are now found in hotels. Though Manhattan lodging tends to be expensive, it often offers unique experiences. Where else can you sleep in Frank Lloyd Wright's former apartment, swim with a view of the Empire State Building, or eat breakfast in bed while watching sea lions at play?

Updated by
Mary Ellen
Schultz

IF ANY SINGLE ELEMENT OF YOUR TRIP to New York City will cost you dearly, it will be your hotel room. Unlike many European cities, New York offers few low-priced lodgings. Real estate is at a premium here, and labor costs are high, so hoteliers start out with a lot of expenses to cover. And there are enough well-heeled visitors to support competition at the premium end of the spectrum. Considering the healthy occupancy rate, market forces are not likely to drive current prices down. Fleabags and flophouses aside, there's precious little here for less than $100 a night. The city no longer has the highest hotel tax in the country (that distinction belongs to Columbus, Ohio), but you should not fail to figure the 13.25% combined taxes plus $2 per room, per night (city occupancy charge) into your calculations. We have scoured the city for good-value hotels and budget properties, but even our $ category includes hotels that run as high as $135 for one night's stay in a double.

Our price categories are based on the "rack rate," or the standard room cost that hotels print in their brochures and quote over the phone. You almost never need to pay this much. If you book directly with the hotel, ask about corporate rates, seasonal special offers, or weekend deals. The latter typically include such extras as complimentary meals, drinks, or tickets to events. Ask your travel agent for brochures, and look for advertisements in travel magazines or the Sunday travel sections of major newspapers such as the *New York Times,* the *Washington Post,* or the *Los Angeles Times.* Of course, booking any all-inclusive package, weekend or longer, will reduce the hotel rate.

If you should be unfortunate enough to arrive in New York City without a hotel reservation, you can also try the most direct method of lowering the room rate: asking. In periods of low occupancy, hotels—especially at the expensive end of the market—will often reduce the price on rooms that would otherwise remain empty.

In general, Manhattan hotels don't measure up to those in other U.S. cities in terms of room size, parking, or outside landscaping. But, this being a sophisticated city, New York hotels usually compensate with fastidious service, sprucely maintained properties, and restaurants that hold their own in a city of knowledgeable diners.

Common sense should tell you not to anticipate the same kind of personal service from even a top-flight convention hotel, such as the New York Hilton, as you would from a smaller, sedate property like the Doral Tuscany, even though both have rooms in the same price range. Know your own taste and choose accordingly.

Women on their own, even at upscale hotels, should be aware that they may be accosted in public areas, either by male guests trying to find companions or by hotel staff trying to chase away the hookers who transact business in hotel lobbies. (Because these "working girls" often look quite respectable, any single woman may be suspect.) You might want to ask the concierge to point out places where you'll feel comfortable relaxing on your own.

Note: Even the most exclusive hotels have security gaps. Be discreet with valuables everywhere, and stay alert in public areas.

236

Algonquin, **50**
Ameritania, **28**
Beekman Tower, **34**
Best Western Seaport Inn, **60**
Beverly, **36**
Carlton Arms, **61**
Carlyle, **7**
Doral Court, **53**
Doral Park Avenue, **55**
Doral Tuscany, **54**
Drake, **22**
Dumont Plaza, **59**
Eastgate Tower, **52**
Essex House, **16**
Excelsior, **1**
Fitzpatrick, **21**
Four Seasons, **20**
Franklin, **3**
Gershwin, **63**
Gramercy Park, **62**
Hotel Beacon, **5**
Hotel Edison, **40**
Hotel Wales, **5**
Hotel Wentworth, **44**
Jolly Madison Towers, **56**
Loews New York, **32**
Lowell, **12**
Mansfield, **48**
Mark, **6**
Marriott Marquis, **42**
Mayfair, **10**
Mayfower, **14**
Michelangelo, **39**
Milburn, **4**
Millenium Hilton, **65**
Morgans, **57**
New York Hilton, **29**
New York Palace, **38**
NewYork Vista, **67**
Omni Berkshire Place, **31**
Paramount, **41**
Park Savoy, **19**
Le Parker Meridien, **23**
Peninsula, **25**
Pickwick Arms, **33**
Pierre, **15**
Plaza, **18**
Plaza Athénée, **11**
Radisson Empire, **13**
Renaissance, **43**
Ritz-Carlton, **17**
Roosevelt, **45**
Royalton, **49**
St. Regis, **24**
San Carlos, **35**
Shelburne, **58**
Shoreham, **26**

Manhattan Lodging

CATEGORY	COST*
$$$$	over $260
$$$	$190–$260
$$	$135–$190
$	under $135

All prices are for a standard double room, excluding 15¼% city and state taxes.

Reservations

New York is constantly full of vacationers, conventioneers, and business travelers, all requiring hotel space. Try to book your room as far in advance as possible, using a major credit card to guarantee the reservation; you might even want to work through a travel agent. Because this is a tight market, overbooking can be a problem, and "lost" reservations are not unheard of. When signing in, take a pleasant but firm attitude; if there is a mix-up, chances are the outcome will be an upgrade or a free night.

Hotels with famous restaurants appreciate it when guests who want to use those facilities book tables when they make their room reservations. All chefs mentioned were in charge at press time. Call to confirm the name under the toque. It can make *all* the difference.

Services

Unless otherwise noted in the individual descriptions, all the hotels listed have the following features and services: private baths, central heating, air-conditioning, private telephones, on-premises dining, valet and room service (though not necessarily 24-hour or short-notice), TV (including cable and pay-per-view films), and a routine concierge staff. Larger hotels will generally have video or high-speed checkout capability.

New York City has finally allowed liquor-stocked minibars to be installed in rooms.

Pools are a rarity, but most properties have fitness centers; we note only those that are on the premises, but other hotels usually have arrangements for guests at nearby facilities, for which a fee is sometimes charged.

Those bringing a car to Manhattan should note the lack of hotel parking. Many properties in all price ranges *do* have parking facilities, but they are often at independent garages that charge as much as $20 or more per day.

Midtown East

$$$$ ⊞ **Four Seasons.** If you shop at Barneys and prefer Woody Allen's Ingmar Bergman imitations to his comedies, you'll love New York's tallest, newest, most expensive hotel. I. M. Pei—he of the Louvre Pyramid, among other modernist icons—designed this limestone-clad, stepped spire amid the prime shops of 57th Street, and he made it big. The guest rooms are big (600 square feet on average) and the lobby is bigger than big. The aptly named Grand Foyer is dauntingly sky-high, and its French limestone pillars, marble, onyx, and acre upon acre of blond wood are a study in earth-toned elegance. What could possibly justify the astronomical rates? Gleaming English sycamore dressing areas with a giant mirror, perhaps, and enough closet space to hold a year's worth of clothing. Wear Armani, Gucci, or Lauren, or you'll feel out of place. ⊠ *57 E. 57th St.,* ☎ *212/758–5700,* ℻ *212/758–5711. 367*

rooms. Restaurant, bar, café, sauna, spa, health club, business services, meeting rooms. AE, DC, MC, V.

$$$$ ⚏ **Omni Berkshire Place.** Just what this town needs, right? *Another* heart-stopping, wallet-emptying place for you to rest following a hard day in the Big Apple. Well, maybe if it's this new sophisticated hotel. Step through the bronze and glass entrance into the two-story atrium lobby and be wowed by the light, the mirrors, the plants, the huge marble fireplace, and the manners of the front desk people, one of whom personally escorts you to your room. Standard rooms are bigger than many small city apartments (375 square feet); are decorated in exquisite palettes of oyster, gold, sage, or burgundy; and feature beamed ceilings, cushiony wing chairs, and ottomans. Three two-line phones; an in-room fax machine; and all-electronic bedside controls for TV, air-conditioning, door privacy sign, radio, and lights make it possible to conduct high-power meetings alone in your room, dressed in a plush terry-cloth robe. The marble bathrooms have tubs you could do laps in. ✉ *21 E. 52nd St.,10022,* ☎ *212/753–5800 or 800/843–6664,* FAX *212/754–5020. 396 rooms, 47 suites. Restaurant, bar, lounge, health club, business services, meeting rooms. AE, DC, MC, V.*

$$$$ ⚏ **The Peninsula.** The Peninsula Group's Hong Kong flagship consis-
★ tently gets top ratings. There's nothing wrong with this one either, with its marble Art Nouveau lobby off 55th Street, gracious afternoon tea service, and unobtrusive, ultraefficient service. Most guest rooms are of a generous size and are deep-carpeted and serenely furnished. They're matched by sumptuous marble baths with bidets, oversize tubs (many of them Jacuzzis), and collectible, Molton Brown English bath products. Even the smaller rooms have graceful sculpted art nouveau–style headboards, desks, and armoires; some also have the same sweeping views down 5th Avenue as the more expensive suites. The rooftop health club has been called the Rolls-Royce of hotel fitness centers; it's truly a knockout. ✉ *700 5th Ave., 10019,* ☎ *212/247–2200 or 800/262–9467,* FAX *212/903–3949. 250 rooms. Restaurant, café, lounge, pool, health club, massage, meeting rooms. AE, DC, MC, V.*

$$$$ ⚏ **St. Regis.** When Sheraton restored this 5th Avenue Beaux Arts landmark, planners set a high standard for themselves with prices to match. Is the experience transporting enough to merit such a splurge? On the plus side is chef Gray Kunz's inspired menu in the very opulent restaurant, Lespinasse (☞ Chapter 6), and the delightful King Cole Bar, home to the famous Maxfield Parrish mural. Guest rooms are filled with Louis XV–style furnishings and expensive amenities. Marble bathrooms, with tubs, stall showers, and double sinks, are outstanding. The fitness center is adequate. ✉ *2 E. 55th St., 10022,* ☎ *212/753–4500 or 800/759–7550,* FAX *212/787–3447. 365 rooms. Restaurant, bar, lounge, health club, meeting rooms, business center. AE, DC, MC, V.*

$$$ ⚏ **The Drake.** This Swissôtel property is favored by many business travelers for its solid service and location just off Park Avenue at 56th Street. The prewar building was originally designed as an apartment house, so the rooms are large enough for refrigerators and other homey touches. Visitors and locals alike thoroughly enjoy Swiss specialties and hard-to-find Swiss wines at the airy Drake Bar. There's more comfort here than spit and polish, more efficiency than character, but the Drake makes a safe choice for a no-nonsense midtown base. ✉ *440 Park Ave., 10022,* ☎ *212/421–0900 or 800/637–9477,* FAX *212/371–4190. 600 rooms. Bar, meeting rooms. AE, DC, MC, V.*

$$$ ⚏ **New York Palace.** This glass monolith with a landmark palazzo at its feet is how many visitors envision New York hotels—big, slightly overwrought, and always busy. Rooms at the Palace are large by Manhattan standards; those on the west side afford views of St. Patrick's Cathedral and Rockefeller Center. All are equipped with fax machines,

irons, and ironing boards. Among the new offerings are an elaborate fitness center and a lobby restaurant. The hotel's big culinary news is the move of the celebrated restaurant Le Cirque to the Villard House—the 100-year-old neo-Renaissance structure that houses many of the hotel's public rooms. ⊠ *455 Madison Ave. 10022,* ☎ *212/888–7000 or 800/697–2522. 900 rooms. 2 restaurants, 2 bars, breakfast room, minibars, no-smoking rooms, room service, beauty salon, health club, spa, dry cleaning, laundry service, concierge, business services, meeting rooms, parking (fee). AE, DC, MC, V.*

$$$ 🏨 **The Tudor.** Run by the London-based Sarova Hotel Group, this charming, medium-size property is close to the United Nations and Grand Central Terminal. Interior spaces are classic and unassuming, with hardwood reproduction furniture upholstered in brocades and velvets, marble floors, and handmade carpets in the public areas. Guest rooms have a fine marble bathroom; the executive rooms and suites have Jacuzzis. Some of these also have a private terrace. The 20-story landmark building dates from the '20s and is part of Tudor City, with its private park and fanciful Englishness. Business travelers are particularly well looked after here, with the requisite two-line phones, fax machines, and business center, and there's a trouser press and minibar in every room. ⊠ *304 E. 42nd St., 10017,* ☎ *212/986–8800 or 800/879–8836,* 𝔽𝔸𝕏 *212/986–1758. 303 rooms. Restaurant, lounge, health club, business services, meeting rooms. AE, DC, MC, V.*

$$$ 🏨 **U.N. Plaza–Park Hyatt.** It's easy to miss the entrance to this favorite
★ among the business and diplomatic set—it's on a quiet side street near (naturally) the United Nations. The striking lobby is small but seems endless thanks to clever designs in dark marble and mirrors; Japanese floral arrangements add warmth and drama. What makes the place special, though, are its guest rooms, all with breathtaking views of Manhattan's East Side. (The delightful rooftop pool also offers such views.) The decor is modern but not sterile, and the color schemes are soothing. Prices here are still reasonable by hotel standards, though the room rates are at the top of this price category. Service throughout the hotel is first-rate. ⊠ *1 United Nations Plaza, 10017,* ☎ *212/758–1234 or 800/223–1234,* 𝔽𝔸𝕏 *212/702–5051. 427 rooms. Restaurant, 2 lounges, pool, health club, meeting rooms. AE, DC, MC, V.*

$$$ 🏨 **Waldorf-Astoria.** This landmark Art Deco masterpiece personifies New York at its most lavish and powerful. The hotel has been kept in great shape, from the original murals and mosaics and elaborate plaster ornamentation to the fine old-wood walls and doors. In the guest rooms, some of which start at the low end of this category, there are new bedspreads and carpets. Bathrooms throughout are old but beautifully maintained and spacious. Of course, in the very private Tower section (well known to heads of state and discerning business travelers), everything is that much grander. Cole Porter wrote many of his famous lyrics on the Steinway grand piano in a suite he kept in the Tower for 25 years. The piano, a gift from the Waldorf, is still played nightly in the hotel lobby. The hotel's richly tinted, hushed lobby is a hub of city life. ⊠ *301 Park Ave., 10022,* ☎ *212/355–3000 or 800/445–8667,* 𝔽𝔸𝕏 *212/421–8103. 1,380 rooms. 4 restaurants, lounge, tea shop, health club, meeting rooms. AE, DC, MC, V.*

$$ 🏨 **The Beverly.** This suite-dominated hotel's plush wood-paneled lobby, with piped Vivaldi, a crystal chandelier, leather couches, mirrored pillars, and a touch-screen information center, inspires confidence in what's upstairs. The spacious accommodations here are popular with visitors to the nearby United Nations, Euro-tourists, and business travelers. About 70 rooms have a rose and green color scheme; most are resplendent in hues of teal and burgundy, with cabbage-rose chintz drapes. The bathrooms often disappoint, however; many are small and dingy with a beige-tone decor. Corner suites (Nos. 1801, 1805, and about six more) cost slightly more but are especially grand, with a terrace and carved wooden beds. There is a complimentary Continental breakfast. ⊠ *125 E. 50th St., 10022,* ☎ *212/753–2700, or 800/223–0945,* FAX *212/759–7300. 187 suites. Restaurant, in-room safes, kitchenettes, beauty salon. AE, DC, MC, V.*

$$ ⊞ **The Fitzpatrick.** This cozy hotel just south of Bloomingdale's, the
★ first American venture for an established Irish company, is a winner in terms of value and charm. More than half of the units are true suites that are priced well below the market average, even on weekdays. Amenities include trouser presses, telephones with voice mail, and subdued traditional furnishings. Though not large, bathrooms are modern and well equipped. The lively bar has become popular with locals. The staff is exceptionally friendly and savvy, which may be why celebs such as Gregory Peck, various Kennedys, Sinead O'Connor, and The Chieftains check in. ⊠ *687 Lexington Ave., 10022,* ☎ *212/355–0100 or 800/367–7701,* FAX *212/308–5166. 92 rooms. Restaurant, bar, meeting room. AE, DC, MC, V.*

$$ ⊞ **Loews New York Hotel.** This moderately priced hotel is lively and fun, attracting visitors from around the globe. Business travelers also find it to their liking. Rooms are comfortable and well designed. Deluxe units (only slightly higher in price than standard) come with such goodies as Godiva chocolates and liquor miniatures. During low-occupancy periods, you can book rooms here for the upper end at less expensive prices; even suites are below $200. ⊠ *Lexington Ave. at 51st St., 10022,* ☎ *212/752–7000,* FAX *212/758–6311. 766 rooms. Restaurant, lounge, health club, meeting rooms. AE, DC, MC, V.*

$$ ⊞ **The Roosevelt.** Practically on top of Grand Central Terminal, this enormous hotel has rooms that are quiet symphonies of beige and green with graceful wood furniture. The squeaky-clean bathrooms are stocked with lush towels and toiletries. The Madison Avenue Lounge and lobby have faded Turkish-style carpets, black-and-white marble tile floors, chandeliers, brocade armchairs, and wrought-iron rails. Both possess a Norma Desmond glamour, which isn't surprising for a dame of the '20s, and a sister of the old, more famous, Biltmore. ⊠ *Madison Ave. at 45th St., 10017,* ☎ *212/661–9600 or 800/223–1870,* FAX *212/687–5064. 1,031 rooms, 57 suites. Restaurant, bar, café, lounge, minibars, meeting rooms. AE, DC, MC, V.*

$$ ⊞ **San Carlos.** This small residential-style property offers basic service, clean modern rooms, and a neighborly atmosphere. Larger suites come with kitchenettes; lone women travelers will feel quite secure here. ⊠ *150 E. 50th St., 10022,* ☎ *212/755–1800 or 800/722–2012. 140 rooms. Restaurant. AE, DC, MC, V.*

$ ⊞ **Pickwick Arms Hotel.** This convenient East Side establishment charges $95 a night for standard doubles and has older singles with shared baths for as little as $45. The marble-clad lobby is often bustling, since this place is routinely booked solid by bargain hunters. Privations you endure to save a buck really start and end with the Lilliputian size of some rooms, all of which are pleasantly if simply furnished. However, the place is well-run and safe, and some rooms and the rooftop garden look over the Manhattan skyline. ⊠ *230 E. 51st St., 10022,* ☎ *212/355–0300 or 800/742–5945,* FAX *212/755–5029. 400 rooms. AE, MC, V.*

$ ⊞ **Vanderbilt YMCA.** Of the various Manhattan Ys offering accommodations, this one has the best location and facilities. Although rooms hold as many as four people, they are little more than dormitory-style cells—you may feel crowded even with only one or two beds to a room. Each room does have a late-model TV, however. There are no private baths; communal showers and toilets are clean. Guests are provided with basics such as towels and soap and good fitness facilities. The Turtle Bay neighborhood is safe, convenient, and interesting (the United Nations is a few blocks away). ⊠ 224 E. 47th St., 10017, ☎ 212/756–9600, FAX 212/752–0210. 430 rooms. Coffee shop, 2 pools, sauna, exercise rooms, gym, indoor-track, coin laundry, meeting rooms. MC, V.

Midtown West

$$$ 🏨 **Le Parker Meridien.** This dramatic, modern, French hotel boasts one of the city's more striking lobbies. Here are two-story arched mirrors with palms and Doric columns, an Islamic-style stained-glass roof, three colors of marble, full-size trees, and a sheer cliff of blond wood at the registration desk. Other standout features are the rooftop swimming pool and comprehensive Club La Raquette fitness center. Upstairs, the rooms are still shipshape, and there is suitably Gallic luxurious Lanvin in the sparkling bathrooms. The service is anything but snooty. ⊠ 118 W. 57th St., 10019, ☎ 212/245–5000 or 800/543–4300, FAX 212/307–1776. 700 rooms. Restaurant, bar, café, pool, health club, nightclub, meeting rooms. AE, DC, MC, V.

$$$ 🏨 **Marriott Marquis.** This giant in the heart of the theater district is one of the places New Yorkers love to hate. It's obvious, brash, and bright. Although it hosts many conventions and groups, more than half its guests are vacationers. As at other Marriotts, the help is ultra-friendly and informative, if not terribly polished. Rooms are *not* the largest in town (though Marriott claims otherwise), but they're large enough. Their color schemes are restful, and their bathrooms perfectly adequate and modern. Some rooms have dramatic urban views. There's a revolving restaurant, the View, on the 46th floor, and a second revolving lounge on the eighth-floor lobby level. ⊠ 1535 Broadway at 45th St., 10036, ☎ 212/398–1900 or 800/843–4898, FAX 212/704–8930. 1,877 rooms. 3 restaurants, café, 3 lounges, health club, theater, business services, meeting rooms. AE, DC, MC, V.

$$$ 🏨 **The Michelangelo.** The Theater District's only true deluxe hotel, having been through several incarnations, is better and friendlier than in the past. A very long, wide, low lobby-lounge caters to Italophiles, with plenty of multihued marble, Vivaldi in the air, and Veronese-esque oil paintings. Upstairs, the rooms are bigger than you'd expect and have either French country decor or a distinctly deco feel (curvy black lacquered or pale oak closets concealing TVs or fitted bar areas in the larger rooms; much chrome and glass). All have king-size beds, multiline phones, and marble bathrooms equipped with bidets, TVs, and phones. The staff is helpful; the concierge is a cut above those found in other New York City hotels. ⊠ 152 W. 51st St., 10019, ☎ 212/765–1900 or 800/237–0990, FAX 212/581–7618. 178 rooms. Restaurant, bar, lounge, health club, meeting rooms. AE, DC, MC, V.

$$$ 🏨 **New York Hilton.** Many consider this the city's premier hotel for professional meetings, large and small. It has a conference center, a business center, and loads of multilingual help. Hilton spends vast sums to keep the hotel trim, and it shows: There's a distinctive landscaped driveway and a sprawling, brassy lobby—more businesslike than beautiful but always buzzing. Considering the size of this property, guest rooms are surprisingly well maintained, if not always spacious or fashionable. All have two telephones, computer hookup, minibar, coffeemaker, hair dryer, and iron/ironing board. If you don't require high levels of personal service or ostentatious elegance, this well-run machine will satisfy. ⊠ 1335 6th Ave., 10019, ☎ 212/586–7000 or 800/445–8667, FAX 212/315–1374. 2,042 rooms. 2 restaurants, café, lounge, sports bar, health club, business center, meeting rooms. AE, DC, MC, V.

$$$ ⊞ **Renaissance.** The former Ramada Renaissance was redone to suit the business community, though vacationers often take advantage of its low off-season rates start and its proximity to Broadway. Elevators lead from street level to the art deco brass and mahogany third-floor lounge-reception area, where service is superfriendly. Rooms have two-line phones (with speaker-phone capability) and marble bathrooms with deep tubs. ⊠ *2 Times Sq., 10036,* ☎ *212/765–7676,* FAX *212/765–1962. 305 rooms, 10 suites. Restaurant, 2 bars, lounge, in-room VCRs, in-room safes, minibars, exercise room, business services, meeting rooms. AE, D, DC, MC, V.*

$$$ ⊞ **The Royalton.** Ian Schrager and the late Steve Rubell's second Man-
★ hattan hotel (Morgan's came first) is a second home to the world's media, music, and fashion biz folk. French designer Philippe Starck—he of the pointy-ended toothbrush and the chrome lemon squeezer on stilts—transformed spaces of intimidating size into a paradise for poseurs, with vividly colored, geometrically challenged but comfy chairs and couches and lots of catwalk-style gliding areas. The bathrooms off the lobby are amalgams of raw slate, brushed steel, and sculpted water (you have to see them to understand that). Rooms are glamorously offbeat, some of them oddly shaped and none too big, but all of them comfortable. The staff here does a good job catering to people who feel it's their lot in life to be waited on. The restaurant, 44, is predictably booked solid by New York–style gurus. ⊠ *44 W. 44th St., 10036,* ☎ *212/869–4400 or 800/635–9013,* FAX *212/869–8965. 170 rooms. Restaurant, bar, lounge, fitness center, library, meeting rooms. AE, DC, MC, V.*

$$ ⊞ **The Algonquin.** This beloved landmark hotel, where the Round Table group of writers and wits once met for lunch, still shelters celebrities, particularly literary types visiting nearby publishing houses or *The New Yorker* magazine offices. Late-night performances continue at the Oak Room. Rooms have Victorian-style fixtures and furnishings; large, firm beds; and such modern conveniences such as computerized phones. The bathrooms are stocked with Caswell-Massey toiletries and the tubs, tiles, and sinks are still—some would say quaintly—old-fashioned. ⊠ *59 W. 44th St., 10036,* ☎ *212/840–6800 or 800/548–0345,* FAX *212/944–1419. 165 rooms. Restaurant, 2 lounges, business services, meeting rooms, free parking on weekends. AE, DC, MC, V.*

$$ ⊞ **The Mansfield.** Built in 1904 as a hotel for well-heeled bachelors, this small hotel is Victorian and clublike. Turn-of-the-century details abound here: from the column-supported coffered ceiling, warm ivory walls, and yellow limestone floor in the lobby to the guest rooms' black marble bathrooms, ebony-stained floors and doors, dark wood venetian blinds, and sleigh beds covered in Belgian all-cotton monogrammed sheets. After the theater, be tempted by the nightly dessert buffet in the lounge. ⊠ *12 W. 44th St., 10036,* ☎ *212/944–60500,* FAX *212/764–4477. 123 rooms, 24 suites. Lounge, concert salon, library. AE, D, DC, MC, V.*

$$ ⊞ **The Shoreham.** This is a miniature, low-attitude version of the Roy-
★ alton—and it's comfortable to boot. Almost everything is metal or metal colored, from perforated steel tables (lit from within and draped in see-through gold organza) to the steel sink and matching beaker in the shiny, tiny bathrooms to the silver-gray carpets. Other touches include black oval night tables with digital gadgetry and a single red rose; and in-room VCRs and CD players. And, darling, those cedar-lined closets are to *die for.* ⊠ *33 W 55th St, 10019,* ☎ *212/247–6700,* FAX *212/765–9741. 84 rooms. Lounge, in-room VCRs and CD players, video and CD library. AE, DC, MC, V.*

$$ ⊞ **The Warwick.** Catercorner from the New York Hilton and well placed for theater and points west, this handsome, cozy classic belongs to a Paris-based chain. The decor is the familiar, comforting hotel version of Regency style, with thick carpets and floral drapes. Amenities include two-line phones, marble bathrooms, and mahogany armoires in surprisingly ample rooms. The lobby-lounge is most inviting, with lots of armchairs, marble floors, a dark green bar, and the huge Tudor murals of the Ciao Europa restaurant. ⊠ *65 W. 54th St.,* ☎ *212/247–2700,* FAX *212/957–8915. 425 rooms, 70 suites. Restaurant, bar, lounge, minibars, meeting rooms. AE, DC, MC, V.*

$ 🏨 **Ameritania.** This converted single-room-occupancy hotel at Broadway and 54th Street is a pleasant choice. Everything about the lobby and the simple rooms is modern and cheerful. Some units have superior baths and amenities. The hotel's proximity to popular nightspots such as the Ritz keep the clientele on the youthful side. ⊠ *1701 Broadway, 10019,* ☎ *212/247–5000,* FAX *212/247–3316. 250 rooms, 12 suites. Restaurant, lounge, exercise room. AE, DC, MC, V.*

$ 🏨 **Hotel Edison.** This offbeat old hotel is a popular budget stop for tour groups from here and abroad. The loan-shark murder scene in *The Godfather* was shot in what is now Sophia's restaurant, and the pink-plaster coffee shop has become a hot place to eavesdrop on show-business gossip. Guest rooms are brighter and fresher than the dark corridors seem to hint. There's no room service, but this part of the Theater District has so many restaurants and delis that it doesn't matter much. The crowd here is perfectly wholesome, so save money on your room and spend the big bucks on theater tickets. ⊠ *228 W. 47th St., 10036,* ☎ *212/840–5000,* FAX *212/596–6850. 1,000 rooms. Restaurant, bar, coffee shop. AE, DC, MC, V.*

$ 🏨 **Hotel Wentworth.** This relatively small prewar hotel is near many theaters, Rockefeller Center, and some of the city's best-known Brazilian restaurants. The lobby is mighty peculiar with its narrow corridor that snakes off for a mile or so around the corner, its school of photorealist cityscape murals, and some rather handsome Art Deco Bakelite lights. The rooms are very plain, but most are well maintained and clean and of a reasonable size, and there's cable TV, direct-dial phones, and mostly new baths. This is a popular stop for South Americans, although you'll see a few U.S. business travelers, too. Single women might find the area eerie at night. ⊠ *59 W. 46th St., 10036,* ☎ *212/719–2300 or 800/223–1900. 250 rooms. AE, DC, MC, V.*

$ 🏨 **The Paramount.** For the forever young and arty, the Paramount is
★   *the* place, completely transformed by the team that owns the Royalton (☞ *above*), and Morgans (☞ *below*). It's so irresistible that it's nearly always full. In the Philippe Starck lobby, a cliff of concrete and a glamorous sweep of staircase lead to a mezzanine gallery of squashy seating, tiny nightclub-style table lamps, and a restaurant—the perfect place to spy on the glitterati below. The staff is welcoming, and there's a perennial scene in the Whiskey Bar off the lobby, which remains packed into the wee hours. Rooms are minute, it's true, but they have wildly patterned covered headboards and conical steel sinks in the bathrooms—all bearing the Starck stamp. ⊠ *235 W. 46th St., 10036,* ☎ *212/764–5500 or 800/225–7474,* FAX *212/354–5237. 610 rooms. 2 restaurants, bar, in-room VCRs, exercise room, business services. AE, DC, MC, V.*

$ 🏨 **Park Savoy.** Follow the mirrored, cherry-wood paneled tunnel directly opposite the Essex House's 58th Street entrance to the Park Savoy's all-purpose registration, information, concierge, and switchboard desk. Of course, there's no bellhop, no room service, no direct-dial phone, no cable channels on the ancient TV, but do you really need all that when your room costs as little as $49 (rates go up to $120) and from it you can smell Central Park, hear Carnegie Hall, and taste the caviar at Petrossian. Room decor is eclectic (William Morris–pattern drapes, wine-color carpet, rock-hard beds, perhaps a print of a little girl in a daisy field, and maybe some peeling paint), but about 20 rooms have fridges, 10 have kitchenettes, and all have adequate closets, clean bathrooms, and more space than rooms in chain hotels that cost twice as much. The staff (OK, the guy at the desk) knows all the guests, and there's a lot of repeat business. ⊠ *158 W. 58th St., 10019,* ☎ *212/245–5755,* FAX *212/765–0668. 96 rooms. AE, MC, V.*

$ ⊞ **Wellington Hotel.** This large, old-fashioned property's main advantages are reasonable prices and a location near Carnegie Hall (both are draws for many budget-conscious Europeans). Rooms are small but clean; baths are serviceable. ⊠ *871 7th Ave. at 55th St., 10019,* ☎ *212/247–3900 or 800/652–1212,* FAX *212/581–1719. 700 rooms. Restaurant, coffee shop, beauty salon. AE, DC, MC, V.*

Central Park South/59th Street

$$$$ ⊞ **Essex House.** The owners, Japan's Nikko Hotels, have done won-
★ ders for this stately Central Park South property. The public areas are Art Deco masterpieces fit for Fred and Ginger. The talented Christian Delouvrier oversees the cuisine, both in the informal Café Botanica, which faces Central Park and resembles a lush prewar English greenhouse, and in the intimate Les Célébrités. Journey's, the hotel's wood-paneled bar, has a working fireplace. Guest rooms resemble those in a splendid English country home, elegant and inviting. Baths are all marble and have double sinks and separate stall showers. The staff is discreet, efficient, and friendly. ⊠ *160 Central Park S (between 6th and 7th Aves.), 10019,* ☎ *212/247–0300,* FAX *212/315–1839. 595 rooms. 2 restaurants, bar, spa, meeting rooms, business services. AE, DC, MC, V.*

$$$$ ⊞ **The Plaza.** Occupying the entire southwest corner of Central Park West and 5th Avenue, with its front-yard fountain and unsurpassed location opposite Central Park and F.A.O. Schwarz, the Plaza is probably the most high-profile of all New York hotels. Donald Trump bought it (in 1988), the fictional Eloise ran riot in it (and her "portrait" adorns the Palm Court), and film upon film has featured it— from *North by Northwest* in the 1950s and *Breakfast at Tiffany's* and *Barefoot in the Park* in the 1960s, through the 1971 *Plaza Suite,* and the more recent *Sleepless in Seattle, Scent of a Woman,* and *Home Alone 2.* And does the institution live up to the hype? Reports are good. Furnishings, though still hotel-like in most units, are of high quality. Bathrooms have fluffy towels and toiletries. An advantage here is the size of guest rooms—only a handful of other classic properties can offer similar spaciousness in nearly all accommodations. One thing's for sure: Even if it's your first time in New York, a quick nip at the dimly lit Oak Bar or a stroll by the fin-de-siècle Palm Court will make you feel part of what makes the city tick. ⊠ *5th Ave. at 59th St., 10019,* ☎ *212/759–3000 or 800/228–3000,* FAX *212/546–5324. 807 rooms. 3 restaurants, 2 bars, café, meeting rooms. AE, DC, MC, V.*

$$$$ ⊞ **Ritz-Carlton.** This property—once hot, then lukewarm—is now
★ back up there in the panoply of Manhattan grands, re-infused with the glamour of the name of Ritz-Carlton. Guest rooms are graced with rich brocades, polished woods, and marble bathrooms. The rooms with Central Park views are preferable, but all accommodations are identical in decor and amenities. The staff is friendly and helpful. ⊠ *112 Central Park S, 10019,* ☎ *212/757–1900 or 800/241–3333,* FAX *212/757–9620. 196 rooms. Restaurant, bar, health club, concierge floor, meeting rooms. AE, DC, MC, V.*

Upper East Side

$$$$ ⊞ **The Carlyle.** The Museum Mile and the tony boutiques of Madison
★ Avenue are on the doorstep of New York's least hysterical grand hotel,

where European tradition and Manhattan swank shake hands. The mood is English manor house. Baths, though more subdued than others in town, are marble and chock-full of de rigueur amenities. Most visitors have heard about the Café Carlyle, where performers such as Bobby Short and Barbara Cook entertain. But the hotel also contains the charming Bemelmans Bar, named after Ludwig Bemelmans, illustrator of the beloved children's book character Madeline and the "twelve little girls in two straight lines"; he created the murals here. There's a jewel of a fitness center that is ultraprivate and luxurious. This is one of the few grand hotels where friendliness and old-school elegance really mix; you don't have to be famous to get a smile or good treatment. The concierge and housekeeping service are exceptional. ⊠ *35 E. 76th St., 10021,* ☎ *212/744–1600,* ℻ *212/717–4682. 190 rooms. Restaurant, bar, café, lounge, kitchenettes and pantries in larger units, health club, meeting rooms. AE, DC, MC, V.*

$$$$ ▦ **The Lowell.** If only we all had rich uncles who would spoil us like this hotel. You may be tempted to curl up all day in the elegant guest rooms, gazing at Chinese porcelains, antiques, and original prints or warming yourself by the working fireplace. More than half the rooms are suites; all have furnished terraces overlooking Park Avenue. Bathrooms are marble with shiny brass hardware; beds have Scandinavian down comforters and king-size feather pillows; and minibars are stocked with gourmet snacks. There's even a suite with its own gym. The Pembroke Room, on the second floor, serves a fine high tea, breakfast, and weekend brunch. ⊠ *28 E. 63rd St., 10021,* ☎ *212/838–1400 or 800/221–4444,* ℻ *212/838–9194. 65 rooms. 2 restaurants, kitchenettes in 56 rooms, minibars, in-room VCRs, health club, concierge. AE, DC, MC, V.*

$$$$ ▦ **The Mark.** You'll find this friendly baby grand hotel a block north
★ of the Carlyle and steps from Central Park. The feeling of calm that pervades the Biedermeier-furnished marble lobby follows you into the deep-green and burgundy bar, where even lone women travelers feel comfortable. The serenity continues at Mark's Restaurant (☞ Chapter 6), where afternoon tea is an institution. Bedrooms are cozy and cosseting, with creamy walls, museum-quality prints, plump armchairs, a potted palm or two, and Belgian bed linens. The Italian black-and-white marble bathrooms have oversize tubs. You may recall the Mark's 15 minutes of infamy in fall 1994, when actor Johnny Depp deconstructed his suite and was arrested. You will not normally encounter this behavior here. ⊠ *25 E. 77th St., 10021,* ☎ *212/744–4300 or 800/843–6275,* ℻ *212/744–2749. 180 rooms. Restaurant, café, lounge, in-room VCRs, health club, meeting rooms. AE, DC, MC, V.*

$$$$ ▦ **Mayfair Hotel.** Managing director Dario Mariotti adds a cheery Italian influence and general manager Michael Blackman an oh-so-civilized Britannic charm to this low-key, gracious hotel. Locals know it for its traditional tea lounge. Even the smallest rooms have marble baths and traditional-style, peach-tone decor with extras such as four-line telephones (with free local calls) and outlets to accommodate portable computers and fax machines. While it may not appear as glitzy as other hotels in this price category, the Mayfair more than makes up for its slightly lived-in feel (which many guests, incidentally, prefer) with friendliness and a lively atmosphere. ⊠ *610 Park Ave., 10021,* ☎ *212/288–0800 or 800/223–0542,* ℻ *212/737–0538. 200 rooms. Restaurant, lounge, meeting rooms. AE, DC, MC, V.*

$$$$ ▦ **The Pierre.** Before Canada's Four Seasons hotel group opened its eponymous flagship on 57th Street, the Pierre was its pride and joy, and it remains a high-profile presence. Quite the opposite of the understated Four Seasons, the Pierre owes a lot to the Palace of Versailles, with its chandeliers and handmade carpets, murals depicting putti, and

Corinthian columns in the Rotunda lounge (great for tea), and much muted damask and mahogany in the rooms. Diners who love dancing cheek-to-cheek between courses can do so in the elegant Cafe Pierre. The hotel manages not to be ostentatious or stuffy, though, and the staff conveys a sense of fun about working in these posh surroundings. ⊠ *5th Ave. at 61st St., 10021,* ☎ *212/838–8000 or 800/332–3442,* FAX *212/940–8109. 202 rooms. Restaurant, bar, tea shop, laundry service, meeting rooms. AE, DC, MC, V.*

$$$$ 🏨 **Plaza Athénée.** The French half of Forte Hotels' New York offerings used to be snooty to noncelebrities, but much of that has changed. What hasn't changed is the quiet elegance of the guest rooms and marble baths. Even small rooms are well thought out, if not opulent, in soothing hues of beige and coral, with French-style mahogany furniture. Walls are covered in fabric, with drapery and bedspreads of hand-printed silks. ⊠ *37 E. 64th St.,* ☎ *212/734–9100 or 800/225–5843,* FAX *212/772–0958. 153 rooms. Restaurant, bar, meeting rooms. AE, DC, MC, V.*

$$$$ 🏨 **The Westbury.** The English half of Forte's Exclusive Hotels' New York empire combines understated British formality with genuine friendliness. Sedate and comfortable, it delivers good service. Rooms and suites are decorated in either masculine "hunt-motif" fabrics or with the more demure traditional English chintz. Some units, though elegant, are small; all baths are less than spacious. Still, all the rooms have luxurious fittings and amenities. ⊠ *69th St. at Madison Ave., 10021,* ☎ *212/535–2000 or 800/321–1569,* FAX *212/535–5058. 235 rooms. Restaurant, lounge, health club, meeting rooms. AE, DC, MC, V.*

$$ 🏨 **The Franklin.** It's "like sleeping in an art installation." This former seedy, low-rent hostel was transformed into its current incarnation as a ravishing, funky, uptown version of the Paramount. The lobby feels like a private club, with black granite, brushed steel, and cherry-wood decor. Rooms can be very, very small (some measuring 11 feet square), but they have pleasant violet carpeting, custom-built steel furniture, and gauzy white canopies over the beds. Bathrooms feature restored cast-iron tubs with amazing hand-held adjustable-force showerheads and stainless-steel sinks set in black granite. ⊠ *164 E. 87th St, 10128,* ☎ *212/369–1000 or 800/428–5252,* FAX *212/369–8000. 53 rooms. Breakfast lounge. AE, D, DC, MC, V.*

$$ 🏨 **Hotel Wales.** This Madison Avenue landmark between 93rd and 94th streets has been lovingly restored to its original, turn-of-the-century ambience from the burgundy striped lobby with its glittering crystal chandelier to the cozy, somewhat small rooms done in soft greens and pinks with oak woodwork and fireplaces. It's folksy, with families and older couples in Birkenstocks, boat shoes, and Lands' End duds, all the better for strolling to the many nearby museums. Guests also enjoy complimentary Continental breakfast. ⊠ *1295 Madison Ave., 10128,* ☎ *212/876–6000 or 800/428–5252,* FAX *212/860–7000. 92 rooms, 5 suites. Restaurant, lounge. AE, D, DC, MC, V.*

Upper West Side

$$ 🏨 **Mayflower.** Step under the green awning into the long, low, wood-
★ paneled lobby—with its leather chesterfields, plants in Asian pots, and gilt-framed oils of tall ships and flowers—take an apple from the basket on the registration desk, and feel truly welcomed to New York. Such is the charm of this venerable hotel on Central Park. Rooms are spacious for midtown, with either two queens or a king-size bed, and most include walk-in pantries with a fridge and sink. Spend an extra $20 for a heartbreakingly spectacular park view. Some rooms feature ultrathick carpeting, fruit-and-flower-print drapes, Regency striped

upholstery, dark wood Colonial-style furniture, and bathrooms done in ivory tile with pink or blue borders. ⊠ *15 Central Park W, 10023,* ☎ *212/265–0060 or 800/223–4164,* FAX *212/265–2026. 365 rooms, 6 suites. Restaurant, bar, exercise room. AE, D, DC, MC, V.*

$$ 🔟 **Radisson Empire Hotel.** The Empire's English country–style lobby is warm and inviting; halls are decorated in soft pastel pink and peach with elegant lamps. Rooms and suites are small, but nicely furnished; special room features include high-tech electronics, and the small but immaculate baths have heated towel racks. New Yorkers in the know frequent the cozy second-floor lounge. This hotel is one of the city's better buys and you can't beat its location across from Lincoln Center. ⊠ *Broadway at 63rd St., 10023,* ☎ *212/265–7400, 800/333–3333,* FAX *212/315–0349. 373 rooms. Restaurant. AE, DC, MC, V.*

$ 🔟 **The Excelsior.** The Excelsior is like one of those faded atmospheric hotels you often find on Parisian backstreets, except that it's in a prime New York location: directly across from the American Museum of Natural History. It faded in exactly the right way, with its cranberry carpet, oak paneling, and collection of clocks showing international time in the lobby. Would that the bedrooms retained such warm color schemes instead of the floor-to-ceiling icy blues, made colder still by the harsh light of electricity-saving bulbs (a room at the front with a park view will offset the chill). Room decor aside, you can't beat the great staff, great neighborhood, and great rates. ⊠ *45 W. 81st St., 10024,* ☎ *212/362–9200 or 800/368–4575,* FAX *212/721–2994. 155 rooms. Coffee shop, kitchenettes in suites. AE, DC, MC, V.*

$ 🔟 **Hotel Beacon.** Three blocks from both Central Park and Lincoln Cen-
★ ter, this exquisite hotel lays on many features it needn't have bothered with, but did anyway. The large rooms and the suites (which cost only $35 more and just bust the $ category) have kitchenettes with coffeemakers, full-size fridges and stoves. The closets are huge; the dark-wood furniture is elegant, and the bathrooms come complete with Hollywood dressing room–style mirrors. You get voice mail on your phone, of which there are two in the suites, as well as two TVs. There is no restaurant or bar, but with so much in the neighborhood, this isn't a problem. Nor does it matter that the only lounge is the tony gold-ceilinged, marble-floored lobby—not when the rooms are so comfortable. ⊠ *2130 Broadway at 75th St., 10023,* ☎ *212/787–1100 or 800/572–4969,* FAX *212/724–0839. 178 rooms. AE, DC, MC, V.*

$ 🔟 **The Milburn.** A mere block from the Hotel Beacon, and convenient
★ to Lincoln Center, Central Park, and Zabar's, this friendly suite hotel is popular with families, artists performing in the neighborhood, and Europeans. Could this be because the lobby looks like a small Bavarian castle with salmon pink walls, black-and-white marble floor, heraldic doodads, and abundant gilt? No, it's probably because of the homey, spacious rooms with kitchenettes equipped with, among other things, a microwave and a coffeemaker. The decor used to be a chaotic but cozy assemblage of, say, burgundy carpet and blue drapes, a glass-top brass table, and framed posters on pink floral walls. A recent installation of matching dark wood furniture, however, has successfully pulled together the decor. Room service you won't find; speed dialing to nearby Chinese and Mexican restaurants you will. ⊠ *242 W. 76th St., 10023,* ☎ *212/362–1006 or 800/833–9622,* FAX *212/721–5476. 89 suites. Kitchenettes, laundry service. AE, DC, MC, V.*

Murray Hill, Gramercy Park, Greenwich Village

$$$ 🔟 **Doral Court, Doral Park Avenue,** and **Doral Tuscany.** These three sis-
★ ters are not only near neighbors in off-the-tourist-map, peaceful Murray Hill, but they allow guests of each to sign for food and drinks at

the others' facilities. Which to choose? All have the feel of a small European hotel: The Park Avenue has amusing neoclassical follies mixed with '20s Art Deco, while the other two have a more sober, wood-paneled, country house decor. The Tuscany is the priciest ($20–$30 a night more than the others), and its rooms have entrance halls, Italian marble baths, dressing rooms with a sink, walk-in closets, and three phones. At the Court, you forego the marble and dress in a mere alcove. At the bargain Park Avenue, the rooms lack a dressing area, but your bathroom is done in marble. ⊠ *Doral Court, 130 E. 39th St., 10016,* ☎ *212/685–1100 or 800/223–6725,* FAX *212/779–0148. 199 rooms. Doral Park Avenue, 70 Park Ave. at 38th St., 10016,* ☎ *212/687–7050 or 800/223–6725,* FAX *212/779–0148. 202 rooms. Doral Tuscany, 120 E. 39th St., 10016,* ☎ *212/686–1600 or 800/223–6725,* FAX *212/779–0148. 121 rooms. Combined: 4 restaurants, 2 bars, health club, meeting rooms. AE, DC, MC, V.*

$$ ▥ **Morgans.** The first hotel in nightclub mavens Ian Schrager and the
★ late Steve Rubell's triumphant triumvirate is the perfect place to stay if you want privacy or you care deeply about style. There's no sign outside, which is a turn-on for many guests, some of them famous. The stunning rooms, created by André Putman, are less wacky than those at the Starck-designed Royalton (☞ *above*) and Paramount (☞ *above*), but from the speckled walls to the window-seat cushions, from the built-in-closet doors to the specially commissioned Mapplethorpe photographs, everything is in black, white, and all shades in between. The exquisite, tiny bathrooms have tile patterns reminiscent of Checker cabs, crystal shower doors, brushed-steel sinks, and Kiehl's toiletries. There's a complimentary breakfast buffet. ⊠ *237 Madison Ave., 10016,* ☎ *212/686–0300,* FAX *212/779–8352. 112 rooms. Breakfast room. AE, DC, MC, V.*

$$ ▥ **Manhattan East Suite Hotels.** These nine midtown properties combine full hotel service with independent pied-à-terre living. They vary in character and price, though all nearly top the $$ category in busy seasons. Best bets are **Beekman Tower** (⊠ 3 Mitchell Pl.), near the United Nations; **Dumont Plaza** (⊠ 150 E. 34th St.); **Surrey Hotel** (⊠ 20 E. 76th St.), which is close to Madison Avenue and borders on truly elegant; **Southgate Tower** (⊠ 371 7th Ave.), which is attractive and secure, is near Madison Square Garden, and has the lowest rates; and **Eastgate Tower** (⊠ 222 E. 39th St.), which has the second-lowest rates. Except for the modern Dumont and the Art Deco Beekman Tower, all have traditional guest-room decor. Most accommodations have completely equipped pantries; larger units have dining areas with full-size tables. Except for the **Shelburne** (⊠ 303 Lexington Ave.), the other hotels in this group are residential with low rates for long stays. The Beekman, Surrey, Shelburne, and Dumont Plaza have restaurants. The Dumont, Southgate, and Shelburne have on-site fitness centers. The older hotels in the group have some disappointing rooms, but overall these properties are outstanding for convenience, location, and space. ⊠ *Sales office, 500 W. 37th St., 10018,* ☎ *212/465–3600 or 800/637–8483,* FAX *212/465–3663. AE, DC, MC, V.*

$ ▥ **Carlton Arms.** It isn't arty, it's art—every wall, ceiling, and other surface is engulfed by murals, commissioned over the years by the hip, friendly managers. They themselves are immortalized on the lobby corridor wall, with the legend: IF YOU THINK IT'S BETTER TO HAVE PARTY THAN NOTHING, YOU WORK HERE. The youthful guests do sometimes "have party," so it can be noisy. But the Carlton Arms is clean, though you'll probably overlook this fact owing to the paintings of roses and auto accidents in cobalt blue by G. Dominguez (Room 4A), the 1987 sunset-colored nudes (Room 11A), or the psychedelic religious symbolism and aquarium bedspread in Room 8A. More recent artistic expressions include the Versailles Room (5A) by Fabian Compton, an outré symphony of faux marble, red walls, classical statues, and gilt cherubs; and the Cow Spot Room (3C) by Heinz Burkhardt, where a Holstein-motif dapples rugs, bedspreads, and walls. Rooms have double-glazed windows but are phoneless, TV-less, almost free of furniture, and sometimes bathless (these start at $44, with a further 10% if you're a student or you book for seven nights). But that's hardly the point. ⊠ *160 E. 25th St., 10010,* ☎ *212/684–8337 or 212/679– 0680 for reservations. 54 rooms. Fans. MC, V.*

$ ⬚ **The Gershwin.** Interclub, the small-scale hoteliers who can see into
★ the soul of the hip backpacker, have packed 'em in at West Coast arts-oriented youth havens for years, and its new East Coast establishment—in a converted 13-story Greek Revival—is ripening nicely. Enter, and be visually assaulted by a giant primary-colored cartoony sculpture, one of many works by house artist, Brad Howe. He also did the little winged light boxes above the bedroom doors, and the faux Lichtensteins by the reception desk (that's a real de Koonig behind it, and there is a real Lichtenstein in the cafeteria). Rooms are all painted in custard yellow and apple green, somewhat crumbly in places, with new (albeit thin) carpets, big closets and venetian blinds. Superior rooms have great Mondrian-style mosaic tiling and possibly a desk, a mural, and great cross-ventilation (important in summer, since there's no air-conditioning). Most dormitories have only four beds and a remarkable $20 rate. You won't be spending much time in your room, however, because of all the activities here: rooftop barbecues, monthly theme parties, and the like. The neighborhood, which is close to Gramercy Park and also Little India, is safe enough to write home about, yet funky enough for fun. ⊠ *7 E. 27th St., 10016,* ☎ *212/545–8000,* ℻ *212/684–5546. 160 rooms. Restaurant, bar, lounge. MC, V.*

$ ⬚ **Gramercy Park.** The terra-cotta-color, Queen Anne–style hotel is al-
★ most the only one in this elegant neighborhood, which boasts the city's least-populated park. The park remains thus because it's locked, but hotel guests can use it. Further advantages to staying here include more peace and quiet than is usual, and a bar straight out of a Cole Porter lyric, with pianist, hot hors d'oeuvres (at happy hour only), and wicked martinis. This hotel holds an annual art fair, a unique event during which guest rooms are turned into minigalleries displaying the work of contemporary artists. Though the rooms are above average for hotels in this price range, don't expect too much from them. ⊠ *2 Lexington Ave., 10010,* ☎ *212/475–4320,* ℻ *212/505–0535. 357 rooms. Bar, lounge. AE, D, DC, MC, V.*

$ ⬚ **Jolly Madison Towers.** Who could resist that name? Actually, it refers not to the ambience here but to the Italian chain that owns the hotel. Prices are reasonable for this tony neighborhood, and the decor, service, and facilities are unobjectionable if unspectacular. Rooms are small but handsome in deep sapphire and dove gray, with dark-wood headboards and desks; king-size beds in the higher priced rooms, queen-size elsewhere. Bathrooms are tiny, with marbleized vanities and white tiles around compact tubs. ⊠ *22 E. 38th St., 10016,* ☎ *212/802–0600,* ℻ *212/447– 0747. 225 rooms. Restaurant, bar, health club. AE, DC, MC, V.*

$ ⬚ **Washington Square Hotel.** This cozy Greenwich Village hotel has a true European feel and style, from the wrought iron and gleaming brass in the small, elegant lobby to the personal attention given by the staff. Rooms and baths are simple but pleasant and well-maintained. Continental breakfast is included in the room rate. There's also a good, reasonably priced restaurant, C3 (☞ Chapter 6). The manager has strong ties to the local jazz community and enjoys providing tips about catching a set at the nearby Blue Note. ⊠ *103 Waverly Pl., 10011,*

☎ *212/777–9515 or 800/222–0418,* FAX *212/979–8373. 160 rooms. Restaurant, bar, lounge. AE, DC, MC, V.*

Lower Manhattan

$$$$ 🏨 **Millenium Hilton.** This sleek black monolith is the class act of downtown, outdoing the elegance of both the Marriott and the Vista. The modern rooms and suites are decorated in beige tones with wood accents. Higher floors have delightful views of landmark buildings and both the Hudson and the East rivers. The health club has an attractive pool with windows that look out on St. Paul's Church. ⊠ *55 Church St., 10007,* ☎ *212/693–2001,* FAX *212/571–2317. 561 rooms. 2 restaurants, bar, pool, health club, business services, meeting rooms. AE, DC, M, V.*

$$$ 🏨 **New York Vista.** When it opened 12 years ago, the Vista was the first major lower Manhattan hotel. Now the West Street Marriott and the classy Millenium have joined it, but the Vista is well up to its newer neighbors. The fabulous skylit lobby has a contemporary green-granite and marble entrance, a grand curved staircase, and a fountain. ⊠ *3 World Trade Center, 10048,* ☎ *212/938–9100,* FAX *212/321–2107. 820 rooms. 2 restaurants, 2 lounges, pool, health club, indoor track, meeting rooms, free parking with weekend packages. AE, DC, MC, V.*

$$ 🏨 **Best Western Seaport Inn.** This thoroughly pleasant, restored 19th-century building is one block from the waterfront—close to South Street Seaport. The decor is between that of a Colonial sea captain's house and that of a chain hotel. The reasonably priced rooms have dark wood, white walls, and floral nylon bedcovers. There's a fine view of Brooklyn Bridge from rooms on the fifth and sixth floors facing Front Street. ⊠ *33 Peck Slip, 10038,* ☎ *212/766–6600 or 800/468–3569,* FAX *212/766–6615. 65 rooms. AE, DC, MC, V.*

Airport

$$$ 🏨 **LaGuardia Marriott Airport Hotel.** A quarter-mile from the airport and—barring traffic—about 20 minutes from Manhattan, this hotel is out of the direct line of most flights. ⊠ *102–05 Ditmars Blvd., East Elmhurst, 11369,* ☎ *718/565–8900 or 800/228–9290,* FAX *718/899–0764. 436 rooms, 3 suites. AE, D, DC, MC, V.*

$$ 🏨 **Newark Airport Marriott.** The Marriott is right on airport premises and provides free 24-hour shuttle service to all terminals; it's only 20 minutes, in light traffic, from Manhattan. Triple-glazed glass doors keep noise to a minimum. ⊠ *Newark International Airport, Newark, NJ 07114,* ☎ *623–0006 or 800/882–1037,* FAX *201/623–7618. 590 rooms, 6 suites. 2 restaurants, 2 lounges, indoor-outdoor pool, hot tub, sauna. AE, D, DC, MC, V.*

$$ 🏨 **Travelodge Hotel.** This is the only hotel on the grounds of the John F. Kennedy International Airport that has free 24-hour shuttle service to all terminals. Considering its proximity to air traffic, it is surprisingly quiet. ⊠ *Kennedy Airport, Queens NY 11430-1613,* ☎ *718/995–9000,* FAX *718/995–9075. 475 rooms. Restaurant, lounge, meeting rooms. AE, D, DC, MC, V.*

Bed-and-Breakfasts

Hundreds of bed-and-breakfast rooms are available in Manhattan and the other boroughs, principally Brooklyn. B&Bs often cost well below $100 a night, though there is also the type with its own kitchen, washer-dryer, whirlpool, and sauna in somebody's priceless brownstone for double or triple that (the price of a room at the Waldorf). But accommodations, amenities, service, and privacy may fall short of what you get in hotels. Sometimes you really do get breakfast, and sometimes you don't. And you usually can't pay by credit card.

A few reservation agencies book B&B accommodations in and near Manhattan. There is no fee for the service, but they advise you to make reservations as far in advance as possible.

Abode Bed and Breakfasts Ltd. (✉ Box 20022, 10128, ☎ 212/472–2000).

Bed and Breakfast Network of New York (✉ 134 W. 32nd St., Suite 602, 10001, ☎ 212/645–8134).

Inn New York (✉ 266 W. 71st St., 10023, ☎ 212/580–1900, FAX 212/580–4437). Unhosted brownstone apartments.

Manhattan Home Stays (✉ Box 20684, Cherokee Station, 10021, ☎ 212/737–3868, FAX 212/265–3561). B&B accommodations and unhosted apartments.

New World Bed and Breakfast (✉ 150 5th Ave., Suite 711, 10011, ☎ 212/675–5600 or 800/443–3800 in the U.S., FAX 212/675–6366).

Urban Ventures (✉ Box 426, 10024, and 38 W. 32nd St, 10001, ☎ 212/594–5650, same phone for both locations, FAX 212/947–9320).

8 Nightlife

*New York has been described as the
city that never sleeps. Its late hours
hold enough delights and diversions to
please the most discerning night owl.
In the same evening you can head for a
classic West Village jazz haunt, a sleek
TriBeCa bar packed with celebrities, a
sophisticated uptown cabaret like the
Café Carlyle, or a grungy East Village
club where you can hip-hop 'til you
drop. Whether your musical tastes are
loud rock, Brazilian beat, blues, or
bluegrass, you can find it somewhere in
Manhattan. Or laugh the night away at
a comedy club.*

OKAY, SO YOU'VE TAKEN THE STATEN ISLAND
ferry, you've lunched at the Plaza, visited the
Met. But don't tuck yourself in just yet. Get
yourself truly attuned to the Big Apple's schedule, which runs more
by New York nocturnal than by eastern standard time. Even if you're
not a night owl by habit, it's worth staying up late at least once, because by night, Manhattan takes on a whole new identity.

Revised by
Andrea Coller

CLUBS AND ENTERTAINMENT

New York nightlife really started to swing in 1914, when a pair of ballroom dancers, Florence and Maurice Walton, took over management
of the Parisian Room, in what is today's Theater District. At Chez Maurice, as their new club was called, the city's café society learned a sen-
sual dance at Tango Teas. Then came the Harlem Renaissance of the
1920s and '30s, and the New York jazz scene shifted north of 110th
Street. In the 1950s, nightspots mushroomed in Greenwich Village and
the East 50s. Along 52nd Street in those years, recalls columnist Pete
Hamill, "you could walk down a single block and hear Art Tatum, Billie Holiday, and Charlie Parker. And you could go to the Latin Quarter and see girls running around with bananas on their heads."

Well, fruit as headgear is out, but night-owling in the look of the moment never will be, and the current nightclub scene is probably more
varied and vital than ever before. It has moved downtown—along with
just about everything else—to drab-by-day East Village dives that
come alive nightly, to classic jazz joints in the West Village, to sleekly
decorated TriBeCa see-and-be-seen traps, and to preppy hangouts
around Wall Street.

There are enough dedicated club-hoppers here to support nightspots
for almost every idiosyncratic taste. But keep in mind that *when* you
go is just as important as where you go in clubland. These days night
prowlers are more loyal to floating parties, DJs, even party promot-
ers, than they are to addresses. A spot is only hot when it's hopping,
and you may find the same club or bar that raged last night completely
empty tonight.

Style can be a tricky issue. An appropriate costume for a night on the
town could include striped platform sneakers, an Armani coat, a Ba-
lenciaga gown—anything from pearls, to chains and leather, to a hip-
hugger rubber mini and belly-button pierced earring. Fortunately,
Velvet Rope Syndrome—that is, gimlet-eyed bouncers arbitrarily pick-
ing and choosing the "right" clientele at the door—has largely gone
the way of the big-money '80s. The atmosphere now is looser and more
accepting. So even if you do wind up wearing the wrong shoes, you
probably won't be left standing out in the cold in them.

For the tattooed and pierced, *Paper* magazine's "P.M. 'Til Dawn" and
bar sections have as good a listing as exists of the roving clubs and the
best of the fashionable crowd's hangouts. *Time Out New York* offers
a comprehensive weekly listing of amusements by category. The more
staid Friday *New York Times*'s "Weekend" section carries a "Sounds
Around Town" column that can clue you in to what's in the air, as can
the *Village Voice*, which probably has more nightclub ads than any other
rag in the world. Or stop by Tower Records (✉ Broadway and E. 4th
St., ☎ 212/505–1500; Broadway and W. 73rd St., ☎ 212/799–2500),
where flyers about coming events and club passes are stacked in the
entry. You may also get good tips from a suitably au courant hotel

concierge. Just remember that what's hot and what's not changes almost weekly. We've tried to give you a rounded sample of reliable hangouts—but clubs have the life span of the tsetse fly, so phone ahead to make sure your target nightspot hasn't closed or turned into a polka hall. Most charge a cover which can range from $2 to $25 or more depending on the club and the night. Take cash, because many places don't accept plastic.

Putting on the Ritz

You are wearing Oscar de la Renta and Armani, your transport is a white stretch limo, and you've just come from dinner at Lutèce. Just remember to hide this guidebook so people won't guess that you're not regulars.

The Carlyle (⊠ 35 E. 76th St., ☎ 212/744–1600). The hotel's discreetly sophisticated Café Carlyle is where Bobby Short plays when he's in town; otherwise, you might find Barbara Cook or Eartha Kitt purring by a piano. Bemelmans Bar, with murals by the author of the Madeline books, regularly stars pianist Peter Mintun.

Oak Room (⊠ Algonquin Hotel, 59 W. 44th St., ☎ 212/840–6800). You'll hear that the Algonquin has faded, but this room still offers yesteryear's charms. Just head straight for the long, narrow club-cum-watering hole; you might find the hopelessly romantic singer Andrea Marcovicci, or pianist Steve Ross playing Berlin or Porter.

Rainbow Room and **Rainbow & Stars** (⊠ 30 Rockefeller Plaza, ☎ 212/632–5000). You can find two kinds of heaven high up on Rockefeller Center's 65th floor. The Rainbow Room serves dinner (☞ Chapter 6) and dancing to the strains of a live orchestra, and occupies a floor right out of an Astaire-Rogers musical. At the intimate Rainbow & Stars, classy singers such as Maureen McGovern and Rosemary Clooney entertain, backlit by twinkling city lights.

Supper Club (⊠ 240 W. 47th St., ☎ 212/921–1940). Note the last four digits of the telephone number. This huge, prix-fixe dinner-and-dancing club specializes in cheek-to-cheek big band sounds on Friday and Saturday nights, complete with a full orchestra.

Clubbing

The city's busiest clubs are as much places to bump and grind as to see and be seen. Revelers come to socialize, to find romance, to scream business deals over the music, to show off their glad rags, or to be photographed rubbing shoulders with stars. Some are cavernous spaces filled with throbbing music and writhing bodies. Others are clubs in a different sense, like parties thrown by a mutual friend for people who don't know one another; comers are drawn by a common interest, a likeness of spirit, that can be created almost anyplace. The venues mentioned below are dance clubs, but parties—with or without dancing—with DJs and themes ranging from '60s bossa nova nights to soul-and-drag galas have been known to crop up at places like **Circa** and **XVI** (☞ Watering Holes, *below*), and **Irving Plaza** and **Coney Island High** (☞ Rock Your World, *below*). So read some rags and make some calls.

Delia's Supper Club (⊠ 197 E. 3rd St., ☎ 212/254–9184). They serve a terrific prix-fixe dinner here on Friday and Saturday nights, but after 11 or so, the chairs are pushed back to create a tiny yet happening dance floor for the cool but not unbearably hip East Village crowd.

Expo (⊠ 124 W. 43rd St., ☎ 212/819–0377). Standing where Xenon, the legendary disco, dominated in the '70s, revelers dance among decorations from the 1939 World's Fair. Spotted: Sylvester Stallone, Traci Lords, and Sandra Bullock, among others.

Le Bar Bat (✉ 311 W. 57th St., ☎ 212/307–7228). This bamboo-en-crusted, multitiered monster of a club fits right in with the Planet Hollywoods on 57th Street's Theme Restaurant Row, but a flashy good time can be had here among the Euro and prepster poseurs.

Limelight (✉ 660 6th Ave., ☎ 212/807–7850). Affectionately known as "Slimelight," this transformed Chelsea church (complete with stained glass, spiral staircases, and catwalks) hosts the gamut of New York club culture, with "alternative" and heavy-metal nights.

Nell's (✉ 246 W. 14th St., ☎ 212/675–1567). Back in vogue, Nell Campbell (of *Rocky Horror* fame) reintroduced sophistication to nightlife with her club. The tone in the upstairs live-music jazz salon is Victorian; downstairs is for tête-à-têtes and dancing to a DJ. The boîte opens at 10 PM and closes at 4 AM nightly.

Palladium (✉ 126 E. 14th St., ☎ 212/473–7171). A native New Yorker hasn't crossed its threshold in years, but it's still a hoot with the suburban bridge-and-tunnel set.

Robots (✉ 25 Ave. B, ☎ 212/995–0968). So it's 3 AM on a Saturday night, and you're all tanked up with no place to go. Stop in at Robots, where the absence of alcohol permits patrons to party all night long. (Yes, it's true, even in the city that never sleeps, bars close at 4 AM.) Work off that buzz to hip hop on the dance floor, or nod off in the upstairs lounge 'til 8 AM—when the club starts serving liquor again.

Roseland (✉ 239 W. 52nd St., ☎ 212/247–0200). This famous old ballroom-dance floor is still open for ballroom dancing from Thursday to Sunday; come and swing to the big bands.

Roxy (✉ 515 W. 18th St., ☎ 212/645–5156). Roller disco on Tuesday and Wednesday nights, dance club Friday and Saturday, this huge hall is gay-centric on Tuesday and Saturday nights, and draws a mixed rave crowd on others.

Sound Factory Bar (✉ 12 W. 21st St., ☎ 212/206–7770). This smaller but still frenetic version of its defunct cousin on 27th Street is into specialized nights (e.g., Industry night, Gay Latin night), but if you call you're sure to find one that suits your style.

Tatou (✉ 151 E. 50th St., ☎ 212/753–1144). This pleasing addition to the supper-club scene offers dinner, dancing, and cabaret under one stylish roof.

Webster Hall (✉ 125 E. 11th St., ☎ 212/353–1600). This fave among NYU students and similar species boasts four floors and five eras of music. Go for the live bands on Thursday, dance DJs on Friday and Saturday—or the trapeze artists any night.

Jazz Notes

Jazz players always come home to Manhattan. Somehow, the city evokes their sound. Greenwich Village is still the mecca, with more than 12 jazz nightclubs, although plenty of others are strewn around town.

Arthur's Tavern (✉ 57 Grove St., ☎ 212/675–6879). The place starts to cook late (say 1 or 2 AM) and eschews all fancy trappings. It offers jazz and blues on the steamy side (Dixieland on Sunday and Monday) until 4 AM.

Birdland (✉ 2745 Broadway, ☎ 212/749–2228). Although way up on the West Side (at 105th St.), this spot is still close to the Village at heart. You'll find lots of up-and-coming groups here—plus dinner.

Blue Note (✉ 131 W. 3rd St., ☎ 212/475–8592). This club is considered by many to be the jazz capital of the world. Just an average week could bring Spyro Gyra, the Modern Jazz Quartet, and Jon Hendricks. Expect a steep music charge, except on Monday, when $7.50 will buy you a ticket to the club's New Artists Night.

Bradley's (⌧ 70 University Pl., ☎ 212/228–6440). With mood lighting and, generally, trios or quartets, this vintage club attracts serious fans of jazz.

Cajun (⌧ 129 8th Ave., ☎ 212/691–6174).This landlocked Chelsea restaurant with a riverboat feel dishes New Orleans–style jazz alongside Cajun-Creole grub. Live music from the likes of former Louis Armstrong clarinetist Joe Muranyi will make you feel like you've ducked in off of Bourbon Street.

Five Spot (⌧ 4 W. 31st St., ☎ 212/631–0100). This three-year-old jazz club features new and established musicians in a sleek restaurant setting. The menu, at press time, was Continental with "limited Japanese."

Knitting Factory (⌧ 74 Leonard St., ☎ 212/219–3055). This eclectic gem of a cross-genre music café in TriBeCa features avant-garde jazz in a homey, funky setting. Check it out.

Red Blazer Too (⌧ 349 W. 46th St., ☎ 212/262–3112). Roaring '20s, Dixieland, and swing are on tap. It's hot post-theater.

Smalls (⌧ 183 W. 10th St., ☎ 212/929–7565). Where can you find jazz 'til dawn and beyond? After the Village Vanguard closes, poke your head around the corner, and you'll find scene newcomer Smalls, where the music keeps coming until 8 AM.

Sweet Basil (⌧ 88 7th Ave. S, ☎ 212/242–1785). A little ritzy, though reliable, this nightspot runs from swing to fusion. Sunday brunch with trumpeter Doc Cheatham is truly a religious experience.

Village Vanguard (⌧ 178 7th Ave. S, ☎ 212/255–4037). This former Thelonius Monk haunt, the prototype of the old-world jazz club, lives on in a smoky cellar, in which jam the likes of Wynton Marsalis and James Carter, among others.

Zinno (⌧ 126 W. 13th St., ☎ 212/924–5182). The food (northern Italian) is actually as good as the jazz (usually duos and trios) at this mellow village club, which boasts a stellar wine list.

Rock Your World

The roots of rock may lie in America's heartland, but New York has added its own spin. Crowds at the Big Apple's rocketerias are young, enthusiastic, and hungry; the noise is often deafening, but you can catch many a rising star in this lively scene.

A.K.A. (⌧ 77 W. Houston St., ☎ 212/673–7325). A sweeping view of the Village makes this SoHo loft space, which specializes in jazz-funk-rap hybrid music, extra special.

The Bitter End (⌧ 147 Bleecker St., ☎ 212/673–7030). This old Village standby still serves up its share of new talent (like Lisa Loeb), as it once did Joan Armatrading and Warren Zevon. Check before arriving; blues, country, rock, and jazz all make appearances here.

Brownie's (⌧ 169 Ave. A, ☎ 212/420–8392). It's catch-as-catch-can at the East Village dive, but the hard thrashing sounds occasionally pull people in off the street to join the greasy-haired throngs.

CBGB & OMFUG (⌧ 315 Bowery, ☎ 212/982–4052). The full name is "Country Blue Grass Blues & Other Music For Uplifting Gourmandizers," which basically means: rock. American punk rock was born here, in this long, black tunnel of a club featuring bands with inventive names: Shirley Temple of Doom, Trick Babies, and Xanax 25.

Coney Island High (⌧ 15 St. Mark's Pl., ☎ 212/674–7959). Murals of Coney Island amusement park sideshow acts don't add much cheer to the black and red walls of this hardcore rock haven, which is not nearly as venerable as its state of decrepitude suggests.

Continental (⌧ 25 3rd Ave., ☎ 212/529–6924). This knockdown version of CBGB appeals to thrifty college kids on their last nickel.

Don Hill's (⊠ 511 Greenwich St., ☎ 212/219–2850). A TriBeCa favorite for bands both popular and not-yet-signed. Squeeze Box parties on Friday nights are genius.

Irving Plaza (⊠ 17 Irving Pl., ☎ 212/777–6800). Looking for Marilyn Manson, Blind Melon, or Faith No More? You'll find them here—except on Sundays, Swing Dance Society night.

Ludlow St. Café (⊠ 165 Ludlow St., ☎ 212/353–0536). In an artsy enclave just across Houston from the East Village, this basement club serves up consistently good blues, rock, and alternative bands.

Mercury Lounge (⊠ 217 E. Houston, ☎ 212/260–4700). With one of the best sound systems in the city, this two-year-old club in the East Village holds a quiet cachet with bands and industry insiders.

New Music Café (⊠ 380 Canal St., ☎ 212/941–1019). Their mission: To promote new music, but they've learned how to schedule the bands from totally green (early in the evening) to new but news (around 10 PM). Look out for Milo-Z and The Authority.

Rock 'n' Roll Café (⊠ 149 Bleecker St., ☎ 212/677–7630). A week's worth of band names should clue you in: Power Windows and the No Future Club.

Wetlands (⊠ 161 Hudson St., ☎ 212/966–5244). If you can ignore the environmental murals and the hokey broken-down-VW bus-cum-gift-shop, this large club rules, mostly because it draws great, often danceable bands. Dave Matthews and Hootie and the Blowfish both "developed" here.

World of Music

A former mayor once called New York a "gorgeous mosaic" for the rich ethnic mix of its inhabitants, and the music in some of its clubs reflects that. Brazilian, Celtic, and of course Latin—salsa, samba, merengue—integrates with the ever-present urban energy of the streets.

Anarchy Café (⊠ 27 3rd Ave., ☎ 212/475–1270). Everything from Afro-funk to Middle Eastern music turns up here, creating musical chaos—and making this East Village spot worth a stop.

Copacabana (⊠ 617 W. 57th St., ☎ 212/582–2672). Music and passion were always in fashion at this legendary nightclub, but now it's in the form of Latin music by such performers as Junior Gonzales, Tito Rodriguez, Jr., and Tito Nieves. Women often pay less, so give a call.

The Knitting Factory (⊠ 74 Leonard St., ☎ 212/219–3055). This cross-genre music café (☞ Jazz Notes, *above*) regularly features performers from far and wide.

Paddy Reilly's Music Bar (⊠ 519 2nd Ave., ☎ 212/686–1210). Irish rock-and-roots hybrid **Black 47** (named for the year of the great famine) has a standing Saturday night gig at this cramped but congenial club. Or stop in on Thursday for a traditional Irish jam session.

SOB's (⊠ 204 Varick St., ☎ 212/243–4940). Since 1982, this has been the—and we mean *the*—place for reggae, Trinidadian carnival, zydeco, African, and especially Latin tunes and salsa rhythms. The initials stand for Sounds of Brazil, just in case you wondered. The decor is à la Tropicana; the favored drink, a Brazilian *caipirinha*.

Down-Home Sounds

If you're in the mood for something acoustic, folksy, bone-warming, or bluesy, there are multiple options all over the Village. Many a lonesome cowboy carrying nothing but a tune has hitched his horse in front of the following saloons.

The Bottom Line (⊠ 15 W. 4th St., ☎ 212/228–7880). Clubs come and go, but this granddaddy prevails. Its reputation is for showcasing talents on their way up, as it did for both Stevie Wonder and Bruce Springsteen. Recent visitors include Buster Poindexter and Leon Redbone.

Chicago Blues (⊠ 73 8th Ave., ☎ 212/924–9755). Big Time Sarah, Jimmy Dawkins, the Holmes Brothers, and others have cozied into this nothing-fancy, just-plain-folksy West Village blues club.

Dan Lynch (⊠ 221 2nd Ave., ☎ 212/677–0911). This divey blues surprise in the East Village bustles with jam sessions on Saturday and Sunday afternoons.

Dan Lynch II (⊠ 29 St. Mark's Pl., ☎ 212/353–0692). Worth a stop because this bar-club is right on the St. Mark's strip, offering seven nights of live blues for no cover to speak of ($2 Friday and Saturday only).

Louisiana Community Bar & Grill (⊠ 622 Broadway, ☎ 212/460–9633). Not exactly the Big Easy, but free Cajun waltz lessons and the lilting zydeco of the Gotham Playboys Sunday night (live music other nights as well) makes this restaurant a down-home good time.

Manny's Car Wash (⊠ 1558 3rd Ave., ☎ 212/369–2583). Powerhouse blues jams on Manhattan's soul-free Upper East Side? Sounds shocking, but such is the scene at Manny's. Jams are only on Sunday, but live bands dish up the blues seven nights.

Rodeo Bar (⊠ 375 3rd Ave., ☎ 212/683–6500). This nightspot has engulfed Albuquerque Eats, the restaurant that used to house it. The Rodeo Bar has turned full-scale Texas roadhouse, complete with barnwood siding and a BBQ/Southern Texan menu, and featuring "music with American roots"—country, rock, rockabilly, and blues.

Sidewalk Bar–Restaurant (⊠ 94 Ave. A, ☎ 212/473–7373). Depending on who's playing, this salon will be packed with bikers, slackers, finger-snapping neo-beatniks, or other fans of the mix of poetry, blues, rock, and folk on tap.

Tramps (⊠ 45 W. 21st St., ☎ 212/727–7788). For more than two decades Tramps has delivered bands like the Dixie Dregs and NRBQ; now they've got Bruce Springsteen and George Clinton. Come for Chicago blues or most any other kind of music around.

Comic Relief

Neurotic New York comedy is known the world over, and a few minutes watching these hilarious Woody Allen types will make your own problems seem laughable. Comedy isn't pretty, nor is it especially cheap. Expect to pay around $15 per person on a weekend, sometimes on top of a drink minimum, and reservations are usually necessary. One warning: Only those skilled in the art of the repartee should sit in the front. The rest are advised to hide in a corner, or be relentlessly heckled. The *Village Voice* covers the comedy scene well, and it's worth checking its listings because lots of music clubs book comedians for periods between sets. The clubs below are devoted exclusively to comedy.

Boston Comedy Club (⊠ 82 W. 3rd St., ☎ 212/477–1000). It's so named because the owner's from Beantown, but comedians come here from all over the country to test their stuff Note: Monday is amateur night. (Just thought you should know.)

Caroline's Comedy Club (⊠ 1626 Broadway, between 49th and 50th Sts., ☎ 212/757–4100). This high-gloss club features established names as well as comedians on the edge of stardom. Richard Jenny, Sandra Bernhard, and Gilbert Gottfried have appeared.

Chicago City Limits (⊠ 1105 1st Ave., ☎ 212/888–5233). This troupe's been doing improvisational comedy for a long time, and it seldom fails to whip its audiences into a laughing frenzy. Chicago City Limits performs in a renovated movie theater and is very strong on audience participation.

Comedy Cellar (✉ 117 MacDougal St., ☎ 212/254–3480). This spot has been running for 14 years now beneath the Olive Tree Café, with a bill that's a good barometer of who's hot.

Comic Strip Live (✉ 1568 2nd Ave., ☎ 212/861–9386). The atmosphere here is strictly corner bar ("More comfortable than a nice pair of corduroys," says daytime manager J. R.). The stage is brilliantly lit but minuscule; the bill is unpredictable but worth checking out.

Dangerfield's (✉ 1118 1st Ave., ☎ 212/593–1650). Since 1969, this has been an important showcase for prime comic talent. It's owned and occasionally visited by comedian Rodney Dangerfield himself.

Freestyle Repertory Theater (various theaters, call 212/642–8202 to find out locations). Here's an improvisational theater group that's a step above the others. On "Spontaneous Broadway" nights, when an audience member shouts out a song title, the troupe will improvise a show tune—and then a whole musical—around it; on other evenings, teams compete to outperform one another in head-to-head "theater sports" matches.

New York Comedy Club (✉ 241 E. 24th St., ☎ 212/696–5233). At just $5 Sunday through Thursday (plus a two "beverage"—that means Pepsi counts—minimum), this intimate club, chock-full of comedy memorabilia and talent such as Brett Butler, Colin Quinn, and Damon Wayans, has been referred to as "the Wal-Mart of comedy."

Original Improvisation (✉ 433 W. 34th St., ☎ 212/279–3446). The Improv, which moved to a bigger home in 1993, is to comedy what the Blue Note is to jazz. Lots of now-famous comedians got their first laughs here, among them Richard Pryor.

Stand-Up NY. (✉ 236 W. 78th St., ☎ 212/595–0850). The Upper West Side option for comedy devotees, this club books bright faces off recent TV gigs. Robin Williams has been known to stop in.

Show and Tell

Cabaret takes many forms in New York City, from a lone crooner at the piano to a full-fledged song-and-dance revue. Various nightspots have stages; here are some of the most consistently entertaining.

Arcimboldo (✉ 220 E. 46th St., ☎ 212/972–4646). This peachy Italian restaurant dishes out more than spaghetti on Sundays, when it offers its "Opera with Taste" entertainment series, serving up singers from the Metropolitan Opera along with a prix-fixe dinner for a mere $40.

Asti (✉ 13 E. 12th St., ☎ 212/741–9105). Even if the hokey notion of opera-singing waiters dampens your appetite, give this place a chance—the professionally trained staff here will knock your socks off.

Danny's Skylight Room (✉ 346 W. 46th St., ☎ 212/265–8133). Housed in Danny's Grand Sea Palace, a fixture on Restaurant Row, this venue offers a little bit of everything: jazz, crooners, ivory-tinklers, and monologuists.

Don't Tell Mama (✉ 343 W. 46th St., ☎ 212/757–0788). At this convivial Theater District spot, composer-lyricist hopefuls and established talents show their stuff until 4 AM. Extroverts will be tempted by the open-mike policy of the piano bar in front.

The Duplex (✉ 61 Christopher St., ☎ 212/255–5438). Catch a singing luminary on the rise, a drop-in fresh from Broadway at the open mike, or a comedienne polishing up her act at this longtime Village favorite on Sheridan Square. At 47, it's New York's oldest continuing cabaret.

Eighty Eight's (✉ 228 W. 10th St., ☎ 212/924–0088). Come here to hear (among other things) songs by the best of Broadway's tunesmiths, and inventively assembled programs.

Fez (✉ 380 Lafayette St., ☎ 212/533–2680). Tucked away in the trendy Time Café, this Moroccan-themed Casbah offers everything from drag shows to readings and jazz amid a polished young crowd.

55 Grove Street (⊠ near Christopher St. and 7th Ave. S, ☎ 212/366–5438). This 50-year-old landmark cabaret offers a piano bar, singers, and sketch comedy above. You may see a Judy Garland impersonator sparring with an Ann Miller impersonator, or a mother-and-daughter team that decided all anyone needs to succeed in show business is nerve—but you'll find good entertainment as well.

Judy's (⊠ 49 W. 44th St., ☎ 212/764–8930). This club in the lobby of the Hotel Iroquois is known for singing pianists in the Michael Feinstein mold.

Michael's Pub (⊠ 211 E. 55th St., ☎ 212/758–2272). Woody Allen often moonlights on the clarinet here on Monday nights. On other evenings, other fine performers such as Mel Tormé take the stage. The crowd is very monied, very uptown.

Nuyorican Poets Café (⊠ 236 E. 3rd St., ☎ 212/505–8183). "Nuyorican" means a New Yorker of Puerto Rican descent, but poets of all backgrounds spout their often amazing stuff at this loud, packed Alphabet City haunt. Open-mike "slam" nights give you a chance to read your works—and hear audience opinions.

Tatou (⊠ 151 E. 50th St., ☎ 212/753–1144). Singers, dancers, celebrity impersonators, and the odd celebrity go down easy on Sundays at this supper club, which turns into a reliable dance hall late at night.

West Bank Café (⊠ 407 W. 42nd St., ☎ 212/695–6909). Below an attractive bistro-type restaurant across from Theater Row, moonlighting musical-comedy triple threats (actor-singer-dancers) show off; on occasion, new plays are read.

BARS

While the health-club craze may have hit New York hard, there's little danger that Manhattanites will abandon their bars. Drinking establishments thrive and multiply, particularly in TriBeCa, where it appears bar design has become a minor art. The city's liquor laws allow bars to stay open until 4 AM, so it's easy to add on a watering stop at the end of an evening's merriment.

Vintage Classics

Algonquin Hotel Lounge (⊠ 59 W. 44th St., ☎ 212/840–6800). This is a venerable spot, not only because it was the site of the fabled literary Round Table, but also for its elegant tone. (☞ also The Oak Room in Putting on the Ritz, *above*).

Café des Artistes (⊠ 1 W. 67th St., ☎ 212/877–3500). This restaurant, as well known for its glorious Art Nouveau murals as for its food (☞ Chapter 6), has a small, warm bar where interesting strangers tell their life stories and the house drink is pear champagne.

Elaine's (⊠ 1703 2nd Ave., ☎ 212/534–8103). The food's nothing special, and you will be relegated to an inferior table, but go to gawk; go late when the stars rise in Elaine's firmament. Woody Allen's favorite table is by the cappuccino machine.

The Four Seasons (⊠ 99 E. 52nd St., ☎ 212/754–9494). Miró tapestries in the lobby greet you as you enter this power bar in the Grill Room (☞ Chapter 6). Watch for Kissingers and Trumps.

Fantino (⊠ 112 Central Park S, ☎ 212/757–1900). Dressy and traditional in the Ritz-Carlton—a very double-martini sort of place.

King Cole Bar (⊠ at the St. Regis Hotel, 2 E. 55th St., ☎ 212/753–4500). The famed Maxwell Parrish mural is a welcome sight at this gorgeous midtown rendezvous spot.

Oak Bar (⊠ at the Plaza Hotel, 5th Ave. and 59th St., ☎ 212/759–3000). Newly bedecked with plush leather chairs and oak walls, this old favorite continues to age well. Its great location draws sophisticates, shoppers, businessmen, tourists in the know, and stars.

Pen Top Lounge (⊠ at the Peninsula Hotel, 700 5th Ave., ☎ 212/247–2200). Drinks are pricey, but the Manhattan views are jaw-dropping at this spectacular, glass-lined penthouse bar.

River Café (⊠ 1 Water St., Brooklyn, ☎ 718/522–5200). An eminently romantic spot hidden at the foot of the Brooklyn Bridge, this restaurant offers smashing views of Wall Street and the East River.

Top of the Tower (⊠ 3 Mitchell Pl., near 1st Ave. at 49th St., ☎ 212/355–7300). There are higher hotel-top lounges, but this one on the 26th floor of the Beekman Tower still feels halfway to heaven. The atmosphere is elegant and subdued.

"21" Club (⊠ 21 W. 52nd St., ☎ 212/582–7200). Famous for its old-time club atmosphere even before it was filmed in *All About Eve,* this isn't exactly a swinging joint, but its conservative environs evoke a sense of connections, power, and prestige. It's tough to get in unless you plan to eat here, too (☞ Chapter 6).

Watering Holes

Exploring neighborhood by neighborhood, you'll find a glut of mahogany-encrusted historic old town taverns in the West Village; chi-chi wine bars in SoHo and TriBeCa; yuppie and collegiate minifrats on the Upper West and East sides; and terribly trendy kitsch bars in the East Village and Alphabet City. Happy hunting.

South of Houston Street

Bridge Café (⊠ 279 Water St., ☎ 212/227–3344). This busy little restaurant flanks the Brooklyn Bridge, a hop, skip, and a jump from South Street Seaport. The bar is abridged, but between lunch and dinner you can pass a pleasant afternoon sipping a good selection of domestic wines or single-malt Scotches at a table.

Broome Street Bar (⊠ 363 W. Broadway at Broome St., ☎ 212/925–2086). A classic hangout, this SoHo standard attracts local artsy types on weekdays, the same from other boroughs on weekends.

Buddha Bar (⊠ 150 Varick St., ☎ 212/255–4433). This discreet yet trendy spot draws the model crowd and their oglers. Sunday is so-called ladies' night; to be admitted, a guy must be accompanied by three women—and pay double the cover. Is it worth it? You be the judge.

Ear Inn (⊠ 326 Spring St., ☎ 212/226–9060). Nothing fancy in this 1817 Federal house. It's the artsy crowd that makes the place, along with Saturday-afternoon poetry readings—"lunch for the ear."

El Teddy's (⊠ 219 W. Broadway, ☎ 212/941–7070). You can't miss the gigantic Lady Liberty crown out front, and the Judy Jetson Goes to Art Camp decor at this former mob haunt. The margaritas (on the rocks, *por favor*) at this enduring TriBeCa bar are phenomenal.

Fanelli's (⊠ 94 Prince St., ☎ 212/226–9412). This is a casual SoHo neighborhood bar where many come on Sundays with the fat *New York Times* under their arms. The food's good, too.

I Tre Merli (⊠ 463 W. Broadway, ☎ 212/254–8699). Happy drinkers spill out of the massive doors of this wide, inviting restaurant-bar.

Lucky Strike (⊠ 59 Grand St., ☎ 212/941–0479). Formerly a see-and-be-seen scene, this SoHo bistro has calmed into a mere scene.

Max Fish (⊠ 178 Ludlow St., ☎ 212/529-3959). This crowded kitsch palace on an artsy East Village strip boasts a twisted image of a grimacing Julio Iglesias over the bar and a pool table in back.

Merc Bar (⊠ 151 Mercer St., ☎ 212/966–2727). Once there were plans to open a classy hotel in SoHo, and this bar was to be the cornerstone. The hotel is not to be, but the martinis here are wonderful.

Naked Lunch (✉ 17 Thompson St., ☎ 212/343–0828). Dazzlingly successful, this Burroughs-inspired, earth-tone SoHo haunt is said to be often graced by Robert De Niro, among others.

Sporting Club (✉ 99 Hudson St., ☎ 212/219–0900). The six 10-foot screens and 11 TV monitors here stay tuned to the evening's major sports event. Aficionados come in after punching out on Wall Street.

Spring Street Bar and Restaurant (✉ 162 Spring St., ☎ 212/219–0157). A sleek bar that attracts an artsy clientele in the heart of SoHo.

Walker's (✉ 16 N. Moore St., ☎ 212/941–0142). First-precinct NYPD detectives, TriBeCa artists, Wall Street types, and the odd celeb somehow all manage to call this cozy restaurant-bar home.

Chelsea and the Village

For perhaps the most bizarre bar crawl Manhattan has to offer, consider a mug-hoisting stroll along the West Village's esoteric and enchanting Washington Street, which is one street east of the West Side Highway. Begin while it's light out at the dingy corner of West 13th Street with a visit to **Hogs & Heifers** (✉ 859 Washington St., ☎ 212/929–0655); this seems to be Gotham's homage to the movie *Deliverance*. Next, walk south through the meat-packing district to **Braque** (✉ 775 Washington St., ☎ 212/255–0709). Have a seat at the outdoor café frequented by the likes of RuPaul, or in a leather club chair in the newly opened adjoining indoor restaurant. Across the street, pop into **Tortilla Flats** (✉ 767 Washington St., ☎ 212/243–1053) and check out the backroom "Vegas Lounge," a tribute to the stars of Vegas, from Lewis and Martin to Siegfried and Roy. Proceed next to the French bistro–inspired **Black Sheep** (✉ 11th and Washington Sts., ☎ 212/242–1010). Then stumble on to the always hopping **Automatic Slim's** (✉ 733 Washington St., ☎ 212/645–8660)—from which you can finish off an A-1 evening by calling a cab.

Chelsea Commons (✉ 242 10th Ave., ☎ 212/924-9424). An old-fashioned pub in front and a small tree-shaded courtyard in back, this West Chelsea bar draws a disparate but friendly crowd of bookworms, sports fans, and slackers.

Chumley's (✉ 86 Bedford St., ☎ 212/675–4449). There's no sign to help you find this place—they took it down during Chumley's speakeasy days—but when you reach the corner of Barrow Street, you're very close. A fireplace warms this relaxed spot where the burgers are hearty and the clientele collegiate.

Cornelia Street Café (✉ 29 Cornelia St., ☎ 212/989–9319). A streetside table on this quaint West Village lane is a romantic spot to share a bottle of Merlot—or two. Inside you can groove to live jazz.

Dix et Sept (✉ 181 W. 10th St., ☎ 212/645–8023). They say they're "*comme à* Paris—without the attitude," but what they mean is they've subbed a New York attitude, which suits this lively spot just fine.

Flight 151 (✉ 151 8th Ave., ☎ 212/229–1868). This popular, unpretentious neighborhood hangout serves lunch, dinner, and a bargain all-you-can-eat brunch on weekends. The polished wood bar, candlelit booths, and friendly staff create a welcoming atmosphere. Don't miss Tuesday's Flip Night—you call it, you win it!

Flowers (✉ 21 W. 17th St., ☎ 212/691–8888). In this ultratrendy model hangout, you, too, can escape your fans by taking to the roof, which overlooks the hip Photo District.

McSorley's Old Ale House (✉ 15 E. 7th St., ☎ 212/473–9148). One of New York's oldest saloons (opened in 1854), this is a must-see for first-timers to Gotham.

Peter MacManus Café (✉ 152 7th Ave., ☎ 212/463–7620). It's known simply as MacManus's to regulars, who like the unpretentiousness. Among them are lots of actors, fresh from neighborhood classes.

Peculier Pub (⊠ 145 Bleecker St., ☎ 212/353–1327). Here, in the heart of the Village, you'll find nearly 400 brands of beer, from Anchor Steam to Zywiec.

Slaughtered Lamb (⊠ 182 W. 4th St., ☎ 212/727–3350). A none-too-subtle haunted mansion is the theme here (the paintings have roving eyes, skeletons are strewn here and there).

White Horse Tavern (⊠ 567 Hudson St., ☎ 212/243–9260). Here's where Dylan Thomas drained his last cup. From April through October, there's outdoor café drinking.

East Village through East 20s

Alcatraz (⊠ 132 St. Mark's Pl., ☎ 212/473–3370). The loudest, hardest, and, some say, best jukebox in New York rears its head at this Tompkins Square landmark.

Bowery Bar (⊠ 358 Bowery, ☎ 212/475–2220). Long lines peer through venetian blinds at the fabulous crowd within. One party person outside looking for a friend within was told by a watchcap-wearing bouncer, "If he misses you, he'll come out." He didn't.

Babyland (⊠ 81 Ave. A ☎ 212/473–7464). From the outside, it looks like a juvenile furnishing store but inside . . . well, there are cribs as chairs and paintings of babies crying on the wall. The customers in this kitschy bar, however, are laughing.

Blue & Gold Bar (⊠ 79 East 7th St., ☎ 212/473–8918). Unassuming and cheap—a neighborhood favorite.

Café Tabac (⊠ 232 E. 9th St., ☎ 212/674–7072). Practice your glare before entering the ground-floor lounge of this pretentious salon, the site of many Madonna visits as well as fights between Christian Slater, Ethan Hawke, and whichever models they are dating at the moment.

Circa (⊠ 103 2nd Ave., ☎ 212/777–4120). Blond and tony, with c-shaped velvet banquettes and high ceilings, Circa supplies a surprising slice of the Upper East Side on ever-gentrifying 2nd Avenue.

Cloister Café (⊠ 238 E. 9th St., ☎ 212/777–9128). With one of Manhattan's largest and leafiest outdoor gardens, the Cloister is a perfect perch for stargazing and elbow-bending.

Coffee Shop (⊠ 29 Union Sq. W, ☎ 212/243–7969). The moonlighting models bringing your food and drinks may not be the fastest waitpeople in the city, but a flashy, gorgeous crowd makes for an unbelievable, if attitudinal, spectacle.

Coyote Ugly (⊠ 153 1st Ave., ☎ 212/477–4431). The name is appropriate for this dive, where the raucous regulars can be heard across the 'hood singing along with the Skynard wailing from the jukebox.

Flamingo East (⊠ 219 2nd Ave., ☎ 212/533–2860). Kidney-shaped sofas, style-mad patrons, and moody lighting make this haute downtown restaurant and bar a cool good time. Upstairs starts late, but the terrace overlooking 2nd Avenue is a treat, and the food is delicious.

Jules (⊠ 65 St. Mark's Pl., ☎ 212/477–5560). A *très* Français, *très* romantique wine bar with a perfect people-watching patio out front.

Lucky Cheng's (⊠ 24 1st Ave., ☎ 212/473–0516). Have a bite beside the goldfish pond downstairs, or mingle amid the gilt and leopard, and be served by lovely waiters and bartenders in drag at this Pacific Rim restaurant-cum-cross-dressing-cabaret.

Nation (⊠ 50 Ave. A, ☎ 212/473–6239). Despite the enormous signs proclaiming "No Dancing" and "Pot Smoking Is Not Allowed," this smoke-saturated bar still manages to feel friendly. Grab a two-top by the window, and watch the parade of passers-by on Avenue A.

No-Tell Motel (⊠ 167 Ave. A, ☎ 212/475–2172). Decorated with tame 1950s porno mags, LPs, black-velvet paintings of JFK and religious icons, this kitsch palace is the East Village at its most ironic.

Old Town Bar and Restaurant (✉ 45 E. 18th St., ☎ 212/529–6732). Proudly unpretentious, this watering hole is heavy on the mahogany and redolent of "old New York." True to its name, the Old Town has been around since 1892.

Pete's Tavern (✉ 129 E. 18th St., ☎ 212/473–7676). This saloon is famous as the place where O. Henry is alleged to have written "The Gift of the Magi" (at the second booth to the right as you come in). These days, it's still crowded with noisy, friendly souls.

Telephone Bar (✉ 149 2nd Ave., ☎ 212/529–5000). Imported English telephone booths and a polite, handsome crowd mark this pub.

Temple Bar (✉ 332 Lafayette St., ☎ 212/925–4242). Romantic and upscale, this unmarked haunt is famous for its martinis and is a treat at any price.

XVI (✉ 16 1st Ave., ☎ 212/255–8366). The upstairs decor largely consists of what appear to be artfully draped sheets, but somehow it all turns out chic in the end. Downstairs doesn't succeed as well; the low-ceilinged space strives for Beat but only makes basement.

Midtown and the Theater District

Barrymore's (✉ 267 W. 45th St., ☎ 212/391–8400). At this pleasantly downscale Theater District spot, you'll see the requisite show posters on the wall. Listen in on the conversations at the bar and you'll hear a few tawdry, true stories of what goes on behind Broadway stage doors.

Café Un Deux Trois (✉ 123 W. 44th St., ☎ 212/354–4148). This old hotel lobby, charmingly converted, is chicly peopled. The bar itself is small, but it's a hot spot before and after the theater.

Century Café (✉ 132 W. 43rd St., ☎ 212/398–1988). An immense vintage neon sign lights up the bar at this trendy, friendly Theater District bistro, where you *won't* find the requisite show posters.

Halcyon Bar (✉ at the Rihga Royal Hotel, 151 W. 54th St., ☎ 212/307–5000). A big, airy hotel bar, with large and well-spaced tables, it's great for a private chat.

Joe Allen (✉ 326 W. 46th St., ☎ 212/581–6464). At this old reliable on Restaurant Row, celebrated in the musical version of *All About Eve,* everybody's en route to or from a show. Its "flop wall" offers a change of pace: The posters that adorn it are from Broadway musicals that quickly bombed.

Landmark Tavern (✉ 626 11th Ave., ☎ 212/757–8595). This aged red-brick pub (opened in 1868) is blessed by the glow of warming fireplaces on each of its three floors.

Sardi's (✉ 234 W. 44th St., ☎ 212/221–8440). "The theater is certainly not what it was," croons a cat in *Cats*—and he could be referring to this venerable spot as well. Still, if you care for the theater, don't leave New York without visiting this establishment.

Top of the Sixes (✉ 666 5th Ave., ☎ 212/757–6662). This bar has an impressive nighttime view of Central Park to the north, from 39 stories up above 5th Avenue.

The Whiskey (✉ at the Paramount Hotel, 235 W. 46th St., ☎ 212/764–5500). A downstairs bar graces this chic, revamped Times Square hotel that's sleek and hip, and ideal après-theater.

East Side

American Trash (✉ 1471 1st Ave., ☎ 212/998–9008). The name refers to the decor, not necessarily to the clientele—old pipes, bike wheels, and golf clubs line the walls and ceilings.

Dakota Bar & Grill (✉ 1576 3rd Ave., ☎ 212/427–8889). A mix of yuppies fresh out of college and neighborhood lifers congregate around the 52-foot, 4-inch bar, one of the longest in Manhattan.

Harglo's (⊠ 974 2nd Ave., ☎ 212/759–9820). The spicy Cajun food and bright neon sign attract white collars who just can't seem to go straight home after a long day at the office.

Jim McMullen's (⊠ 1341 3rd Ave., ☎ 212/861–4700). A young, quintessentially Upper East Side watering hole, McMullen's has a large, busy bar decked with bouquets of fresh flowers. Here you'll find lots of Gold Cards, tennis talk, and alumni-fund gatherings.

Live Psychic (⊠ 207 E. 84th St., ☎ 212/744–5003). The clientele, in their late twenties and thirties, pay the on-hand psychics to advise them about life, love, and the other patrons at the bar.

P. J. Clarke's (⊠ 915 3rd Ave., ☎ 212/759–1650). New York's most famous Irish bar, this establishment comes complete with the requisite mirrors and polished wood. Lots of after-workers like unwinding here, in a place that recalls the days of Tammany Hall.

Polo Lounge (⊠ Westbury Hotel, 840 Madison Ave., ☎ 212/439–4835). This place is, in a word, classy; it's frequented by European royalty and Knickerbocker New York.

Twins (⊠ 1712 2nd Ave., ☎ 212/987–1111). Owned by twin sisters Debbie and Lisa Ganz and actor Tom Beringer, this spot employs 37 additional pairs of twins. The customers enjoy the double-chocolate fondue—as well as some singular food delights.

Water Club (⊠ 500 E. 30th St., ☎ 212/683–3333). Right on the East River, with a pleasing outside deck (you're not on a boat, but you'll somehow feel you are), this is a special-occasion kind of place—especially for those who've already been to all the special landlocked spots in town.

Upper West Side

On the Yupper West Side, as it's sometimes referred to, Amsterdam Avenue between 79th and 86th streets is a promenade for young revelers, most still wearing their college sweatshirts. Weave up and down the Avenue, and be sure to stop in at the classy, racially mixed **Shark Bar** (⊠ 307 Amsterdam Ave., ☎ 212/874-8500). Then try **Hi-Life** (⊠ 83rd St. and Amsterdam Ave., ☎ 212/787–7199), big with the nabe's bon vivants.

Black Bass (⊠ 370 Columbus Ave., ☎ 212/362–3559). Every night is a big, nasty fraternity party that leaves you smelling like a beer-sodden cigarette the next day—hence its popularity.

Chaz & Wilson's (⊠ 201 W. 79th St., ☎ 212/769–0100). There must be a reason for the line out the door of this otherwise unremarkable but enduringly popular bar. Perhaps it's the live music Wednesdays and Sundays, or the possibility of forging a formidable connection.

China Club (⊠ 2130 Broadway, ☎ 212/877–1166). If you don't spot someone famous here within 30 minutes, you just aren't trying hard enough. On Monday night it's the place to be on the Upper West Side.

Iridium (⊠ 44 W. 63rd St., ☎ 212/582–2121). The owners spent untold sums to make this lavish restaurant and jazz club near Lincoln Center stand out, which it does. If nothing else, take a look inside.

Lucy's Retired Surfer Bar (⊠ 503 Columbus Ave., ☎ 212/787–3009). One of the many bars to claim to be "Home of the Jello Shot," this playful beach hut is a hit with young Upper West Siders, who pack themselves in and sometimes even manage to dance.

Museum Café (⊠ 366 Columbus Ave., ☎ 212/799–0150). Trendy, overdesigned joints on Columbus Avenue come and go, but this oasis across from the American Museum of Natural History endures thanks to nice street-side windows and high, airy ceilings.

O'Neal's Lincoln Center (⊠ 49 W. 64th St., ☎ 212/787–4663). Mike O'Neal, the owner of the beloved but now defunct Ginger Man, has moved the bar from that establishment down the street and created a series of rooms (one with a fireplace) serving good pub food.

The Saloon (✉ 1920 Broadway, ☎ 212/874–1500). The menu goes on and on; the bar is large and informal; and the waitresses and waiters cruise around on roller skates. It may be gimmicky, but the spirit of fun is infectious, and the people-watching is second to none.

Theme Dreams

In some ways, concept restaurants are as un-New York as it gets. Things that come on strong with a gimmick but can't back up the bluster tend to get eaten alive in the Big Apple, while the true hot spots are all action, no talk (just buzz). While these after dark theme parks may be tacky and touristy, they do draw some famous faces—if, perhaps, not as many as they'd like you to think—and a visit to one (or several) can become a classically campy evening's adventure.

Fashion Café (✉ 51 Rockefeller Plaza, ☎ 212/765-3131). Why supermodels Elle MacPherson, Claudia Schiffer, Naomi Campbell, and Christie Turlington would open the kind of restaurant that they would otherwise never grace will remain a mystery for the ages.

Hard Rock Cafe (✉ 221 W. 57th St., ☎ 212/459–9320). Formerly embraced by the kids of stars—now, in fact, its clientele seems to be eternally prepubescent kids accompanied by muttering parents who find it big, crowded, and far too noisy for talk.

Harley-Davidson Cafe (✉ 1370 6th Ave., ☎ 212/245–6000). Motorcycles are not allowed to park outside, which should give you an idea of the authenticity of this upholstered showroom-size restaurant. Still, rock stars and other biker fans do drop in on occasion.

Jekyll & Hyde Club (✉ 1409 6th Ave., ☎ 212/541–9505). "A restaurant and social club for eccentric explorers and mad scientists," this multiple-story eating and ogling extravaganza features 250 varieties of beer and actors dressed as horror meisters.

Planet Hollywood (✉ 140 W. 57th St., ☎ 212/333–7827). It's touristy, it doesn't take reservations, and waiting lines are long. Still, the place has cachet, an undeniable star quality, and such movie memorabilia as C3PO and Dorothy's red shoes.

Gay and Lesbian Bars

For advice on the bar scene, health issues, and other assorted quandaries, call the **Gay and Lesbian Switchboard** (☎ 212/777–1800) or stop by the **Lesbian and Gay Community Services Center** (✉ 208 W. 13th St., ☎ 212/620–7310). Check out *HomoExtra, Next* magazine, *Sappho's Isle,* the *Village Voice,* or *Paper* for what's what.

Dance Clubs

Clit Club (✉ Friday at the Bar Room, 432 W. 14th St., 212/366–5680). Leather-vested and well-pierced Harley dykes as well as lipstick lesbians dance the night away. Call first, because this club roves.

Lick It! (✉ Limelight, 47 W. 20th St., ☎ 212/807–7850). On Wednesday and Friday, Chelsea's church of sin turns up the heat. Music-wise it's nothing special; cruise-wise it's an action-packed adventure, replete with go-go boys.

1984 (✉ Crowbar, 339 E. 10th St., ☎ 212/420–0670). The tiny dance floor here pulses and throbs every Friday to a fabulous array of new wave syntho-trash.

The Roxy (✉ 515 W. 18th St., ☎ 212/645–5156). Saturday night is boys' night, but girls "won't be turned away" from this huge roller disco-cum-club.

Men's Bars

The Break (⊠ 232 8th Ave., ☎ 212/627–0072). The scene is usually quite young, and swells according to the number and generosity of the night's drink specials.

Cleo's 9th Avenue Saloon (⊠ 656 9th Ave., ☎ 212/307–1503). Near the Theater District, this small, narrow neighborhood bar draws a convivial, laid-back older crowd.

Crowbar (⊠ 339 E. 10th St., ☎ 212/420–0670). Gay grungers and NYU students mingle happily at this East Village hot spot. Very big on Wednesday and Friday (☞ 1984, *above*).

The Eagle (⊠ 142 11th Ave., ☎ 212/691–8451). This leather-and-Levi's bar is serious about three things: drinking, glaring, and shooting pool.

The Monster (⊠ 80 Grove St., ☎ 212/924–3558). Upstairs, the tone-deaf gather and sing around the piano; downstairs, the rhythm-impaired gyrate in a campy pitch-black disco. This place has been at it for 13 years, though, and continues to draw a busy mix of ages, races, and genders.

Nuts & Bolts (⊠ 101 7th Ave. S, ☎ 212/620–4000). Upscale gents converge on this classy lounge, which features live performances and a video lounge.

Rawhide (⊠ 212 8th Ave., ☎ 212/242–9332). The older Wild West crowd of this Chelsea nook is mostly local and usually leathered-up.

The Spike (⊠ 120 11th Ave., ☎ 212/243–9688). Here, at the ultimate parade of black leather, chains, and Levi's, the bark is always bigger than the bite.

Splash Bar (⊠ 50 W. 17th St., ☎ 212/691–0073). The staggering popularity of this hangout is due as much to its size as to anything else. Most nights go-go dancers writhe in translucent shower-cubicles.

Stonewall (⊠ 53 Christopher St., ☎ 212/463–0950). An odd mix of tourists chasing down gay history and down-to-earth locals, the scene is everything but trendy.

The Townhouse (⊠ 236 E. 58th St., ☎ 212/754–4649). On good nights it's like stepping into a Brooks Brothers catalog—cashmere sweaters, Rolex watches, distinguished-looking gentlemen—and it's surprisingly festive.

Ty's (⊠ 114 Christopher St., ☎ 212/741–9641). Though its clientele is close-knit and fiercely loyal, this small, jeans-and-flannel neighborhood saloon never turns away friendly strangers.

The Works (⊠ 428 Columbus Ave., ☎ 212/799–7365). Whether it's Thursday's $1 margarita party or just a regular Upper West Side afternoon, the crowd is usually J. Crew–style or disco hangover at this bar, newly renovated in honor of its 15th anniversary.

Women's Bars

Crazy Nanny's (⊠ 21 7th Ave. S, ☎ 212/366–6312). The crowd is wide-ranging—from urban chic to shaved head—and tends toward the young and the wild.

Henrietta Hudson (⊠ 438 Hudson St., ☎ 212/924–3347). A little more upscale than Crazy Nanny's, with two huge rooms and a pool table.

Julie's (⊠ 204 E. 58th St., ☎ 212/688–1294). Popular with the sophisticated-lady, upper-crust crowd, this brownstone basement has a piano bar—and dancing on Sunday and Wednesday nights.

Shescapes (various locations, ☎ 212/645–6479). This roving dance party is probably the most popular of Manhattan's lesbian soirées.

9 Outdoor Activities and Sports

New Yorkers are stopped by nothing in their passion for sports: You can see them jogging in the park when it's sleeting, or heading for a tennis bubble on the most blustery of Sunday winter afternoons. From boccie to croquet, no matter how esoteric the sport, there's a place to pursue it in New York.

YOU'LL FIND OASES OF GREENERY YOU'D NEVER imagine here (13% of the city, in fact, is parkland). And if you strike up a conversation while waiting to rent a boat or a bike at the Loeb Boathouse, or while stretching before a jog around the Reservoir in Central Park, you'll discover a friendly, relaxed side of New Yorkers that you might not otherwise get the chance to see.

By Karen Cure

Updated by
Margaret
Mittelbach

Just one word before you set out: Weekends are very busy. If you need to rent equipment or secure specific space—for instance, a tennis court—go very early or be prepared to wait.

BEACHES

Fine weather brings sun-worshiping New Yorkers out in force. Early in the season, the nearest park or even a rooftop is just fine for catching rays, but later on everyone heads for New York City beaches. Before you go, call to check on swimming conditions.

City Beaches

The tame waves of **Coney Island** (☎ 718/946–1353) are the closest many New Yorkers get to a surf all year. The last stop in Brooklyn on the B, D, F, and N lines, the beach here, which has the boardwalk and the famous amusement-park skyline of the Cyclone and the Wonder Wheel as its backdrop, is busy every day that the sun shines. If you want to see surfers riding the waves in wet suits, venture out on the A train to the beaches in the **Rockaways** section of Queens—at 9th Street, 23rd Street, or 80–118th streets.

Long Island

New Yorkers' favorite strand may be **Jones Beach** (☎ 516/785–1600), one of the great man-made beaches of the world, built during the era of the famous parks commissioner Robert Moses. In summer the Long Island Railroad (☎ 718/217–5477) runs regular trains from Penn Station to Freeport, where you can catch a bus to the beach. On the western end of Fire Island, there's a good beach at **Robert Moses State Park** (☎ 516/669–0449), which can be reached in summer via the Long Island Railroad (☎ 718/217–5477).

PARTICIPANT SPORTS

For information about athletic facilities in Manhattan as well as a calendar of sporting events, pick up a complimentary copy of *Metrosports* magazine at sporting goods stores and health clubs.

Bicycling

Although space comes at a premium in Manhattan apartments, many locals keep a bicycle around for a few of the glorious rides that this city has to offer. A sleek pack of dedicated racers zooms around Central Park at dawn and at dusk daily, and on weekends, parks swarm with recreational cyclists. **Central Park** has a 7.2-mile circular drive that is closed to traffic in summer and fall from 10 AM to 3 PM and 7 to 10 PM on weekdays, and from 7 PM Friday to 6 AM Monday. On holidays it's closed from 7 PM the night before until 6 AM the day after. In **Riverside Park,** the promenade between 72nd and 110th streets, with its Hudson River view, gets an easygoing crowd of slow-pedaling cyclists—many of them with training wheels. The **Hudson River bike path** runs along the waterfront from Little West 12th Street down to the **Hudson River Park promenade.** From there cyclists will enjoy exploring the **Wall Street** area, which is deserted on weekends. The winding roads in Brooklyn's beautiful **Prospect Park** are closed to cars on the weekends in summer from 10 AM to 3 PM and 7 to 10 PM on weekdays.

Bike Rentals

Expect to leave a deposit or a credit card when renting a bike. **AAA Bikes in Central Park** (✉ Loeb Boathouse, mid-park, near E. 74th St., ☎ 212/861–4137) provides cycles for the whole family. **87th Street Bicycles** (✉ 1690 2nd Ave., ☎ 212/722–2201) features 10-speeds, mountain bikes, and "hybrids" designed for city riding. **Metro Bicycles** (✉ 1311 Lexington Ave. at 88th St., ☎ 212/427–4450) offers only 7-speed hybrids, a good choice for urban cycling. **Pedal Pusher** (✉ 1306 2nd Ave., between 68th and 69th Sts., ☎ 212/288–5592) has everything from clunky 3-speeds to racing bikes to hybrids.

Group Trips

For organized rides with other cyclists, call or write before you come to New York. **Transportation Alternatives** (✉ 92 St. Mark's Pl., New York, NY 10009, ☎ 212/475–4600) can provide an ongoing update of group rides throughout the metropolitan area. The **Staten Island Bicycling Association** (☎ 718/815–9290) sponsors trips in New York's most countrified borough, as well as other pretty spots.

Billiards

It used to be that pool halls were dusty, grimy, sticky places—and there are still a few of those around. But they've been joined by a group of oh-so-chic spots with deluxe decor, high prices, and even classical music or jazz in the background. Most halls are open late.

Amsterdam Billiard Club (✉ 344 Amsterdam Ave., between 76th and 77th Sts., ☎ 212/496–8180) is particularly fashionable and part-owned by comedian David Brenner.

Billiard Club (✉ 220 W. 19th St., between 7th and 8th Aves., ☎ 212/206–7665) in Chelsea; has a classy look.

Chelsea Billiards (✉ 54 W. 21st St., between 5th and 6th Aves., ☎ 212/989–0096) has 48 tables on two floors.

East Side Billiard Club (✉ 163 E. 86th St., between 3rd and Lexington Aves., ☎ 212/831–7665) serves up pizza and beer.

Julian's Famous Poolroom (✉ 138 E. 14th St., ☎ 212/598–9884) has 25 tables, a giant-screen TV, and a jukebox.

West Side Billiard Club (✉ 601 W. 50th St. at 11th Ave., ☎ 212/246–1060) has 14 pool tables and eight Ping-Pong tables.

Bird-Watching

Manhattan's green parks and woodlands provide habitats for thousands of birds, everything from fork-tailed flycatchers to common nighthawks. Since the city is on the Atlantic flyway, a major migratory route, you can see birds that nest as far north as the High Arctic. May is the best season, since the songbirds are in their freshest colors—and so many are singing at once that you can hardly distinguish their songs. To find out what's been seen where, call the Rare Bird Alert (☎ 212/979–3070). For information on best bird-watching spots in various parks, call the **Urban Park Rangers,** a uniformed division of the Parks Department: Manhattan (☎ 212/427–4040); the Bronx (☎

718/885–3466); Brooklyn (☎ 718/287–5252); Queens (☎ 718/699–4204); and Staten Island (☎ 718/667–6042).

Birders will like the 1,146-acre **Van Cortlandt Park** in the Bronx, with its varied habitats, including freshwater marshes and upland woods. In Brooklyn, **Green-Wood Cemetery** (call superintendent at 718/768–7300 for permission to enter grounds) features Victorian-era headstones, as well as a nice woodland that attracts hawks and songbirds. The Ramble in Manhattan's **Central Park** is full of warblers in springtime, and may attract as many birders as it does birds. In Queens, try **Jamaica Bay Wildlife Refuge,** where birds are drawn to the 9,155 acres of salt marshes, fresh and brackish ponds, and open water (stop by the visitor center, ✉ Crossbay Blvd., Broad Channel, Queens, ☎ 718/474–0613, to get a permit). In Staten Island, head for the fairly undeveloped 317-acre **Wolfe's Pond Park** (☎ 718/984–8266), where the pond and the nearby shore can be dense with geese and ducks during the annual migrations.

Guided Walks
The **New York City Audubon Society** (✉ 71 W. 23rd St., ☎ 212/691–7483) has occasional bird-watching outings; call Monday–Thursday 1–4 PM for information. Also check with the Urban Park Rangers at the numbers listed above.

Boating

The boating available on New York City's ponds and lakes conjures up 19th-century images of a parasol-twirling lady rowed by her swain.

In **Central Park,** the boats are rowboats (plus one Venetian gondola for nighttime glides in the moonlight) and the rowing terrain is the 18-acre Central Park Lake. Rent your boat at **Loeb Boathouse** (☎ 212/517–4723), near 74th Street, from spring through fall.

Boccie

This pinless Italian version of bowling thrives in New York, with 100 city courts. The easiest to get to from midtown are at 96th Street and 1st Avenue; at East River Drive and 42nd Street; and at the Thompson Street Playground (at Houston St.) in Greenwich Village. There's also a boccie court at **Il Vagabondo** (✉ 351 E. 62nd St., ☎ 212/832–9221), a vintage Italian restaurant east of Bloomingdale's.

Bowling

The **Leisure Time Bowling & Recreation Center** (✉ 625 8th Ave. at 42nd St., ☎ 212/268–6909) offers 30 lanes on the second floor of the Port Authority Bus Terminal. **Bowlmor** (✉ 110 University Pl., ☎ 212/255–8188) is a funky 44-lane operation frequented by a colorful Village crowd; many stay until closing time: 4 AM on weekends.

Boxing

The recent trendiness of the sport is reflected in its availability to the casual participant. **Chelsea Piers Sports Center** (✉ 23rd St. and the Hudson River, ☎ 212/336–6000) has a boxing ring and equipment circuit. Day passes are $26. **Crunch Fitness** (✉ 404 Lafayette St., ☎ 212/614–0120; 54 E. 13th St., ☎ 212/475–2018) has a boxing ring at its Lafayette Street location and kickboxing classes at its gym on East 13th St. The **Broadcast Boxing Club** (✉ 41 W. 57th St., ☎ 212/319–4142), also known as Geraldo Rivera's gym, has coed boxing instruction. Brooklyn's venerable **Gleason's** (✉ 75 Front St., ☎ 718/

797–2872), home of 106 world champs, including Jake LaMotta and Muhammad Ali, also instructs visitors.

Chess and Checkers

In **Central Park,** the Chess & Checkers House is picturesquely situated atop a massive stone outcrop. Ten tables are available for indoor play on weekends, 11:30–4:30, and 24 outdoor tables are available during all daylight hours. Bring your own or pick up playing pieces at the **Dairy** (mid-park at 64th St., ☎ 212/794–6565) 11–4, Tues.–Sun.; there is no charge, but a $20 deposit is required.

Downtown in Greenwich Village, the **Village Chess Shop** (✉ 230 Thompson St., between Bleecker and W. 3rd Sts., ☎ 212/475–9580) is always an active spot. Uptown, the **Manhattan Chess Club** (✉ 353 W. 46th St., between 8th and 9th Aves., ☎ 212/333–5888) sponsors tournaments and exhibitions.

Dance and Aerobics

Naturally enough, New York gives birth to many a new fitness trend, and an aerobics class here may turn out to be executed on in-line skates or to the accompaniment of live gospel singing. **Crunch Fitness** (✉ 404 Lafayette St., ☎ 212/614–0120; 54 E. 13th St., ☎ 212/475–2018; and 162 W. 83rd St., ☎ 212/875–1902) offers everything from straight-up aerobics to African dance and body sculpting. **Equinox** (✉ 344 Amsterdam Ave., ☎ 212/721–4200, and 897 Broadway, between 19th and 20th Sts., ☎ 212/780–9300) has yoga and meditation, along with general fitness classes. The **Vanderbilt YMCA** (✉ 224 E. 47th St., ☎ 212/756–9600) schedules more than 100 different drop-in aerobics and exercise classes every week. None requires membership for classes.

Golf

Bethpage State Park (☎ 516/249–0700), in the Long Island town of Bethpage, about one hour and 20 minutes from Manhattan, is home to five golf courses, including its 7,065-yard par-71 Black, generally ranked among the nation's top 25 public courses. Reservations for tee times are accepted 24 hours a day on the course's automated reservation hot line (☎ 516/249–0707). Reservations can be made up to four days in advance. However, getting a tee time is often a matter of luck, since all five courses are busy seven days a week.

Of the 13 city courses, the 6,215-yard Split Rock in **Pelham Bay Park,** the Bronx, is considered the most challenging (☎ 718/885–1258). Slightly easier is its sister course, the 6,405-yard Pelham, which has fewer trees to contend with. **Van Cortlandt Park** in the Bronx has the nation's first municipal golf course, established in 1895—the hilly 6,052-yard Van Cortlandt (☎ 718/543–4595). Queens has a 5,431-yard course at **Forest Park** in Woodhaven (✉ Park La. S and Forest Pkwy., ☎ 718/296–0999). Staten Island has the links-style 5,891-yard **Silver Lake** golf course (✉ 915 Victory Blvd., one block south of Forest Ave., ☎ 718/447–5686).

Driving Range

In midtown you can take lessons or practice your swing in netted cages, with bull's-eye backdrops, at the **Richard Metz Golf Studio** (✉ 425 Madison Ave. at 49th St., 3rd Floor, ☎ 212/759–6940). Jutting right out into the river, the **Golf Club at Chelsea Piers** (✉ 23rd St. and the Hudson River, ☎ 212/336–6400) has a 200-yard artificial turf fairway, a computerized tee-up system, and heated hitting stalls—so you can keep right on swinging even in winter.

Miniature Golf

At **Hackers, Hitters & Hoops** (⊠ 123 W. 18th St., ☎ 212/929–7482), you can outsmart the obstacles on all 18 holes.

Horseback Riding

A trot on the bridle path around Central Park's Reservoir provides a pleasant look at New York. The carefully run **Claremont Riding Academy** (⊠ 175 W. 89th St., ☎ 212/724–5100) is the city's oldest riding academy and the only riding stable left in Manhattan. Experienced riders can rent horses, at $33 per hour, for an unescorted walk, trot, or canter in nearby Central Park; call ahead to reserve.

Hotel Health Clubs

Although space is tight in Manhattan hotels, most of them offer some kind of fitness facility, even if it's just an arrangement enabling guests to use a nearby health club.

Doral Fitness Center (⊠ 90 Park Ave., ☎ 212/370–9692) is available to guests of the **Doral Park Avenue, Doral Court,** and **Doral Tuscany.** This serious health club offers a number of workout programs. The **Four Seasons** (⊠ 57 E. 57th St., ☎ 212/758–5700) has a spacious and high-tech facility, including an aerobics room with video, free weights, StairMaster, and Cybex machines. **Holiday Inn Crowne Plaza** (⊠ 1605 Broadway at 49th St., ☎ 212/977–8880) has a fitness center operated by the New York Sports Club, with a lap pool, weights and cardiovascular equipment, and an aerobics studio. **The Peninsula** (⊠ 700 5th Ave., ☎ 212/247–2200) reserves floors 21–23 for its health club, with a pool on the 22nd floor, plus exercise machines and a poolside dining terrace. **Sheraton Manhattan** (⊠ 790 7th Ave. at 51st St., ☎ 212/581–3300) has a health club including a large pool, aerobics and aquatic exercise equipment, swimming lessons, and a sundeck. **The Millenium Broadway** (⊠ 145 W. 44th St., ☎ 212/768–4400) offers a fitness center with Lifecycles, treadmills, StairMaster, and a sauna.

Ice-Skating

Each of the city's rinks has its own character, but all have scheduled skating sessions. Lockers, skate rentals, music, and snack bars complete the picture. Major rinks include the outdoor one in **Rockefeller Center** (⊠ 50th St. at 5th Ave., lower plaza, ☎ 212/332–7654), which is fairly small yet utterly romantic, especially when the enormous Christmas tree towers above it. The beautifully situated **Wollman Memorial Rink** (⊠ 6th Ave. at 59th St., ☎ 212/396–1010) offers skating in the open air beneath the lights of the city. Be prepared for crowds on weekends. **Sky Rink** (⊠ 23rd St. and the Hudson River, ☎ 212/336–6100) has two year-round rinks in the Chelsea Piers complex.

In-Line Skating

New York is wild over in-line skating. **Peck & Goodie** (⊠ 917 8th Ave. at 54th St., ☎ 212/246–6123) sells and rents skates. **Blades** has several Manhattan stores, including: East (⊠ 160 E. 86th St., ☎ 212/996–1644), 2nd Avenue (⊠ 1414 2nd Ave., ☎ 212/249–3178), Downtown (⊠ 659 Broadway, ☎ 212/477–7350), and West (⊠ 120 W. 72nd St., ☎ 212/787–3911); they give lessons and sell and rent skates along with all the appropriate protection. In TriBeCa, **NYC Skates** (⊠ 128 Chambers St., ☎ 212/964–1944) can furnish you with everything you'll need to skate in Hudson River Park.

Those who think skates should be used for disco dancing can be found, whirling and twirling and wearing headphones, weekends in Central Park between the Mall and Bethesda Fountain. Two outdoor roller rinks at the **Chelsea Piers** complex (⊠ 23rd St. and the Hudson River, ☎ 212/336–6200) have free-skates, classes, Rollaerobics™, and hip-hop dance parties. The **Roxy** (⊠ 515 W. 18th St., ☎ 212/645–5156), a downtown dance club, goes roller-disco on Tuesday and Thursday.

Jogging and Racewalking

Jogging
In New York, dog-walkers jog, librarians jog, rock stars jog, and parents jog (sometimes pushing their toddlers ahead of them in speedy Baby Jogger strollers). Publicity notwithstanding, crime is not a problem as long as you jog when and where everybody else does. On Manhattan streets, figure 20 north–south blocks per mile.

In Manhattan, **Central Park** is the busiest spot, specifically along the 1.58-mile track circling the **Reservoir**. A runners' lane has been designated along the park roads, which are closed to traffic weekdays 10–3 and 7–10, and from 7 PM Friday to 6 AM Monday. A good 1.72-mile route starts at Tavern on the Green along the West Drive, heads south around the bottom of the park to the East Drive, and circles back west on the 72nd Street park road to your starting point. **Riverside Park,** along the Hudson River bank in Manhattan, is glorious at sunset. You can cover 4½ miles by running from 72nd to 116th streets and back.

Other favorite Manhattan circuits are around **Gramercy Park** (⅓ mile), **Washington Square Park** (½ mile), the **Battery Park City Esplanade** (about 2 miles), and the **Hudson River Esplanade** (about 1½ miles). In Brooklyn, try the **Brooklyn Heights Esplanade,** facing the Manhattan skyline, or the loop in **Prospect Park** (about 6 miles).

A year-round schedule of races and group runs is organized by the **New York Road Runners Club** (⊠ 9 E. 89th St., ☎ 212/860–4455), including group runs at 6:30 PM and 7:15 PM on weekdays and at 10 AM Saturday, starting at the club headquarters. One of the most popular events is the 5-mile Runner's World Nike Midnight Run, held on New Year's Eve with many of the runners wearing inventive costumes.

Racewalking
Elbows pumping vigorously at their sides, racewalkers can move as fast as some joggers, the great difference being that their heels are planted firmly with every stride. A number of competitive racewalking events are held regularly; for information, contact the **Park Walker's Club** (⊠ 320 E. 83rd St., ☎ 212/628–1317).

Swimming

The **Carmine Street Recreation Center** (⊠ 7th Ave. S and Clarkson St., ☎ 212/242–5228), which has a 23-yard indoor pool and a 105-yard outdoor pool. For the $25 membership fee, you can use the pool daily while you're in town, but you have to bring your own padlock and towel. **Asphalt Green** (⊠ York Ave., between 90th and 92nd Sts., ☎ 212/369–8890) is a fairly new facility with a pool and some fitness equipment; drop-in fee for the day is $15. **Chelsea Piers Sports Center** (⊠ 23rd St. and the Hudson River, ☎ 212/336–6000) has a six-lane, 25-yard lap pool, with an adjacent whirlpool. Day passes are $26. The

U.N. Plaza-Park Hyatt (⊠ 1 United Nations Plaza, ☎ 212/702–5016) has a lovely rooftop swimming pool that can be used by nonguests for a $25-a-day fee. The **YWCA** (⊠ 610 Lexington Ave. at 53rd St., ☎ 212/755–4500) has a sparkling 75-foot lap pool available at $10 to members of all YWCAs and $15 to nonmembers .

Tennis

The New York City Parks Department maintains scores of tennis courts. Some of the most scenic are the 26 clay courts and four hard courts in **Central Park** (mid-park, near 94th St., ☎ 212/280–0206), set in a thicket of trees with the skyline beyond. Same-day admissions are available for $5 an hour per person.

You can also play where Pete Sampras and Andre Agassi do: at the **USTA National Tennis Center** (☎ 718/760–6200) in Flushing Meadows–Corona Park, Queens, site of the U.S. Open Tournament. The center has 29 outdoor and nine indoor courts, all Deco Turf II. Reservations are accepted up to two days in advance, and prices range from $14 to $40, depending on when you play.

Several local clubs will book courts to nonmembers:

Crosstown Tennis (⊠ 14 W. 31st St., ☎ 212/947–5780) has four indoor hard courts that are air-conditioned in summer.

Midtown Tennis Club (⊠ 341 8th Ave. at 27th St., ☎ 212/989–8572) provides lessons and sponsors a tennis camp. It's best to make reservations for one of their eight courts a couple of days in advance.

HRC Tennis (⊠ Piers 13 and 14, East River at Wall St., ☎ 212/422–9300) has eight Har-Tru courts under two bubbles, which are air-conditioned in summer. HRC Tennis also owns **Village Tennis Courts** (⊠ 110 University Pl., between 12th and 13th Sts., ☎ 212/989–2300), with two hard rubber courts that are air-conditioned in summer.

Manhattan Plaza Racquet Club (⊠ 450 W. 43rd St., ☎ 212/594–0554) offers five hard surface courts on which WTA and U.S. Open players have been known to practice—not to mention a soap opera star or two, since many actors live in special housing near the club.

Roosevelt Island Racquet Club (⊠ 281 Main St., Roosevelt Island, ☎ 212/935–0250) has 12 air-conditioned green clay courts, group and private lessons, clinics, tennis parties, and game arranging.

SPECTATOR SPORTS

Many sporting events—ranging from boxing to figure skating—take place at **Madison Square Garden** (⊠ 7th Ave., between 31st and 33rd Sts.); tickets can be ordered by phone through the box office (☎ 212/465–6000) or Ticketmaster (☎ 212/307–7171). Both of New York's professional football teams and one of its basketball teams perform across the Hudson River at the **Meadowlands** (⊠ Rte. 3, East Rutherford, NJ; for box office and information, ☎ 201/935–3900). When events are sold out, you can sometimes pick up a ticket on the day of the game outside the venue from a fellow sports fan whose guests couldn't make it at the last minute. Ticket agencies, listed in the Manhattan Yellow Pages phone directory and the sports pages of the *Daily News* can be helpful—for a price.

Baseball

The **New York Mets** play at Shea Stadium (☎ 718/507–8499) at the penultimate stop on the No. 7 subway in Flushing, Queens. The **New York Yankees** have their home at Yankee Stadium (☎ 718/293–6000), accessible by the No. 4, D, or C subway to the 161st Street station in the Bronx. The baseball season runs from April through October.

Basketball

Currently, the **New York Knickerbockers** (the "Knicks") arouse intense hometown passions, which means tickets for home games at Madison Square Garden (✉ 7th Ave., between 31st and 33rd Sts.) are *extremely* hard to come by. For up-to-date game roundups, phone the New York Knickerbockers Fan Line (☎ 212/465–5867). The **New Jersey Nets,** New York's second NBA team, plays at the Meadowlands in the Brendan Byrne Arena (✉ Rte. 3, East Rutherford, NJ). For tickets—which are remarkably easy to obtain—call the Meadowlands box office (☎ 201/935–3900) or TicketMaster (☎ 201/507–8900). The basketball season is late-October–April.

Boxing and Wrestling

Major and minor **boxing** bouts are staged in Madison Square Garden (✉ 7th Ave., between 31st and 33rd Sts., ☎ 212/465–6000). **Wrestling,** a more frequent presence at Madison Square Garden (✉ 7th Ave., between 31st and 33rd Sts., ☎ 212/465–6000) since the days of "Gorgeous" George and "Haystack" Calhoun in the late '50s, is stagy and outrageous, drawing a rowdy but enthusiastic crowd.

Football

The enormously popular **New York Giants** play at Giants Stadium in the Meadowlands sports complex (✉ Rte. 3, East Rutherford, NJ; ☎ 201/935–8111). All seats for Giants games are sold on a season-ticket basis—and there's a waiting list for those. The struggling **New York Jets** play at Giants Stadium (✉ Rte. 3, East Rutherford, NJ; ☎ 516/538–6600). Although they're as scarce as Giants tickets, most Jets tickets are snapped up in August before the season opener. The football season runs September–December.

Hockey

The Stanley cup–winning **New York Rangers** play at Madison Square Garden (✉ 7th Ave., between 31st and 33rd Sts., ☎ 212/465–6741, or call the Rangers hot line at 212/308–6977). The **New York Islanders** skate at Nassau Veterans Memorial Coliseum in Uniondale, Long Island (for tickets call 516/888–9000). The area's third hockey team, the **New Jersey Devils,** fights for the puck at the Brendan Byrne Arena at the Meadowlands (✉ Rte. 3, East Rutherford, NJ; ☎ 201/935–3900). Tickets for the Islanders and Devils are usually available at game time; Rangers tickets are more difficult to find. The hockey season runs from October through April.

Horse Racing

Modern **Aqueduct Racetrack** (✉ 110th St. and Rockaway Blvd., Ozone Park, Queens, ☎ 718/641–4700), with its spate of lawns and gardens, holds Thoroughbred races late-October–early May from Wednesday–Sunday. In May the action moves from Aqueduct Racetrack to **Belmont Park** (✉ Hempstead Turnpike, Elmont, Long Island, ☎ 718/641–4700), home of the third jewel in horse racing's triple crown, the Belmont Stakes. The horses run here May–July, every day except Tuesday. Then after a few weeks upstate at Saratoga, they return to Belmont from late-August through October.

The **Meadowlands** (⊠ Rte. 3, East Rutherford, NJ, ☎ 201/935–8500), generally a trotting venue, also has a flat-racing season from Labor Day through December.

Yonkers Raceway (⊠ Central Ave., Yonkers, NY, ☎ 718/562–9500) features harness racing every evening except Wednesday and Sunday year-round. The **Meadowlands** (⊠ Rte. 3, East Rutherford, NJ, ☎ 201/935–8500) has both trotters and pacers late December–mid-August.

Running

The **New York City Marathon** has taken place annually on a Sunday in early November since 1970, and New Yorkers love to cheer on the pack of 25,000 (some 16,000 of them finish). Racewalkers, "jogglers," oldsters, youngsters, and disabled competitors help to make this what former Olympic Organizing Committee president Peter V. Ueberroth called "the best sporting event in the country." Spectators line rooftops and sidewalks, promenades, and terraces all along the route—but don't go near the finish line in Central Park around 2 PM unless you relish mob scenes. Contact the **New York Road Runners Club** (☎ 212/860–4455).

Tennis

The annual **U.S. Open Tournament,** held from late-August through early September at the U.S.T.A. National Tennis Center (⊠ Flushing Meadow/Corona Park, Queens, ☎ 718/760–6200), is one of the high points of the tennis buff's year, and tickets to watch the late rounds are some of the hottest in town. Early-round matches are entertaining, too, and with a stadium-court ticket you can also view matches in outlying courts—where the bleachers are so close you can almost count the sweat beads on the players' foreheads—and in the grandstand, where bleacher seating is first-come, first-served. During early rounds, ushers may help you move down to better seats in the stadium court or the grandstand (you may wish to consider giving a gratuity of $5 or $10). Wherever you sit, the eclectic mix of casual visitors, tennis groupies, and celebrities makes for terrific people-watching. Tickets go on sale in May through Telecharge (☎ 800/524–8440).

The tennis year winds up with the **WTA Tournament,** a major women's pro event held at Madison Square Garden (⊠ 7th Ave., between 31st and 33rd Sts., ☎ 212/465–6000) in mid-November. Tickets go on sale in September.

10 Shopping

More than ever before, New York is the place to shop—from its small boutiques and retro-style salons to its larger discount-chain stores. Welcome the era of the superstore and the specialty boutique, flourishing side by side in the city. In fact, each complements the other in an ever-changing market. And such singular variety makes the retail landscape of New York an eyeful.

THERE'S SOMETHING FOR EVERYONE, in every price range in New York. You can hunt for gift baskets that look like French paintings (**Manhattan Fruitier,** ✉ 105 E. 29th St.), special paper products (**Kate's Paperie,** ✉ 561 Broadway, ☎ 212/941–9816), ooh-la luscious gifts and home furnishings (**La Maison Moderne,** ✉ 144 West 19th St.,), and even skeletons and fossils (**Maxilla & Mandible,** ✉ 451 Columbus Ave., between 81th and 82nd Sts.).

By Karen Cure

Updated by
Clair Berg

Another big Manhattan shopping lure is the bargain. Major intersections are instant markets as street peddlers hawk fake Gucci and Cartier watches at $15–$25 each. (These may just possibly last a year or two.) There are thrift shops and resale shops where well-known socialites send their castoffs and movie stars snap up antique lace. At off-price and discount stores, mark-offs result in substantial savings, and the sales are even better. Designers' showroom sales allow you to buy cheap at the source; auctions promise good prices as well.

Sales

Sales take place late June and July (for summer merchandise) and late December and January (for winter wares); these sales are announced in the papers. Sales of special merit may end up in *New York* magazine's "Sales and Bargains" column. These often include sales in manufacturers' showrooms that are otherwise never promoted to the public. If your visit is planned for April or October, when most take place, you might phone your favorite designer and ask whether one is in the offing. Find out before you go whether the seller requires cash or accepts credit cards and checks (whether local or out-of-state).

Shopping Neighborhoods

New York shops are, for the most part, collected in neighborhoods rather than in malls, so there's nothing more pleasant than shop-crawling when the weather is fine. The following sections single out shopping highlights in each neighborhood. Addresses for shops, if not included here, can be found in store listings below.

South Street Seaport

The Seaport's shops are located along the cobbled, pedestrians-only extension to Fulton Street; in the Fulton Market building, the original home of the city's fish market; and on the three levels of Pier 17. You'll find many outstanding retailers: **Ann Taylor** for women's clothing, **Brookstone** for gadgets and hardware, **Caswell-Massey** for fragrances, and **Sharper Image** for high-tech gimmickry. The big catalogue house **J. Crew** chose the Seaport as the location for its first Manhattan retail outlet. There are also few-of-a-kind shops, notably **Bowne & Co.,** an old-fashioned print shop; **Mariposa** for rare butterflies mounted under glass; and **Next Stop South Pole** for penguin-themed gifts.

World Financial Center

Although the nearby World Trade Center bills its concourse as the city's busiest shopping center, the World Financial Center in Battery Park City is a shopping destination to reckon with, thanks to stores such as **Barneys New York** for clothing, **Godiva Chocolatier** for chocolates, **Platypus** for unique gifts, **Ann Taylor,** and **Caswell-Massey. Rizzoli** has books and magazines stocked on handsome wooden shelves, and **Quest Toys** has a wonderful selection of wooden and educational playthings. Most are open on Sundays.

Lower East Side/East Village

Once home to millions of Jewish immigrants from Russia and Eastern Europe, the Lower East Side is New Yorkers' bargain beat. The center of it all is narrow, unprepossessing Orchard Street, which is crammed with tiny, no-nonsense clothing and shoe stores ranging from kitschy to elegant. Don't expect to schmooze with salespeople, especially on Sunday, the busiest day of the week (On, Saturday shops in the Orchard Street area are closed). Start at Houston Street, walk down one side as far as Canal Street, then walk back up. Essential stops include **Fine & Klein** for handbags; **Forman's** for women's clothing; and **Lace-Up Shoes.** Grand Street (off Orchard Street, south of Delancey Street) is chockablock with linens, towels, and other items for the home; the Bowery (between Grand Street and Delancey Street), with lamps and lighting fixtures. The East Village offers diverse, off-beat specialty stops including **Little Rickie** for collectible kitsch.

SoHo

On West Broadway, SoHo's main drag, and on Broadway and Wooster, Greene, Mercer, Prince, Spring, Broome, and Grand streets, major art galleries keep company with chic clothing stores such as **Yohji Yamamoto** and **Agnès B.** Some well-known stops include **Wolfman-Gold & Good Company** for decorative items; **Dean & DeLuca,** a gourmet food emporium; **Zona,** full of well-designed home furnishings and gifts; **Williams-Sonoma Grande Cuisine** for kitchenware and gourmet specialties; and the remarkable **Enchanted Forest** toy store. On Lafayette Street below Houston, a hip new strip includes shops outside the mainstream, mainly dealing in home furnishings. Many stores in SoHo are open seven days a week.

Lower 5th Avenue/Chelsea

Fifth Avenue south of 23rd Street along with the streets fanning east and west are home to some of New York's hippest shops and a lively downtown crowd. Many of the locals sport clothes from the neighborhood—a mix of the hip like **Emporio Armani, Paul Smith,** and **Matsuda** (for Japanese designer clothing) as well as discount clothiers such as **BFO** and **Moe Ginsburg.** The antique-replica and nostalgia-packed world of **B. Shackman & Company, Inc.** is also popular. A block away in the same latitudes on 6th Avenue are a cluster of superstores, including **Barnes & Noble, T. J. Maxx, Filene's Basement, Burlington Coat Factory,** and **Old Navy,** as well as the colossal **Bed, Bath & Beyond,** which now has a café. **Barneys, Williams-Sonoma,** and **Pottery Barn** are within walking distance on nearby 7th Avenue.

Herald Square

Reasonable prices prevail at this intersection of 34th Street and Avenue of the Americas (6th Avenue). Giant **Macy's** has traditionally been the linchpin. Opposite is Manhattan's first **Toys "R" Us.** Next door on 6th Avenue, the seven-story Manhattan Mall is anchored by **Stern's** department store, which makes for wonderful browsing, as do **Lechter's,** for home furnishings; **HMV** for its large music selection; and **Mouse N' Around,** for cartoon-emblazoned merchandise. The concentration of shops in a small area makes it a good bet in nasty weather.

5th Avenue

The boulevard that was once home to some of the biggest names in New York retailing is not what it once was, that role having been usurped by Madison Avenue north of 57th Street. But 5th Avenue from Central Park South to Rockefeller Center still shines with **F.A.O. Schwarz** and **Bergdorf Goodman** (both the main store and **Bergdorf Goodman Men** are at 58th St.), **Tiffany** and **Bulgari** jewelers (at 57th St.), **Ferragamo** and other various luxury stores in **Trump Tower** (at 56th St.), **Steuben**

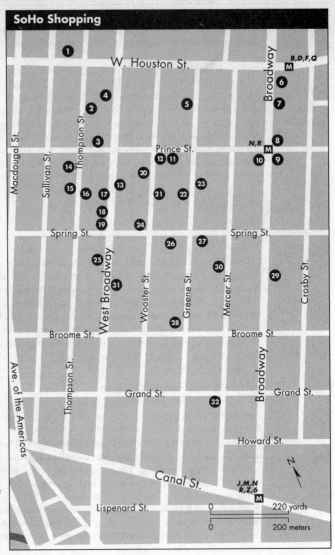

SoHo Shopping

crystal (at 56th St.), **Henri Bendel,** across the street, **Takashimaya** (at 54th St.), **Cartier** jewelers (at 52nd St.), and so on down to **Saks Fifth Avenue** (at 50th St.). **Rockefeller Center** itself provides a plethora of shops. To the south (at 47th St.) is the shiny 575 atrium mall, named for its 5th Avenue address, and the venerable **Lord & Taylor** department store (at 39th St.).

57th Street

The thoroughfare of Carnegie Hall, Planet Hollywood, and the Hard Rock Cafe supports stores that sell everything from remaindered books to $50,000 diamond-and-platinum bracelets. Begin at the **Compleat Strategist** game store (between 8th and 9th Aves.) and head eastward, via the **Pottery Barn, Coliseum Books,** and **Jerry Brown** and **Paron** fabric stores. At 5th Avenue you'll come to **Bergdorf Goodman's** two stores, one on each corner on the south side of the street. On the northeast corner of 57th Street and 5th Avenue, you'll find the glittery, glassy **Warner Bros. Studio Store**, with its state-of-the-art interactive elements,

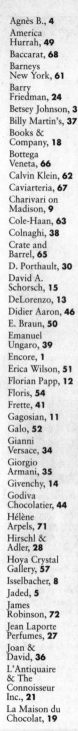

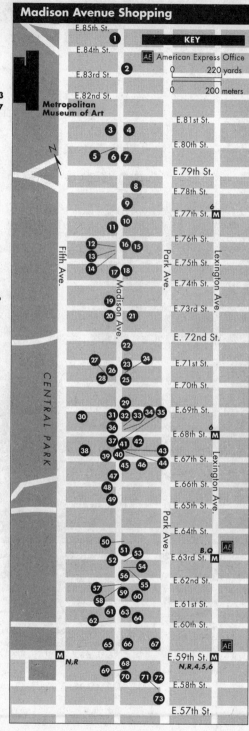

57th Street/5th Avenue Shopping

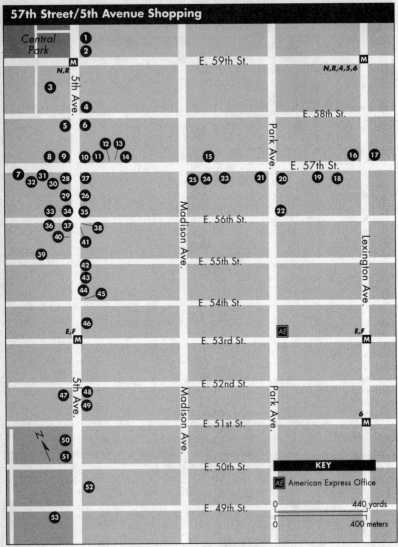

A La Vieille Russie, **2**
Alfred Dunhill of London, **21**
André Emmerich Gallery, **15**
Ann Taylor, **11**
Asprey, **35**
Bergdorf Goodman, **5, 6**
Blum Helman, **31**
Buccellati, **23**
Bulgari, **28**
Burberrys, **13**
Cartier, **48**
Chanel, **12**
Charivari 57, **30**
Cole-Haan, **50**
Christian Dior, **42**

David Webb, **20**
Dempsey & Carroll, **19**
F.A.O. Schwarz, **4**
Façonnable, **45**
Felissimo, **36**
Fortunoff, **46**
Gazebo, **18**
Geoffrey Beene, **1**
Godiva Chocolatier, **43**
H. Stern, **49**
Hammacher Schlemmer, **17**
Harry Winston, **37**
Henri Bendel, **40**
Hermès, **14**
Ikea's Manhattan Outpost, **16**

Israel Sack, **29**
J.N. Bartfield, **7**
Kinokuniya Bookstore, **53**
Librairie de France/Libraria Hispanica, **51**
Louis Féraud, **34**
Manolo Blahnik, **39**
Neuchatel Chocolates, **3**
Norma Kamali O.M.O., **33**
Pace Gallery, **25**
Rizzoli, **8**
Saks Fifth Avenue, **52**
Salvatore Ferragamo, **38**
Steuben, **41**

Susan Bennis Warren Edwards, **32**
T. Anthony, **22**
Takashimaya New York, **44**
Teuscher Choclates, **50**
Tiffany & Co., **27**
Tower Records and Videos, **26**
Traveller's Bookstore, **47**
Trump Tower, **26**
Van Cleef & Arpels, **9**
Victoria's Secret, **24**
Warner Bros. Studio Store, **10**

animation art, and vast array of children's merchandise, as well as such exclusive stores as **Chanel, Burberrys, Hermès,** and **Alfred Dunhill of London** for men's clothing and cigars (at the corner of Park Ave.). Above these stores are top art galleries such as **André Emmerich** and **Pace.**

Columbus Avenue

Between 66th and 86th streets, this former tenement district is now home to some of the city's glitziest stores. Shops are mostly modern in design, upscale but not top-of-the-line. Clothing runs the gamut from traditional for men and women (**Frank Stella Ltd.**) to high funk (**Betsey Johnson**) and high style (**Charivari**).

Upper East Side

On Madison and Lexington avenues, roughly between 57th and 79th streets, New York branches of world-renowned designer boutiques are joined by spirited retailers who fill their stores with the unique and stylish. **Calvin Klein**'s retail store opened its doors recently on Madison and 60th St., carrying men's and women's fashion as well as tableware and sheets. On the Upper East Side, domestic and imported items for the home, fine antiques, and wonderful clothing predominate—and the prices aren't always sky-high. **Ikea,** for instance, now has a Manhattan outpost here.

Blitz Tours

Get your subway tokens ready, and save enough cash for cab fare to lug all your packages home from these shopping itineraries. They're arranged by special interest; addresses, if not included here, can be found in the store listings below.

Antiques

Spend two hours at the **Manhattan Art & Antiques Center** on 2nd Avenue (at 55th St.), then swing over to 57th Street for an even posher array of European, American, and Asian treasures. Stroll westward across 57th Street, stopping at **Lillian Nassau** of Tiffany lamp and Art Nouveau furniture fame and **Israel Sack,** nearby on 5th Avenue, with superb American antique furniture. Then head up Madison to **America Hurrah** (at 65th St.), **Didier Aaron** (on 67th St.), **Thomas K. Woodard** (near 69th St.), **Leigh Keno** (on 74th St.), **Stair & Company** (near 74th St.), **DeLorenzo** and **Leo Kaplan** (near 75th St.), **David A. Schorsch** (on 76th St.), **Florian Papp** (at 76th St.), and **Barry Friedman** (at 83rd St.).

Bargains

Start early at **Century 21** or **Syms** in lower Manhattan. Take a cab to Hester and Orchard streets and shop along Orchard to Houston Street. (Prowl along Grand Street if you're more interested in goods for your home than in clothing.) Leave at 2:30 and take a cab to **S&W** in Chelsea; shop the new Chelsea discounters—**Old Navy, T. J. Maxx,** and others, for everything from clothes to housewares; then take the subway uptown to **Loehmann's** (open until 9 PM) in the Bronx. But remember: On Saturdays, most shops on the Lower East Side are closed.

Cook's Tour

Browse in **Zabar's** (⊠ 2245 Broadway at W. 80th St.) for a couple of hours beginning at 8 AM; then go across town to **Kitchen Arts & Letters** bookstore (⊠ 1435 Lexington Ave., between 93rd and 94th Sts.) and proceed down to **Bridge Kitchenware** (⊠ 214 E. 52nd St.). Order an enchanting fruit basket from **Manhattan Fruitier** (⊠ 105 E. 29th St.). Head downtown to hit **Balducci's** in the Village; **Williams-Sonoma Grande Cuisine** (⊠ 580 Broadway, between Houston and Prince Sts.), **Dean & DeLuca** (⊠ 560 Broadway at Prince St.), and **Broadway Panhandler** (⊠ 477 Broome Street, between Greene and Wooster Sts.) in

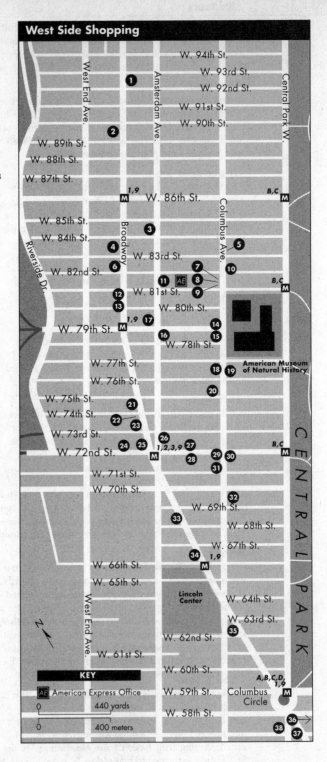

West Side Shopping

KEY

AE American Express Office

0 — 440 yards

0 — 400 meters

SoHo; and **Kam-Man** (⊠ 200 Canal St.,) in Chinatown. Or head up-town to **Macy's Cellar.** If you live in a landlocked area, make your last stop in New York **Citarella** (⊠ 2135 Broadway at 75th St.), and have some great fish packed in ice to go.

Home Furnishings

For a French accent, start at the luscious, two-story, petite **La Maison Moderne** (⊠ 144 West 19th St.) for distinctive home furnishings, ele-gant decor, and one-of-a-kind gifts, also complimentary espresso and cappuccino; on weekends, mimosas. Stop at **Barneys New York** (⊠ 7th Ave. and 17th St.), and visit its Chelsea Passage. Head to Greenwich Village to **William–Wayne & Co.** (⊠ 40 University Place; also uptown at 846 and 850 Lexington Ave. at 64th St.) for elegant decorative gifts for the home and garden. Then take a cab to SoHo and stroll around, making sure not to miss **Wolfman–Gold & Good Company** (⊠ 116 Greene St.) and **Zona** (⊠ 97 Greene St.). Cab it back uptown to **Ikea's Man-hattan Outpost** (⊠ 131 E. 57th St.) and **Crate & Barrel** (⊠ 650 Madi-son Ave. at 59th St.) for great selection, and finally over to **Bloomingdale's,** open late on Thursdays, and to **Macy's,** open late Mon-days, Thursdays, and Fridays.

Department Stores

Most of these stores keep regular hours on weekdays and are open late (8 or 9) at least one night a week. Many have personal shoppers who can walk you through the store at no charge.

ABC Carpet & Home (⊠ 888 Broadway at 19th St., ☎ 212/473–3000). This huge emporium has just about everything for the home, from an-tique armoires to modern, state-of-the-art TVs and stereos.

Barneys New York (⊠ 106 7th Ave. at 17th St., ☎ 212/593–7800; ⊠ Madison Ave. at 61st St., ☎ 212/826–8900; ⊠ World Financial Cen-ter, ☎ 212/945–1600). Founded as a menswear discounter some 60 years ago, Barneys is still the place to see what's hot. The still-exten-sive selection of menswear ranges from made-to-measure and Euro-pean and American designer labels to mass-market natural-shouldered suits; the women's department is a showcase of current fashion.

Bergdorf Goodman (⊠ 754 5th Ave., between 57th and 58th Sts., ☎ 212/753–7300). Good taste reigns in an elegant and understated set-ting. The Home Department is room after exquisite room of wonder-ful linens, tabletop items, and gifts. The expanded men's store, across the street, occupies the former home of the giant F.A.O. Schwarz toy store (⊠ now at 767 5th Ave.).

Bloomingdale's (⊠ 1000 3rd Ave. at 59th St., ☎ 212/355–5900). Only a handful of department stores occupy an entire city block; Macy's is one, and this New York institution is another. The main floor is a stu-pefying maze of cosmetic counters, mirrors, and black walls; else-where the racks are overfull and the salespeople overworked. Still, selections are dazzling at all but the lowest price points, and the mark-downs on top-of-the-line designer goods can be extremely rewarding.

Henri Bendel (⊠ 712 5th Ave., between 55th and 56th Sts., ☎ 212/247–1100). Bendel's continues to charm with its stylish displays and so-phisticated boutiques. The second-floor café is a delight.

Lord & Taylor (⊠ 424 5th Ave., between 38th and 39th Sts., ☎ 212/391–3344). This store can be relied upon for the wearable, the fashionable, and the classic in clothes and accessories for women. It's refined, well stocked, and never overwhelming.

Macy's (⊠ Herald Sq., Broadway at 34th St., ☎ 212/695–4400). No less than a miracle on 34th Street, Macy's main store is the largest re-tail store in America. Over the past two decades, it has grown chic and much more au courant in the style department, but its main floor is reassuringly traditional. Estate Jewelry offers fine antique pieces. And for cooking gear and housewares, the Cellar nearly outdoes Zabar's.

Saks Fifth Avenue (✉ 611 5th Ave., between 49th and 50th Sts., ☎ 212/753–4000). This wonderful store still embodies the spirit of service and style with which it opened in 1926. Saks believes in good manners, the ceremonies of life, and dressing for the part; the selections for men, women, and children affirm this quality.

Stern's (✉ 33rd St. and 6th Ave., ☎ 212/244–6060). What was the old Gimbel's, a block south of Macy's, lives again as home to an atrium mall, whose nine floors are anchored by Stern's, working hard to become as well established here as in the outer boroughs. The sales are some of the best in town.

Takashimaya New York (✉ 693 5th Ave., between 54th and 55th Sts., ☎ 212/350–0100). This pristine branch of Japan's largest department store carries stylish clothes and fine household items, all of which reflect a combination of Eastern and Western designs.

Specialty Shops

Antiques

Antiquing is fine sport in Manhattan. Goods run the gamut from rarefied museum-quality to wacky and eminently affordable. Premier shopping areas are on Madison Avenue north of 57th Street, 57th Street east of 5th Avenue, and 60th Street between 2nd and 3rd avenues, where more than 20 shops, dealing in everything from 18th-century French furniture to Art Deco lighting fixtures cluster on one block. Around 11th and 12th streets, between University Place and Broadway, a tantalizing array of settees, tables, bedsteads, and rocking chairs can be seen in the windows of about two dozen dealers, many of whom have TO THE TRADE signs on their doors; a card from your hometown architect or decorator, however, may get you inside. Most dealers are open on Saturdays.

Many small dealers cluster in two antiques "malls."

Manhattan Art & Antiques Center (✉ 1050 2nd Ave., between 55th and 56th Sts., ☎ 212/355–4400). More than 100 dealers stocking everything from paisley and Judaica to satsuma, scientifica, and samovars jumble the three floors here. The level of quality is not, as a rule, up to that of Madison Avenue, but then neither are the prices.

Metropolitan Arts and Antiques Pavilion (✉ 110 W. 19th St., between 6th Ave. and 7th Aves., ☎ 212/463–0200). Good for costume jewelry, off-beat bric-a-brac, and '50s kitsch, this antiques mall holds regularly scheduled auctions and specialty shows featuring rare books, photography, tribal art, Victoriana, and other lots.

AMERICAN AND ENGLISH

America Hurrah (✉ 766 Madison Ave., between 65th and 66th Sts., 3rd Floor, ☎ 212/535–1930). Superb American patchwork quilts and other Americana can be found here.

David A. Schorsch (✉ 30 E. 76th St., No. 11A, ☎ 212/439–6100). This specialist in Early American furniture and folk art sees clients by appointment only.

Florian Papp (✉ 962 Madison Ave., between 75th and 76th Sts., ☎ 212/288–6770). This store has an unassailed reputation among knowledgeable collectors.

Hyde Park Antiques (✉ 836 Broadway, between 12th and 13th Sts., ☎ 212/477–0033). This store features English decorative arts from the 18th and 19th centuries.

Kentshire Galleries (⊠ 37 E. 12th St., ☎ 212/673–6644). There are eight floors of elegant furniture displayed in room settings, with an emphasis on formal English pieces from the 18th and 19th centuries, particularly the Georgian and Regency periods.

Leigh Keno American Antiques (⊠ 980 Madison Ave., 2nd Floor, ☎ 212/734–2381). Before he was 30, Leigh Keno set a new auction record in the American antiques field by paying $2.75 million for a hairy-paw-foot Philadelphia wing chair. He has a good eye and an interesting inventory.

Steve Miller American Folk Art (⊠ 17 E. 96th St., ☎ 212/348–5219). This gallery is run by one of the country's premier folk-art dealers, the author of *The Art of the Weathervane.*

Israel Sack (⊠ 730 5th Ave., between 56th and 57th Sts., ☎ 212/399–6562). This is widely considered one of the very best places in the country for 18th-century American furniture.

Stair & Company (⊠ 942 Madison Ave., between 74th and 75th Sts., ☎ 212/517–4400). Period rooms stylishly show off fine 18th- and 19th-century English mahogany and other pieces.

Thomas K. Woodard (⊠ 799 Madison Ave., between 67th and 68th Sts., 2nd Floor, ☎ 212/794–9404). Americana and antique quilts are among the specialties of this prestigious dealer.

ECLECTIC

Newel Art Galleries (⊠ 425 E. 53rd St., ☎ 212/758–1970). Located near the East Side's interior-design district, this gallery, the city's biggest antiques store, has a huge collection that roams from the Renaissance to the 20th century.

EUROPEAN

Artisan Antiques (⊠ 81 University Pl. at 11th St., ☎ 212/751–5214). Art Deco chandeliers come in merry profusion, along with lamps, sconces, and other lighting fixtures from France.

Barry Friedman (⊠ 851 Madison Ave., between 70th and 71st Sts., ☎ 212/794–8950). Wiener Werkstätte, Bauhaus, De Stijl, Russian Constructivist, and other European avant-gardists star.

DeLorenzo (⊠ 958 Madison Ave., between 75th and 76th Sts., ☎ 212/249–7575). Come here to explore the sinuous curves, strongly articulated shapes, and highly polished surfaces of French Art Deco furniture and accessories at their best.

Didier Aaron (⊠ 32 E. 67th St., ☎ 212/988–5248). This highly esteemed gallery specializes in superb 18th- and 19th-century French furniture and paintings.

L'Antiquaire & The Connoisseur, Inc. (⊠ 36 E. 73rd St., ☎ 212/517–9176). Proprietress Helen Fioratti has written a guide to French antiques, but she is equally knowledgeable about the Italian and Spanish furniture and decorative objects from the 15th through the 18th centuries, as well as the medieval arts, that comprise her stock.

Leo Kaplan Ltd. (⊠ 967 Madison Ave., between 75th and 76th Sts., ☎ 212/249–6766). The impeccable items here include Art Nouveau glass and pottery, porcelain from 18th-century England, stunning antique and modern paperweights, and Russian artwork, including creations by Fabergé.

Malmaison Antiques (⊠ 253 E. 74th St., ☎ 212/288–7569). This gallery has the country's largest selection of Empire furniture and decorative arts.

Pierre Deux Antiques (⊠ 369 Bleecker St. at the corner of Charles St., ☎ 212/243–7740). The company that brought French provincial to a provincial America still offers an excellent selection.

FUN STUFF

Back Pages Antiques (⊠ 125 Greene St., ☎ 212/460–5998). To acquire an antique jukebox or slot machine, just drop in.

Darrow's Fun Antiques (⊠ 1101 1st Ave., between 60th and 61st Sts., ☎ 212/838–0730). The first of the city's nostalgia shops, the store is full of whimsy: antique toys, animation art, and other collectibles.

John T. Johnston's Jukebox Classics (⊠ 6742 5th Ave., near 68th St., Brooklyn, ☎ 718/833–8455). You'll find oodles of vintage jukeboxes, pinball machines, gum ball machines, slot machines, and other goodies, all expertly restored.

Art Galleries

America's art capital, New York has numerous wealthy collectors, so many galleries are minimuseums that welcome browsing.

André Emmerich Gallery (⊠ 41 E. 57th St., ☎ 212/752–0124). Located in the Art Deco Fuller Building, this gallery displays major works by major modern artists.

Art in General (⊠ 79 Walker St., ☎ 212/219–0473). Come here for works in a variety of mediums by emerging contemporary artists.

Blum Helman (⊠ 20 W. 57th St., ☎ 212/245–2888). Contemporary art by Brian Hunt, Robert Moskowitz, Joe Andoe, and Ellsworth Kelly, among others, is displayed here.

A Clean, Well-Lighted Place (⊠ 363 Bleecker St., ☎ 212/255–3656). Prints by well-known artists, including Sean Scully, Susan Rothenberg, Robert Motherwell, and David Hockney, are displayed here.

Colnaghi (⊠ 21 E. 67th St., ☎ 212/772–2266). This is the New York outpost of one of London's preeminent fine art galleries, offering European and English paintings and objets d'art.

First Peoples Gallery (⊠ 114 Spring St., ☎ 212/343–0166). Paintings, sculpture, and magnificent pottery by many of the country's top Native American artists are showcased here.

Gagosian (⊠ 980 Madison Ave., between 76th and 77th Sts., ☎ 212/744–2313; ⊠ 136 Wooster St., ☎ 212/228–2828). Works on display are by such artists as Richard Serra, Willem de Kooning, Jasper Johns, Frank Stella, Warhol, David Salle, and Philip Taaffe.

Hirschl & Adler (⊠ 21 E. 70th St., ☎ 212/535–8810). A respected dealer of American painting and sculpture, this gallery also offers American decorative arts. Among the celebrated artists whose works are featured: Thomas Cole, Childe Hassam, Ralston Crawford, John Storrs, and William Merritt Chase.

Isselbacher (⊠ 41 E. 78th St., ☎ 212/472–1766). This gallery offers prints by late-19th- and 20th-century masters such as Henri Toulouse-Lautrec, Henri Matisse, Marc Chagall, Joan Miró, Pablo Picasso, and Edvard Munch.

Leo Castelli (⊠ 420 W. Broadway, between Prince and Spring Sts., ☎ 212/431–5160; ⊠ 578 Broadway, near Prince St., ☎ 212/431–6279). He's the man who discovered Pop. Look for works by Jasper Johns, Roy Lichtenstein, Ed Ruscha, and Ed Rosenquist.

Margo Feiden Galleries (⊠ 699 Madison Ave., between 62nd and 63rd Sts., ☎ 212/677–5330). The specialty here is drawings and prints by theatrical caricaturist Al Hirschfeld, who has been delighting readers of the *New York Times* for more than 60 years.

Mary Boone (⊠ 734 5th Ave., ☎ 212/752–2929). A hot '80s gallery, it's now uptown and still intriguing, with such artists as Eric Fischl and Richard Tuttle.

Multiple Impressions (⊠ 128 Spring St., ☎ 212/925–1313). Twentieth-century American, European, and South American paintings and prints are offered here at reasonable prices.

O. K. Harris (✉ 383 W. Broadway, ☎ 212/431–3600). The oldest gallery in SoHo, opened in 1969, O. K. Harris showcases paintings, sculpture, and photography by contemporary artists.

Pace Gallery (✉ 32 E. 57th St., ☎ 212/421–3292). This gallery features such well-known modern and contemporary artists as Picasso, Alexander Calder, and Julian Schnabel.

Paula Cooper (✉ 155 Wooster St., ☎ 212/674–0766). Exhibits include contemporary paintings and sculpture. At press time, the gallery had plans to move to Chelsea in late 1996.

Pat Hearn Gallery (✉ 530 W. 22nd St., ☎ 212/727–7366). Emerging and established artists are showcased here.

Spanierman (✉ 45 E. 58th St., ☎ 212/832–0208). More than a half-century old and now in handsome quarters, this gallery deals in 19th- and early 20th-century American painting and sculpture.

Books

With so many of the country's publishing houses, magazines, and writers based here, there is an abundance of bookshops, small and large. Of course, all the big national chains are here—**Barnes & Noble, B. Dalton, Brentano's, Doubleday, Waldenbooks**—with branches all over town.

Biography Bookshop (✉ 400 Bleecker St., ☎ 212/807–8655). Published diaries, letters, biographies, and autobiographies fill this neighborly store.

Books & Company (✉ 939 Madison Ave., between 74th and 75th Sts., ☎ 212/737–1450). A comfy upstairs sofa and broad book selection invites lingering here.

Coliseum Books (✉ 1771 Broadway at 57th St., ☎ 212/757–8381). This supermarket of a bookstore has a huge, quirky selection of remainders, best-sellers, and scholarly works.

Corner Bookstore (✉ 1313 Madison Ave. at 93rd St., ☎ 212/831–3554). This friendly small shop has been a favorite with local book lovers for years.

Drama Book Shop (✉ 723 7th Ave., between 48th and 49th Sts., ☎ 212/944–0595). The comprehensive stock here includes scripts, scores, and libretti.

Gotham Book Mart (✉ 41 W. 47th St., ☎ 212/719–4448). The late Frances Steloff opened this store years ago with just $200 in her pocket, half of it on loan. But she helped launch James Joyce's *Ulysses,* D. H. Lawrence, and Henry Miller and is now legendary among bibliophiles, as is her bookstore, an oasis for those who love to read.

Irish Bookshop (✉ 580 Broadway at Prince St., 11th Floor, ☎ 212/274–1923). Here you'll find the country's widest selection of books about Ireland, both current and out-of-print titles.

Kinokuniya Bookstore (✉ 10 W. 49th St., ☎ 212/765–1461). Come here for everything you ever wanted to read about Japan—in English and Japanese.

Librairie de France/Libraria Hispanica (✉ 610 5th Ave., in Rockefeller Center, ☎ 212/581–8810). These huge collections of foreign-language books and periodicals, some in quite exotic tongues, are among the country's largest. Books in French and Spanish predominate.

Madison Avenue Bookshop (✉ 833 Madison Ave., between 69th and 70th Sts., ☎ 212/535–6130). Serious contemporary fiction and biographies are sold here in pleasant surroundings.

Rizzoli (✉ 31 W. 57th St., ☎ 212/759–2424; ✉ 454 W. Broadway, ☎ 212/674–1616; ✉ World Financial Center, ☎ 212/385–1400). Uptown, an elegant marble entrance, oak paneling, chandeliers, and classical music accompany books and magazines on art, architecture, dance, design, photography, and travel; the downtown stores come with fewer frills.

Shakespeare & Co. (⊠ 939 Lexington Ave., between 68th and 69th Sts., ☎ 212/570–0201; ⊠ 2259 Broadway at 81st St., ☎ 212/580–7800; ⊠ 716 Broadway at Washington Pl., ☎ 212/529–1330). The stock here represents what's happening in publishing today in just about every field. Late hours are a plus.

CHILDREN'S BOOKS

Bank Street College Bookstore (⊠ 2875 Broadway at 112th St., ☎ 212/678–1654). Operated by the famed teachers college, here's a miniemporium of politically correct children's books, cassettes, games, and videos. More than 30,000 titles are available.

Books of Wonder (⊠ 132 7th Ave. at 18th St., ☎ 212/989–3270). This store offers an excellent stock of children's books—including antique and out-of-print books—for all reading levels. Oziana is a specialty. Sunday-morning story hours present authors and artists.

Twinkleberry and Nutkin (⊠ 311 E. 81st St., ☎ 212/794–2565). Besides its thoughtful selection of children's books, the shop stocks educational and book character–related toys and gifts.

GAY AND LESBIAN

A Different Light (⊠ 151 W. 19th St., between 6th and 7th Aves., ☎ 212/989–4850). A popular source for fiction, nonfiction, periodicals, calendars, posters, and information about gay life in New York.

Oscar Wilde Memorial Bookshop (⊠ 15 Christopher St., ☎ 212/255–8097). Opened in 1967, this was the first gay and lesbian bookstore in the city. It's just steps away from the site of the Stonewall riots.

MUSIC

Carl Fischer (62 Cooper Sq., ☎ 212/777–0900). This landmark in the East Village is known for its excellent selection of sheet music for all instruments, including music for choir and band.

Colony Music (⊠ 1619 Broadway at 49th St., ☎ 212/265–2050). Sheet music of popular songs can be found here.

Joseph Patelson Music House (⊠ 160 W. 56th St., ☎ 212/582–5840). A huge collection of scores has long made this the heart of the music lover's New York.

MYSTERY AND SUSPENSE

Whodunits are the specialty at **Murder Ink** (⊠ 2486 Broadway, between 92nd and 93rd Sts., ☎ 212/362–8905); **Mysterious Bookshop** (⊠ 129 W. 56th St., ☎ 212/765–0900); and **Partners & Crime** (⊠ 44 Greenwich Ave., between 10th and 11th Sts., ☎ 212/243–0440).

RARE AND USED BOOKS

Academy Book Store (⊠ 10 W. 18th St., ☎ 212/242–4848). Out-of-print, used, antiquarian, scholarly, and art books overflow here. Academy also deals with autographs and carries a selection of classical and jazz records and CDs.

Argosy Bookstore (⊠ 116 E. 59th St., ☎ 212/753–4455). This sedate landmark, established in 1921, keeps a scholarly stock of books and autographs.

Bauman Rare Books (⊠ The Waldorf-Astoria, lobby level, 301 Park Ave. at 50th St., ☎ 212/759–8300). This very successful Philadelphia firm now offers New Yorkers the most impossible-to-get titles, first editions, and fine leather sets.

J. N. Bartfield (⊠ 30 W. 57th St., 3rd floor, ☎ 212/245–8890). This legend in the field offers old and antiquarian books distinguished by binding, author, edition, or content.

Pageant Book and Print Shop (⌧ 114 W. Houston St., ☎ 212/674–5296). This old, reliable shop carries a broad selection of used books, prints, and maps.

Skyline Books & Records, Inc. (⌧ 13 W. 18th St., ☎ 212/675–4773). Come here for out-of-print and unusual books in all fields. The store handles literary first editions, as well as jazz and rock records.

Strand (⌧ 828 Broadway at 12th St., ☎ 212/473–1452; ⌧ 159 John St., ☎ 212/809–0875). Eight miles of shelves house more than 2 million books at this biggest of Manhattan's used-book stores.

TRAVEL BOOKS

Complete Traveller Bookstore (⌧ 199 Madison Ave. at 35th St., ☎ 212/685–9007). Old and new titles are sold here.

Traveller's Bookstore (⌧ 22 W. 52nd St., ☎ 212/664–0995). The stock includes essays and novels, as well as maps and guides.

Cameras and Electronics

Bi-Rite (⌧ 20 E. 39th St., ☎ 212/685–2130). Once your turn comes, this tiny discounter's Hasidic salesmen offer good service, great prices. Take model numbers; there's no showroom.

47th Street Photo (⌧ 115 W. 45th St., ☎ 212/389–1530). Prices can be better elsewhere, but this store, manned by Hasidic Jews, is a heavyweight among electronics discounters. Note Friday afternoon and Saturday closings.

Harvey Electronics (⌧ 2 W. 45th St., ☎ 212/575–5000; ⌧ 888 Broadway at 19th St. inside ABC Carpet & Home, ☎ 212/982–7191). A well-informed staff offers top-of-the-line audio equipment.

Willoughby's (⌧ 136 W. 32nd St., ☎ 212/564–1600). Calling itself the world's largest camera store, Willoughby's rates high among amateurs and pros for selection and service.

CDs, Tapes, and Records

The city's best record stores provide browsers with a window to New York's hipper subcultures.

Bleecker Bob's Golden Oldies (⌧ 118 W. 3rd St., ☎ 212/475–9677). The staff sells punk, new wave, progressive rock, reggae, and R&B until the wee hours.

Footlight Records (⌧ 113 E. 12th St., ☎ 212/533–1572). Stop here to browse through New York's largest selection of old and new musicals and movie soundtracks, as well as a good choice of jazz and popular recordings.

Gryphon Record Shop (⌧ 251 W. 72nd St., 2nd Floor, ☎ 212/874–1588). *New York* magazine called this the city's best rare-record store, citing its 90,000 out-of-print and rare LPs.

HMV (⌧ 57 W. 34th St., ☎ 212/629–0900; ⌧ 2081 Broadway at 72nd St., ☎ 212/721–5900; ⌧ 1280 Lexington Ave. at 86th St., ☎ 212/348–0800; ⌧ 5th Ave. at 46th St., ☎ 212/681–6700). These state-of-the-art record superstores stock 800,000 discs, tapes, and videos.

House of Oldies (⌧ 35 Carmine St., ☎ 212/243–0500). The specialty here is records made between 1950 and the late 1980s—45s and 78s, as well as LPs; there are more than a million titles.

Jazz Record Center (⌧ 236 W. 26th St., 8th Floor, ☎ 212/675–4480). Here is the city's only jazz-record specialist.

J&R Music World (⌧ 23 Park Row, ☎ 212/732–8600). This store offers a huge selection with good prices on major releases. Jazz recordings are sold at 25 Park Row, classical at No. 33.

Midnight Records (⌧ 263 W. 23rd St., ☎ 212/675–2768). This rock specialist stocks obscure artists from the '50s onward.

Tower Records and Videos (✉ 692 Broadway at 4th St., ☎ 212/505–1500; ✉ 2107 Broadway at 74th St., ☎ 212/799–2500; ✉ 725 5th Ave., basement level of Trump Tower, ☎ 212/838–8110). The selection of CDs and tapes can get overwhelming here. The scene is pure New York: At the Village branch, you'll see many customers in head-to-toe black; the Upper West Side outlet has a good selection but a more traditional clientele.

Children's Clothing

Need red-sequined shoes for the baby? Or a sunbonnet? Try one of these:

Bébé Thompson (✉ 1216 Lexington Ave., ☎ 212/249–4740). Downtown style is evident here: plenty of black-and-white and jungle prints among the embroidered treasures. Look for sales.

Ibiza Kidz (✉ 42 University Pl., ☎ 212/505–9907) and **Ibiza** (✉ 46 University Pl., ☎ 212/533–4614). Come here for clothing handmade from beautiful materials, plus shoes and toys.

Greenstones et Cie (✉ 442 Columbus Ave., between 81st and 82nd Sts., ☎ 212/580–4322). **Greenstones Too!** (✉ 1184 Madison Ave., between 86th and 87th Sts., ☎ 212/427–1665). Catering to junior yuppies, these stores offer some handsome clothes, particularly sweaters.

Little Eric (✉ 1331 3rd Ave. at 76th St., ☎ 212/288–8987; ✉ 1118 Madison Ave. at 83rd St., ☎ 212/717–1513). Moms who love Eric can introduce their daughters to this happy footwear shop that's styled in an adult mode.

Oilily (✉ 870 Madison Ave., between 70th and 71st Sts., ☎ 212/628–0100). Brightly colored play and school clothes designed in Holland.

Space Kiddets (✉ 46 E. 21st St., ☎ 212/420–9878). Casual trendsetting clothes for kids are carried here.

Wicker Garden's Children (✉ 1327 Madison Ave., near 93rd St., ☎ 212/410–7001). Top-of-the-line pretties for boys, girls, and babies.

RESALE SHOPS

Once Upon a Time (✉ 171 E. 92nd St., ☎ 212/831–7619) and **Second Act Children's Wear** (✉ 1046 Madison Ave. at 80th St., ☎ 212/988–2440) offer gently worn children's wear, sizes 0–14.

Crystal

Three peerless sources are **Baccarat** (✉ 625 Madison Ave., between 58th and 59th Sts., ☎ 212/826–4100); **Hoya Crystal Gallery** (✉ 689 Madison at 61st St., ☎ 212/223–6335); and **Steuben** (✉ 717 5th Ave. at 56th St., ☎ 212/752–1441). **Rogaska** (✉ 685 Madison Ave., between 61st and 62nd Sts., ☎ 212/980–6200) offers understated classic wares made in Slovenia at relatively modest prices.

Food

CAVIAR

Macy's and **Zabar's** (☞ *below*) feature good deals on caviars, especially when they're battling each other during their periodic "caviar wars." **Caviarteria** (✉ 502 Park Ave. at 59th St., ☎ 212/759–7410) and **Petrossian** (✉ 182 W. 58th St., ☎ 212/245–2217) are specialists.

CHOCOLATE AND CANDY

Elk Candy Company (✉ 240 E. 86th St., ☎ 212/650–1177). This is a marzipan fantasy and a chocoholic's sweet dream.

Black Hound (✉ 149 1st Ave. at 9th St., ☎ 212/979– 9505. The hottest new place to buy truffles and unusual sweets for the sweet is found in the East Village.

Godiva Chocolatier (✉ 793 Madison Ave. at 67th St., ☎ 212/249–9444; ✉ 701 5th Ave., between 54th and 55th Sts., ☎ 212/593–2845; ✉ 560 Lexington Ave. at 50th St., ☎ 212/980–9810; ✉ 33 Maiden

La., ☎ 212/809–8990). This famous maker features cleverly molded chocolates—and embossed gold boxes.

La Maison du Chocolat (✉ 25 E. 73rd St., ☎ 212/744–7117). This is the New York branch of the famous Parisian chocolatier, whose bonbons have been described in *Vogue* as "the most refined and subtle in the world."

Li-Lac Chocolates (✉ 120 Christopher St., ☎ 212/242–7374). This charming nook feeds the Village's sweet tooth with homemade selections in the French tradition.

Neuchatel Chocolates (✉ 2 W. 59th St., in the Plaza Hotel, ☎ 212/751–7742). Velvety chocolates come in five dozen varieties here—all made in New York to approximate the Swiss chocolates.

Teuscher Chocolates (✉ 620 5th Ave., in Rockefeller Center, ☎ 212/246–4416; ✉ 25 E. 61st St., ☎ 212/751–8482). Fabulous chocolates made in Switzerland are flown in weekly for sale in these jewel-box shops, newly decorated each season.

COFFEE

Empire Coffee and Tea Company (✉ 592 9th Ave., between 42nd and 43rd Sts., ☎ 212/586–1717). The selection here numbers almost 90 different beans, plus an extensive array of loose teas.

McNulty's Tea & Coffee Company (✉ 109 Christopher St., ☎ 212/242–5351). Antique wood paneling says "Old New York"—indeed, this is the city's oldest coffee and tea emporium. The barrels of beans say "Timor," "Java," and "New Guinea."

Porto Rico Importing Company (✉ 201 Bleecker St., ☎ 212/477–5421; ✉ 40½ St. Mark's Pl., ☎ 212/533–1982). The dark, old-fashioned, and highly aromatic store on Bleecker Street has been a local coffee source since 1907; the East Village branch has a smaller selection.

Sensuous Bean (✉ 66 W. 70th St., ☎ 212/724–7725). Exotic, confectionery-like flavorings such as banana split and linzertort are a specialty.

GOURMET MARKETS

Balducci's (✉ 424 6th Ave. at 9th St., ☎ 212/673–2600). In this former mom-and-pop food shop, now one of the city's finest food stores, mounds of baby carrots keep company with frilly lettuce, feathery dill, and superlative meats, fish, cheeses, chocolates, baked goods, pastas, vinegars, oils, and Italian specialties.

Dean & DeLuca (✉ 560 Broadway at Prince St., ☎ 212/431–1691). This huge SoHo trendsetter, splendidly bright white, has an encyclopedic selection, from the heady array at the cheese counter to the shelves of crackers and the display cases of prepared foods.

Kam-Man (✉ 200 Canal St., ☎ 212/571–0330). The city's premier Chinese market, Kam-Man is filled with exotic foods, the staccato sound of Chinese, and mysterious smells.

Murray's Sturgeon Shop (✉ 2429 Broadway, between 89th and 90th Sts., ☎ 212/724–2650). A longtime favorite for smoked fish.

Greenmarket Farmers' Market (✉ Union Square, 17th St., between Broadway and Park Ave. S). Farms truck organic produce to this outdoor bastion of fresh food. Home-baked breads, Pennsylvania Dutch pretzels, fish, and local vineyard wine are also for sale. Open Monday, Wednesday, Friday, and Saturday year-round.

Zabar's (✉ 2245 Broadway at 80th St., ☎ 212/787–2000). Enjoy the atmosphere of one of New York's favorite food markets. Dried herbs and spices, chocolates, and assorted bottled foods coexist with a fragrant jumble of fresh breads and the cheese, meat, and smoked-fish counters. Upstairs is a large selection of kitchenware.

SPICES

Aphrodisia (✉ 264 Bleecker St., between 6th and 7th Aves., ☎ 212/989–6440). You'll find more than 700 herbs and spices from all over the world in help-yourself glass canisters.

Kalustyn (✉ 123 Lexington Ave., between 28th and 29th Sts., ☎ 212/685–3451). Spices and delicacies from India and the Mideast abound here.

WINE

Acker Merrall & Condit (✉ 160 W. 72nd St., ☎ 212/787–1700). Known for its selection of red burgundies, this store has knowledge-able, helpful personnel.

Garnet Wines & Liquors (✉ 929 Lexington Ave., between 68th and 69th Sts., ☎ 212/772–3211). Its fine selection includes champagne at prices that one wine writer called "almost charitable."

Morrell & Company (✉ 535 Madison Ave., near 54th St., ☎ 212/688–9370). Peter Morrell is a well-regarded and very colorful figure in the wine business; his store reflects his expertise.

Sherry-Lehmann (✉ 679 Madison Ave., between 61st and 62nd Sts., ☎ 212/838–7500). It's a New York institution.

Union Square Wine & Spirits (✉ 33 Union Sq. E, ☎ 212/675–8100). The store stocks a great selection and has a regular schedule of wine seminars and special tasting events.

Sokolin (✉ 178 Madison Ave., between 33rd and 34th Sts., ☎ 212/532–5893). Knowledgeable oenophiles have been shopping here for more than 50 years.

Fragrance Shops

Aveda Environmental Lifestyle Store (✉ 140 5th Ave. at 19th St., ☎ 212/645–4797)and **Aveda Aromatherapy Esthetique** (✉ 509 Madison Ave., between 52nd and 53rd Sts., ☎ 212/832–2416; ✉ 456 W. Broadway, between Prince and Houston Sts., ☎ 212/473–0280). Con-coct your own perfumes from the impressive selection of essential oils.

Body Shop (✉ 773 Lexington Ave. at 61st St., ☎ 212/755–7851; ✉ 485 Madison Ave. at 52nd St., ☎ 212/832–0812; ✉ the World Trade Center, ☎ 212/488–7595; and other Manhattan locations). Stop here for clean, green goodies for skin and hair.

Caswell-Massey (✉ 518 Lexington Ave. at 48th St., ☎ 212/755–2254). The original displays its fragrant toiletries in polished old cases; branches are in the World Financial Center and at South Street Seaport.

Essential Products Company (✉ 90 Water St., ☎ 212/344–4288). This company, established in 1895, sells "interpretations" of famous fra-grances at a fraction of the original price tags.

Floris (✉ 703 Madison Ave., between 62nd and 63rd Sts., ☎ 212/935–9100). Floral English toiletries beloved of such beauties as Cher and Catherine Deneuve fill this re-creation of the cozy London original.

Jean Laporte Perfumes (✉ 870 Madison Ave., between 70th and 71st Sts., ☎ 212/517–8665.) Exquisite French scents and antique perfume bottles make a splendid array.

Kiehl's (✉ 109 3rd Ave., near 13th St., ☎ 212/475–3400). A favored haunt of top models and hairstylists, it's been a purveyor of quality skin and hair products since 1851.

Fun and Games

These are stores by adults, for adults, but with such humor and whimsy that kids will like them, too.

B. Shackman & Company, Inc. (✉ 85 5th Ave. at 16th St., ☎ 212/989–5162.). Opened in 1898, this gem of a store is filled with hard-to-find

Victoriana and other fun items, including paper dolls, flip books, toys, and games.

Compleat Strategist (✉ 11 E. 33rd St., ☎ 212/685–3880; ✉ 320 W. 57th St., ☎ 212/582–1272). All kinds of strategy games are supplied for the serious enthusiast.

Darts Shoppe Ltd. (✉ 30 E. 20th St., ☎ 212/533–8684). Exquisitely crafted English darts and boards are sold here.

Flosso Hornmann (✉ 45 W. 34th St., Room 607, ☎ 212/279–6079). This modest magic shop offers museum-class memorabilia, including a hand-painted crate used by Harry Houdini.

Game Show (✉ 474 6th Ave., between 11th and 12th Sts., ☎ 212/633–6328; ✉ 1240 Lexington Ave., between 83rd and 84th Sts., ☎ 212/472–8011). The mix here includes board games, box games, and card games.

Little Rickie (✉ 49½ 1st Ave. at 3rd St., ☎ 212/505–6467). This fun spot is packed with wacky novelties and vintage treasures.

Marion & Co. (✉ 147 W. 26th St., ☎ 212/727–8900). Playing cards come in all shapes and sizes here. Also a source for chips and dice.

Only Hearts (✉ 386 Columbus Ave., between 78th and 79th Sts., ☎ 212/724–5608). Heart-shape waffle irons, anyone?

Star Magic (✉ 745 Broadway, between 8th St. and Astor Pl., ☎ 212/228–7770; ✉ 275 Amsterdam Ave. at 73rd St., ☎ 212/769–2020; ✉ 1256 Lexington Ave., between 84th and 85th Sts., ☎ 212/988–0300). Astronomy meets New Age in a clutter of crystals, star charts, and other celestial playthings.

Tannen Magic Co. (✉ 24 W. 25th St., ☎ 212/929–4500). You'll find sword chests, dove-a-matics, magic wands, and crystal balls, not to mention the all-important top hats with rabbits, at this six-decades-old magicians' supply house.

Uncle Futz (✉ 408 Amsterdam Ave. at 79th St., ☎ 212/799–6723; ✉ 1054 Lexington Ave. at 75th St., ☎ 212/535–4686). These delicious toy shops are crammed with supercool puzzles, board games, and souped-up yo-yos.

Gadgets

Hammacher Schlemmer (✉ 147 E. 57th St., ☎ 212/421–9000). The store that offered America its first pop-up toaster still ferrets out the outrageous, the unusual, and the best-of-kind in-home electronics.

Sharper Image (✉ Pier 17, South St. Seaport, ☎ 212/693–0477; ✉ 4 W. 57th St., ☎ 212/265–2550; ✉ 900 Madison Ave., between 72nd and 73rd Sts., ☎ 212/794–4974). This retail outlet of the catalog company stocks gifts for the pampered executive who has everything.

Home Decor and Gifts

Aris Mixon & Co. (✉ 381 Amsterdam Ave., between 78th and 79th Sts., ☎ 212/724–6904). The intrigue here is in the mix of newly manufactured, handmade, and antique.

Avventura (✉ 463 Amsterdam Ave. at 82nd St., ☎ 212/769–2510). Glory in Italian design in all its streamlined beauty here. Tabletop items and handblown glass accessories are all stunning.

Bed, Bath & Beyond (✉ 620 6th Ave., between 19th and 20th Sts., ☎ 212/255–3550). This huge Chelsea emporium has some 80,000 different household items at reasonable prices.

Be Seated (✉ 66 Greenwich Ave., near 11th St., ☎ 212/924–8444). Manhattan's source for new and vintage African and Asian baskets also stocks cotton fabrics from India and Indonesia.

Charlotte Moss & Co. (✉ 1027 Lexington Ave., between 73rd and 74th Sts., ☎ 212/772–3320). Within what looks like a vine-wrapped, chintz-cozy English country house, you'll find charming pieces, such as a replica of Lady Nancy Astor's button-tufted slipper chair.

Crate & Barrel (⊠ 650 Madison Ave. at 59th St., ☎ 212/308–0011). At this fabulous emporium, you'll find one of the best selections of practically everything imaginable for the home and kitchen, including glassware, kitchen and bath items, and stylish furniture.

Felissimo (⊠ 10 W. 56th St., ☎ 212/247–5656). Spread over four stories of a Beaux Arts town house are unusual items, many handcrafted either in the United States or abroad, that reconcile classic European and modern Asian sensibilities.

Gazebo (⊠ 114 E. 57th St., ☎ 212/832–7077). Quilts and wicker overflow at this bastion of American country style.

William-Wayne & Co. (⊠ 40 University Pl., ☎ 212/533– 4711; ⊠ 846 Lexington Ave., ☎ 212/737–8934; and ⊠ 850 Lexington Ave., ☎ 212/288–9243.) The highly tasteful, irresistible selection of gifts for home and garden here includes many collectibles with a monkey theme.

La Maison Moderne (⊠ 144 West 19th St., ☎ 212/691– 9603). This inviting two-level store is a sumptuous stop filled with elegant gifts for the home and bath.

Lexington Gardens (⊠ 1011 Lexington Ave., between 72nd and 73rd Sts., ☎ 212/861–4390). A favorite source for some of New York's top decorators, this delightful shop offers new and antique ornaments for both city terraces and country gardens.

Let There Be Neon (⊠ 38 White St., between Broadway and Church St., ☎ 212/226–4883). Browse among the terrific collection of new and antique neon signs, clocks, and tabletop accessories.

Mabel's (⊠ 849 Madison Ave., between 70th and 71st Sts., ☎ 212/734–3263). Enchanting animal lovers is the business of this Noah's Ark of knickknacks in animal shapes.

Miya Shoji Interiors (⊠ 109 W. 17th St., ☎ 212/243–6774). This shop offers a superb selection of beautifully crafted Japanese folding screens.

The Pillowry (⊠ 132 E. 61st St., ☎ 212/308–1630). The selection of decorative, one-of-a-kind pillows is vast. (☉ Weekdays at 11:30; otherwise by appointment.)

Pottery Barn (⊠ 600 Broadway at Houston St., ☎ 212/219–2420); ⊠ 117 E. 59th St., ☎ 212/753–5424; ⊠ 2109 Broadway, between 73rd and 74th Sts., ☎ 212/595–5573; ⊠ 250 W. 57th St., ☎ 212/315–1855; ⊠ 231 10th Ave., between 23rd and 24th Sts., ☎ 212/206–8118; and other locations). Come here for contemporary-style items for setting the table. The new SoHo concept store features a unique home-design studio and a new bath line. Overstocks are discounted at the 10th Avenue location.

Scully & Scully (⊠ 504 Park Ave., between 59th and 60th Sts., ☎ 212/755–2590). The style here is high WASP, whether it's the leather footstools in animal shapes, the small pieces of reproduction antique furniture, or the vast display of Herend figurines made in Hungary.

Wolfman-Gold & Good Company (⊠ 116 Greene St., ☎ 212/431–1888). Half antique and half contemporary in spirit, this chic SoHo shop, a major New York trendsetter, is all white, with touches of blond wood and wicker. Tableware is the focus.

Zona (⊠ 97 Greene St., ☎ 212/925–6750). SoHo's airy, high-ceilinged bastion offers Solieri bells, earth-toned textiles, expensive furniture, and terra-cottas, all artfully displayed.

LINENS

Luxurious linens enchant at **D. Porthault** (⊠ 18 E. 69th St., ☎ 212/688–1660), **E. Braun** (⊠ 717 Madison Ave., between 63rd and 64th Sts., ☎ 212/838–0650), **Frette** (⊠ 799 Madison Ave., between 67th and 68th

Sts., ☎ 212/988–5221), and **Pratesi** (✉ 829 Madison Ave. at 69th St., ☎ 212/288–2315). Chic prevails at lower prices at **Ad Hoc Softwares** (✉ 410 W. Broadway at Spring St., ☎ 212/925–2652). For bargains, check out the Lower East Side's dry-goods merchants (most on Grand St.), notably **Harry Levy** (✉ 278 Grand St., ☎ 212/226–8102), which counts many celebrities among the polyglot clientele, and **Century 21** (✉ 22 Cortlandt St., between Broadway and Church St., ☎ 212/227–9092; ✉ 472 86th St., Bay Ridge, Brooklyn, ☎ 718/748–3266).

Jewelry, Watches, and Silver

Most of the world's premier jewelers have retail outlets in New York, and the nation's wholesale jewelry center is on 47th Street.

A La Vieille Russie (✉ 781 5th Ave., between 59th and 60th Sts., ☎ 212/752–1727). Stop here to behold bibelots by Fabergé and others, enameled or encrusted with jewels.

Asprey (✉ 725 5th Ave. at 56th St., ☎ 212/688–1811). The only branch of the distinguished London jeweler, which holds three royal warrants, this store is just the place to go when seeking crystal, silver, leather goods or, perhaps, a brooch fit for a queen.

Beads of Paradise (✉ 16 East 17th St., ☎ 212/620–0642. Enjoy a startlingly rich selection of African bead necklaces, earrings, and rare artifacts. Also, you can create your own designs.

Buccellati (✉ 46 E. 57th St., ☎ 212/308–5533). The exquisite, Florentine-finish Italian jewelry here makes a statement.

Bulgari (✉ 730 5th Ave. at 57th St., ☎ 212/315–9000; ✉ 2 E. 61st St., in the Pierre Hotel, ☎ 212/486–0326). The expertly crafted jewelry here has an understated, tailored look.

Camilla Dietz Bergeron (✉ Upper East Side, ☎ 212/794–9100). Estate jewelry is the specialty here. Men dote on the antique cufflinks that date back to the Roaring '20s. (☉ By appointment only.)

Cartier (✉ 2 E. 52nd St., ☎ 212/446–3400). Simple but superb pieces are displayed in the former mansion of the late yachtsman and socialite Morton F. Plant.

David Webb (✉ 445 Park Ave. at 57th St., ☎ 212/421–3030). Featured here are gem-studded pieces, often enameled and in animal forms.

Robert Lee Morris (✉ 400 W. Broadway, ☎ 212/431– 9405). Striking originals in silver, gold, and gold plate can be discovered at this SoHo jewelry and accessory mecca.

Fortunoff (✉ 681 5th Ave., between 53rd and 54th Sts., ☎ 212/758–6660). Good prices on gold and silver jewelry, flatware, and hollowware draw crowds to this large store.

Harry Winston (✉ 718 5th Ave. at 56th St., ☎ 212/245–2000). The moneyed clientele here appreciates this store's oversize stones and impeccable quality.

H. Stern (✉ 645 5th Ave., between 50th and 51st Sts., ☎ 212/688–0300). Gemstones in contemporary settings are the specialty of this Brazilian firm.

James Robinson (✉ 480 Park Ave. at 58th St., ☎ 212/752–6166). This family-owned business sells handmade flatware, antique silver, fine estate jewelry, and 18th- and 19th-century china.

Jean's Silversmiths (✉ 16 W. 45th St., ☎ 212/575–0723). Where to replace the butter knife that's missing from your great-aunt's set? Try this dusty, crowded shop.

Tiffany & Co. (✉ 727 5th Ave. at 57th St., ☎ 212/755–8000). A shiny robin's-egg-blue box from this venerable New York jeweler announces the contents as something very special. Along with the $80,000 platinum-and-diamond bracelets, a lot is affordable on a whim.

Van Cleef & Arpels (✉ 744 5th Ave. at 57th St., ☎ 212/644–9500). The jewelry here is sheer perfection.

COSTUME JEWELRY

The Accessory Shop (✉ 2 East 22nd St., ☎ 212/254–3511) carries costume and semiprecious jewelry in bold colors, as well as custom-made ladies accessories. **Gale Grant Ltd.** (✉ 485 Madison Ave., ☎ 212/752–3142) features enamels and tailored looks that travel well from day into evening. Jewelry inspired by Etruscan, Renaissance, and Baroque designs is the specialty of **Jaded** (✉ 1048 Madison Ave. at 80th St., ☎ 212/288–6631; ✉ 1048 Madison Ave., near 80th St., ☎ 212/288–6631).

Luggage and Leather Goods

Altman Luggage (✉ 135 Orchard St., between Delancey and Rivington Sts., ☎ 212/254–7275). Come here for reasonable prices.

Bottega Veneta (✉ 635 Madison Ave., between 59th and 60th Sts., ☎ 212/371–5511). The superb Italian goods here are for people who know real quality.

Crouch & Fitzgerald (✉ 400 Madison Ave. at 48th St., ☎ 212/755–5888). Since 1839, this store has offered a terrific selection in hard- and soft-sided luggage, as well as handbags.

Fine & Klein (✉ 119 Orchard St., ☎ 212/674–6720). Fabulous handbags are discounted here.

Peter Hermann Leathergoods (✉ 118 Thompson St., ☎ 212/966–9050). The stock includes chic leather goods for men and women.

Lederer Leather Goods (✉ 613 Madison Ave. at 58th St., ☎ 212/355–5515). The excellent selection here includes exotic skins.

North Beach Leather (✉ 772 Madison Ave. at 66th St., ☎ 212/772–0707). High-fashion leather wear comes in many colors here.

T. Anthony (✉ 445 Park Ave. at 56th St., ☎ 212/750–9797). This store's hard- and soft-sided luggage of coated fabric with leather trim has brass fasteners that look like precision machines.

Menswear

Alfred Dunhill of London (✉ 450 Park Ave. at 57th St., ☎ 212/753–9292). Corporate brass comes here for finely tailored clothing, both ready-made and custom-order, and smoking accessories; the walk-in humidor stores top-quality tobacco and cigars.

Brooks Brothers (✉ 346 Madison Ave. at 44th St., ☎ 212/682–8800). Here's an American-menswear institution, with conservative styles in both suits and sportswear.

Façonnable (✉ 689 5th Ave. at 54th St., ☎ 212/319–0111). Designed in France, the well-made traditional clothing and sportswear has an international appeal.

Frank Stella Ltd. (✉ 440 Columbus Ave. at 81st St., ☎ 212/877–5566; ✉ 1388 6th Ave., between 56th and 57th Sts., ☎ 212/757–2295). Classic clothing with subtle variations is offered here.

J. Press (✉ 7 E. 44th St., ☎ 212/687–7642). This store emphasizes the oxford-cloth shirt, natural-shoulder suit, madras-patch Bermuda shorts, and amusing club tie.

Paul Smith (✉ 108 5th Ave. at 16th St., ☎ 212/627–9770). Dark mahogany Victorian cases display downtown styles.

Paul Stuart (✉ Madison Ave. at 45th St., ☎ 212/682–0320). The fabric selection is interesting, the tailoring superb, and the look traditional but not stodgy.

Saint Laurie, Ltd. (✉ 895 Broadway at 20th St., 3rd Fl., ☎ 212/473–0100). This family-owned business sells suits manufactured on the premises in lovely fabrics.

New York men looking for bargains rely on **BFO** (✉ 149 5th Ave. at 21st St., ☎ 212/254–0059); **Eisenberg and Eisenberg** (✉ 85 5th Ave. at 16th St., ☎ 212/627–1290); **Moe Ginsburg** (✉ 162 5th Ave. at 21st St., ☎ 212/242–3482); **Rothman's** (✉ 200 Park Ave. S at 17th St., ☎ 212/777–7400); **Syms** (✉ 42 Trinity Pl., ☎ 212/797–1199; cash or store credit card only); and **Today's Man** (✉ 625 6th Ave., ☎ 212/924–0200; and various locations in Manhattan).

MEN'S HATS

Worth & Worth (✉ 331 Madison Ave. at 43rd St., ☎ 212/867–6058). Come here for elegant handmade head wear—everything from driving caps to fedoras.

MEN'S SHOES

Billy Martin's (✉ 812 Madison Ave. at 68th St., ☎ 212/861–3100). Quality hand-tooled and custom-made boots are carried here.
Church's English Shoes (✉ 428 Madison Ave. at 49th St., ☎ 212/755–4313). This store has been selling beautifully made English shoes since 1873.
Cole-Haan (✉ 620 5th Ave. at Rockefeller Center, ☎ 212/765–9747; and ✉ 667 Madison Ave. at 61st St., ☎ 212/421–8440). The look in both dress and casual shoes is smart and stylish, yet not at all trendy.
Stuart Weitzman (✉ 625 Madison Ave., ☎ 212/750–2555). The stock specializes in hard-to-find sizes and widths. This store carries the designer's entire line.
Tip Top (✉ 155 W. 72nd St., ☎ 212/787–4960). You'll find comfortable walking shoes and sandals here.
To Boot (✉ 256 Columbus Ave., between 71st and 72nd Sts., ☎ 212/724–8249). Here you'll find stylish shoes and boots for a fashionable business look.
Tootsie Plohound (✉ 137 5th Ave., ☎ 212/460–8650; ✉ 413 W. Broadway, between Prince and Spring Sts., ☎ 212/925–8931). These shops are tops for "downtown" shoes: fun, funky, and cool. They carry women's styles, too.

Needlecraft

FABRIC

Seamstresses prize the selection and prices at shops in the upper 30s and on 40th Street, between Broadway and 8th Avenue, such as **U.S. Liberty Fabric** (✉ 250 W. 39th St., ☎ 212/354–9360). Luxurious imports fill **Tessuti** (✉ 228 W. 39th St., ☎ 212/730–2866), **Paron Fabrics** (✉ 56 W. 57th St., ☎ 212/247–6451), **Paron Fabrics West** (✉ 206 W. 40th St., ☎ 212/768–3266), which discounts remnants, and **Weller** (✉ 24 W. 57th St., ☎ 212/247–3790). Good buys can be had at the fabric shops on Orchard Street between Delancey and Houston streets.

TRIMMING

Dingy 38th Street between 5th and 6th avenues is a treasure chest. Jewelers include **Hyman Hendler & Sons** (✉ 67 W. 38th St., ☎ 212/840–8393), the ribbon king, since 1900; and **Tinsel Trading** (✉ 47 W. 38th St., ☎ 212/730–1030), for new and antique trims and tassels. Nearby **M & J Trimming** (✉ 1008 6th Ave., near 37th St., ☎ 212/391–9072) stocks more than 100 styles of tassels and tiebacks. Uptown, buttons overflow the charming **Tender Buttons** (✉ 143 E. 62nd St., ☎ 212/758–7004).

YARNS

Erica Wilson (✉ 717 Madison Ave., between 63rd and 64th Sts., 2nd Floor, ☎ 212/832–7290). The eponymous British-born needlepoint authority is a top resource.

Wallis Mayers Needlework (⊠ 30 E. 68th St., ☎ 212/861–5318). Have fun choosing among oodles of yarns and offbeat hand-painted canvases.

Paper, Greeting Cards, Stationery
Dempsey & Carroll (⊠ 110 E. 57th St., ☎ 212/486–7526). Supplying New York's high society for a century, this firm is always correct but seldom straitlaced.

Kate's Paperie (⊠ 561 Broadway at Prince St., ☎ 212/941–9816; ⊠ 8 W. 13th St., ☎ 212/633–0570). These wonderful spots feature fabulous wrapping papers, some handmade; bound blank books; and more.

Untitled (⊠ 159 Prince St., ☎ 212/982–2088). The stock here includes thousands of tasteful greeting cards and art postcards.

Performing-Arts Memorabilia
Actor's Heritage (⊠ 262 W. 44th St., ☎ 212/944–7490). Collectors will love the theater posters, scripts of plays old and new, and soundtracks of big Broadway musicals past and present.

Motion Picture Arts Gallery (⊠ 133 E. 58th St., 10th Floor, ☎ 212/223–1009). Vintage posters enchant collectors here.

Movie Star News (⊠ 134 W. 18th St., ☎ 212/620–8160). The film memorabilia emphasizes Hollywood glamour.

One Shubert Alley (⊠ Shubert Alley, between 44th and 45th Sts. west of Broadway, ☎ 212/944–4133). Souvenirs from past and present Broadway hits reign at this Theater District shop.

Richard Stoddard Performing Arts Books (⊠ 18 E. 16th St., Room 305, ☎ 212/645–9576). This veteran dealer who offers out-of-print books also has the largest stock of old Broadway *Playbill*s in the world.

Triton Gallery (⊠ 323 W. 45th St., between 8th and 9th Aves., ☎ 212/765–2472). Theatrical posters large and small can be found here for hits and flops.

Souvenirs of New York City
Ordinary Big Apple souvenirs can be found in and around major tourist attractions. More unusual items can be found at:

Citybooks (⊠ 61 Chambers St., ☎ 212/669–8245). Discover all kinds of books and pamphlets that have to do with New York City's government and its various departments (building, sanitation, etc.), as well as pocket maps, Big Apple lapel pins, and sweatshirts featuring subway-token motifs. Closed on weekends.

New York Bound Bookshop (⊠ 50 Rockefeller Plaza, in lobby of Associated Press Bldg., ☎ 212/245–8503). New and old New York books, photographs, maps, and prints are the specialty.

Think New York (⊠ 875 7th Ave., between 55th and 56th Sts., ☎ 212/957–8511). Here you'll find New York City landmarks featured on mugs, aprons, and many other objects, some surprising and unusual.

Transit Museum Gift Shop (⊠ Grand Central Terminal, main concourse, near Vanderbilt Ave. entrance, ☎ 212/682–7572). Coffee mugs, T-shirts, and other items emblazoned with the transit-system logos are the stock in trade here, along with banks in the form of city buses, motormen's hats, and jewelry made of old subway tokens.

Toys
Many toy companies are headquartered here, and the windows of the Toy Center at 23rd Street and 5th Avenue display the latest thing, especially during February's Toy Week, when all the out-of-town buyers come to place orders for the next Christmas season (☞ *also* Fun and Games, *above*).

Big City Kite Co. (⊠ 1210 Lexington Ave. at 82nd St., ☎ 212/472–2623). Kites of all sizes and shapes are found here.

Enchanted Forest (⊠ 85 Mercer St., between Spring and Broome Sts., ☎ 212/925–6677). Fancy reigns in this shop's stock of unique hand-made items.

F.A.O. Schwarz (⊠ 767 5th Ave. at 58th St., ☎ 212/644–9400). You will be hooked on this sprawling two-level children's store from the minute you walk through the door and one of the costumed staff members—a donkey, a clown, a cave woman, or a mad scientist—extends a welcome. Beyond a wonderful mechanical clock with many dials and dingbats are all the stuffed animals in the world, dolls large and small, things to build with (including blocks by the pound), computer games, toy cars (including a multi-thousand dollar Ferrari), and more.

Kidding Around (⊠ 60 W. 15th St., ☎ 212/645–6337; 68 Bleecker St., ☎ 212/598–0228). This unpretentiously smart shop is full of old fashioned wood toys, fun gadgets, craft and science kits, and a small selection of infant clothes. A great place to browse and find special gifts.

Penny Whistle Toys (⊠ 448 Columbus Ave., between 81st and 82nd Sts., ☎ 212/873–9090; ⊠ 1283 Madison Ave., between 91st and 92nd Sts., ☎ 212/369–3868). Meredith Brokaw, wife of TV anchorman Tom Brokaw, has an intriguing selection of quality toys here.

West Side Kids (⊠ 498 Amsterdam Ave. at 84th St., ☎ 212/496–7282). The shrewd selection here mixes educational toys with a grab bag of fun little playthings.

DOLLS AND MINIATURES

Dollhouse Antics (⊠ 1343 Madison Ave. at 94th St., ☎ 212/876–2288). This is a miniaturist's paradise, with infinitesimal accessories such as a small *New York Times.*

Iris Brown's Victorian Doll and Miniature Shop (⊠ 253 E. 57 St., ☎ 212/593–2882.) A sweet, knowledgeable owner presides over the antique dolls, dollhouses, miniatures, and Christmas ornaments.

TRAINS AND MODELS

Railroad aficionados will be dazzled by the vast selections at **America's Hobby Center** (⊠ 146 W. 22nd St., ☎ 212/675–8922) and **Red Caboose** (⊠ 23 W. 45th St., basement level, ☎ 212/575–0155).

Women's Clothing

The department stores' collections are always good: **Saks** for its designers; **Macy's** for its breadth; **Bloomingdale's** for its extremes; **Barneys** and **Henri Bendel** for their trendy chic; and **Lord & Taylor** for its classicism. **Bergdorf Goodman** offers a range from updated classics to up-to-the-minute, all of the highest quality. The following add another dimension.

CLASSICISTS

Ann Taylor (⊠ 2015–2017 Broadway, near 69th St., ☎ 212/873–7344; ⊠ 2380 Broadway at 87th St., ☎ 212/721–3130; ⊠ 4 Fulton St., ☎ 212/480–4100; ⊠ 805 3rd Ave. at 50th St., ☎ 212/308–5333; ⊠ 3 E. 57th St., ☎ 212/832–2010; and other locations). These stores provide what the elegant young woman with a sense of style needs for work and play.

Burberrys (⊠ 9 E. 57th St., ☎ 212/371–5010). The look is classic and conservative—and nobody does a better trench coat.

DESIGNER SHOWCASES

Betsey Johnson (⊠ 130 Thompson St., ☎ 212/420–0169; 251 E. 60th St., ☎ 212/319–7699; ⊠ 248 Columbus Ave., between 71st and

72nd Sts., ☎ 212/362–3364; ✉ 1060 Madison Ave., between 80th
and 81st Sts., ☎ 212/734–1257). The look here is still hip and quirky.
Calvin Klein (✉ 654 Madison Ave. at 60th St., ☎ 212/292–9000). This
huge, stark store showcases Calvin Klein's latest design collection.
Chanel (✉ 5 E. 57th St., ☎ 212/355–5050). The classic designs here
never go out of style; neither do those wonderful Chanel perfumes.
Christian Dior (✉ 703 5th Ave. at 55th St., ☎ 212/223–4646). An elegant, two-level, gray-hued outpost of one of France's most venerable
fashion houses, this shop offers both daytime and evening clothes, plus
all the accessories (and scents) to enhance them.
Comme des Garçons (✉ 116 Wooster St., ☎ 212/219–0660). This SoHo
shop showcases Japanese designer Rei Kawakubo.
Emanuel Ungaro (✉ 792 Madison Ave. at 67th St., ☎ 212/249–
4090). The style here is body-conscious, but it's never flashy.
Emporio Armani (✉ 110 5th Ave., between 16th and 17th Sts., ☎ 212/
727–3240). The Italian designer's casual line is featured.
Geoffrey Beene (✉ 783 5th Ave., between 59th and 60th Sts., ☎ 212/
935–0470). A splendid-looking boutique houses exquisite day and
evening wear by America's master designer.
Gianni Versace (✉ 817 Madison Ave., between 68th and 69th Sts., ☎
212/744–6868). An Italian maestro of color and form continues to dazzle with his daring.
Giorgio Armani (✉ 815 Madison Ave., between 68th and 69th Sts.,
☎ 212/988–9191). In this lofty blond-and-beige space with grand,
arched windows and doors, Armani's high-end line looks oh-so-chic.
Givenchy (✉ 954 Madison Ave. at 75th St., ☎ 212/772–1040). This
designer is famous for timeless elegance.
Hermès (✉ 11 E. 57th St., ☎ 212/751–3181). Patterned silk scarves
and the so-called "Kelly" handbags are hallmarks.
Louis Féraud (✉ 3 W. 56th St., ☎ 212/956–7010). The couturiers deft
hand is seen in the superb cut and colorations at the only freestanding boutique bearing his name in North America.
Matsuda (✉ 156 5th Ave., between 20th and 21st Sts., ☎ 212/645–
5151). Kudos go out for wonderful cuts and fine muted hues.
Missoni (✉ 836 Madison Ave. at 69th St., ☎ 212/517–9339). Wonderfully textured knits, suits, and sportswear stand out.
Nicole Miller (✉ 780 Madison Ave., between 66th and 67th Sts., ☎
212/288–9779; ✉ 134 Prince St, ☎ 212/343–1360). Sexy and colorful, these clothes for a woman by a woman are spirited and sassy.
Norma Kamali O.M.O. (✉ 11 W. 56th St., ☎ 212/957–9797). The look
here ranges from sweatshirts to evening gowns.
Polo/Ralph Lauren (✉ 867 Madison Ave. at 72nd St., ☎ 212/606–
2100). Lauren's flagship store is one of New York's most distinctive
shopping experiences, in a grand, carefully renovated turn-of-the-century town house.
Todd Oldham (✉ 123 Wooster St., ☎ 212/219–3531). The cutting-
edge designer has opened his first freestanding shop in SoHo.
Valentino (✉ 823 Madison Ave., between 68th and 69th Sts., ☎ 212/
744–0200). The mix here is at once audacious and beautifully cut, with
the best of France and Italy on its racks.
Vera Wang (✉ 991 Madison Ave. at 77th St., ☎ 212/628–3400). Sumptuous, made-to-order bridal and evening wear is shown here by appointment only. Their periodic prêt-à-porter sales offer designer dresses
for a (relative) song.
Yohji Yamamoto (✉ 103 Grand St., ☎ 212/966–9066). Severe, beautifully cut fashions come from fashion's Zen master.

Yves St. Laurent Rive Gauche (✉ 859 Madison Ave., between 70th and 71st Sts., ☎ 212/517–7400). The looks range from chic to classic for day and evening.

DISCOUNT

Aaron's (✉ 627 5th Ave. at 17th St., Park Slope, Brooklyn, ☎ 718/768–5400). If your taste runs to expensive labels, you'll appreciate the significant savings. You'll have your own salesperson assigned to you.

Century 21 (✉ 22 Cortlandt St., between Broadway and Church St., ☎ 212/227–9092; ✉ 472 86th St., Bay Ridge, Brooklyn, ☎ 718/748–3266). Spiffy quarters make bargain-hunting a pleasure, and there are fabulous buys on very high fashion. Note that there are no try-ons.

Daffy's (✉ 111 5th Ave. at 18th St., ☎ 212/529–4477; ✉ 335 Madison Ave. at 44th St., ☎ 212/557–4422). Cheap stuff is priced cheaper, and pricey stuff is marked way down. Only for the most patient.

Forman's (✉ 82 Orchard St., ☎ 212/228–2500; ✉ 145 E. 42nd St., between Lex. and 3rd Aves., ☎ 212/681–9800). This is an unexpectedly attractive longtime mainstay of the Lower East Side.

Loehmann's (✉ 236th St. and Broadway, the Bronx, ☎ 718/543–6420). The flagship store of this premier off-price outlet is an institution among shopaholics.

S&W (✉ 165 W. 26th St., ☎ 212/924–6656). Prices here are good to great on coats, suits, shoes, handbags, and accessories.

T. J. Maxx (✉ 620 6th Ave. at 19th St., ☎ 212/229–0875) The first New York location for this chain is filled to the max, for less.

ETHNIC LOOKS

April Cornell Company (✉ 860 Lexington Ave., between 64th and 65th Sts., ☎ 212/570–2775; ✉ 487 Columbus Ave., between 83rd and 84th Sts., ☎ 212/799–4342). In addition to the frocks in Provençal, African, and Indian prints, the stores carry table and bed linens in similar fabrics. The color combinations here are luscious.

Putumayo (✉ 341 Columbus Ave., between 76th and 77th Sts., ☎ 212/595–3441; ✉ 147 Spring St., ☎ 212/966–4458). There's cool cotton clothing here, much of it crinkly and easy to pack.

HIP STYLES

A/X: Armani Exchange (✉ 568 Broadway, near Prince St., ☎ 212/431–6000). Here's Giorgio Armani's answer to the Gap.

Canal Jean (✉ 504 Broadway, between Spring and Broome Sts., ☎ 212/226–1130). Casual funk draws hip shoppers.

The Limited (✉ 691 Madison Ave. at 62nd St., ☎ 212/838–8787). Considering the address, prices are moderate for well-styled though not outrageous clothing, much of it casual.

Limited Express (✉ 7 W. 34th St., ☎ 212/629–6838; and other locations). Mass-market chic includes great leggings, sweaters, and microscopic dresses—all with a Gallic accent.

Reminiscence (✉ 74 5th Ave., between 13th and 14th Sts., ☎ 212/243–2292). The theme is strictly '50s and '60s.

Trash and Vaudeville (✉ 4 St. Mark's Pl., ☎ 212/982–3590). Black, white, and electric colors are the focus here.

Women's Workout Gear (✉ 121 7th Ave., between 17th and 18th Sts., ☎ 212/627–1117). Come here for exercise wear in all colors.

LINGERIE

Exquisite little things in silk and lace, both naughty and nice, are found at **Joovay** (✉ 436 W. Broadway, ☎ 212/431–6386). Treat yourself or someone special to fine lingerie at **La Petite Coquette** (✉ 52 University Pl., ☎ 212/473–2478); **Montenapoleone** (✉ 789 Madison Ave. at 67th

St., ☎ 212/535–2660); and **Victoria's Secret** (✉ 34 E. 57th St., ☎ 212/758–5592; ✉ 693 Madison Ave. at 62nd St., ☎ 212/838–9266).

ROMANTICS

Laura Ashley (✉ 398 Columbus Ave. at 79th St., ☎ 212/496–5110). Old-fashioned English frocks abound here.

TRENDSETTERS

Agnès B. (✉ 116 Prince St., ☎ 212/925–4649; ✉ 13 E. 16th St., ☎ 212/741–2585); ✉ 1063 Madison Ave., ☎ 212/570–9333). This Euro-style boutique has maintained its SoHo popularity for several years.
Charivari (✉ 2315 Broadway, between 83rd and 84th Sts., ☎ 212/873–1424). Since Selma Weiser founded this store on the Upper West Side, she has made a name for herself internationally for her eagle eye on the up-and-coming and avant-garde. The branches, too, take a high-style approach: **Charivari 72** (✉ 257 Columbus Ave. at 72nd St., ☎ 212/787–7272); **Charivari 57** (✉ 18 W. 57th St., ☎ 212/333–4040); and **Charivari** on **Madison** (✉ 1001 Madison Ave. at 78th St., ☎ 212/650–0078).
Patricia Field (✉ 10 E. 8th St., ☎ 212/254–1699). This store collects the essence of the downtown look.

VINTAGE

Harriet Love (✉ 126 Prince St., ☎ 212/966–2280). This is the doyenne of the city's vintage clothing scene.
Screaming Mimi's (✉ 382 Lafayette St., between 4th and Great Jones Sts., ☎ 212/677–6464). Vintage clothes and the avant-garde go together here.

Women's Shoes

DESIGNER SHOES

Hèléne Arpels (✉ 470 Park Ave., between 57th and 58th Sts., ☎ 212/755–1623). The grande dame of fine footwear for the well-heeled features everything from basic pumps in exotic leathers to the most delicate of evening slippers in silks and satins.
Manolo Blahnik (✉ 15 W. 55th St., ☎ 212/582–3007). It's possibly the hautest—and costliest—footwear in town, by England's top shoe designer.
Peter Fox (✉ 105 Thompson St., ☎ 212/431–7426 and 212/431–6359; ✉ 806 Madison Ave., between 67th and 68th Sts., ☎ 212/744—8340). Looks here are outside the fashion mainstream—really fun.
Robert Clergerie (✉ 41 E. 60 St., ☎ 212/207–8600). Exquisite, high-style French footwear includes the chicest platform sandals imaginable.
Salvatore Ferragamo (✉ 725 5th Ave. at 56th St., ☎ 212/759–3822). No stylistic gimmicks here, just beautiful shoemaking.
Susan Bennis Warren Edwards (✉ 22 W. 57th St., ☎ 212/755–4197). Here you'll find alligator, silk, satin, suede, canvas, and buttery-soft leather exquisitely worked.
Tanino Crisci (✉ 795 Madison Ave., between 67th and 68th Sts., ☎ 212/535–1014). Well-made shoes in classic styles and subtle variations of basic colors are the highlight here. All are made in Italy.

DISCOUNT AND LOWER-PRICE SHOES

Discounters dot Reade Street between Church and West Broadway, including **Anbar** (✉ 60 Reade St., ☎ 212/227–0253). Several Orchard Street stores discount uptown shoe styles; try **Lace-Up Shoes** (110 Orchard St., ☎ 212/475–8040) for moderate discounts on very high-style shoes.

MODERATELY PRICED SHOES

The shoes at these stores tend toward the classic, in a good range of colors and styles: **Sacco** (✉ 324 Columbus Ave., between 75th and 76th

Sts., ☎ 212/799–5229; ⊠ 94 7th Ave., between 15th and 16th Sts., ☎ 212/675–5180; ⊠ 111 Thompson St., ☎ 212/925–8010; and other locations); **Galo** (⊠ 825 Lexington Ave. at 63rd St., ☎ 212/832–3922; ⊠ 692 Madison Ave., between 62nd and 63rd Sts., ☎ 212/688–6276); **Joan & David** (⊠ 816 Madison Ave. at 68th St., ☎ 212/772–3970; ⊠ 104 5th Ave. at 16th St., ☎ 212/627–1780); **Maraolo** (⊠ 782 Lexington Ave., between 60th and 61st Sts., ☎ 212/832–8182); **Ritz** (⊠ 14 W. 8th St., between 5th and 6th Aves., ☎ 212/228–4137; ⊠ 505 Park Ave. at 59th St., ☎ 212/838–2556); **Shoe Express** (⊠ 1420 2nd Ave. at 74th St., ☎ 212/734–3967); and **Vamps** (⊠ 1421 2nd Ave. at 74th St., ☎ 212/744–0227).

Secondhand Shops

Resale Shops

To find top-of-the-line designs at secondhand prices, try: **Encore** (⊠ 1132 Madison Ave., between 84th and 85th Sts., upstairs, ☎ 212/879–2850); **Exchange Unlimited** (⊠ 563 2nd Ave. at 31st St., ☎ 212/889–3229); **Michael's** (⊠ 1041 Madison Ave., between 79th and 80th Sts., ☎ 212/737–7273); and **Renate's** (⊠ 235 E. 81st St., ☎ 212/472–1698).

Thrift Shops

Affluent New Yorkers donate castoffs to thrift shops run for charity. And, oh, such castoffs! Hours are limited, so call ahead.

Arthritis Foundation Thrift Shop (⊠ 246 E. 84th St., ☎ 212/439–8373).

Council Thrift Shop (⊠ 767 9th Ave., between 51st and 52nd Sts., ☎ 212/757–6132).

Everybody's Thrift Shop (⊠ 261 Park Ave. S, between 20th and 21st Sts., ☎ 212/674–4298).

Housing Works Thrift Shop (⊠ 143 W. 17th St., ☎ 212/386–0820; ⊠ 202 E. 77th St., ☎ 212/772–8461). These shops benefit housing services for people with AIDS.

Irvington Institute for Medical Research Thrift Shop (⊠ 1534 2nd Ave. at 80th St., ☎ 212/879–4555).

Memorial Sloan-Kettering Cancer Center Thrift Shop (⊠ 1440 3rd Ave., between 81st and 82nd Sts., ☎ 212/535–1250).

Spence-Chapin Thrift Shop (⊠ 1430 3rd Ave., between 81st and 82nd Sts., ☎ 212/737–8448).

Flea Markets

The season runs from March or April through November or December at most of these markets in school playgrounds and parking lots.

Annex Antiques Fair and Flea Market (⊠ 6th Ave. at 26th St., ☎ 212/243–5343), weekends.

The Garage (⊠ 112 W. 25th St., between 6th and 7th Aves., ☎ 212/647–0707). The newest flea market in town, this one is indoors in a 23,000-square-foot, two-story former parking garage. Weekends.

IS 44 Market (⊠ Columbus Ave., between 76th and 77th Sts., ☎ 212/721–0900 evenings), Sunday.

PS 183 Market (⊠ 67th St., between York and 1st Aves.), Saturday.

11 Portraits of New York City

The New York Babel

Books and Videos

THE NEW YORK BABEL

F PARIS SUGGESTS INTELLIGENCE, if London suggests Experience, then the word for New York is Activity. York itself is an almost intolerably famous name, but adding New to it was one of the lucky prophetic insights of nomenclature, for newness, from day to day, was to be the moral essence of the place. There is no place where newness is so continuously pursued.

What is not naturally active in New York soon has to turn to and become so. There is not an inactive man, woman, or child in the place. It might be thought that a contemplative, passive New Yorker, one who is inhabited by his feelings and his imaginings, who lives in an inner world, or was born torpid, must be immune to the active spirit. This is not so in New York, where states like passivity, contemplation, vegetativeness, and often sleep itself are active by prescription. Pragmatism sees to that. The prime example is the bum or derelict. There he lies asleep or drunk on the doorstep or props himself against a wall in the Bowery, an exposed, accepted, but above all an established figure of a 51st state. In a city where all activity is specialized, he has his specialty: he must act in protest against activity, which leads him from time to time on a chase for alcohol, a smoke, or a coin as persistent as a salesman's, but in solitude. Virginia Woolf used to ask where Society was; the notion was metaphysical to her. But Skid Row exists as a recognized place. You go there when the thing comes over you. You graduate in dereliction. You put in a 20-hour day of internal fantasy-making in your studied rejection of the New York norm. The Spanish mendicant has his rights and takes his charity with condescension; the bum grabs with resentment. He is busy. You have upset his dream. The supremely passive man in theory, he will stop in the middle of the street as he crosses the Bowery, holding up his dirty hand at the traffic, and scream in the manner of madness at the oncoming driver. Screaming like that—and New York is dotted with screamers on a scale I have seen in no other city

in the world, though Naples has its share—reveals the incessant pressure of the active spirit.

For ourselves who are trying to settle first what we see before our eyes, this active, practical spirit has curious manifestations. New York City is large, but Manhattan is small in extent, so small that a large part of its population has to be pumped out of it every night by bridges and tunnels. Despite the groans about the congestion of its traffic, it is easy to dash from one end to the other of the island and to drive fast all around it. And most people do dash. The only real difficulty is in the downtown tangle of named streets in old New York; the grid has settled the rest. The grid is an unlovely system. It is not originally American: Stuttgart and Berlin hit upon this method of automatically extending cities in the 17th century. By the 18th century Europe had discovered that cities must be designed before they are extended: mere pragmatism and planning will not do. It absolutely will not do if left to engineers, soldiers, or what are called developers. The makers of the New York grid confused the idea that parallel lines can be projected into infinity without meeting, with the idea of design. The boredom this has inflicted upon the horizontal life of Manhattan has turned out to be endurable to the primarily active man who is impatient of the whole idea of having neighbors. The striping, unheeding avenues of the grid have given one superb benefit. They cut through long distances, they provide long vistas that excite the eye, and these are fine where the buildings are high, if they are featureless where the buildings are low. No other city I can think of has anything like the undulating miles that fly down Park Avenue from 96th Street to Grand Central, blocked now though it is by the brutal mass of the Metropolitan Life Building—a British affront to the city and spoken of as a revenge for Suez—or the longer streak of Madison. These two avenues impress most as a whole, other avenues in part, by their assurance as they cleave their way through the cliffs.

OF COURSE, BEING A stranger, you have been living it up, for if you want a night city, this is preeminently the one. There is a large fluorescent population of pale faces—who is that old man sitting alone in the Automat at this late hour? Where are all those taxis streaking to endlessly through the night? You have been listening to the jazz in Birdland perhaps, listening to the long drumming that says "Encroach, encroach, encroach, encroach, overcome, come!" or to that woman with the skirling voice which is shoving, pushing, and struggling cheerfully to get all her energy out of her body and into her mouth as she sings what is really the theme song of the city: "And it's good. It's all good, good, good." She was wired in to some dynamo.

Those words never fade from the mind. In sleep you still hear them. You are a receiving station for every message Babel sends out day and night. The sirens of the police cars, the ambulances and fire engines, mark the hours, carrying the mind out to fantasies of disaster. I say "fantasies," for surely all these speeding crews are studiously keeping alive the ideal of some ultimate dementia while the rest of us sleep. New York demands more than anything else that one should never fail to maintain one's sense of its drama; even its social manners, at their most ceremonious, have this quality. Where the crowds of other cities are consolidating all day long, filling up the safes and cellars of the mind, the New York crowd is set on the pure function of self-dispersal. A couple of cops idling through the night in a police car will issue their noise as if it were part of the uniform and to keep up their belief in their own reality and in the sacred notion of the Great Slaying or the Great Burglarization. Then there is light traffic on the highways, with its high, whipping, cat-gut whine. On 104th Street on the West Side I used to have the sensation of being flayed alive all night by knives whipping down Riverside Drive; it was not disagreeable. City life is for masochists. On many other avenues the trucks bulldozed the brain. There were bursts of noctambulist shouting off Madison and 60th at 3 or 4; followed by the crowning row of the city, the clamor of the garbage disposers, successors to Dickens's gentlemanly swine, that fling the New York garbage cans across the pavement and grind the stuff to bits on the spot. Often I have sat at my window to watch these night brutes chew up the refuse. The men have to rush to keep up with its appetite. As a single producer of shindy this municipal creature is a triumph.

The only way of pinning some sort of identity onto the people is to think of them as once being strangers like yourself and trace them to their districts. The man who used to bring my breakfast, saying, every morning, "Lousy day," was a 115th Street Puerto Rican, of five years' standing. You learn to distinguish. You know where the Ukrainians, the Sephardic Jews, early and late Italians, degrees of Irish, live. You build up a map of the black and Puerto Rican pockets. You note the Germans are at 86th Street and yet the Irish are there, too; that, at the bottom, on East End Avenue, the neighborhood has become suddenly fashionable. The Greenwich Village Italians are pretty fixed; the several Harlems have established their character, for they have stuck to their district for 60 years, which must be a record for New York. You know the Greeks are on 9th Avenue. The Lower East Side, now largely transformed, is Jewish and Puerto Rican. But large groups break away; poor give place to poorer. Sometimes poor give place to rich. In Sutton Place they cleared the poor away from that pleasant little cliff on the East River. But one must not understand these quarters as being the old parishes or the ancient swallowed-up villages of European cities, though they were sometimes the sites of farms. Topographically they are snippings of certain avenues and cross streets. For the avenues stripe the city and the groups live on a block or two along or across the stripe. One would have to analyze New York street by street, from year to year, to know the nuances of racial contact.

Statistics deceive, but it is clear that the oldest American stock of Dutch, British, and German, though dominant in wealth and traditional influence, is a small minority in New York. The question no one can answer is how far the contents of the melting pot have really melted and whether a new race has yet been created. For a long time the minorities resist, huddle into corners. Some foreign groups of New Yorkers melt slowly or not at all. O. Henry in his time called Lower Manhattan "Bagdadon-the-Subway," thinking then of the unchanging Syrians and Armenians around Rector Street, but they have almost vanished. The Ukrainians still have their shops and churches near Avenue A. The Russian Orthodox priest walks down the street. The Poles shout from their windows or sit on the cagelike fire escapes east of Greenwich Village. Slowly these people, no doubt, merge; but the tendency for social classes to be determined by race is marked. Many groups of Orthodox Jews remain untouched. Over in Williamsburg you see a sect wearing beards, the men in black hats and long black coats, their hair often long, with curls at the ears, walking with a long loping shuffle as if they traveled with knees bent. They look like a priesthood, and the boys, curled in the same way, might be their acolytes. You will meet them with their black cases of treasure between their feet standing on the pavement outside the diamond markets of 47th Street.

THE FOREIGN ARE TENACIOUS of their religions—there must be more Greek Orthodox and Russian Orthodox churches than in any other city outside of Europe—and of their racial pride. The old Romanian who cleans your suit has never seen Romania, but he speaks with his old accent; as one looks at his settled, impersonal, American face, one sees the ghost person of another nation within its outlines, a face lost, often sad and puzzled. The Italian cop stands operatically in the full sun at the corner of Union Square; the nimble Greek with his four pairs of hands in the grocer's has the avidity of Athens under that slick, standard air of city prosperity. It occasionally happens that you go to restaurants in New York kept by the brother-in-law or uncle, say, of the man who has the founding place in London, Naples, or Paris; you fall into family gossip, especially with Italians, who are possibly more recent but who are still entangled in the power politics of the European family system. I once talked to an Irish waiter who rushed away into the bar crying, "D'ye see that bloody Englishman? He knows me father." I didn't, but I did know that his father was a notorious leader of one of those "columns" of the IRA in the Irish Civil War.

In this quality of being lost and found there is the mixture of the guilt, the sadness, the fading mind of exile with the excited wonder at life which is an essential New York note. New York tolerance allows the latitude to civilization. People are left alone and are less brutally standardized than in other cities. "Clearly"—these foreigners tell you with resignation—"this is not Europe. But"—they suddenly brighten, tense up, and get that look of celebration in their eyes—"it is New York." That is to say, the miracle. Although New Yorkers of all kinds curse the city for its expense and its pressures, and though all foreigners think it is the other foreigners who make it impossible, they are mad about the place. There is no place like it in the world. And although a Londoner or a Parisian will think the same about their cities, here the feeling has a special quality: that of a triumphant personal discovery of some new thing that is getting bigger, richer, higher, more various as every minute of the day goes by. They have come to a ball. And this is felt not only by the New Yorker with the foreign strain, but also by the men and women who come in from the other states, drawn by its wealth but even more by the chances, the freedom, and the privacy that a metropolis offers to human beings. Its very loneliness and ruthlessness are exciting. It is a preemptive if not a literal capital. Scott Fitzgerald speaks of his wife Zelda coming up because she wanted "luxury and largeness beyond anything her world provided," and that precisely describes the general feeling of many a newcomer.

—V. S. Pritchett

One of the great living masters of English prose, V. S. Pritchett expounds delightfully on his impressions of the city in New York Proclaimed. *Here are some choice passages from the book.*

BOOKS AND VIDEOS

Suggested Books

Some of the best full-length accounts are *Christopher Morley's New York,* a mid-1920s reminiscence; *Walker in the City* by Alfred Kazin; and *Apple of My Eye,* a 1978 recollection of writing a New York guidebook, by Helene Hanff. Dan Wakefield recalls his early literary days in *New York in the 50s. Back Where I Came From* brings together essays on the city that

A. J. Liebling wrote for *The New Yorker*. *Up in the Old Hotel* is a collection of stories by another *New Yorker* writer, Joseph Mitchell, who etches memorable portraits of several colorful city characters. Other recent literary memoirs include *New York Days,* by Willie Morris, and *Manhattan When I Was Young,* by Mary Cantwell. And don't forget E. B. White's excellent 1949 essay "Here Is New York."

FOR A WITTY EARLY HISTORY of New York, turn to the classic *Knickerbocker's History of New York,* by Washington Irving. The heavily illustrated *Columbia Historical Portrait of New York,* by John Kouwenhoven, provides a good introduction to the city. Another profusely illustrated history of the metropolis is Eric Homberger's *The Historical Atlas of New York City,* full of maps, photographs, drawings, and charts. *You Must Remember This,* by Jeff Kisseloff, is an oral history of ordinary New Yorkers early in this century.

Fiorello H. LaGuardia and the Making of Modern New York, by Thomas Kessner, is a biography of the charismatic Depression-era mayor. Robert Caro's *The Power Broker* relates the fascinating story of parks commissioner Robert Moses. In *Prince of the City,* Robert Daley covers New York police corruption. Highly critical accounts of recent politics can be found in *The Streets Were Paved with Gold,* by Ken Auletta; *The Rise and Fall of New York City,* by Roger Star; *Imperial City,* by Geoffrey Moorhouse; and *City for Sale,* by Jack Newfield and Wayne Barrett. *A License to Steal,* by Benjamin J. Stein, concerns Wall Street's Michael Milken, as does *Den of Thieves,* by James B. Stewart.

Theater lovers will want to look at *Act One,* the autobiography of playwright Moss Hart, *The Season* by William Goldman, and David Mamet's *The Cabin. From Manet to Manhattan,* by Peter Watson, explores the city's art world. *Literary New York,* by Susan Edmiston and Linda D. Cirino, traces the haunts of famous writers, neighborhood by neighborhood. Shaun O'Connell's *Remarkable, Unspeakable New York, A Literary History* discusses writers who wrote about the city. *The Heart of the World,* by Nik Cohn, is a vivid block-by-block account of the high- and low-life of Broadway.

AIA Guide to New York City, by Elliot Willensky and Norval White, is still the definitive guide to the city's myriad architectural styles; Paul Goldberger's *The City Observed* describes Manhattan building by building.

Many writers have set their fiction here. Jack Finney's *Time and Again* is a delightful time-travel story illustrated with 19th-century photos; *Winter's Tale,* by Mark Helprin, uses surreal fantasy to create a portrait of New York's past. Novels set in 19th-century New York include Henry James's *Washington Square,* Edith Wharton's *The Age of Innocence,* Stephen Crane's *Maggie, A Girl of the Streets,* and two more recent works: *The Alienist,* by Cabel Carr, and *The Waterworks,* by E. L. Doctorow. O. Henry's short stories depict the early years of this century, while Damon Runyon's are set in the raffish underworld of the 1930s and 1940s. F. Scott Fitzgerald (*The Beautiful and the Damned*), John Dos Passos (*Manhattan Transfer*), John O'Hara (*Butterfield 8*), and Mary McCarthy (*The Group*) all wrote about this city. J. D. Salinger's *Catcher in the Rye* partly takes place here, as does Thomas Pynchon's *V.* Truman Capote's 1958 novella *Breakfast at Tiffany's* is a favorite of many New Yorkers.

John Cheever, Bernard Malamud, Grace Paley, and Isaac Bashevis Singer have written many wonderful short stories celebrating New York and its singular inhabitants. More current New York novels include *Bonfire of the Vanities,* by Tom Wolfe; *The Mambo Kings Play Songs of Love,* by Oscar Hijuelos; *The New York Trilogy,* by Paul Auster, and *People Like Us,* by Dominick Dunne.

The black experience in Harlem and New York City has been chronicled in Ralph Ellison's *Invisible Man,* James Baldwin's *Go Tell It on a Mountain,* and Claude Brown's *Manchild in the Promise Land.* For a portrait of 1920s Harlem, try *When Harlem Was in Vogue,* by David Levering Lewis. The history of New York's Jewish population can be traced in such books as *World of Our Fathers,* by Irving Howe; *Call It Sleep,* by Henry Roth; *The Promise,* by Chaim Potok; and *Our Crowd,* by Stephen Birmingham.

Greenwich Village and How It Got That Way is an affectionate investigation by Terry Miller. Francine Prose's novel *Household Saints* uses Little Italy as its setting. *The New Chinatown,* by Peter Kwong, is a recent study of the community across Canal Street. Kate Simon's memoir *Bronx Primitive,* Laura Cunningham's autobiographical *Sleeping Arrangements,* and E. L. Doctorow's novel *World's Fair* are all set in the Bronx. Brooklyn's history is lovingly unfolded in *Brooklyn: People and Places, Past and Present,* by Grace Glueck and Paul Gardner. Part of William Styron's novel *Sophie's Choice* takes place in 1940s Brooklyn.

Mysteries set in New York City range from Dashiell Hammett's urbane 1933 novel *The Thin Man* to Rex Stout's series of Nero Wolfe mysteries. More recent picks include *While My Pretty One Sleeps,* by Mary Higgins Clark; *Greenwich Killing Time,* by Kinky Friedman; *Dead Air,* by Mike Lupica; and *Unorthodox Practices,* by Marissa Piesman.

Suggested Videos

Perhaps the quintessential New York City movie is *Breakfast at Tiffany's* (1961), directed by Blake Edwards and based on Truman Capote's novella. Anyone who sees the film cannot forget the opening scene, in which Audrey Hepburn as party-girl Holly Golightly, dressed in a long black Givenchy evening gown, window-shops at Tiffany's jewelry store at dawn. *On the Town* (1949) stars Gene Kelly and Frank Sinatra as sailors on a 24-hour leave; directed by Kelly and Stanley Donen, this was one of the first Hollywood musicals to be shot on location.

Filmmaker Woody Allen has photographed many of his movies in Manhattan, and many of his characters are shown walking the city streets. *Annie Hall* (1977), *Manhattan* (1979), *Broadway Danny Rose* (1985), *Hannah and Her Sisters*

(1987), *Another Woman* (1988), *Crimes and Misdemeanors* (1989), *Alice* (1990), *Manhattan Murder Mystery* (1993), *Bullets Over Broadway* (1994), and *Mighty Aphrodite* (1995) are a few.

Director Martin Scorsese, who attended New York University's film school, has made his best films in New York. *Mean Streets* (1973) and *Taxi Driver* (1976), both starring Robert De Niro and Harvey Keitel, show a darker side of the city.

Sidney Lumet films often deal with misfits and police corruption. Look for *Serpico* (1973), starring Al Pacino, *Dog Day Afternoon* (1975), *Prince of the City* (1981), and *Q&A* (1990).

Some of director Paul Mazursky's most entertaining films have New York settings: *Next Stop, Greenwich Village* (1976), *An Unmarried Woman* (1978), *Moscow on the Hudson* (1984), and *Enemies, A Love Story* (1989), based on the novel by Isaac Bashevis Singer.

Neil Simon films with city locations are *Barefoot in the Park* (1967), *The Odd Couple* (1968), *The Sunshine Boys* (1975), *The Goodbye Girl* (1977), and *Brighton Beach Memoirs* (1986).

Joan Micklin Silver portrays the Lower East Side in *Hester Street* (1975) and *Crossing Delancey* (1988). For a look at the African-American experience in Manhattan and Brooklyn, try the films of Spike Lee: *She's Gotta Have It* (1988), *Do the Right Thing* (1990), *Jungle Fever* (1991), and *Crooklyn* (1994). *I Like It Like That* (1994), directed by Darnell Martin, deals with a Latino woman in the Bronx.

Other NYC-set movies include *Sweet Smell of Success* (1957), *Love with a Proper Stranger* (1963), *A Thousand Clowns* (1965), *Up the Down Staircase* (1967), *Wait Until Dark* (1967), *Midnight Cowboy* (1969), *Kramer Vs. Kramer* (1979), *Fame* (1980), *Tootsie* (1982), *Moonstruck* (1987), *New York Stories* (1989), *Sea of Love* (1989), *Household Saints* (1993), and *City Hall* (1996).

INDEX

✕ = restaurant, 🏨 = hotel

NOTES

NOTES

NOTES

NOTES

NOTES

Escape to ancient cities and

journey to *exotic islands with*

CNN Travel Guide, a wealth of valuable advice. Host

Valerie Voss will take you to

all of your favorite destinations,

including those off the beaten

path. Tune-in to your passport to the world.

CNN TRAVEL GUIDE
SATURDAY 12:30 PMET   SUNDAY 4:30 PMET

CNN®

Fodor's Travel Publications

Available at bookstores everywhere, or call 1–800–533–6478, 24 hours a day.

Gold Guides

U.S.

Alaska	Florida	New Orleans	Santa Fe, Taos, Albuquerque
Arizona	Hawai'i	New York City	Seattle & Vancouver
Boston	Las Vegas, Reno, Tahoe	Pacific North Coast	The South
California	Los Angeles	Philadelphia & the Pennsylvania Dutch Country	U.S. & British Virgin Islands
Cape Cod, Martha's Vineyard, Nantucket	Maine, Vermont, New Hampshire	The Rockies	USA
The Carolinas & the Georgia Coast	Maui & Lāna'i	San Diego	Virginia & Maryland
Chicago	Miami & the Keys	San Francisco	Washington, D.C.
Colorado	New England		

Foreign

Australia	Europe	Montréal & Québec City	Scotland
Austria	Florence, Tuscany & Umbria	Moscow, St. Petersburg, Kiev	Singapore
The Bahamas	France	The Netherlands, Belgium & Luxembourg	South Africa
Belize & Guatemala	Germany	New Zealand	South America
Bermuda	Great Britain	Norway	Southeast Asia
Canada	Greece	Nova Scotia, New Brunswick, Prince Edward Island	Spain
Cancún, Cozumel, Yucatán Peninsula	Hong Kong	Paris	Sweden
Caribbean	India	Portugal	Switzerland
China	Ireland	Provence & the Riviera	Thailand
Costa Rica	Israel	Scandinavia	Tokyo
Cuba	Italy		Toronto
The Czech Republic & Slovakia	Japan		Turkey
Eastern & Central Europe	London		Vienna & the Danube
	Madrid & Barcelona		
	Mexico		

Fodor's Special-Interest Guides

Caribbean Ports of Call	Halliday's New Orleans Food Explorer	Sunday in New York	Where Should We Take the Kids? Northeast
The Complete Guide to America's National Parks	Healthy Escapes	Sunday in San Francisco	Worldwide Cruises and Ports of Call
Family Adventures	Kodak Guide to Shooting Great Travel Pictures	Walt Disney World, Universal Studios and Orlando	
Gay Guide to the USA	Net Travel	Walt Disney World for Adults	
Halliday's New England Food Explorer	Nights to Imagine	Where Should We Take the Kids? California	
	Rock & Roll Traveler USA		